Michaela Kreyenfeld • Dirk Konietzka
Editors

Childlessness in Europe: Contexts, Causes, and Consequences

Editors
Michaela Kreyenfeld
Hertie School of Governance
Berlin, Germany

Max Planck Institute for Demographic
  Research
Rostock, Germany

Dirk Konietzka
Department of Social Sciences
Braunschweig University of Technology
Braunschweig, Germany

DOI 10.1007/978-3-319-44667-7

Preface

In recent decades, levels of childlessness have been increasing rapidly in most European countries. German-speaking countries seem to be at the forefront of this development, as more than 20 % of the women living in Germany, Switzerland, and Austria who are now reaching the end of their reproductive period will remain childless. But other European countries, such as the UK and Finland, also report high levels of childlessness. Eastern and Southern Europe did not have high levels of childlessness a decade ago, but are now seeing steady increases. This book provides an overview of the recent trend toward a "life without children" across Europe. It seeks answers to questions like: What are the determinants of childlessness in the twenty-first century? Is there an unbroken trend in childlessness, or is there evidence of trend reversals? How does the likelihood of remaining childless differ across social strata? To what extent do economic uncertainties affect childlessness? How do fertility desires evolve over the life course? To what extent does the situation of a woman's partner affect her fertility decisions? How far can we push the biological limits of fertility? What role can assisted reproduction play in reducing childlessness? How many men fail to have children of their own? What impact can family policies have on fertility decisions? Can governments reverse the trend toward childlessness—and, if so, should they?

This book builds on the 2nd edition of the book *Ein Leben ohne Kinder*, published by Springer VS in Germany in 2013. It contains six updated and completely rewritten chapters of its German-language predecessor. Additionally, this volume contains ten new chapters by internationally renowned authors. Scholars from various European countries and the USA have contributed to the completion of this volume. We regret that we were unable to include any country study of a Southern European country. Unfortunately, the planned contribution on Italy was not ready on time for this edition. The "hot phase" of the editing process was in the summer of 2015, when the weather—at least in Berlin—was also very hot. During this phase, the editors exchanged numerous e-mails with the authors. Even though we were bothering our authors during their well-deserved summer vacation, it was always a joy to read and edit the papers. We would like to express our appreciation and thanks to the authors of this book for their diligence, patience, and support.

It is not possible to complete such a complex volume without the support of people who provide a wide range of essential services. The editors want to express their gratitude to Miriam Hils, who greatly helped us with the language editing of the book. We thank Tom Hensel for taking on the nitty-gritty work of ensuring that the text and the figures are properly formatted. We also wish to thank Hannes Laichter, who checked the reference lists. This book project was generously funded by the Max Planck Institute for Demographic Research in Rostock. We would like to thank Frans Willekens and James Vaupel, who greatly supported this endeavor. Last but not least, we thank Evelien Bakker and Bernadette Deelen-Mans from Springer SBM NL, who initially suggested that we publish this book—many thanks for pushing us in the right direction.

Berlin, Germany   Michaela Kreyenfeld
Braunschweig, Germany   Dirk Konietzka
January 2016

Contents

Contributors

Marco Albertini Department of Political and Social Sciences, University of Bologna, Bologna, Italy

Gunnar Andersson Demography Unit, Stockholm University, Stockholm, Sweden

Laura Bernardi LIVES, Faculty for the Social and Political Sciences, University of Lausanne, Lausanne, Switzerland

Ann Berrington Department of Social Statistics & Demography, University of Southampton, Southampton, UK

Gesche Brandt German Centre for Higher Education Research and Science Studies, Deutsches Zentrum für Hochschul- und Wissenschaftsforschung (DHZW), Hanover, Germany

Marion Burkimsher Independent researcher affiliated with the University of Lausanne, Lausanne, Switzerland

Christin Czaplicki Research and Development, German Pension Insurance, Berlin, Germany

Tomas Frejka Independent researcher and consultant, Sanibel, FL, USA

Michael Grotheer German Centre for Higher Education Research and Science Studies, Deutsches Zentrum für Hochschul- und Wissenschaftsforschung (DHZW), Hanover, Germany

Jan M. Hoem Demography Unit, Stockholm University, Stockholm, Sweden

Katya Ivanova University of Amsterdam, Amsterdam, The Netherlands

Sylvia Keim Institute of Sociology and Demographic Research, University of Rostock, Rostock, Germany

Renske Keizer Department of Sociology, Erasmus University of Rotterdam, Rotterdam, The Netherlands

Department of Child Development, University of Amsterdam, Amsterdam, The Netherlands

Martin Kohli Department of Social and Political Sciences, European University Institute, Florence, Italy

Bremen International Graduate School of Social Sciences, Bremen, Germany

Dirk Konietzka Department of Social Sciences, Braunschweig University of Technology, Braunschweig, Germany

Katja Köppen Institute of Sociology and Demographic Research, University of Rostock, Rostock, Germany

Michaela Kreyenfeld Hertie School of Governance, Berlin, Germany

Max Planck Institute for Demographic Research, Rostock, Germany

Anne-Kristin Kuhnt Institute of Sociology, University of Duisburg-Essen, Duisburg, Germany

Magali Mazuy French Institute for Demographic Studies (INED), Paris, France

Anneli Miettinen Population Research Institute, Väestöliitto, Finland

Tatjana Mika Research and Development, German Pension Insurance, Berlin, Germany

Melinda C. Mills Department of Sociology and Nuffield College, University of Oxford, Oxford, UK

Gerda Neyer Demography Unit, Stockholm University, Stockholm, Sweden

Patrick Präg Department of Sociology and Nuffield College, University of Oxford, Oxford, UK

Anna Rotkirch Population Research Institute, Väestöliitto, Finland

Hildegard Schaeper German Centre for Higher Education Research and Science Studies, Deutsches Zentrum für Hochschul- und Wissenschaftsforschung (DHZW), Hanover, Germany

Tomáš Sobotka Vienna Institute of Demography, Austrian Academy of Sciences and Wittgenstein Centre for Demography and Global Human Capital, Vienna, Austria

Laurent Toulemon French Institute for Demographic Studies (INED), Paris, France

Heike Trappe Institute of Sociology and Demographic Research, University of Rostock, Rostock, Germany

Kryštof Zeman Vienna Institute of Demography, Austrian Academy of Sciences and Wittgenstein Centre for Demography and Global Human Capital, Vienna, Austria

Part I
Childlessness in Europe: An Overview

Chapter 1
Analyzing Childlessness

Michaela Kreyenfeld and Dirk Konietzka

1.1 Introduction

Increasing childlessness is only one of the many shifts in demographic behavior that have been occurring in Europe in recent decades, but in the public debate, it is probably the most ideologically charged of these developments. Some commenters have characterized increasing childlessness as an outgrowth of an individualistic and ego-centric society (Siegel 2013; The Guardian 2015), or have blamed childless women for the rapid aging of the population and for the looming decay of social security systems (Focus 2013; Last 2013). Meanwhile, commenters on the other side of this debate have called for a "childfree lifestyle" and have recommended "bypassing" parenthood (Mantel 2013; Walters 2012). From a feminist perspective, the decision to remain childless has been described as an expression of a self-determined life, as in previous generations a woman's life had been constructed around the roles of wife and mother (Correll 2010; Gillespie 2003).

While this heated public debate has been simmering for years, scholarly research has provided a more neutral and fact-based assessment of the evolution and consequences of childlessness in contemporary societies. The key topics in this area of research are, among others, the social stratification of childlessness (Beaujouan et al. 2015; Koropeckyj-Cox and Call 2007; Wood 2016), the consequences of childless-

M. Kreyenfeld (✉)
Hertie School of Governance, Berlin, Germany

Max Planck Institute for Demographic Research, Rostock, Germany
e-mail: kreyenfeld@hertie-school.org

D. Konietzka
Department of Social Sciences, Braunschweig University of Technology, Braunschweig, Germany
e-mail: d.konietzka@tu-braunschweig.de

© The Author(s) 2017
M. Kreyenfeld, D. Konietzka (eds.), *Childlessness in Europe: Contexts, Causes, and Consequences*, Demographic Research Monographs,
DOI 10.1007/978-3-319-44667-7_1

ness for labor market outcomes (Budig et al. 2012; Correll et al. 2007; Gash 2009), health (Kendig et al. 2007), and old-age well-being (Dykstra and Wagner 2007; Huijts et al. 2013; Klaus and Schnettler 2016; Zhang and Hayward 2001). Because of data limitations, most past research focused on female childlessness. However, the analysis of "male childlessness" has recently advanced to become a key area of research, too (Gray et al. 2013; Keizer 2010; Keizer et al. 2010; Nisen et al. 2014; Schmitt and Winkelmann 2005). Many of the prior longitudinal studies on childlessness and the evolution of fertility desires had been conducted using data from the US (Thomson 1997). Meanwhile, Europe is catching up with the US, as large-scale panel data are now available for many European countries. These data enable researchers to study how fertility desires change across the life course, how they are influenced by the partnership situation, and how they are related to the other domains of the life course (Berrington and Pattaro 2014; Keizer et al. 2007; Kuhnt and Trappe 2015). Moreover, methodological and technical innovations have given rise to advances in the field. The longstanding interest in explaining the trajectories that lead to childlessness (Hagestad and Call 2007) can now be satisfied through the use of software packages, many of which now include sequence analysis techniques (Mynarska et al. 2013; Jalovaara and Fasang 2015). The biological limits of fertility and the scope of assisted reproduction in alleviating involuntary childlessness are also emerging as research topics (Sobotka et al. 2008; Velde et al. 2012).

This volume adds to the abovementioned research by presenting detailed country reports on long-term trends and socio-demographic differences in female and male childlessness. It also includes reports of results from recent European panel studies that map the evolution of fertility desires across the life course. Moreover, several of the chapters provide new evidence on the prevalence of assisted reproduction, and examine the consequences of childlessness for economic and psychological well-being. In this introductory chapter, we sketch the major conceptual issues that tend to arise in the analysis of childlessness (Sect. 1.2), and present a more detailed outline of the contents of this volume (Sect. 1.3).

1.2 Analyzing Childlessness – Issues and Conceptual Problems

1.2.1 Is Childlessness a (Post)Modern Phenomenon?

Since the mid-twentieth century, many western European countries have seen radical changes in demographic behavior, including increasing shares of permanently childless women and men. It seems tempting to regard this development as a distinctly new and "post-modern" phenomenon. While previous generations were pressed into parenthood by the influence of social norms and religious doctrines—and by the lack of efficient birth control methods—the ability of current generations to "choose" whether to have children seems to be an achievement of post-modern life course conditions (Burkart 2007; Gillespie 2001; Mayer 2004). But is "voluntary" childlessness really a new development? Can we actually draw a line between "voluntary" and "involuntary" childlessness? And how do current trends line up with long-term historical developments?

Historical demography tells us that in many European regions in the 19th and early 20th centuries, 20 % or more of women remained childless. Childlessness used to be an integral part of what Hajnal (1965) described as the "Western European marriage pattern." A relatively high age at marriage was typical for the western European family system, in which young adults left the parental household to work as servants and maids in the households of their employers (Wall 1998: 45). During that time they were obliged to remain single and childless (Ehmer 2011: 29; Mitterauer 1990). A high prevalence of childlessness has also been observed for the North American family system, where "the single adult was a significant part of the American population in the nineteenth and early twentieth century" (Rindfuss et al. 1988: 61).

However, it is not only in pre-industrial times that we observe high levels of childlessness. There is also considerable evidence that a large share of the women who were born around 1900 remained childless. According to Morgan (1991: 782), 25 % of US women of these cohorts were permanently childless. Rowland (1998: 20) estimates for Australia that about 30 % of the women of the 1891–1906 cohorts had no children. Similar estimates are reported for European countries for female cohorts born at the beginning of the twentieth century (see also Berrington, Chap. 3; Burkimsher and Zeman, Chap. 6; Kreyenfeld and Konietzka, Chap. 5; or Sobotka, Chap. 2, in this volume). It is commonly argued that childlessness among these cohorts is related to the social and economic upheavals that followed the Great Depression of the 1920s (Rowland 1998). Although economic deprivation probably contributed to this development, other factors also played a role. For example, the heavily distorted sex ratios caused by World War II help to explain high levels of female childlessness among the cohorts born around 1920 (see Burkimsher and Zeman, Chap. 6, in this volume, who report childlessness by gender for these cohorts).

The following cohorts, born in the 1930s and 1940s, entered their reproductive ages in the 1950s and early 1960s, a period that has been retrospectively labeled the "Golden Age of Marriage" (Festy 1980). These cohorts married much earlier than the previous generations, and childlessness dropped to historically low levels: "Marriage had not been so close to universal nor taken at such an early age in Western Europe for at least two centuries" (Festy 1980: 311). The increase in marriage and fertility rates during the 1950s and the early 1960s is commonly explained by a revival of traditional family values after wartime. The scholars of that time were nevertheless puzzled by that development (Parsons 1955). Veevers (1973: 203) even spoke of a "paradoxical decline of rates of childlessness."

Starting with the birth cohorts born around 1950, the prevalence of childlessness increased (again) in many parts of Europe, and particularly in West Germany, Austria, Switzerland, the Netherlands, and England/Wales (see Sobotka, Chap. 2, in this volume, for an overview see also Miettinen et al. 2015; OECD 2016). In other parts of Europe, and especially in southern and eastern European countries, widespread permanent childlessness is a relatively recent phenomenon. In these countries the shares of women who remain childless have been increasing rapidly. In Italy, for example, childlessness skyrocketed to 20 % among the cohorts born around 1965 (Tanturri and Mencarini 2008). Meanwhile, in Belgium, France, and the Scandinavian countries, childlessness has remained comparatively low. An exceptional case is Finland: in the Nordic context, Finland has always had relatively high levels of childlessness. Recent data for Finland show that childlessness in that country is still rising; thus, it appears that the gap between Finland and the rest of the Nordic states is expanding (see Rotkirch and Miettinen, Chap. 7, in this volume).

In his broad overview of fertility trends in 28 European countries, Sobotka (Chap. 2, in this volume) concludes that because of the recent increase in childlessness in southern Europe and in the former state-socialist central and eastern European countries, childlessness is converging at high levels in Europe. From a global perspective, significant developments can be observed in Asian countries, and particularly in Japan, too, where childlessness has been increasing among recent birth cohorts (Frejka et al. 2010; Raymo et al. 2015). However, we also see some signs of a reversal of this trend, as childlessness appears to be gradually declining among the younger cohorts in a number of countries, including the UK (see Berrington, Chap. 3, in this volume). The US also had high levels of childlessness for decades, but recent evidence indicates that the trend is reversing in this country as well (see Frejka, Chap. 8, in this volume).

1.2.2 Childlessness Across the Life Course

Research on childlessness has always faced challenges in formulating a clear definition of "permanent childlessness." In qualitative studies, respondents who stated that they firmly reject parenthood were often categorized as childless, even if they were still of childbearing age at the time of the interview (Gillespie 2000: 228; Black und Scull 2005). But earlier quantitative studies also did not use any age limitations in the analysis of childlessness (De Jong and Sell 1977; Baum 1983). The conclusion from these investigations that "childlessness is temporary and that childbearing may occur later in life" (1977: 132) seemed self-evident. The studies that followed failed to use universal definitions of permanent childlessness. In principle, researchers have to wait until female cohorts have passed a certain age before drawing firm conclusions about the childlessness levels in these cohorts. However, the temptation to predict the childlessness levels of cohorts who are close to the end of their reproductive period is strong. The inability to imagine further increases in childbearing at later ages has led many researchers to use cut-off ages that are too low. As a consequence, these scholars overstated childlessness levels for the younger cohorts. The measurement of permanent childlessness among men is even more complicated, because a man's reproductive period is less clearly defined than a woman's. In addition, concerns have been raised about the collection of male fertility histories in social science surveys (Rendall et al. 1999).

In the literature, researchers commonly distinguish between "voluntary" and "involuntary" childlessness (Höpflinger 1991; Kelly 2009; Noordhuizen et al. 2010; Somers 1993; Veevers 1979; Wilcox and Mosher 1994). This distinction is often used to differentiate between biological and other reasons for childlessness, although many early studies also assigned unmarried women to the category of "involuntarily childless" (Veevers 1979: 3). Due to the strong relationship between age and fecundity, and because whether an individual has a child depends not only on his or her own reproductive capacity, but also on the ability of his or her partner to conceive or father a child, it is cumbersome to generate clear-cut estimates on "involuntary childlessness" at the individual level. Survey data can also be problematic because people do not necessarily know whether they are able to have children. The growing availability of assisted reproduction has softened the boundaries between "voluntary" and "involuntary" childlessness even further. Despite these caveats, it has been estimated that about five to 10 % of each cohort remain childless for biological reasons (Leridon 1992, see also Berrington, Chap. 3 and Trappe, Chap. 13, in this volume).

An issue that has been debated in the literature is the relationship between fertility postponement and childlessness. While some scholars have claimed that childlessness can be best understood as an unintended series of fertility postponements (Rindfuss et al. 1988; Morgan 1991), others have argued that childlessness is a clear and conscious lifestyle choice. In the feminist debate, efforts have been made to eliminate the term childlessness and to replace it with the term "childfree." According to these scholars, the term "childless" has negative connotations because the suffix "less" implies that "something is lacking, deprived, unfortunate" (Underhill 1977: 307); whereas the term "childfree" implies that childlessness is a deliberate choice to not have children (Gillespie 2000; Hoffman and Levant 1985). The recent availability of large-scale panel data has made it easier to generate more solid evidence on the evolution of fertility desires across the life course (see Berrington, Chap. 3, in this volume).

1.3 Patterns, Causes, and Consequences of Childlessness

This book provides an overview of recent trends in childlessness in European countries and the US. In Chap. 2, Tomáš Sobotka assembles data from 28 European countries and describes long-term trends in childlessness. He critically evaluates the potential of the different types of data (censuses, social science surveys, vital statistics) that are commonly used to generate shares of childlessness. The paper shows elevated levels of childlessness for the cohorts born around 1900, and lower levels thereafter. In most countries, the 1940s cohorts had the lowest levels of childlessness ever recorded. In several of the western European countries, childlessness levels increased among the younger cohorts. The former socialist and southern

European countries are laggards in this development, but Sobotka observes some convergence, as childlessness also appears to be increasing in the CEE countries. Moreover, signs of a trend reversal have been reported. Switzerland and England/ Wales were among the first countries where childlessness increased. For these countries, we see that childlessness is leveling off at values of around 20 %. These findings suggest that the increase in childlessness in contemporary societies may have limits. However, Sobotka cautions against projecting childlessness for the cohorts who are still of childbearing age.

Chapters 3, 4, 5, 6, and 7 in this volume contain country studies for major European countries. The first paper in this larger section is by Ann Berrington, who explores trends in childlessness in the UK. The UK has long had high levels of childlessness, but also relatively high cohort fertility rates. This pattern suggests that fertility behavior in this country is relatively polarized, with significant shares of people either remaining childless or having a large family. Berrington provides fresh evidence showing that the increase in childlessness rates has stopped, or may have even "gone into reverse" starting with the cohorts born in 1970. Using additional evidence from survey data, Berrington explores people's stated reasons for remaining childless: while career planning is seldom given as a reason for remaining childless, "not having found the right partner" is often cited. Berrington also presents evidence on the evolution of fertility intentions across the life course. She shows that the share of people who categorically reject parenthood is low. However, there is a significant share of people who are still childless at age 42, despite having said they intend to have children at age 30. It seems likely that a large fraction of these people are "lulled" into childlessness through ongoing postponement.

In the following chapter, Katja Köppen, Magali Mazuy, and Laurent Toulemon investigate long-term trends in female and male childlessness in France. They examine how childlessness varies by level of education and occupation. Compared to the UK, levels of permanent childlessness are rather low in France. It is also shown that highly educated women are more likely to be childless than their less educated counterparts. By contrast, childlessness does not differ greatly by level of education or occupation among men. Less educated men are, however, slightly less likely to have children; a finding the authors attribute to the difficulties these men face in finding a partner. As in the study by Berrington for the UK, Köppen and her coauthors emphasize the role of partnership dynamics in permanent childlessness. While rates of childlessness are low among people who have ever entered a union, many of the men and women who have never entered a union remain childless at later ages.

In the next chapter, Kreyenfeld and Konietzka explore trends in childlessness in East and West Germany. West Germany was among the "vanguards" of childlessness in post-war Europe. Starting with the 1950s birth cohorts, childlessness increased continuously, reaching levels of more than 20 % for the female cohorts born around 1965. In state-socialist East Germany, childlessness remained low. For the recent East German birth cohorts who entered their reproductive ages after German unification, permanent childlessness has been increasing gradually; a trend that is comparable to the patterns found in other former state-socialist countries.

The most significant development is most likely the narrowing of the differences in childlessness levels by women's educational attainment among recent West German cohorts. An investigation based on survey data explores the typical pathways into childlessness for recent cohorts (1971–1973) of women and men. The findings of this analysis support the evidence from France and the UK that particularly for men, the lack of a partner often leads to childlessness at later ages.

Marion Burkimsher and Kryštof Zeman provide an overview of the development in childlessness in Austria and Switzerland. Together with (West) Germany, they are among the western European countries that report having high levels of childlessness and low cohort fertility rates. In Austria and Switzerland, childlessness increases strongly with level of female education. As the authors have access to data on long-term trends, they are also able to provide estimates on childlessness by level of education for the cohorts born around 1900. Very few of these women progressed to tertiary education, and if they did, they mostly remained childless. According to the authors, for these cohorts of women tertiary education was a "life calling similar to the calling to commit to a celibate life in the church." For the subsequent cohorts in Austria and Switzerland, educational differences in childlessness levels have narrowed considerably. However, some differences in female childlessness by educational attainment remain: for example, for the cohorts born around 1960, about 35 % of the tertiary educated women have remained childless. Estimates of childlessness among men show only small differences by education. Again, less educated men are more likely to be childless than highly educated men.

Anna Rotkirch and Anneli Miettinen explore trends in childlessness in Finland. In the European context, Finland's childlessness patterns have long been seen as paradoxical. While the other Scandinavian countries—Norway, Sweden, Iceland, and Denmark—have regularly reported low levels of childlessness, Finland has historically had elevated levels of childlessness. The recent findings presented in this chapter provide further evidence of this trend, as the authors show that about 20 % of the women who are now reaching the end of their reproductive period have remained childless. Childlessness levels are highest among the least educated women and men, and have increased the most for this group in recent years. Thus, in Finland the educational patterns in childlessness are much more similar for men and women than in other European countries. However, the authors also show that in Finland the lack of a (marital) partner is strongly correlated with remaining childless. However, childlessness within unions has been increasing over time, too.

The following chapter by Tomáš Frejka is the only paper in this volume that goes beyond European borders to present evidence for the United States. The author shows that as in many European countries, in the US childlessness was elevated for the cohorts born around 1900. Black women of these cohorts were particularly likely to have remained childless. Frejka attributes the elevated childlessness levels among these women to their economic, social, and health-related disadvantages. Among the subsequent cohorts, childlessness dropped for all groups, and especially for the black population. Starting with the cohorts born in the 1940s, black women have been more likely to have children than white women. Among the cohorts born in the 1960s, childlessness has gradually declined, particularly for white women.

Within the context of this volume, this chapter provides important insights into long-term developments in childlessness in industrialized countries. It is important that we understand whether the trend reversal is unique to the US, or whether the patterns in the US indicate that childlessness is about to start declining in other "high childlessness countries" as well.

While the previous chapters provided long-term overviews, Chaps. 9, 10, 11, 12, 13 and 14 examine the determinants of childlessness in contemporary Europe. The contribution by Gerda Neyer, Jan Hoem, and Gunnar Andersson explores the association of education and childlessness in Austria and Sweden. While prior analyses often used broad categories to group different levels of education, these authors take a more nuanced view, and investigate how field of education relates to childlessness. While in Sweden childlessness does not greatly vary by level of education, it is possible to single out professions with very high levels of childlessness. For example, librarians and hotel and restaurant workers are particularly likely to be childless. Conversely, women who are educated in the field of health seldom remain childless. In Austria, we find a very strong educational gradient in childlessness. Among tertiary-educated women of the 1955–1959 cohorts, about 30 % have remained childless. In Austria, some heterogeneity has been found within the different educational groups. Among the highly educated social scientists, for example, childlessness is almost 40 %.

In their study, Hildegard Schaeper, Michael Grotheer, and Gesche Brandt take a dynamic perspective on the relationship between education and fertility. The data for this analysis come from the panel studies of higher education graduates conducted by the German Centre for Research on Higher Education and Science Studies (DZHW). The data contain detailed monthly employment histories of East and West German women who graduated from a university in Germany. The findings indicate that East Germans are more likely to have children during education, and that East German university graduates are significantly younger at first birth than their West German counterparts. However, Schaeper and her coauthors also report a convergence of behavior among the cohort who graduated from university in 2009. The multivariate analysis, which draws on event history modeling, shows that stable employment is generally seen as a prerequisite for family formation by highly educated women in Germany. However, there is also a group of women who have a first child despite being subject to "long periods of precarious employment and insecure occupational prospects."

In the following study, Kuhnt, Kreyenfeld, and Trappe also applied a longitudinal perspective to the analysis of fertility in Germany. Using data from the first six waves of the German Family Panel, they explore how "fertility ideals" vary across the life course. Fertility ideals were operationalized by asking respondents to report their desired number of children "under ideal circumstances." On average, people said they want to have about two children. However, the authors show that the desired number of children declines more rapidly with age for women than for men. The further multivariate analysis explored the factors that lead to a change in fertility ideals. The most important factor that is found to influence fertility ideals is the birth of a child; thus, people seem to adjust their fertility ideals as their family grows. Interestingly, economic factors do not seem to have much influence on fertility ideals.

Laura Bernardi and Sylvia Keim present evidence from a qualitative study in East and West Germany. The sample was made up of women who were highly qualified and in full-time employment. At the time of the interview the women were still childless, but wanted to have children. They were asked to report on their attitudes toward having children and combining work and family life. The results show that East and West Germans have very different ideas about how they wish to organize their future family life. The typical "male breadwinner model" was more prevalent in the narratives of the West German respondents, whereas the East German women took it for granted that they would continue to work after becoming a parent. The chapter provides evidence that different perceptions of what constitutes parenthood and family life have persisted after German unification.

The contribution by Heike Trappe explores the prevalence of assisted reproductive technologies (ART) in Germany. The author notes that in 2012 about 14,000 children in Germany were born following the application of assisted reproduction technologies. While acknowledging that the use of assisted reproduction has increased over time in Germany, Trappe argues that the German legal context has inhibited the wider use of ART. She observes, for example, that some groups—including cohabiting couples, same-sex couples, and singles—do not have the same access to ART as married couples.

Patrick Präg and Melinda C. Mills complement the chapter by Trappe by providing a rich overview of the prevalence of ART and the related rules and regulations in Europe. They show that access to and the prevalence of assisted reproduction vary greatly across countries. The most liberal of the European countries are Denmark and Belgium, where the costs of couples and individuals undergoing ART are largely covered. The restrictions imposed in other European countries can be evaded by crossing borders and seeking out ART in more liberal countries. However, the authors raise concerns about social justice, as people with lower incomes may be unable to travel to access ART. Furthermore, they point out that the high levels of ART that are available in some countries of Europe demonstrate that ART can influence levels of total fertility.

The last three chapters of this volume address the psychological and economic consequences of childlessness for later life outcomes. Renske Keizer and Katya Ivanova investigate the consequences of having children for men and women in the Netherlands. Children seem to impact men's life satisfaction indirectly. A deterioration in partnership quality seems to affect the well-being of childless men more strongly than that of men with children. It appears that having children buffers some of the adverse effects that being in a low-quality partnership can have on physical and mental ill health.

Tatjana Mika and Christin Czaplicki investigate the role of motherhood for old-age income in East and West Germany. Using linked survey and register data, they show that having children can greatly affect a woman's lifetime employment profile. The differences in employment directly transfer into differences in old-age income. The authors of this study observe a significant motherhood penalty for old-age income in West Germany, but not in East Germany. In Germany, women's pension are highly subsidized, as a woman automatically collects pension points for each birth. Although these transfers are rather generous, they are not sufficient to close the gap in old-age income between mothers and childless women.

Marco Albertini and Martin Kohli investigate how the elderly receive and give support within their social networks, and the extent to which they are engaged in charity work. The authors make distinctions between the elderly based on parental status. Their findings indicate that childless elderly people greatly contribute to the functioning of their social networks, and that—contrary to widely held stereotypes—they do not receive a disproportionate share of transfers. Instead, they are actively involved in charity work and in maintaining their social networks. By contrast, the people who have children, but have lost contact with them, are shown to be the most likely to be in need of support.

Literature

Baum, F. E. (1983). Orientations towards voluntary childlessness. *Journal of Biosocial Science, 15*, 153–164.

Beaujouan, E., Brzozowska, Z., & Zeman, K. (2015). *Childlessness trends in twentieth-century Europe: Limited link to growing educational attainment* (VID Working Paper 6).

Berrington, A., & Pattaro, S. (2014). Educational differences in fertility desires, intentions and behaviour: A life course perspective. *Advances in Life Course Research, 21*, 10–27.

Black, R., & Scull, L. (2005). *Beyond childlessness*. London: Rodale.

Budig, M. J., Misra, J., & Boeckmann, I. (2012). The motherhood penalty in cross-national perspective: The importance of work-family policies and cultural attitudes. *Social Politics, 19*, 163–193.

Burkart, G. (2007). Eine Kultur des Zweifels. Kinderlosigkeit und die Zukunft der Familie [A culture of doubt. childlessness and the future of the family]. In D. Konietzka & M. Kreyenfeld (Eds.), *Ein Leben ohne Kinder* (pp. 401–423). Wiesbaden: Springer VS.

Correll, L. (2010). *Anrufungen zur Mutterschaft. Eine wissenssoziologische Untersuchung von Kinderlosigkeit* [Calls for motherhood. A scientific study of childlessness]. Münster: Verlag Westfälisches Dampfboot.

Correll, S. J., Benard, S., & Paik, I. (2007). Getting a job: Is there a motherhood penalty? *American Journal of Sociology, 112*, 1297–1338.

De Jong, G. F., & Sell, R. R. (1977). Changes in childlessness in the United States: A demographic path analysis. *Population Studies, 31*, 129–141.

Dykstra, P. A., & Wagner, M. (2007). Pathways to childlessness and late-life outcomes. *Journal of Family Issues, 28*, 1487–1517.

Ehmer, J. (2011). The significance of looking back: Fertility before the fertility decline. *Historical Social Research, 36*, 11–34.

Festy, P. (1980). On the new context of marriage in Western Europe. *Population and Development Review, 6*, 311–315.

Focus. (2013). Kinderlose Sozialschmarotzer oder Betreuungsgeld kassierende Muttis. Wer ist egoistischer? [Childless or mothers receiving child care benefits: Who is more egoistic?]. *Focus Online (18/11/2014)* http://www.focus.de/familie/erziehung/familie/gegensaetzliche-lebensentwuerfe-kinderlose-sozialschmarotzer-oder-betreuungsgeld-kassierende-muttis-wer-ist-egoistischer_id_4282162.html. Accessed 15 Jan 2016.

Frejka, T., Jones, G. W., & Sardon, J.-P. (2010). East Asian childbearing patterns and policy developments. *Population and Development Review, 36*, 579–606.

Gash, V. (2009). Sacrificing their careers for their families? An analysis of the penalty to motherhood in Europe. *Social Indicators Research, 93*, 569–586.

Gillespie, R. (2000). When no means no: Disbelief, disregard and deviance as discourses of voluntary childlessness. *Women's Studies International Forum, 23*, 223–234.

Gillespie, R. (2001). Contextualizing voluntary childlessness within a postmodern model of reproduction: Implications for health and social needs. *Critical Social Policy, 21*, 139–159.

Gillespie, R. (2003). Childfree and feminine: Understanding the gender identity of voluntarily individualistic and ego-centric society. *Gender & Society, 17*, 122–136.

Gray, E., Evans, A., & Reimondos, A. (2013). Childbearing desires of childless men and women: When are goals adjusted? *Advances in Life Course Research, 18*, 141–149.

Hagestad, G. O., & Call, V. R. A. (2007). Pathways to childlessness. A life course perspective. *Journal of Family Issues, 28*, 1338–1361.

Hajnal, J. (1965). European marriage patterns in perspective. In D. V. Glass & D. E. C. Eversley (Eds.), *Population in history: Essays in historical demography* (pp. 101–143). London: Edward Arnold.

Hoffman, S. R., & Levant, R. F. (1985). A comparison of childfree and child-anticipated married couples. *Family Relations, 34*, 197–203.

Höpflinger, F. (1991). Neue Kinderlosigkeit. Demographische trends und gesellschaftliche Spekulationen (New childlessness. Demographic trends and societal speculations). *Acta Demographica, 1*, 81–100.

Huijts, T., Subramanian, S. V., & Kraaykamp, G. (2013). Childlessness and psychological well-being in context: A multilevel study on 24 European countries. *European Sociological Review, 29*, 32–47.

Jalovaara, M., & Fasang, A. E. (2015). Are there gender differences in family trajectories by education in Finland? *Demographic Research, 33*, 1241–1256.

Keizer, R. (2010). *Remaining childless. Causes and consequences from a life course perspective.* Dissertation, Utrecht University.

Keizer, R., Dykstra, P. A., & Jansen, M. D. (2007). Pathways into childlessness: Evidence of gendered life course dynamics. *Journal of Biosocial Science, 40*, 863–878.

Keizer, R., Dykstra, P. A., & Poortman, A.-R. (2010). Life outcomes of childless men and fathers. *European Sociological Review, 26*, 1–15.

Kelly, M. (2009). Women's voluntary childlessness: A radical rejection of motherhood? *Women's Studies Quarterly, 3*, 157–172.

Kendig, H., Dykstra, P. A., van Gaalen, R. I., & Melkas, T. (2007). Health of aging parents and childless individuals. *Journal of Family Issues, 38*, 1457–1486.

Klaus, D., & Schnettler, S. (2016). Social networks and support for parents and childless adults in the second half of life: Convergence, divergence, or stability? *Advances in Life Course Research* (online first).

Koropeckyj-Cox, T., & Call, V. R. A. (2007). Characteristics of older childless persons and parents cross-national comparisons. *Journal of Family Issues, 28*, 1362–1414.

Kuhnt, A.-K., & Trappe, H. (2015). Channels of social influence on the realization of short-term fertility intentions in Germany. *Advances in Life Course Research* (online first).

Last, J. V. (2013). *What to expect when no one's expecting: America's coming demographic disaster.* New York: Encounter Books.

Leridon, H. (1992). Sterility and subfecundity from silence to impatience? *Population (English Selection), 4*, 35–54.

Mantel, H. (Ed.). (2013). *No kidding. Women writers on bypassing motherhood.* Berkely: Seal Press.

Mayer, K.-U. (2004). Whose lives? How history, societies, and institutions define and shape life courses. *Research in Human Development, 3*, 161–187.

Miettinen, A., Rotkirch, A., Szalma, I., Donno, A., & Tanturri, M.-L. (2015). *Increasing childlessness in Europe: Time trends and country differences* (Families and Societies Working Paper No. 33).

Mitterauer, M. (1990). Servants and youth. *Continuity and Change, 5*, 11–38.

Morgan, S. P. (1991). Late nineteenth- and early twentieth-century childlessness. *American Journal of Sociology, 97*, 779–807.

Mynarska, M., Matysiak, A., Rybińska, A., Tocchioni, V., & Vignoli, D. (2013). Diverse paths into childlessness over the life course. *Advances in Life Course Research, 25*, 35–48.

Nisen, J., Martikainen, P., Silventoinen, K., & Myrskylä, M. (2014). Age-specific fertility by educational level in the Finnish male cohort born 1940–50. *Demographic Research, 31*, 119–136.

Noordhuizen, S., de Graaf, P., & Sieben, I. (2010). The public acceptance of voluntary childlessness in the Netherlands: From 20 to 90 per cent in 30 years. *Social Indicators Research, 99*, 163–181.

OECD. (2016). OECD family database. http://www.oecd.org/els/family/database.htm#structure

Parsons, T. (1955). The American family. In T. Parsons & R. F. Bales (Eds.), *Family, socialization and interaction process* (pp. 3–33). Glencoe: Free Press.

Raymo, J. M., Park, H., Xie, Y., & Yeung, W.-J. J. (2015). Marriage and family in East Asia: Continuity and change. *Annual Review of Sociology, 41*, 471–492.

Rendall, M. S., Clarke, L., Peters, H. E., Ranjit, N., & Verropoulou, G. (1999). Incomplete reporting of men's fertility in the United States and Britain: A research note. *Demography, 36*(1), 135–144.

Rindfuss, R. R., Morgan, P. S., & Swicegood, G. (1988). *First births in America: Changes in the timing of parenthood.* London: University of California Press.

Rowland, D. T. (1998). The prevalence of childlessness in cohorts of older women. *Australian Journal on Ageing, 17*, 18–23.

Schmitt, C., & Winkelmann, U. (2005). Wer bleibt kinderlos? Was sozialstrukturelle Daten über Kinderlosigkeit bei Frauen und Männern verraten [Who remains childless? What socio-economic data say about childdlessness]. *Zeitschrift für interdisziplinäre Frauen- und Geschlechterforschung, 23*, 9–23.

Siegel, H. (2013). Why the choice to be childless is bad for America. *Newsweek (2/19/13)* http://europe.newsweek.com/why-choice-be-childless-bad-america-63335?rm=eu. Accessed 15 Jan 2016.

Sobotka, T., Hansen, M. A., Jensen, T. K., Pedersen, A. T., Lutz, W., & Skakkebæk, N. E. (2008). The contribution of assisted reproduction to completed Fertility: An analysis of Danish data. *Population and Development Review, 34*, 79–101.

Somers, M. D. (1993). A comparison of voluntarily childfree adults and parents. *Journal of Marriage and the Family, 55*, 643–650.

Tanturri, M. L., & Mencarini, L. (2008). Childless or childfree? Paths to voluntary childlessness in Italy. *Population and Development Review, 34*, 51–77.

The Guardian. (2015). Pope Francis: Not having children is selfish (11/02/2015). http://www.theguardian.com/world/2015/feb/11/pope-francis-the-choice-to-not-have-children-is-selfish. Accessed 15 Jan 2016.

Thomson, E. (1997). Couple childbearing desires, intentions, and births. *Demography, 34*, 343–354.

Underhill, L. D. (1977). 'Childfree' Semantics. *Science News, 111*, 307.

Veevers, J. E. (1973). Voluntary childlessness: A neglected area of family study. *The Family Coordinator, 22*, 199–205.

Veevers, J. E. (1979). Voluntary childlessness: A review of issues and evidence. *Marriage and Family Review, 2*, 1–24.

Velde, E. T., Habbema, D., Leridon, H., & Eijkemans, M. (2012). The effect of postponement of first motherhood on permanent involuntary childlessness and total fertility rate in six European countries since the 1970s. *Human Reproduction, 27*, 1179–1183.

Wall, R. (1998). Characteristics of European family and household systems. *Historical Social Research, 20*, 44–66.

Walters, K. D. (2012). *Kidfree & Lovin' it! Whether by choice, chance or circumstance: The complete guide to living as a non-parent.* Summerland: Serena Bay.

Wilcox, L. S., & Mosher, W. D. (1994). Characteristics associated with impaired fecundity in the United States. *Family Planning Perspectives, 26,* 218–221.

Wood, J. (2016). *European fertility.* Dissertation, Universiteit Antwerpen.

Zhang, Z., & Hayward, M. D. (2001). Childlessness and the psychological well-being of older persons. *Journal of Gerontology: Series B, 56,* 311–320.

Chapter 2
Childlessness in Europe: Reconstructing Long-Term Trends Among Women Born in 1900–1972

Tomáš Sobotka

2.1 Introduction

In most parts of Europe, childlessness and non-marriage were common phenomena during the course of the demographic transition (Rowland 2007), and contributed to the fertility decline in the late nineteenth century and in the first four decades of the twentieth century. More recently, the decline in fertility among the cohorts of women born in the 1950s and 1960s has been accompanied by rising childlessness levels (e.g., Frejka and Sardon 2004). Most of the social, economic, and cultural trends of the last 45 years appear to steer women away from having children. Easy access to modern contraception—including to emergency post-coital contraception, which first became available in the late 1990s—has vastly expanded the ability of couples to decide whether and when to become parents, and has arguably made it more likely that they will choose to remain childless (van de Kaa 1997). While the educational attainment of women lagged behind that of men well into the 1980s, women are now more likely than their male counterparts to earn a tertiary degree in all countries of Europe except Switzerland (VID 2014). Moreover, women currently have relatively high rates of labour participation, even in the countries of southern Europe, where in the past the majority of women remained outside of the labour market (OECD 2011; Thévenon 2009). While young women now almost universally expect to be employed throughout their life (Goldin 2006), family policies and employers have only partly adjusted to women's new aspirations. Also their male partners have yet to fully adjust: although men are now more involved in parenting, cooking, and housework than in the past (Hook 2006), there is still a large gap in the

T. Sobotka (✉)
Vienna Institute of Demography, Austrian Academy of Sciences and Wittgenstein Centre for Demography and Global Human Capital, Welthandelsplatz 2, Level 2, Vienna 1020, Austria
e-mail: tomas.sobotka@oeaw.ac.at

© The Author(s) 2017
M. Kreyenfeld, D. Konietzka (eds.), *Childlessness in Europe: Contexts, Causes, and Consequences*, Demographic Research Monographs,
DOI 10.1007/978-3-319-44667-7_2

amount of unpaid work done by men and women, and especially by fathers and mothers. This "incomplete gender revolution" (Esping-Andersen 2009) forces some women to make difficult choices between having a career and being a parent (Thévenon 2009). The nature of the labour market has also changed in recent decades: as the market has become more competitive, more demanding, and less secure, younger women and men are often working in temporary and poorly paid stop-gap jobs (McDonald 2002; Mills and Blossfeld 2005). This lack of secure employment had led many young adults to postpone marriage and parenthood.

In addition, the broad-based shift in values related to reproduction and marriage, and the related changes in partnership behaviour known as the "second demographic transition" (Lesthaeghe 2010), can also be expected to lead to higher rates of childlessness. In their analysis of European survey data, Merz and Liefbroer (2012) found that approval of voluntary childlessness was closely related to the progression of the second demographic transition, with respondents in Norway, Denmark, and the Netherlands expressing the most positive views on voluntary childlessness.

Some observers have suggested that childlessness has become the status most compatible with contemporary society. A single individual unhindered by family commitments is the winner in the race for the greatest career and material success in life (McDonald 2002). According to Beck (1992: 116), "the ultimate market society is a childless society." Such an alarmist perspective can, however, be countered by pointing to the low shares of survey respondents who declare that childlessness is their reproductive ideal (Miettinen and Szalma 2014; Sobotka and Beaujouan 2014; see also Kuhnt et al., Chap. 11, in this volume). In most countries, the share of younger men and women surveyed who express a firm intention to remain childless stays low. In their analysis of Eurobarometer data, Miettinen and Szalma (2014) reported that between 2008 and 2011 the share of female respondents aged 18–40 across the European Union who said they did not intend to have children was unchanged, at 5 % (see, however, Sobotka and Testa 2008 for some contrasting examples based on a different survey). Rather than being consistently planned from a young age, childlessness is often driven by a mix of adverse circumstances and adjustments to unforeseen events, such as infertility, poor health, not having a right partner, and partnership dissolution (Gray et al. 2013; Heaton et al. 1999). Many women and men of reproductive age therefore adopt a strategy of perpetually postponing childbearing (Berrington 2004), which increases the likelihood that they will gradually become adapted to their "childfree" lifestyle, and will eventually lose interest in having a child (Rindfuss et al. 1988; Veevers 1980). On the whole, it appears to be much more common for childless adults to express uncertainty about their reproductive plans than to claim they have chosen to be childless (Ní Bhrolcháin and Beaujouan 2011).

But are the theoretical expectations about rising childlessness in Europe actually supported by empirical trends? Is childlessness reaching unprecedented levels, as alarmist warnings that Europeans are no longer willing to reproduce appear to suggest? And is the prevalence of permanent childlessness becoming increasingly the same across Europe? Although a vast body of literature has examined period and cohort fertility trends across Europe, empirical research on childlessness among women and men is typically limited to studies of individual countries. Several cross-country studies published in the past decade generated broad evidence that may be used to address these questions. These studies were based on census and register data (Rowland 2007), cohort data derived from reconstructed series of period fertility rates (Dorbritz and Ruckdeschel 2007; Frejka and Sardon 2004), or a mixture of different data sources (Miettinen et al. 2015). In this study, I take advantage of the rapid growth in recent years in the availability of data on cohort fertility and cohort parity distribution. By combining different datasets, I aim to provide the most detailed evidence to date on childlessness in Europe. I reconstruct the long-term development of childlessness in 30 European countries among women who were born between the beginning of the twentieth century and 1972. I discuss the trends in individual countries and broader European regions, the degree of historical continuity, and the main reversals in trends. I also analyse shifts in the geographic differentiation in childlessness, as until recently there was a clear east-west divide, with central and eastern Europe having unusually low childlessness levels. I focus on permanent childlessness among women, as the available data on men are much more limited, and are of uncertain quality (see below). In conclusion, I suggest that the childlessness levels among women born around 1970 are not unusually high when compared with those of their counterparts born in the early twentieth century.

2.2 Data and Methods

2.2.1 Reliability of Childlessness Estimates

Data on childlessness can be derived from different sources, including census and survey data that ask respondents about their number of children ever born, register data that include the childbearing or parenthood histories of the resident population, and vital statistics data on births by birth order that make it possible to reconstruct cohort fertility trends over long periods of time. Because each of these sources has potential advantages and drawbacks, there has been considerable uncertainty about childlessness estimates. Even very similar data sources (such as two consecutive censuses) can yield large differences in estimates of final childlessness in the same cohort of women. These discrepancies have been attributed to slight differences in the questions asked about the number of children, migration between censuses, differential mortality, and selective non-response.

Because the degree of uncertainty about the prevalence of final childlessness is particularly high among men, who can reproduce for a much longer period of their life than women, and for whom the relevant data are frequently missing, this study concentrates on childlessness among women. Even among women, a key issue is deciding at what point in their life course childlessness can be seen as permanent or almost final (Kreyenfeld and Konietzka 2007). Because of advances in assisted reproduction, European women are now more often having their first child after age 40, and a few women have even given birth in their 50s or 60s. The Eurostat database (2015) recorded 334 cases of women having a child at age 50 or older in 2013; such cases were much rarer until the early 2000s. But the important question is at what age the number of first births becomes so small that it no longer makes a real difference in childlessness estimates. The same dataset shows that of the first births in the European Union in 2013, 15.4 % were to a mother over age 35, and 2.8 % were to a mother over age 40; this share falls to 1.1 % after age 42 and 0.1 % after age 46. Thus, it can be argued that childlessness among women is virtually permanent by age 46, and that, with a small degree of uncertainty, the final number can be established among women by age 42, when 99 % of first births have been realised.

As census data are available for some countries up to 2011, and vital statistics data are available up to 2013 or 2014, childlessness can be reliably estimated for women who were born around 1970 or earlier. Thus, the current analysis does not look at the experiences of the more recent cohorts, who have been in their peak reproductive years since around 2000. A number of previous studies attempted to make projections of final childlessness for the cohorts of women who, at the time, were in their late 30s or even younger, typically using the most recent period first birth rates to estimate the share of women who would have their first child in the future (e.g., Dorbritz and Ruckdeschel 2007; Frejka and Sardon 2004; Morgan and Chen 1992; Sobotka 2005). The accuracy of these predictions was mixed, with many studies overestimating the levels of final childlessness in recent cohorts. The biggest challenge researchers faced was in capturing the process of the recovery of postponed first birth rates at late childbearing ages, as the number of first births among women who were over age 35 was rising. The simplest projection method used—i.e., freezing the most recently observed period first birth rates—typically resulted in an underestimation of the first birth rates at these ages, and thus an overestimation of the levels and rates of increase of childlessness among the youngest cohorts. It can therefore be argued that predicting cohort childlessness is problematic, as the results are often misleading (Rindfuss et al. 1988). However, these studies often employed projection methods that were too simple, and relatively little effort has been put into determining which projection methods yield the most reliable estimates (the paper by Morgan and Chen 1992 is the main exception).

2.2.2 Data Sources on Permanent Childlessness: Drawbacks and Advantages

Before discussing the data used in this study, I outline the general advantages and disadvantages of different data sources on childlessness. These observations pertain to most of the historical data analysed here. In recent years, these distinctions between different data sources have been becoming more artificial, as register-based data are increasingly used to generate population census results (register-based censuses) as well as vital statistics records.

Population Census Data which include responses to the question on the number of children ever born, usually cover the entire female population of reproductive and post-reproductive ages (typically, ages 15+). These data also constitute the most accessible source of information on permanent childlessness. They typically cover the whole population (although some censuses, e.g., the Polish census of 2002, asked only a selected sample of women about family and reproduction), and thus allow detailed cohort-by-cohort comparisons of childlessness. As the censuses often collect information on a large number of socio-economic and demographic characteristics of the population, these data can also be used to conduct a detailed analysis of the main factors associated with childlessness (e.g., Burkimsher and Zeman, Chap. 6, in this volume), including educational attainment (Brzozowska et al. 2016).

Census data can, however, be affected by higher or lower mortality among childless women, giving a distorted picture of permanent childlessness among older women, especially if they experienced higher mortality during their reproductive ages or lived through wars and major upheavals. Because census data (like survey and register data) provide only a snapshot of the "current population", they offer no information on women who left the country, while providing data on family size of women who recently moved into the country, including children they gave birth to before migrating. The influence of migration can be addressed with more detailed analyses that take into account women's migration status, but the data needed to conduct such analyses are often not published or available. Moreover, in a census a woman may misreport the total number of children she has (especially if one or more of her children died in infancy or childhood), or may fail respond to the question on the number of children she has ever had. The rate of non-response is often not proportionally distributed with respect to parity: especially in countries where childlessness is perceived as being undesirable, childless women often do not respond to the question on the number of children they have.[1] Whether there is a bias in reporting can be determined by checking the correlation between the share of women who are childless and the non-response rate in the data. When this correlation is strong, it is safe to assume most of the non-responses are due to childless women who failed to report their status. If it is assumed that all of the missing responses came from childless women, a simple adjustment can be made (El-Badry 1961). As this adjustment is likely to produce estimates of childlessness that are unrealistically high, more sophisticated imputation methods, including those based on regression techniques, are preferable. Such methods have, for example, been used to estimate childlessness in German micro-census surveys (e.g., Statistisches Bundesamt 2015). Finally, population censuses only rarely ask men about the number of children they have.

---

[1] This bias can be further strengthened by the questionnaire design. For instance, in the Czech Republic, childless women frequently leave the response on children ever born blank instead of writing "0" in the respective box (Zeman 2013).

Survey Data Generally, survey data have the same strengths as census data, but have additional weaknesses. As these data are often based on a small sample of the population (typically, several thousand respondents), cohort childlessness estimates made on the basis of these data are unstable and unsuitable for more detailed analyses. In addition, because many survey samples are not representative of the total female population with respect to family size, they may provide biased estimates of childlessness. In particular, survey non-response can produce distorted estimates of childlessness. The challenges of collecting survey data on childlessness are best illustrated by a discussion by Murphy (2009) and Ní Bhrolcháin et al. (2011). They attempted to explain a sudden rise in childlessness reported in some rounds of the UK General Household Surveys, and discussed a range of possible explanations, including differential response rates, changing non-response rates, changing sample designs, deliberate misreporting, and changes in survey procedures. Overall, it is preferable to use large-scale surveys with low non-response rates, as these surveys can eliminate the biases typical of surveys with smaller sample sizes.

Collecting data on childlessness among men is even more challenging, partly because men tend to underreport their children from previous marriages and partnerships (Rendall et al. 1999), and partly because they have a longer reproductive period. Thus, the only sources of data on childlessness among men are often smaller scale surveys, such as the Fertility and Family Surveys (FFS) conducted in the 1990s and the Generation and Gender Surveys (GGS) conducted since the early 2000s (e.g., Miettinen et al. 2015).

Population Register Data In Europe, a number of countries, including Nordic countries, Baltic countries, the Netherlands and Slovenia, have established population registers that contain records on demographic events for all of the residents in the country. These are in theory the most accurate and efficient sources of information on childlessness. Because they can be merged with other registers, they provide a broad scope for detailed analyses of the determinants of childlessness (for an excellent analysis of the educational gradient in childlessness and cohort fertility in the Nordic countries, see Andersson et al. 2009). However, using demographic register data for analysing childlessness has two main limitations. The first is that it is difficult to cover the reproductive histories of the entire population, especially those of migrant women, for whom the number of children they gave birth to before arriving in the country may not be known or reported. A partial solution to this problem is to measure fertility and childlessness only among women who were born in the country. The second limitation pertains to data access: to ensure the protection of data and confidentiality, many countries make accessing their register data difficult, and often also costly. Thus, obtaining register-based data on childlessness is not easy in countries that do not routinely publish these estimates.

Vital Statistics Data Statistical offices of almost all European countries now collect data on live births by age of the mother, year of birth of the mother, and birth order of the child. In combination with the official estimates of the female population by age and year of birth, these data can be used for estimating fertility rates by the child's birth order and age of the mother. These data can then be cumulated over long periods of time and used to estimate cohort childlessness and parity distribution. This approach has often been used in the past, including by Frejka and colleagues (e.g., Frejka and Sardon 2004, 2006, 2007; Frejka et al. 2010), Heuser (1976), Sobotka (2005), and Dorbritz and Ruckdeschel (2007). The estimates of childlessness and parity distribution based on period vital statistics data are also featured in the Human Fertility Database.

However, approaches based on cumulating time series of period vital statistics to obtain childlessness data also have several drawbacks. The first one is obvious: to reconstruct the entire childbearing history of a single birth cohort, it is necessary to accumulate over 30 years of fertility data, starting from around age 15. Such long time series often are not available, either because birth order is not continually reported in birth records, or because in the past many countries collected birth order information only for women who gave birth within marriage. Several countries, including Germany and the United Kingdom, have only recently started collecting data on biological birth order. Childlessness estimates derived from the period data are also very sensitive to the quality of birth order statistics. Data quality problems, such as a high share of births with an unknown birth order, the publication of the birth order for 5-year age groups only (this practice was common in the past in some of the countries of the former Yugoslavia and the Soviet Union), and the incorrect or inconsistent reporting of biological birth order (this practice is common in France) make the resulting cohort childlessness estimates volatile and often useless. Furthermore, period data only contain the records on births that took place in the country: fertility for emigrants is included, but only before the date when they left the country, and the reproductive histories of immigrants are ignored up to the date when they arrived in the country. Thus, the cohort fertility histories created in this way are somewhat artificial, and may not reflect the actual childlessness of the residents in countries with high immigration or emigration, especially if the fertility behaviour of migrants differs from the behaviour of the "stayers". Finally, the estimates of the female population distribution by age might be strongly affected by incomplete reporting of migration. For instance, incomplete reporting of emigration can affect statistics on the entire female population of reproductive age (as is the case for some countries of central and eastern Europe (CEE) with high levels of emigration, including Poland) or of specific population groups, such as immigrant women (as is the case for Germany; Pötzsch 2016). This in turns inflates the registered number of women of reproductive age, which leads to an underestimation of period and cohort fertility rates, and, consequently, to an overestimation of childlessness. For these reasons, childlessness estimates based on period vital statistics should be used with caution. While such estimates may accurately reflect the average level of childlessness in the long run, they may be unstable or have implausibly low values for some cohorts. This is, for instance, the case in the estimated time series of lifetime childlessness in the Human Fertility Database for some CEE countries, including Bulgaria and Estonia (HFD 2015a).

Census or large sample survey data are often used in combination with the subsequent vital statistics. This approach, which is frequently used in this chapter, makes use of the comprehensive picture of childlessness among many different cohorts provided in the censuses, and then extends it using more recent data covering the period for which the census records are not available.

To illustrate the extent to which different data sources often yield different estimates of final childlessness, let us consider the data for Romania and Spain presented in Fig. 2.1, or the different estimates of childlessness for the United States discussed by Frejka (Chap. 8, in this volume). The data for Romania are mostly drawn from censuses taken between 1977 and 2011, although the data from the 2002 census are combined for the younger cohorts with the vital statistics data for 2002–2013. While the censuses of 1992 and 2002 closely overlap and give very similar estimates of final childlessness, the census of 1977 gives lower childlessness estimates for the women born in the 1920s, whereas the most recent census of 2011 gives much higher estimates of childlessness for the women born in the 1920s–1950s. For instance, women born in 1927 had a childlessness rate of 15 % in the 1977 census, of 18 % in the censuses of 1992 and 2002, and of 23 % in the most recent census of 2011. It is unlikely that selective emigration plays a role in this discrepancy (as it is implausible that women with children would have been leaving the country at a higher rate than childless women). Likewise, it is unlikely that women with children would have had a mortality rate that was so much higher than that of childless women that their share in the population of older woman would have declined so rapidly. Similar discrepancies can be found in the data for Spain: the more recent census data for 2011 show higher rates of childlessness than the 1991 census data, and the childlessness rates reconstructed from vital statistics records are much lower (and are also less stable) than they are in both census datasets. In this case, immigration might have played some role, as Spain experienced an unprecedented wave of immigration between the late 1990s and 2010 (Verdugo and Swanson 2011): the higher childlessness estimates in the more recent census likely reflect the fact that many female immigrants to Spain were childless when they arrived in the country.

2.2.3 Country Coverage, Data, and Assumptions Employed

This study presents childlessness estimates for European countries with populations over one million; in total I have assembled datasets for 30 countries. I could not find reliable data or longer time series for Albania, Bosnia and Herzegovina, Kosovo, Latvia, Macedonia, and Serbia; these countries are therefore not included in the analysis. For the United Kingdom, data are available for England and Wales only. Because eastern and western Germany were separate countries in 1949–1990, and continue to have distinct fertility patterns, I analyse the data for these two regions separately, alongside the dataset for Germany as a whole. To capture the main differences between major parts of Europe, I also study trends for six larger European

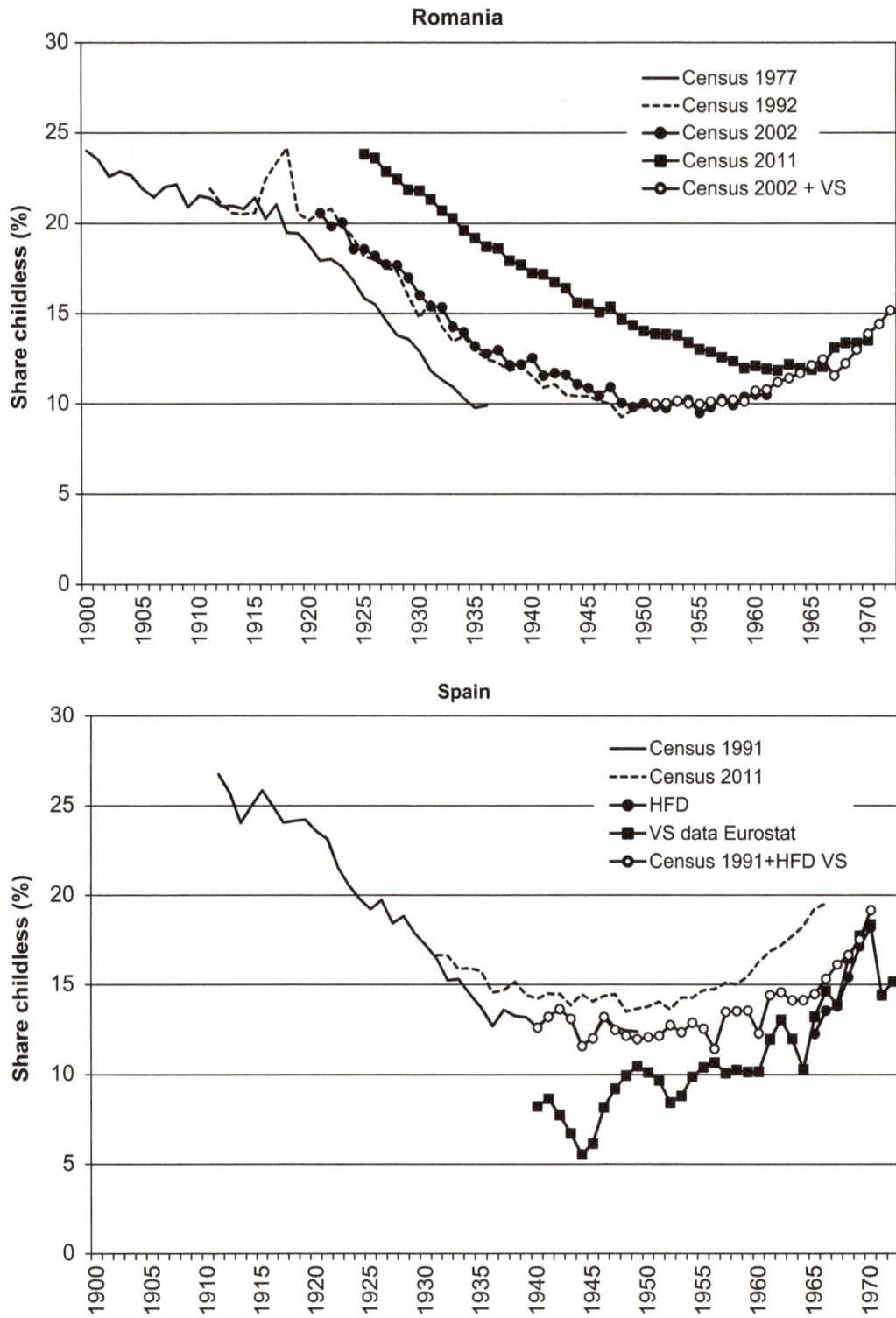

Fig. 2.1 Estimates of permanent childlessness in Romania and Spain among women born in 1900–1972; a comparison of different data sources. Notes: *HFD* Human Fertility Database (2015b), *VS* vital statistics (Sources: see Appendix 1)

regions that have had distinct fertility patterns in the past (Sobotka 2013): western Europe, the Nordic countries, southern Europe, the predominantly German-speaking countries of Europe (Austria, Germany, and Switzerland), central Europe, and a broad region of eastern and south-eastern Europe. The latter two regions are composed of the former state-socialist countries of central and eastern Europe (CEE).

For most of the countries, I have found multiple datasets on permanent childlessness (see the examples for Romania and Spain in Fig. 2.1). Combining them allowed me to reconstruct long-term series of cohort childlessness. However, having multiple datasets for identical cohorts also meant that I had to select some datasets over others, as I present only one figure for each of the analysed cohorts in each country.[2] In the selection procedure I followed a set of simple rules, which were based in part on the data issues and preferences outlined above. The selected datasets are listed in Appendix 1. The selection rules are as follows:

- Longer data series that show permanent childlessness for many cohorts are preferred.
- The time series that overlap closely with other available data (e.g., Romanian census data for 1992 and 2002 in Fig. 2.1) are preferred.
- The more stable datasets that show "plausible" ranges of childlessness are preferred (specifically, datasets that exclude data suggesting that childlessness levels are below 4 %, as these levels are implausible given that the permanent sterility is 2–3 %). This means giving preference to census data over vital statistics-based estimates. The drawback of this approach is that the availability of census data for the most recent round of censuses in 2011 is limited, as many countries either switched to conducting the census based entirely on population registers and other administrative registers, which often do not allow for the reconstruction of the parity structure of women (e.g., in Austria); or the organisers decided not to include the question on the number of children ever born in the census.
- Survey data are used only when the datasets are large, and only for countries where population-based datasets were unavailable (France and Germany).
- A hybrid approach of combining census data (mostly for the censuses around 1991 and 2001) and the time series based on vital statistics for the subsequent period is used to derive an estimate of childlessness for the most recent period (usually for 1 January 2014).

Age Ranges I present childlessness estimates as "final" when they pertain to women aged 42 or older; for some CEE countries, I have also included data for women aged 41, as these countries still have very low first birth rates among women at higher ages. In six countries (Austria, the Czech Republic, England and Wales, Italy, Spain, and Switzerland) I have used a simple trend projection based on the first birth probabilities by age to estimate permanent childlessness among women

---

[2] I considered the option of presenting multiple datasets for the same cohort, but this would make cross-country and regional comparisons more difficult, and would also require much more space for data presentation, exceeding the scope of this study.

who were born prior to 1972, and for whom the data were available up to ages 40 or 41. At these ages the potential margin of error for such a projection is very small—well below the degree of uncertainty in estimates of childlessness levels based on different data sources. The census and survey data considered in the analysis were for women who were under age 80 at the time of the census, as above that age the selectivity due to differential mortality was assumed to be too large.

Redistributing Women with Unknown Parity When the number of women with unknown parity was available in the published datasets, they were usually assumed to have the same parity distribution as the women whose parity was recorded. Therefore, childlessness was computed only for the women for whom the parity distribution was reported. Usually, this assumption was not critical for estimating childlessness, as in most countries the share of women with unknown parity was typically below 1 %. However, in many of the available datasets the number of women with unknown parity distribution was not reported, and it is often unclear whether any specific assumptions for these women were applied by the national statistical offices that processed and published these data. Finally, some census data show that there is a close correlation between the share of childless women and the share of women with unknown or unreported birth order; in these cases, all of the women with unknown birth order are assumed to be childless (see Appendix 1).

Main Data Sources The data sources selected for each of the countries are detailed in Appendix 1. For some countries, the data came from census tabulations or other estimates published by national statistical offices or were provided by the researchers working with these datasets (see Appendix 1 and the acknowledgements). Here I outline the main sources, which were used for multiple countries. For the census data, there are two key sources: the census-based tabulations of the parity distribution of women provided in the input datasets in the Human Fertility Database (HFD 2015b), and the tabulations of the parity distribution of women aged 40–80 by cohort and education provided in the Cohort Fertility and Education database (CFE 2015; Zeman et al. 2014). The HFD census-based tabulations were available for 11 countries and territories: Belarus, Bulgaria, the Czech Republic, Estonia, eastern Germany, Lithuania, Portugal, Russia, Slovakia, Slovenia, and Ukraine.[3] The CFE data were available for Croatia, the Czech Republic, Hungary, Ireland, Poland, Romania, Russia, Slovakia, and Spain.

In addition to the census data, the HFD also contains annual register-based or official estimates of the parity composition of women by age for Finland, Hungary, the Netherlands, Norway, and Sweden. These estimates were used for selected years in this study (Appendix 1). The key sources of the childlessness estimates based on vital statistics are the Human Fertility Database (2015a) and the author's own

---

[3] These data are not part of the main HFD "output" datasets, as their purpose is to provide estimates of the parity distribution of women of reproductive age, serving as an input for constructing fertility tables in the database.

computations based on the Eurostat online database (2015). In theory, the time series of period data on fertility by birth order from the Human Fertility Collection (HFC 2015) can also be used to generate estimates of lifetime childlessness, but for most European countries these estimates either cover relatively few cohorts or are too unstable to be used for that purpose.

2.3 Long-Term Developments in Childlessness in Europe: Evidence for 30 Countries

The presentation of long-term developments in childlessness in 30 European countries is nested within six broader regions that reflect the major geographic and cultural divisions of Europe, but also the geopolitical division of east and west that prevailed in Europe until 1989. These divisions are apparent in European fertility patterns, including childlessness (e.g., Sobotka 2011). In the next section, I summarise the major regional differences and discuss the between-country heterogeneity in childlessness in Europe.

In western Europe, childlessness trends have followed an asymmetric U-shaped pattern, starting from very high levels among women born in the first quarter of the twentieth century, reaching low levels among women born in the mid-1940s, and then rising again, especially among women born in the 1950s (Fig. 2.2). The level of childlessness reached around 25 % among French women born around 1900, Belgian woman born in 1910, and Irish women born in 1925 (earlier data are not available). Childlessness levels then declined substantially, to 10–14 % among the early- to mid-1940s cohorts, most of whom had their first child in the 1960s, i.e., during the later stages of western European baby boom. The subsequent increases in childlessness were steepest in the Netherlands and England and Wales, whereas in France the level of childlessness rose gradually; today France has the lowest childlessness rate in the region, of 14 % among women born in the second half of the 1960s. Among the 1960s cohorts there was a clear stabilisation in childlessness levels, with England and Wales even reporting a decline; among the late 1960s cohorts, 16–19 % of women in Belgium, Ireland, the Netherlands, and England and Wales remained childless (see also Berrington, Chap. 3, in this volume).

The childlessness patterns were similar in the Nordic countries, starting from high levels around 25 % among women born around 1910 (data available for Finland and Sweden only) and reaching much lower levels among those born in the 1940s. As in France, childlessness levels then increased gradually (see Köppen et al., Chap. 4, in this volume). Among women in Denmark, Norway, and Sweden who were born in 1970, the childlessness levels are 12–14 %. In Finland childlessness rates rose more sharply, with one out of five women born in 1968 remaining childless (see Rotkirch and Miettinen, Chap. 7, in this volume).

The three predominantly German-speaking countries, together with southern Europe, make up the group of countries with the highest levels of childlessness in

Western Europe

Nordic countries

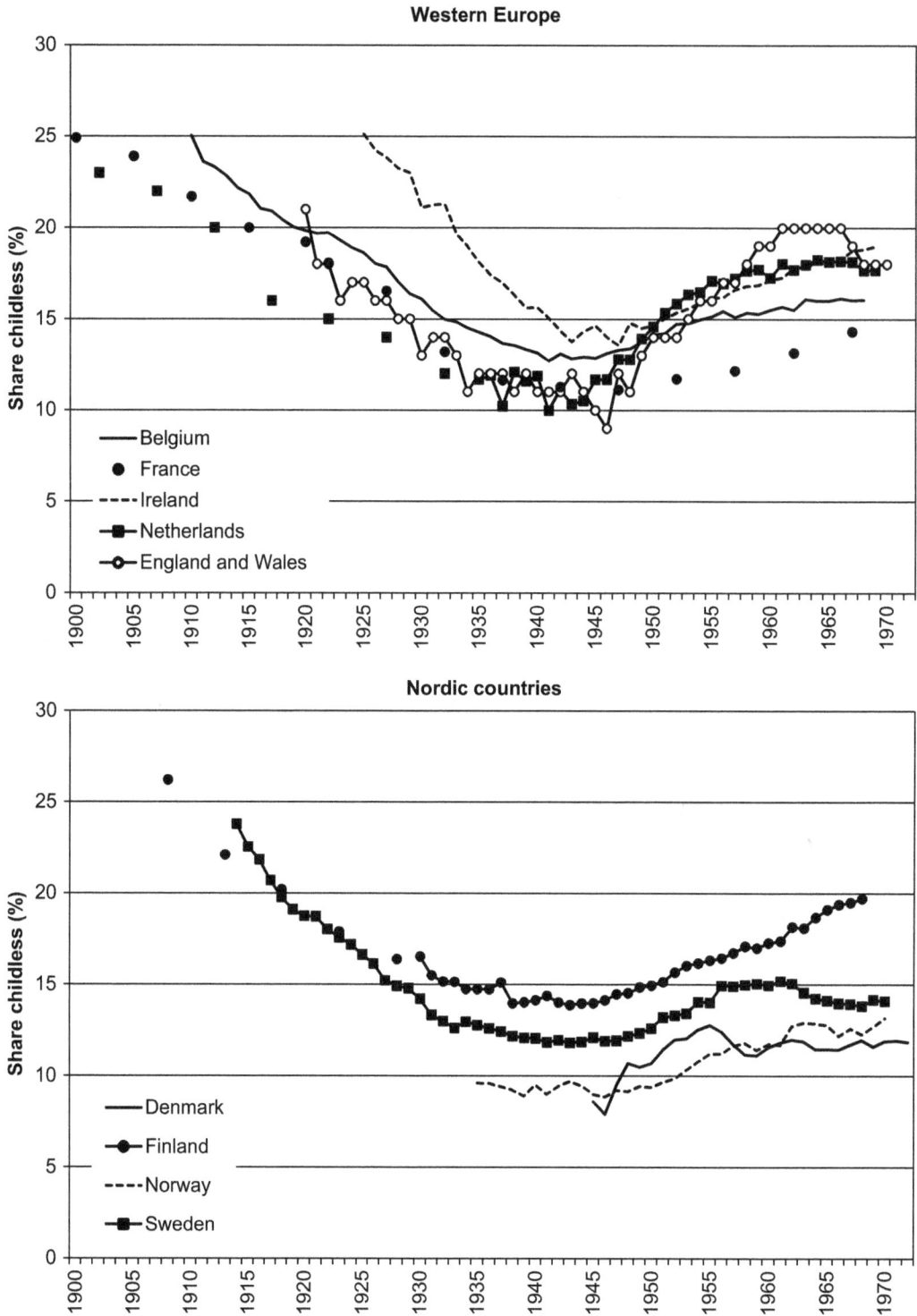

Fig. 2.2 Childlessness among women born in 1900–1972; western European and Nordic countries (in %). Notes: For each country and cohort only one data source was selected; the alternative datasets are not shown (see Sect. 2.2.3). For women who were born in the late 1960s and the early 1970s a small portion of their first birth rates (after age 42) is either estimated or disregarded (Sources: detailed sources by country are listed in Appendix 1)

Europe. In the German-speaking countries, childlessness increased sharply among women who were born in the 1950s and 1960s, and has been especially prevalent among women who have a tertiary education (Sobotka 2012). In Switzerland and Germany, the rates of childlessness exceeded 20 % in the late 1960s cohorts. In Germany, the fertility patterns in the eastern and in the western parts of the country have long been distinct, partly mirroring the broader differences between the former state-socialist countries and other regions of Europe (Goldstein and Kreyenfeld 2011; Kreyenfeld 2004; see also Bernardi and Keim-Klärner, Chap. 12, in this volume). Until recently, levels of childlessness were far lower in eastern than in western Germany: just 8–12 % of eastern German women born between the 1930s and the early 1960s were childless. While the results of the micro-census surveys of 2008 and 2012 indicate that this east-west gap had become much smaller among the 1960s cohorts (Fig. 2.3), western German women of the late 1960s cohorts had the highest childlessness levels in Europe; of around 25 % among those born in 1969. Over the past century, childlessness trends in western Germany have followed a U-shaped pattern: the level was around 26 % among the cohorts born in the early twentieth century, declined to less than 13 % among the mid-1940s cohorts, and then almost doubled among the women born over the next 25 years. But while recent estimates showing that 23–24 % of German women born in the late 1960s have remained childless seem high, these figures are actually lower than many estimates based on the smaller sample survey data analysed prior to the recent rounds of the micro-census surveys (e.g., Dorbritz and Ruckdeschel 2007). In Switzerland, it appears that childlessness levels peaked at around 22 %, and were lower among women born around 1970. However, these estimates are partly based on vital statistics, and are not fully in line with evidence from other data sources (for a more detailed analysis, see Burkimsher and Zeman, Chap. 6, in this volume).

In southern Europe, the long-term childlessness trends in the two largest countries, Italy and Spain, were similar: the childlessness levels were around 25 % among the cohorts born in the early twentieth century, declined gradually to around 11–12 % among the cohorts born in the early 1950s, and then increased sharply among the cohorts born in the 1960s and early 1970s, surpassing 20 %. This pattern reflects that the decline in fertility in southern Europe occurred later than the decreases observed in western and northern Europe, but also that the decline has been more severe in the south: among women born in 1972, the completed fertility rates in Italy and Spain are estimated to be the lowest in Europe, at 1.45 and 1.43 children per woman, respectively. Greece appears to be on a similar trajectory. By contrast, the level of childlessness in Portugal is considerably lower, estimated at around 12 % among women born in 1968. While the country currently has the lowest period total fertility rate in Europe, of 1.21 in 2013, this development is not yet reflected in the childlessness trends examined here. In addition, it appears that the cohort fertility decline in Portugal has mainly been characterised by a rapid spread of one-child families, with an estimated 36 % of women born in 1968 having only one child (computations based on Human Fertility Database).

In central, eastern, and south-eastern Europe, childlessness trends differed sharply from those in other parts of Europe among women born in the 1940s to

Austria, Germany, Switzerland

Southern Europe

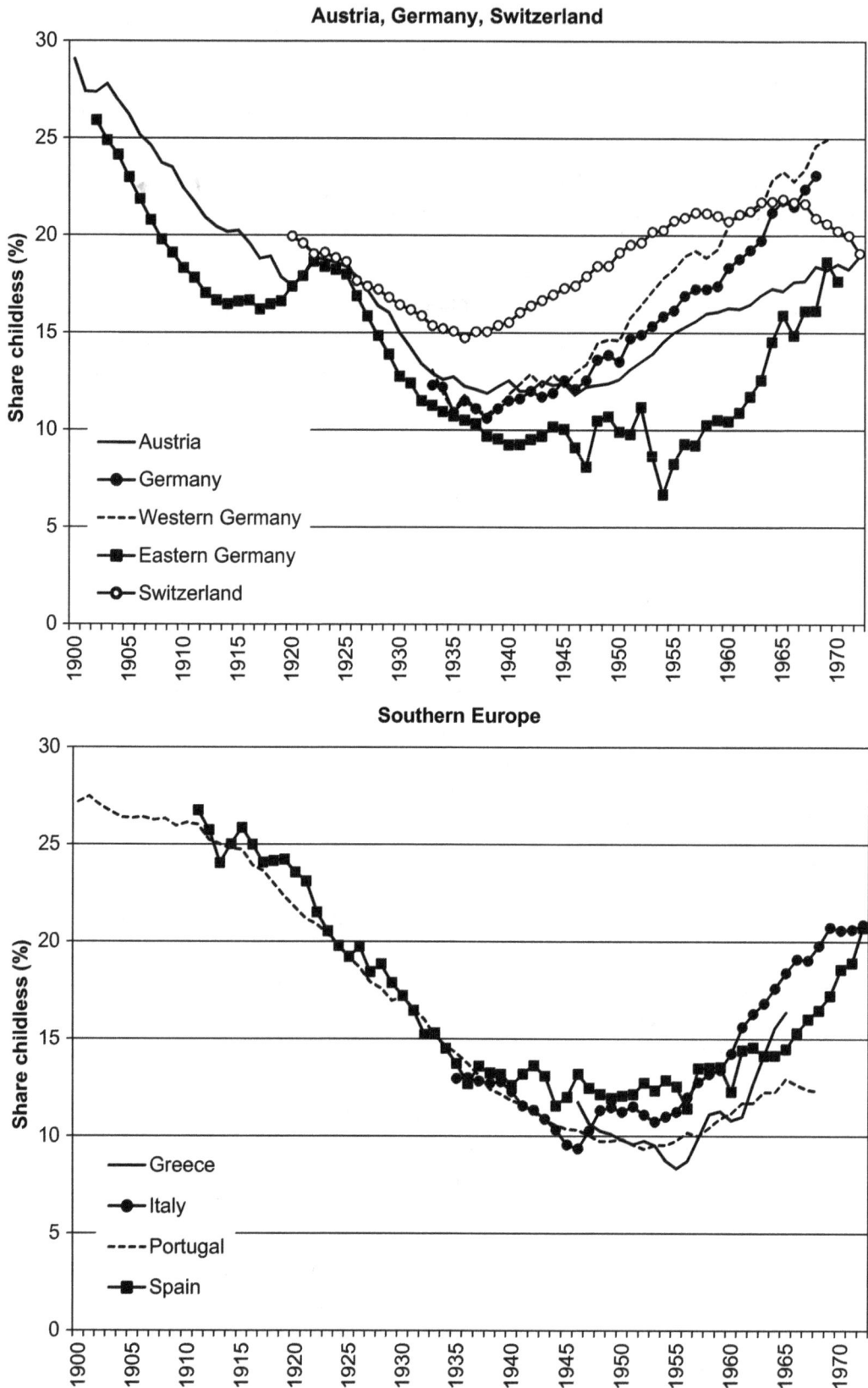

Fig. 2.3 Childlessness among women born in 1900–1972; Austria, Germany, Switzerland, and southern Europe (in %) (Notes and sources: see Fig. 2.2)

mid-1960s. Among these cohorts, childlessness levels were not only very low (estimated in most countries at 5–10 %); they were also much more stable than in the rest of Europe, where childlessness was rising. This pattern can be seen as one of the key features of reproduction under state socialism in the CEE region in the 1950–1980s. A wide range of social and economic factors contributed to this pattern of universal family formation: low average age at marriage and childbearing, negative attitudes towards childlessness, insufficient availability of modern contraception (which resulted in large numbers of unplanned pregnancies and "shotgun marriages"), the relative predictability of the life course, the lack of labour market competition, and the relatively consistent availability of institutional childcare (Sobotka 2011, 2015). With some exceptions (especially in Romania), childlessness was rare among women of all educational groups, suggesting that labour market participation did not pose a major barrier to family life in the region (Brzozowska et al. 2016).

Some CEE countries stand out for their particularly low levels of childlessness: among women in Belarus, Bulgaria, Czech Republic, and Russia who were born in the 1950s (and thus had their first child mainly in the 1970s or the 1980s) the levels of childlessness were 5–6 %; or just a few percentage points above the estimated level of lifetime sterility (Leridon 2008). The highest childlessness levels in the CEE countries among these cohorts, of around 9–10 %, were recorded in Estonia, Romania, and Slovakia. These levels were, however, still well below those in most other parts of Europe. However, childlessness levels are higher among the youngest CEE women analysed, especially among those born at the turn of the 1960s and 1970s, who realised most of their reproduction in the post-communist transition era of the 1990s. While childlessness has been rising in all of the CEE countries, particularly sharp increases have been observed in Romania: according to a recent estimate, around 15 % of Romanian women born in the early 1970s are childless. This estimate is, however, tentative, as it is based on cohort fertility rates reconstructed from period vital statistics. These computations involve estimating the female population of reproductive age who are resident in the country in each year, which can be particularly challenging in countries with high rates of emigration, such as Poland and Romania (Sect. 2.2.2) (Fig. 2.4).

2.4 Diversity and Contrasts in Childlessness Trends: Countries and Broader European Regions

The analysis of childlessness trends for all countries presented above may not clearly illustrate the main differences between broader European regions. Figure 2.5 shows changes in childlessness in Europe, averaging data for all available countries, and also depicts regional averages of childlessness for the six broader regions analysed above. These regional averages are based on data for selected countries for which long-term series were available. This analysis is also accompanied by selected

Central Europe

Eastern & Southeast Europe

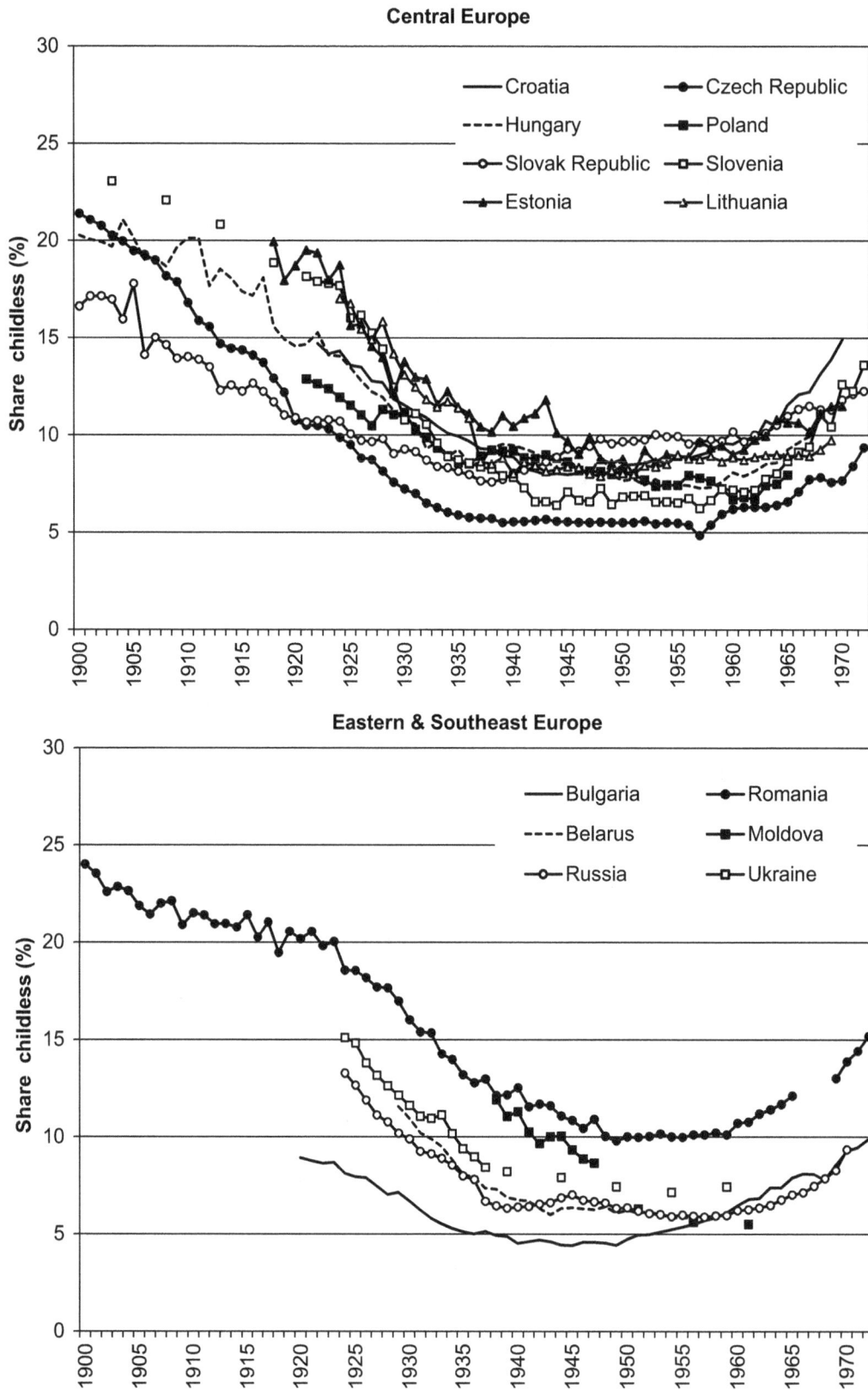

Fig. 2.4 Childlessness among women born in 1900–1972; central, eastern, and south-eastern Europe (in %) (Notes and sources: see Fig. 2.2)

European regions

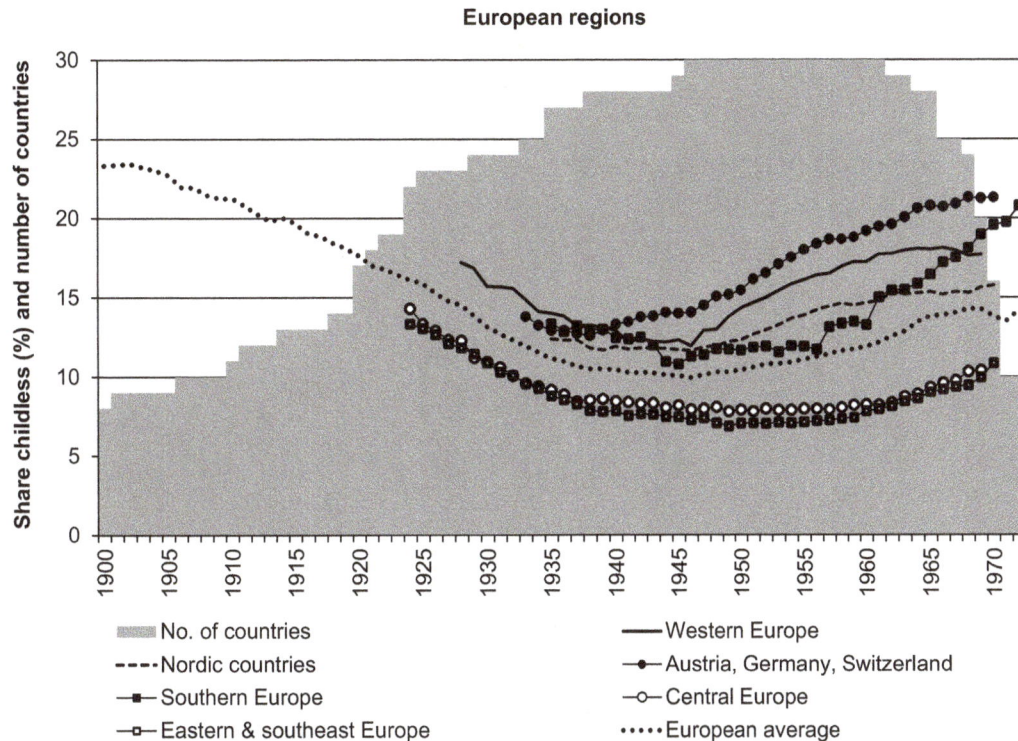

Fig. 2.5 Childlessness in Europe among women born in 1900–1972 (average for all countries with available data, in percent) and in six broader European regions (average for selected countries). Notes: European average is an average level of childlessness in all countries for which data were available in a given year. The regional data are unweighted averages based on selected countries for which longer time series of data were available. The selected countries are as follows: western Europe: Belgium, England and Wales, Ireland, and the Netherlands; Nordic countries: Finland, Norway, and Sweden; southern Europe: Italy and Spain; central Europe: Croatia, Czech Republic, Estonia, Hungary, Lithuania, Poland, Slovakia, and Slovenia; eastern and south-eastern Europe: Bulgaria, Romania, and Russia (Sources: detailed sources by country are listed in Appendix 1)

summary indicators of cross-country heterogeneity in childlessness in Europe in selected cohorts born between 1900 and 1968 (Fig. 2.6).

These data provide clear evidence that childlessness levels were high across Europe in the course of the demographic transition, in line with the findings of Rowland (2007). Women who were born in the early twentieth century had very high childlessness levels, as the family formation plans of many women were disrupted by the economic depression of the 1930s and by a lack of male partners after the First World War. Childlessness levels of women born between 1900 and 1911 approached or exceeded 20 % in all of the 13 countries with available data except Slovakia.

In various European countries and regions, the pattern of childlessness over the past century was U-shaped. In most countries, the lowest levels are observed among women born around 1940. These women were starting a family in the prosperous era of the early- to mid-1960s; a time when most women still fully embraced the "traditional" family model based on marriage and the strong division of gender roles. On average, only around 10 % of European women of these cohorts remained

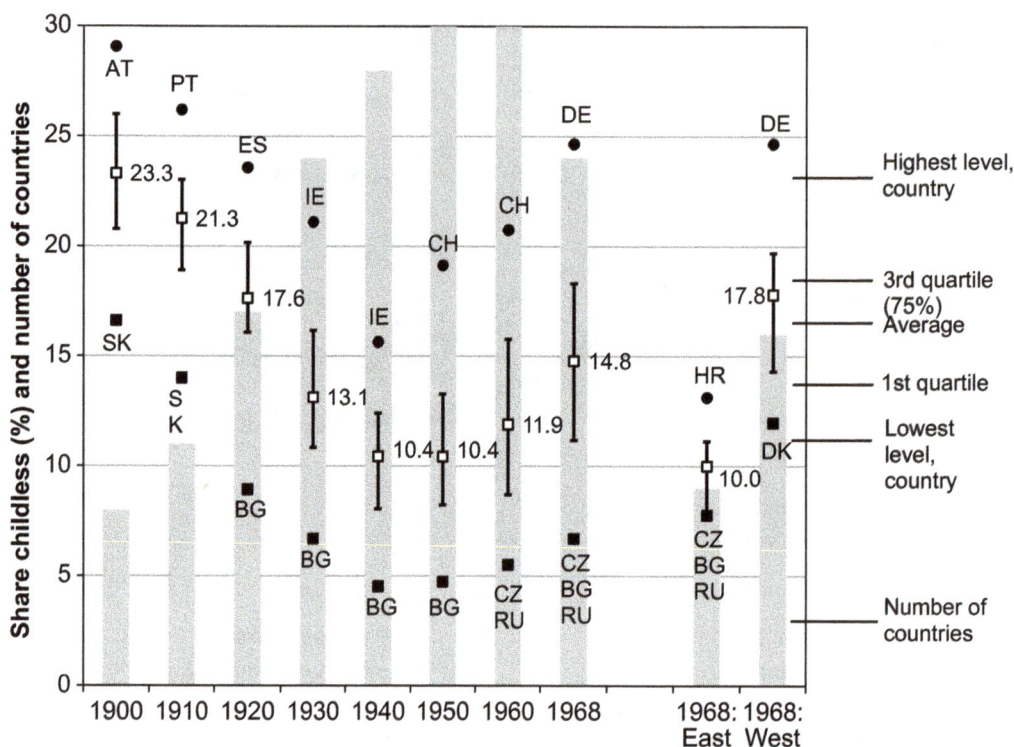

Fig. 2.6 Selected indicators of cross-country differences in childlessness in Europe (average, lowest and highest levels, 25 and 75 % of the childlessness distribution). Women born in 1900–1968, selected cohorts, in percent (Notes and sources: Indicators are computed for all European countries with populations over one million for which data were available for a given year; for the countries and the cohorts included, see also Figs. 2.2, 2.3, and 2.4 and Appendix 1). Country codes: *AT* Austria, *BG* Bulgaria, *CH* Switzerland, *CZ* Czech Republic, *DE* Germany, *DK* Denmark, *ES* Spain, *IE* Ireland, *PL* Poland, *PT* Portugal, *RU* Russia, *SK* Slovakia

childless (Fig. 2.6). A higher childlessness rate, of around 14 %, can be observed in only three countries: Ireland, Finland, and Switzerland. Paradoxically, the lowest levels of childlessness were reached at the same time among the cohorts who were experiencing the baby boom in western countries, and among the cohorts in eastern Europe whose fertility rates were declining to low levels (van Bavel et al. 2015).

The regional trajectories in Fig. 2.5 also suggest that some of the differences in childlessness between the eastern and the western parts of Europe preceded the geopolitical division of the continent that emerged after World War II. The CEE countries consistently had childlessness levels that were below European average, including among women who were born in the mid-1920s, many of whom had their first child before the new reproduction patterns of the state-socialist era were established during the 1950s.

While childlessness eventually increased in all of the regions, the timing of this rise differed considerably. In western Europe, including in Austria, western Germany, and Switzerland, the increase in childlessness began among women born in the 1940s. In the Nordic countries, the increase started among women born in the early 1950s, and then progressed much more slowly. In the south, the rise in childlessness started among women born in the 1960s. In the CEE countries, childlessness first started to rise among the cohorts born in the late 1960s (Fig. 2.5). Because of these differences in the onset of the increase in childlessness, the east-west gap in child-lessness levels was most pronounced among women born between 1950 and 1965, although the differences between countries were large (Fig. 2.6). For an illustration, consider regional differences observed among women born in 1968: the average level of childlessness in the CEE countries (10 %) is below the lowest childlessness level in other parts of Europe (12 % in Denmark), and is well below the average level across non-CEE countries (18 %). These differences are also observed in the ranking of European countries with the lowest and the highest childlessness levels among women born in 1940 and 1968 (see Fig. 2.7): all of the countries with the lowest childlessness levels are located in the CEE, with Bulgaria, the Czech Republic and Russia having the lowest levels.

Finally, a distinction can be made between regions where childlessness seems to be levelling off or even declining slightly among the cohorts born in the late 1960s and early 1970s (western European countries, Nordic countries, Austria, Germany, and Switzerland), and regions where childlessness has been rising rapidly, and is likely to continue to increase (southern European and CEE countries).

How closely is childlessness correlated with completed fertility? Do countries with high childlessness rates also have low cohort fertility rates? Previous research has suggested that among women who were born in the early and mid-1960s, there is a weak correlation between low fertility rates and high levels of childlessness (Dorbritz and Ruckdeschel 2007: Figure 9, Miettinen et al. 2015: Figure 10c). In Fig. 2.8 we can see that among women who were born in 1968, the strength of this correlation varies by region: no correlation can be observed in the CEE countries (or if there is a correlation, it runs in the opposite direction), while in the rest of Europe the expected correlation is found, but it is not very strong. The main outlier is Ireland, which has both a high completed fertility rate (2.17) and a relatively high childlessness rate (19 %).

2.5 Discussion and Conclusions

This study has provided the most detailed reconstruction to date of long-term childlessness trends among women in Europe. But because the analysis is based on diverse datasets, the cross-country comparisons cannot be precise, and a degree of uncertainty about the exact levels of childlessness remains, especially in countries where different datasets provide contrasting estimates of childlessness, and in coun-tries that have been experiencing intensive migration. It is beyond the scope of this article to give a detailed account of all of the alternative datasets available, but these uncertainties should be taken into account when analysing the presented data.

This limitation notwithstanding, the main findings of the analysis are robust and clear. Europe has experienced a U-shaped pattern in permanent childlessness among women born between 1900 and 1972. Among the cohorts born in the early twentieth century, the childlessness rates were high (typically more than 20 %) in all of the countries for which data are available except Slovakia. Childlessness levels then

Women born 1940

Bulgaria	4.5
Czech Republic	5.5
Russia	6.4
Belarus	6.7
Slovenia	7.8
European avg	10.4
Spain	12.6
Belgium	13.1
Finland	14.1
Switzerland	15.5
Ireland	15.6

Lowest childlessness

Highest childlessness

Women born 1968

Bulgaria	7.8
Czech Republic	7.8
Russia	7.9
Lithuania	9.3
Hungary	10.9
European avg	14.5
Ireland	19.0
Finland	19.7
Italy	19.8
Switzerland	20.9
Germany	23.1

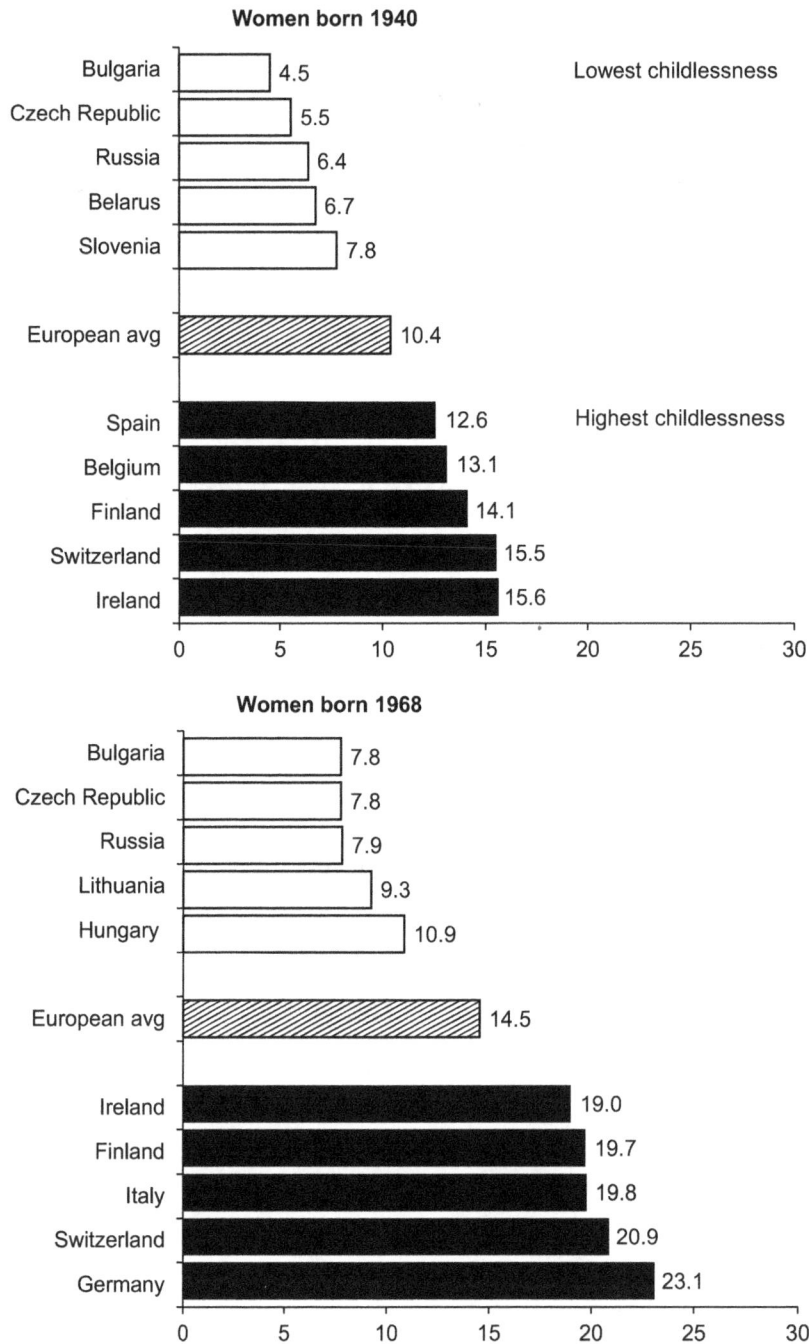

Fig. 2.7 European countries with the highest and the lowest childlessness levels among women born in 1940 and 1968 (Notes and sources: Ranking based on European countries with populations over one million for which data were available for a given year; for the data sources, the countries, and the cohorts included, see also Figs. 2.2, 2.3, and 2.4 and Appendix 1)

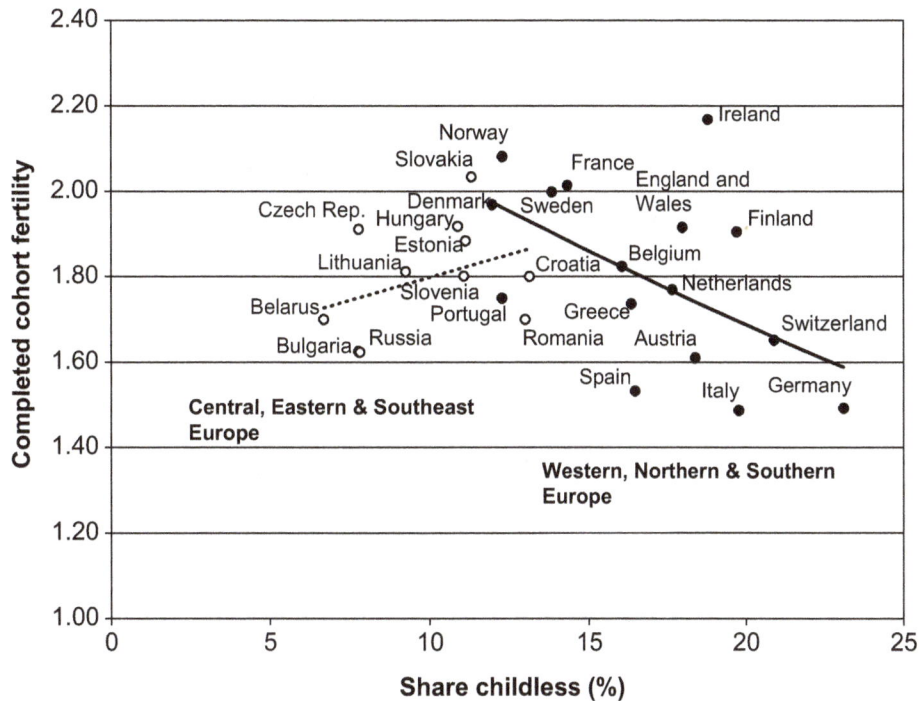

Fig. 2.8 Permanent childlessness and completed cohort fertility rates in Europe, women born in 1968. Notes: The data are for 28 European countries with populations over one million and available data on childlessness. The childlessness data for France are for the 1965–1969 cohorts, the data for Belarus and Greece are for the 1965 cohort, and the data for Romania are for the 1969 cohort (Sources: Childlessness: see Appendix 1; completed fertility: European Demographic Data Sheet 2010 (VID 2010) and own computations)

steadily declined, and were lowest among the 1940s cohorts. Relative to the childlessness levels among both the older and the younger cohorts, the levels among these cohorts were low (Rowland 2007). The timing and the intensity of the subsequent increase in childlessness varied substantially by region. One clear and persistent regional difference was between the former state-socialist countries, where childlessness was rare, and the other regions of Europe, where childlessness was much more common. Although the CEE countries did not have high cohort fertility rates, motherhood was almost universal there, and voluntary childlessness was not normatively approved. However, the data for women born in the late 1960s and the early 1970s, who reached adulthood in the period when the state-socialist political systems in the CEE were collapsing, suggest this long-standing difference is now eroding. Some of the CEE countries, including Croatia, Hungary, and Romania, have experienced rapid increases in childlessness, matched only by the sharp upturns in childlessness in southern Europe. In contrast, the trend towards increasing levels of childlessness appears to be levelling off—and in some cases (e.g., in Switzerland and England and Wales) even reversing—in much of western Europe, the Nordic countries, and the three predominantly German-speaking countries of Europe.

I have not analysed the specific factors that have contributed to the between-country differences in childlessness levels, and to the increase in childlessness among women born in the 1950s and 1960s. Very generally, it appears that the factors that have contributed to declines in cohort fertility have also been driving trends in childlessness. Two broad sets of institutional influences can be highlighted. First, whenever women face difficulties in combining paid employment with parenthood because of limited childcare, inflexible work conditions, long work hours, and unhelpful partners, childlessness is likely to increase. Highly educated women, who have the strongest career prospects, and who thus face the steepest opportunity costs if they have children, are especially likely to remain childless under these conditions. Countries such as Germany and Spain—and to some extent the United Kingdom, where the cost of childcare is very high—fit this pattern. Second, child-lessness is also on the rise in countries where labour market conditions are poor: i.e., unemployment is high, a large percentage of the working-age population are in temporary employment, a large share of young adults are neither in education nor working, and the rate of self-employment is high. Under these circumstances, many couples postpone and even forgo parenthood and they often cannot afford the type of housing they would need to start a family. Until recently, these conditions were mainly found in the countries of southern Europe (Adserà 2004). Now, however, these conditions are also prevalent in many ex-socialist countries of central and eastern Europe.

At the same time, however, childlessness trends appear to have a stronger norma-tive underpinning than changes in cohort fertility: in countries where voluntary childlessness is not generally accepted, childlessness is still relatively infrequent, especially among women, who often face strong social pressure to have at least one child. This normative pressure was widespread in CEE countries until recently (see, e.g., Merz and Liefbroer 2012; Sobotka 2016), but it also helps to explain the low childlessness levels observed among some religious and ethnic minorities in coun-tries where childlessness is otherwise relatively common and accepted. The broad acceptance and prevalence of voluntary childlessness is closely linked with low religiosity (e.g., Abma and Martinez 2006; Tanturri and Mencarini 2008; Burkimsher and Zeman, Chap. 6, in this volume). In addition, there is a high degree of historical and cultural continuity in childlessness levels over time (Morgan 1991), which sug-gests that countries where childlessness was widespread in the past are also likely to have high childlessness rates in the future, as younger women and men are socialised in conditions in which childlessness is common and generally accepted.

Will childlessness rates continue to increase; and, if so, by how much? It is important to note that recent childlessness levels are still well below the historical highs in most of the analysed countries, and that current childlessness levels are not as high as might be anticipated, considering the range of interconnected factors outlined in the introduction that may be expected to encourage women and men to remain childless. Among the women born in the 1970s and the early 1980s, child-lessness is likely to increase especially in southern and central-eastern Europe, whereas it may stabilise in other regions. Childlessness levels are likely to be high-est in the southern European countries, especially in Italy and in Spain; and possibly in Greece, for which reliable recent data are unavailable. In these countries childlessness levels are over 20 % among the early 1970s cohorts, and may eventually reach 25 % if the increase in childbearing intensity at higher reproductive ages slows down or stops. Outside of Europe these high childlessness levels may be exceeded in some East Asian societies, especially in Japan, for which Frejka et al. (2010) have estimated that childlessness levels are close to 30 % in the late 1960s cohorts.

Future research should examine more rigorously the reliability of different data sources on childlessness, and the main sources of errors and distortions in these datasets. An important source of uncertainty about future childlessness lies in the interplay between fertility postponement and the ability of couples and individuals to realise their childbearing plans later in life. The mean age at first birth among women has exceeded 30 in Italy, Spain, and Switzerland; and is approaching this boundary in many other European countries. The share of women who are still childless at ages 35–40, when infertility becomes an important limiting factor (Menken et al. 1986), has risen rapidly in much of Europe. For instance, in Spain 35 % of women aged 35 were childless in 2011, up from 16 % in 1991 (computations are based on census data). Many of them are likely to experience infertility by the time they decide to start a family, and thus may need to use assisted reproduction, which is costly and rather ineffective at higher reproductive ages (e.g., Wang et al. 2008; see also Trappe as well as Präg and Mills, Chap. 14, in this volume). This trend is likely to contribute to an increase in involuntary childlessness. This pattern of "perpetual postponement" may also be associated with stronger fluctuations in childlessness levels in the future. Compared to past generations of women, most of whom had their first child at a relatively young age, and thus could postpone parenthood decision in difficult times, the current cohorts of women will have less "extra space" left for postponing motherhood if they encounter adverse circumstances. When times are tough, many women might be running a race against the biological clock that they are likely to lose.

Acknowledgements This research was funded by the European Research Council under the European Union's Seventh Framework Programme (FP7/2007–2013)/ERC Grant agreement n° 284238 (EURREP project). I wish to extend my thanks to Kryštof Zeman, who provided computations of cohort childlessness based on the data in Human Fertility Collection, and provided assistance with accessing the datasets used for several countries. I also gratefully acknowledge the help of colleagues who have provided census or survey data on childlessness for individual countries, especially Karel Neels (Belgium), Éva Beaujouan (France), Martin Bujard (Germany), Zuzanna Brzozowska (Poland), Marion Burkimsher (Switzerland), Anna Rotkirch and Anneli Miettinen (Finland), and Glenn Sandström (Sweden). I would like to thank the many colleagues and institutions who have provided census-based and register-based data on cohort parity distribution to the Human Fertility Database and Completed Fertility and Education database. I also wish to thank Michaela Kreyenfeld for her insightful comments on the first draft of this paper.

Appendices

Appendix 1

Data sources by country

Country	Cohorts	Data	Reference period	Source	Note
Austria	1900–1940	C 1991	15 May 1991	CFE (2015)	Parity on 1 Jan. 2014 computed by Kryštof Zeman for Geburtenbarometer (2014); First births realised after 2013 projected (trend projection)
	1941–1964	C 2001	15 May 2001	CFE (2015)	
	1965–1972	& VS 2001–2013	up to 31 Dec. 2013	See note	
Belarus	1929–1957	C 1999	16 Feb. 1999	HFD (2015b)	Data available for 5-year cohorts only
	1959–1963, 1964–1968	C 2009	October 2009	HFD (2015b)	
Belgium	1910–1950	C 2001	31 Dec. 2000	See note	Computations by Karel Neels from individual data obtained by Statistics Belgium
	1951–1968	C 2001	31 Dec. 2000	See note	Computations by Karel Neels from individual data obtained by Statistics Belgium
		& VS 2001–1910	up to 31 Dec. 2010	Eurostat (2015)	Own computations; First births realised after 2013 projected (trend projection)
Bulgaria	1920–1972	C 2001	1 Mar. 2001	HFD (2015b)	No unknown birth order reported
		& VS for 2001–2013	Up to 31 Dec. 2013	Eurostat (2015)	

(continued)

Country	Cohorts	Data	Reference period	Source	Note
Croatia	1922–1945	C 2001	31 Mar. 2001	CFE (2015)	Unknown birth order proportionally redistributed
	1946–1970	C 2011	22 Mar. 2011	CFE (2015)	Unknown birth order proportionally redistributed
Czech Republic	1900–1919	C 1961	1 Mar. 1961	HFD (2015b)	
	1920–1960	C 2001	3 Mar. 1991	HFD (2015b)	
	1961–1972	VS up to 2013	up to 31 Dec. 2013	HFD (2015b) & Eurostat (2015) for 2012, 2013	Own computations based on HFD + Eurostat data First births realised after 2013 projected (trend projection)
Denmark	1945–1949	R 2013		Statistics Denmark (2014)	
	1950–1972	VS 1968–2013	Up to 31 Dec. 2012	Eurostat (2015) and older Eurostat data	Own computations
Estonia	1918–1936	C 1979	17 Jan. 1979	HFD (2015b)	
	1937–1943	C 1989	12 Jan. 1989	HFD (2015b)	
	1944–1970	C 2011	31 Dec. 2011	HFD (2015b)	Women with unknown birth order assumed to be childless
Finland	1930–1934	R 1986	Up to 31 Dec. 1986	HFD (2015b)	
	1935–1949	R 1999	Up to 31 Dec. 1999	HFD (2015b)	
	1950–1968	R 2009	Up to 31 Dec. 2009	HFD (2015b)	

Country	Cohorts	Source	Date	Reference	Note
France	1900,1905,10,15,20	INSEE surveys		Daguet (2000, T. 1)	
	1920–1924 to 1965–1969	Surveys 1982, 1990, 1999, 2011		See note	Data computed for 5-year cohorts by Éva Beaujouan from survey data obtained by INED and INSEE; Results based on combining several available surveys
Germany	1933–1968	Microcensus (MC) 2008,12		CFE (2015)	For most cohorts data computed by combining results from both MC surveys to obtain more robust results
Germany/ Eastern Germany	1902–1940	C 1981		HFD (2015b)	
	1941–1958	Microcensus (MC) 2008		Statistisches Bundesamt (2015)	Data computed by Martin Bujard
	1959–1970	Microcensus (MC) 2012		Statistisches Bundesamt (2015)	Data computed by Martin Bujard
Germany/ Western Germany	1901–1905 to 1926–1930	Census 1970		Schwarz (2003: Table 8)	Data computed for 5-year cohorts
	1933–1969	Microcensus (MC) 2008,12		CFE (2015)	For most cohorts data computed by combining results from both MC surveys to obtain more robust results
Greece	1946–1965	VS 1960–2008	up to 31 Dec. 2008	HFC (2015)	Computations by Kryštof Zeman
Hungary	1900–1919	C 1970	1 Jan. 1970	IPUMS/CFE (2015)	5 % sample of the census data available
	1920–1929	C 1970 + 90	1 Jan. 1990	IPUMS/CFE (2015)	5 % sample of the census data, average of two censuses used
	1930–1949	C 1990 + 2000	2 Feb. 2000	IPUMS/CFE (2015)	5 % sample of the census data, average of two censuses used
	1950–1968	R 2010	up to 1 Jan. 2010	HFD (2015)	
Ireland	1925–1948	C 2006	23 Apr. 2006	CFE (2015)	Unknown birth order proportionally redistributed
	1949–1969	C 2011	10 Apr. 2011	CFE (2015)	Unknown birth order proportionally redistributed

(continued)

Country	Cohorts	Data	Reference period	Source	Note
Italy	1935–1972	VS 1950–2013	up to 31 Dec. 2013	data provided by ISTAT for HFD	First births realised after 2013 projected (trend projection)
Lithuania	1924–1936	C 1979	17 Jan. 1979	HFD (2015b)	Unknown birth order proportionally redistributed
	1937–1969	C 2011	1 Mar. 2011	HFD (2015b)	Unknown birth order proportionally redistributed
Moldova	1938–1947	C 1989	12 Jan. 1989	Statistics Moldova	Tabulated data obtained from Statistics Moldova
	1949–1953 to 1959–1963	C 2004	October 2004	Statistics Moldova (2006)	Data available for 5-year cohorts only
Netherlands	1900–2004 to 1930–1934			Rowland (2007, T. 1)	Data computed for 5-year cohorts, assembled by Pearl Dykstra
	1935–1969	R 2013	Up to 31 Dec. 2012	CBS (2015)	Data for cohorts 1965–69 up to age 43, small adjustment (−0.15 %) added
Norway	1935–1939	R 1985	Up to 1 Jan. 1985	HFD (2015b)	
	1940–1944	R 1990	Up to 1 Jan. 1990	HFD (2015b)	
	1945–1949	R 1995	Up to 1 Jan. 1995	HFD (2015b)	
	1950–1954	R 2000	Up to 1 Jan. 2000	HFD (2015b)	
	1955–1959	R 2005	Up to 1 Jan. 2005	HFD (2015b)	
	1960–1970	R 2012	Up to 1 Jan. 2012	HFD (2015b)	

		C + VS	1 Jan. 1990	Bolesławski (1993)	
Poland	1921–1927				
	1927–1960	C/S 2002	June 2002	CFE (2015)/Brzozowska (2014)	Census survey (1.7 % of female pop.); results smoothed (3-years moving avg.)
	1961–1965	& VS 2002–2013	Up to 31 Dec. 2013	Eurostat (2015)	Figures for cohorts 1966–72 were implausibly low and are not shown
Portugal	1900–1929	C 1981	16 Mar. 1981	HFD (2015b)	
	1930–1948	C 1991	15 Apr. 1991	HFD (2015b)	
	1949–1968	& VS 1991–2013	Up to 31 Dec. 2013	Eurostat (2015)	
Romania	1900–1918	C 1977		IPUMS/CFE (2015)	10 % sample of the census data available
	1919–1920	C 1992		IPUMS/CFE (2015)	10 % sample of the census data available
	1921–1972	C 2002	17 Mar. 2002	INSSE (2003)	No unknown birth order reported
		& VS for 2002–2013		Eurostat (2015)	
Russian Federation	1924–1936	C 1979	17 Jan. 1979	HFD (2015b)	
	1937–1970	C 2010	October 2010	Data provided for CFE (2015)	Unknown birth order proportionally redistributed
Slovak Republic	1900–1914	C 1961	1 Mar. 1961	HFD (2015b)	Unknown birth order proportionally redistributed
	1915–1929	C 1991	3 Mar. 1991	HFD (2015b)	Unknown birth order proportionally redistributed
	1930–1972	C 2001	1 Mar. 2001	HFD (2015b)	Women with unknown birth order assumed to be childless
		& VS for 2001–2013	31 Dec. 2013	Eurostat (2015)	Own computations
Slovenia	1901–1905 to 1916–1920	C 1971	31 Mar. 1971	HFD (2015b)	Data available for 5-year cohorts only
	1921–1927	C 1971	31 Mar. 1971	HFD (2015b)	
	1928–1972	C 2002	31 Mar. 2002	HFD (2015b)	
		& VS for 2002–2013	31 Dec. 2013	Eurostat (2015)	Own computations

(continued)

Country	Cohorts	Data	Reference period	Source	Note
Spain	1911–1930	C1991	1 Mar. 1991	CFE (2015)	
	1931–1964	C 2011	3 Nov. 2011	CFE (2015)	
	1965–1972	VS up to 2013	Up to 31 Dec. 2013	& VS 2011–13	Own computations based on Eurostat data; first births realised after 2013 projected (stable rates projection)
Sweden	1914–1923	R 1969	Up to 31 Dec. 1969	HFD (2015b)	
	1924–1933	R 1979	Up to 31 Dec. 1979	HFD (2015b)	
	1934–1943	R 1989	Up to 31 Dec. 1989	HFD (2015b)	
	1944–1953	R 1999	Up to 31 Dec. 1999	HFD (2015b)	
	1954–1970	R 2011	Up to 31 Dec. 2011	HFD (2015b)	
Switzerland	1920–1949	Census 2000	5 Dec. 2000	CFE (2015)	Data provided by Marion Burkimsher
	1950–1972	& VS 2001–2012	Up to 31 Dec. 2012	HFD (2015b) and Eurostat (2015)	Own computations; HFD data used for 2000–2011
UK/England and Wales	1920–1970	R + S	up to 2013	ONS (2014)	
Ukraine	1924–1937	C 1979	17 Jan. 1979	HFD (2015b)	Data available for 5-year cohorts only;
	1937–1941 to 1957–1961	C 2001	5 Dec. 2001	HFD (2015b)	Unknown birth order proportionally redistributed

Note: Types of data sources: *VS* vital statistics, *C* census, *R* population register, *S* survey

Appendix 2

Childlessness among women, selected cohorts (1900–1972), by country and region

Country	Cohort 1900	1910	1920	1930	1940	1950	1960	1965	1968	1970	1972
Western Europe											
Belgium	–	25.0	19.8	16.1	13.1	14.1	15.5	16.0	16.1	–	–
France	24.9	21.7	19.2	13.2 (1930–1934)	11.3 (1940–1944)	11.7 (1950–1954)	13.2 (1960–1964)	–	14.3 (1965–1969)	–	–
Ireland	–	–	–	21.1	15.6	14.7	17.1	18.0	18.8	–	–
Netherlands	23 (1900–1904)	20 (1910–1914)	15 (1920–1924)	12 (1930–1934)	11.9	14.6	17.3	18.1	17.7	–	–
England and Wales	–	–	21.0	13.0	11.0	14.0	19.0	20.0	18.0	18.0	–
Nordic countries											
Denmark	–	–	–	–	–	10.7	11.6	11.5	12.0	11.9	11.9
Finland	–	26.2 (1906–1910)	20.2 (1916–1920)	16.5	14.1	14.9	17.3	19.1	19.7	–	–
Norway	–	–	–	–	9.5	9.4	11.7	12.8	12.3	13.2	–
Sweden	–	23.8 (1914)	18.7	14.2	12.1	12.6	15.0	14.1	13.8	14.1	–
Austria, Germany, Switzerland											
Austria	29.1	22.4	17.4	15.0	12.5	12.6	16.3	17.2	18.4	18.5	19.0
Germany	–	–	–	–	11.5	13.5	18.4	21.8	23.1	–	–
Western Germany (FRG)		22 (1906–1910)	18 (1916–1920)	14 (1926–1930)	11.8	14.6	20.6	23.3	23.6 (1966–1970)	–	–

(continued)

Country	Cohort										
	1900	1910	1920	1930	1940	1950	1960	1965	1968	1970	1972
Eastern Germany (GDR)	25.9 (1902)	18.3	17.4	12.8	9.2	9.9	10.5	15.9	16.1	17.7	–
Switzerland	–	–	20.0	16.4	15.5	19.1	20.7	21.9	20.9	20.2	19.1
Southern Europe											
Greece	–	–	–	–	–	9.8	10.8	16.4	–	–	–
Italy	–	–	–	–	12.3	11.2	14.2	18.4	19.8	20.6	20.9
Portugal	27.2	26.1	21.8	17.2	11.8	9.8	11.2	12.9	12.3		20.7
Spain	–	26.7 (1911)	23.6	17.2	12.6	12.1	12.3	14.5	16.5	18.6	
Central Europe											
Croatia	–	–	–	11.5	8.9	8.5	9.5	11.5	13.1	14.9	–
Czech Republic	21.4	16.8	10.7	7.2	5.5	5.5	6.2	6.6	7.8	7.7	9.4
Hungary	20.3	20.1	14.6	10.7	9.5	7.7	8.1	9.3	10.9	–	–
Poland	–	–	12.9 (1921)	11.2	9.2	8.1	6.7	8.0	–		
Slovak Republic	16.6	14.0	10.9	9.3	8.0	9.7	10.2	11.0	11.3	11.8	12.3
Slovenia	23.1 (1901–1905)	22.2 (1906–1910)	18.2 (1921)	10.8	7.8	6.8	7.2	8.7	11.1	12.6	13.6
Estonia	–	–	18.7	13.8	10.5	8.8	9.0	10.6	11.1	11.5	–
Lithuania	–	–	–	13.1	8.0	8.0	8.8	8.9	9.3	–	–

Eastern & South-eastern Europe

Bulgaria	–	21.5	8.9	6.7	4.5	4.7	6.5	7.9	7.8	9.3	9.9
Romania	24.0	–	20.2	16.0	12.5	10.0	10.7	12.1	–	13.9	15.2
Belarus	–	–	–	10.9	6.7	6.2	5.8 (1959–1963)	6.7 (1964–1968)	–	–	–
Moldova	–	–	–	–	11.3	6.3 (1949–1953)	5.5 (1959–1963)	–	–	–	–
Russia	–	–	–	9.9	6.4	6.3	6.2	7.0	7.9	9.3	–
Ukraine	–	–	–	11.6	8.2 (1939)	7.4 (1947–1952)	7.4 (1957–1961)	–	–	–	–
Europe – average	23.3	20.7	17.5	13.1	10.5	10.6	12.4	14.1	14.8	14.3	15.2

Literature

Abma, J. C., & Martinez, G. M. (2006). Childlessness among older women in the United States: Trends and profiles. *Journal of Marriage and Family, 68*, 1045–1056.

Adserà, A. (2004). Changing fertility rates in developed countries. The impact of labour market institutions. *Journal of Population Economics, 17*, 1–27.

Andersson, G., Rønsen, M., Knudsen, L. B., Lappegård, T., Neyer, G., Skrede, K., Teschner, K., & Vikat, A. (2009). Cohort fertility patterns in the Nordic countries. *Demographic Research, 20*, 313–352.

Beck, U. (1992). *Risk society. Towards a new modernity*. London: Sage Publications.

Berrington, A. (2004). Perpetual postponers? Women's, men's and couples fertility intentions and subsequent fertility behaviour. *Population Trends, 117*, 9–19.

Bolesławski, L. (1993). *Polskie tablice dzietności kobiet 1971–1992. Polish fertility tables 1971–1992*. Warsaw: Główny urząd statystyczny.

Brzozowska, Z. (2014). Fertility and education in Poland during state socialism. *Demographic Research, 31*, 319–336.

Brzozowska, Z., Beaujouan, E., & Zeman, K. (2016). The limited effect of increasing educational attainment on childlessness trends in twentieth-century Europe, women born 1916–65. *Population Studies*. Published online 21 August 2016. http://dx.doi.org/10.1080/00324728.2016.1206210.

CBS. (2015). *Online table of the share of childless women by cohort (1935 and younger)*. Statistics Netherlands. http://statline.cbs.nl. Accessed 10 June 2015.

CFE. (2015). *Cohort Fertility and Education database. Census data on cohort parity distribution for Croatia, Czech Republic, Hungary, Ireland, Poland, Romania, Slovakia, and Spain*. http://www.cfe-database.org. Accessed 7 July 2015.

Daguet, F. (2000). L'évolution de la fécondité des générations nées de 1917 à 1949: analyse par rang de naissance et niveau de diplôme. *Population, 55*, 1021–1034.

Dorbritz, J., & Ruckdeschel, K. (2007). Kinderlosigkeit in Deutschland. Ein europäischer Sonderweg? Daten, Trends und Gründe. In D. Konietzka & M. Kreyenfeld (Eds.), *Ein Leben ohne Kinder* (pp. 45–81). Wiesbaden: VS Verlag für Sozialwissenschaften.

El-Badry, M. A. (1961). Failure of enumerators to make entries of zero: Errors in recording childless cases in population censuses. *Journal of the American Statistical Association, 56*, 909–924.

Esping-Andersen, G. (2009). *The incomplete revolution. Adapting to women's new roles*. Cambridge: Polity Press.

Eurostat. (2015). *Data on first births by age of mother and on female population by age in European countries in 1960–2013*. http://ec.europa.eu/eurostat/data/database. Accessed 8 July 2015.

Frejka, T., & Sardon, J.-P. (2004). *Childbearing trends and prospects in low-fertility countries: A cohort analysis. European studies of population* (Vol. 13). Dordrecht: Kluwer Academic Publishers.

Frejka, T., & Sardon, J.-P. (2006). First birth trends in developed countries: Persistent parenthood postponement. *Demographic Research, 15*, 147–180.

Frejka, T., & Sardon, J.-P. (2007). Cohort birth order, parity progression ratio and parity distribution trends in developed countries. *Demographic Research, 16*, 315–374.

Frejka, T., Jones, G. W., & Sardon, J.-P. (2010). East Asian childbearing patterns and policy developments. *Population and Development Review, 36*, 579–606.

Geburtenbarometer. (2014). *Geburtenbarometer: Monitoring of fertility in Austria and Vienna*. Annual report for 2013 http://www.oeaw.ac.at/vid/barometer/downloads/Geburtenbarometer_Ergebnis_2013.pdf. Accessed 25 Nov 2014.

Goldin, C. (2006). The quiet revolution that transformed women's employment, education, and family. *American Economic Review, 96*, 1–21.

Goldstein, J. R., & Kreyenfeld, M. (2011). Has East Germany overtaken West Germany? Recent trends in order-specific fertility. *Population and Development Review, 37*, 453–472.

Gray, E., Evans, A., & Reimondos, A. (2013). Childbearing desires of childless men and women: When are goals adjusted? *Advances in Life Course Research, 18*, 141–149.

Heaton, T. B., Jacobson, C. K., & Holland, K. (1999). Persistence and change in decisions to remain childless. *Journal of Marriage and the Family, 61*, 531–539.

Heuser, R. L. (1976). *Fertility tables for birth cohorts by color.* U. S. Department of Health, Education, and Welfare. DHEW Publication No. (HRA)76-1152.

HFC. (2015). *Human Fertility Collection, data on period first birth rates by age of mother in selected European countries.* www.fertilitydata.org. Accessed 11 Feb 2015.

HFD. (2015a). *Human fertility database.* Summary indicators. www.humanfertility.org/Docs/HFDLite/CCH.xlsx. Accessed 08 June 2015.

HFD. (2015b). *Human fertility database.* Input data tables on women by age and parity (selected censuses and register-based data for Belarus, Bulgaria, Czech Republic, Estonia, Finland, eastern Germany, Hungary, Lithuania, Norway, Portugal, Russia, Slovakia, Slovenia, Sweden, and Ukraine). www.humanfertility.org. Accessed 13 July 2015.

Hook, J. L. (2006). Care in context: Men's unpaid work in 20 countries, 1965–2003. *American Sociological Review, 71*, 639–660.

INSSE. (2003). *Romania, Census 2002. Female population aged 15+ by year of birth and number of children ever born (in Romanian).* Bucharest: National Institute of Statistics. http://www.insse.ro/cms/files/RPL2002INS/vol1/titluriv1.htm. Accessed 31 May 2015.

Kreyenfeld, M. (2004). Fertility decisions in the FRG and GDR: An analysis with data from the German Fertility and Family Survey. *Demographic Research, Special Collection, 3*, 275–318.

Kreyenfeld, M., & Konietzka, D. (2007). Kinderlosigkeit in Deutschland. Theoretische Probleme und empirische Ergebnisse. In D. Konietzka & M. Kreyenfeld (Eds.), *Ein Leben ohne Kinder* (pp. 11–41). Wiesbaden: VS Verlag für Sozialwissenschaften.

Leridon, H. (2008). A new estimate of permanent sterility by age: Sterility defined as the inability to conceive. *Population Studies, 62*, 15–24.

Lesthaeghe, R. (2010). The unfolding story of the second demographic transition. *Population and Development Review, 36*, 211–251.

McDonald, P. (2002). Sustaining fertility through public policy: The range of options. *Population (English Edition), 57*, 417–446.

Menken, J., Trussell, J., & Larsen, U. (1986). Age and infertility. *Science, 233*, 1389–1394.

Merz, E. M., & Liefbroer, A. C. (2012). The attitude toward voluntary childlessness in Europe: Cultural and institutional explanations. *Journal of Marriage and Family, 74*, 587–600.

Miettinen, A., & Szalma, I. (2014). Childlessness intentions and ideals in Europe. *Finnish Yearbook of Population Research, 49*, 31–55.

Miettinen, A., Rotkirch, A., Szalma, I., Donno, A., & Tanturri, M.-L. (2015). *Increasing childlessness in Europe: Time trends and country differences.* Families and Societies Project, Working Paper 33. www.familiesandsocieties.eu/wp-content/uploads/2015/03/WP33MiettinenEtAl2015.pdf. Accessed 29 June 2015.

Mills, M., & Blossfeld, H.-P. (2005). Globalization, uncertainty and the early life course. A theoretical framework. In H. P. Blossfeld, E. Klijzing, M. Mills, & K. Kurz (Eds.), *Globalization, uncertainty and youth in society* (pp. 1–24). London/New York: Routledge Advances in Sociology Series.

Morgan, S. P. (1991). Late nineteenth and early twentieth century childlessness. *The American Journal of Sociology, 97*, 779–807.

Morgan, S. P., & Chen, R. (1992). Predicting childlessness for recent cohorts of American women. *International Journal of Forecasting, 8*, 477–493.

Murphy, M. (2009). Where have all the children gone? Women's reports of more childlessness at older ages than when they were younger in a large-scale continuous household survey in Britain. *Population Studies, 63*, 115–133.

Ní Bhrolcháin, M. N., & Beaujouan, É. (2011). Uncertainty in fertility intentions in Britain, 1979–2007. *Vienna Yearbook of Population Research, 2011*, 99–129.

Ní Bhrolcháin, M. N., Beaujouan, E., & Murphy, M. (2011). Sources of error in reported childlessness in a continuous British household survey. *Population Studies, 65*, 305–318.

OECD. (2011). *Doing better for families*. Paris: OECD Publishing.

ONS. (2014). *Childbearing for women born in different years, England and Wales, 2013*. London: Office for National Statistics. http://www.ons.gov.uk/ons/rel/fertility-analysis/childbearing-for-women-born-in-different-years/2013/stb-cohort-fertility-2013.html. Accessed 16 Apr 2015.

Pötzsch, O. (2016). Fertility in Germany before and after the 2011 Census: Still no Trend Reversal in Sight. *Comparative Population Studies, 41*, 87–118.

Rendall, M. S., Clarke, L., Peters, H. E., Ranjit, N., & Verropoulou, G. (1999). Incomplete reporting of men's fertility in the United States and Britain: A research note. *Demography, 36*, 135–144.

Rindfuss, R. R., Morgan, S. P., & Swicegood, G. (1988). *First births in America. Changes in the timing of parenthood*. Berkeley: University of California Press.

Rowland, D. T. (2007). Historical trends in childlessness. *Journal of Family Issues, 28*, 1311–1337.

Schwarz, K. (2003). Betrachtungen eines Demographen zu Ehe und Familie um das Jahr 2000. *Zeitschrift für Bevölkerungswissenschaft, 28*, 423–442.

Sobotka, T. (2005, March 31–April 2). *Childless societies? Trends and projections of childlessness in Europe and the Unites States*. Paper presented at the 2005 PAA Annual Meeting, Philadelphia.

Sobotka, T. (2011). Fertility in Central and Eastern Europe after 1989: Collapse and gradual recovery. *Historical Social Research, 36*, 246–296.

Sobotka, T. (2012). Fertility in Austria, Germany and Switzerland: Is there a common pattern? *Comparative Population Studies, 36*, 263–304.

Sobotka, T. (2013). *Pathways to low fertility: European perspectives*. Expert Paper No. 2013/8, United Nations Department of Economic and Social Affairs, Population Division. http://www.un.org/en/development/desa/population/publications/pdf/expert/2013-8_Sobotka_Expert-Paper.pdf. Accessed 5 Jan 2014.

Sobotka, T. (2016). Birth control, reproduction, and family under state socialism in Central and Eastern Europe. Forthcoming in L. Niethammer & S. Satjukow (Eds.), Gender relations and birth control in the age of the »Pill« (pp. 87–116). Göttingen: Wallstein Verlag.

Sobotka, T., & Beaujouan, É. (2014). Two is best? The persistence of a two-child family ideal in Europe. *Population and Development Review, 40*, 391–419.

Sobotka, T., & Testa, M. R. (2008). Attitudes and intentions towards childlessness in Europe. In C. Höhn, C. D. Avramov, & I. E. Kotowska (Eds.), *People, population change and policies: Lessons from the population policy acceptance study* (Vol. 1, pp. 177–211). Berlin: Springer.

Statistics Denmark. (2014). *Number of childless women by age and time*. www.statbank.dk/statbank5a/default.asp?w=1680. Accessed 19 Mar 2014.

Statistics Moldova. (2006). *Moldova, Census 2004. Female population aged 15+ by age group and number of live-born children by region*. www.statistica.md/pageview.php?l=ro&idc=295&id=2234. Accessed 30 July 2015.

Statistisches Bundesamt. (2015). *Daten zu Geburten, Familien und Kinderlosigkeit. Ergebnisse des Mikrozensus 2012 – Tabellen mit neuer Hochrechnung anhand der Bevölkerungsfortschreibung auf Basis des Zensus 2011 – Ausgabe 2015*. www.destatis.de/DE/Publikationen/Thematisch/Bevoelkerung/HaushalteMikrozensus/GeburtentrendsTabellenband5122203159015.xlsx?__blob=publicationFile. Accessed 31 Mar 2015.

Tanturri, M. L., & Mencarini, L. (2008). Childless or childfree? Paths to voluntary childlessness in Italy. *Population and Development Review, 34*, 51–77.

Thévenon, O. (2009). Increased women's labour force participation in Europe: Progress in the work-life balance or polarization of behaviours? *Population (English Edition), 64*, 235–272.

van Bavel, J., Klesment, M., Beaujouan, É., Brzozowska, Z., Puur, A., Reher, D., Requena, M., Sandström, G., Sobotka, T., & Zeman, K. (2015, April 30–May 2). *Women's education and cohort fertility during the baby boom*. Paper presented at the 2015 PAA annual meeting, San Diego. http://paa2015.princeton.edu/uploads/150211. Accessed 22 Apr 2015.

Van de Kaa, D. J. (1997). Options and sequences: Europe's demographic patterns. *Journal of the Australian Population Association, 14*, 1–29.

Veevers, J. E. (1980). *Childless by choice*. Toronto/Vancouver: Butterworth & Co.

Verdugo, R. R., & Swanson, D. (2011). Immigration and its effects on demographic change in Spain. *The Open Demography Journal, 4*, 22–33.

VID. (2010). *European demographic data sheet 2010*. Vienna: Vienna Institute of Demography and IIASA.

VID. (2014). *European demographic data sheet 2014*. Box on "Female advantage and the reversed gender gap in tertiary education in Europe." Vienna Institute of Demography and IIASA/Wittgenstein Centre for Demography and Global Human Capital. www.oeaw.ac.at/vid/data-sheet/DS2014/DS2014_index.shtml. Accessed 29 June 2015.

Wang, Y. A., Healy, D., Black, D., & Sullivan, E. A. (2008). Age-specific success rate for women undertaking their first assisted reproduction technology treatment using their own oocytes in Australia, 2002–2005. *Human Reproduction, 23*, 1633–1638.

Zeman, K. (2013). *Human Fertility Database documentation: The Czech Republic*. http://www.humanfertility.org/Docs/CZE/CZEcom.pdf. Accessed 12 July 2015.

Zeman, K., Brzozowska, Z., Sobotka, T., Beaujouan, E., & Matysiak, A. (2014). *Cohort Fertility and Education database. Methods protocol*. www.eurrep.org/wp-content/uploads/EURREP_Database_Methods_Protocol_Dec2014.pdf. Accessed 29 June 2015.

Part II
Country Studies

Chapter 3
Childlessness in the UK

Ann Berrington

3.1 Introduction

Interest in Britain in the causes and consequences of childlessness has grown since the 1980s in response to the increase in voluntary childlessness from very low levels in the 1960s and early 1970s (e.g., Baum and Cope 1980; Campbell 1985; Kiernan 1989). Some early authors characterised childlessness as "a mode of ultimate feminism" (McAllister and Clarke 2000), and early studies focused on women who had been married for at least 10 years but had had no children (e.g., Kiernan 1989). More recently, scholars have used a life course approach to investigate the parental background and life course factors associated with fertility intentions and outcomes (McAllister and Clarke 2000; Berrington 2004; Kneale and Joshi 2008; Simpson 2009; Berrington and Pattaro 2014). From the outset, researchers in this area have struggled with the difficulties inherent in defining and measuring voluntary and involuntary childlessness, in differentiating between those who wish to postpone childbearing and those who do not want children, and in understanding how individuals' viewpoints change across the life course (Baum and Cope 1980; Iacovou and Travares 2011).

Relative to the rest of Europe, Britain is a particularly interesting case because it is one of the countries where overall aggregate levels of fertility are high (with a completed family size of around 1.9 births per woman), but levels of childlessness are also high (at around 20 %) (Coleman 1996; Berrington et al. 2015). This chapter provides new empirical evidence for Britain which can help us better understand this apparent contradiction. We add to the existing knowledge on this topic in a number of ways. First, we examine how the educational gradient of childlessness

A. Berrington (✉)
Department of Social Statistics & Demography, University of Southampton, Southampton, UK
e-mail: A.Berrington@soton.ac.uk

© The Author(s) 2017
M. Kreyenfeld, D. Konietzka (eds.), *Childlessness in Europe: Contexts, Causes, and Consequences*, Demographic Research Monographs, DOI 10.1007/978-3-319-44667-7_3

has changed over birth cohorts. Second, we examine childlessness trends for both men and women using a unique cohort study of individuals born in Britain in one week of April 1970. Using prospective data collected from this cohort during their adult years, we investigate how the childbearing intentions of individuals who are childless at age 30 are associated with the likelihood of remaining childless at age 42. Finally, we examine the reasons given for not (yet) having had children among those who are childless at age 42.

3.1.1 A Continuum of Childlessness

Traditionally, a distinction has been made between people who are involuntarily childless as a result of biological infertility, and people who are voluntarily child-less. However, this distinction is not necessarily clear-cut, since, for example, individuals who are not fertile may be accepting of their childless situation (McAllister and Clarke 2000). Involuntary childlessness can arise for reasons other than health problems. The terms "childless by circumstance" or "social infertility" (which describe those who do not have a suitable partner, or who have a partner who does not want children) are used both in academic research (e.g., Carmichael and Whittaker 2007) and more generally (e.g., Black and Scull 2005; Day 2013). Indeed, while one member of a couple may be infertile or choose not to have children, for the other member this inability or unwillingness to have children may represent a circumstance which he or she has not chosen (Carmichael and Whittaker 2007). Several authors have suggested that there is a continuum of childlessness (Letherby 2002; McAllister and Clarke 2000). On one end of the continuum is a small group who report from a young adult age that they do not want to have children; the so-called "early articulators" (Houseknecht 1987). Qualitative research has suggested that such women often feel they do not have an affinity for babies or young children. There is less support for the idea that these women are making their decision to remain childless to protect a high-powered career (McAllister and Clarke 2000; Carmichael and Whittaker 2007). At the other extreme are women who are childless due to a medical condition. In between is a group of women who intended to have children, but who ended up with no children because of their circumstances (McAllister and Clarke 2000; Carmichael and Whittaker 2007; Keizer et al. 2008). There is also a category of women who never made a conscious decision about whether to have children. These women have sometimes been referred to as being "ambivalent" about childbearing. For these ambivalent women, childlessness is the consequence of having chosen to follow a particular life pattern, rather than of a decision made at an easily identified point in time.

Of particular relevance in the UK context is the association between the rise in childlessness and the increased mean age at entry into parenthood, particularly among more educated women (Berrington et al. 2015). As more couples delay childbearing, the issue of declining reproductive capacity with age becomes increasingly important. In addition, as more young adult women spend extended periods in education or pursuing career opportunities that have recently opened up to women, they may repeatedly decide to postpone childbearing, and thus drift into childlessness (Merz and Liefbroer 2012). Such individuals, who express a positive fertility intention but postpone childbearing until it is "too late", are described by Berrington (2004) as "perpetual postponers". Recent UK data confirm that very few individuals report that they wish to remain childless, including people who are still childless in their thirties (Ní Bhrolcháin et al. 2010; Berrington and Pattaro 2014). Some of these men and women will not be able to have the children they desire, due to age-related infecundability. It is difficult to quantify exactly what proportion of women who try to have their first baby at older ages will not succeed. Recent estimates show that rates of sterility rise after age 35 and especially after age 40, and that this increase is due not only to difficulties in conceiving, but to increased rates of fetal loss at higher ages (Leridon 2008; Eijkemans et al. 2014).

In summary, childless men and women are a very heterogeneous group. Both "active" and "passive" decision-making occurs across the life course which results in some individuals not having children (Gillespie 1999). Individuals can move along the childlessness continuum over time as their own life course develops (Baum and Cope 1980; McAllister and Clarke 2000). As Miettinen (2010: 20) noted: "For many, the decision not to have children may be a consequence of a process, where childbearing is postponed due to reasons related to relationship, personal considerations as well as financial and work-related constraints until it is too late to have children."

There is a risk when studying childlessness that the researcher will inadvertently characterise men and women without children as somehow lacking or as deviating from the norm. Some commentators prefer to use the term "childfree" rather than "childless", thereby emphasising that many couples who decide not to have children are making a positive choice to, for example, have more freedom and disposable income than families with children typically have (McAllister and Clarke 2000; Carmichael and Whittaker 2007). In this chapter, I use the term childlessness in its demographic sense to describe a person who has not had a biological child of his or her own, while noting that many individuals, especially men, act as social parents to children who may not be their own biological children.

Much of the previous work on childlessness has focused on women only. This is partly due to data constraints. The data published within the vital registration system generally only links births to the mother's characteristics (ONS 2014), while in many surveys (e.g., the British General Household Survey) only female respondents are asked questions about their past fertility. It is, however, important to consider men's experiences of childlessness as well (Jamieson et al. 2010). Choosing not to become a parent may not be equally socially acceptable for men and women (Rijken and Merz 2014). Furthermore, the factors associated with remaining childless are likely to differ by gender, as there are gender differences in, for example, the opportunity costs of childbearing. Moreover, although decisions about childbearing are often made jointly by a couple, the interaction of the partners' desires and intentions is rarely examined. Qualitative research for the UK suggests that ambivalent women can be swayed either way by their partner's views (McAllister and Clarke 2000), while quantitative research using longitudinal data indicates that when the intentions of the partners conflict, the probability of having further children is reduced (Berrington 2004). Among childless couples, research has generally shown that women's intentions are stronger predictors of entry into parenthood than men's intentions.

3.1.2   Aims of This Chapter

This chapter provides new insights into trends in childlessness by using an approach which compares findings for men and women and for individuals with different educational backgrounds. The following research questions are examined: How have childlessness levels changed across birth cohorts of women, and how do rates differ according to level of education? What proportion of childless individuals in their thirties say they intend to have children? Does this share differ by gender or level of education? What proportion of these "postponers" go on to have a child by age 42? How does this share vary by gender, education, and partnership history? What reasons do people give for not having had a child by age 42? How do these reasons vary by gender, level of education, and partnership history?

3.2   Data Sources

Three data sources are used: vital registration data, retrospective fertility histories from a series of cross-sectional surveys, and longitudinal prospective data collected within a national birth cohort study. Below, we describe the latter two data sources in more detail. The vital registration data are a long time series of data on the proportions of individuals who remain childless. The data, which are provided by the Office for National Statistics (ONS 2014), are based on births registered in England and Wales. However, these data are available for women only, and are not broken down according to any socio-economic characteristics.

3.2.1   Retrospective Fertility Histories from the General Household Survey and the United Kingdom Household Longitudinal Study

In order to examine how educational differentials in childlessness have changed over cohorts, we use a specially constructed dataset which combines data from repeated retrospective surveys of women carried out between 1979 and 2009 (General Household Survey Time Series dataset (Beaujouan et al. 2014)). This dataset is augmented by retrospective fertility data for recent cohorts collected within the first wave of the United Kingdom Household Panel Survey (UKHLS) (Knies 2014). Both the General Household Survey and the UKHLS collect information on respondents' educational attainment upon leaving full-time education and their retrospective childbearing histories, and both surveys have been used to examine educational differentials in the timing and quantum of fertility in Britain (Ní Bhrolcháin and Beaujouan 2012; Berrington et al. 2015).[1] Childlessness estimates are based on responses from women aged 40–49 at the time of the survey. Women's highest qualification upon first leaving education (i.e., at the end of continuous education) provides the best available indication of educational attainment prior to entry (or potential entry) into motherhood.[2] The analyses presented here use four categories of education: less than secondary level, secondary level, advanced level, and academic degree or equivalent. A secondary-level qualification is equivalent to a school-leaving qualification typically earned at age 16. An advanced-level qualification is typically earned at age 18, and is generally required for entry into a tertiary (university) educational institution. The interpretation of changing educational differentials in fertility over time is made more complex by the changing composition of the British population by education. The proportion of the female population who have either no qualifications or who failed to earn any secondary-level qualifications at the end of compulsory schooling (generally at age 16) decreased from 64 % of women born in 1940–1949 to just 18 % of women born in 1960–1968. Over the same cohorts, the proportion of women who earned an academic degree or another higher-level qualification increased from 9 to 20 %.

3.2.2 Prospective Data from 1970 British Birth Cohort

Prospective longitudinal data are needed to examine fertility intentions and their association with subsequent fertility behaviour. The UK is fortunate to have a number of birth cohort studies that have followed respondents from birth to adulthood. Data collected from people born in Britain in 1946 and 1958 have provided us with new insights into the parental background and life course factors associated with intentions to remain childless and childbearing outcomes (Kiernan 1989; Kneale and Joshi 2008; Berrington and Pattaro 2014). In this chapter, we use data for men and women born in Britain in one week of April 1970 (BCS70) who have been followed up in multiple waves of data collection through childhood and early

---

[1] The data are weighted to take account of survey design and non-response (Beaujouan et al. 2011; Knies 2014).

[2] We recognise that the level of educational attainment among some women is a result of their childbearing patterns: i.e., some of the youngest mothers may have had to leave full-time education as a result of becoming pregnant.

adulthood to age 42 (Elliott and Shepherd 2006).[3] We focus on individuals who were childless at age 30 (3209 childless men and 2603 childless women). Overall, 60 % of men and 46 % of women born in 1970 were childless at age 30, but far higher proportions of academic degree-educated men and women were childless at age 30 (80 % of academic degree-educated men and 69 % of academic degree-educated women). This gap reflects the tendency among individuals with a higher level of education to postpone childbearing.

At age 30, the respondents were asked the following question: "Do you intend to have any children?" The possible answers were: "yes", "no", and "don't know". At age 42, the respondents were asked to provide details of their achieved fertility. The analyses in which we compare fertility intentions with outcomes are restricted to the respondents who were present in both the age 30 and the age 42 waves. Of those respondents who reported being childless at age 30, 73 % of the men and 80 % of the women also participated in the survey at age 42.[4] The respondents who were childless at 42 were given a showcard of possible reasons for not having had children (see Appendix). The respondents were invited to tick as many reasons as were applicable. Those who ticked more than one reason were then asked to identify the reason they consider most important. In this chapter, I focus on the most important reason given.

3.3   Childlessness Trends in the UK

3.3.1   Historical Trend in Childlessness

Figure 3.1 shows for England and Wales the percentages of women born between 1920 and 1983 who were childless at age 30 and at the end of their reproductive period. Levels of childlessness at the end of the childbearing period were very low among women born in the 1940s. Childlessness started rising among later cohorts, and then stabilised among women born in the 1960s. For example, just 9 % of women in the 1946 birth cohort, but 18 % of women born in 1968 (the most recent cohort to reach age 45), had not had a child by the end of their childbearing years. Childlessness first started to increase among the cohorts born in the 1950s, who were also the cohorts who first started postponing childbearing (Office for National Statistics 2014). These two trends are related, and later in this chapter we examine the achievement of fertility intentions among "postponers".

---

[3] Since this is a birth cohort study of those born in Britain in 1970, the sample is primarily white British. No attempt is therefore made to examine ethnic differences in childlessness. Further details of the on-going study can be found here: http://www.cls.ioe.ac.uk/

[4] Response rates were slightly higher among degree-educated men and women (80 % and 85 %, respectively). Thus, more advantaged socio-economic groups may be over-represented in the reasons for childlessness.

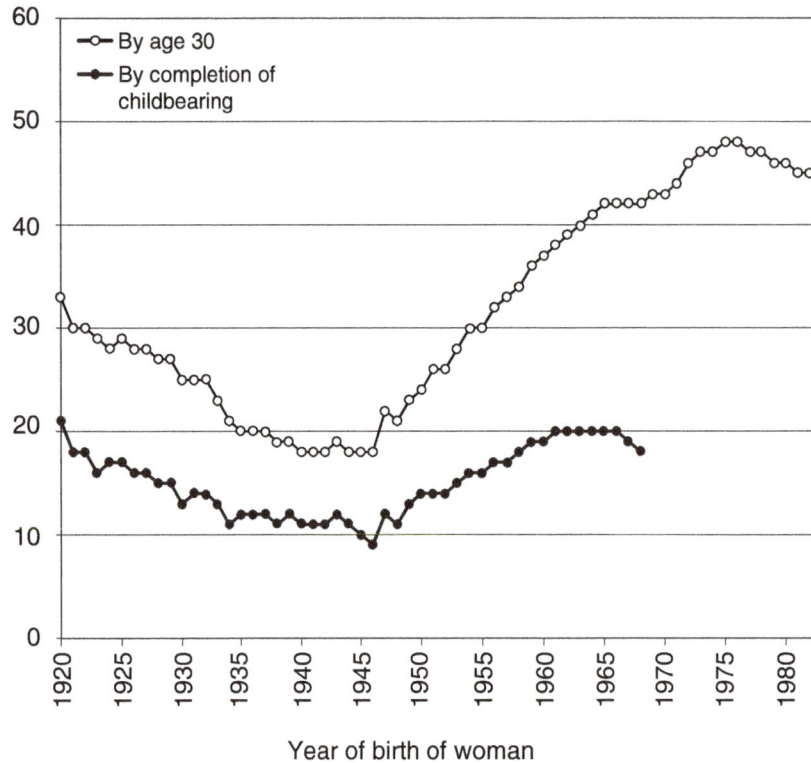

Fig. 3.1 Share of women who were childless at their 30th birthday and upon completion of childbearing, by year of birth of woman. England and Wales, in per cent (Source: ONS (2014))

The current levels of childlessness are not, however, historically unprecedented. As has been shown for many other European countries (Dykstra 2009) and the United States (Morgan 1991), there is evidence in the UK of a U-shaped pattern of childlessness among birth cohorts. Historically, more than one-fifth of the population of England and Wales were childless, largely as a result of non-marriage (Hajnal 1965).

Historically in Britain, there was a tradition of late marriage, and high proportions of the population never married. These trends were characteristic of the West European Marriage Pattern, as described by Hajnal (1965). In the early twentieth century, high levels of non-marriage were associated with imbalances in the sex ratio resulting from excess male emigration and male mortality during the First World War (Kiernan 1988; Dykstra 2009). Additionally, as noted by Holden (2005), non-marriage may have become economically feasible for middle- and upper-class women due to the availability of jobs in light industry, services, and businesses in urban areas.

What differentiates the patterns of contemporary cohorts from those of historical cohorts is that today the high levels of childlessness at age 30 are associated with the postponement of the start of parenthood to older ages. The share of women who were childless at age 30 rose from 18 % of those born in 1946, to 42 % of those born in 1968, and to 46 % of those born in 1983. The data suggest, however, that levels of postponement and childlessness are no longer increasing, and may have even gone into reverse, with the proportion women who are childless at 30 peaking among those born in the mid-1970s.

3.3.2   Educational Differentials in Childlessness in the UK

Figure 3.2 shows the proportions of British women who were childless at age 40 according to birth cohort and highest educational level upon first leaving full-time education. The positive educational gradient in childlessness existed in all birth cohorts starting with women born in the 1940s. The proportion childless among respondents with a tertiary education is roughly double that among respondents with no or less than secondary qualifications (i.e., the least educated). Over time, the educational gradient has increased very slightly as a result of faster increases in childlessness among women with tertiary education. Thus, among British women born in the 1960s, 22 % of university graduates, and 10 % of the least educated group remained childless.

These strong educational differences have tended to fuel discussions in the media, with commentators frequently asserting that many highly educated women

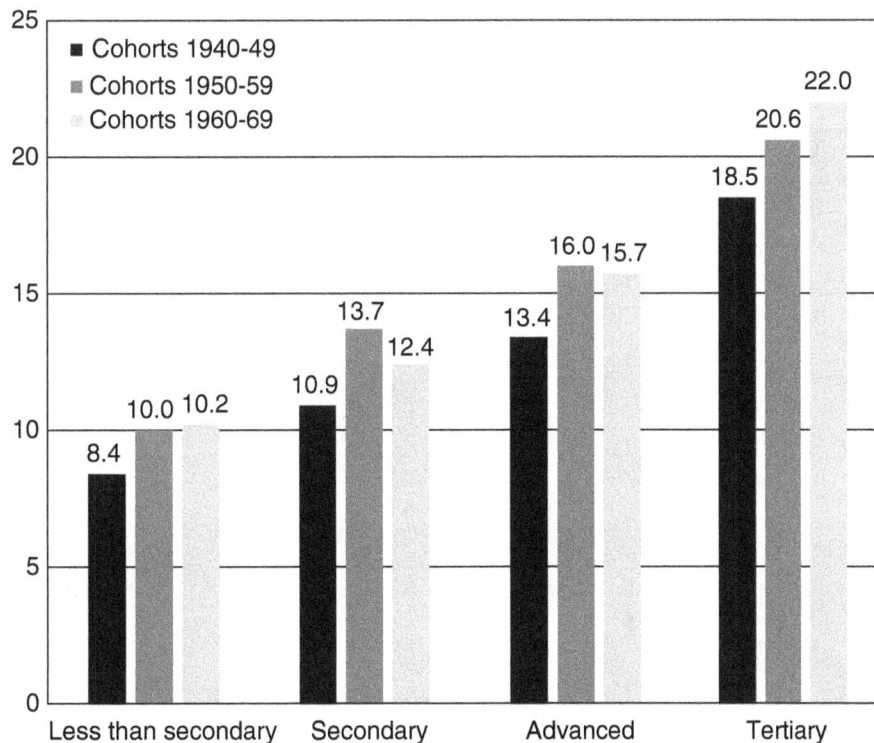

Fig. 3.2 Childlessness by birth cohort and highest level of education. British women aged 40–49 born 1940–1969, in per cent (Source: Author's analysis of CPC General Household Survey Time Series and UKHLS)

in Britain are choosing to remain childless in order to "pursue a career", or that they have postponed starting a family in response to the conflicting demands of their career, and "have left it too late" to have a child (McAllister and Clarke 2000; Hadfield et al. 2007). In the following sections, we examine the likelihood that highly educated women intend to remain childless, and how their intentions compare with those of their male counterparts.

3.4 Fertility Intentions and Childlessness

3.4.1 Fertility Intentions

Studies using a number of different data sources have consistently shown that very few British men and women intend to remain childless—at least if we take survey responses on intentions at face value (Berrington 2004; Ní Bhrolcháin et al. 2010; Berrington and Pattaro 2014). Research indicates that the proportion of individuals who intend to remain childless increases with age, as individuals adjust their intentions according to their lived experiences (Berrington 2004; Iacovou and Tavares 2011). Nevertheless, in the UK a large share of individuals who are still childless in their thirties express a strong desire to have children. This is consistent with the notion that individuals are postponing their childbearing to later ages, rather than rejecting parenthood altogether (Ní Bhrolcháin et al. 2010; Berrington and Pattaro 2014). Table 3.1 below presents the childbearing intentions at age 30 of childless men and women born in Britain in 1970, according to their highest level of qualification.

Table 3.1 Intention to have a child according to highest level of education among 1970 British Cohort Study members who were childless at age 30. Row per cent

	Yes	Don't know	No	Self/partner not able to have children	Number of cases
Men					
Less than secondary	57.2	22.8	16.3	3.7	754
Secondary	62.6	21.5	13.1	2.8	1044
Advanced	64.1	22.0	11.5	2.4	460
Tertiary	69.3	19.3	10.2	1.3	945
Total	63.5	21.2	12.8	2.5	3203
Women					
Less than secondary	58.1	18.9	15.0	8.1	434
Secondary	63.2	14.3	14.4	8.0	810
Advanced	66.8	17.1	11.8	4.3	397
Tertiary	67.6	19.5	9.7	3.1	958
Total	64.5	17.4	12.4	5.7	2599

Source: Author's analysis of BCS70

Around 3 % of men and 6 % of women said that either they or their partner were unable to have children. The percentage who reported infertility problems was much higher among respondents with lower levels of education, reflecting a selection effect whereby less educated men and women who remain childless at age 30 are a select subset of the population with lower levels of education, who typically start their childbearing at earlier ages (Kneale and Joshi 2008; Berrington et al. 2015).

Overall, the respondents' childbearing intentions at age 30 differed little by gender: around two-thirds of both men and women who were childless expressed an intention to have at least one child, 12 % said they do not intend to have a child, while around 20 % said they are unsure. Tertiary-educated childless men and women were more likely to express a positive intention, while those with the least education were more likely to express a negative intention. The majority can therefore be classified as postponers i.e., they have a positive intention to have a child, but they remain childless. However, the fact that 20 % of the group are uncertain suggests that circumstances could easily play a role in shaping their decision.

3.4.2 Fertility Outcomes

Figure 3.3 examines the question of whether the respondents who were childless at age 30 had entered parenthood by the time they were interviewed in 2012, when they were age 42. Once again, there is remarkable consistency in the findings for childless men and women. Fertility intentions at age 30 were a good predictor of fertility outcomes: around 30 % of those who said they intend to have a child remained childless at age 42, compared to around one-half of those who said they are uncertain in their intentions, and around three-quarters of those who said they do not intend to have a child. Half of both male and female postponers—i.e., those who said they intend to have children—went on to have two or more children. Of those who did not intend to have any children, 11 % of men and 18 % of women went on to have at least one child. Thus, the fertility intentions of the respondents were both under- and overachieved, but the levels of underachievement were higher. Men and women with uncertain intentions appear to have behaved in a similar fashion: compared to respondents with positive intentions, they were more likely to have remained childless or to have had just one child, and they were less likely to have had a second child. In further analyses (not shown) highly educated men and women are found to be more likely than less educated individuals to achieve their positive intentions for childbearing at older ages. This is consistent with earlier findings (Berrington 2004; Berrington and Pattaro 2014), and is likely to be related to the selection effect whereby individuals from lower educational groups who remain childless at age 30 are more likely to have other socio-demographic characteristics (e.g., health problems) associated with a lower likelihood of becoming a parent.

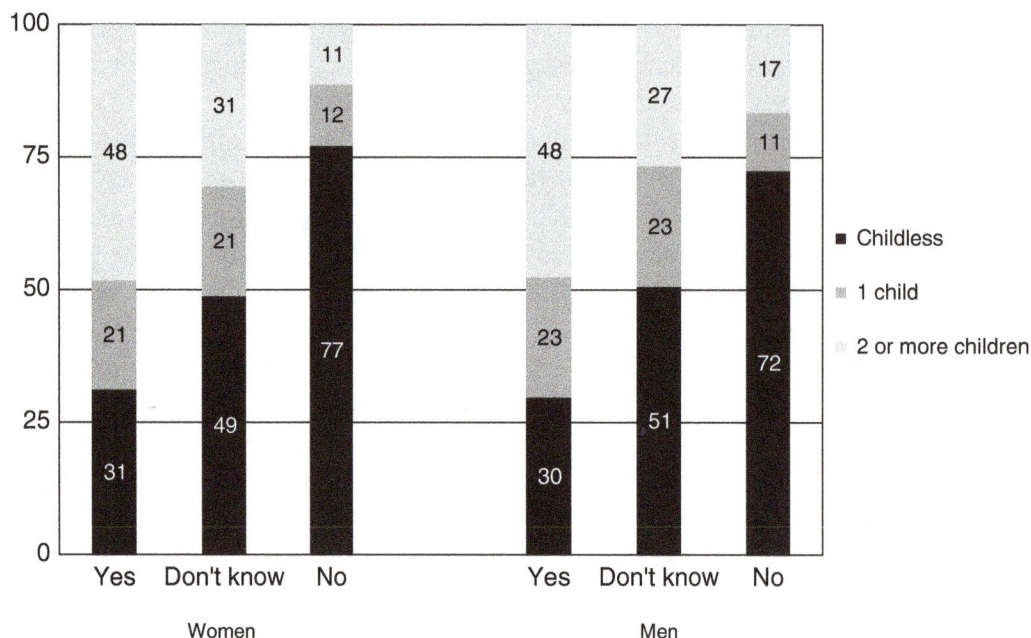

Fig. 3.3 Distribution of achieved family size at age 42, according to intentions at age 30. 1970 British Cohort Study members who were childless at age 30, in per cent. Sample size for men is: 1359 Yes, 441 Don't know, 280 No. Sample size for women is: 1260 Yes, 345 Don't know, 246 No (Source: Author's analysis of BCS70)

Table 3.2 Percentage childless according to partnership status at age 42. 1970 British Cohort Study members who were childless and had never had a co-residential union at age 30. In per cent

	Men	Women
Never married no partner	92	81
Never married currently cohabiting	50	52
Currently married	20	23
Divorced, separated, widowed, currently no partner	43	27
Divorced, separated, widowed, currently cohabiting	40	75
Civil partnership/ex civil partnership	100	50

Source: Author's analysis of BCS70

3.4.3 Partnership Experience and the Likelihood of Achieving Intentions

An important pathway through which positive fertility intentions remain unrealised is partnership experience (McAllister and Clarke 2000; Berrington 2004; Carmichael and Whittaker 2007; Berrington and Pattaro 2014). To gain a better understanding of this dynamic, let us look at BCS70 cohort members who were childless and had never lived in a co-residential union at age 30, but who had a positive intention to have a child. Table 3.2 shows the percentage of this group who remained childless by their partnership status at age 42. Of course, we cannot tell from these data the extent to which partnership status had a *causal* effect on childlessness, since both partnership formation and childbearing are likely to be influenced by other factors, such as the respondent's health status, work ambitions, and attitudes regarding family formation. Nevertheless, the table clearly shows that partnership experience plays a key role in childlessness over the life course. The vast majority (nine out of ten men and eight out of ten women) of those who were never married and did not have a co-residential partner at age 42 remained childless. By comparison, about half of those who were in a cohabiting relationship at age 42 remained childless. The group most likely to have achieved their fertility intentions were those who married after age 30 and remained married at 42; only one-fifth of this group remained childless. In comparison, levels of childlessness were higher among those who married after age 30 but subsequently separated.

3.5 Reasons for Remaining Childless

Of the BCS70 respondents at age 42, one-quarter of the men and just under one-fifth of the women had never had a biological child of their own. Consistent with our earlier findings for women based on the General Household Survey/Understanding Society Survey (Sect. 3.3.2), we observe a strong positive educational gradient in the proportion childless among women: one-quarter of female university graduates born in 1970 remained childless, compared to 15 % of women with less than secondary qualifications.[5] However, among the male cohort members, the differences by educational level in the proportion childless were much smaller (27 % of male university graduates were childless at 42, compared to 23 % of men with less than secondary-level qualifications).

3.5.1 *Work and Careers Not Reported as the Main Reason*

Table 3.3 shows the reasons given by childless respondents at age 42 for why they had not (yet) had children. Recall that respondents were asked to tick the possible reasons, which are shown in the Appendix. Three main reasons dominate the responses. The most common reason was that the respondent had not wanted children (cited by 28 % of men and 31 % of women). The second most common reason was that the respondent had never met the right person (cited by 23 % of men and 19 % of women). A similar share of women cited health reasons: i.e., that they or their partner were infertile, or had some other health problem. Men were less likely to cite their own infertility as a reason for childlessness.

---

[5]For this analysis only, educational attainment is measured at age 42 so as to maximise sample size.

Table 3.3 Most important reason for remaining childless. 1970 British Cohort Study members who remained childless at age 42. Column per cent

	Men	Women
Not wanted children	28	31
Never met right person	23	19
Own infertility	3	12
Other health reason	2	4
Partner's infertility	4	3
Wanted children but not got around to it	6	5
Partner did not want children	3	4
I have been focused on my career	3	2
Financial/housing situation would have made it difficult	2	2
Other reason	2	2
Partner has been sterilised/vasectomy/hysterectomy	1	1
Partner already has children & does not want more	1	1
In a same-sex partnership[a]	1	0
Did not want to compromise relationship	1	0
No particular reason	18	12
Don't want to answer	2	3
Total	976 (100 %)	845 (100 %)

Source: Author's analysis of BCS70
[a]"In a same-sex partnership" was one of the write-in responses that respondents added to the list of possible answers (see the Appendix)

Other reasons were less prevalent. A small share of respondents (3 % of men and 4 % of women) said their partner did not want children, which reminds us of the importance of the couple in childbearing behaviour. A significant minority, 18 % of male and 12 % of female childless respondents, did not tick any reason.

Some respondents agreed with the statement that they had wanted children, but had not got around to it, which suggests ambivalence about childbearing. Just 3 % of men and 2 % of women cited being focused on their career as their main reason for remaining childless. In further analyses (not shown), we compare the reasons given according to the highest level of education. While childless university graduates were slightly more likely than others to have responded that they were focused on their career, the shares were still only 4 % of men and 3 % of women. These findings are in stark contrast to the prevailing tone of media discussions, which often portray childless women as being too focused on their career.

In fact, we see two main differences in the distribution of reasons for childlessness based on the highest level of education. First, health reasons were cited by a higher proportion of the least educated women. Second, both male and female university graduates had a greater tendency than respondents with less education to report that they had never met the right person: 30 % of male and 34 % of female university graduates gave this response, compared with 19 % of men and 28 % of women with less than a secondary education.

Table 3.4 Most important reason for remaining childless according to legal marital status at age 42. Female 1970 British Cohort Study members who were childless at age 42. Column per cent

	Married	Div./Wid./Sep.	Never married
Not want children	34	26	30
Health reasons[a]	32	24	12
Wanted but not got round to it	5	5	5
Partner did not want children	3	6	3
Never met the right person	2	14	31
I have been focused on career	3	4	1
No particular reason	10	11	12
Other & don't know[b]	6	8	4
Don't want to say	4	3	2
Total	264 (100 %)	111 (100 %)	452 (100 %)

Source: Author's analysis of BCS70
[a]Health reasons includes "own and partner's infertility"
[b]Other includes "financial and housing worries", "partner already had children", "did not want to compromise relationship", and "in a same-sex partnership"

3.5.2 The Importance of Having a Partner

Table 3.4 presents the reasons for remaining childless by legal marital status at age 42. We show the pattern for women only, since the findings for men are very similar. Those women who had been married but who had remained childless were more likely than women who had never married to say either that they had not wanted to have children, or that there were health reasons that had prevented them from having children. By contrast, among those who had never married, almost one-third said they had never met the right person, and another 30 % said they had not wanted to have children. Interestingly, the proportion of respondents who reported that their partner had not wanted children was slightly higher among those who were divorced or separated; at around 6 %. The divorced, separated, and widowed group were also quite likely to say they had not met the right person.

3.6 Discussion

This chapter has provided new insights into childlessness in Britain by showing how the overall trend masks considerable educational differences in the likelihood of not having children. Unlike in some other European countries, such as the Netherlands (van Agtmaal-Wobma and van Huis 2008) and Norway (Andersson et al. 2009), educational differentials in childlessness are not narrowing over time, but remain large, and are even increasing slightly. Today, tertiary-educated women are roughly twice as likely as women with low levels of education to remain childless.

The co-existence in Britain of relatively large completed family sizes (of around 1.9 children per woman) with high levels of childlessness results from different childbearing patterns within different sub-groups of the population (Berrington et al. 2015). High levels of childlessness among tertiary-educated women are being offset by relatively high rates of progression to third and fourth births, especially among mothers with the lowest levels of education (Berrington et al. 2015). The cohort fertility rates for women born in the 1980s suggest that childlessness, both at age 30 and upon completion of childbearing, may no longer be increasing. Thus, we may not see in Britain the very high levels of childlessness currently observed in countries like Austria and Italy.

Levels of childlessness, at least at age 42, are higher among British men than among British women, although it is of course possible for men to enter fatherhood at older ages. Nevertheless, a significant minority of men will remain childless. Educational differentials in childlessness are much smaller among men than among women. The proportion of men without children is high both among more educated and less educated men, though we might speculate that the pathways through which this occurs differ according to socio-economic status. Consistent with Demey et al. (2014), we see a significant minority of socio-economically disadvantaged men who are not given the opportunity for family formation. Quantitative evidence from the 1970 and previous 1958 British cohorts (Berrington and Pattaro 2014) and qualitative evidence from Jamieson et al. (2010) suggest that for some men (particularly socio-economically disadvantaged men), finding a partner can be very difficult, which leads indirectly to unfulfilled childbearing intentions. While some women with low levels of education are unable to fulfil their childbearing intentions between ages 30 and 42, the share among women is much smaller than it is among men.

Our findings regarding fertility intentions and outcomes for the 1970 British birth cohort suggest that relatively few men and women are rejecting parenthood. In terms of the "continuum of childlessness", this so-called "certain group" (or "early articulators") who declare that they do not intend to have children are a minority (around about one in eight of those who are childless at age 30).[6] The majority of both men and women are "postponers", as at age 30 just under two-thirds of childless men and women express a positive intention to have a child. There is a substantial group of childless men and women who report having uncertain fertility intentions. Some of these respondents would probably fall into the "ambivalent group", as described by McAllister and Clarke (2000), who have not explicitly considered whether they intend to have children. Other uncertain respondents may have considered their ideal family size, but remain uncertain about having a child because they are unsure of their situation. For example, they may not know whether they will have a suitable partner who also wants children, or whether childcare will be available. The significance of uncertainty in fertility intentions has not received the attention it should (although see Berrington 2004; Ní Bhrolcháin et al. 2010;

---

[6] We note that there may be a social desirability effect whereby British respondents may be unwilling to express a desire to remain childless, as British society and media tend to have a pro-natalist bias (Hadfield et al. 2007).

Ní Bhrolcháin and Beaujouan 2011). Evidence from the 1970 cohort suggests that those who are uncertain have an intermediate chance of having a first birth: i.e., in between those who have a negative intention and those who have a positive intention. Thus, if those who were uncertain had been included in the group with positive fertility intentions, there would have been a lower level of agreement between intentions and outcomes. Moreover, uncertain intentions might reflect the fact that intentions for childbearing can be affected by period circumstances, such as partnership status and the availability of childcare, some of which could be affected by social policy changes.

Consistent with findings from earlier UK and US cohorts, respondents both under- and overachieve their intended fertility (Morgan and Rackin 2010; Berrington and Pattaro 2014), but childless postponers are more likely to underachieve: overall, 30 % of those who were childless at age 30 and who said they intend to have a child were still childless at age 42. Interestingly, this share is almost identical for male and female postponers. It is of course possible that the respondents' intentions were modified between ages 30 and 42 in response to circumstances such as partnership experiences and work situations. Consistent with Berrington (2004), we find that the percentage of postponers who achieved their intentions was higher among men and women with higher levels of education and those who married (and stay married). Over one-third of postponing men with no or secondary-level qualifications remained childless at age 42.

Morgan (1991) cautioned against viewing childlessness as a modern phenomenon, and suggested that the reasons why people are childless today may not be very different from those of previous generations. In this British cohort, childless respondents gave a variety of reasons for not having had a child at age 42: around three in ten said they "had not wanted children", and two in ten said they had "never met the right person". Health issues were also frequently cited, especially by women, who were more likely than men to have reported their own infertility problems. It would be useful to know the extent to which these health problems were associated with the postponement of fertility and age-related declines in fecundability. If health played an important role, the association between increased postponement and increased childlessness among cohorts born from the 1950s onwards may be partially causal.

Comparatively few men and women reported that they had not had children because they had "not got round to it" or were "focused on career". The finding that career demands do not play a large role in the decision to remain childless is consistent with previous research for the UK, Australia, and Finland (McAllister and Clarke 2000; Carmichael and Whittaker 2007; Miettinen 2010). The reported reasons for childlessness are similar across genders and levels of education, but differ more by partnership history. Finding and staying together with an appropriate partner appears to be a key element in childbearing decisions.

This study has a number of limitations. The type of evidence collected in quantitative surveys is limited, and individuals' statements about the number of children they want are likely to be subject to social desirability effects and post-hoc rationalisations. The chapter presents intentions as measured at age 30, and outcomes at age

42. It would be interesting to know how individuals' intentions change between ages 30 and 42 in response to life course events. Second, while this study is novel in that childlessness data are available for both men and women, the data do not provide information about couples. As childbearing is generally a couple-level activity, one would ideally want to investigate the preferences and constraints of both partners. Finally, many of the reasons offered to respondents in the BCS70 questionnaire for not having had children are negative, such as being in poor health or not having found the right partner. Ideally, the reasons offered should also include positive pull factors of being childfree, such as having more freedom and disposable income (Gillespie 2003). Around 30 % of childless women ticked the "not wanted to have children" box but this still leaves open the question of why they did not want to have children.

In summary, childlessness increased first among the cohorts born in the 1950s, who were also the first cohorts to start postponing childbearing. Postponement and childlessness may be causally related, e.g. through reduced fecundity with age, but both are also manifestations of underlying changes in women's lives, such as opportunities for women to develop a career, the availability of reliable contraception, and increased partnership postponement and instability (Murphy 1993; Hobcraft and Kiernan 1995; Thomson et al. 2012).

Acknowledgements This work is part-funded by the ESRC Centre for Population Change (CPC). CPC is a joint initiative of the Universities of Southampton, St Andrews, Edinburgh, Stirling, Strathclyde; in partnership with the Office for National Statistics, and National Records for Scotland. The Centre is funded by the Economic and Social Research Council (ESRC) grant number RES-ES/K007394/1. The General Household Survey is conducted by the Office for National Statistics. The United Kingdom Household Longitudinal Study is conducted by the Institute for Social and Economic Research at the University of Essex. The CPC GHS time series data-file was constructed in collaboration with Máire Ní Bhrolcháin, Éva Beaujouan and Mark Lyons Amos. The 1970 British Birth Cohort (BCS70) is conducted by the Centre for Longitudinal Studies, Institute for Education, London. Access to all data is provided by the UK Data Archive. Neither the original data creators, depositors, or funders bear responsibility for the further analysis or interpretation of the data presented in this study. Thanks are due to Juliet Stone and Éva Beaujouan who commented on early versions of this work.

Appendix

Most Important Reason for Remaining Childless Showcard.
  1970 British Birth Cohort Study, Age 42 Questionnaire.

1. Infertility problems
2. Partner sterilized, had vasectomy/hysterectomy
3. Other health reasons
4. I have not wanted to have children
5. I have wanted to have children but not got round to it
6. I have been focused on my career

7. I have never met the right person to have children with
8. My partner has not wanted to have children
9. My partner already has children and has not wanted more
10. I have not wanted to compromise my relationship with my partner
11. My financial situation would have made it difficult
12. My housing situation would have made it difficult
13. No particular reason
14. Other reason – please write in:_____

Literature

Andersson, G., Knudsen, L. B., Neyer, G., Teschner, K., Rønsen, M., Lappegård, T., Neyer, G., Skrede, K., Teschner, K., & Vikat, A. (2009). Cohort fertility patterns in the Nordic countries. *Demographic Research, 20*, 313.

Baum, F., & Cope, D. R. (1980). Some characteristics of intentionally childless wives in Britain. *Journal of Biosocial Science, 12*, 287–300.

Beaujouan, E., Brown, J., & Ní Bhrolcháin, M. (2011). Reweighting the general household survey, 1979–2007. *Population Trends, 145*, 119–145.

Beaujouan, E., Berrington, A., Lyon-Amos, M., & Ní Bhrolcháin, M. (2014). *User guide to the Centre for Population Change GHS database 1979–2009* (CPC working paper 47). Southampton: ESRC Centre for Population Change.

Berrington, A. M. (2004). Perpetual postponers? Women's, men's and couple's fertility intentions and subsequent fertility behaviour. *Population Trends, 117*, 9–19.

Berrington, A., & Pattaro, S. (2014). Educational differences in fertility desires, intentions and behaviour: A life course perspective. *Advances in Life Course Research, 21*, 10–27.

Berrington, A., Stone, J., & Beaujouan, E. (2015). Educational differentials in timing and quantum of fertility: Evidence from 1940–1969 cohorts. *Demographic Research, 33*, 26.

Bhrolcháin, N., & Beaujouan, E. (2011). Uncertainty in fertility intentions in Britain, 1979–2007. *Vienna Yearbook of Population Research, 9*, 99–129.

Black, R., & Scull, L. (2005). *Beyond childlessness: For every woman who ever wanted to have a child – And didn't.* London: Rodale International Ltd.

Campbell, E. (1985). *The childless marriage: An exploratory study of couples who do not want children.* London: Tavistock Publications.

Carmichael, G. A., & Whittaker, A. (2007). Choice and circumstance: Qualitative insights into contemporary childlessness in Australia. *European Journal of Population, 23*, 111–143.

Coleman, D. (1996). *Europe's population in the 1990s.* Oxford: Oxford University Press.

Day, J. (2013). *Rocking the life unexpected: 12 weeks to your Plan B for a meaningful and fulfilling life without children.* Seattle: CreateSpace Independent Publishing Platform.

Demey, D., Berrington, A., Evandrou, M., & Falkingham, J. (2014). Living alone and psychological well-being in mid-life: Does partnership history matter? *Journal of Epidemiology and Community Health, 68*, 403–410.

Dykstra, P. A. (2009). Childless old age. In P. Uhlenberg (Ed.), *International handbook of population aging* (pp. 671–690). Dordercht: Springer.

Eijkemans, M. J., van Poppel, F., Habbema, D. F., Smith, K. R., Leridon, H., & te Velde, E. R. (2014). Too old to have children? Lessons from natural fertility populations. *Human Reproduction, 29*, 1304–1312.

Elliott, J., & Shepherd, P. (2006). Cohort profile: 1970 British birth cohort (BCS70). *International Journal of Epidemiology, 35*, 836–843.

Gillespie, R. (1999). Voluntary childlessness in the United Kingdom. *Reproductive Health Matters, 7*, 43–53.

Gillespie, R. (2003). Childfree and feminine: Understanding the gender identity of voluntarily childless women. *Gender & Society, 17*(1), 122–136.

Hadfield, L., Rudoe, N., & Sanderson-Mann, J. (2007). Motherhood, choice and the British media: A time to reflect. *Gender and Education, 19*, 255–263.

Hajnal, J. (1965). European marriage patterns in perspective. In D. V. Glass & D. E. C. Eversley (Eds.), *Population in history*. London: Arnold.

Hobcraft, J. N., & Kiernan, K. E. (1995, September). Becoming a parent in Europe. Plenary paper for European population conference (pp. 27–65). In *EAPS/IUSSP Proceedings of European population conference Milan*.

Holden, K. (2005). Imaginary widows: Spinsters, marriage, and the "lost generation" in Britain after the Great War. *Journal of Family History, 30*, 388–409.

Houseknecht, S. K. (1987). Voluntary childlessness. In B. Marvin & S. K. Steinmetz (Eds.), *Handbook of marriage and the family* (pp. 369–395). New York: Plenum Press.

Iacovou, M., & Tavares, L. P. C. (2011). Yearning, learning, and conceding: Reasons men and women change their childbearing intentions. *Population and Development Review, 37*, 89–123.

Jamieson, L., Milburn, K. B., Simpson, R., & Wasoff, F. (2010). Fertility and social change: The neglected contribution of men's approaches to becoming partners and parents. *The Sociological Review, 58*, 463–485.

Keizer, R., Dykstra, P. A., & Jansen, M. D. (2008). Pathways into childlessness: Evidence of gendered life course dynamics. *Journal of Biosocial Science, 40*(06), 863–878.

Kiernan, K. E. (1988). Who remains celibate? *Journal of Biosocial Science, 20*, 253–264.

Kiernan, K. E. (1989). Who remains childless? *Journal of Biosocial Science, 21*, 387–398.

Kneale, D., & Joshi, H. (2008). Postponement and childlessness: Evidence from two British cohorts. *Demographic Research, 19*. http://www.demographic-research.org/Volumes/Vol19/58/. Accessed 28 July 2015.

Knies, G. (2014). *The UK household longitudinal study waves 1–4. User manual.* https://www.understandingsociety.ac.uk/documentation/mainstage. Accessed 28 July 2015.

Leridon, H. (2008). A new estimate of permanent sterility by age: Sterility defined as the inability to conceive. *Population Studies, 62*, 15–24.

Letherby, G. (2002). Childless and bereft?: Stereotypes and realities in relation to 'voluntary' and 'involuntary' childlessness and womanhood. *Sociological Inquiry, 72*, 7–20.

McAllister, F., & Clarke, L. (2000). Voluntary childlessness: Trends and implications. In G. R. Bentley & C. G. Mascie-Taylor (Eds.), *Infertility in the modern world. Present and future prospects* (pp. 189–237). Cambridge: Cambridge University Press.

Merz, E. M., & Liefbroer, A. C. (2012). The attitude toward voluntary childlessness in Europe: Cultural and institutional explanations. *Journal of Marriage and Family, 74*, 587–600.

Miettinen, A. (2010). Voluntary or involuntary childlessness? Socio-demographic factors and childlessness intentions among childless Finnish men and women aged 25–44. *Finnish Yearbook of Population Research, 45*, 5–24.

Morgan, S. P. (1991). Late nineteenth-and early twentieth-century childlessness. *American Journal of Sociology, 97*, 779–807.

Morgan, S. P., & Rackin, H. (2010). The correspondence between fertility intentions and behavior in the United States. *Population and Development Review, 36*, 91–118.

Murphy, M. (1993). The contraceptive pill and women's employment as factors in fertility change in Britain 1963–1980: A challenge to the conventional view. *Population Studies, 47*, 221–243.

Ní Bhrolcháin, M., & Beaujouan, E. (2012). Fertility postponement is largely due to rising educational enrolment. *Population Studies, 66*, 311–327.

Ní Bhrolcháin, M., Beaujouan, E., & Berrington, A. M. (2010). Stability and change in fertility intentions in Britain 1991–2007. *Population Trends, 141*, 13–35.

ONS (Office for National Statistics). (2014). *Childbearing for women born in different years, England and Wales, 2013.* http://www.ons.gov.uk/ons/rel/fertility-analysis/childbearing-for-women-born-in-different-years/2013/stb-cohort-fertility-2013.html#tab-Childlessness. Accessed 28 July 2015.

Rijken, A. J., & Merz, E. M. (2014). Double standards: Differences in norms on voluntary childlessness for men and women. *European Sociological Review, 30,* 470–482.

Simpson, R. (2009). Delayed childbearing and childlessness in Britain. In J. Stillwell, D. Kneale, & E. Coast (Eds.), *Fertility, living arrangements, care and mobility: Understanding population trends and processes* (Vol. 1, pp. 23–40). Dordrecht: Springer.

Thomson, E., Winkler-Dworak, M., Spielauer, M., & Prskawetz, A. (2012). Union instability as an engine of fertility? A microsimulation model for France. *Demography, 49,* 175–195.

van Agtmaal-Wobma, E., & van Huis, M. (2008). De relatie tussen vruchtbaarheid en opleidingsniveau van de vrouw [The relationship between fertility and educational level of women]. *Bevolkingtrends, 56,* 32–41.

Chapter 4
Childlessness in France

Katja Köppen, Magali Mazuy, and Laurent Toulemon

4.1   Introduction

Current discussions on decreasing birth rates, high rates of childlessness, and a lack of support for working parents in some European countries often cite France as an example of a country with a successful family policy. Compared with most other western European countries, France not only has higher maternal labour force participation rates; it also has higher fertility rates. As the average French woman has two children, the birth rate in France is higher than in any other European country, except for Iceland and Ireland (Eurostat 2012a). Less than 15 % of women in France remain childless; a share which is considerably lower than those of women in neighbouring countries like England, Switzerland, or Germany. In this article, we will attempt to explain why parenthood is still a standard part of the biography among French men and women. After providing an overview of the institutional regulations and family policies, we will present the most important demographic indicators of childlessness, and look at how they differ by social group.

K. Köppen (✉)
Institute of Sociology and Demographic Research, University of Rostock, Rostock, Germany
e-mail: katja.koeppen@uni-rostock.de

M. Mazuy • L. Toulemon
French Institute for Demographic Studies (INED), Paris, France
e-mail: mazuy@ined.fr; toulemon@ined.fr

© The Author(s) 2017

M. Kreyenfeld, D. Konietzka (eds.), *Childlessness in Europe: Contexts, Causes, and Consequences*, Demographic Research Monographs, DOI 10.1007/978-3-319-44667-7_4

4.2 Institutional Framework and Family Policies

When seeking to explain the high fertility rates and comparatively low childlessness rates in France, scholars often cite the country's extensive and well-developed child care system and generous family benefit system, which provide tax deductions and financial support to families with many children (Ehmann 1997; Becker 2000; Fagnani 2002; Letablier 2002; Köppen 2006; Thévenon and Luci 2012). These high levels of state support and family-friendly measures can be traced back in history. France experienced a rapid drop in fertility much earlier than most countries, as birth rates were falling even in the nineteenth century. French women born in the middle of the nineteenth century had an average of 3.4 children. During the same period, women in France' neighbouring country Germany had an average of 5.4 births, which was higher than the European average (Festy 1979: 49). Since then family policy in France has always had strong pro-natalistic elements. Even today, this bias is apparent in the promotion of large families and the relative neglect of one-child families in French family policy (Schultheis 1988: 92).

Some contemporary family benefits in France can also be traced back to charity programmes of Catholic enterprises during the nineteenth century: for example, child allowances, support of proprietary, and the work-free family Sunday evolved from voluntary benefits offered by employers (Spieß 2004: 51). During this period, so-called compensation funds were established to compensate wage earners for the burdens associated with rearing and caring for children. After employees went to court and demanded that these initially voluntary benefits were made mandatory in work contracts, the benefits became a standard part of regular wage employment, and these programmes increasingly came under state control. First, family compensation funds, which took over the payment of family benefits from companies, were founded in 1920. A large proportion of employees had to join these funds in 1932. In response to the on-going decline in the population, the *Code de la Famille* standardised and regulated the hitherto non-governmental, corporate-based family policy in 1939. Today, family benefits are organised and financed through the *Caisse Nationale d'Allocation Familiale* (CNAF), the bureaus in charge of distributing family benefits. One-third of the funding of the CNAF comes from the government, and two-thirds comes from employer contributions and tobacco tax proceeds (Spieß 2004).

Another factor that helps to explain contemporary family policies in France is French laicism. The state in France has a strong legal mandate to intervene and participate in family matters and childcare arrangements. In particular, childcare is supported and subsidised by the state. There are historical reasons for this high degree of government involvement in family arrangements. To attenuate the influence of the Catholic Church on family and education and to ensure that children were raised as loyal republican citizens, the French government took over control of the educational system in the late nineteenth century. In 1881 a public educational system based on republican-secularist principles was established in France (Veil 2002: 1). As children are seen in France as the "future of the nation" (Letablier

2002: 171), the state is considered responsible for their well-being, health, and education. The government aims to provide equal opportunities to all children, regardless of their parents' income. The principle that childcare should be state-supported is also based in moral concepts regarding the relationship between state and church. The church lobbied for Catholic and conservative values, whereas the state advocated republican values: i.e., the principles of *égalité et liberté*. To ensure that women do not have to leave the labour market when they become mothers, the state supports them by providing adequate childcare (Letablier 2002).

Having children is not seen as a reason for quitting work or reducing work hours. Although attendance is not obligatory, currently almost all French children between the ages of three and six attend preschool, the *écoles maternelles*. Thus, preschool is an established institution in France. The majority of children attend preschool between 8.30 a.m. and 4.30 p.m., and some preschools offer care after those hours (the so-called *garderie*). Most of the *écoles maternelles* are state-run and free of charge; however, parents have to pay a small amount for lunch and care after the official closing time (Letablier 2002: 172). In addition to public services, there are other forms of childcare in France. Childcare for children younger than 3 years of age is especially diverse, and is dominated by privately organised domestic childcare arrangements. The government provides financial allowances and tax deductions that offset the costs of employing a registered day-care professional (*assistante maternelle agree*). These benefits are available for dual-earner parents with children under 6 years of age who employ a registered day-care professional. Parents can also engage a nanny (*nourrice*), who may perform household work in addition to providing childcare. In this case as well, parents can apply for governmental assistance and make use of tax deductions (Becker 2000: 231f.). Children in compulsory education in France attend school all day. School starts at 8.30 a.m. and usually finishes at 4.00 or 4.30 p.m., interrupted by a break for lunch, which is paid for in part by the parents. Children in pre- or primary schools may attend after-school care programmes. However, as there is no school on Wednesday afternoons, parents may be forced to find alternative childcare arrangements, work part-time, or use the 35-h limit on working hours in France to take a half-day off on Wednesdays.

The cost of childrearing is reduced in France and parents are encouraged to return to work soon after giving birth not just by a comprehensive system of childcare, but also by a system of monetary benefits for families. In France, monetary incentives to remain home after the birth of the first child are comparatively low. Child benefits and paid parental leave have long been available to two-child families only. Before 1994, only families with at least three children were eligible for these allowances. However, since 2004 parents with one child also receive a basic allowance for the first 3 years and paid parental leave.

In France, under the principle of family splitting, the family's tax burden is reduced based on the number of children. In this system families with at least three children and high-income households have the highest level of tax relief (Dingeldey 2000: 76). Thus, large families with dual-earner parents benefit the most from tax deductions.

This historically evolved system of comprehensive and reasonably priced childcare, lower taxes for large families, and high levels of acceptance of and appreciation for children in French society are among the reasons why France has relatively high birth rates, but also high levels of labour market attachment among women, and among mothers in particular. The dilemma of how to combine work and family that many women still have to face is thus less pronounced in France, but also the social pressure to have children is stronger in France than in most other western European countries (Debest and Mazuy 2014).

4.3 Female Employment

In recent decades the share of women who have a high level of education has been increasing in Europe. At the same time, female employment rates have been rising continuously. Table 4.1 displays the development of maternal employment in France for the years 1990, 1995, 2000, and 2013. Labour force participation rates increased steadily over this period, even among mothers with three and more children. In 2000 there is a noticeable decline in the rate of employment among mothers with two children, including those with one child under age three. This decrease has been attributed to changing parental leave regulations. Since 1994 women who gave birth to a second child could apply for paid parental leave. Before this point, only women with at least three children were eligible for paid leave. Younger and less educated women in particular took advantage of the paid leave option, and one-third of the applicants have been unemployed (Reuter 2002: 19).

The abovementioned changes in parental leave were apparently introduced to encourage women to withdraw from the labour market, at least for the years immediately after the birth of their second child (Reuter 2002: 19). In this context, another aspect worth mentioning is the high unemployment rate among French women. Unemployment is higher among women than among men, even though women are more likely to work in the public sector, which tends to be less affected than other sectors by unemployment (Toulemon and de Guibert-Lantoine 1998: 4). Young women in particular are at risk of becoming unemployed. In 2010, 23.7 % of all French women younger than age 25 were unemployed (Mansuy and Wolff 2012). In

Table 4.1 Labour force participation rates of mothers who live in a partnership, by number of children and age of youngest child, 1990, 1995, 2000, 2013

	1990		1995		2000		2013	
	Under 3	3–5	Under 3	3–5	Under 3	3–5	Under 3	3–5
No. of children								
One child	76.6	83.2	79.8	82.9	81.3	85.5	83.0	89.8
Two children	66.3	75.7	68.0	78.3	56.5	81.4	68.6	86.9
Three and more children	31.7	43.8	32.6	56.2	36.1	60.2	43.6	73.0
All	61.2	68.0	64.3	72.6	61.6	76.2	68.9	84.1

Source: Avenel and Roth (2001) and Guggemos and Vidalenc (2014)

contrast, the unemployment rate of this particular group of women in Germany (eastern and western Germany combined) was just 8.8 % (Federal Statistical Office of Germany 2012).

However, in France a comparatively large share of women are in full-time employment. During the first half of the 1990s, less than 25 % of French women worked part-time, and almost 30 % of these women would have preferred to work full-time if given the choice. Recently, female part-time employment rates have increased slightly in France, but they are still lower than those in many other European countries (Eurostat 2012b).

4.4 Fertility and Ideal Family Size

As in most western European countries, a rather traditional view of family life dominated in French society until the 1970s: a family consisted of a male breadwinner who had to provide for his wife and at least three children. Since the beginning of the 1980s, alternative forms of private living arrangements have become increasingly important, and non-marital unions with children have become a permanent feature of everyday life. Almost 58 % of all children born in the year 2014 had non-married parents. In this respect, France and Scandinavia are quite similar: i.e., becoming a parent is no longer automatically associated with marriage.

France has one of the highest birth rates in Europe. Since 1975 the total fertility rate has been rather stable, at an average of 1.8 children per woman, and recent numbers indicate that the TFR has risen to two children per woman (Fig. 4.1). Even from a cohort perspective, French fertility is exceptionally high. For French women

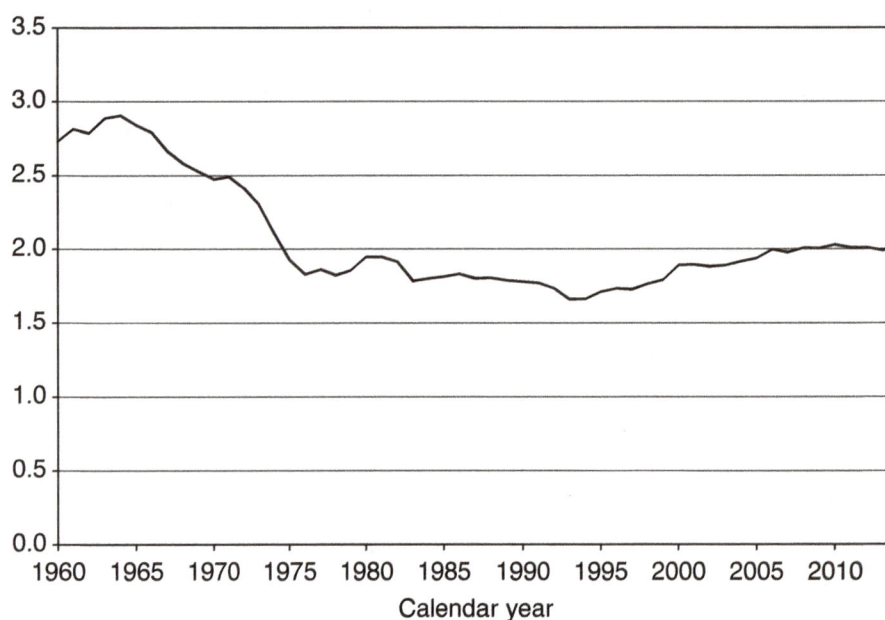

Fig. 4.1 Total fertility rate, France 1960–2014, provisional numbers for 2013 and later (Source: Council of Europe (2004), Richet-Mastain (2006) and Bellamy and Beaumel (2015))

born in 1960, the cohort fertility rate is 2.1, which is basically replacement-level fertility (Mazuy et al. 2014). Moreover, childbearing intentions, as reported in social science surveys, are comparatively high in France. When people are asked about their ideal number of children, the scores are highest in France, Ireland, Finland, and Great Britain (Toulemon and Leridon 1999; Goldstein et al. 2003). In France, most men and women say two or three is the ideal number of children, and the average preferred family size is 2.6. Less than 5 % of French respondents see childlessness as the most favourable living arrangement (Toulemon 2001b). By contrast, the ideal family size in Germany is below two; the lowest number in Europe (Dorbritz and Ruckdeschel 2012).

4.5 Childlessness

4.5.1 How Is Childlessness Measured in France?

Three sources are available to estimate childlessness in France: the census, official registration, and survey data. We encounter certain problems when seeking to measure childlessness in France. The registration office in France does not register the births by their biological order (Toulemon 2001a). Therefore, vital statistics data do not provide information on the evolution of childlessness. Yet it is possible to get comparatively reliable information on the development of childlessness for France. Since 1982 the National Institute for Statistic and Economics Studies (INSEE) has conducted a series of surveys on family life in which 1–2 % of all women in France are interviewed. These women are also asked about their number of births. On the basis of these surveys it is possible to estimate the complete fertility histories of women born during the twentieth century. However, reliable information about the final number and order of births can be obtained only for women aged 45 and older, and with a small degree of uncertainty for women above age 40. For cohorts born after 1975 only estimations can be made, since they have not yet completed their fertility. In addition to these surveys, a yearly census has been conducted in France since 2004. Previously, census data had been collected every 8–9 years, and the last census year was 1999. Due to the survey structure of the census (a rolling system in which only part of the population are interviewed each year), the initial results were published in 2008, and have since been updated each year.

For most of the following analyses, we use the *enquête Famille et logements*, a representative survey on family life which has been conducted parallel to the 2011 census, and contains life histories of around 360,000 men and women. For the period estimates of mean age at first child birth, we used combined information from the 1999 family survey, the civil registration system, and the French census.

Table 4.2 Mean age at first childbirth, France 1960–2010

Calendar year	Mean age at first childbirth
1960	24.1
1965	23.8
1970	24.0
1975	24.4
1980	24.9
1985	25.7
1990	26.6
1995	27.4
1998	27.7
2010	28.1

Source: Numbers for France 1996–1998: INSEE, enquête Étude de l'Histoire Familiale 1999 – Toulemon and Mazuy (2001); numbers for France 2010: INSEE, civil registration and population estimates – Davie (2012)

4.5.2 Development of Childlessness

In a first step, we display the mean age at first childbirth as an indicator of the postponement in childbearing. Subsequently, the focus will be on the development of childlessness in France.

When we look at the mean age at which women became mothers for the first time, we can clearly see a postponement to higher ages: the mean age at first childbirth increased from 24 years in the 1970s to 27.7 years in 1998 and to 28.1 years in 2010 (Table 4.2). Despite this shift to having children at older ages, the postponement of childbirth has not been associated with increasing shares of childlessness: 11–13 % of all women born 1960 in France remained childless (Toulemon and Mazuy 2001; Masson 2013). France not only holds a top position in overall fertility; it also has the lowest share of childlessness in western Europe.

Figure 4.2 displays the development of family size according to a fertility projection (Toulemon and Mazuy 2001). This projection is based on the 1999 family survey, and is updated here using the 2011 estimates.[1] For women born between 1935

---

[1] According to the 2011 survey, the proportion of women who are childless is higher than we would have predicted given the results of the 1999 EHF survey. In the 2011 survey a minimum of 12 % is reached for cohorts 1935 and 1955, and infertility increases to 13 % for women born in 1960 and to 14 % for those born in 1965. However, based on the 1999 survey we assumed that the proportion childless would be as low as 10 % among the 1940–1960 cohorts. We believe that the 1999 survey partly overestimated cohort fertility due to a non-response bias (whereby childless women are more prone to avoid filling out a form). On the other hand, the data for the cohorts born before 1950 may become less reliable in 2011, when cohorts were 12 years older than in 1999, due to differential mortality and out-migration. We thus transformed our projection using the mean of both surveys estimates for the 1920 cohort, the 2011 estimate for the 1960 cohort, and similar assumptions on trends for more recent cohorts. For the sake of simplicity, we use the 2011 survey only when we compare subgroups within the population, as for older cohorts the social differences are similar.

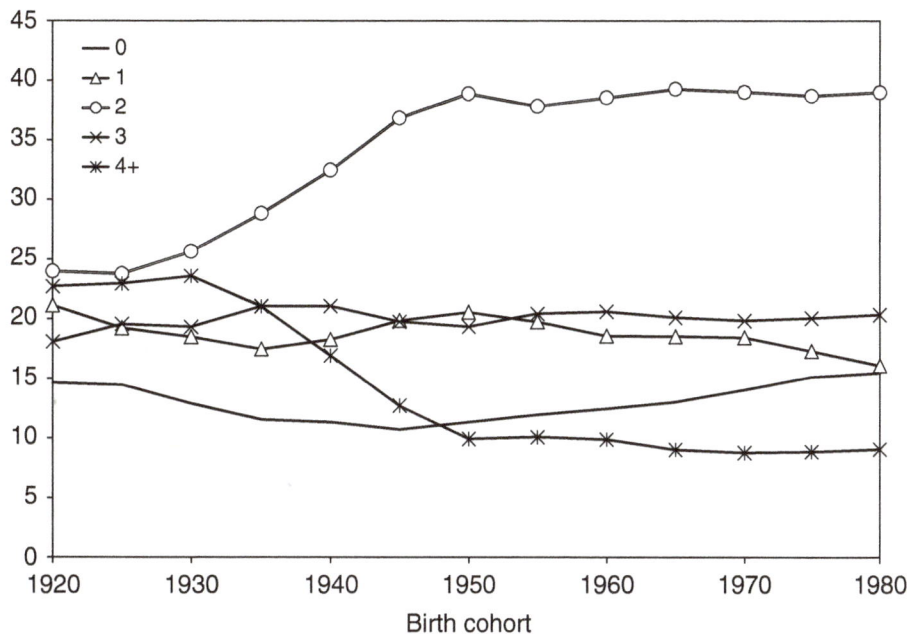

Fig. 4.2 Number of children, women in France, birth cohorts 1920–1960, in per cent (Source: INSEE, enquêtes Étude de l'Histoire Familiale 1999 and Famille et logements 2011; Toulemon and Mazuy (2001) and authors' update)

and 1955, childlessness stabilises at around 12 % (11 % for cohorts around 1945). A slight increase can be observed for women born after 1960, and the proportion childless increases to 15 % among women born in 1980. The majority of women in France have at least two children. Starting with the 1930 cohort, the share of women with large families (four or more children) has been decreasing, and the share with two children has been increasing. However, smaller shares of women born after 1960 had only one child than had three children. The high number of three-child families can most likely be explained by French policies that support large families.

Figure 4.3 displays the shares of women who are childless by birth cohort and age. Due to the lack of men after the First World War (Onnen-Isemann 2003), almost one-quarter of the women born at the beginning of the twentieth century remained childless. Childlessness decreased to constant and stable low levels in the following cohorts, and started to increase again among women born after 1960. However, reliable numbers for the final shares of women who are childless cannot be estimated since not all women born during the 1970s had reached the end of their reproductive life in 2011. Nonetheless, it appears that rates of childlessness are lower in France than in most European countries, and that the increase in childlessness has slowed due to the increase in fertility in the 2000s (Toulemon et al. 2008).

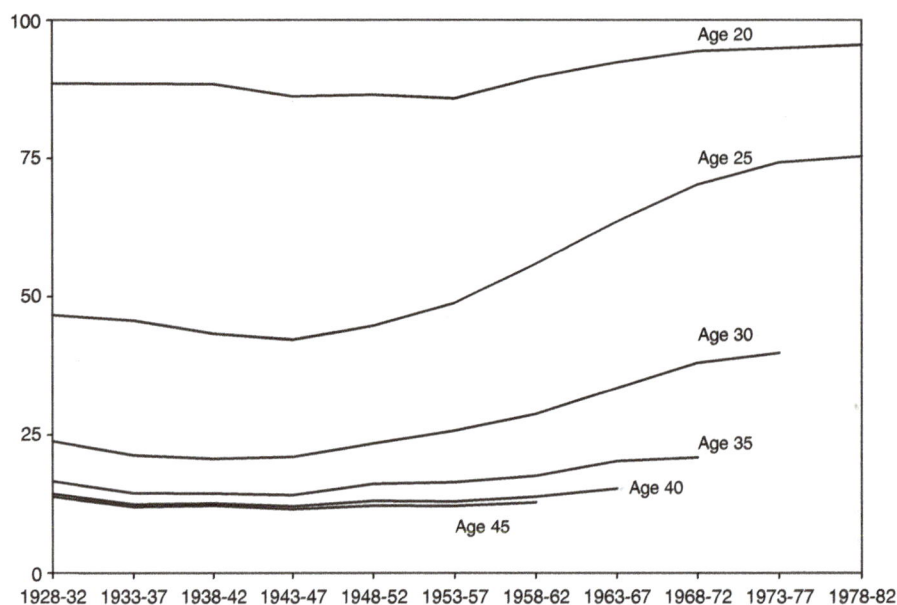

Fig. 4.3 Share of childless women in France at ages 20, 25, 30, 35, 40, 45, and 50, birth cohorts 1928–1982, in per cent (Source: INSEE, enquête Famille et logements (2011), own estimations)

4.5.3 Differences in Childlessness by Education and Occupation of Women

The transition to parenthood differs by education. Compared to women with higher levels of education, less educated women become mothers earlier and more frequently. Women with less education also have a high probability of having a child in a first union, whereas highly educated women are more likely to have a child in the second or third partnership episode. Lone parenthood after first childbirth is also more common among less educated women. The higher the level of education, the longer the duration of the partnership is likely to be before the birth of the first child (Mazuy 2006). As in other countries, women with a university degree are most likely to be childless.[2] The high proportion of university graduates who are childless is not a novelty, as highly educated women who were born before World War II also had high rates of childlessness (Fig. 4.4a). The exceptionally high rates of childlessness among highly educated women are partly attributable to their tendency to have their first child at a higher age, but also to the amount of time they live without a partner. These women tend to be older at their first union, and are more likely than less educated women to remain single (Robert-Bobée and Mazuy 2005; Masson 2013). In the more recent cohorts, women with low levels of education have higher

[2] French levels of education are defined as follows: (1) Collège = first 4 years of secondary education from the ages of 11–15; 2. CAP-BEP = vocational high school after collège, duration 2–3 years; (3) Baccalauréat = baccalauréat diploma that leads to higher education studies or directly to professional life; (4) Sup = all higher education studies such as bachelor's, master's, or doctoral programmes.

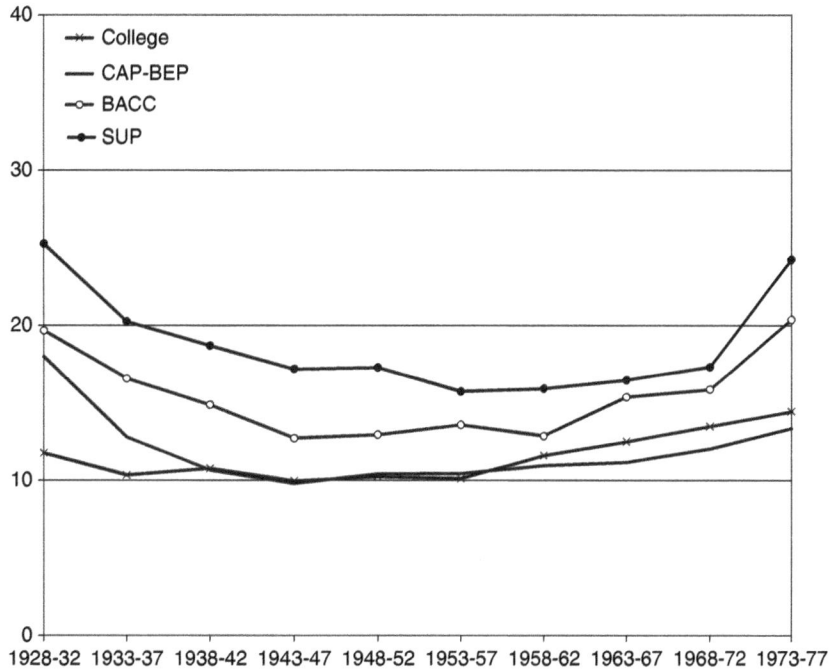

Fig. 4.4a Proportion of childless women in France by level of education (in per cent), birth cohorts 1928–77 (Source: INSEE, enquête Famille et logements (2011), own estimations). Among cohorts born after 1972 (under age 38 at 1-1-2011), the proportions childless or who never lived in a union may decline after the survey

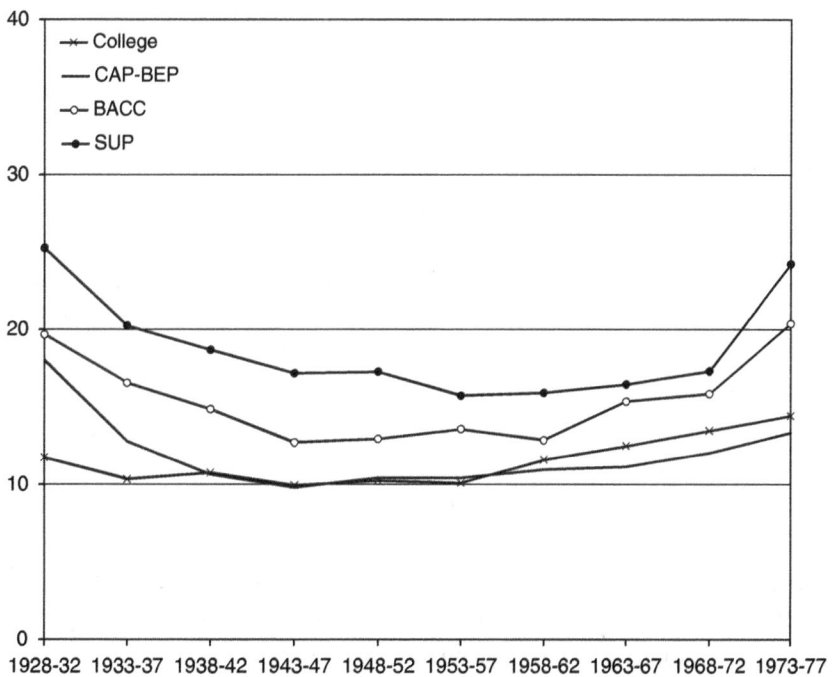

Fig. 4.4b Proportion of childless women in France (in per cent), among women who have ever lived as a couple by level of education, birth cohorts 1928–1977 (Source: INSEE, enquête Famille et logements (2011), own estimations)

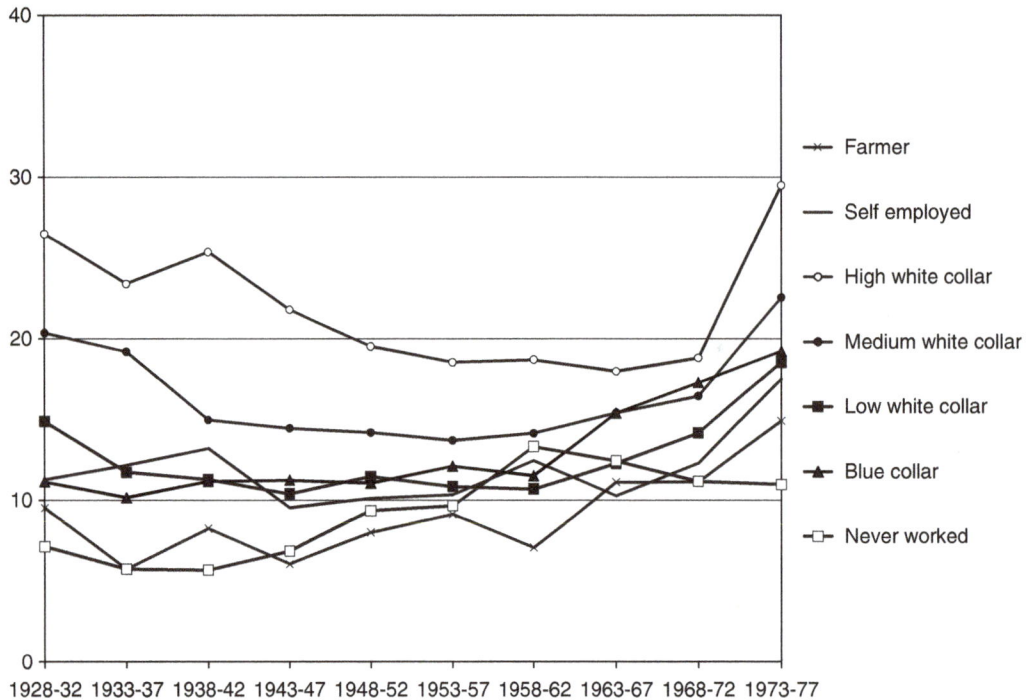

Fig. 4.5 Proportion of childless women in France by occupation, birth cohorts 1928–1977 (Source: INSEE, enquête Famille et logements (2011), own estimations)

rates of childlessness than women with short secondary education. This appears to be because the least educated make up a growing proportion of the women who never enter a union.

If we only consider women who are living or have ever lived as a couple, the degree of childlessness decreases for all women, regardless of the level of education. However, the proportion of childlessness is still higher for women with a university degree (Fig. 4.4b). The data for the cohorts born in 1973–1977, who were aged 33–37 at the time of the survey, are still provisional, especially for more educated women, who may have a first child after the survey.

Childlessness varies not only by level of education, but also by occupation. White-collar employees are more likely to remain childless than blue-collar workers, self-employed women, or women who have never been in employment. The lowest level of childlessness is observed among women who have never been employed or who work as farmers (Fig. 4.5). Again, the overall share of women who are childless decreases when we exclude women who have never been in a union (Fig. 4.6). But although the relative differences in childlessness between the single occupational groups become smaller when only women who ever lived as a couple are considered, the rates of childlessness are still higher among women in higher-level occupations than among women with a lower occupational status.

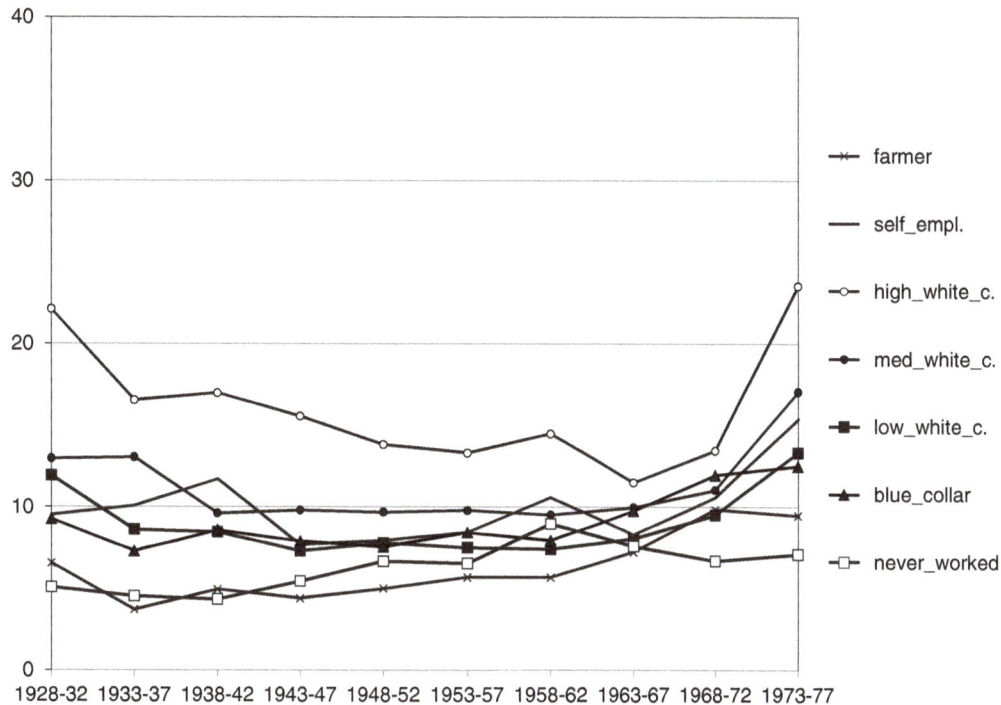

Fig. 4.6 Proportion of childless women in France, among women who have ever lived as a couple by occupation, birth cohorts 1928–1977 (Source: INSEE, enquête Famille et logements (2011), own estimations)

4.5.4 Men and Childlessness

When we try to interpret permanent childlessness among men, certain problems arise. Whereas births can almost always directly be assigned to the respective mother, this is not always the case for men. Around 2 % of all children are not recognized by their biological father. On the basis of survey data, this results in an overestimation of biological childlessness for men (Toulemon and Lapierre-Adamcyk 2000). In addition, our analyses confirm that men tend to be older than women at first child-birth. Moreover, after a union disruption men may lose touch with their children, and may then become reluctant to refer to them in the survey, especially if they have almost never lived with their children or have no contact with them. Almost 60 % of women born around 1945 have been mothers at age 25, but only 40 % of men had a first child at this age (Fig. 4.7). The gender differences are estimated at around 2 % for the birth cohorts 1930–1945, and increase for younger cohorts.

Another reason for gender differences in childlessness are imbalanced partner markets, in which either men or women are overrepresented. Men born in France after 1940 remained childless to the same extent as women if they had ever lived as a couple. However, single men displayed a much higher rate of childlessness. A major reason for this pattern may be gender-specific immigration patterns. In the past, more men than women migrated to France, resulting in an excess of male

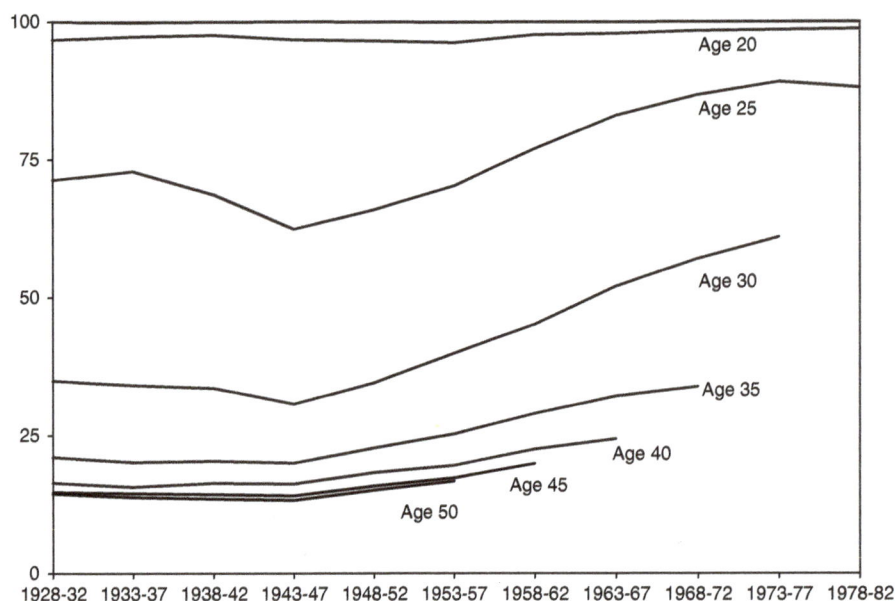

Fig. 4.7 Share of childless men in France at ages 20, 25, 30, 35, 40, 45, and 50; birth cohorts 1928–1982 (Source: INSEE, Famille et logements (2011), own estimations)

marriage partners of reproductive ages. Among cohorts born after 1955, migration by sex is more balanced. Nevertheless, more men than women remain single (whereby more men than women experience many unions), which in turn leads to higher rates of childlessness among men. Moreover, union disruptions are more frequent among men, and some men lose touch with their children (Toulemon 1996: 8).

Among men, the effect of education on childlessness is the opposite of that among women. Like for women, the data for the cohorts born in 1973–1977 are still provisional. There are almost no differences in the levels of childlessness by education, except among men with a low level of education, who tend to be more likely to remain childless (Fig. 4.8). If men who have never lived in a couple relationship are excluded, less qualified men are as likely as better educated men to become fathers (Fig. 4.9). The high proportion of men with a low level of education who are childless is mainly due to their partnership status. They are more likely to be excluded from the marriage market, which hampers their chances of starting a family; while the opposite used to be the case for less educated women (Toulemon and Lapierre-Adamcyk 2000; Mazuy 2002). Over time, social differences based on the level of education are decreasing more rapidly among men than among women. Among recent cohorts, women with a low level of education have reduced risks of entering a union, and, as a consequence, are more likely to remain childless than women with secondary or tertiary education (Fig. 4.4a, Toulemon 2014). This trend is related to the increasing proportion of couples in which the woman is more educated than the man; a trend that has been observed in many countries around the world (Esteve et al. 2012). As it has become increasingly necessary to have two incomes to maintain a household, women with only a basic level of education and

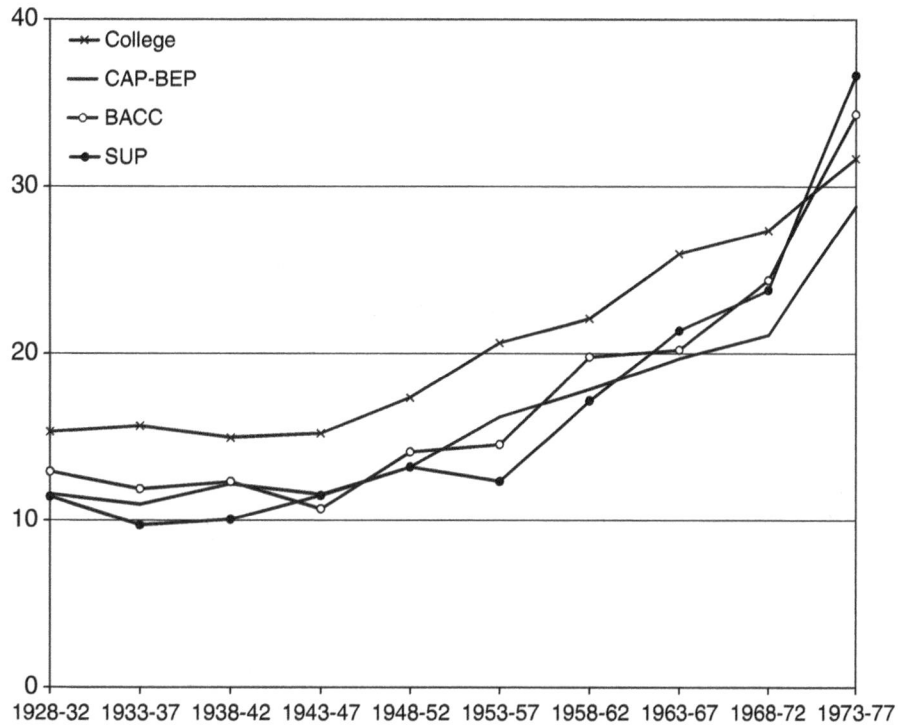

Fig. 4.8 Proportion of childless men in France by level of education, birth cohorts 1928–1977 (Source: INSEE, enquête Famille et logements (2011), own estimations). Among cohorts born after 1972 (aged less than 38 years at 1-1-2011), the proportions childless or who never lived in a union may decline after the survey

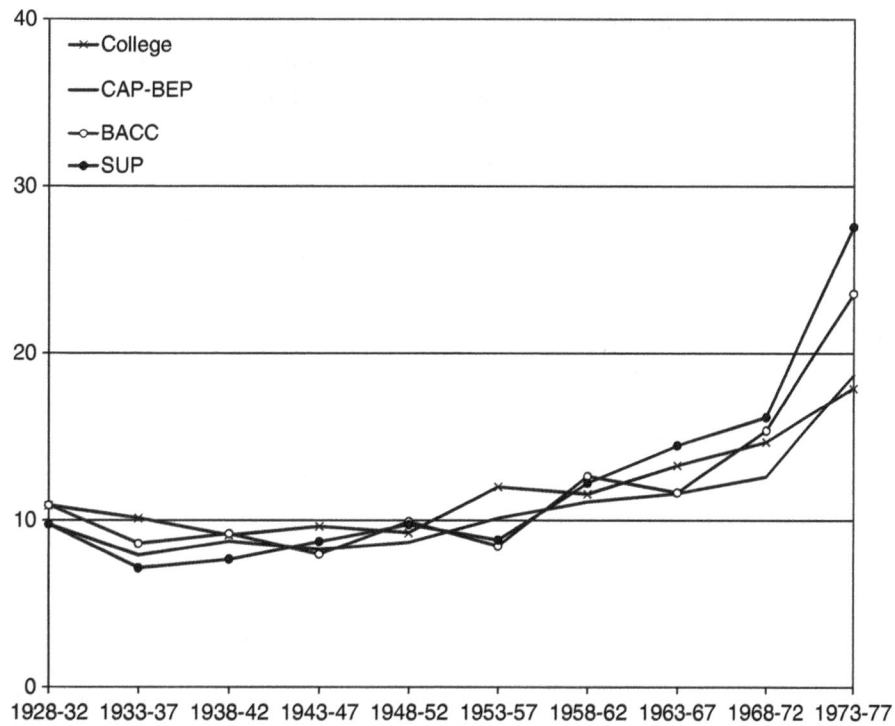

Fig. 4.9 Proportion of childless men in France who have ever lived as a couple by level of education, birth cohorts 1928–1977 (Source: INSEE, enquête Famille et logements (2011), own estimations)

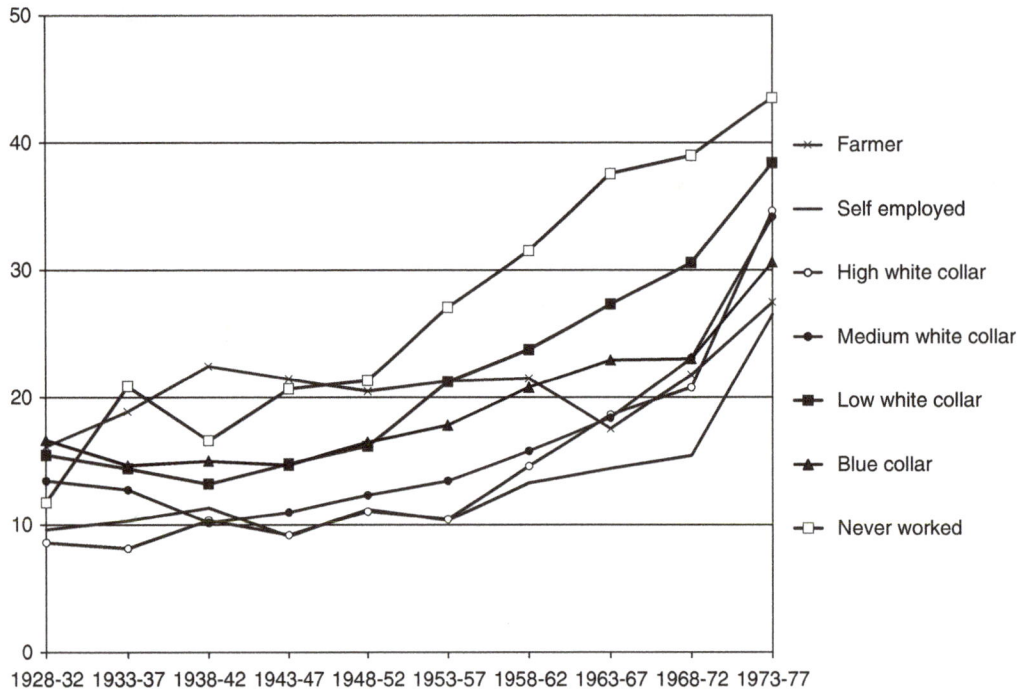

Fig. 4.10 Proportion of childless men in France by occupation, birth cohorts 1928–1977 (Source: INSEE, enquête Famille et logements (2011), own estimations)

comparatively bad income prospects have lower chances of finding a suitable partner and eventually becoming a mother.

There are marked differences in the levels of childlessness of different occupational groups. The higher a man's occupational status, the less likely he is to remain childless[3] (Fig. 4.10). Men who are farmers, blue-collar workers, or low-level white collar workers are more likely to remain childless than men who are self-employed or who work in higher-level white-collar occupations. In recent cohorts, childlessness has increased in all of the groups except for farmers, as this group is getting smaller, more selected, and more educated (a secondary diploma is now required to get the necessary loans for farming). While in the past a large share of farmers remained unmarried, this is no longer the case among recent cohorts. The differences between the various occupation groups have become smaller and the share of men who are childless has decreased, if only the men who have ever lived as a couple are considered (Fig. 4.11). Thus, it is again the elevated share of single men that contributes to the increase in childlessness in most occupational groups.

---

[3] More than half of all men who have never been employed remain childless. Due to a strong selection of these men who have never worked and due to the very small sample size, we do not display them in the graph.

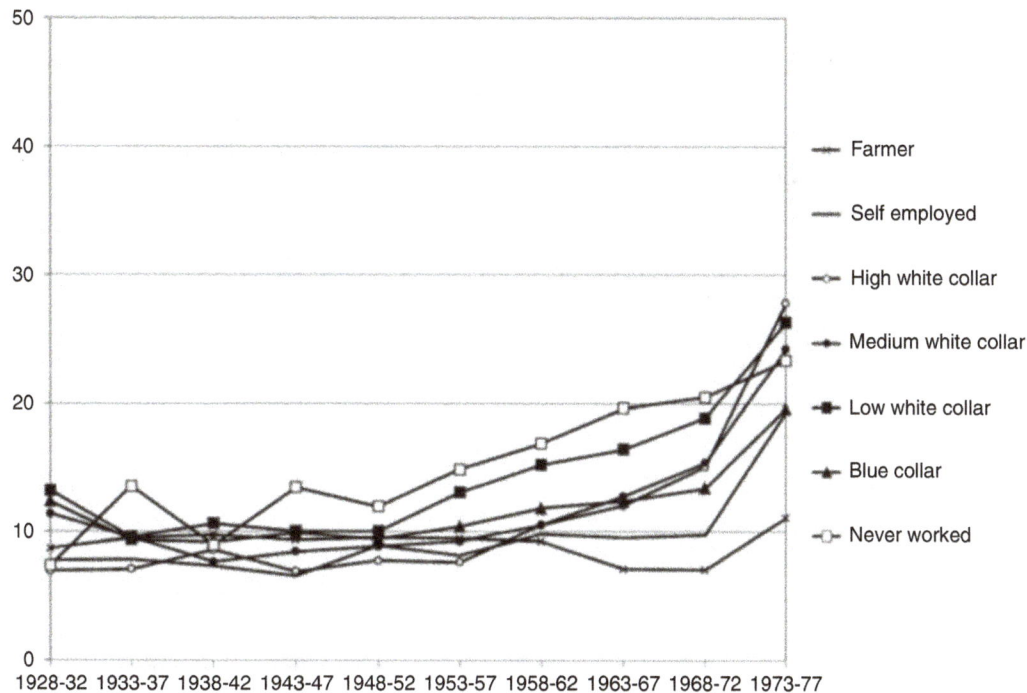

Fig. 4.11 Proportion of childless men in France who have ever lived as a couple by occupation, birth cohorts 1893–1966 (Source: INSEE, enquête Famille et logements (2011), own estimations)

4.6 Conclusion

Our aim in this article was to present an overview of the development of childlessness in France, and to describe some of the underlying institutional trends. In western Europe, France has some of the smallest proportions of men and women who remain childless. When asked about their ideal number of children, only a very small share of French men and women say they do not want to have any children at all (Debest and Mazuy 2014). This is probably related to France's system of state-supported family benefits and its well-developed childcare system. The French state and French society strongly promote and support the reconciliation of work and family life, but the social pressure to have children also remains strong.

However, the extent of childlessness differs between social groups: i.e., between birth cohorts, between men and women, and between different educational and occupational groups. For men and for women, childlessness is increasing in younger birth cohorts independent of their level of education or their occupational status. Whether this increase in childlessness is permanent or is due to a postponement of the first childbirth is not yet entirely clear. While the age at first birth in France has been increasing, birth rates have not been decreasing. Thus, it is possible that a non-negligible share of those men and women who are still childless at ages 35+ may still have children in the future.

One of the reasons why the childlessness rate is higher among men than among women is that problems arise when measuring the number of children men have. Imbalances in the partner market can also account for the higher rate of childlessness among men. Yet married men are as likely as married women to remain childless. Partnership status is thus a decisive parameter of the extent of childlessness. Men and women who have never lived in a couple relationship (either a marriage or a non-marital union) are much more likely to remain childless than those who live in or have lived in a union. Since more than 90 % of all men and women are or have been in a relationship, a large share of childlessness can be traced back to those 10 % who have been without a partner or remained single until the time of interview.

Despite the family-friendly conditions that help women combine work and family life, highly educated women in France are still more likely than less educated women to be childless, despite the fact that they now as likely to live in a couple relationship. During the period of life in which many women start a family, women who are earning a university degree are still in education or are trying to establish a career. The older they get, the more likely it is that their initial desire to have children, if any, will turn into involuntary childlessness due to infertility, or will be given up in favour of pursuing other goals. However, the differences by education are currently becoming smaller in France, mainly because the least educated women are more likely to remain childless.

In contrast, there are only slight differences in rates of childlessness by education among men. Men with low qualifications are more likely to remain single, and for that reason are also more likely than highly educated men to remain childless. This pattern can be observed for different occupational groups as well: blue-collar workers and low-level white-collar workers are the most likely to remain childless, as they are more likely than other occupational groups to have a precarious employment status or a low income. Among men in France, having an unstable economic situation leads to the postponement of marriage and family formation, which may result in childlessness (Oppenheimer 1988; Mills and Blossfeld 2003; Pailhé and Solaz 2012). Persistent high unemployment, an increase in the prevalence of part-time jobs, and the economic demand for dual-earner households may exacerbate feelings of economic uncertainty. This insecurity could lead young people to postpone childbearing, which may in turn lead to an increase in childlessness among younger cohorts.

Literature

Avenel, M., & Roth, N. (2001). Les enfants moins de 6 ans et leurs familles en France métropolitaine. *Recherches et Prévisions, 63*, 91–97.

Becker, A. (2000). *Mutterschaft im Wohlfahrtsstaat. Familienbezogene Sozialpolitik und die Erwerbsintegration von Frauen in Deutschland und Frankreich.* Berlin: Wissenschaftlicher Verlag Berlin.

Bellamy, V., & Beaumel, C. (2015). Bilan démographique 2014. Des décès moins nombreux, Insee première, 1532, 4 pages. http://www.insee.fr/fr/themes/document.asp?reg_id=0&ref_id=ip1532. Accessed 30 Mar 2015.

Council of Europe. (2004). *Recent demographic developments in Europe: Demographic Yearbook 2003*. Strasbourg: Council of Europe.

Davie, E. (2012). Un premier enfant à 28 ans. *INSEE Première* 1419. Paris: INSEE. http://www.insee.fr/fr/ffc/ipweb/ip1419/ip1419.pdf. Accessed 25 Mar 2015.

Debest, C., Mazuy M., & Fecond Team. (2014) Childlessness: A life choice that goes against the norm. *Population & Societies, 508,* http://www.ined.fr/en/resources_documentation/publications/pop_soc/bdd/publication/1671/. Accessed 30 Mar 2015.

Dingeldey, I. (2000). *Begünstigungen und Belastungen familialer Erwerbs- und Arbeitszeitmuster in Steuer- und Sozialversicherungssystemen. Ein Vergleich zehn europäischer Länder.* Gelsenkirchen: Institut Arbeit und Technik.

Dorbritz, J., & Ruckdeschel, K. (2012). Kinderlosigkeit – differenzierte Analysen und europäische Vergleiche. In: D. Konietzka & M. Kreyenfeld (Eds.), *Ein Leben ohne Kinder. Ausmaß, Strukturen und Ursachen von Kinderlosigkeit* (pp. 253–278). Wiesbaden: Springer.

Ehmann, S. (1997). *Familienpolitik in Frankreich und Deutschland: Ein Vergleich.* Frankfurt/Main: Peter Lang.

Esteve, A., Garcia, J., & Permanyer, I. (2012). Union formation implications of the gender gap reversal in education: The end of hypergamy. *Population and Development Review, 38,* 535–546.

Eurostat. (2012a). *Basic figures on the EU: Autumn 2012 editing.* Luxemburg: Eurostat.

Eurostat. (2012b). *Datenbank Beschäftigung und Arbeitslosigkeit: Teilzeitbeschäftigung als Prozentsatz der gesamten Beschäftigung, nach Geschlecht und Alter.* Luxemburg: Eurostat.

Fagnani, J. (2002). Why do French women have more children than German women? Family policies and attitudes towards child care outside the home. *Community, Work and Family, 5,* 103–120.

Federal Statistical Office of Germany. (2012). *Statistisches Jahrbuch* (p. 356). Wiesbaden: Federal Statistical Office of Germany.

Festy, P. (1979). *La Fécondité des pays occidentaux de 1870 à 1970.* Paris: Presses Universitaires de France, INED.

Goldstein, J., Lutz, W., & Testa, M. R. (2003). The emergence of sub-replacement family size ideals in Europe. *Population Research and Policy Review, 22,* 479–496.

Guggemos, F., & Vidalenc, J. (2014). *Activité des couples selon l'âge quinquennal, le nombre et l'âge des enfants de moins de 18 ans.* Paris: INSEE. http://www.insee.fr/fr/publications-et-services/irweb.asp?id=irsoceec12. Accessed 25 Mar 2015.

Köppen, K. (2006). Second births in western Germany and France. *Demographic Research, 14,* 295–330.

Letablier, M.-T. (2002). Kinderbetreuungspolitik in Frankreich und ihre Rechtfertigung. *WSI Mitteilungen, 55,* 169–175.

Mansuy, A., & Wolff, L. (2012). *Une photographie du marché du travail en 2010, INSEE Première, 1391.* Paris: INSEE. http://www.insee.fr/fr/ffc/ipweb/ip1391/ip1391.pdf. Accessed 25 Mar 2015.

Masson, L. (2013). Avez-vous eu des enfants ? Si oui, combien ? *France Portrait social,* 93–109. http://www.insee.fr/fr/themes/document.asp?reg_id=0&id=4062. Accessed 30 Mar 2015.

Mazuy, M. (2002). Situations familiales et fécondité selon le milieu social. Résultats à partir de l'enquête EHF de 1999. INED, Documents de travail n°114. https://www.ined.fr/fichier/s_rubrique/19428/114.fr.pdf. Accessed 25 Mar 2014.

Mazuy, M. (2006). *Être prêt-e, être prêts ensemble? Entrée en parentalité des hommes et des femmes en France.* Thèse de Doctorat en démographie, Université Paris 1.

Mazuy, M., Barbieri, M., & d'Albis, H. (2014). Recent demographic trends in France: The number of marriages continues to decrease. *Population-E, 69,* 273–322.

Mills, M., & Blossfeld, H.-P. (2003). Globalization, uncertainty and changes in early life courses. *Zeitschrift für Erziehungswissenschaft, 6,* 188–218.

Onnen-Isemann, C. (2003). Familienpolitik und Fertilitätsunterschiede in Europa: Frankreich und Deutschland. *Aus Politik und Zeitgeschichte Beilage zur Wochenzeitung Das Parlament B, 44*(03), 31–38.

Oppenheimer, V. K. (1988). A theory of marriage timing. *American Journal of Sociology, 94,* 563–591.

Pailhé, A., & Solaz, A. (2012). The influence of employment uncertainty on childbearing in France: A tempo or quantum effect? *Demographic Research, 26,* 1–40.

Reuter, S. (2002). *Frankreichs Wohlfahrtsstaatsregime im Wandel? Erwerbsintegration von Französinnen und familienpolitische Reformen der 90er Jahre.* ZES-Arbeitspapier Nr. 12, Bremen: Zentrum für Sozialpolitik.

Richet-Mastain, L. (2006). Bilan démographique 2005, *INSEE Première 1059.* Paris: INSEE. http://www.insee.fr/fr/ffc/docs_ffc/IP1059.pdf. Accessed 25 Mar 2015.

Robert-Bobée, I., & Mazuy, M. (2005). Calendriers de constitution des familles et âge de fin des études. In: C. Lefevre & A. Filhon (Eds.), *Histoires de familles, histoires familiales, Les Cahiers de l'Ined, 156,* 175–200.

Schultheis, F. (1988). *Familien und Politik. Formen wohlfahrtsstaatlicher Regulierung von Familie im deutsch-französischen Gesellschaftsvergleich.* Konstanz: UVK.

Spieß, K. (2004). *Parafiskalische Modelle zur Finanzierung familienpolitischer Leistungen.* Berlin: DIW.

Thévenon, O., & Luci, A. (2012). Reconciling work, family and child outcomes: What implications for family support policies? *Population Research and Policy Review, 31,* 855–882.

Toulemon, L. (1996). Very few couples remain voluntarily childless. *Population: An English Selection, 8,* 1–28.

Toulemon, L. (2001a). How many children and how many siblings in France in the last century? *Population and Societies, 374,* Paris: INED. http://www.ined.fr/fichier/s_rubrique/173/pop_and_soc_english_374.en.pdf. Accessed 25 Mar 2015.

Toulemon, L. (2001b). Why fertility is not so low in France. Paper presented at the IUSSP seminar on International Perspectives on Low Fertility: Trends, Theories and Policies, Tokyo, 21–23 March 2001.

Toulemon, L. (2014), Single low-educated women and growing female hypogamy. A major change in the union formation process. 2014 Quetelet Seminar: 40th edition Fertility, childlessness and the family: A pluri-disciplinary approach. http://www.uclouvain.be/478889.html. Accessed 30 Mar 2015.

Toulemon, L., & de Guibert-Lantoine, C. (1998). *Fertility and family surveys in countries of the ECE region. Standard country report France.* New York: United Nations.

Toulemon, L., & Lapierre-Adamcyk, E. (2000). Demographic patterns of motherhood and fatherhood in France. In: C. Bledsoe, S. Lerner, & J. Guyer (Eds.), *Fertility and the male life cycle in the era of fertility decline* (pp. 293–330). Oxford: University Press.

Toulemon, L., & Leridon, H. (1999). La famille idéale: combien d'enfants, à quel âge? *INSEE Première* 652, Paris: INSEE. http://www.insee.fr/fr/ffc/docs_ffc/ip652.pdf. Accessed 25 Mar 2015.

Toulemon, L., & Mazuy, M. (2001). Les naissances sont retardées mais la fécondité est stable. *Population, 56,* 611–644.

Toulemon, L., Pailhé, A., & Rossier, C. (2008). France: High and stable fertility. *Demographic Research, 19,* 503–556. Special Collection 7: Childbearing Trends and Policies in Europe. http://www.demographic-research.org/volumes/vol19/16/. Accessed 30 Mar 2015.

Veil, M. (2002). Ganztagsschule mit Tradition: Frankreich. *Aus Politik und Zeitgeschichte, Beilage zur Wochenzeitung Das Parlament,* B 41/02, 29–37.

Chapter 5
Childlessness in East and West Germany: Long-Term Trends and Social Disparities

Michaela Kreyenfeld and Dirk Konietzka

5.1 Introduction

It is a well-established historical fact that childlessness has been a frequent phenomenon in Western Europe for centuries. Historical demography has found ample evidence that it was not uncommon for 20 % or more of a cohort to never marry, and in most cases these unmarried people remained childless (Hajnal 1965). In Germany during the seventeenth and eighteenth centuries, the feudal order restricted the marriage behavior of the serfs, who needed to seek the consent of their "seigneurial lords" to get married (Mitterauer 1990). In the nineteenth century, when the feudal order had been overthrown in many of the German states, opportunities to get married improved. Nonetheless, the authorities continued to restrict access to marriage for people who were "considered to be in an unfavorable economic situation or otherwise socially undesirable" (Knodel 1967: 280; Matz 1980). The formation of the German Empire and the introduction of civil marriage in 1876 did not provide universal access to marriage, either. Marriage restrictions (*Ehebeschränkungen*) were not abolished in Germany until 1919 (Knodel 1967). In addition to the legal regulations that governed marriage and fertility behavior, economic and political conditions heavily influenced historical trends in childlessness. The significant events of the first half of the twentieth century that contributed to high levels of

M. Kreyenfeld (✉)
Hertie School of Governance, Berlin, Germany

Max Planck Institute for Demographic Research, Rostock, Germany
e-mail: kreyenfeld@hertie-school.org

D. Konietzka
Department of Social Sciences, Braunschweig University of Technology, Braunschweig, Germany
e-mail: d.konietzka@tu-braunschweig.de

M. Kreyenfeld, D. Konietzka (eds.), *Childlessness in Europe: Contexts, Causes, and Consequences*, Demographic Research Monographs, DOI 10.1007/978-3-319-44667-7_5

childlessness among the relevant cohorts were the Great Depression and the World Wars I and II (Schwarz 1991).

In Germany, as in other parts of Europe, a range of legal, economic, and social conditions shaped historical trends in childlessness. What makes the German case interesting is the more recent history since the mid-twentieth century, when Germany was divided into two opposing political systems. In the state-socialist German Democratic Republic (GDR), the centrally planned economy guaranteed stable and predictable employment paths. Furthermore, social and family policies that were often ridiculed in the West as being "pro-natalistic" encouraged early childbearing and the full-time integration of mothers into the labor market. West Germany's social policies were geared towards the male breadwinner model, and the trade unions adhered to the principle of family wages for male employees. Family policies, in particular the system of joint taxation and the coverage of non-working spouses in the public pension and health care systems, are the key characteristics of a regime that was never seriously interested in the integration of mothers into the labor market. Pro-natalism was rejected in West Germany, not only because it was misused during the Nazi period, but also because the government wanted to take a clear political stance against the pro-natalist orientation of East Germany's family policies. A statement by the first West German chancellor Konrad Adenauer reflects the attitudes towards family policies that were prevalent among West German politicians during that period: *Kinder bekommen die Leute immer* ("People will always have children").

When Adenauer made his famous statement, the fertility patterns in the two parts of Germany were quite similar. In the 1960s, the age at first birth was low, and the total fertility rate was around replacement level in both East and West Germany. However, the behavioral patterns in the two parts of the country started to diverge in the 1970s; and, from a cohort perspective, for women and men born in 1950 onwards. Among the cohorts born in 1950–1964, the share of women in East Germany who would remain childless held steady at around 10 %, whereas the share increased from 10 % to around 20 % in West Germany. The growth in childlessness in West Germany was accompanied by a steady rise in the age at first birth, a postponement of marriage, and an upsurge in cohabitation. Retrospectively, West Germany emerges as one of the "vanguard countries" in Europe in the trend towards high levels of childlessness. Other countries—and especially the countries of Southern Europe—started following this pattern later (see Sobotka in this volume).

The legacy of having lived under two very different regimes is still deeply entrenched in the fertility patterns and living arrangements that we observe in contemporary Germany. Compared to West Germans, East Germans are less likely to remain childless, are younger at first birth, and are far more likely to have children in a cohabiting union or as a single parent (Huinink et al. 2012). The correlation between socioeconomic characteristics and childlessness also differs between East and West. In East Germany, there are only small differences in childlessness rates by women's level of education; whereas in West Germany, highly educated women were far more likely than less educated women to remain childless. This elevated childlessness of the West German female academics has attracted considerable public and media attention, and was probably an important motivation for recent policy reforms, including the expansion of public childcare and the reform of the parental leave benefit system (*Elternzeit*). However, there is also evidence that behavioral patterns have shifted among the most recent cohorts, and that the educational disparities are narrowing for the younger cohorts of West German women.

In this paper, we aim to describe recent developments and to integrate them into a larger historical, economic, and social-political framework. The reminder of this paper is structured as follows. In the next section (Sect. 5.2) we present data from census and vital registration systems that elucidate long-term trends in childlessness in East and West Germany. In Sect. 5.3 we analyze the disparities in female childlessness between different socioeconomic groups using micro-census data. Due to the paucity of information on male fertility in the official data, we complement the official data with estimates on the number of children by gender based on social science survey data, and illustrate the major pathways that have led to childlessness among recent birth cohorts in Germany. In Sect. 5.4 we draw a conclusion.

5.2 Childlessness in German Census and Micro-census Data: Long-Term Trends in Childlessness

There is a dearth of official data on childlessness in (West) Germany. Census data, including the recent register based census of 2011, do not include the number of biological children ever born. Moreover, the only census that surveyed the number of children of *married* women is the one conducted in 1970. Although estimates of childlessness from these data may be too high because they do not include births to unmarried women, the census of 1970 is one of the rare sources that gives us an impression of the long-term trends in childlessness in West Germany.[1] The estimates from these data show that childlessness was elevated for women born in the late nineteenth and early twentieth centuries. Further evidence that there were elevated levels of childlessness among the cohort born around 1900 comes from East German statistics (also Table 5.1). Unlike the censuses in West Germany, the East German census of 1981 collected the number of children ever born for the entire population, regardless of marital status.[2] These data confirm that more than 20 % of the East German women born in 1902–1909 were childless.

---

[1] Fertility estimates of census data have limitations. Most importantly, they do not cover the fertility behavior of the people who had died or had emigrated prior to the date of the interview. While this is a well-known problem of estimates based on census or micro-census data, it is aggravated for the West German census of 1970 because of the high death rates during World War II (including the mass killings of the Jewish population), large-scale resettlement (particularly from the former eastern German territories), and the high rates of emigration during and following the war.

[2] Like the West German census of 1970, the East German census of 1971 collected the number of children for married women only.

Table 5.1 Childlessness of women in per cent, West German census of 1970 and East German census of 1981

Cohorts	1895–1904	1905–1909	1910–1914	1915–1919	1920–1924	1925–1929	1930–1934	1935–1939	–
West Germany	33	33	28	25	25	25	22	18	–
Cohorts	–	1902–1909	1910–1914	1915–1919	1920–1924	1925–1929	1930–1934	1935–1939	1940–1944
East Germany	–	22	17	17	18	16	12	10	9

Note: West German data come from the Volkszählung 1970 BRD (own estimates conducted by Sebastian Böhm at GESIS, Mannheim). Only marital births were queried in these data. Furthermore, because foreigners were not asked in the census about their number of children, this group was eliminated from the analysis. The East German data come from the Volkszählung 1981 DDR. These data were provided upon request by Olga Pötzsch (Federal Statistical Office Germany)

The cohorts born around 1900 (in both East and West Germany) experienced economic deprivation in the aftermath of World War I and the Great Depression. While having experienced economic and social hardship certainly played a role in the high levels of childlessness in these cohorts, deprivation was not the only contributing factor. A potential factor that is seldom mentioned in this context is female emancipation. This is surprising, as the scholars of that time were very concerned about the growing share of women who were "earning their own livelihood" (Brentano 1910: 376). The cohorts born in the late nineteenth century would have entered adulthood during a period when new employment opportunities for young women were emerging in the growing service sector in the Weimar Republic of Germany (Zeeb 1915).

The most significant event that affected the life course of the following cohorts was World War II. As a result of the upheavals during and after the war—including resettlements, mass emigration, high rates of imprisonment, and the excess death rates among soldiers—the sex ratio among these cohorts was highly distorted. For example, for the West German cohort born in 1920, there were only 73 men to 100 women at age 36 (Human Mortality Database 2016). Thus, the lack of a marital partner was probably a key element in the family behavior of this generation of women.

Apart from censuses, long-term trends in childlessness are commonly generated based on vital statistics data. Among the prerequisites for using such data are that the biological order is available from the vital registration system, and that this information is collected for a sufficiently long period of time. Unfortunately, West German vital statistics do not fulfill these criteria.[3] In the absence of better

---

[3] The vital statistics were not changed to include biological birth order in the registers until 2008. Since 2009, the new registration system has been fully implemented. Although this reform modernized German vital statistics system, it does not enable the system to generate cohort estimates of childlessness until several decades in the future. In order to estimate the share of ultimate childlessness by birth cohort among women, order-specific birth information for the reproductive histories of an entire cohort must be collected. This means that the German registration system will produce the first estimates of childlessness for the cohorts born in 1994 who reached age 15 in

Table 5.2 Number of children by birth cohorts of women (in per cent) and mean number of children. Vital statistics (East Germany) and combined vital statistics and survey data (West Germany)

Cohorts	1940	1945	1950	1955
East Germany				
Childless	11	8	7	8
One child	26	29	30	27
Two children	35	42	47	48
Three and more children	28	21	16	18
Total	100	100	100	100
Mean number of children	**1.98**	**1.87**	**1.79**	**1.84**
West Germany				
Childless	11	13	14	19
One child	26	30	31	27
Two children	34	35	35	36
Three and more children	29	22	20	18
Total	100	100	100	100
Mean number of children	**1.97**	**1.78**	**1.70**	**1.62**

Source: For East Germany, data were provided upon request by Jürgen Dorbritz (Bundesinstitut für Bevölkerungsforschung). Data for West Germany are estimates based on Kreyenfeld (2002)
Note: For the West German 1955 cohort, the estimates are up to age 40 only

alternatives, researchers had estimated childlessness by combining survey and vital statistics data (Birg et al. 1990; Kreyenfeld 2002). For East Germany, superior data are available, as the vital statistics of the GDR had included biological birth order. It is one of the ironies of German unification that this practice was discontinued in 1990 because East Germany had to adopt the German Federal Statistics Law. Nevertheless, during its 40 years of existence, the vital statistics of the GDR produced data for a period that is long enough to allow us to calculate the share of ultimately childless women for several cohorts of women. These data, together with the estimates from the West German data, are presented in Table 5.2. They show that in East Germany 11 % of the 1940 cohort were childless, and that this share declined to less than 10 % for the subsequent cohorts. In West Germany, by contrast, 11 % of the 1940 cohort remained childless, but childlessness increased gradually among the subsequent cohorts, reaching 19 % for the 1955 cohort.

Micro-census data are a further source for generating fertility indicators, including the prevalence of childlessness by birth cohorts of women (and, ideally, of men).[4] In the German micro-census, women aged 15–75 are asked every 4 years

---

2009, when the reform was first implemented. Thus, the first official estimates on ultimate childlessness from the German registration system will be generated in 2043, when this birth cohort reaches age 49.

[4] In Germany, the questionnaire of the micro-census is governed by law, and requires the approval of the German *Bundesrat*. The inclusion of the question on the number of children was preceded by a lengthy debate over the sensitivity of the item. Among the arguments that were made against

how many biological children they have.[5] The question about the number of children was included in the micro-census for the first time in 2008, and for the second time in 2012 (see also: Bujard 2015; Bujard et al. 2015; Dorbritz 2015; Naderi 2015). The parity distribution that is generated using these data is displayed in Table 5.2. The table shows that childlessness has been rising in West Germany starting with the 1940s cohorts. Of the most recent cohorts, those born in 1965–1969, 22 % have remained childless, which suggests that childlessness has increased steadily starting with the cohorts born in the 1940s. By contrast, in East Germany female childlessness levels stalled for the 1940–1959 cohorts, and increased only slightly thereafter. Hence, childlessness levels in East Germany are still substantially lower than those of West Germany. However, the increase in childlessness among the recent birth cohorts indicates that the differences in the birth patterns of the two parts of Germany have become smaller.

Examining the childlessness trends in East Germany is instructive when seeking to understand how radical changes on the macro level transfer into cohort-specific behavioral patterns. The cohorts who were most affected by the economic and political transformation in the aftermath of unification were those born between 1965 and 1969. They experienced the early stages of their employment careers in the 1990s, and thus during the period when the East German economy was being privatized. In the course of privatization, many factories were closed, unemployment was high, and work schedules were reduced. Yet despite these challenging economic conditions, only 17 % of these cohorts were childless; a considerably smaller share than that of their West German counterparts. One explanation for this relatively low level of childlessness is that many of the women in these cohorts had their first child before German unification; while a second explanation is that these cohorts were still in the mid- or late twenties when the Berlin Wall came down, and could thus delay childbearing without getting to close to the biological limits of fertility. The East German case illustrates that even severe economic upheavals do not necessary lead to an increase in childlessness, and that the extent to which economic conditions affect childlessness depends on the "fertility regime". Since the fertility regime of East Germany was characterized by universal and early childbearing, childless women had the "biographical leeway" to postpone childbearing until conditions improved.

---

the inclusion of this question were, for example, that the micro-census is a household survey. The opponents also argued that during the interview situation a man (or a woman) may be forced to report having a child whom he had, up to that point, successfully concealed from his spouse. Still other opponents raised concerns that a question on the number of children would create distress for people with deceased children. A further argument was that a woman who had deposited her child in a "baby hatch" would be forced to report a birth she would like to keep anonymous.

[5] Unfortunately, the question on the number of children is one of the few non-obligatory questions in the German micro-census. Unlike most of the other questions, which respondents are required to answer by law, people are free to choose whether to provide this information. Missing cases were largely imputed by the German statistical office, but sensitivity analyses of competing imputation methods have, unfortunately, never been conducted. Nevertheless, compared to estimates from social science surveys, estimates from micro-census data are presumably relatively reliable due to the high case numbers and the low unit non-response of these data.

5.3 Social Disparities in Childlessness

5.3.1 Childlessness by Level of Education

In the public debate, concerns have been raised about the elevated rates of childlessness among female university graduates in West Germany. Some of these estimates—e.g., that 40 % or more of these women are childless (see e.g.: Der Spiegel 2005)—are greatly exaggerated. Nevertheless, there is firm evidence from multiple sources that female university graduates in West Germany are more likely to remain childless than their less educated counterparts (see e.g., Duschek and Wirth 2005; Schmitt and Winkelmann 2005). In Table 5.3 we provide new evidence on female childlessness by level of education in East and West Germany based on an analysis of data from the German micro-census of 2012. Migrants have been omitted from

Table 5.3 Number of children by birth cohorts of women (in per cent) and mean number of children. German micro-census 2012

	1940–1944	1945–1949	1950–1954	1955–1959	1960–1964	1965–1969[a]
Germany						
Childless	12	13	15	18	20	22
1 child	25	27	27	25	24	25
2 children	40	40	41	40	39	37
3 and more	24	20	17	18	17	16
Total	100	100	100	100	100	100
Mean number of children	**1.89**	**1.76**	**1.69**	**1.67**	**1.60**	**1.54**
East Germany						
Childless	10	10	10	10	13	17
1 child	28	30	29	27	32	34
2 children	40	44	47	48	43	36
3 and more	22	17	14	16	13	13
Total	100	100	100	100	100	100
Mean number of children	**1.87**	**1.73**	**1.72**	**1.75**	**1.61**	**1.52**
West Germany						
Childless	12	14	17	20	22	24
1 child	23	27	26	24	22	23
2 children	40	39	39	38	38	37
3 and more	25	21	19	19	18	17
Total	100	100	100	100	100	100
Mean number of children	**1.90**	**1.76**	**1.68**	**1.64**	**1.59**	**1.54**

Note: East Germany, including East Berlin
[a]Aged 43–47 in 2012
Course: Micro-census 2012 (own estimates)

this analysis because migration background is an important confounder in the association between education and fertility (see also Naderi 2015, and Table A2 in the
Appendix for a calculation by migrant status). We distinguish between women with
a tertiary degree, with a vocational training degree, and with none of these certificates. This distinction differs slightly from the ISCED classification that is commonly used in cross-national comparisons, but it is particularly well suited for
mapping differential labor market opportunities in Germany, which tend to reward
tertiary education and vocational education and training more than general secondary education (Konietzka 2003).

The findings displayed in the table support the notion that childlessness levels
are indeed high among female university graduates, especially among the cohorts
born in 1940–1944: 25 % of the women with tertiary education, but only 13 % of
those with a vocational training degree and 9 % of those without a degree remained
childless. It is, however, important to note that only a small fraction of the women
in these cohorts received tertiary education (see Table A1 in the Appendix), whereas
the women of the following cohorts greatly profited from the educational expansion
in Germany. Even though in all of the cohorts women with a university degree were
the most likely to remain childless, the table shows significant changes in this pattern over time. Most importantly, it is clear that for the youngest cohorts the levels
of childlessness among university educated women have not been increasing, even
though the levels have been rising among the other educational groups, and especially among those who did not earn a degree. This means that educational differences in levels of childlessness are narrowing over time. The West German cohort
born in 1965–1969 will probably be the first for whom female education explains
only a very small share of the differences in childlessness at later ages.

In East Germany, the differences in childlessness rates by level of education are
small. We even see that women without a degree are more likely to remain childless
than women with a university or vocational training degree. It is important to note,
however, that East Germany was a much more homogeneous society than West
Germany. On the one hand, the state-socialist policies pushed people to earn at least
a vocational training degree. Thus, the share of individuals who never earned a
degree was very low, and represented a selective group of people who probably also
suffered from health impairments (see Table A1 in the Appendix). On the other
hand, access to university education was highly rationed and directed by the state
authorities. Despite the selectivity of the university graduates in the older East
German cohorts, levels of childlessness were very low among female university
graduates. Even among the 1965–1969 cohorts, East German women with a university degree are less likely to be childless than less educated West German women.

Table 5.5 reports the results from analyses based on alternative operational definitions of education. In order to guarantee significant case numbers of individual
categories, we grouped the 1960–1964 and 1965–1969 cohorts into a single group
and restricted the analysis to the West German sample. The upper part of the table
contains the results by whether the woman has a vocational or a university degree.
Similar to the results from Table 5.4, educational differences are small. When the
analysis of women's childlessness is based on their school-leaving certificates (sec-

Table 5.4 Childlessness of women by birth cohorts and education (in per cent). Women without migration background. German micro-census 2012

	1940–1944	1945–1949	1950–1954	1955–1959	1960–1964	1965–1969[a]
West Germany						
No degree	9	12	15	18	21	25
Vocational degree	13	14	17	19	21	22
Tertiary degree	25	24	28	31	32	31
East Germany						
No degree	9	13	17	26	28	29
Vocational degree	9	9	8	8	10	14
Tertiary degree	13	16	13	14	18	23

Note: [a]Aged 43–47 in 2012. Women with a migrant background were excluded from this table
Course: Micro-census 2012 (own estimates)

Table 5.5 Childlessness in per cent. West German women without a migration background. Cohorts 1960–1969

Vocational or university education	
No degree	23
Vocational degree	22
University degree	32
School level degree	
Low (*Hauptschule* or less)	20
Medium (*Realschule*)	22
High (*Fachhochschulreife, Abitur*)	30
Combined degrees	
No degree & low schooling	22
No degree & medium schooling	21
No degree & high schooling	32
Vocational degree & low schooling	19
Vocational degree & medium schooling	22
Vocational degree & high schooling	29
University degree	32

Source: Micro-census 2012 (own estimates)

ond part of the table), we find a clear negative educational gradient. In the last part of this table, we have combined the two types of operational definitions of education into seven different categories. This system of classification results in a very uneven pattern: in addition to women with a university degree, women whose highest degree was the *Abitur* are found to have high levels of childlessness. It is likely that the educational careers of women who have the *Abitur*, but who never earned a vocational training or university degree, were disrupted. These women may have entered and exited education, and never settled into a stable employment career, and for this reason remained childless.

Table 5.6 Childlessness by education. West German Cohorts 1971–1973. German Family Panel (pairfam). Column per cent

	Women	Men
No degree	20	36
Vocational degree	25	36
University degree	25	28
All	25	33
Sample size	800	617

Note: The sample includes women and men aged 40 and older at the time of the interview. Migrants are excluded from this analysis. Estimates are weighted by the combined designs and post-stratification weight d1ca1weight
Source: German Family Panel pairfam, waves 1–6 (years 2008/2009–2013/2014)

5.3.2 Childlessness Among Men and Women

To further explore the socioeconomic gradient in childlessness, we analyzed estimates from the German Family Panel pairfam, the results of which are shown in Table 5.6 (for details on this data see: Huinink et al. 2011; Kreyenfeld et al. 2012). The sample was restricted to West German men and women of the 1971–1973 cohorts who were at least 40 years old at the last interview (on average age 41) and who were born in Germany. Although the German Family Panel oversamples East Germans, the number of childless East Germans of these cohorts is too small for a meaningful investigation. Thus, as a separate analysis of the East German patterns was not feasible using these data, the table shows the results for the West German respondents only. The findings presented in the table only partially support the prior evidence of the micro-census, as women without a degree are found to be substantially less likely to remain childless than the other two groups. This difference may stem from the different operational definitions of education in these data. It should also be noted that these cohorts are, on average, age 41 at the time of censoring. It seems likely that the highly educated have a greater probability of having children at higher ages; thus, the differences in childlessness levels between the less educated and the highly educated may narrow further over time.

With regard to gender differences in childlessness, we observe that 25 % of the women, but 33 % of the men are childless at age 41 (which is the average age at censoring in the sample). It is well known that men start the family formation process later than women, and the biological limits of fertility are often considered to be less fixed for men than for women. Thus, there is every reason to believe that the male respondents are more likely than the female respondents to have children past the date of the interview. Other potential explanations for the gender difference are that childless men are not well covered in the survey data, and that when they are covered they are more likely than women to provide faulty reports on their number of children (Rendall et al. 1999). Because we have no external sources to validate male fertility, we can only raise this concern, but have no remedy to cure it. More clarity exists regarding the educational gradient in childlessness. The findings displayed in the table suggest that there is a negative educational gradient in childlessness among men. While a large share of the men with a vocational degree or with no degree have no biological children, the percentage of university educated men who are childless is substantially lower.

Unlike other types of demographic behavior, such as divorce, teenage pregnancy, or non-marital childbearing, childlessness cannot be inherited, and thus passed on to the next generation. However, the number of brothers and sisters a person has may influence his or her ideas about family behavior. Thus, in Table 5.7 we display the results of an analysis of the degree of childlessness by the number of siblings. We find that there is indeed a strong association between these two parameters. Women and men who come from larger families are less likely to remain childless than women and men who were raised as only children. This evidence suggests that a decline in the number of children in each family could result in an increase in childlessness among the next generation. However, this is only an association that does not control for the many characteristics that may be correlated with the number of siblings, such as parental education and the value orientations of the parents and their children.

A characteristic that must be considered in this context is religious affiliation, which has been shown in prior investigations to explain fertility differences in contemporary as well as in past societies (Berghammer 2012). The data from the German Family Panel support this association (see Table 5.8). If we look at the female respondents, we can see that 32 % of those who have no religious affiliation, but just 23 % of those who have a religious affiliation, are childless. A more subtle analysis in a multivariate framework (not shown here) indicates that the effect of religiosity is stable to the inclusion of further covariates, such as education and number of siblings. For men, the differences in levels of childlessness by religiosity are smaller, and insignificant. An aspect that this simple cross-tabulation does not explore is the interaction of having children and religious practices and affiliations over the life course (for a longitudinal analysis of religiosity in Germany, see Lois 2010).

Table 5.7 Childlessness by number of siblings. West German cohorts 1971–1973. German Family Panel (pairfam). Column per cent

	Women	Men
No siblings	33	44
1 sibling	23	35
2 siblings	32	31
3 and more siblings	16	25
Sample size	800	618

Note: The sample includes women and men aged 40 and older at the time of the interview. Migrants are excluded from this analysis. Estimates are weighted by the combined designs and post-stratification weight d1ca-1weight

Source: German Family Panel pairfam, waves 1–6 (years 2008/2009–2013/2014)

Table 5.8 Childlessness by religious affiliation. West German cohorts 1971–1973. German Family Panel (pairfam). Column per cent

	Women	Men
Religious affiliation	23	32
No religious affiliation	32	36
Sample size	801	618

Note: The sample includes women and men aged 40 and older at the time of the interview. Migrants are excluded from this analysis. Estimates are weighted by the combined designs and post-stratification weight d1ca1weight

Source: German Family Panel pairfam, waves 1–6 (years 2008/2009–2013/2014)

Table 5.9 Childlessness by marital status. West German cohorts 1971–1973. German Family Panel (pairfam)

	Women	Men
Never married	68	77
Married	12	13
Divorced or widowed	21	16
Sample size	800	611

Note: The sample includes women and men aged 40 and older at the time of the interview. Migrants are excluded from this analysis. Estimates are weighted by the combined designs and post-stratification weight d1ca1weight

Source: German Family Panel pairfam, waves 1–6 (years 2008/2009–2013/2014)

In most cases, childlessness is not the result of a single decision, but is instead the outcome of an accumulation of actions and decisions in the various domains of the life course (Hagestad and Call 2007; Jalovaara and Fasang 2015). In addition to his or her employment and educational careers, an individual's partnership process is likely to affect whether he or she remains childless. Thus, in Table 5.9 we show the results of the analysis on levels of childlessness by marital and partnership status. It is hardly surprising that men and women who were single at the time of the interview have a much higher probability of being childless than married women and men. Marriage and childbearing are "tied events" (Hoem and Kreyenfeld 2006; Nave-Herz 2006) in West Germany, and people often get married in anticipation of having children. While it may seem obvious that there is a strong correlation between marriage and childlessness, it is surprising to see how closely the two are correlated: 12 % of the married women and 13 % of the married men are childless, whereas among the never married, about 75 % of the men and almost 70 % of the women are childless.

5.3.3 Pathways to Childlessness

Marriage and the partnership status in the abovementioned analyses refer to the characteristics of the respondent at the date of the last interview. Because parents may be more hesitant to dissolve a union than childless couples, being single at the time of the interview may not be the cause, but the consequence of not having children. In order to explore how the marital and partnership trajectories relate to later life childlessness, we present sequence index plots in the following (Abbott 1995). To improve the comparability of the plots, we have drawn a sample of men, women, childless individuals, and individuals with children. All four groups contain 50 randomly selected cases. Their union histories are displayed in Fig. 5.1. In the figure we distinguish between episodes (a) of being single; (b) of being in a cohabiting union without being married; (c) of being separated, widowed, or divorced; and (d) of being in a marital union, irrespective of whether the partner lives in the same household.

The figure shows that childlessness is closely related to the individual's partnership biography. The childless women, and particularly the childless men, were single for much of their twenties and thirties. Only a small fraction of the childless men have been married over a longer period of time (for a detailed study on childlessness of married couples, see Rupp 2005). In addition to observing that a large share of the childless individuals are permanently single, we can see that a large fraction of the childless men and women moved in and out of a (cohabiting or marital) union. Overall, there seem to be two dominant pathways to childlessness: having a turbulent partnership biography and being permanently single. The latter pathway is more typical for men than for women.

While the patterns for childless men and women differ, this is not the case for men and women with children. The primary difference between the sexes in this context is that men tend to enter cohabitation later than women. For both sexes, periods of cohabitation are typically of short duration. The large majority of the men and women who eventually have children turn their cohabitation into a marriage in West Germany.

5.4 Summary

In this paper, we have provided an overview of the long-term trends in childlessness in East and West Germany. We have also explored the socioeconomic differences in childlessness and how they have changed over time. For East Germany, we find only little differences in childlessness by female education. East German women of the birth cohorts 1940–1969 mostly had their children before unification when childbearing was almost universal and women integrated into the labor market full-time. In West Germany, there is a strong educational gradient of female childlessness. University educated women are substantially more likely to remain childless than

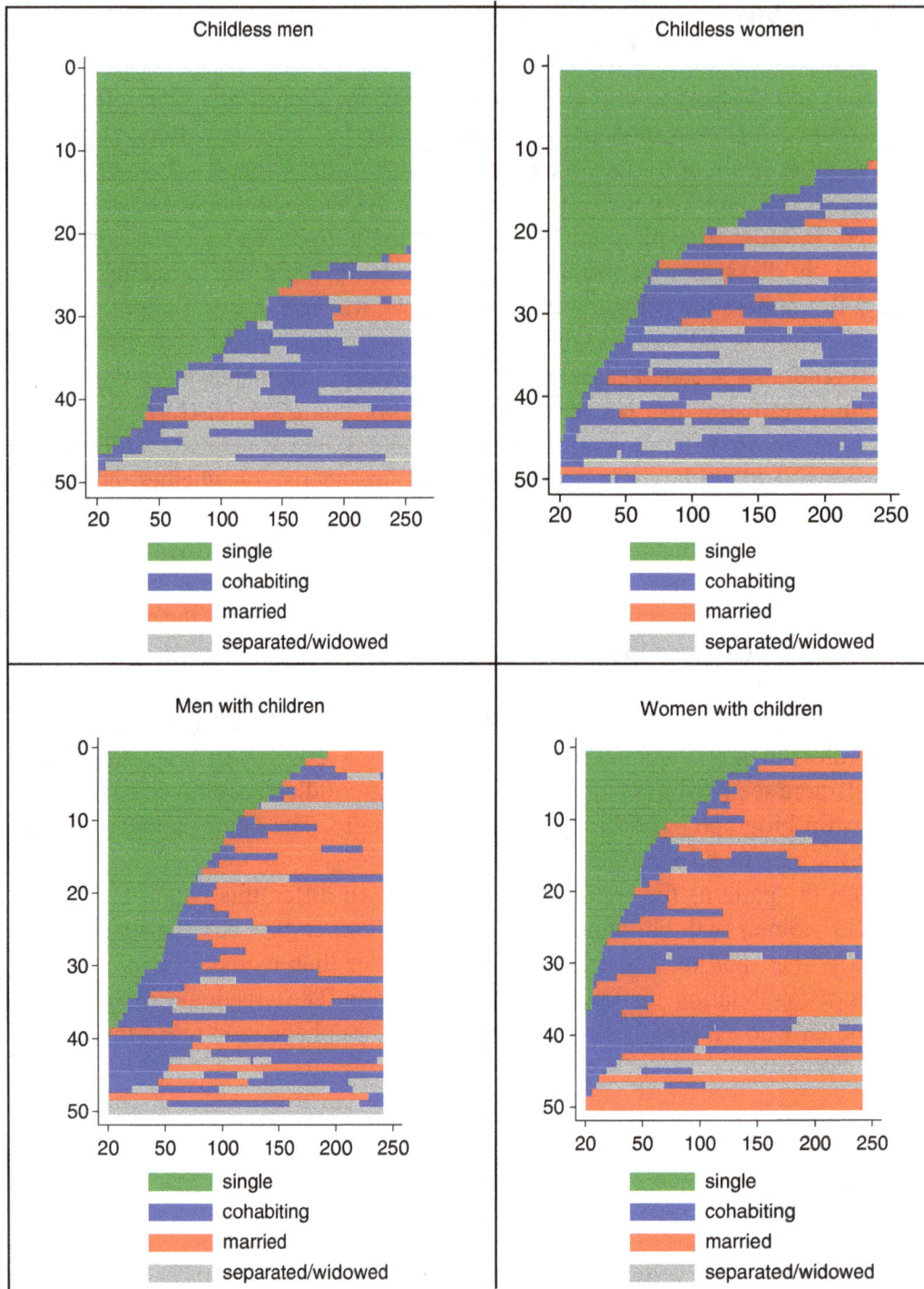

Fig. 5.1 Sequence index plots of the partnership trajectories for West German men and women (x-axis: time since age 20 in months, y-axis: number of cases)

medium or lowly educated women. A very significant development is, however, the narrowing of childlessness by education among the recent female birth cohorts in West Germany. While childlessness among the highly educated has stalled for the recent cohorts, it has continued to increase among the other educational groups, and particularly among women who never earned a university or a vocational training degree. A possible explanation for this finding is that highly educated women have profited more than less educated women from recent policy reforms, such as the expansion of public day care and the reform of the parental leave benefit system in 2007. It may also be the case that less educated women are gradually losing out on the partner market. This finding would appear to confirm evidence from other countries that the lack of a partner often leads to childlessness among less educated women (Jalovaara and Fasang 2015, see also Berrington in this volume). If this interpretation was correct, it would stand in contrast to prior speculations that the lack of a partner was the typical pathway into childlessness for the highly educated women in Germany (Der Spiegel 2005).

The investigations that have been presented in this paper have many limitations. One of the limitations is that findings were sensitive to the classification of education. Moreover, education was only measured at interview and did not capture the educational biographies that may or may not have led to a specific educational outcome. Related to that we have pointed out the problems of correctly classifying a person who got a high school degree (*Abitur*), but never continued to receive a university or vocational training certificate. These people are very often childless, most likely because of their disruptive educational careers.

Some of the findings that we have generated in this paper were hard to interpret. In particular, it seems difficult to understand why childlessness is continuously increasing among West German women with a vocational training degree. More nuanced analyses by type of education would certainly lead to a better understanding for the elevated childlessness among this large group of women (see Neyer et al. in this volume for analyses by field of education using Swedish and Austrian data). We also explored pathways into childlessness my means of sequence analysis in this paper. It was shown that permanent singlehood as well as turbulences in the partnership history are strongly associated with childlessness. However, this part of the analysis remained very explorative. The results confirm that a partnership is a prerequisite for having children, but the causal direction, in particular how fertility preferences influence partnership dynamics, was not explored.

Appendix

Table A1 Level of education by birth cohorts (in per cent). Women without migration background. German micro-census 2012

	1940–1944	1945–1949	1950–1954	1955–1959	1960–1964	1965–1969*
West Germany						
No degree	30	23	18	14	13	11
Vocational degree	63	68	69	72	72	73
Tertiary degree	7	9	13	14	15	17
Total	100	100	100	100	100	100
East Germany						
No degree	12	7	6	5	4	4
Vocational degree	79	82	78	79	80	80
Tertiary degree	9	11	15	15	16	16
Total	100	100	100	100	100	100

Source: Micro-census 2012 (own unweighted estimates)
Note: *Aged 43–47 in 2012

Table A2 Childlessness of women by birth cohorts and education (in per cent). All women (including those without migration background.) German micro-census 2012

		West Germans		East Germans
	All	No migration background	Migration background	No migration background
No degree	17	23	8	28
Vocational degree	19	22	12	12
Tertiary degree	28	32	21	21

Source: Micro-census 2012 (own un-weighted estimates)
Note: Due to the small numbers of migrants in East Germany, we did not distinguish the East German sample by migration background

Literature

Abbott, A. (1995). Sequence analysis: New methods for old ideas. *Annual Review of Sociology, 21*, 93–113.

Berghammer, C. (2012). Family life trajectories and religiosity in Austria. *European Sociological Review, 28*, 127–144.

Birg, H., Filip, D., & Flöthmann, E.-J. (1990). Paritätsspezifische Kohortenanalyse des generativen Verhaltens in der Bundesrepublik Deutschland nach dem 2. Weltkrieg. *IBS-Materialien 16*.

Brentano, L. (1910). The doctrine of Malthus and the increase of population during the last decades. *The Economic Journal, 20*, 371–393.

Bujard, M. (2015). Kinderlosigkeit in Deutschland: Wie interagieren Bildung, Wohnort, Migrationshintergrund, Erwerbstätigkeit und Kohorte? *Zeitschrift für Familienforschung, 3,* 255–269.

Bujard, M., Dorbritz, J., Herter-Eschweiler, R., & Lux, L. (2015). Das unterschätzte Potenzial hoher Fallzahlen – Stärken und Limitierungen des Mikrozensus am Beispiel von Fertilitätsanalysen. *Zeitschrift für Familienforschung, 3,* 343–872.

Der Spiegel. (2005). *Über 40 Prozent kinderlos: "Akademikerinnen finden oft keinen Partner".* (07.09.2005). Accessed 15 Jan 2016.

Dorbritz, J. (2015). Paritätsverteilungen nach Geburtsjahrgängen, Lebensformen und Bildung bei besonderer Beachtung von Kinderlosigkeit und Kinderreichtum: Eine demografisch-soziologische Analyse. *Zeitschrift für Familienforschung, 3,* 297–321.

Duschek, K.-J., & Wirth, H. (2005). Kinderlosigkeit von Frauen im Spiegel des Mikrozensus. Eine Kohortenanalyse der Mikrozensen 1987 bis 2003. *Wirtschaft und Statistik* (8), 800–820.

Hagestad, G. O., & Call, V. R. A. (2007). Pathways to childlessness. A life course perspective. *Journal of Family Issues, 28,* 1338–1361.

Hajnal, J. (1965). European marriage patterns in perspective. In D. V. Glass & D. E. C. Eversley (Eds.), *Population in history: Essays in historical demography* (pp. 101–143). London: Edward Arnold.

Hoem, J. M., & Kreyenfeld, M. (2006). Anticipatory analysis and its alternatives in life-course research. Part 2: Two interacting processes. *Demographic Research, 15,* 485–498.

Huinink, J., Brüderl, J., Nauck, B., Walper, S., Castiglioni, L., & Feldhaus, M. (2011). Panel analysis of intimate relationships and family dynamics (pairfam): Framework and design of pairfam. *Zeitschrift für Familienforschung, 23,* 77–101.

Huinink, J., Kreyenfeld, M., & Trappe, H. (Eds.). (2012). *Familie und Partnerschaft in Ost- und Westdeutschland: Ähnlich und doch immer noch anders.* Leverkusen: Babara Budrich.

Human Mortality Database. (2016). West Germany, Population size (1-year). In V. Shkolnikov, M. Barbieri, & J. Wilmoth (Eds.), http://www.mortality.org/

Jalovaara, M., & Fasang, A. E. (2015). Are there gender differences in family trajectories by education in Finland? *Demographic Research, 33,* 1241–1256.

Knodel, J. (1967). Law, marriage and illegitimacy in nineteenth-century Germany. *Population Studies, 20,* 279–294.

Konietzka, D. (2003). Vocational training and the transition to the first job in Germany. New risks at labor market entry? In D. Bills (Ed.), *The sociology of job training. Research in the sociology of work* (pp. 161–195). Amsterdam: Elsevier.

Kreyenfeld, M. (2002). Parity specific birth rates for West Germany: An attempt to combine survey data and vital statistics. *Zeitschrift für Bevölkerungswissenschaft, 27,* 327–357.

Kreyenfeld, M., Huinink, J., Trappe, H., & Walke, R. (2012). DemoDiff: A dataset for the study of family change in Eastern (and Western) Germany. *Schmollers Jahrbuch, 132,* 653–660.

Lois, D. (2010). Wie verändert sich die Religiosität im Lebensverlauf? Eine Panelanalyse unter Berücksichtigung von Ost-West-Unterschieden. *Kölner Zeitschrift für Soziologie und Sozialpsychologie, 63,* 83–110.

Matz, K.-J. (1980). *Pauperismus und Bevölkerung: Die gesetzlichen Ehebeschränkungen in den süddeutschen Staaten während des 19. Jahrhunderts.* Stuttgart: Klett-Cotta.

Mitterauer, M. (1990). Servants and youth. *Continuity and Change, 5,* 11–38.

Naderi, R. (2015). Kinderzahl und Migrationshintergrund. Ein Vergleich zwischen Frauen türkischer Herkunft mit oder ohne eigene Wanderungserfahrung sowie Frauen ohne Migrationshintergrund in Westdeutschland. *Zeitschrift für Familienforschung, 3,* 322–342.

Nave-Herz, R. (2006). *Ehe- und Familiensoziologie.* Weinheim/München: Juventa.

Rendall, M. S., Clarke, L., Peters, H. E., Ranjit, N., & Verropoulou, G. (1999). Incomplete reporting of men's fertility in the United States and Britain: A research note. *Demography, 36,* 135–144.

Rupp, M. (2005). Kinderlosigkeit in stabilen Ehen. *Zeitschrift für Familienforschung, 17,* 21–40.

Schmitt, C., & Winkelmann, U. (2005). Wer bleibt kinderlos? Was sozialstrukturelle Daten über Kinderlosigkeit bei Frauen und Männern verraten. *Zeitschrift für interdisziplinäre Frauen- und Geschlechterforschung, 23*, 9–23.

Schwarz, K. (1991). Die Kinderzahl der Frauen der Geburtsjahrgänge 1865–1955. *Zeitschrift für Bevölkerungswissenschaft, 17*, 149–157.

Zeeb, F. B. (1915). The mobility of the German woman. *American Journal of Sociology, 21*.

Chapter 6
Childlessness in Switzerland and Austria

Marion Burkimsher and Kryštof Zeman

6.1 Introduction

For several reasons, Switzerland and Austria are of interest to researchers analysing the factors that influence levels of childlessness. The countries are similar in terms of population size, standard of living, and socio-economic setting. The Alpine regions have traditionally had rather high levels of childlessness, with a significant proportion of women and men remaining single (Viazzo 1989). The current population of Switzerland is about 8.2 million, of whom 65 % are German-speaking, 23 % are French-speaking, and 8 % are Italian-speaking. As each canton has its own official religion and language(s), there are French- and German-speaking Catholic, Protestant, and secular cantons. In the age range 20–39 a third of the population has foreign citizenship. These immigrants come not only from the neighbouring countries of Germany, France, and Italy, but also from ex-Yugoslavia, Portugal, and Spain. Austria has a slightly larger population, at 8.6 million, and the official language is German, with 89 % of the population speaking German as their mother tongue. The proportion of foreigners in the country is less than half that of Switzerland, with immigrants from Germany and the countries of ex-Yugoslavia and Turkey being the most numerous. Around 20 % of women in Switzerland who have reached the end of their reproductive years have no children, while the corresponding figure in Austria is a little lower, at around 18 %. In Switzerland, the share

M. Burkimsher (✉)
Independent researcher affiliated with the University of Lausanne, Lausanne, Switzerland
e-mail: drmarionb@gmail.com

K. Zeman
Vienna Institute of Demography, Austrian Academy of Sciences and Wittgenstein Centre for Demography and Global Human Capital, Vienna, Austria
e-mail: krystof.zeman@oeaw.ac.at

© The Author(s) 2017
M. Kreyenfeld, D. Konietzka (eds.), *Childlessness in Europe: Contexts, Causes, and Consequences*, Demographic Research Monographs, DOI 10.1007/978-3-319-44667-7_6

of the population who are childless has never been lower than 14 % even for the cohorts who lived through the baby boom years, whereas in Austria it dropped to around 12 %. These levels and trends are similar to those of some countries in western Europe (the United Kingdom, Germany, the Netherlands) and a few overseas developed countries (the United States, Japan), but are very different from central and eastern Europe, which have much lower rates of childlessness.

This chapter examines the differentials in fertility outcomes across subpopulations in the two countries, drawing on census and survey data. Specifically, we examine the variations in levels of childlessness by cohort, educational attainment, religion, migration background, and current place of residence in the country. We also provide insights into differences in fertility desires in the two countries.

6.2 Institutional Setting and Data

6.2.1 Institutional Setting

In Austria, the parental leave period is up to 3 years, and because the conditions for taking this leave are relatively generous,[1] it is widely used. Only one-third of mothers with children under age three are in the labour force, well below the OECD average of 41 % (OECD 2014). Just 21 % of children under age three were in public day-care in Austria in 2012, which is the lowest proportion among all of the western European countries. As childcare in Austria is administered by municipalities, there are big disparities in childcare provision between the regions. The availability of day-care has been increasing in Vienna, and the proportion of children under age 3 who are enrolled has grown from 17 % in 1995 to 35 % currently. Participation rates have generally been high for children aged 4–5, and have recently increased considerably among 3-year-olds, from 40 to 50 % in the 1990s to 81.5 % in the 2012/13 school year (Statistics Austria 2013a). Women in Austria have a legal right to reduce their working hours to part-time after having a child, and many women take advantage of this option. Among couples with children ages 0–14, the proportion of families in Austria with one parent working full-time and the other working part-time was 44 % in 2011, the highest share amongst all OECD countries except for the Netherlands with 60 % (OECD 2014). Public spending on the family is very biased towards cash benefits (such as parental leave and child allowances) rather than services (pre-school childcare, or policies to help parents combine work and childrearing). As Neyer and Hoem (2008: 94) noted, "Austria represents a conservative, gendering welfare state which supports mother's absence from the labor market".

In Switzerland, by contrast, there is less public support for new families. Maternity leave is only 14 weeks and childcare facilities are scarce and expensive, especially in the German- and Italian-speaking areas of the country. High incomes

---

[1] Since 2008 parental leave in Austria has been made more flexible, with three variants of duration of 18/24/36 months, which offer different levels of monthly allowances, of 800/624/436 EUR.

and the widespread availability of part-time jobs only partially offset the challenges facing couples with small children; the opportunity costs of a break in employment to have a child are higher in Switzerland than in most other countries. The female labour force participation rate of women aged 25–39 has been increasing, and was 85 % in 2014. While 80 % of employed women living in a household with child(ren) under the age of 15 are working part-time, the corresponding proportion of men with young families who are working part-time remains low, but increased from 3 % in 1992 to 10 % in 2014 (Federal Statistical Office 2015a).

6.2.2 Data

In this chapter, the primary data source for Switzerland is the full population census taken in the year 2000. The census asked both women and men to state the number of children they had ever borne or fathered. The question on number of children was not compulsory, and around 3 % of women did not respond. This proportion was a little higher for men, and was markedly higher among young and elderly people, who may have considered the question irrelevant. Foreigners also had an elevated non-response rate, of around 7 %.

Austria has similar census data, which in 1981, 1991, and 2001 included fertility data. Women aged 16 and over were asked to report the number of live-born children they had ever had. Because of the way the census question was posed, there were some discrepancies in the proportion of respondents who said they were childless among comparable cohorts between the 1981 survey and subsequent surveys (Zeman 2011). For this chapter, we mainly use the 2001 census data.[2]

Birth registration data for the years since the last census, together with population estimates from registers, allow for the calculation of age- and birth order-specific fertility rates, and thus enable us to make on-going estimates of cohort fertility. For Switzerland and Austria, these base data are available in the Human Fertility Database (2015).

Surveys of various sizes and spheres of interest are used to complement the census and birth registration data for both Switzerland and Austria. In 1994, Switzerland participated in the multi-national Fertility and Families Survey (FFS). More up-to-date information was gathered in 2013 with the Families and Generations Survey (FGS). This survey, which had a sample size of over 17,000, included information on family sizes and fertility intentions, along with many other demographic variables. Another on-going survey that offers insights into fertility in Switzerland is the Swiss Household Panel (SHP). In Austria, a micro-census of around 22,500 households is performed four times a year, and includes many socio-economic variables, with a focus on the labour market. Special modules asking about the number of

---

[2] Census data on parity by level of education, origin, and cohort are available in the Cohort Fertility and Education database (Zeman et al. 2014).

children and fertility intentions (*Kinderwunsch*) are included about every 5 years (1986, 1991, 1996, 2001, 2006, and 2012). In this chapter we use the individual micro-data from the micro-census wave of the fourth quarter of 2012.

6.3 Childlessness by Socio-economic Characteristics

6.3.1 Changing Levels of Childlessness by Birth Cohort

Figure 6.1 shows the trends in cohort fertility for Austria and the corresponding proportions of women born between 1920 and 1960 who were childless. In earlier generations, the rates of childlessness were even higher: among the cohorts born in the 1880s and 1890s, around one-third of the women remained childless in both Switzerland and Austria (Viazzo 1989). In traditional societies a substantial proportion of the population did not marry for a variety of reasons. For example, many people were discouraged or prohibited from marrying by family inheritance systems; poverty and the inability to raise enough money to marry; choosing to enter into religious orders; or legal restrictions on the right to marry for members of the lower classes (Mantl 1999). In addition, a significant proportion of married women remained childless because, for example, they suffered from infectious diseases or were infertile, their pregnancies ended in miscarriage or still-birth, or they were widowed or separated from their partner for long periods of time (Ehmer 2011).

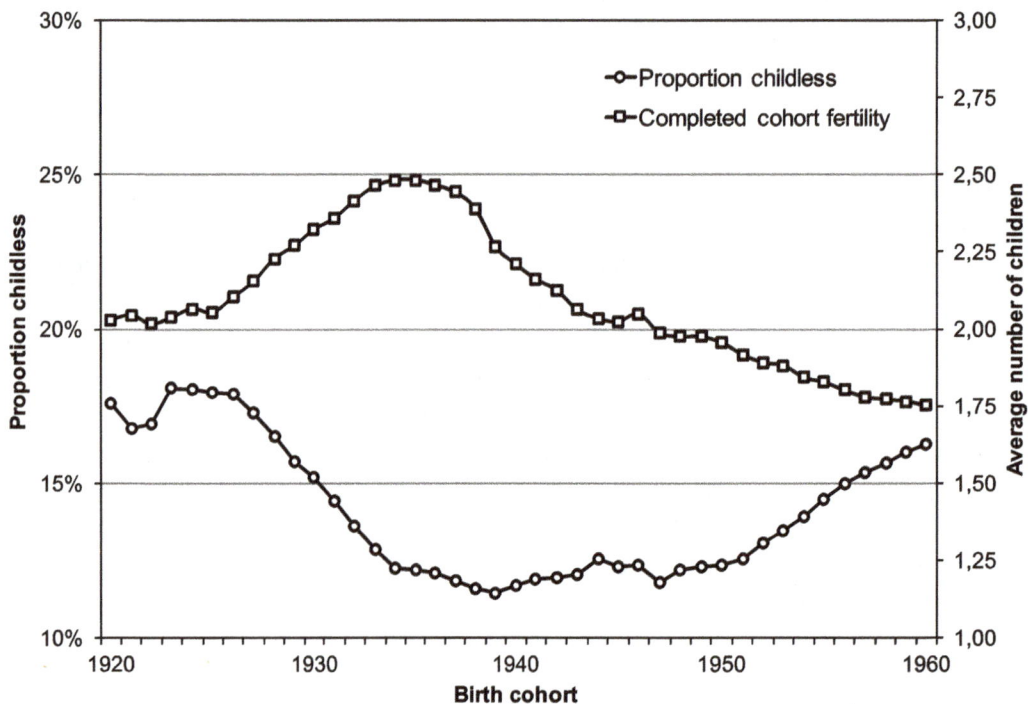

Fig. 6.1 Proportion of women who were childless, cohorts 1920–1960 (*left scale*) and completed cohort fertility (*right scale*) by birth cohort, Austria (Source: Census 2001, own estimates)

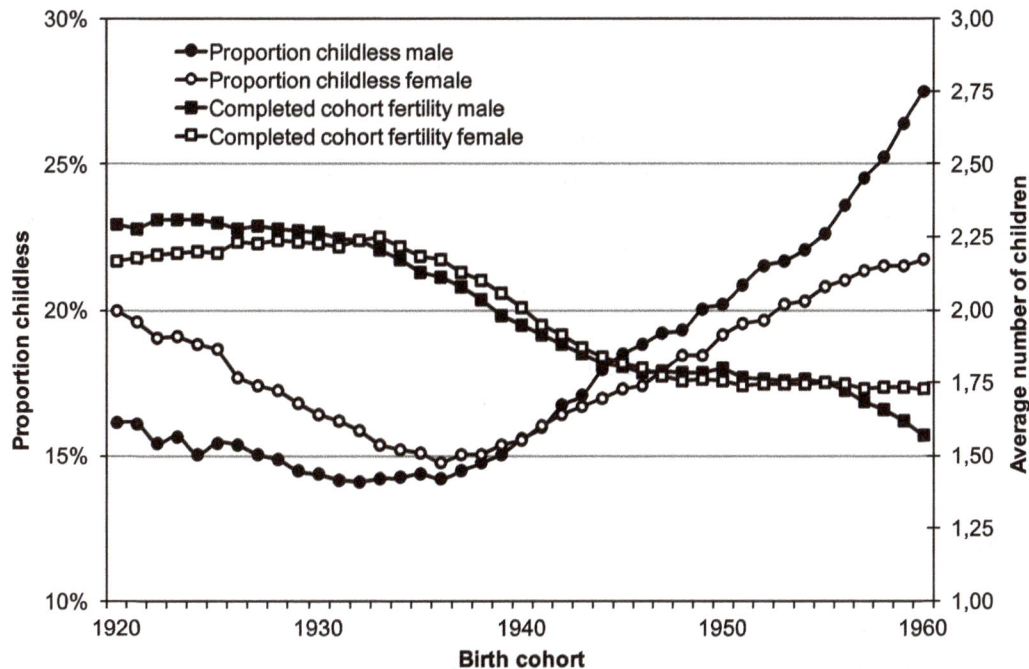

Fig. 6.2 Proportion of men and women who were childless, cohorts 1920–1960 (*left scale*) and completed cohort fertility (*right scale*), Switzerland (Source: Census 2000, own estimates)

The lowest level of childlessness in Austria, at around 12 %, was reached for women born in 1938. The childlessness rates among subsequent cohorts increased steadily, rising to around 18 % for women born around 1970. In 1984, only 11 % of first births occurred after age 30, and just 0.3 % of births occurred after age 40. In 2013, the corresponding figures were 45 % and 2.3 %, which represents a significant shift. As women are postponing the birth of their first child to increasingly high ages, the risk of infertility is rising, and is only partially offset by the increasing availability of assisted reproductive technology (ART). In Austria, public health care provides subsidised ART to infertile women, and 2 % of live births resulted from the use of ART in 2010 (ESHRE 2014).

Switzerland has fertility data for both men and women (see Fig. 6.2), and while the levels and trends in Switzerland are similar to those of Austria, they are not identical. The lowest childlessness rates were for the 1932 male cohort and the 1936 female cohort. It is interesting to note that for the cohorts born before 1940 childlessness was higher for women, but among the more recent cohorts childlessness has been higher for men. There is no clear explanation for this shift. It is possible that men of earlier generations would seek a new partner if their first wife did not bear them a child, as the pressure to produce an heir, especially in rural communities, may have been significant. Among more recent generations, the situation may be reversed, as an increasing proportion of less skilled men are failing to find a partner. The different life courses and work constraints of male and female immigrants and low skilled workers, and how they have changed over time, may also explain the differential.

The baby boom was associated with a double peak in period fertility rates. In Austria, the highest TFRs were 2.75 in 1940 and 2.82 in 1963, while Switzerland's peak TFRs were a little lower, at 2.62 in 1946 and 2.68 in 1964. An upsurge in early births was a major cause of the temporal peaks in period fertility; whilst postponement, together with the decline in large families, has depressed period rates since the baby boom. Although the period trends were similar in Austria and Switzerland, the cohort fertility trends in the two countries were rather different. In Austria there was a peak of 2.5 children on average, for women born in the mid-1930s, followed by a decline to 1.75 for the 1960 cohort (Fig. 6.1). In Switzerland the average family size was quite stable at around 2.2 children for the cohorts born up to the mid-1930s. Subsequent cohorts then experienced declines to the current level of around 1.75.

6.3.2   *Childlessness by Education*

A large number of studies have shown that, for women, having more education is associated with lower overall fertility and higher rates of childlessness (for a general overview, see Skirbekk 2008; for Austria, see Neyer and Hoem 2008, Prskawetz et al. 2008, Sobotka 2011; for Switzerland, see Coenen-Huther 2005, Sauvain-Dugerdil 2005, and Mosimann and Camenisch 2015; for other countries, see Wood et al. 2014). For an analysis of the link between childlessness and field of education, see the chapter by Neyer et al. in this volume.

Over the past century, educational levels have been rising, particularly for women. In Switzerland, for example, the proportion of women who have tertiary-level education increased from 6 % of those born in 1930, to 13 % of those born in 1950, to 21 % of those born in 1970, and it is still rising. The corresponding figures for men born in 1930, 1950, and 1970 are 24 %, 30 %, and 33 %, respectively. We might expect to find that with higher education becoming more prevalent, the reproductive behaviour of highly educated women would become less differentiated from that of less educated women. Interestingly, Austria has seen such a convergence (Fig. 6.3), whereas Switzerland has seen a divergence (Fig. 6.4). Austria differs from most other developed countries in that men are still more likely than women to enrol in tertiary education; whereas in most other European countries, including in Switzerland, women now outnumber men in higher education.

The 1981 Austrian census showed that around 60 % of the women born in the 1890s and early 1900s who had a tertiary education were childless: thus, their decision to pursue a higher education was effectively a "life calling" similar to the calling to commit to a celibate life in the church. Among the cohorts born after the Second World War in Austria, there has been a convergence in childlessness rates between women at the upper two educational levels, and between women at the lower two educational levels; the differentiating factor is whether or not a woman graduated from secondary school with a high school diploma (*Matura*) (Fig. 6.3). This pattern may be caused by Austria's early educational streaming of pupils after the fourth year of elementary school into either vocational training or a higher

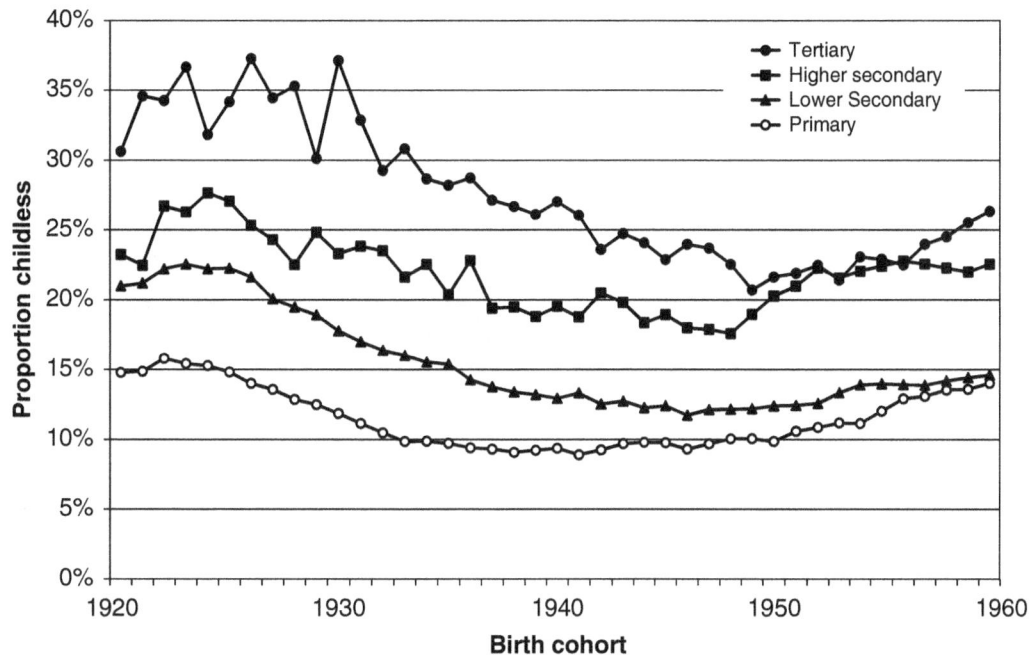

Fig. 6.3 Proportion of women who were childless by birth cohort and level of education, Austria. Note: The primary level includes ISCED 1997 levels 0–2; the lower secondary level includes ISCED levels 3B and 3C; the higher secondary level includes ISCED levels 3A and 4; and the tertiary level includes all ISCED levels of 5 and 6 (Source: Census 2001, own estimates)

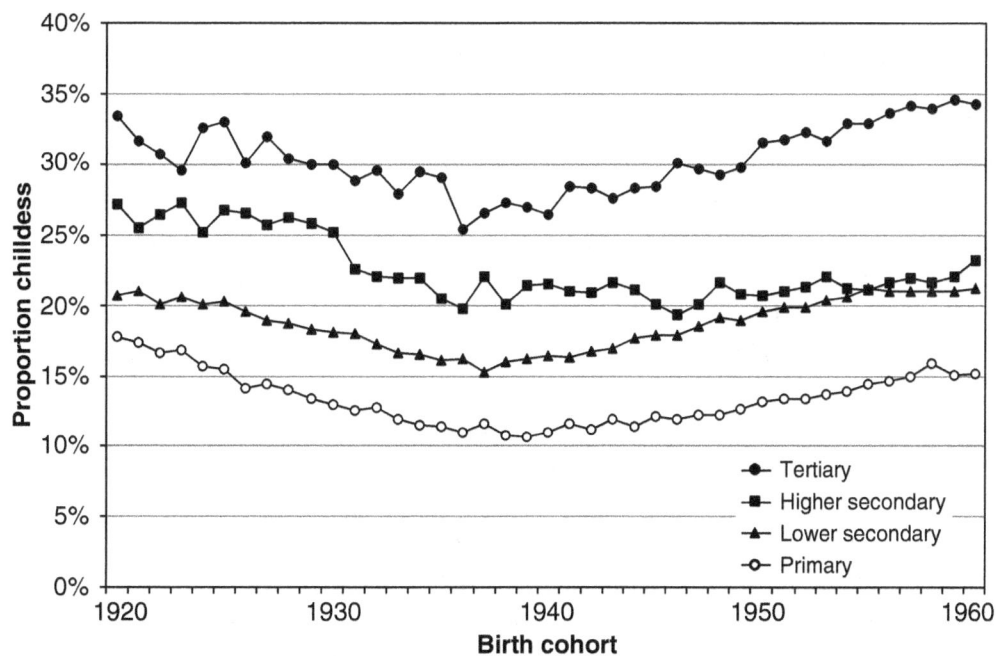

Fig. 6.4 Proportion of women who were childless by birth cohort and level of education, Switzerland. Note: The primary level includes ISCED 1997 levels 0–2; the lower secondary level includes ISCED levels 3B and 3C; the higher secondary level includes ISCED level 3A; and the tertiary level includes all ISCED levels of 5 and 6 (Source: Census 2000, own estimates)

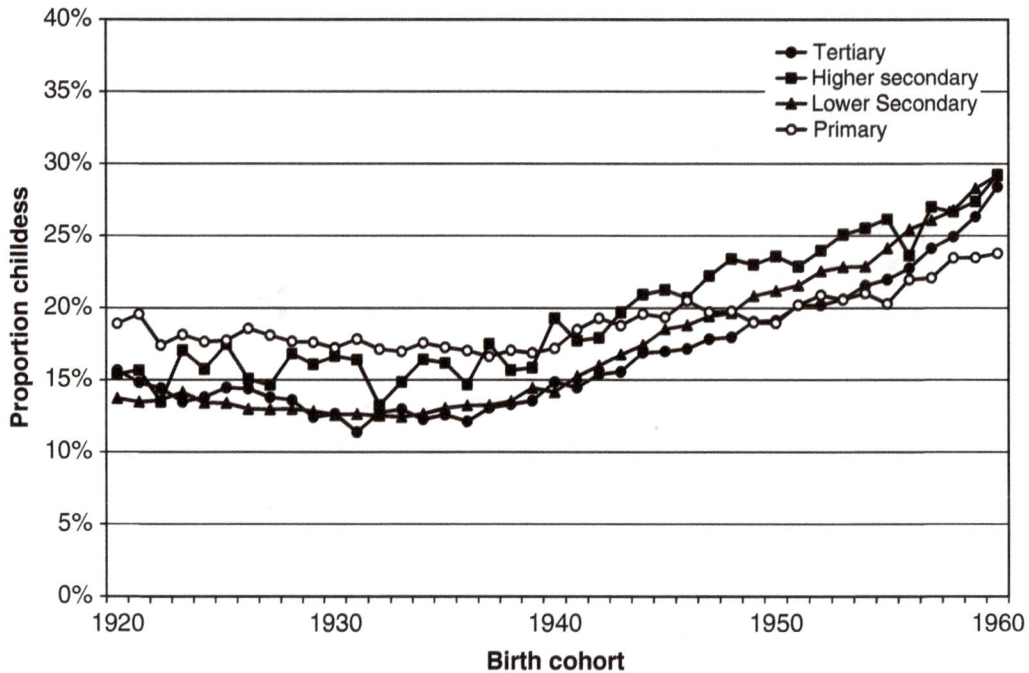

Fig. 6.5 Proportion of men who were childless by birth cohort and level of education, Switzerland. Note: The primary level includes ISCED 1997 groups 0–2; the lower secondary level includes ISCED levels 3B and 3C; the higher secondary level includes ISCED levels 3A and 4; and the tertiary level includes all ISCED levels of 5 and 6 (Source: Census 2000, own estimates)

secondary and university track, with limited opportunities to transfer between the two. This educational system has been described as being "segregated by gender and social class" (Neyer and Hoem 2008: 107).

Figure 6.4 shows the incidence of childlessness for women of different educational levels in Switzerland. Among women with a low educational level, the rates are similar for Switzerland and Austria, at around 15 % of the current generation completing their childbearing. However, for women with tertiary education, the rates of childlessness differ considerably between the two countries: one-third of these women in Switzerland are childless; whereas in Austria only around one-quarter are childless, which is similar to the rate for women with higher secondary education. Moreover, unlike in Austria, in Switzerland the two secondary education groups recently converged at a level of about 20 %. In Austria there are now two distinct groups: moderate rates of childlessness among women with primary or lower secondary education, and higher rates of childlessness among women with tertiary or higher secondary education. In Switzerland, however, three groups have emerged: moderate rates of childlessness among women with primary education, higher rates of childlessness for those with secondary education, and the highest rates of childlessness for women with tertiary education.

The differentials in childlessness by education for men are much smaller than those for women (see Fig. 6.5 for Swiss data). Among the older generations, lower educated men had the highest rates of childlessness, most likely caused by poverty.

There is a transposition in ranking among younger men, with an intermediate level of academic attainment being associated with the highest levels of childlessness. It was still possible that the men born after 1955 (who were under age 45 at the time of the census) could father a child.

6.3.3 Childlessness by Religion

Back in 1994, the Swiss FFS found that religiosity was associated with different views on the benefits of having children (Coenen-Huther 2005). The findings indicated that compared with respondents who were active in their faith, those with no religious affiliation were less likely to believe that having children offers benefits such as joy and satisfaction, partnership consolidation, and continuation of the family line. In addition, the respondents who did not attend religious services were less likely to see children as a potential support when elderly, or as a continuation of life after their death. It is, therefore, not surprising that religiosity has an impact on fertility outcomes.

Both Austria and Switzerland are more religious than many other western European countries, with up to one-quarter of all adults regularly attending a religious service. In Austria the majority religion is Catholic; 61 % of Austrians are members of the Catholic Church, whilst around 5 % are members of Protestant churches. In Switzerland there is a more even split between the Catholic and the Reformed (Protestant) denominations, and affiliation with these churches is mixed across both regional and linguistic lines. In both countries the proportion of the population with no religious affiliation is growing, and young people attend religious services much less frequently than older people (Burkimsher 2014). In Switzerland, religious affiliation was recorded in the 2000 census. For Austria, census data from 2001 is available for women in Vienna, obtained as part of the WIREL project (see Acknowledgements).

There is a close relationship between educational level and religious affiliation. Most notably, those who classify themselves as having "no religion" have, until recently, been more concentrated among the highly educated. Recent evidence suggests, however, that among the younger generations (those born after the 1960s) this link is weakening or even reversing.

In general, the differences between Catholics and Protestants in rates of childlessness are slight in both Switzerland and Austria. However, very significant differences appear when we look at the non-religious. Holding other factors constant, the childlessness rate of the non-religious is about double that of Catholics and Protestants in Switzerland. This result contradicts the findings of Baudin (2008) for France: that (non-)religiosity has a significant effect on family size, but not on the likelihood of remaining childless. The differential between Catholics and those with no religion is not quite as marked in Austria (Vienna) as in Switzerland, but it is still significantly large.

Vienna is a very heterogeneous city in which all the major religions are represented. In the 2001 census the level of childlessness for 45–54-year-old women was 20 % for both Catholics and Protestants. Among Muslim and Orthodox women the childlessness levels were significantly lower, at 8 % and 9 %, respectively. In contrast, the childlessness level for women with no religious affiliation was significantly higher, at 26 %. When we take into account country of birth and education in our analysis, the distinctiveness of Muslim and Orthodox women becomes weaker, which suggests that the very low levels of childlessness among these women is attributable in part to their migration background and low educational attainment. In Vienna, the factors of education and country of birth have greater effects on childlessness than religion *per se*.

In a recent study that focused on women scientists in Austria, Buber-Ennser and Skirbekk (2015) found that education (along with age and marital status) was the most important determinant of *actual* childlessness; and that religious affiliation, whilst still having significant explanatory power, had a weaker effect. In contrast to *actual* childlessness, differentials by religiosity in the *intention* to remain childless were large. However, there were no significant differentials in fertility intentions by education when religion was taken into account (but a significant proportion of highly educated women fail to achieve their fertility ambitions). The same pattern was found for men and women in the FGS in Switzerland: i.e. the non-religious were much more likely than the religious to say they did not want to have a child, but the differentials in actual childlessness were smaller.

In Switzerland, the effects of having a higher education and no religious affiliation are multiplicative: for women born in the 1960s, almost 45 % of those who were both tertiary educated and had no religious affiliation were childless. From the 1920s cohort to the 1960s cohort an increasing proportion of the population (4–12 % of women) embraced the "no religion" position. At the same time, their fertility behaviour, perhaps surprisingly, became increasingly differentiated from that of women who were traditional Catholics/Protestants. But among younger cohorts there are indications that the patterns in Switzerland and Austria are becoming increasingly similar to those observed in Britain (Dubuc 2009): i.e. as the lower educated increasingly describe themselves as having no religion, the historical association between having no religion and a high rate of childlessness is starting to break down.

In contrast to the traditionally Christian background of the local population, the Muslim (predominantly immigrant) communities are distinctive in their partnering and fertility behaviour (Fig. 6.6). Almost all Muslims marry, and within marriage childlessness is rare; probably around the biological minimum. There is a norm of early marriage and childbearing: at age 30 (in 2000) only 6 % of Muslim women were still unmarried, and 84 % had had at least one child.

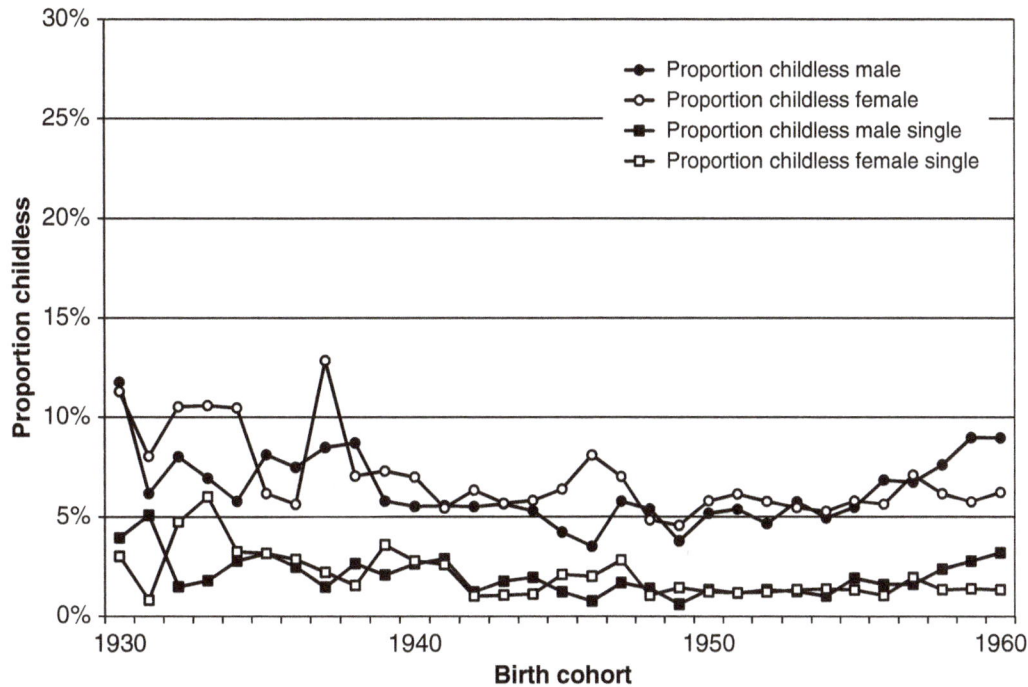

Fig. 6.6 Proportion of Muslim men and women who are single or childless by cohort, Switzerland (Source: Census 2000, own estimates)

6.3.4 Childlessness by Country of Birth

In Switzerland, and to a lesser extent in Austria, very high proportions of the young adult population were born outside of the country. Their reasons for being in the country, as well as the strong influences of education and religion, as already discussed, affect their levels of childlessness.

On average, immigrants have a lower rate of childlessness than the native-born. However, closer investigation reveals that there are big differentials by country of origin. Censuses record either current citizenship (Austria in 1981 and 1991) or country of birth (Austria in 2001); or they record both (Switzerland in 2000). These categories are not directly equivalent, as the relative ease or difficulty of naturalisation determines how many immigrants acquire citizenship; it is easier to become a citizen in Austria than in Switzerland, and it is easier for some nationalities than others to acquire citizenship in both countries. In both Switzerland and Austria, being born in the country does not confer the automatic right to that country's citizenship. Table 6.1 shows the proportion of the total population by citizenship, and by whether they were born in the country.

In general, people with foreign citizenship have a younger age profile than all people "born abroad", because immigrants who stay in the country longer often aspire to citizenship. Having children in the country also tends to be associated with settling or remaining for a longer period of time. The outcome of these factors in terms of childlessness is illustrated in Table 6.1 for Austria. The 1981 census showed

Table 6.1 Proportion of population (men and women) in 2013 by current citizenship and country of birth

	Switzerland	Austria
Swiss/Austrian citizenship, born in the country	67.2 %	82.0 %
Foreign citizenship, born in the country	4.6 %	1.8 %
Swiss/Austrian citizenship, born abroad	9.0 %	6.1 %
Foreign citizenship, born abroad	19.2 %	10.1 %

Sources: Swiss data from Population and Households Statistics, STATPOP (Federal Statistical Office, 2015b), Austrian data from Statistics Austria (2013b)

that the childlessness level of women with *foreign citizenship* was ten per cent higher than that of Austrian women. This reflects the fact that in the 1960s and 1970s many immigrants came from Western Europe for short- and medium-term work, and they made up a very small share of the population (1.5–3 % of the 1920–1940 cohorts). In the 2001 census, when *country of birth* was recorded, the differentials were much lower, and among women younger than age 50 there was a reversal, with immigrants having lower levels of childlessness than the native-born. The reason for this shift is that in the 1990s more immigrants came from the war-torn countries of former Yugoslavia, and later from Turkey; and these migrants, who were especially likely to settle and have a family in Austria, had higher fertility rates than the native population. These immigrants also made up a much larger share of the population than other groups of foreign citizens (10–14 % of the 1920–1940 cohorts) (Fig. 6.7).

For Switzerland, we have more detailed information on childlessness rates by country of birth from the 2000 census. Table 6.2 shows the rates for a selection of countries and regions to illustrate certain factors that have a bearing on childlessness. A higher rate of childlessness is associated with coming from a culture in which childlessness is quite common, especially amongst highly educated women. This can explain the high rates for women from the Anglo-Saxon countries, Finland, Germany, and the Netherlands; as well as from the developed countries of the Far East, including Japan, South Korea, and Taiwan. In contrast, childlessness is low among women from southern Europe, the Balkans, and Turkey, as in those countries childlessness is rare. However, the high rates of childlessness among women from the ex-communist countries are surprising, as the rates were traditionally very low in these countries.

For some immigrants, the constraints imposed by their specific work conditions in Switzerland can have a significant impact on their rates of marriage and childbearing. The high levels of childlessness among women from the Philippines, Thailand, and Latin America is likely attributable to the fact that many come to work as maids or nannies. The childlessness rates are significantly lower for men from these countries than for women. Immigrants from some countries find a restricted "marriage market" in the country, caused by a gender mismatch in the number of immigrants from the same culture. As was already mentioned, this mismatch partly explains the higher rates of childlessness for women than men from

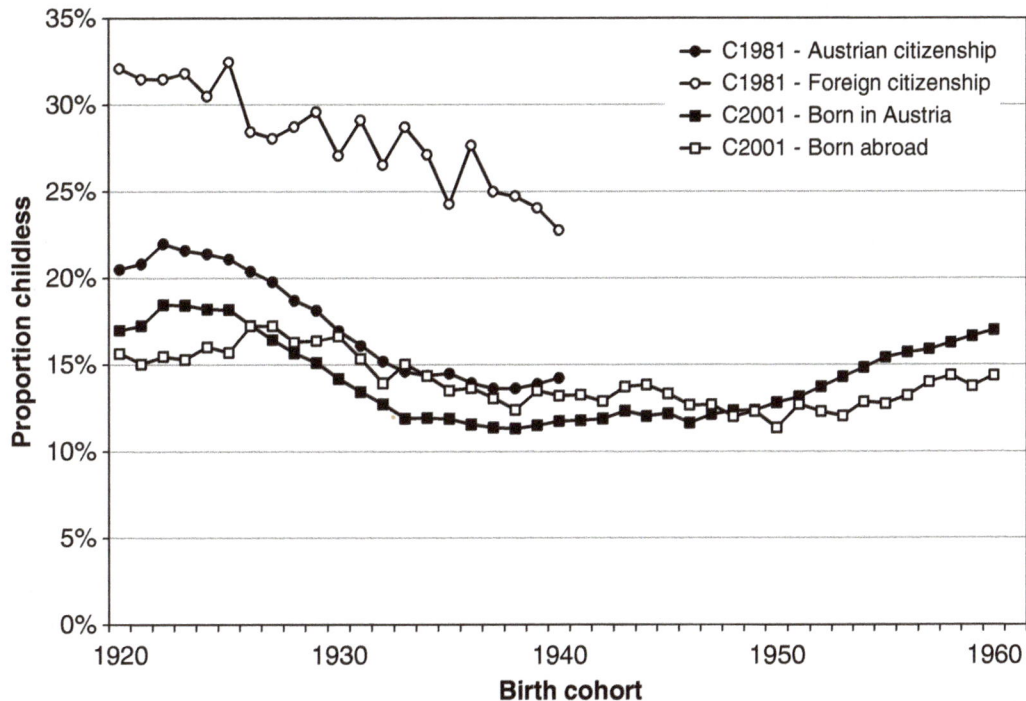

Fig. 6.7 Proportion of women who were childless by birth cohort, citizenship, and migration background, Austria (Source: Census 1981 and 2001, own estimates)

less developed countries. Similarly, it explains why childlessness is higher for men compared to women coming from Spain and Italy. Many single young men come from these countries to work in physically demanding jobs, often on a short- or medium-term basis; if they marry, they often return to their home countries.

We can see the influence of these factors playing out if we compare German, French, and Italian speakers by their respective places of birth: i.e., Switzerland, Germany, France, or Italy (Figs. 6.8, 6.9, and 6.10).

As we noted earlier, the childlessness level for Germans is rather high, and the differential between native Swiss-Germans and immigrant Germans is getting larger with younger cohorts. Childlessness is particularly common for German women living in Switzerland: it is nearly 35 % for the 1960 cohort, compared to "only" 25 % for the Swiss-Germans of the same cohort.

The graph for French speakers (Fig. 6.9) is quite different from that for German speakers in Switzerland. The childlessness rates for French speakers are lower than the rates for German speakers, and the differences by country of birth (France or Switzerland) are much smaller. For men the gap between the two groups is insignificant, although for women immigrating from France, the rate is a couple of percentage points higher.

Figure 6.10, which shows the patterns of childlessness for Italian speakers, is different again. Immigrants from Italy have very low levels of childlessness; lower even than those of native Italians in Italy. The proportion of native-born Italian speakers–most of whom live in the canton of Ticino–who are childless is even

Table 6.2 Proportion of childless women (cohort 1930–1960) and childless men (cohort 1930–1950) by country of birth, Switzerland

Country of birth	Women		Men	
	Per cent childless	N	Per cent childless	N
Far East developed*	26 %	1565	17 %	277
Philippines & Thailand	25 %	4858	18 %	3217
Anglo-Saxon*	24 %	12,894	20 %	5060
Finland	24 %	1887	14 %	191
Germany	23 %	58,107	19 %	29,790
Netherlands	21 %	5193	17 %	2162
Latin America*	20 %	8185	15 %	1485
Ex-communist*	20 %	14,680	19 %	8586
France	20 %	27,914	17 %	12,605
Switzerland	19 %	961,364	18 %	576,147
Austria	17 %	21,499	17 %	9075
Italy	9 %	65,973	10 %	60,440
Spain	9 %	17,636	13 %	10,302
Ex-Yugoslavia & Albania	8 %	40,875	6 %	17,671
Portugal	8 %	12,095	6 %	3406
Turkey	5 %	8273	6 %	4301

Source: Census 2000, own estimates
Note: *Far East developed = Japan, South Korea, Taiwan; Anglo-Saxon = UK, Ireland, USA, Canada, Australia, New Zealand; Latin America = Mexico, Brazil, Argentina, Chile, Colombia, Peru; Ex-communist = Hungary, Czech Republic, Poland, Romania, Slovakia, Russia, Bulgaria

higher than in the German-speaking parts of the country. In this Alpine region, there is a long-established tradition of marrying late, and a high rate of singlehood. This may be an adaptation to life in a rugged region, where population pressures were mitigated by a division into high-fertility "family" women and men, and those who remained single and had other specific roles to play in society (Viazzo 1989). The low, though steadily increasing rates of childlessness among Italian immigrants may be explained by their origin in southern Italy, where fertility behaviour follows the southern European pattern.

6.3.5 Geographical Variations in Childlessness and the Process of Concentration

Childlessness has traditionally been considerably higher in Vienna than in the rest of Austria, for two main reasons: first, a large proportion of the city's population are single, many of them students or seasonal migrants; and, second, there is selective outmigration of young families to the periphery of Vienna, which is mostly in the province of Lower Austria. Table 6.3 gives the proportion of women who are

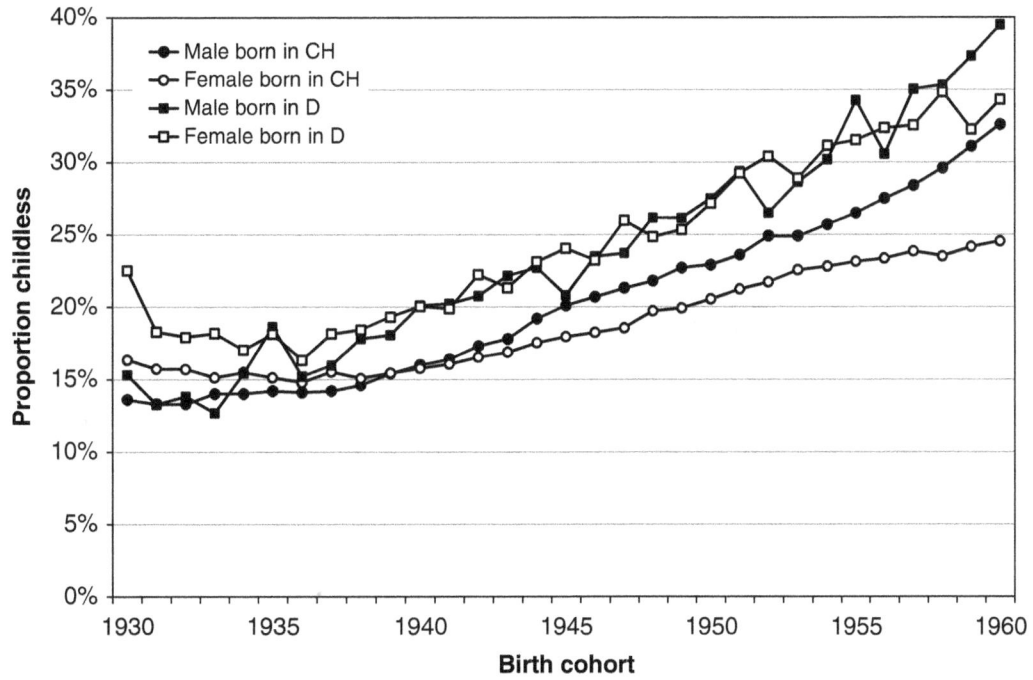

Fig. 6.8 Proportion of German-speaking women and men in Switzerland who are childless, whether born in Switzerland or Germany (Source: Census 2000, own estimates)

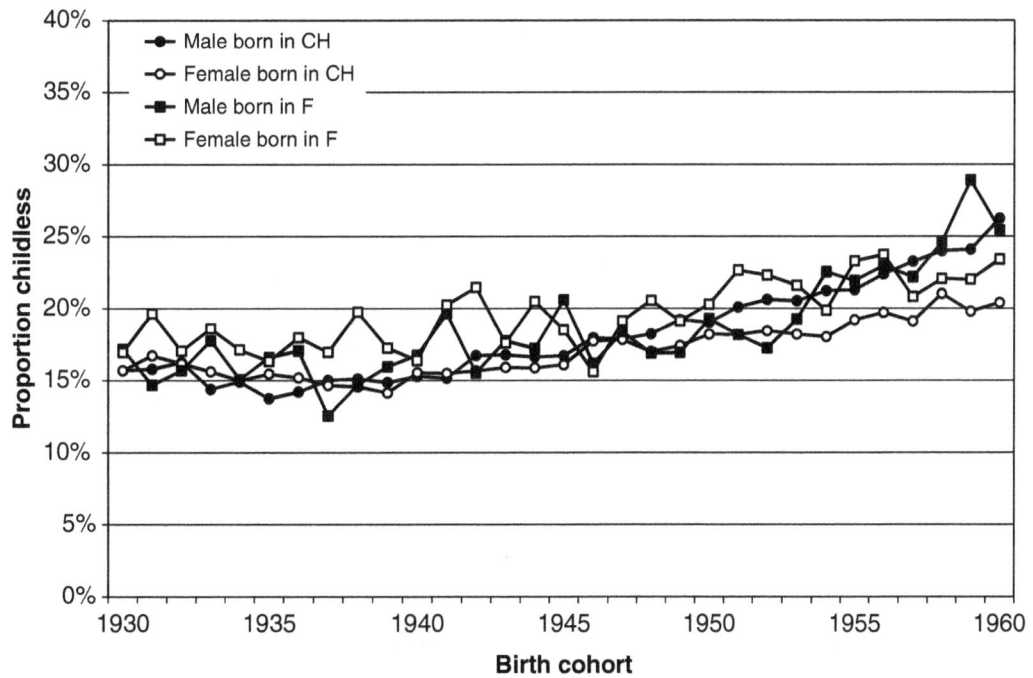

Fig. 6.9 Proportion of French-speaking women and men in Switzerland who are childless, whether born in Switzerland or France (Source: Census 2000, own estimates)

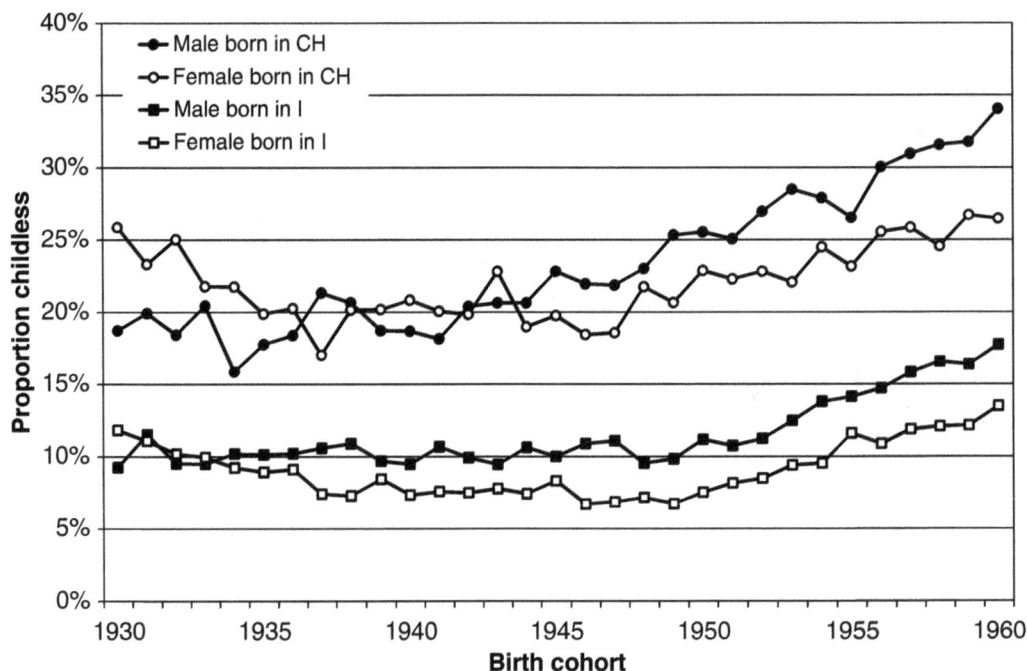

Fig. 6.10 Proportion of Italian-speaking women and men in Switzerland who are childless, whether born in Switzerland or Italy (Source: Census 2000, own estimates)

Table 6.3 Proportion of women who are childless, by province (Bundesland), cohorts 1958–1967 (aged 45–54), Austria

Bundesland	Childlessness
AUSTRIA	15.4 %
Styria	11.2 %
Upper Austria	12.7 %
Carinthia	13.2 %
Vorarlberg	13.6 %
Tyrol	14.4 %
Salzburg	15.4 %
Lower Austria	15.6 %
Burgenland	19.8 %
Vienna	25.6 %

Source: Mikrozensus Q4/2012, own estimates
Note: The childlessness level of 15.4 % for Austria as a whole, as shown in this table, is lower than that estimated from census and *Geburtenbarometer* data due to the specificity of the micro-census respondents

childless at ages 45–54 (i.e., the birth cohorts of 1958–1967) by province (*Bundesland*) based on the micro-census Q4/2012 data. Most of the regions have a childlessness level of around 11–15 %, whereas in Vienna it is nearly 26 %. Another region with high rates of childlessness is Burgenland, a small region of mixed ethnicity in the Vienna outer commuter belt bordering Hungary and Slovenia: there, the childlessness level is nearly 20 %.

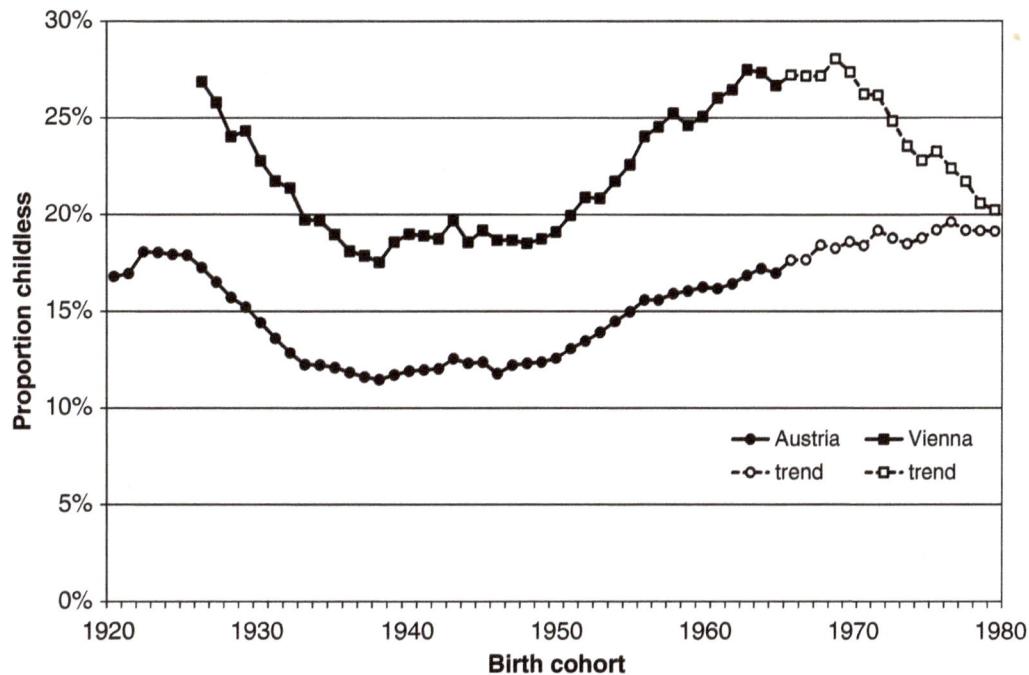

Fig. 6.11 Childlessness among women in Vienna and Austria as a whole: Known rates and projections extrapolating current trends of age-specific fertility rates, Austria and Vienna (Source: Geburtenbarometer (2014), own estimates)

Using data from the Geburtenbarometer (2014), and extrapolating the trends in age-specific fertility rates, we can project that any increase in childlessness will be modest, reaching perhaps 19 % for Austria as a whole. In Vienna, on the other hand, childlessness is forecast to decline, from 27 % to 21 %. Figure 6.11 shows this expected convergence. Among the 19–29 age group, the mean intended family size for women in Vienna is identical to that of Austria as a whole, at 1.8; and the proportion of women who intend to stay childless is also the same, at 12 % (Mikrozensus Q4/2012).

When we analyse variations by type of settlement, we can see that for women aged 45–54 the childlessness rate was around 8–9 % in agricultural areas, 12 % in rural areas, 15 % in small towns, 19 % in larger towns, and 27 % in Vienna. A similar pattern has been found in Switzerland (Wanner 2000). The 2013 FGS showed that the proportion of women aged 45–54 who were childless was 27 % in the major cities (Zürich, Geneva, Basel, Lausanne, Bern, and Winterthur), 20 % in other towns, and 18 % in rural areas. Among men of the same age, the childlessness rate was 43 %, 22 %, and 20 % for the respective areas. When we look at the map derived from the Swiss census data of 2000, which shows the relative levels of childlessness for 45–49-year-old women (Fig. 6.12), we can see clear concentrations of childlessness in the major urban areas, especially around Zürich and Bern, across much of the canton of Ticino, and in some pockets of the high Alpine areas.

Fig. 6.12 Relative proportion of women who were childless at age 45–49 by local area, Switzerland (Source: Map prepared by Christoph Freymond (Swiss Federal Statistical Office) and Tom Hensel (MPIDR))

6.4 Fertility Intentions

Respondents are asked about their ideal family size in many social surveys, and the results indicate that the two-child family ideal is still widespread across Europe (Sobotka and Beaujouan 2014). However, for many young people this is a hypothetical question, with a distinction between general family ideals and individual fertility intentions or desires. There are several major hurdles individuals have to clear before they can consider having a child: finding a (suitable) partner, resolving any conflicts between life goals, and being able to offer a child a good start in life (by having access to, for example, adequate housing, sufficient income, employment security, and child care). For women, all of these conditions have to be met while they are still in their reproductive years. It is, therefore, not surprising that expressed desires are fluid until the reproductive clock has finally stopped ticking. Even if a significant proportion of children are still unplanned, most people will seek to fulfil at least some of the pre-requisites before becoming parents.

From the 1994 Fertility and Family Survey (FFS) of Switzerland it was apparent that the desire to have children changes as people move through their adult life (Gabadinho and Wanner 1999). While 7 % of female respondents in their early twenties said they intended to remain childless, this figure fell to 2 % for respondents aged 25–29, before rising again for respondents in their 1930s. Among male respondents, the proportion who said they plan to remain child-free was slightly higher than that of women until they reached their late thirties. At that life stage, most of the women who had not had children accepted that they were unlikely to become a mother because of the path their life had taken; whereas some men, who are fecund for longer, indicated that they still hoped to become a father. The Swiss census confirmed that a few men do become first-time fathers even in their sixties and seventies.

The results of the Families and Generations Survey (FGS), which was undertaken in Switzerland in 2013, confirm these patterns and provide additional insights. As was shown by Mosimann and Camenisch (2015), having a low educational level appears to be associated with a reduced desire to have a child among young men, or it may reflect their limited potential for finding a partner. Among women, there is no difference based on educational level in the expressed intention to remain childless. Although women with a tertiary education are much more likely to end up childless, this does not reflect their stated aspirations when they were younger.

In Austria, family size ideals are below replacement level (Goldstein et al. 2003), with a relatively high proportion of women opting to remain child-free. According to the Eurobarometer 2011 survey, the mean intended number of children at ages 15–39 was 1.78, far lower than in any other country of Europe: the mean number was 1.9 in Romania and was two or more in all other countries, with an average of 2.3 across all of the surveyed countries (OECD 2014). For young men in Austria the intended number was even lower, at 1.55. At 11 %, the share of women in Austria who said they intend to remain childless was the highest among all of the countries in the survey. Educational level has been found to have a significant effect on fertility desires. Data from the micro-census Q4/2012 show that, at ages 19–34, the proportion of women who said they intend to stay childless was 7 % for those with low education, 10–12 % for those with completed secondary education, and 15 % for those with tertiary qualifications. By contrast, the final rates of childlessness for women aged 45–54 for these educational levels were 13–14 %, 16 % and 27 % respectively. This indicates that the differences in fertility intentions by level of education are smaller than the differences in fertility outcomes. A study by Buber et al. (2011) showed that, amongst a sample of 196 female scientists aged under 35 (PhD diploma holders who had applied for a grant at the Austrian Academy of Sciences), 11 % said they intended to remain childless, while the actual level of childlessness of similar women at age 45 was 44 %. Among the most important obstacles to childbearing cited were strong work commitment, the need to be geographically mobile, and the high prevalence of living-apart-together (LAT) relationships. The same sentiment was expressed by women in the Swiss Family and Fertility Survey, that their primary reason for not wanting to have a child was the problem of having to reconcile work and family (Coenen-Huther 2005).

The Swiss Household Panel survey sheds more light on the ambivalent fertility desires of individuals. From 2002 onwards the same group of respondents have been asked each year how many children they would ideally like to have. As they have been followed, it has become apparent that stated fertility intentions are volatile across the life course. Out of a sample of over 4000 respondents, for whom at least three survey waves were available and who were under age 38 in 2002, only 4

(0.1 %) stated they wished to have no children across all of the survey years. There was more stability in the responses of those who said they wanted to have at least one child, with over 57 % of the respondents falling into this category. However, a significant minority sometimes express the desire to have children and at others times say they do not (this does include some who actually have children). We can therefore deduce that while, on average, 11 % of respondents in any specific survey wave say they want no children, this is not a fixed trait: the blossoming (or breakup) of a romantic relationship may change their opinion (see Kuhnt et al. in this volume 11). The approach of menopause may increase the desire to have a child for some women, or extinguish it for others. The conflicting appeal of career versus motherhood—when there is a perception that these roles are incompatible—will influence the choice of a significant number of childless women (Mosimann and Camenisch 2015).

6.5 Conclusions and Discussion

Austria and Switzerland (along with Germany) share a pattern of low rates of fertility and high rates of childlessness which distinguishes them from other countries of Europe. Not all (developed) countries with relatively high levels of childlessness have low overall fertility. In some countries, such as the Nordic countries and the UK, the significant proportion of larger families compensates for the rather high levels of childlessness (see Berrington in this volume 3). In a western context, the countries that have a wide range of family forms and family sizes (including childlessness), and that allow for flexibility in the timing of childbearing, currently have higher fertility rates than countries in which fertility behaviour is more uniform. In Austria and Switzerland traditional norms tend to dominate.

Medical advances have changed patterns of childbearing, as women are able to postpone parenthood with the use of efficient contraceptives, and older women are able to have children using ART. However, many constraints remain, as the previous sections in this chapter have shown. Among these constraints are the varying degrees of desire to have a child. For example, German speakers are somewhat less family-oriented than French and Italian speakers. Moreover, the desire to have a child is not always fulfilled: for example, people who live in the Italian-speaking part of Switzerland apparently find it more difficult to meet their fertility goals. They have a low desire for childlessness, yet actual levels of childlessness are similar to those of the German-speaking region. It is unclear whether this gap is mainly attributable to the limited childcare facilities in Ticino, or to the legacy of traditional Alpine family formation patterns, as described by Viazzo (1989). In contrast, marriage rates in the French-speaking parts of Switzerland are lower than in the German- and Italian-speaking areas, yet childlessness is also less common: this reflects the higher incidence of extramarital fertility in the French-speaking region, which resembles that of France to some extent.

Men and women who classify themselves as having "no religion" have a much lower desire to have children than the religiously affiliated, and have lower marriage rates; as a consequence, they are more likely to remain childless. In addition, the Swiss census shows that a very high proportion—about one-third—of non-religious *married* men and women (secondary- and tertiary-educated) are childless. It would appear that the declaration of having no religion reflects life priorities that are different from those of people who are affiliated with religion to some degree. However, in Austria level of education and country of birth are more important explanatory characteristics of childlessness than religion itself, at least amongst women. In Switzerland, the influence of having no religion on childlessness has varied across cohorts, with the largest effect seen in women born in the 1950s, for whom the influence of being non-religious was even greater than that of having a tertiary education. Among men, education has a much smaller effect on the likelihood of being childless, with religion being the primary determinant across all cohorts.

At younger ages, the majority of women, regardless of their level of education, say they want two children (Mosimann and Camenisch 2015). It appears, however, that as life passes, highly educated women in particular face mounting constraints on their ability to fulfil their earlier expectations: they experience difficulties in finding a suitable life partner, reconciling the demands of a career and motherhood, and managing the practical issues of childcare.

The future trajectory of fertility in Austria and Switzerland will depend on whether women and men maintain their fertility intentions; whether partnering, marriage, and divorce patterns evolve; and whether the current hurdles faced by (for example) highly educated women can be overcome. The trends in the United States would suggest that the future could be brighter than is sometimes anticipated, as childlessness has been declining and fertility has been increasing amongst the highly educated (Livingston 2015 and Frejka, Chap. 8 in this volume). Where America is trending today, will Europe follow tomorrow? The projections for childlessness, calculated by Sobotka (in this volume), suggest that childlessness will indeed decline in Switzerland if current trends are maintained, and will rise only modestly in Austria, to around 20 %. Whether the differentials by sub-population are sustained remains to be seen.

Acknowledgements This paper uses data collected in the Swiss Household Panel (SHP), based at the Swiss Centre of Expertise in the Social Sciences FORS, University of Lausanne. The SHP is financed by the Swiss National Science Foundation. The Families and Generations Survey (FGS) was carried out by the Swiss Federal Statistical Office (SFSO). Funding for the supply of the Swiss Census data of 2000 and the FGS data from the SFSO was provided by the Institut de sciences sociales des religions contemporaines, University of Lausanne.

Zeman's contribution to this chapter was funded by the European Research Council (ERC) under the EU's Seventh Framework Programme (FP7/2007–2013)/ERC Grant agreement no. 284238. The data for Vienna from the Census of 2001 were obtained through the WIREL project on "Past, present and future religious prospects in Vienna 1950–2050" funded by WWTF, the Vienna and Science Technology Fund (2010 Diversity-Identity Call).

Literature

Baudin, T. (2008). *Religion and fertility: The French connection* (Working paper of the Centre de l'Economie de la Sorbonne). https://halshs.archives-ouvertes.fr/halshs-00348829/document Accessed 2 Sept 2015.

Buber, I., Berghammer, C., & Prskawetz, A. (2011). *Doing science, forgoing childbearing? Evidence from a sample of female scientists in Austria* (VID Working Paper 01/2011).

Buber-Ennser, I., & Skirbekk, V. (2015). Researchers, religion and childlessness. *Journal of Biosocial Science, 47*, 1–15.

Burkimsher, M. (2014). Is religious attendance bottoming out? An examination of current trends across Europe. *Journal for the Scientific Study of Religion, 53*, 432–445.

Coenen-Huther, J. (2005). Le souhait d'enfant: un ideal situé. In J.-M. Le Goff, C. Sauvain-Dugerdil, C. Rossier, & J. Coenen-Huther (Eds.), *Maternité et parcours de vie: L'enfant a-t-il toujours une place dans les projets des femmes en Suisse?* (pp. 85–133). Berne: Peter Lang.

Dubuc, S. (2009). *Fertility and religion in the UK: Trends and outlook.* Paper presented at the population association of America conference 2009, Detroit.

Ehmer, J. (2011). The significance of looking back. Fertility before the "fertility decline". *Historical Social Research, 36*, 11–34.

ESHRE. (2014). *Results generated from European registers by ESHRE Human Reproduction, 29, 2099–2113 – Supplementary data.* https://humrep.oxfordjournals.org/content/suppl/2014/07/27/deu175.DC1/deu175_suppl.pdf. Accessed 20 Oct 2016.

Federal Statistical Office. (2015a). *On the way to Gender Equality. Current situation and developments. Economic and social Situation of the Population 619–1300.* http://www.bfs.admin.ch/bfs/portal/en/index/themen/20/05/blank/key/Vereinbarkeit/01.html Accessed 19 Oct 2016.

Federal Statistical Office. (2015b). *Population résidente permanente et non permanente selon Année, de population, Lieu de naissance et Nationalité.* http://www.bfs.admin.ch Accessed 2 Sept 2015.

FFS. (1999). *Fertility and family survey. Switzerland. Population activities unit, Economic Commission for Europe.* Geneva: United Nations.

Gabadinho, A., & Wanner, P. (1999). *Fertility and family surveys in countries of the ECE region. Standard country report: Switzerland.* New York/Geneva: United Nations Economic Commission for Europe.

Geburtenbarometer. (2014). *Vienna Institute of Demography.* http://www.oeaw.ac.at/vid/data/geburtenbarometer-austria-and-vienna/. Accessed 20 Oct 2016.

Goldstein, J., Wolfgang, L., & Testa, M. R. (2003). The emergence of sub-replacement family size ideals in Europe. *Population Research and Policy Review, 22*, 479–496.

Human Fertility Database. (2015). *Max Planck Institute for Demographic Research (Germany) and Vienna Institute of Demography (Austria).* www.humanfertility.org Accessed 17 Feb 2015.

Livingston, G. (2015). *Childlessness falls, family size grows among highly educated women.* Pew Research Center; Social & Demographic Trends. http://www.pewsocialtrends.org/2015/05/07/childlessness-falls-family-size-grows-among-highly-educated-women/ Accessed 19 Oct 2016.

Mantl, E. (1999). Legal restrictions on marriage: Marriage and inequality in the Austrian Tyrol during the nineteenth century. *The History of the Family, 4*, 185–207.

Mikrozensus. (2012). Kinderwunsch – Zusatzfragen zur Mikrozensus-Arbeitskräfteerhebung Q4/2012. Statistics Austria.

Mosimann, A., & Camenisch, M. (2015). *Families and generations survey 2013: First results.* Federal Statistical Office, Neuchâtel, 7–8.

Neyer, G., & Hoem, J. M. (2008). Education and permanent childlessness: Austria vs. Sweden. A research note. In J. Surkyn, P. Deboosere, & J. van Bavel (Eds.), *Demographic challenges for the 21st century. A state of art in demography* (pp. 91–114). Brussels: VUBPRESS.

OECD. (2014). *OECD family database.* Paris: OECD. www.oecd.org/social/family/database.htm Accessed 2 Sept 2015.

Prskawetz, A., Sobotka, T., Buber, I., Engelhardt, H., & Gisser, R. (2008). Austria: Persistent low fertility since the mid-1980s. *Demographic Research, 19*, 293–360. Special Collection 7: Childbearing trends and policies in Europe childbearing trends and policies in Europe. http://www.demographic-research.org/volumes/vol19/12/19-12.pdf Accessed 7 Sept 2015.

Sauvain-Dugerdil, C. (2005). La place de l'enfant dans les projets de vie. In J.-M. Le Goff, C. Sauvain-Dugerdil, C. Rossier, & J. Coenen-Huther (Eds.), *Maternité et parcours de vie: L'enfant a-t-il toujours une place dans les projets des femmes en Suisse?* (pp. 281–316). Berne: Peter Lang.

Skirbekk, V. (2008). Fertility trends by social status. *Demographic Research, 18*, 145–180. http://www.demographic-research.org/Volumes/Vol18/5/18-5.pdf Accessed 19 Oct 2016

Sobotka, T. (2011). Fertility in Austria, Germany and Switzerland: Is there a common pattern? *Comparative Population Studies, 36*, 263–304.

Sobotka, T., & Beaujouan, E. (2014). Two Is best? The persistence of a two-child family ideal in Europe. *Population and Development Review, 40*, 391–419.

Statistics Austria. (2013a). *Kindertagesheimstatistik 2012/13*. Vienna: Statistics Austria.

Statistics Austria. (2013b). *Bevölkerungsstand 1.1.2013.*. Vienna: Statistics Austria.

Viazzo, P. P. (1989). *Upland communities: Environment, population and social structure in the Alps since the sixteenth century*. Cambridge: Cambridge University Press.

Wanner, P. (2000). L'organisation spatiale de la fécondité dans les agglomérations. Le cas de la Suisse, 1989–1992. *Geographica Helvetica, 55*, 238–250.

Wood, J., Neels, K., & Kil, T. (2014). The educational gradient of childlessness and cohort parity progression in 14 low fertility countries. *Demographic Research, 31*, 1365–1416. http://www.demographic-research.org/volumes/vol31/46/31-46.pdf Accessed 19 Oct 2016

Zeman, K. (2011). Human fertility database documentation: Austria. Human Fertility Database.

Zeman, K., Brzozowska, Z., Sobotka, T., Beaujouan, E., & Matysiak, A. (2014). *Cohort fertility and education database*. Methods Protocol. Available at www.cfe-database.org Accessed 18 Feb 2015.

Chapter 7
Childlessness in Finland

Anna Rotkirch and Anneli Miettinen

7.1 Introduction

"– Well, life didn't turn out as expected."

Recently, I (the first author of this chapter) attended a school reunion where I caught up with former classmates, many of whom I had not seen for decades. When I spoke to one of the attendees, I was intrigued by her frank answer, quoted above, to my general question about how she was doing. Finns have preserved the touching habit of taking small talk seriously. So I asked her what she meant.

"– For a start, I have no children."

Since my former classmates are now approaching 50, it was clear that the childbearing years were over for the women in the room. Most of the people gathered had a couple of teenagers at home, while some had older children who had already moved out. Some of the men had paired up with younger women and had toddlers. As so often in such social situations, how the children are doing emerged as the easiest, safest discussion topic in the noisy room. Even if the children have problems, they can be shared anecdotally, or glossed over by a superficial answer.

The topic of childlessness is much more sensitive. Finns are liberal and secular in their attitudes towards family life. As early as in the 1980s, over 70 % of Finnish women surveyed said they did not believe that a woman has to have children in order to be fulfilled (Nikander 1992), and only 20 % said they thought that a person could not be completely happy unless he or she has children (Paajanen et al. 2007). Although there is no strong stigma associated with childlessness in Finland, it is still not easy to ask people why they are childless, in part because the reasons they might

A. Rotkirch (✉) • A. Miettinen
Population Research Institute, Väestöliitto, Finland
e-mail: anna.rotkirch@vaestoliitto.fi; anneli.miettinen@vaestoliitto.fi

© The Author(s) 2017
M. Kreyenfeld, D. Konietzka (eds.), *Childlessness in Europe: Contexts, Causes, and Consequences*, Demographic Research Monographs,
DOI 10.1007/978-3-319-44667-7_7

give are so varied. Did my acquaintance have a partner? She indicated that she had been in a stable relationship for a long period of time. Was her partner unwilling to have children? Or had they experienced medical problems? Or, like the "perpetual postponers" found across Europe, had they avoided the decision about whether to have a child until it was biologically too late for her to conceive (Berrington 2004)? Had she acknowledged long ago that she was never going to become a mother, or had she only recently recognized that she would be childless?

I did not find out, as we were soon interrupted. Still, it may be the brevity and vagueness of our conversation that best captures the essence of childlessness in contemporary Finland. Like most Finns, my former classmate indicated that she had expected to become a mother. Indeed, most of our peers had two or three—or, more rarely, only one—child. But for my former classmate and a substantial and growing minority of the Finnish population things had not "turned out as planned" when it came to childbearing. Currently, 25 % of men and 20 % of women aged 40–45 do not have a child of their own.

In this chapter we describe the general trends in childlessness among both women and men in Finland, focusing on the generations born after the Second World War. In particular, we are interested in investigating how the prevalence of lifetime childlessness among people of different educational levels has changed, and how marriages and cohabitations relate to childlessness. We also discuss the childbearing intentions of childless Finns, and the extent to which these intentions are reflected in their actual childbearing behaviour. The term childless is used for all adults who have no children of their own, whether through birth or adoption. We recognise that this definition excludes important family ties individuals may have to a child, e.g., through step-parenting or foster care.

7.2 Data and Methods

Two types of data are used: register data obtained from Statistics Finland, and nationally representative survey data collected by the Population Research Institute at Väestöliitto. The survey data were also linked to register data on subsequent births.

7.2.1 Register Data

Statistics Finland provides register data on births and family life indicators. Some indicators span more than a century, and many are available at the Statistics Finland website, www.stat.fi. Birth statistics are collected for children born to women resident in Finland; we refer to these children and their parents as "Finns". The majority of residents of Finland are ethnically Finnish and Finnish nationals. When we cite Statistics Finland as the data source, the data cover the entire Finnish population.

We also use the FINNUNION dataset, an 11 % sample drawn from the population registers by Statistics Finland. The register database covers the entire population of Finland from 1970 to 2010, and links data from a longitudinal population register, including data on vital events with registers of employment and educational qualifications. From 1987 onwards, the register-based union histories cover not only marriages, but also cohabitations, which is widespread in Finland (Coleman 2014). FINNUNION contains data on around 471,000 individuals born in 1930–1990 and their marital and cohabiting partners. When we cite the FINNUNION dataset as the data source, it refers to this particular register dataset. We divide individuals into 5-year birth cohorts, and denote each cohort—unless otherwise specified—by the first year of the 5 years. Thus, for example, a reference to birth cohorts 1950 and 1965 would refer to the birth cohorts 1950–1954 and 1965–1969, respectively.

7.2.2 Survey Data

The Well-Being and Social Relationships Survey is a nationally representative Finnish survey that was conducted in 2008 by the Population Research Institute at Väestöliitto (the Finnish Family Federation). The questionnaires were mailed to 7000 Finnish residents aged 25–44 years who had no or only one child (Miettinen and Rotkirch 2008; Miettinen 2010). The response rate was 44 %. The questionnaire asked the respondents about various aspects of their personal and marital well-being, attitudes and expectations towards work, relationship quality, family and social relationships, and childbearing ideals and intentions.[1] Here we use only the answers provided by the childless respondents ($N = 1244$). For more details, see Miettinen (2010) and Miettinen et al. (2011).

In 2011, these survey data were combined with register data from the Population Register Centre of Finland for those respondents who gave their permission. The combined data enabled us to examine the effect of fertility intentions and other survey measures including relationship quality on actual births during the period 2008–2011. The number of respondents in the combined data is 1981, of whom 922 were childless at the time of the survey in 2008; for more information, see Lainiala (2011, 2012).

7.3 General Trends in Fertility and Childlessness: Finland as the Northern European Outlier

Compared to other European countries, Finland has relatively high overall fertility levels: completed cohort fertility has remained quite stable and even risen, from 1.86 for women born in 1950 to 1.90 for the 1970 birth cohort (Myrskylä et al.

---

[1] The questionnaire is available in English at http://www.vaestoliitto.fi/in_english/population_research_institute/family_research/late_fertility/

2013). However, compared to elsewhere in Europe, the share of the population who are childless is very high in Finland (see Sobotka, Chap. 2, in this book). A recent study that compared the childlessness rates of 40–44-year-old men and women across 20 European countries found that men in Finland had the highest level of childlessness, while women in Finland had the third-highest level of childlessness, after Italy and Switzerland. Finland has also seen its childlessness levels increase more rapidly in recent decades than most other European countries (Miettinen et al. 2015).

Finland's fertility regime and childbearing patterns are similar in many respects to those of the other Nordic countries (Andersson et al. 2009). Thus, the cohort fertility rate in Finland is close to the rate in Denmark of around 1.90 (for women born in 1950–1970), and is somewhat lower than the rates in Norway and Sweden of slightly higher than two (Myrskylä et al. 2013). These Nordic welfare states share a number of historical and social policy characteristics, and are the global leaders in social and gender equality (Kautto 2001). However, when we look at the distribution of the number of children born to each woman, we can see that the polarization of fertility, or the reproductive skew, is pronounced in Finland (Fig. 7.1).

As Fig. 7.1 shows, around 30 % of Finnish women currently in their 40s have three or more children. Together, these high-parity women produce half of the children born. By contrast, throughout the twentieth century, 15–25 % of Finnish women had no children. This distinguishes Finland from Scandinavia, where the reproductive skew is milder, mothers with more than two children are more scarce (Eurostat 2015) and childlessness is also lower (Andersson et al. 2009).

Among the women who were born in the early twentieth century in Finland, the proportion who were childless was as high as 25 % (Fig. 7.1). This share then declined to around 15 % among women born in the mid-twentieth century, and has since risen to around 20 % for the last cohort of women who have reached the end of their childbearing years. By comparison, among the women born in 1935–1949 in Norway, the share who were childless at age 40 was less than 10 %, and the corresponding figure for Sweden was 12 % (Andersson et al. 2009: 323).

Across the cohorts, lifetime childlessness in Finland has clearly been more prevalent among men than among women. Figure 7.2 shows the proportions of both women and men born between 1930 and 1975 who were childless at ages 40–44.

Although men can have children at later ages, very few of them do, as most Finnish men have a partner who is around the same age. Around 80 % Finnish couples have an age difference of 5 years or less, and less than 0.5 % have an age difference of 20 years or more (Nikander 2010). Consequently, men of the 1940–1950 birth cohort reached a 95 % level of achieved cohort fertility by ages 41–42 (Nisén, Martikainen et al. 2014: 127). It is of course possible for a man to have fathered a child even though his paternity is not recognised by the authorities. Currently, only 1.9 % of all children born have no registered father (THL 2015). Since not all of these cases involve men who are otherwise childless, the current proportion of men who have sired children but are not recognised as the father of any of those children—and are thus considered childless—can be estimated at no more than 1 %.

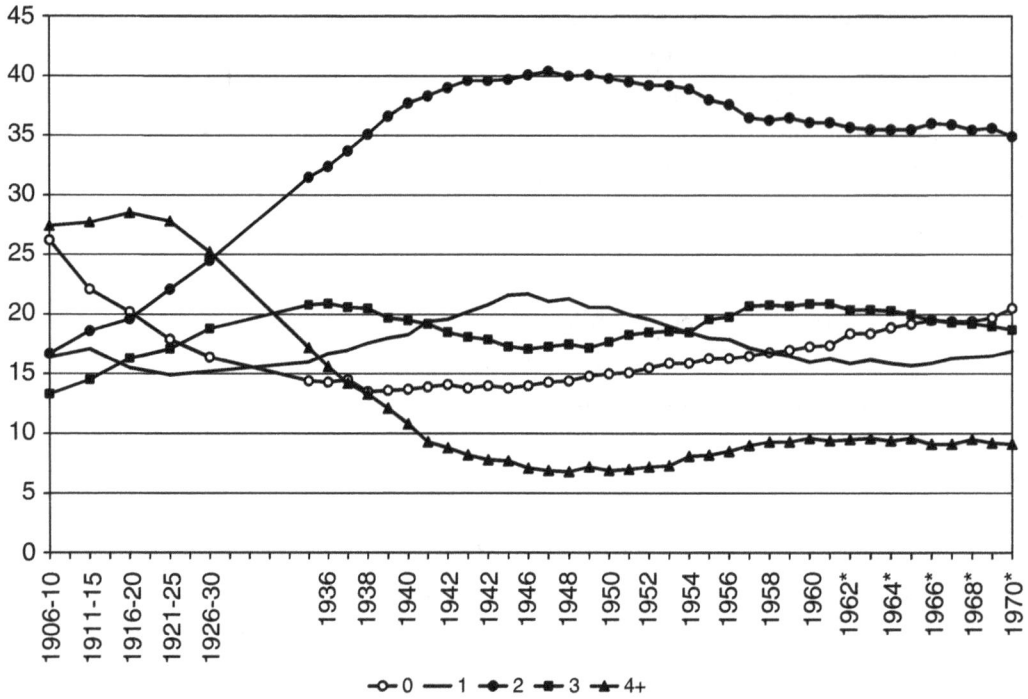

Fig. 7.1 Proportions of women by numbers of children, in per cent, female cohorts born in 1906–1970 (women at age 45/50). Note: *Asterisk* indicates cohorts who are still of reproductive age (Source: Statistics Finland and Population Research Institute, Väestöliitto (own calculations based on register data))

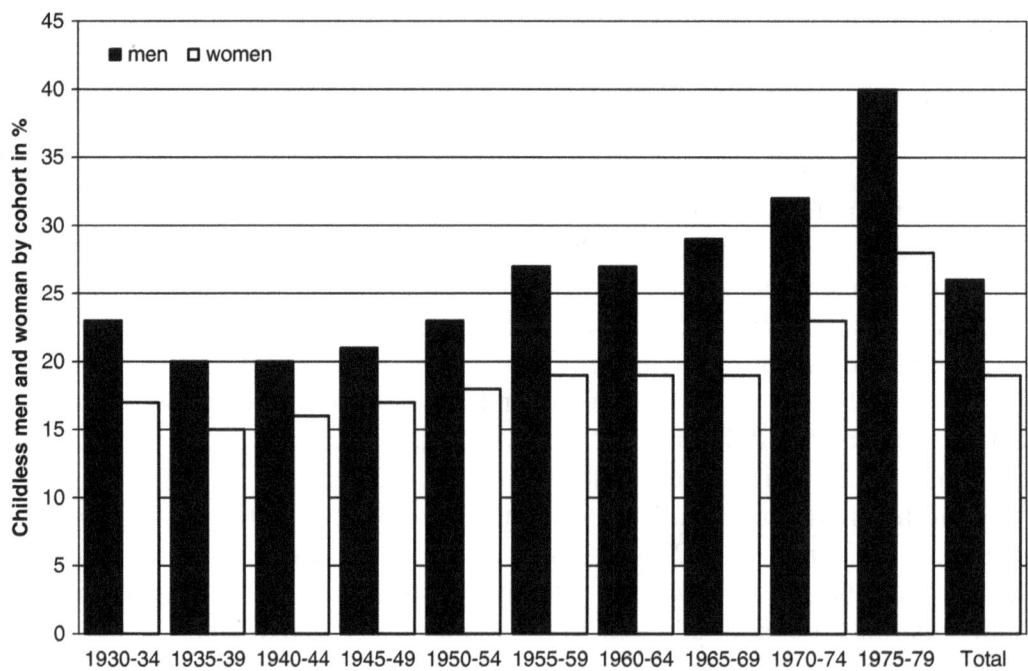

Fig. 7.2 Proportions of childless men and women in Finland at ages 40–44, in per cent, cohorts born in 1930–1975. Note: The last two cohorts have not reached the end of their childbearing years (Source: Statistics Finland, FINNUNION register dataset, and Population Research Institute, Väestöliitto (own calculations))

The historical data suggest that in preindustrial Finland childlessness was common among both men and women. Among agrarian Finns, who were largely neo-local, couples were not supposed to marry and have children until they were sufficiently independent to live and manage on their own (Therborn 2004). Consequently, the ages at marriage and first birth were relatively high, at around 25–26 years for women and a couple of years higher for men (see Lahdenperä et al. 2004 for the eighteenth century, Liu et al. 2012 for the nineteenth century). Data from four Finnish parishes in 1760–1849 indicate that among individuals who reached adulthood, lifetime childlessness was 34 % among men and 26 % among women. Among ever married adults, childlessness was 15.5 % among men and 14 % among women (Courtiol et al. 2012; Pettay, personal communication).

In European societies of the late nineteenth century and early twentieth century it was not unusual for 20–25 % of women to be childless. However, unlike in most of the rest of Europe, in Finland childlessness rates remained high throughout the twentieth century (Rowland 2007). While in most countries childlessness rates fell among the cohorts born in 1940–1950, in Finland the decrease was less marked. The lack of a "low dip" in childlessness levels in the mid-twentieth century can be attributed in part to the huge losses the country experienced during the Second World War and the ensuing relocation of a large share of the population. Finland lost 82,000 men in battle, a figure that is 13 times larger than the corresponding figures in the other Nordic countries. Moreover, 410,000 Finnish Karelians, or 12 % of the population, had to be relocated from Karelia to other parts of the country after 1940. In the 1960s, emigration especially to Sweden meant the loss of over half a million Finns from the population.

When the first cohorts studied were born (1940–1950), Finland was a relatively poor country that had only recently been industrialised, and was suffering from the effects of the Second World War. In the decades that followed, living standards improved, and the country made a rapid transition to being a post-industrial and wealthy welfare state. Traditionally, the labour force participation rates of Finnish women, including of mothers with children, have been high, and both women and men tend to work full-time (see, e.g., Haataja and Nyberg 2006).

7.4 Increase in Childlessness in Unions

While family formation and reproduction patterns have changed considerably in Finland in recent decades, being in a partnership continues to be an important pre-requisite for childbearing (Spéder and Kapitány 2009; Miettinen et al. 2015). Like in many other developed countries, in Finland men are more likely than women to remain outside a marital or cohabiting union throughout their life. For both men and women, having socio-economic resources—such as high educational attainment, steady employment, and a reliable source of income—promotes union formation (Jalovaara 2012).

The age at first union formation in Finland appears to have changed little in recent decades. Among the cohorts who were born in the 1970s, half of the women were cohabiting or married by age 22, and almost half of the men were in a union by age 25. By the age of 33, 90 % of women and 83 % of men had formed a union (Jalovaara 2012: 75).

These relatively young ages at union formation are supported by the welfare state, which provides housing benefits and income support, and by the prevailing cultural ethos, which favours early independence from the family home. By contrast, the mean age at entering parenthood increased in recent decades: women who were born in the 1960s had their first child 2–3 years later than those who were born in the 1950s, and the mean age at first birth is now around 28.6 years (Official Statistics of Finland 2014). Thus, it appears that today Finns live in unions for longer periods of time before having a child. Does this mean that the association between having a partner and having a child has weakened?

Childlessness is indeed less tied to formal marriage today than it was in the past. Figure 7.3 shows how marital status (i.e., being never married, married, divorced, or separated) is related to being childless in different birth cohorts. We can see that among individuals who are in their early forties, childlessness is much more common among those who never married than among those who married, but that among men and women who never married the shares who were childless have

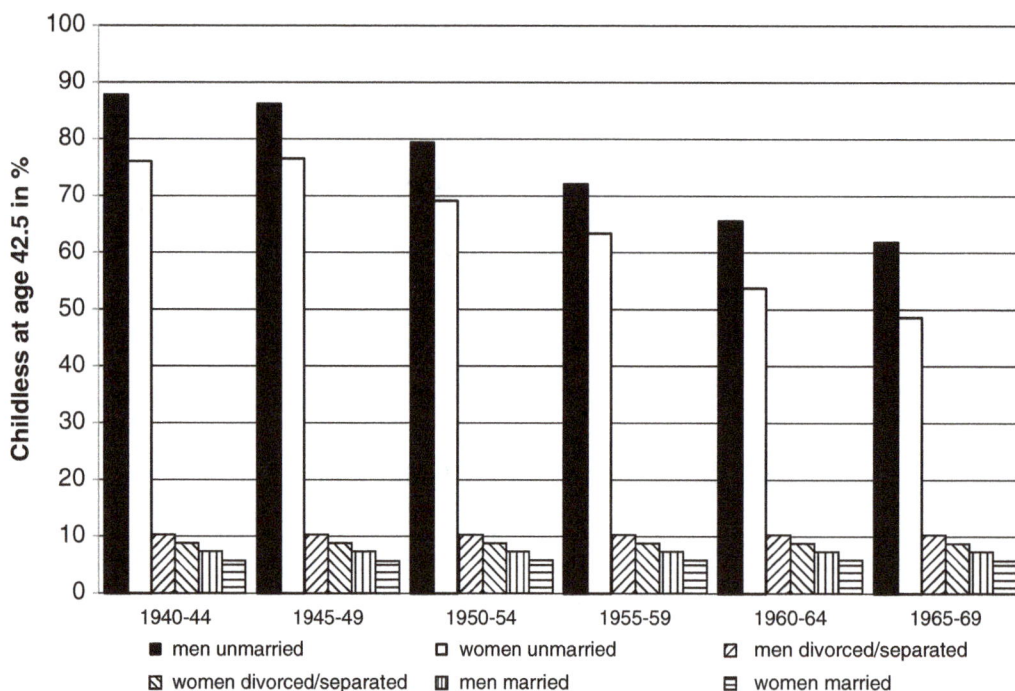

Fig. 7.3 Proportion of childless men and women in Finland at age 42.5 by marital status and birth cohort, in per cent. Note: Widowed persons (0.2 % among 42.5-year-old-men, 1.0 % among 42.5-year-old women) are included in the "married" category. Marital status as measured at age 42.5. Unmarried = person has never married (by age 42.5) (Source: Statistics Finland, FINNUNION register dataset, and Population Research Institute, Väestöliitto (own calculations))

steadily declined across birth cohorts: 88 % of never married men and 76 % of never married women born in 1940–1944 were childless in their early forties, compared to 66 % of men and 54 % of women born 20 years later, in 1960–1964.

The decreasing levels of childlessness among never married individuals across cohorts is related to the popularity of cohabitation in Finland. Nowadays the first union is usually cohabitation, and the first birth is typically to cohabiting parents. If cohabiting couples do not break up, they usually marry at some point in their life span. However, the wedding may be postponed considerably. Most couples with one child go on to have a second child, and they often get married at that stage, if they have not done so earlier (Miettinen and Rotkirch 2008). Thus, unlike in more traditional countries where cohabitation is less common, in Finland parenthood leads to marriage, rather than the other way around.

Being married is known to promote childbearing, especially compared to being single, but also compared to cohabiting (Coleman 1996). Also in Finland, married individuals have stronger intentions to become parents than cohabiting couples (Miettinen and Rotkirch 2008). However, even among married individuals childlessness has increased, from around 6 % to 8 % among men and from 5 % to 7 % among women (Fig. 7.3). This increase of around 2 % among married individuals accounts for less than 1.5 % of the overall rise in childlessness. Changes in the proportions of childless individuals among those who were married but later divorced or separated across birth cohorts have been even more modest, especially among women, for whom no time trend can be observed.

7.5   Childlessness Increases Among the Less Educated

In Finland as in many other countries, the relationship between socio-economic status and number of children is positive among men, largely because childlessness is more common among less educated men (Barthold et al. 2012). Figure 7.4 shows the proportions of men and women who are childless by level of education across birth cohorts. Among Finnish men, the proportion who are childless has clearly increased in all educational groups, while the educational gradient has persisted over cohorts (Fig. 7.4a).

Among Finnish women, the situation differs compared to men (Fig. 7.4b). In the oldest cohorts studied here, born during or immediately after World War II, the proportions of childless individuals are highest among women with a high level of education. Beginning with the female cohorts born in 1950, however, childlessness is highest among the least educated. In a wider context, this pattern is unusual: highly educated women are often the most likely to remain childless (see the chapters on the US and the UK in this book). However, in the Nordic countries motherhood has become increasingly common among highly educated women. Thus, the correlation between female educational levels and childbearing has become mixed or even positive in these countries (Kravdal and Rindfuss 2008; Persson 2010), including in Finland.

a

b

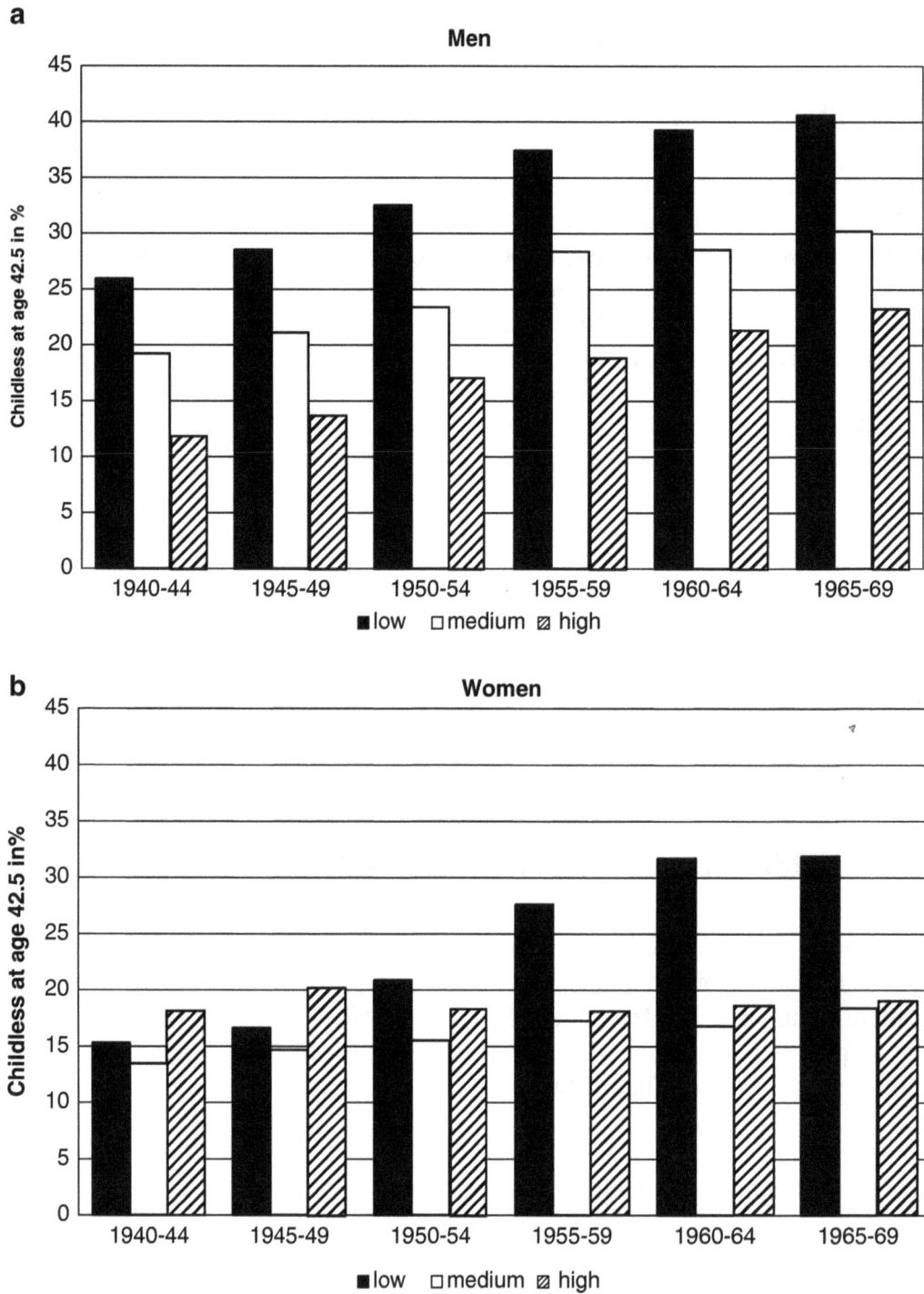

Fig. 7.4 (**a and b**) Proportion of Finns aged 42.5 who are childless by educational level, men (**a**) and women (**b**), in per cent. Note: For individuals born after 1967, at age 40–41. Education level: *Low* ISCED 1–2, *Medium* ISCED 3–4, *High* ISCED 5–6 (Source: FINNUNION register dataset, Population Research Institute, Väestöliitto (own calculations))

Figure 7.4b illustrates how women with a high level of education are somewhat more likely to be childless at age 42 than are women with a middle level of education in all birth cohorts. Childlessness slightly decreases among women with a high level of education, from 20 % in the 1945–1949 birth cohort, to around 18–19 % in the younger cohorts. By contrast, childlessness is most common among women with the least education during the last decades. Being childless has also increased twofold in this group during the period studied, from around 15 % to over 30 %. Also among women with mid-level education, childlessness has increased, but more moderately, from 13 to 18 %.

A comparison of childlessness levels across the entire population over the past decade shows a similar pattern to our analysis above: between 2004 and 2012, childlessness rates have increased the most among the least educated men and women (Fig. 7.5a and b).

When interpreting these results, one should keep in mind that the average level of education in Finland has increased: 26 % of men and 21 % women born in 1943–1972 and 18 % of men and 10 % of women born in 1973–1982 are in the lowest educational group (MED 2010).

It is also important to note that despite statistical associations between educational levels and childlessness, education is probably rarely the direct "cause" for childbearing behaviour. A study of childlessness among Finnish twins born in the 1950s found that the factors linking education to both male and female childlessness were shared by twins, and that these factors were genetic rather than environmental. For instance, cognitive abilities, personality traits or attitudes to parenthood may influence both the educational pathways and childbearing behaviour of individuals. The study found no evidence for a direct causal pathway linking childlessness in this cohort to lower education among men and higher education among women (Nisén et al. 2013).

7.6 Associations of Having a Spouse, Education and Childlessness

Is the increase in childlessness among less educated men and women associated with the lack of a partner? Above, we showed that being married remains linked to the probability of becoming a parent (Fig. 7.3). We further investigated how having ever had a spouse was associated with remaining childless in different educational groups. Having a spouse is defined as having lived in cohabitation or marriage at least once.

Never having had a spouse was clearly more frequent among men and women with little education compared to other educational groups (Table 7.1). Among those with least education, 24 % of men and 17 % of women had had no spouse. The more educated the men were, the more often they had had at least one spouse, so that only 7 % of highly educated men had not had any spouse. Among women, by

a

Men

■ 2004 □ 2012

b

Women

■ 2004 □ 2012

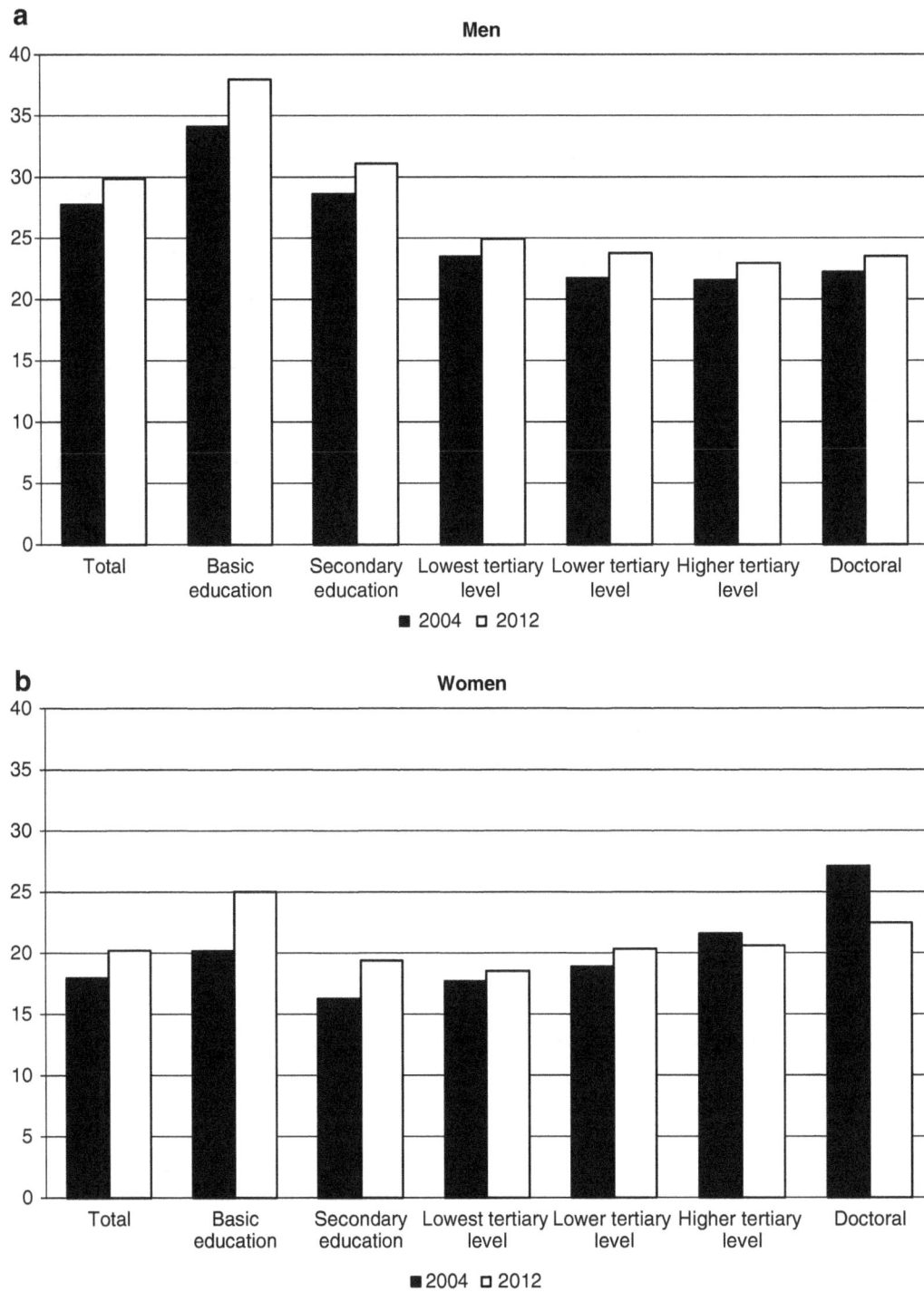

Fig. 7.5 (**a** and **b**) Proportion of childless people at ages 40–44 in 2004 and 2012 by educational level, men (**a**) and women (**b**), in per cent, entire Finnish population (Source: Statistics Finland and Population Research Institute, Väestöliitto (own calculations based on register data))

Table 7.1 Childlessness by having ever had a spouse (through marriage or cohabitation), Finnish men (N = 95,331) and women (N = 91,528) born 1945–1964, column per cent

		Having had no spouse	Childlessness among individuals with no spouse	Childlessness among individuals with at least one spouse	Proportion of childless individuals with no spouse of all childless individuals
Men	Low	24.1	92.1	17.0	63.3
	Middle	12.6	93.3	14.6	47.8
	High	6.5	94.8	11.3	37.8
	All men	14.8	92.8	14.3	53.0
Women	Low	17.4	84.1	12.2	59.2
	Middle	7.0	79.1	9.9	37.6
	High	9.5	86.4	12.2	42.6
	All women	10.8	83.6	11.3	47.3

Source: FINNUNION register dataset, Population Research Institute, Väestöliitto (own calculations)

Note: Educational level: Low = ISCED 1–2; Medium = ISCED 3–4; High = ISCED 5–6

contrast, those with highest education had somewhat more often not had any spouse than those with mid-level education.

Lifetime childlessness is strongly linked to not having had any spouse. Among men with no spouse ever, over 90 % were childless in all educational groups. Among men who had had a spouse, proportions of childless individuals ranged from 11 to 17 % in different educational groups and were most common among those with least education. Among women with no spouse, proportions of childlessness varied between 79 % among those with mid-level education to around 85 % among those with either low or high education. Of women who had ever cohabited or been married, those with mid-level education had the lowest proportions of childless individuals while women with either low or high education had similar levels of childlessness. Table 7.1 further shows that the concentration of childlessness among individuals with no spouse, compared to the overall childlessness in a particular educational group, also varied. Among men and women with middle or high education, between 40 and 50 % of childlessness was found among individuals with no spouse. Among men and women with low education, however, around 60 % of childless individuals had had no spouse.

We also entered these same variables into a regression (not shown in table; controlling for the effect of birth cohort). When taking into the account the effect of having had any spouse, differences in male childlessness by educational groups diminished, but remained highly statistically significant. Also among women, the educational differences in childlessness in women remained after controlling for having had any spouse, albeit less accentuated and only marginally statistically significant for the difference between women with low and high education. In other words, the lack of spouse explains much but not all of differences in childlessness between educational groups. Having ever had a spouse accounts for most of the differences between women with high and low education.

Thus Finnish men with a low level of education were most likely never to have had a spouse, and also to be childless if they had had at least one spouse. Women with low education were also most likely never to have had a spouse, but as likely as those with a high level of education to have a child with or without a spouse. If having ever had a spouse would not affect childbearing, women with a low and women with a high level of education would be about as likely ever to become mothers. In this respect, it is Finnish women with a mid-level education who appear to be unusual, since they have lower levels of childlessness whether they had ever married or cohabited or not.

7.7 Regional and Occupational Effects

Region of residence and occupational status also affect the likelihood that an individual will enter a union or start a family. Finland has a small population, and the density of the population is low: there are around 5.5 million Finnish citizens and only 18 inhabitants per square kilometre. Thus, the population density in Finland is much lower than in Sweden and Denmark, although still higher than in Norway and Iceland. As a consequence of urbanisation and the high proportion of women who are educated, the sex ratios at age 20 in Finnish municipalities have become more skewed over the last three decades. Currently, half of the 20–29-year-olds live in a sub-region with a male surplus in that age range; with 10 out of 18 sub-regions having a sex ratio above 1.1 (Lainiala and Miettinen 2013).

Sex ratios are associated with childlessness. Higher sex ratios or a male surplus in a certain age group appears to accentuate the reproductive skew, especially among Finnish men. In Finnish municipalities where the proportion of young males is higher than the proportion of young females, a larger share of women are likely to partner earlier, and go on to have children earlier, than in areas with less skewed sex ratios. This may raise overall fertility levels in those municipalities. However, a larger share of men remain unmarried in these municipalities, contributing to increased male childlessness (Lainiala and Rotkirch 2015).

Childlessness has also been shown to be more common among some occupational groups. In a study of Finnish men and women born between 1940 and 1950 that used register data, Nisén, Myrskylä et al. (2014) investigated the effects of family background on fertility, including on childlessness. They found that women who were from families headed by an administrative or professional worker were more likely to have remained childless than women who were from a family headed by a manual worker or farmer. After various family background variables, such as the number of siblings and the family type, were taken into account, having a manual labour family background was still shown to be associated with female childlessness (ibid.).

7.8 Low Voluntary Childlessness

Is the growth in childlessness due to a preference for a childfree lifestyle? It is widely assumed that voluntary childlessness, or the decision to have a childfree lifestyle, is the main explanation for the increase in childlessness in contemporary western societies. While there is some evidence that young adults feel more free to express less traditional views on having children today than in the past, recent studies have shown that voluntary childlessness is still relatively rare in most countries. This seems to be the case in Finland, as well (Miettinen and Paajanen 2005).

We here define voluntary childlessness as a personal ideal and intention to have no children (Miettinen 2010). We also distinguish between childless individuals who say they intend to have children in the future, and those who say they do not expect to have children, whether voluntarily or not.

The results of several national and international surveys indicate that most Finns want to have children, and seldom choose to be childless. The average ideal and intended numbers of children cited by respondents in Finland have been around 2.5 since the 1970s (Miettinen and Rotkirch 2008). In the Eurobarometer 2011, the average ideal number of children cited was 2.5 among Finnish women and 2.1 among Finnish men (Testa 2011). The average intended number of children was, at 2.3 among women and 2.1 among men, somewhat lower than the average ideal number, but was still clearly higher than the actual fertility rate. In the same survey, 0 % of the women aged 25–54 said their ideal number of children was to have none, while 6 % of the 15–24-year-old women and 2 % of the women above age 55 said they did not wish to have children. Among men, childlessness as an ideal declined with age: from 10 % among 15–24-year-olds, to 6 % among 25–34-year-olds, to 5 % among 50–54-year-olds, and, finally, to 2 % among those aged 55 and above. Compared to the childbearing ideals expressed in other Nordic countries, Finnish fertility ideals Finland tend to be similar or somewhat higher (Testa 2011).

The Well-Being and Social Relationships Survey conducted by Väestöliitto in 2008 had a larger sample of childless individuals than the Eurobarometer. In this survey, the fertility intentions among the childless respondents aged 25–44 were as follows: among men, 4 % had a pregnant partner, 9 % had a partner who was trying to get pregnant, 38 % wanted to have children at some point, 22 % were unsure, and 27 % did not intend to have a child. Among women, 3 % were pregnant, 15 % were trying to become pregnant, 36 % wanted to have a child at some point, and 25 % did not plan to have children at all (Lainiala 2012).

Among those who did not intend to have children, the personal ideal number of children was often larger than one, indicating that voluntary childlessness was not very common (Fig. 7.6). Among the 25–29-year-old respondents who were childless, 5 % of the women and 3 % of the men stated that they did not intend to have any children, and preferred to have a life without children. Among the 35–44-year-old respondents, 14 % of the women and 10 % of the men were classified as voluntarily childless using the same criteria (Miettinen 2010).

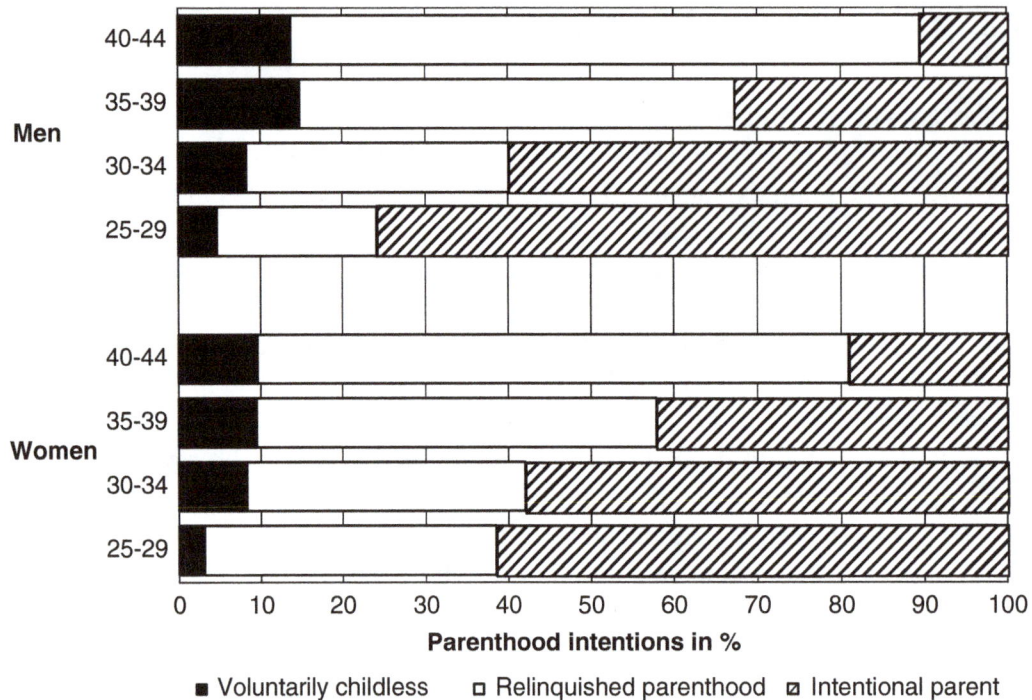

Fig. 7.6 Parenthood intentions among childless 25–44-year-old men and women in Finland in 2008, in per cent, *N* = 1244. Note: Reprinted from Miettinen (2010) (Source: Finnish Well-Being and Social Relationships Survey 2008, Väestöliitto)

If we take into account the proportion of all 40–44-year-olds who are childless, we can estimate that less than 3 % of Finnish men and women who have reached or are close to reaching the end of their reproductive age span can be said to be voluntarily childless.

7.9 Delays in Planned Childbearing

While fertility intentions feed into actual behaviour, there is a gap between ideals and intentions, on the one hand, and actual childbearing, on the other hand. In Finland, this gap is among the highest in Europe, mostly due to the proportions of childless people who would have wished for around two children (Goldstein et al. 2003). We combined data from the Well-Being and Social Relationships Survey with register data on births to find out whether the fertility intentions expressed by the childless respondents had been realised during the 3 years following the survey (Lainiala 2011, 2012). The results showed that of the 25–44-year-old men and women who had not yet had a child in 2008, 35 % had become a parent by 2011. Of the respondents who had said they intended to have a child within 2 years, 44 % had realised their plans. Thus, the majority of childless Finns who had wanted to have a child in the near future had not been able to do so.

The probability of becoming a parent was, unsurprisingly, positively related to fertility intentions. Among those who already tried to achieve pregnancy at the time of the survey, around two thirds had succeeded in having a child during the next years. Among those who were uncertain about having a child, however, less than 10 % had become a parent during the follow-up period. Finally, among those who said they did not want to have a child, only very few had nevertheless become a parent; this was the case among 0 % of men and 2 % of women (Lainiala 2012: 26). Why would this last group have changed its mind? Lainiala (2012) found that having a spouse who wanted a child in some cases changed a woman's (but no man's) fertility plans, so that they became parents although they had earlier declared they did not intend to do so.

Lainiala (2011) also investigated how relationship satisfaction at the time of the survey related to childbearing intentions, and to actually having a first child. For a male respondent, relationship satisfaction was a stronger predictor of actual fatherhood than his own fertility intentions. For a female respondent, relationship satisfaction was not as important for fertility, as a high degree of satisfaction with the spouse was related to both increased and decreased actual childbearing.

Other factors that negatively influenced the transition to a first child were age, being in education or unemployed, and for men, lack of a permanent job (Lainiala 2012).

7.10 Infertility

Of the Finnish men and women studied who remained childless in the Relationship and Wellbeing Survey, the share who had no children because they were suffering from primary infertility was around 10 % (Miettinen and Rotkirch 2008). This would represent around 5 % of the whole adult population. Notkola (1995), using retrospective data on female cohorts born in 1938–1965, found that 3 % of women remained childless due to primary infertility. However, the proportion of couples who suffer from infertility may have increased in recent years due to both the postponement of family formation and the spread of health conditions that can lead to infertility, such as obesity. On the other hand, assisted reproduction technologies have become increasingly sophisticated and available, countering the rise in childlessness due to primary infertility (Miettinen 2011). As the efficacy of treatments has improved, more couples will be able have the child they want with the help of technology. In 2013, 13,500 IVF-treatment cycles were started in Finland. From these treatments, 2473 live children were born, representing 4.4 % of live births in Finland in that year (National Institute for Health and Welfare 2015).

7.11 Conclusions: Many Shades of Childlessness

For decades, Finland has had some of the highest rates childlessness in Europe among both men and women. An unusual feature of childlessness in Finland is that it is particularly prevalent among both men and women from the least educated groups of society. This pattern has become even more pronounced in recent decades, as we have shown here. Part of the explanation is that men and women in the least educated group are also less likely to have had any spouse.

Like the other Nordic countries, Finland has generous family policies and high levels of gender equality—characteristics that are often associated with comparatively high fertility levels (Rønsen and Skrede 2010, see also Section 2.5). The availability of childcare has also been shown to increase fertility at all parities (Rindfuss et al. 2010). It has also been suggested that during the severe economic recession in the early 1990s in Finland, family policies that provided child homecare allowances helped to sustain fertility levels (Vikat 2004). Whereas in the UK and the US childlessness rates are low among less educated women because unwanted pregnancies are common, the Nordic welfare state is highly successful at preventing unwanted pregnancies. Nevertheless, both overall and involuntary forms of childlessness have increased in Finland, even as cohort fertility has been rising and family benefits have become increasingly broad and generous.

There are some clear-cut reasons for not becoming a parent: the lack of partner, not wanting to have a child, or being unable to conceive. Of these reasons, not having a partner remains the strongest single reason for not having children, in Finland and elsewhere. When we compare European countries, we can see that the proportion of the population who have ever married remains positively correlated with lower levels of childlessness, and the results for Finland are in line with this broader picture (Miettinen et al. 2015). It is also increasingly more common for an individual to be childless even though he or she has a partner.

Most childless Finns approaching the end of their reproductive lives are not childless by choice or through infertility. Around 4–5 % of the whole population say they do not want to have children. At the other "extreme" of the childlessness spectrum, infertility affects about the same proportion of the population. Thus, for most Finns who are not parents, childlessness is not attributable to a single, clear-cut reason, but rather appears to result from various choices about love, work, and contraceptive use made at different stages of life.

Finland's history of having higher levels of childlessness than the other Nordic countries may be attributable to both geographical and historical factors. Although comparative data are lacking, it is likely that Finland had more skewed national and local sex ratios because of the country's losses in the Second World War, mass emigration, and the low density of the population. These demographic challenges combine with the diverging educational trajectories of young men and women. Compared to the other Nordic countries, Finland has had a larger proportion of women with tertiary education, and this gap has widened over time.

The policies that successfully promote family formation may not be identical to those that would be most effective in preventing childlessness. Most worrying is the finding that childlessness—and consequently, proportions of persons without any close relatives in the old age—is increasing among the least educated men and women, who may be disadvantaged in terms of their access to health services, infertility treatments, and counselling.

Acknowledgments We thank Statistics Finland for providing us with register data, and Jenni Pettay and Virpi Lummaa for sharing their results on historical Finns. The authors are grateful for funding from Kone Foundation ("Precarious family formation"—research project), and wish to thank the Alli Paasikivi foundation for funding the fertility survey. The research leading to these results has received funding from the European Union's Seventh Framework Programme (FP7/2007-2013) under grant agreement no. 320116 for the research project FamiliesAndSocieties and from the Academy of Finland 266898.

Literature

Andersson, G., Rønsen, M., Knudsen, L., Lappegård, T., Neyer, G., Skrede, K., Teschner, K., & Vikat, A. (2009). Cohort fertility patterns in the Nordic countries. *Demographic Research, 20*, 313–352.

Barthold, J. A., Myrskylä, M., & Jones, O. R. (2012). Childlessness drives the sex difference in the association between income and reproductive success of modern Europeans. *Evolution and Human Behavior, 33*, 628–638.

Berrington, A. M. (2004). Perpetual postponers? Women's, men's and couple's fertility intentions and subsequent fertility behaviour. *Population Trends, 117*, 9–19.

Coleman, D. (1996). *Europe's population in the 1990s*. Oxford: Oxford University Press.

Coleman, D. (2014). Partnership in Europe. Its variety, trends and dissolution. *Finnish Yearbook of Population Research, 48*, 5–49.

Courtiol, A., Pettay, J. E., Jokela, M., Rotkirch, A., & Lummaa, V. (2012). Natural and sexual selection in a monogamous historical human population. *Proceedings of the National Academy of Sciences, 109*, 8044–8049.

Eurostat. (2015). *Women in the EU gave birth to their first child at almost 29 years of age on average*. Eurostat newsrelease 85/2015.

Goldstein, J., Lutz, W., & Testa, M. R. (2003). The emergence of sub-replacement family size ideals in Europe. *Population Research and Policy Review, 22*, 479–496.

Haataja, A., & Nyberg, A. (2006). Diverging paths? The dual-earner/dual-carer model in Finland and Sweden in the 1990s. In A. L. Ellingsaeter & A. Leira (Eds.), *Politicising parenthood in Scandinavia. Gender relations in welfare states* (pp. 217–240). Oxford: Oxford University Press.

Jalovaara, M. (2012). Socio-economic resources and first-union formation in Finland, cohorts born 1969–81. *Population Studies, 66*, 69–85.

Kautto, M. (2001). *Nordic welfare states in the European context*. London: Psychology Press.

Kravdal, Ø., & Rindfuss, R. R. (2008). Changing relationships between education and fertility: A study of women and men born 1940 to 1964. *American Sociological Review, 73*, 854–873.

Lahdenperä, M., Lummaa, V., Helle, S., Tremblay, M., & Russell, A. F. (2004). Fitness benefits of prolonged post-reproductive lifespan in women. *Nature, 428*, 178–181.

Lainiala, L. (2011). The impact of relationship quality on childbearing in Finland. *Finnish Yearbook of Population Research, 46*, 31–47.

Lainiala, L. (2012). *Toiveesta toteutukseen. Suomalaisten lastenhankintaa selittäviä tekijöitä* [From dream to reality. Factors explaining childbearing in Finland.]. E 44. Helsinki: Family Federation of Finland, The Population Research Institute.

Lainiala, L., & Miettinen, A. (2013). Childlessness and the skewed regional sex ratios in Finland. *Finnish Yearbook of Population Research, 48*, 51–63.

Lainiala, L., & Rotkirch, A. (2015, June 24). *Sex ratios and family formation: Combining micro- and macro-level register data from Finnish municipalities.* Paper presented at the workshop Sex ratios and family formation, Nuffield College, Oxford.

Liu, J., Rotkirch, A., & Lummaa, V. (2012). Maternal risk of breeding failure remained low throughout the demographic transitions in fertility and age at first reproduction in Finland. *PLoS ONE, 7*, e34898.

Miettinen, A. (2010). Voluntary or involuntary childlessness? Socio-demographic factors and childlessness intentions among childless Finnish men and women aged 25–44. *Finnish Yearbook of Population Research, 45*, 5–24.

Miettinen, A. (2011). *Äidiksi tai isäksi hedelmöityshoidolla. E40.* Helsinki: Family Federation of Finland, The Population Research Institute.

Miettinen, A., & Paajanen, P. (2005). Yes, no, maybe: Fertility intentions and reasons behind them among childless Finnish men and women. *Yearbook of Population Research in Finland, 41*, 165–184.

Miettinen, A., & Rotkirch, A. (2008). *Milloin on lapsen aika? Lastenhankinnan toiveet ja esteet* [When is the right time for children. Expectations and barriers to childbearing]. E 34. Helsinki: Family Federation of Finland, The Population Research Institute.

Miettinen, A., Basten, S., & Rotkirch, A. (2011). Gender equality and fertility intentions revisited: Evidence from Finland. *Demographic Research, 24*, 469–496.

Miettinen, A., Rotkirch, A., Szalma, I., Donno, A., & Tanturri, M. (2015). *Increasing childlessness in Europe: Time trends and country differences.* Families and Societies Working Papers 33. Available at: http://www.familiesandsocieties.eu/?page_id=3226

Ministry of Education and Culture (MED). (2010). *Suomen väestön koulutustason vahvuudet ja heikkoudet.Opetus- ja kulttuuriministeriön politiikka-analyyseja 2010–2013.* http://www.min-edu.fi/export/sites/default/OPM/Julkaisut/2010/liitteet/okmpol03.pdf?lang=en. Accessed 21 May 2015.

Myrskylä, M., Goldstein, J. R., Cheng, Y. A., & Yeh-Hsin, A. C. (2013). New cohort fertility forecasts for the developed world: Rises, falls, and reversals. *Population and Development Review, 39*, 31–56.

National Institute for Health and Welfare. (2015). Assisted fertility treatments 2013–2014. http://urn.fi/URN:NBN:fi-fe201504297845. Accessed 8 Aug 2015.

Nikander, T. (1992). *Suomalaisnaisen perheellistyminen* [Family formation among Finnish women]. Population 1992:10. Helsinki: Statistics Finland.

Nikander, T. (2010). Avioliiton suosio on hitaasti kasvanut. *Hyvinvointikatsaus, 2*, 2010.

Nisén, J., Martikainen, P., Kaprio, J., & Silventoinen, K. (2013). Educational differences in completed fertility: A behavioral genetic study of Finnish male and female twins. *Demography, 50*, 1399–1420.

Nisén, J., Martikainen, P., Silventoinen, K., & Myrskylä, M. (2014a). Age-specific fertility by educational level in the Finnish male cohort born 1940–50. *Demographic Research, 31*, 119–136.

Nisén, J., Myrskylä, M., Silventoinen, K., & Martikainen, P. (2014b). Effect of family background on the educational gradient in lifetime fertility of Finnish women born 1940–50. *Population Studies, 68*, 321–337.

Notkola, I.-L. (1995). Uutta tietoa hedelmättömyyden yleisyydestä [New information on the prevalence of infertility]. *Suomen Lääkärilehti, 50*, 865–870.

Official Statistics of Finland (OSF). (2014). Births [e-publication]. ISSN = 1798-2413. 2013. Helsinki: Statistics Finland. Access method: http://www.stat.fi/til/synt/2013/synt_2013_2014-04-08_tie_001_en.html. Accessed 15 July 2015.

Paajanen, P., Miettinen, A., & Jääskeläinen, M. (2007). *Mielipiteitä ja näkemyksiä väestönkehityksestä, perheestä ja perheellistymisestä Suomessa 2002* [Attitudes and opinions related to population development, family and family formation in Finland 2002]. Helsinki: Family Federation of Finland, The Population Research Institute.

Persson, L. (2010, April 1–6). *Trend reversal in childlessness in Sweden* (EUROSTAT Working Papers 11).

Rindfuss, R. R., Guilkey, D. K., Morgan, S. P., & Kravdal, Ø. (2010). Child-care availability and fertility in Norway. *Population and Development Review, 36*, 725.

Rønsen, M., & Skrede, K. (2010). Can public policies sustain fertility in the Nordic countries? Lessons from the past and questions for the future. *Demographic Research, 22*, 321–346.

Rowland, D. T. (2007). Historical trends in childlessness. *Journal of Family Issues, 28*, 1311–1337.

Spéder, Z., & Kapitány, B. (2009). How are time-dependent childbearing intentions realized? Realization, postponement, abandonment, bringing forward. *European Journal of Population, 25*, 503–523.

Testa, M. R. (2011). *Family sizes in Europe: Evidence from the 2011 Eurobarometer Survey.* European Demographic Research Papers.

Therborn, G. (2004). *Between sex and power: Family in the world 1900–2000.* London: Routledge.

THL. (2015). *Child maintenance and custody 2014.* http://www.julkari.fi/handle/10024/126139. Accessed 28 Aug 2015.

Vikat, A. (2004). Women's labor force attachment and childbearing in Finland. *Demographic Research, 3*, 175–212.

Chapter 8
Childlessness in the United States

Tomas Frejka

8.1 Introduction

In recent decades, childlessness among women in the United States has attracted a considerable amount of attention in the professional literature, and is frequently discussed in newspapers and on radio and television talk shows. This does not come as a surprise, as the percentage of women who do not have any children by the end of their reproductive years doubled between the mid-1970s and the mid-2000s, from about 10 to 20 %. Since then, however, the share of women who remain childless has been declining: in 2010–2012, the share was around 15 % (Table 8.1).[1] While establishing the levels of and the trends in childlessness is relatively simple, determining the circumstances and reasons which lead women and couples to remain childless is more complex.

Three different sources of statistical data on childlessness are available in the U.S. This wealth of data is almost as much a curse as it is a blessing. However, using data from all three sources one can obtain a good approximate idea of the levels of and the trends in childlessness. Yet because each source provides somewhat different data, it is difficult to determine which one most closely reflects reality. On balance the positive aspect of good approximate information prevails. Moreover, the overall perception provided by the three sources of data is consistent. Not only that. The available sources offer various types of information, including some kinds which are relatively rare. One of the sources contains a time series spanning an

---

[1] The levels of and trends in childlessness among women are based primarily on data from the Current Population Surveys in Table 8.1, which is generally corroborated by data from the cohort fertility tables (Fig. 8.2, 1970 cohort) and from the National Surveys of Family Growth (Table 8.2, latest years).

T. Frejka (✉)
Independent researcher and consultant, Sanibel, FL, USA
e-mail: tfrejka@aol.com

© The Author(s) 2017
M. Kreyenfeld, D. Konietzka (eds.), *Childlessness in Europe: Contexts, Causes, and Consequences*, Demographic Research Monographs, DOI 10.1007/978-3-319-44667-7_8

Table 8.1 Shares of childless women at ages 40–44, all, white, white non-Hispanic, black, and Hispanic women, 1976–2012, United States

Survey year	Percent of women childless					Effect of Hispanic on White childlessness (in % points)
	All	White	White non-Hispanic	Black	Hispanic	
1976	10.2	n.a.	n.a.	n.a.	n.a.	n.a.
1980	10.1	n.a.	n.a.	n.a.	n.a.	n.a.
1985	11.4	n.a.	n.a.	n.a.	n.a.	n.a.
1990	16.0	n.a.	n.a.	n.a.	n.a.	n.a.
1994	17.5	18.0	n.a.	14.3	13.0	n.a.
1995	17.5	18.1	n.a.	15.1	10.1	n.a.
1998	19.0	19.5	20.1	17.0	14.5	−0.6
2000	19.0	19.2	20.3	17.7	10.9	−1.1
2002	17.9	17.9	18.5	19.2	13.1	−0.6
2004	19.3	19.1	20.0	21.3	13.8	−0.9
2006	20.4	21.2	22.5	16.4	14.4	−1.3
2008	17.8	18.0	17.9	18.0	18.9	0.1
2010	18.8	19.1	20.6	17.2	12.4	−1.5
2012	15.1	15.3	16.4	15.4	10.9	−1.1

Source: U.S. Census Bureau, Current Population Survey for selected years, June 1976 to June 2012

entire century, which is also broken down by race. Another source provides data not only by race, but also for Hispanics. A third source contains data on whether women are temporarily, voluntarily, or non-voluntarily childless, as well as information about women's personal characteristics and selected attitudes to work and family. These data are available for a span of close to four decades. Knowledge which can be gleaned from all three sources of data is likely to be expanded in the future.

Following this introduction, the sources of data are discussed. In Sect. 8.3 levels of and trends in childlessness are outlined. Section 8.4 deals with motivations and reasons for childlessness. Section 8.5 discusses trends and circumstances of black childlessness. The chapter concludes with an epilogue.

8.2 Sources of Data

The three sources of statistical data on childlessness are *cohort fertility tables* (National Center for Health Statistics of the Centers for Disease Control and Prevention), the *biannual supplements on fertility of the Current Population Survey* (Census Bureau and Bureau of Labor Statistics), and the *National Survey of Family Growth* (National Center for Health Statistics of the Centers for Disease Control and Prevention [NCHS]).

8.2.1 The Cohort Fertility Tables

The Cohort Fertility Tables consist of two sets. The first set is based on recorded period fertility data for the years 1917–1973, and was prepared by Robert L. Heuser (1976). It provides information on childbearing of complete and incomplete birth cohorts of 1868–1959. The second set uses period data for 1960–2005, and was prepared by Brady E. Hamilton in collaboration with Candace M. Cosgrove (2010). Hamilton and Cosgrove updated this set with period fertility data for 2006–2009. It provides information on childbearing of complete and incomplete birth cohorts of 1911–1995. The Heuser tables can be linked with the Hamilton and Cosgrove tables to create a series of data on childlessness for 93 consecutive birth cohorts.

8.2.2 The Fertility Supplement of the Current Population Survey

The Fertility Supplement of the Current Population Survey is one of 20 supplements sometimes included in the *Current Population Survey* (CPS), a monthly survey of households conducted by the U.S. Census Bureau for the Bureau of Labor Statistics. The CPS collects and maintains a comprehensive body of labor force data, including information on employment, unemployment, hours of work, earnings, and other demographic and labor force characteristics. The periodic fertility supplement provides data on the number of children women aged 15–50 have ever had, and their characteristics. It is usually conducted every 2 years, but the intervals have varied from 1 to 4 years (see Table 8.1 and Fig. 8.3). Since the mid-1990s data on the U.S. Hispanic population[2] have been provided (Bachu 1995).

8.2.3 The National Survey of Family Growth

The National Survey of Family Growth (NSFG) gathers information on family life, marriage and divorce, pregnancy, infertility, use of contraception, and men's and women's health; i.e. data on fertility and on the intermediate factors that explain fertility. The NSFG was conducted by the National Center for Health Statistics (NCHS) in 1973, 1976, 1982, 1988, 1995, and 2002. The most recent NSFG covered the years 2006–2010 (Martinez et al. 2012). In these surveys childless women

---

[2] The Office of Management and Budget (OMB) defines Hispanic or Latino as "a person of Cuban, Mexican, Puerto Rican, South or Central American, or other Spanish culture or origin, regardless of race." In data collection and presentation, federal agencies are required to use a minimum of two ethnicities: "Hispanic or Latino" and "Not Hispanic or Latino."

are comprised of three categories defined as follows (Abma and Martinez 2006; Martinez et al. 2012):

Temporarily Childless women are those who have not had any live births and expect a birth in the future.

Involuntarily Childless women are those with a fecundity impairment who reported to be sterile for non-contraceptive reasons; subfecund, i.e. they reported difficulty conceiving or delivering a baby or difficulty for partner to father a baby; or a doctor advised the woman never to become pregnant because of a medical danger to her, her fetus or both; married or cohabiting women that have had a 3 year period of unprotected sexual intercourse with no pregnancy.

Voluntarily Childless women are those who do not expect to have any children, and are either fecund or surgically sterile for contraceptive reasons.

Note that the cohort fertility tables are based on data from administrative birth records, whereas the other two data sources are based on sample surveys. The sample surveys provide information on the characteristics of mothers and their children which are not available in birth records. However, the estimates of common measures based on the sample surveys are not precisely the same as those based on administrative birth records.

8.3 Levels of and Trends in Childlessness

8.3.1 Cohort Fertility Tables

In any given birth cohort, the youngest women bear few children. With each passing year, these women will have borne more children, and the share of women who remain childless declines. To ensure the comparability of the rates of childlessness between cohorts, the data on the proportion of childless women at the end of their childbearing years are assembled for each cohort. Figure 8.1 depicts the shares of all U.S. childless women, and of white and black women at age 50 in the Heuser (1976) and in the Hamilton and Cosgrove (2010) cohort fertility tables.

Among the 40 cohorts born between the late 1860s and the early 1910s, around 20 % of white women remained childless. Women who lived through the main years of their childbearing period during the core years of the historic economic depression of the 1930s—cohorts born between 1906 and 1911—experienced relatively high rates of childlessness, about 21 %. However, this was not dramatically more than most of the preceding 40 cohorts. A rapid decline in the share of childless women started with the 1913 birth cohort and lasted through the 1925 cohort that reached a childless rate of 9 %. A low share of childlessness among white women fluctuating between 8 and 10 % was retained for almost 20 cohorts from the 1925

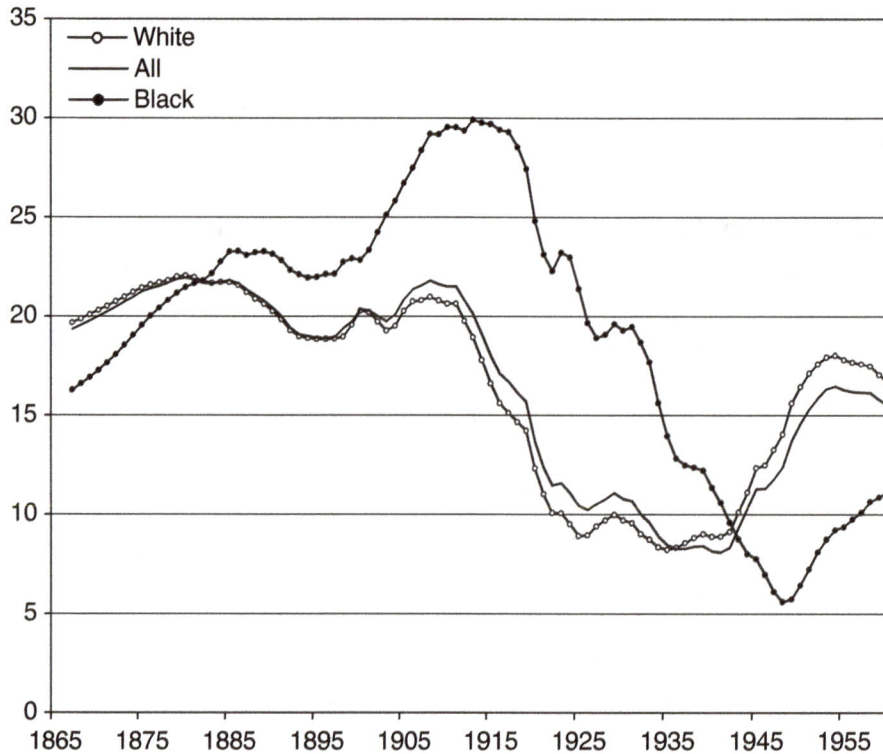

Fig. 8.1 Shares of childless women at age 50, all, *white* and *black* women, birth cohorts 1867–1960, United States (Sources: Heuser (1976); Hamilton and Cosgrove (2010))

through the 1943 birth cohort. A pronounced increase in the shares of childless women ensued, from 10 % among the 1943 cohort to 18 % among the 1953 cohort. The childless rate at age 50 was close to 18 % for a few cohorts and then started to decline to around 17 % in the 1959 and 1960 cohorts (Fig. 8.1).

The long-term trends in the shares of childless black women differed from those of white women. For about 60 cohorts, starting with those of the mid-1880s through those of the mid-1940s, black women experienced higher rates of childlessness than white women. Notably, almost one-third of black women who were in their most fertile years during the Great Depression of the 1930s remained childless. With a time lag of about five cohorts shares of childless black women declined from 29 % among women born in 1916 for more than 30 cohorts to a low of 6 % in the 1948 birth cohort. Thereafter, the share of childless black women increased reaching a share of 11 % in the 1960 cohort (Fig. 8.1).

Although numbers of births after age 40 have increased in recent years (Sobotka 2009), these still tend to be relatively small. Consequently, trends in the shares of childless women at age 40 are essentially the same as trends in the shares of childless women at age 50 (Fig. 8.2). Thus the delineation of trends can be extended for 10 additional cohorts, namely for U.S. women trends of childless women can be obtained by observing trends of shares at age 40 for the 1960s birth cohorts. These women concluded their childbearing during the 2010s, and their principal period of childbearing was during the mid- to late 1980s and early 1990s.

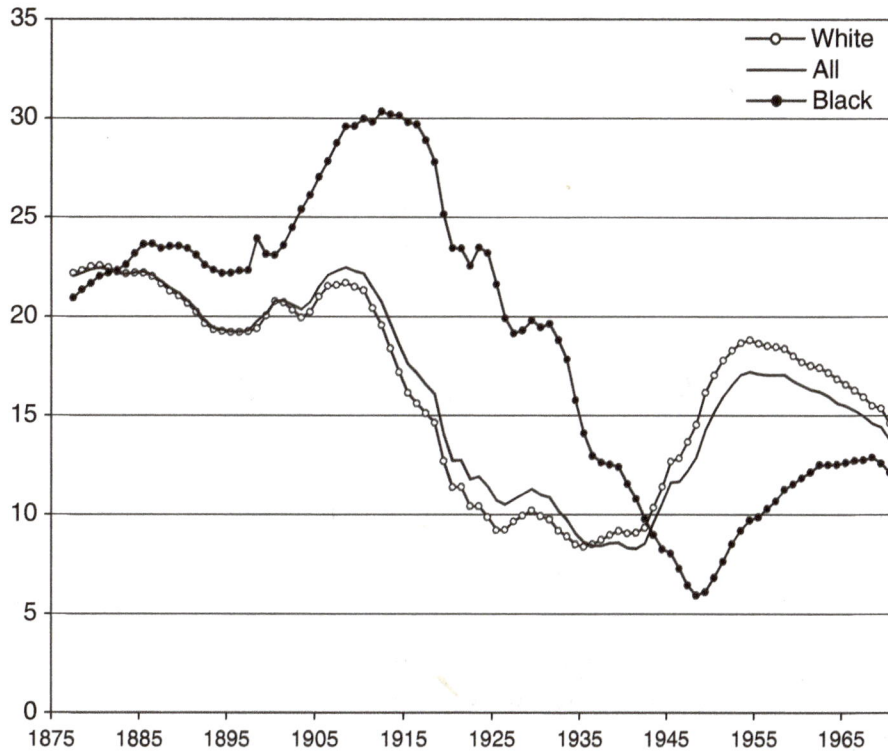

Fig. 8.2 Shares of childless women at age 40 (in per cent), all, *white* and *black* women, birth cohorts 1877–1970, United States (Sources: Heuser (1976); Hamilton and Cosgrove (2010))

Among white women the declining trend of childless women extended into the 1960s cohorts. The share of childless women in the 1960 birth cohort at age 40 was 17.7 % and declined to 14.6 % in the 1970 birth cohort (Fig. 8.2). This implies that around 13 % of white women in the 1970 cohort will be childless at age 50. The rising trend in childlessness among black women of the 1950s cohorts stalled among the 1960s cohorts. The share of women who were childless at age 40 was 11.9 % among the 1960 birth cohort, and 12.1 % among the 1970 birth cohort (Fig. 8.2). This implies that around 11 % of black women in the 1970 cohort will be childless.

It appears that shares of white and black childless women in the 1970 cohort will be quite similar. The difference in the shares of white and black childless women in the 1950 cohort at age 40 was 10.2 percentage points which declined to 5.8 points in the 1960 cohort and to 2.5 points in the 1970 birth cohort.

Levels and trends of *overall* shares of childless women follow the levels and trends of white women quite closely. This is not surprising, as the majority of the U.S. population was and still is white, although the percentage of whites has been declining. In 1900 about 88 % of the U.S. population was white and 12 % was black (U.S. Bureau of the Census 1975). These percentages were essentially maintained through 1970. As of 2000, whites comprised about 82 % and blacks 13 % of the population (U.S. Census Bureau 2012). The effect of black childlessness on the overall levels and trends is nonetheless discernable. When black childlessness is high the overall curve is above the white one, and *vice versa*.

The share of all childless women at age 50 in the 1960 cohort was 15.5 % and at age 40–16.5 %, a difference of exactly 1.0 percentage point. The share of all childless women at age 40 in the 1970 cohort was 13.8 %. Thus it is virtually assured that the overall share of childless women in the 1970 cohort at age 50 will be below 13 %, because the difference in the 10 years younger cohort was 1.0 percentage point and this difference of childlessness between ages 40 and 50 in a particular birth cohort was growing.

8.3.2 Fertility Supplements of the Current Population Survey

In the *fertility supplements of the Current Population Surveys* parity distributions— and thus also the shares of childless women—are provided for 5-year age groups. Until recently the oldest age group for whom these data were available was 40–44. Since 2012 the age group 45–50 has been added. Table 8.1 and Fig. 8.3 are based on data for the 40–44 age group. Although childbearing does not end at age 44, this cut off was necessary to obtain long-term time series.

According to these data the average share of all childless women aged 40–44 in the United States increased from 10 % around 1980 to almost 20 % in the 2000s, i.e. the proportion of childless women increased almost twofold within 20 years. Toward the end of the 2000s and the early 2010s, childlessness declined (Table 8.1).

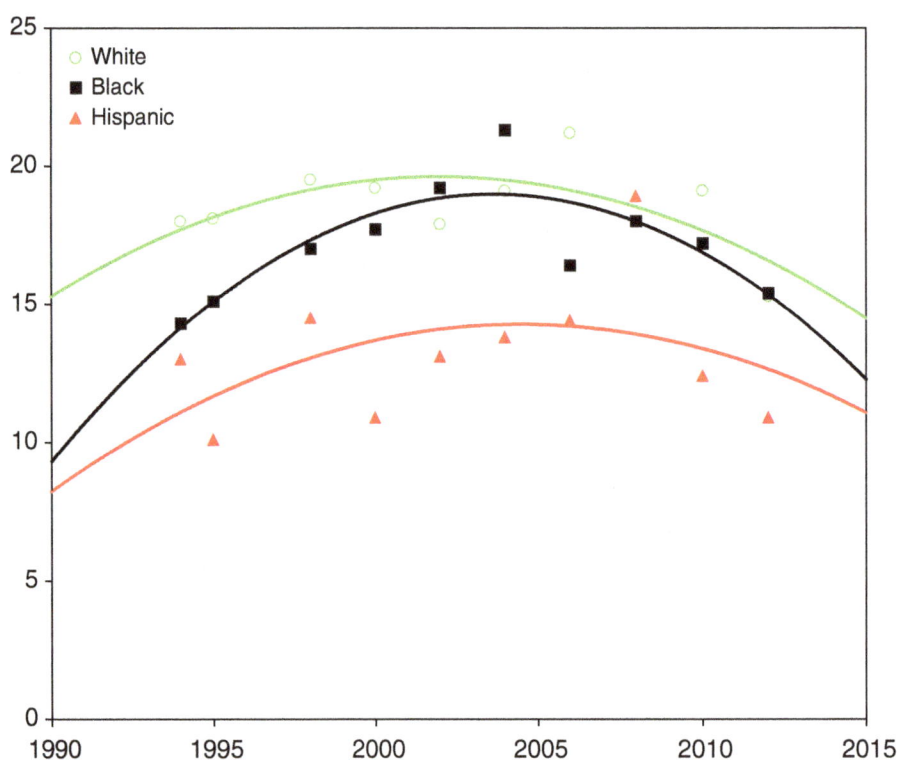

Fig. 8.3 Shares of childless women ages 40–44, *white*, *black*, and Hispanic women, 1976–2012, United States (Source: U.S. Census Bureau, Current Population Survey for selected years, June 1976 to June 2012)

In the mid-1990s the shares of white childless women were almost 10 % higher than those of black women. By 2008–2012 the differences between white and black women in the rates of childlessness had diminished (Fig. 8.3 and Table 8.1).

When comparing childlessness of Hispanic women with childlessness among white and black women one has to keep in mind that in U.S. statistics Hispanics are included in the categories of "white" and "black." Hispanics are considered an ethnic minority, not a race. It is nonetheless possible to get an idea of the effect of Hispanic childlessness on overall levels of childlessness of the race categories. Even though the Hispanic childlessness rate (5th numerical column in Table 8.1) is on average about 30 % lower than childlessness of non-Hispanic white women (3rd col.), the difference between the shares of all white childless women (2nd col. which includes white Hispanic women) and non-Hispanic white women is relatively small, on average this difference is only 0.9 percentage points (last col. in Table 8.1). The reason for such a small difference is that in 2010, for instance, Hispanic women constituted only about 18 % of white women, although the share of Hispanics in the population was increasing (U.S. Census Bureau 2011: Table 6). The effect of Hispanic black childlessness on total black childlessness was even smaller as the proportion of Hispanics among blacks was only about 5 % in 2010.

8.3.3   The National Surveys of Family Growth (NSFG)

Shares of childless women ages 40–44 rose from 7 % in the 1973–1976 rounds to 18 % in the 1995 round of the NSFG. In the rounds conducted during the 2000s, the shares of childless women had settled at 15 % (Table 8.2 and Fig. 8.4). Among childless women ages 40–44 the smallest shares were experienced by the temporarily childless. If the measurements had been taken at the end of women's reproductive period, as was done in the cohort fertility tables, there would not be any temporarily childless women. As women ages 40–44 is the oldest category that can be analyzed, the temporarily childless women have a significant impact on the overall trends in childlessness. Since women are postponing births to higher ages, a larger amount of births are borne by older women; thus, an increasing proportion of women in the 40–44 age group still expect to bear children. While the share of temporarily childless older women has been increasing steadily, it still represents only 3 % of all women and around one-fifth of all childless women. The share of all women who are involuntarily childless has been relatively stable at an average of 5 %. In the 1973–1976 rounds, the share of involuntarily childless women as a proportion of all childless women was 60 % because the overall numbers of childless women were relatively small. In the latest rounds, about one-third of childless women would probably want to have children, but for one reason or another—primarily related to a health issue—they have been unable to achieve this goal.

The NSFG definitions used to distinguish between voluntary and involuntary childlessness appear to be straightforward and clear (see Sect. 8.2.3 above). However, scholars have pointed out that an unknown segment of the women who at

Table 8.2 Women aged 40–44 and their childless status, National Survey of Family Growth, in per cent, United States

All women	1973–1976	1982	1988	1995	2002	2006–2010
One or more children	93	88	86	82	85	85
Childless	7	12	14	18	15	15
Total	100	100	100	100	100	100
All women	1973–1976	1982	1988	1995	2002	2006–2010
One or more children	93	88	86	82	85	85
Voluntarily childless	2	5	8	10	6	8
Involuntarily childless	4	4	5	5	6	5
Temporarily childless	1	1	1	3	2	3
Total	100	100	100	100	100	100
Childless women	1973–1976	1982	1988	1995	2002	2006–2010
Voluntarily	31	53	55	59	44	49
Involuntarily	60	38	36	26	40	30
Temporarily	9	9	10	16	16	21
Total	100	100	100	100	100	100

Sources: Abma and Martinez (2006), Martinez et al (2012), Mosher and Bachrach (1982), author's calculations

Note: Sub-categories of childless do not add up to total due to rounding

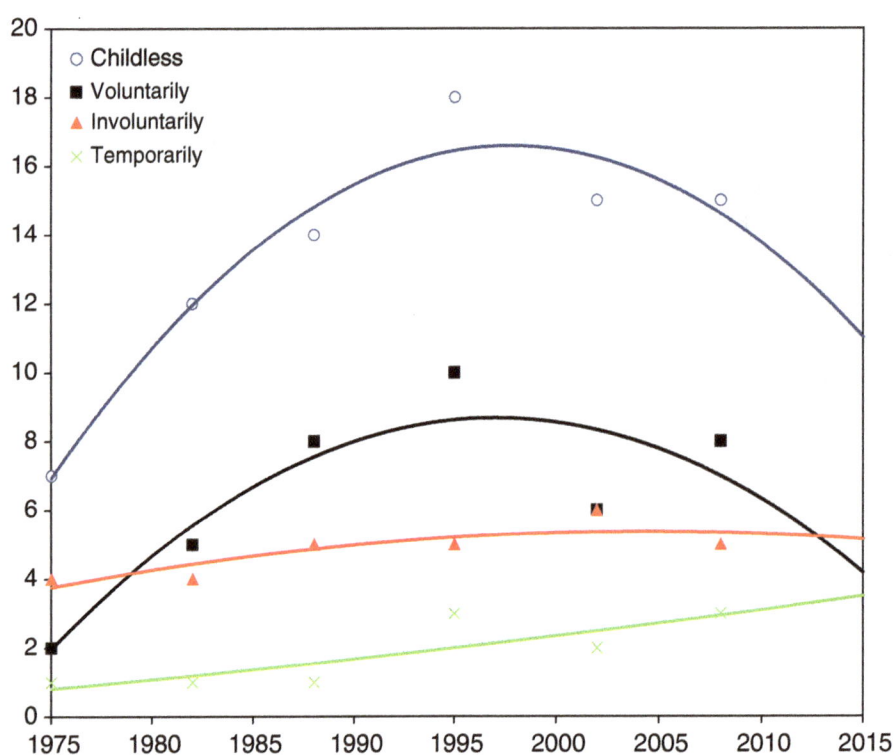

Fig. 8.4 Percent distribution of childless women aged 40–44 by childless status, National Survey of Family Growth, United States (Sources: Abma and Martinez (2006); Martinez et al (2012); Mosher and Bachrach (1982), author's calculations)

the end of their reproductive period report being voluntarily childless or having become involuntarily childless were postponing childbearing for various reasons until it became too late for them to bear children (Rindfuss et al. 1988: throughout). In other words, some, possibly many, women wind up being unintentionally childless as a result of having postponed childbearing. Regardless of how the childlessness occurred, using NSFG definitions, the percentage of the voluntarily childless increased from one-third in the 1970s rounds to approximately one-half of childless women in subsequent rounds (Table 8.2).

8.3.4 Personal Characteristics and Attitudes of Childless Women

There is ample evidence from several rounds of the NSFG that childless women, and particularly the voluntarily childless, are disproportionately white, are employed full-time, and have a higher education; and are less likely to be currently or formerly married and are less religious (Abma and Martinez 2006). For example, data from the 2002 round show that among women aged 35–44, 69 % of the voluntarily childless had some college or higher education, compared to 17 % among all women of that age; 76 % of the voluntarily childless were working full-time, compared to 51 % among all women; 79 % were non-Hispanic white, compared to 71 % among all women; and 35 % never attended religious services, compared to 17 % among all women (Abma and Martinez 2006).

Among the women aged 35–44, the voluntarily childless also differed from the temporarily and involuntarily childless in terms of economic characteristics. They had the highest individual and family incomes, the most extensive past work experience, and were the most likely to be employed in professional and managerial occupations. For example, according to the results of the 1995 round, 57 % of the voluntarily childless had individual annual earnings of over US$25,000, compared to 41 % of the temporarily childless and 36 % of the involuntarily childless; and 84 % had worked more than 15 years, compared with 72 % of the temporarily childless and 77 % of the involuntarily childless (Abma and Martinez 2006).

On the whole, the voluntarily childless tend to differ from women who have children and from the temporarily or the involuntarily childless in terms of their attitudes regarding gender egalitarianism, work, and family. For example, in their responses to questions in the 1995 round, 82 % of voluntarily childless versus 72 % of women with children disagreed with the statement "a man can make long-range plans, a woman cannot;" and 84 % of the voluntarily childless versus 75 % of the women with children agreed with the statement "young girls are entitled to as much independence as boys." The voluntarily childless also stood out in their response to the question of whether "women are happier if they stay at home and take care of their children;" 87 % of them disagreed, compared with around 76 % of the women who had children or were temporarily or involuntarily childless (Abma and Martinez 2006).

8.4 Reasons and Motivations for Remaining Childless

In a discussion of the biological factors which contribute to childbearing motivations, Foster (2000: 227) argued that because of their genetic predisposition to nurture and the effects of hormones, "most women, motivated by a genetically developed desire to nurture, will choose to have at least one child, given reasonably favorable circumstances." Moreover, McQuillan et al. (2008: 17) established that motherhood is valued by mothers and non-mothers alike, and that "there is no evidence that valuing motherhood is in conflict with valuing work success among non-mothers, and among mothers the association is positive." Yet for prolonged periods a fifth of U.S. women, i.e. around 20 %, remained childless. Why?

In the first place about 5 % of women cannot or should not bear children; they are involuntarily childless, mostly due to fecundity impairments or health issues (Fig. 8.4 and Table 8.2). Then there are the temporarily childless, i.e. those that are still expecting to have a child. However, these women can no longer be considered temporarily childless once they have reached the end of their childbearing period. The remainder of women remains childless for a wide variety of reasons.

People grow up and live in differing social, cultural, and economic circumstances which influence their decisions regarding childbearing. They live aided or obstructed by a material world, and are affected by an array of social norms. They may also have their own independent reasons for not having children. Both the material conditions and the norms affecting their decisions may change over time. If we were to accept the notion that every woman has a natural desire to have children, irrespective of her surroundings, there would not be any voluntary childlessness. Indeed, there was a time in U.S. history when only around 8 % of white women and only about 5 to 6 % of black women were childless. Among these women, the rates of voluntary childlessness must have been negligible. The 1973–1976 round of the NSFG found that only 2 % of women reported being voluntarily childless, which implies that this share might have been even lower during the 1960s among white women. Moreover, the 5–6 % rate of childlessness among black women leaves very little room for voluntary childlessness. On the other hand, as was pointed out above, at certain points in time around 20 % of white women and almost 30 % of black women were childless, which implies that the shares of "voluntary" childlessness were large.

The basic explanation for these extreme high and low childlessness rates is the fact that the former occurred at a time of economic hardship and psychological stress for large strata of the population affecting family life during the Great Depression which started in 1929 and lasted through the early to mid-1930s. Conversely, the low childlessness rates occurred when a majority of the population experienced favorable economic and social conditions for childbearing after the Second World War. In his recently published book, *Labor's Love lost: The Rise and Fall of the Working-Class Family in America,* Cherlin (2014) masterfully describes in great detail changes in American family life over the past two centuries. He characterizes "the Great Depression [as] a cataclysmic event in the United States in its depth and duration" (Cherlin 2014: 60). Based on contemporary sociological research of Komarovsky (1940), Cherlin discusses the effect of the Depression, *inter alia*, on reproductive behavior.

> Their sex lives often deteriorated: in twenty-two out of thirty-eight families for which adequate information was collected, the frequency of sexual relations declined--including four families in which sex stopped altogether. In some cases, however, couples reduced sexual activity not because of emotional strain but in order to lower the chance that the wife would become pregnant. Without modern means of birth control such as the pill or the IUD, financially struggling couples did what they could to avoid having another mouth to feed. One parent said, "It is a crime for children to be born when the parents haven't got enough money to have them properly" (Cherlin 2014: 79).

The low shares of childlessness make clear sense in light of Cherlin's characterization of the living conditions of American families in the post-World War II years.

> Why did young couples have so many children? One reason lay in the unique life histories of the generation who were in their twenties and thirties. They experienced the Great Depression as children or adolescents and then a world war erupted as they reached adulthood. After enduring these two cataclysmic events, the "great generation," as they are sometimes called, was pleased in peacetime to turn inward toward home and family. ... Family life was the domain in which they found ... security. Raising children provided a sense of purpose to adults who had seen how fragile the social world could be. ... Moreover, conditions were favorable for family formation and fertility: unemployment rates were low, wages were rising, and the government had enacted the GI Bill, which offered low-interest home mortgage loans to veterans so that they could buy single-family homes. ... Employers in the rapidly expanding American economy were forced to offer higher wages in order to attract new workers because they were in short supply (Cherlin 2014:115).

What remains to be clarified are the social, cultural, and economic circumstances shaping childlessness levels and trends prior to the Great Depression of the 1930s and the levels and trends unfolding during the two to three last decades of the twentieth century, as well as the peak and subsequent decline in childlessness in the early twenty-first century.

It could be considered odd that for 40 years (or 40 birth cohorts, i.e. 1867–1907) childlessness was at a similar level as during the Great Depression (Fig. 8.1). Morgan (1991) has argued that the period of high childlessness in late nineteenth and early twentieth centuries was mainly due to a strong motivation to delay marriage and childbearing, which eventually resulted in many women remaining childless, even though that was not their initial intention. Childbearing delays were significantly more pronounced in the economically more advanced states of the northeast. Many young women working in mills "may have been important income earners. Pressure for them to marry may have been replaced by pressure to continue supporting the family" (Morgan 1991: 801). Furthermore, the harsh conditions of the economic depression of the 1890s might have had an impact similar to that of the Great Depression of the 1930s, even though it was not as long or as deep. In addition, the risk of remaining childless would have been greater when childbearing was delayed, as sub-fecundity and sterility increases among women in their thirties. Finally, growing numbers of women were entering professions during this period, and these women tended not to marry; or, if they married, they often remained childless.

Turning our attention to the end of the twentieth century and the early twenty-first century, numerous societal developments have been taking place simultaneously, each of which has played a role in shaping contemporary childbearing behavior, and has thus contributed to trends in childlessness. These include:

- The re-emergence of marriage and childbearing postponement (Kohler et al. 2002; Hašková 2007; Goldstein et al. 2009; Frejka 2011)
- Rising female labor force participation rates, which are now almost as high as those of men (Oppenheimer 1994; Bianchi 2011)
- The work-family dilemma for employed women (Bianchi 2011)
- The status of the childcare infrastructure (Laughlin 2013)
- The increase in women's earnings, and the growth in their income relative to that of men (Cherlin 2014: 126; Wang et al. 2013)
- The growing empowerment of women (Anonymous 2009)
- High rates of incarceration (Tsai and Scommenga 2012)
- The deployment of men and women in wars (Adams 2013)
- Technological developments in production and communication, and their impact on the composition of the work force (Karoly and Panis 2004; Economist Intelligence Unit 2014)
- The hollowing out of the work force (Cherlin 2014: 124–125)
- Changes in the class structure of society, with education playing the decisive role (Cherlin 2014)
- Growing job insecurity, particularly among the less educated (Farber 2010)
- Changing marriage and cohabitation patterns (Cherlin 2009)
- Changing income and wealth distribution patterns (Saez and Zucman 2014)
- Income stagnation among a large share of the population (Krugman 2007; Fry and Kochhar 2014)

The above developments may influence women and their partners—in various ways, at different stages, and to differing degrees—in their inadvertent or conscious deliberations about whether to remain childless.

On the other hand there are those, including professionals such as psychologists and physicians, who have argued that some women and men decide to remain childless for their own subjective reasons. These individuals presumably engage in an independent decision-making process in which they focus on their personal motivations and preferences, rather than allowing themselves to be influenced by their circumstances. Scott (2009: 75–110; 222) reported the results of a survey of childless individuals which found that the six most compelling motivation statements for not having children were:

- I love our life, our relationship, as it is, and having a child won't enhance it.
- I value freedom and independence.
- I do not want to take on the responsibility of raising a child.
- I have no desire to have a child, no maternal/paternal instinct.

- I want to accomplish/experience things in life that would be difficult to do if I was a parent.
- I want to focus my time and energy on my own interests, needs, or goals.

Taking into account the wide range of circumstances and personal subjective reasons which can affect people's decisions about whether to have children can help us to better understand the increase in the share of women who remained childless which occurred during the final decades of the twentieth century and into the twenty-first century. However, the reasons for the apparent reversal in this trend in the early years of the twenty-first century have yet to be explored. That is a topic for discussion and research in the near future, especially if this trend continues.

8.5 Black Childlessness: Trends and Explanations

For almost 60 birth cohorts (1883–1942) childlessness was higher among black than among white women (Fig. 8.1). At its peak black childlessness was 2.4 times higher than it was among white women – in the 1924 and 1925 birth cohorts. Starting with the cohorts born in the early 1940s, this trend was reversed, and black women became less likely than white women to be childless. Among the youngest cohorts, those born in the late 1950s and the 1960s, the shares of black and of white Americans who are childless are converging at around 12–15 % (Figs. 8.1 and 8.2). The relatively low childlessness among black women and the convergence with white childlessness since the end of the twentieth century is generally confirmed by data from the *Fertility Supplements of the Current Population Survey* as well as the *National Surveys of Family Growth*.

The basic reasons for high black childlessness were analogous to those shaping white childlessness, namely difficult economic and social settings, psychological stress and social norms. In addition, living conditions of black Americans were incomparably more difficult than those of whites. Racial segregation, discrimination, and inequalities have been basic features of American society throughout its history (Massey 2011), and are reflected in virtually all aspects of life, such as economic opportunities, remuneration, schooling, housing, and access to health and reproductive services.

Farley (1970: 217–226) was the first to analyze deteriorating health conditions of blacks systematically, and their effect on reproductive behavior during the first three decades of the twentieth century. An increase in the prevalence of venereal diseases, such as syphilis and gonorrhea may have been an important factor generating the fertility decline and the increase in childlessness among blacks, which culminated in the 1930s. Farley was criticized by McFalls (1973: 18) and others who argued in favor of "a more conservative interpretation of the importance of VD in the natality history of the black population." Yet McFalls (1973: 18) conceded that "health factors undoubtedly played a more significant role" than other societal factors.

But what explains the decline in black childlessness and the crossover from relatively high to relatively low levels of childlessness from the 1941 to the 1942 birth cohorts? The decline in the childlessness rate of black women started with the cohorts most affected by the Great Depression, namely those born around 1915, and lasted until the 1948 cohort, from a share of 30 % to 6 % (Figs. 8.1 and 8.2). The childlessness decline among blacks took more than twice as long as that for white women, 33 compared to 14 cohorts. The childlessness descent for white women also started with the cohorts most affected by the depression of the 1930s, but stopped when living conditions started to improve significantly after the Second World War and essentially settled at that level for over 20 birth cohorts. Among black women childlessness stopped declining temporarily for a few birth cohorts – those born between 1926 and 1931 – but then resumed its decline with new force. Black childlessness declined from 20 % in the 1931 cohort to 6 % in the 1948 cohort.

The passage of the Social Security Act in 1935 strengthened government support for health activities (Farley 1970: 230–235). Title VI of that act appropriated money "for the purpose of assisting States, counties…. in establishing and maintaining adequate public health service, including the training of personnel for State and local health work…" This was an important element in the development of the health system. The resulting improvements in the health of the black population in turn led to declines in childlessness.

Moreover, there may be some justification to assume that improvements in living conditions and educational attainment levels among the black population during the second half of the twentieth century were associated with the long-term decline in childlessness. This progress was both absolute as well as relative to that of the white population. While living conditions for blacks remained inferior to those of whites, the disparities were narrowing as blacks were catching up. On average, incomes of blacks were rising faster than those of whites, especially during the 1990s (Fig. 8.5). Rates of poverty among blacks were also improving. Based on the definition of poverty of the U.S. Census Bureau, the ratio of blacks to whites who were living in poverty declined from 3.4 in 1970 to 2.1 in 2010 (DeNavas-Walt et al. 2012: Table B-1). In addition, educational attainment levels of blacks were increasing faster than those of whites. Between 1960 and 2009, the shares of blacks aged 25 and older who had graduated from high school rose from 20.1 to 84.1 %, whereas the corresponding shares of whites increased from 43.2 to 87.1 % (U.S. Census Bureau 2012: Table 225). Over the same period, the shares of blacks aged 25 and older who had graduated from college grew from 3.1 to 19.3 %, while the corresponding shares of whites increased from 8.1 to 29.9 % (U.S. Census Bureau 2012: Table 225).

What might be the reasons for the most recent turnaround – the doubling in black childlessness from 6 % in the 1948 birth cohort to 12 % in the 1968 cohort? The numerous societal developments shaping childlessness that have been taking place around the turn of the century listed above, together with the subjective motivations of women for not having children, surely played a role in influencing contemporary childbearing behavior and thus contributed to the increase in childlessness of black women.

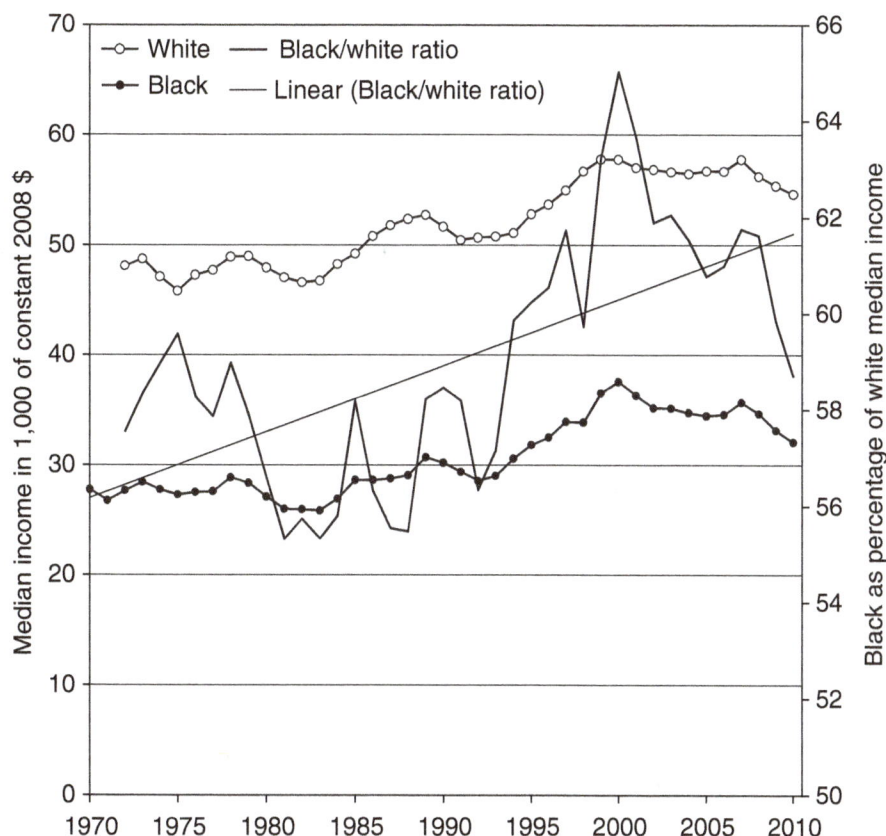

Fig. 8.5 Households by total money income (in 1000 of constant 2008 U.S. dollars) and race of householder, black as percent of white income, 1967–2010 (Source: DeNavas-Walt et al. (2012), Table A-2)

Other important factors which might have influenced the recent rise in black childlessness are changes in union formation and marital trends, and in fertility trends within unions. According to Cherlin (2009: 169), "the larger story for African Americans is a sharp decline in marriage that is far greater than among other groups." In 2010 the share of black married women over age 18 was a mere 31 % compared to 61 % in 1960. In contrast, among white women this share declined from 74 to 55 % (Cohn et al. 2011). These developments are in line with the findings of Espenshade (1985: 209), who concluded that "at least since 1960 in the United States, a weakening of marriage has been under way. The fading centrality of marriage in the lives of American men and women is more noticeable for blacks than for whites." Only 24 % of black women aged 15–44 were married compared with 46 % of white non-Hispanic women according to the NSFG 2006–2010 round (Copen et al 2012: 12).

A comprehensive, albeit complex, set of explanations for declining marriage rates among blacks has been revealed by research conducted by Banks (2011). Most black women want to marry and have children, as getting married is seen as a marker of status and social prestige, and remains an aspiration. Almost all black women would prefer to have a partner of the same race, as they are acculturated to date and marry black men, and rarely marry across racial lines. In the African American community, however, there is a considerable shortage of successful black men who are educated, employed, and have respectful earnings. One reason for this shortfall is the extraordinarily high rate of incarceration of black men (Massey 2011:10; Tsai and Scommenga 2012). Second, black men are up to three times more likely than black women to marry a person of a different race. Third, at all educational levels men's attendance and attainment rates are far below those of women. In these circumstances, many black women remain single or marry less educated black men. In such unions, women tend to be better educated and earn more money than their spouse, which can result in tensions over gender roles. Such marriages have a high potential to dissolve. Hence a high divorce rate among blacks is another reason why their marriage rates are low.

Data on trends in the types of first unions for women aged 15–44 confirm the decline in percentages of women who are married. Shares of marriages in first unions declined from 25.2% in 1995 to 12.5% in the 2006–2010 round of the National Survey of Family Growth (Table 8.3). Over the same period, the share of unions which were cohabitations increased from 35.4 to 49.2%. Consequently, the percentages of black women of reproductive age who were not in any union hardly changed between the 1995 and the 2006–2010 NSFG rounds, i.e. instead of getting married a large share of black women were living in a consensual union. That implies that the recent increase in childlessness of black women does not appear to be associated with a decline in the percentage of women who are in a union. The combined shares of cohabiting and married women were 60.6 and 61.7% in 1995 and 2006–2010, respectively.

What did change dramatically between 1995 and 2013 was the fertility rate of unmarried black women; it declined by 17%, from 74.5 to 61.7 births per 1000 unmarried black women (Table 8.4). It was this significant decline in the fertility rate which was associated with the rise in black childlessness between the 1948 and the 1968 birth cohorts (Fig. 8.2). It is worth noting that the fertility rate of unmarried black women was almost twice the rate of unmarried white non-Hispanic women. Nonetheless, the decline in black fertility, overall and especially of unmarried –

Table 8.3 Type of first unions, women ages 15–44, United States

Year	No union	Cohabitation	Marriage	Total
1995	39.4	35.4	25.2	100
2006–2010	38.4	49.2	12.5	100

Source: Copen et al. (2013) and Martin et al. (2015)

Table 8.4 Births per 1000 women ages 15–44, by race, United States

Year	All black women	Black unmarried women	White non-Hispanic unmarried women
1995	71.0	74.5	28.1
2006	71.4	70.7	32.4
2013	64.7	61.7	31.7

Source: Copen et al. (2013) and Martin et al. (2015)

cohabiting and never married – women, was apparently the decisive factor in the recent rise of black childlessness.

8.6   Epilogue

More than ever in U.S. history, women and couples can regulate their fertility. They have access to a wide variety of means to prevent childbearing, and there is over 20 years of experience with assisted reproductive technologies (ART) which can alleviate the burden of infertility. A *Division of Reproductive Health* at the *Centers for Disease Control* has a long history of surveillance and research in women's health and fertility, adolescent reproductive health, and safe motherhood. In response to a congressional mandate, CDC has started to strengthen existing data collection efforts initiated by the *American Society for Reproductive Medicine* (ASRM) and the *Society for Assisted Reproductive Technology* (SART), and to develop a national system for monitoring ART use and outcomes.

The facts, i.e. the childlessness levels and trends since the late nineteenth century, are reasonably well known. But often the mechanisms that shaped the facts have not been thoroughly deciphered, although some of the basic circumstances affecting levels and trends of childlessness are quite obvious, namely the concurrent economic and social conditions and cultural norms.

The U.S. population has experienced periods of very high and very low childlessness. The challenging living conditions in the 1930s appear to have been the main cause of the high levels of childlessness observed in that period. In contrast, the favorable living standards and enlightened public policies of the 1940s, 1950s, and 1960s were instrumental in maintaining low levels of childlessness.

Living conditions of African Americans were far more difficult than those of white Americans; hence higher black than white childlessness during much of the twentieth century. Subsequently black childlessness declined to levels below those of whites which in part was likely to have been due to improvements in the health and living conditions of blacks, even though these conditions continued to be inferior to those of whites.

In the recent past, i.e. since the 1970s through the late 1990s/early 2000s, the three independent sources of data indicate that the overall childlessness rate doubled (Figs. 8.1, 8.2, 8.3 and 8.4 and Tables 8.1 and 8.2). This was the case among white as well as among black women, although not quite for identical birth cohorts (Fig. 8.2).

While history provides a general understanding of the principal causes of childlessness, the experience of the past few decades points to the complexity inherent in identifying more specific factors shaping levels and trends of childlessness. In Sect. 8.4 above, 15 such societal factors discussed in the literature are listed. In addition, people claim to have personal motivations and preferences for not having children. Six of the most compelling ones were also listed above. What appears lacking is an overall picture of the interaction of the elements which shape childlessness, and how these change over time.

As of the early 2010s, around 12–16 % of U.S. white and black women over age 40 remained childless. Among Hispanic women this share was lower, about 11 % were childless. Whether these percentages will increase or decline is impossible to predict. It depends on whether the material world will be aiding or obstructing family formation, and how cultural norms and personal attitudes will change over time.

Literature

Abma, J. C., & Martinez, G. M. (2006). Childlessness among older women in the United States: Trends and profiles. *Journal of Marriage and Family, 68*, 1045–1056.

Adams, C. (2013, March 14). Millions went to war in Iraq, Afghanistan, leaving many with life-long scars. *McClatchy Newspapers*, http://www.mcclatchydc.com/news/nation-world/national/article24746680.html. Accessed 27 July 2015.

Anonymous. (2009, December 30). Female power. *The Economist*, http://www.economist.com/node/15174418. Accessed 27 July 2015.

Bachu, A. (1995). *Fertility of American Women: June 1994. U.S. Bureau of the Census. Current population reports, populations characteristics (P20-482)*. Washington, DC: U.S. Government Printing Office.

Banks, R. R. (2011). *Is marriage for White people? How the African American marriage decline affects everyone*. New York: Dutton.

Bianchi, S. M. (2011). Changing families, changing workplaces. *Future of Children, 21*, 15–36.

Cherlin, A. J. (2009). *The marriage-go-round: The state of marriage and the family in America today*. New York: Vintage Books.

Cherlin, A. J. (2014). *Labor's love lost: The rise and fall of the working-class family in America*. New York: The Russell Sage Foundation.

Cohn, D'V., Passel, J. S., Wang, W., & Livingston, G. (2011). *Barely half of U.S. adults are married. A record low*. Pew Research Center. http://www.pewsocialtrends.org/2011/12/14/barely-half-of-u-s-adults-are-married-a-record-low/. Accessed 27 July 2015.

Copen, C. E., Daniels, K., Vespa, J., & Mosher, W. D. (2012). First marriages in the United States: Data from 2006–2010 National Survey of Family Growth. *National Health Statistics Reports, 49*, 1–21.

Copen, C. E., Daniels, K., & Mosher, W. D. (2013). First premarital cohabitation in the United States: 2006–2010 National Survey of Family Growth. *National Health Statistics Reports, 64*, 1–15.

DeNavas-Walt, C., Proctor, B. D., & Smith, J. C. (2012). *Income, poverty, and health insurance coverage in the United States: 2011 (P60-243)*. Washington, DC: U.S. Government Printing Office.

Economist Intelligence Unit (EIU). (2014). *What's next: Future global trends affecting your organization – Evolution of work and the worker*. SHRM Foundation.

Espenshade, T. J. (1985). Marriage trends in America: Estimates, implications, and underlying causes. *Population and Development Review, 11*, 193–246.

Farber, H. S. (2010). Job loss and the decline in job security in the United States. In K. G. Abraham, J. R. Spletzer, & M. Harper (Eds.), *Labor in the new economy* (pp. 223–262). Chicago: Chicago Press.

Farley, R. (1970). *Growth of the black population*. Chicago: Markham Publishing Co.

Foster, C. (2000). The limits to low fertility: A biosocial approach. *Population and Development Review, 26*, 209–234.

Frejka, T. (2011). The role of contemporary childbearing postponement and recuperation in shaping period fertility trends. *Comparative Population Studies – Zeitschrift für Bevölkerungswissenschaft, 36*, 927–958.

Fry, R., & Kochhar, R. (2014). *America's wealth gap between middle-income and upper-income families is widest on record.* Pew Research Center. http://www.pewresearch.org/fact-tank/2014/12/17/wealth-gap-upper-middle-income/. Accessed 27 July 2015.

Goldstein, J., Sobotka, T., & Jasilioniene, A. (2009). The end of lowest-low fertility? *Population and Development Review, 35*, 663–700.

Hamilton, B. E., & Cosgrove, C. M. (2010). *Central birth rates, by live-birth order, current age, and race of women in each cohort from 1911 through 1991: United States, 1960–2005.* Hyattsville: National Center for Health Statistics. [2012 addition with 2006–2009 data] http://www.cdc.gov/nchs/nvss/cohort_fertility_tables.htm. Accessed 27 July 2015.

Hašková, H. (2007). Fertility decline, the postponement of childbearing and the increase in childlessness in Central and Eastern Europe: A gender equity approach. In R. Crompton, S. Lewis, & C. Lyonette (Eds.), *Women, men, work and family in Europe* (pp. 76–85). Basingstoke/Hampshire: Palgrave Macmillan.

Heuser, R. L. (1976). *Fertility tables for birth cohorts by color: United States, 1917–73.* Rockville: U.S. Department of Health, Education, and Welfare, National Center for Health Statistics. http://www.cdc.gov/nchs/data/misc/fertiltbacc.pdf. Accessed 27 July 2015.

Karoly, L., & Panis, C. W. A. (2004). *The 21st century at work forces shaping the future workforce and workplace in the United States.* Santa Monica: RAND Corporation.

Kohler, H.-P., Billari, F. C., & Ortega, J. A. (2002). The emergence of lowest-low fertility in Europe during the 1990s. *Population and Development Review, 28*, 641–680.

Komarovsky, M. (1940). *The unemployed man and his family.* New York: Octagon Books.

Krugman, P. (2007). *The conscience of a liberal.* New York: W. W. Norton.

Laughlin, L. (2013). *Who's minding the kids? Child care arrangements: Spring 2011* (Current population reports P70-135). Washington, DC: U.S. Census Bureau.

Martin, J. A., Hamilton, B. E., Osterman, M. J. K., Curtin, S. C., & Mathews, T. J. (2015). *Births: Final data for 2013. National vital statistics reports. 64..* Hyattsville: National Center for Health Statistics.

Martinez, G., Daniels, K., & Chandra, A. (2012). *Fertility of men and women aged 15–44 years in the United States: National survey of family growth, 2006–2010.* National Health Statistics Report 51. Hyattsville: National Center for Health Statistics.

Massey, D. S. (2011). The past and future of American civil rights. *Daedalus, 140*, 33–54.

McFalls, J. A. (1973). Impact of VD on the fertility of the US black population, 1880–1950. *Social Biology, 20*, 2–19.

McQuillan, J., Greil, A. L., Scheffler, K. M., & Tichenor, V. (2008). *The importance of motherhood among women in the contemporary United States.* Lincoln: University of Nebraska.

Morgan, S. P. (1991). Late nineteenth- and early twentieth-century childlessness. *American Journal of Sociology, 97*, 779–807.

Mosher, W. D., & Bachrach, C. A. (1982). Childlessness in the United States. *Journal of Family Issues, 3*, 517–543.

Oppenheimer, V. K. (1994). Women's rising employment and the future of the family in industrial societies. *Population and Development Review, 20*, 293–342.

Rindfuss, R. R., Morgan, S. P., & Swicegood, G. (1988). *First births in America: Changes in the timing of parenthood.* Berkeley: University of California Press.

Saez, E., & Zucman, G. (2014). *Wealth inequality in the United States since 1913: Evidence from capitalized income tax data* (Working Paper 20625). New York: National Bureau of Economic Research.

Scott, S. S. (2009). *Two is enough: A couple's guide to living childless by choice.* Berkeley: Seal Press.

Sobotka, T. (2009). Shifting parenthood to advanced reproductive ages: Trends, causes, and consequences. In J. Tremmel (Ed.), *A young generation under pressure?* (pp. 129–154). Berlin/Heidelberg: Springer.

Tsai, T., & Scommenga, P. (2012). *U.S. has world's highest incarceration rate*. Washington, DC: Population Reference Bureau.

US Bureau of the Census. (1975). *Historical statistics of the United States, colonial times to 1970*. Washington, DC: Bicentennial Edition.

US Census Bureau. (2012). *The 2012 statistical abstract*. http://www.census.gov/compendia/statab/. Accessed 27 July 2015.

Wang, W., Parker, K., & Taylor, P. (2013). *Breadwinner moms: Mothers are the sole or primary provider in four-in-ten households with children; public conflicted about the growing trend*. Pew Research Center. http://www.pewsocialtrends.org/2013/05/29/breadwinner-moms/. Accessed 27 July 2015.

Part III
Women's Education and Childlessness

Chapter 9
Education and Childlessness: The Influence of Educational Field and Educational Level on Childlessness among Swedish and Austrian Women

Gerda Neyer, Jan M. Hoem, and Gunnar Andersson

9.1   Introduction

Demographic research has long paid considerable attention to the connections between education and childlessness. For western countries it has regularly been shown that ultimate childlessness increases with a woman's educational level (see, e.g., Berrington et al., or Kreyenfeld and Konietzka in this volume). Researchers normally focus on individual-level explanations for this pattern, and there are competing interpretations of it. Economic theory holds that for women with more education, motherhood entails increased opportunity costs: i.e., compared to less educated women, highly educated women lose more income and human capital by concentrating on motherhood and on caregiving tasks. As a consequence, economists expect childlessness to increase with a woman's educational level (Becker 1960; Cigno 1991). Some feminist demographers have argued that having more education provides women with more economic independence and personal autonomy, and that highly educated women are therefore less likely to marry than less educated women (Oppenheimer 1994). Since unmarried women are more likely to remain childless than their married counterparts, the share of women who are childless should be higher among those who are highly educated (Kiernan 1989; Blossfeld and Huinink 1991; Hobcraft and Kiernan 1995). Theories that focus on changes in

This contribution is a modified version of the German texts by Neyer et al. (2013) and Neyer (2009). The latter were developed from Hoem et al. (2006) and Neyer and Hoem (2008). We thank Demographic Research, Zeitschrift für Familienforschung, and VUBpress for permission to use our graphs, tables, and other materials which we previously published in their journal or book.

G. Neyer (✉) • J.M. Hoem • G. Andersson
Demography Unit, Stockholm University, Stockholm, Sweden
e-mail: gerda.neyer@sociology.su.se; jan.hoem@sociology.su.se; gunnar.andersson@sociology.su.se

© The Author(s) 2017
M. Kreyenfeld, D. Konietzka (eds.), *Childlessness in Europe: Contexts, Causes, and Consequences*, Demographic Research Monographs, DOI 10.1007/978-3-319-44667-7_9

culture, values, and norms provide a third type of explanation. Researchers who take this perspective regard increasing childlessness as a consequence of a broadening range of life choices (van de Kaa 1996; Surkyn and Lesthaeghe 2004). They maintain that having more education offers women a wider spectrum of opportunities for organising their life, and that having children may thus become less important than other options (Rindfuss et al. 1996). The life course perspective offers yet another type of reasoning to explain the same general pattern: i.e., that because they spend longer periods of time in education and start employment later, women postpone motherhood, possibly up to an age at which physical fecundity may be reduced. Thus, childlessness may be expected to be higher among women who spend longer periods of time in education (Rindfuss and Bumpass 1976; Gustafsson 2001; Kravdal 2001).

However, empirical findings on childlessness for the former communist countries of Eastern Europe call into question the assumption of a monotonic relationship between educational level and childlessness. In these countries, women with more education do not necessarily have higher rates of childlessness than women with less education (Kantorova 2004; Kreyenfeld 2004). A similar conundrum is found in the Nordic countries (Andersson et al. 2009). Studies of the relationship between educational field and childlessness further complicate the picture. Findings for Sweden (Hoem et al. 2006), Norway (Lappegård and Rønsen 2005), Spain (Martín-García and Baizán 2006), Greece (Bagavos 2010), the Netherlands (Begall and Mills 2012), Germany (Maul 2012; Rösler 2012), the U.S. (Michelmore and Musick 2014), and European countries in general (Van Bavel 2010) indicate that women who have been educated to work in the education or health sector are significantly less likely to be childless than women who have been educated to work in other fields. In some cases the connection between educational field and childlessness is even stronger than the association between educational level and childlessness (Hoem et al. 2006; Van Bavel 2010).

We argue in this paper that a purely individual-level approach is not sufficient to resolve these apparent discrepancies. To find a valid explanation for the similarities and the differences in patterns of childlessness across educational groups and across countries, we need to take an institutional approach. We furthermore show that the demographic focus on family policies as the core institutional factor shaping childbearing patterns in highly developed countries is also not sufficient for explaining patterns of childlessness. We call for a comprehensive view of institutions that considers the educational system, the labour market, and family and gender policies, as well as the interactions between these institutions.

Based on this reasoning, we compare the ultimate levels of childlessness of women born in 1955–1959 in Sweden and in Austria, according to their educational level and their educational field.[1] While the institutions of Sweden and Austria are similar in a number of ways, there are also essential differences in the educational

---

[1] In this contribution we use the terms educational field, educational orientation, and type of education interchangeably. The same applies to level of childlessness, rates of childlessness, and per cent childless.

systems and in the labour market, in gender and family policies of the two countries. We contend that these differences have contributed to the marked differences we observe in the rates of childlessness among Austrian and Swedish women. To provide background information in support of this position, we briefly sketch in the following section the relevant country-specific aspects of the Swedish and the Austrian educational systems, and of the two countries' labour market, gender, and family policies (Sect. 9.2). We limit the information presented to the period 1970–1990s, when the women who were born in 1955–1959 were 15–40 years old, and were thus in their main childbearing years. In Sect. 9.3 we briefly describe the data and the methods we use in our analysis, and we present our main findings. We conclude the paper with our reflections on the possible institutional and individual-level explanations for our empirical results, and the implications of our findings for further research (Sect. 9.4).

9.2 Sweden and Austria – Institutional Commonalities and Differences

Because of their similarities and differences, Sweden and Austria are particularly suitable for a comparison of women's childlessness according to educational attainment. Both countries have small populations, a factor that influences their politics and policy formation process (Katzenstein 1985). Both have a long welfare tradition and can be regarded as strong welfare states in which social policies have had considerable influence on social structures. Both countries have coordinated market economies with strong employment protections for workers and employees (Estévez-Abe et al. 2001; Hall and Soskice 2001). In the 1970s and early 1980s, the Austrian federal social democratic government looked to Sweden's welfare state as a model in its efforts to modernise Austrian society (Hoem et al. 2001). The two countries have also undertaken similar family policy reforms. For example, both countries have introduced individual (rather than family-level) taxation, established legal equality between marital and non-marital children, legalised abortion in the first months of pregnancy, amended their parental leave regulations to increase women's employment, and actively promoted gender equality in many areas of public life. Moreover, in the late 1960s and early 1970s both countries reformed their educational systems to make higher education available to all social groups.

Despite these commonalities, the educational, gender, family, and social policies in Sweden and in Austria differ fundamentally in terms of their content and their aims. In political science, Sweden is classified as a proto-typical universalistic welfare state whose public policies are designed to achieve greater social and gender equality (Esping-Andersen 1990; Korpi 2000). By contrast, Austria is seen as a proto-typical conservative welfare state whose policies are designed to preserve social status differentials and perpetuate gender inequality (op cit., Marten et al. 2012). These basic orientations permeate all of the policy areas relevant to childbearing.

9.2.1 Sweden

Since the 1960s, Swedish labour market and social policies have actively promoted the integration of all adults into the employment system, and particularly of mothers with (small) children. Institutional day-care facilities for children of all age groups were gradually expanded to guarantee each child a place in public child care. As a consequence, for the past 50 years Sweden has been among the European countries with the highest public childcare coverage rates for children of all age groups (Bergqvist and Nyberg 2002; Neyer 2003). Maternity protection was replaced by a gender-neutral system of parental leave which grants both parents an individual right to paid parental leave. The (paid) leave was extended successively from 6 months (1974) to 12 months (1989), and an extra non-transferable "daddy month" was added in 1995 to promote a gender-equal division of care (for details, see Duvander and Ferrarini 2010). Until the child's eighth year of life, each parent has the flexibility to take this leave on a part-time or a full-time basis, continuously or in segments, or even as individual days. Parental leave may also be combined with periods during which the parent is attending (further) education. While on parental leave, each mother or father receives an income-dependent benefit which replaces a large percentage of his or her previous income. The income replacement rate was about 90 % in the 1970s and 1980s and was 80 % thereafter, up to a fixed income ceiling. In addition to making it easier for parents to combine employment and family, Sweden has implemented comprehensive regulations to enhance gender and economic equality across all social groups. This includes the active promotion of equality in employment, wages and salaries, career advancement, professional and political representation, and education (Bergqvist et al. 1999).

The Swedish educational system is designed to be open, flexible, and supportive of social equality. It is oriented towards life-long learning (for details see Henz 2001; Halldén 2008). To ensure that as many people as possible have access to higher education, the system does not channel pupils into segregated educational streams early in their educational career. It is also relatively easy for pupils to later revise their early educational choices. Swedish primary schools provide 9 years of compulsory comprehensive education for children between the ages of seven and 16. The curriculum is largely the same for all pupils at this level. After primary school the majority of pupils enter (voluntary) upper-secondary education. If there is competition for places in certain upper-secondary programmes, the pupils' grades determine which programmes they can choose from (Erikson and Jonsson 1996). For the cohorts born in 1955–1959, upper-secondary education still encompassed both 2-year and 3-year lines of education; the 2-year lines were converted into a 3-year line in the 1990s. The focus of the 3-year line is on theoretical knowledge. After successfully completing upper-secondary school pupils are entitled to enrol in tertiary education. The focus of most of the 2-year (and now converted 3-year) lines is on occupational and semi-occupational training. However, to ensure that students have the opportunity to change to other lines of education, a large share of the coursework is in general subjects, while practical vocational training in firms makes up only a small part of the course of study. By taking additional courses pupils in 2-year lines could earn the 3-year qualification needed to enrol in the tertiary educational system (Halldén 2008). Since the 1970s, admission to tertiary education has been regulated by a numerus clausus. Standardised eligibility and admission regulations are applied to all tertiary programmes and to all levels (Erikson and Jonsson 1996). Tertiary education has three levels: (1) 2- to 3-year lines of study that mainly offer advanced vocational education, (2) lines of study of at least 3–4 years that lead to a bachelor's or a master's degree, and (3) further studies that lead to a licentiate or a doctoral degree. The third level is intended to prepare the student for a scientific career.

Despite the selection process applied to upper-secondary-level and tertiary-level programmes, the Swedish educational system aims to equalise educational attainment and reduce class differentials (Erikson and Jonsson 1996). It is flexibly organised, highly permeable, and has special procedures to allow for late entry into (higher) education. Interruptions in education, moves out of and back into education, and changes in the educational line are always possible, and are often used. Individuals have a right to interrupt their employment to further their education. An extensive system of adult education and of active labour market policies facilitates and promotes (re-)education, training, and skill enhancement. Education is tuition free. A generous system of financial support, consisting of grants and loans, for individuals in higher education encourages and facilitates educational participation throughout the life course. This has resulted in high levels of educational participation and the widespread use of opportunities to earn new or improved qualifications on a flexible basis (Tesching 2012).

9.2.2 Austria

Austria has remained a conservative corporatist welfare state in spite of the reforms of the 1970s and early 1980s (Neyer 2003; Obinger and Tálos 2010). The education, employment, and welfare systems are not aligned as closely with the equality principles as the Swedish systems are. Austrian labour and social politics have focused more on securing the branch- and occupation-specific rights of workers and employees and on supporting the male breadwinner model than on ensuring the gender-equal integration of women into the labour market or on reducing gender, social, and economic inequality (Biffl 1997). Fertility-related family policies were designed to make it easier for mothers to leave the labour market and focus full-time on caring for their children. Until 1990, parental leave lasted until the child's first birthday, and was for mothers only. In 1990, parental leave was extended to the child's second birthday, and restricted options for part-time leave and father's leave were introduced. Under a 1996 amendment 6 months of the parental leave were reserved for fathers. During the leave, previously employed mothers and fathers received a low, flat rate benefit which was independent of their previous income, but dependent on their partnership status. Because of the low benefit level and the complicated regulations on part-time work and on how the leave could be split between the mother and the father, parental leave was almost exclusively taken by women as full-time leave (Hoem et al. 2001; Neyer 2010).[2] Until recently, there were very few childcare places for children under age three or for children of school age (Statistik Austria 2014: Table 19). Thus, many women leave their job after taking parental leave or interrupt their employment for several years.

The Austrian school system has three distinct features: the early streaming of pupils into a complex set of educational paths, the "dual system" of apprenticeship and its separation from the main educational system, and the limited options for revising previous educational choices. As in Sweden, compulsory education in Austria lasts 9 years. However, in Austria the common primary school lasts only 4 years, up to the age of ten. Thereafter, the educational lines separate, with pupils being channelled into an upper level of primary school or a lower secondary school (Hauptschule), both lasting 4 years; or into an 8-year high school (Gymnasium) with a lower-secondary and an upper-secondary level. Pupils' grades determine which type of school they can attend. To attend a Gymnasium, the pupils of our cohorts also had to pass an entrance exam. The Gymnasium and the Hauptschule are further subdivided. In the Hauptschule the pupils are grouped according to educational attainment (usually grades). In the Gymnasium pupils have to choose a specific subject line for their upper-secondary level education, such as a concentration on humanities, natural science/mathematics education, or home economics.

Pupils who have completed the Volksschule or Hauptschule or who have left the Gymnasium after completing its lower-secondary level have several options for continuing their education: (1) They can go on to a vocational middle school (berufsbildende mittlere Schule), which generally lasts 3–4 years and offers both vocational and general courses. (2) They can choose an apprenticeship (Lehre), which usually takes 3 years. The programme consists primarily of vocational training in firms, complemented by occupation-specific theoretical education in special vocational schools ("dual system"). Apprenticeships are not integrated into the "regular" educational system.[3] (3) Pupils with good grades can transfer to an upper-secondary high school (Oberstufenrealgymnasium), which is a Gymnasium that only offers the upper-secondary level.[4] (4) Pupils can transfer to a vocational upper-secondary high school (Berufsbildende höhere Schule) that takes 5 years to complete, and that offers vocational training together with a programme of general

---

[2] In 2002 a 3-year childrearing benefit for all mothers (or fathers) replaced the 2-year parental leave benefit for working mothers (or fathers). The regulations were subsequently amended several times, so that parents can now choose between five different variants of payment length with four flat rate benefits and one income-dependent benefit. The longest variant is the most popular one, and fathers on leave are still a minority (for details, see Marten et al. 2012).

[3] Unlike the general school system, which is under the auspices of the ministry of education, education for apprentices is governed by the ministry of economic affairs and the social partners, particularly the regional economic chambers (Graf et al. 2012).

[4] In principle, a pupil can also transfer to the upper-secondary level of a Gymnasium, but due to the different curricula in the Hauptschule and the lower-secondary level of a Gymnasium, this is rarely done.

education equivalent to that of the upper-secondary level of a Gymnasium. (5) Pupils who do not make use of any of the options above can attend a 1-year poly-technical school that offers a preparatory vocational education programme. Upon completion of the Gymnasium, the Oberstufenrealgymnasium, or the berufsbil-dende höhere Schule students take a special maturation exam (Matura). After earning their Matura qualification, students can enrol in a tertiary education institution (a university or a post-secondary vocational college).

Austria has an open university system. Most tertiary education programmes have no numerus clausus, entrance exams, or other selection processes; and students are free to choose any line of study (irrespective of their Matura grades). There are also no formal restrictions on doctoral studies. Universities do not charge tuition, and students may qualify for financial support in the form of a non-repayable scholarship, depending on their own and their parents' income. While there have been efforts to provide special scholarships to former students to resume their studies, these programmes have been less systematically developed in Austria than in Sweden.

Having the Matura diploma is an important pre-requisite for many subsequent educational options. Not only does it open the way to tertiary education; it is also a precondition for many kinds of qualified work, particularly in the public sector. The Matura thus serves as a marker that keeps educational groups and classes apart. Individuals who have completed a course of study that did not finish with the Matura have the option of attending special schools or programmes which prepare them for taking the Matura examination. Individuals may also be admitted to specific lines of tertiary education without having earned the Matura, provided they can prove (e.g., based on their employment history) that they have the qualifications for the chosen line, and pass a special admission examination. However, the availability of preparatory courses for the Matura (outside of high schools) or for the special admission examination varies from region to region, and taking them often involves considerable effort and cost.

9.2.3   Sweden and Austria – A Comparison of Their Institutions

There are certain aspects of the Swedish and the Austrian institutions that should be highlighted here because they appear to have especially strong effects on the relationship between education and childlessness:

First, the Austrian educational system segregates pupils at an early age, and is not organised with the purpose of giving as many people as possible access to higher education. This is mirrored in the distribution of Swedish and Austrian women born in 1955–1959 across educational levels (Table 9.1). In Austria, 31 % of all women in these birth cohorts have completed no more than compulsory education. In Sweden the corresponding figure is as low as 17 %. Conversely, 80 % of the Austrian

Table 9.1 Distribution of Swedish and Austrian women born in 1955–1959, by educational level

Sweden	Percentage	Austria	Percentage
Compulsory school[a]	16.6	Primary School[b]	31.3
Upper-secondary school, 2 years	36.0	Apprenticeship	27.1
		Vocational middle school	20.7
Upper-secondary school, 3 years	14.7	*Gymnasium*[c]	7.9
Post-secondary vocational college; shorter university	20.6	Post-secondary vocational college	6.2
University level[d]	12.1	University[e]	6.7

Sources: Neyer and Hoem (2008) and Neyer (2009)

Note:

[a] Comprehensive school up to age 16

[b] Primary school, lower-secondary school *(Hauptschule),* poly-technical school (up to age 15)

[c] *Gymnasium* proper, upper-secondary high school (*Oberstufenrealgymnasium*), vocational high school (*berufsbildende höhere Schule*)

[d] University, upper tertiary and research degree

[e] University, all levels of completion

women have no upper-secondary (Matura), post-secondary, or tertiary education, while in Sweden the corresponding figure is 53 %. Only 13 % of the Austrian women of these cohorts have completed post-secondary or tertiary education, while among Swedish women the corresponding figure is 33 %.

Second, in Sweden vocational education is integrated into the educational system. It prioritises the transmission of general, "transportable" skills over occupation-specific vocational training. A considerable share (30 %) of vocational education is at the tertiary level (Culpepper 2007). Having transportable and higher-level skills makes it easier to move between the various lines of study, and facilitates occupational mobility in the labour market (Estévez-Abe et al. 2001). By contrast, the Austrian apprenticeship system is largely segregated from the general school system (Graf et al. 2012). It offers a high level of occupation-specific vocational training, but little general, non-occupation-specific or transportable coursework. Thus, pupils in Austria have difficulties moving from an apprenticeship to a general course of study or switching between apprenticeships. Only 4 % of vocational education is offered at the tertiary level (Culpepper 2007). On the other hand, having firm-based training, which tends to be high-quality and standardised, can greatly ease a pupil's transition from school to work. As a consequence, unemployment rates among young people, and particularly among those who complete apprenticeships, have been much lower in Austria than in Sweden (Lindahl 2011; Lassnig 2013).

Third, the Swedish educational system is oriented towards life-long learning, and therefore provides a broader spectrum of flexible options for participating in educational programmes, for leaving and re-entering education, and for earning new qualifications or enhancing existing qualifications over the life course. Austria has a more closed system, and limits participation in education to children and young adults to a much greater extent than Sweden.

Fourth, the Swedish school system is oriented towards promoting class and gender equality, and towards minimising corresponding differentials. Despite this aim, levels of sex segregation by field of education have remained high (Jonsson 1999). Sex segregation is even more pronounced in Austria, where special educational lines directed at women were maintained for much longer than in Sweden. Almost one-third of all of the women who attended the Gymnasium in the 1970s and early 1980s, and more than half of all of the women who attended a vocational middle school or enrolled in an apprenticeship, were in an educational stream in which almost all of the pupils (95 %) were female. These streams had curricula with gender-stereotypical content oriented towards family work (Lassnig and Paseka 1997).

Finally, Austrian family, social, and labour market policies have been designed to encourage women to leave the labour force when they have children. Yet employment protection, social security rights and benefits, and opportunities for promotion in the labour market have largely been tied to having an uninterrupted (and mostly full-time) career. By contrast, Sweden has more consistently pursued policies aimed at helping both parents balance family and work, and at ensuring that men and women have equal career opportunities throughout the life course.

We might expect to find that such national differences influence the connection between educational attainment and childlessness. In particular, we would expect to observe that rates of childlessness are higher in Austria than in Sweden, simply because it is harder to have children and pursue employment in Austria. On the other hand, we might also expect to find that childlessness rates are lower in Austria than in Sweden because of the large share of highly educated women in Sweden and the prevalence of feminised educational fields in Austria. Moreover, it is not clear whether women with similar educational paths in the two countries have similar levels of childlessness. Rates of childlessness among women with all types of education may differ between the two countries because of institutional differences. But if we assume that preferences are more important than institutional conditions, we would expect to observe the same levels of childlessness by educational field in both countries. In the following chapters, we investigate these assumptions by analysing childlessness by educational field and educational level in greater detail.

9.3 Childlessness According to Educational Field and Educational Level in Sweden and in Austria

For our empirical investigation we make use of Swedish register data and of Austrian census data.[5] Both provide individual-level information. We concentrate on the cohorts born in 1955–1959, because at the point in time when we carried out our analyses this was the "youngest" cohort for whom we could get data that allow us to determine whether women were childless at the end of their reproductive years (age 40 or above). The Swedish data are extracts from the country's national educa-

---

[5] For details of data content and data handling, see Hoem et al. 2006; and Neyer and Hoem 2008.

tional and population registers. The educational register contains data on all of the levels of education by field that each woman completed up to 1998. The population register lists all births through 2002. For Austria, we used the national census of 2001. It contains (self-reported) information on each woman's field and highest level of education, and on her births. For both countries, our datasets contained the entire resident female population; the datasets were large enough to allow us to also study the ultimate levels of childlessness among women who had chosen educational lines with comparatively few graduates. We combined the roughly 2600 Swedish and 650 Austrian educational fields into 60 educational groups for each country.[6] The groups largely correspond to the International Standard Classification of Education (ISCED) of 1997. This process made our Swedish and Austrian educational groups generally comparable.[7] Because of the differences in the educational systems, the levels of education were not harmonised. In particular, Sweden does not have the Austrian differentiation between vocational middle school (berufsbildende mittlere Schule) and apprenticeship (Lehrberuf). Conversely, the Austrian data contained no differentiation of degrees at the tertiary level, while the Swedish data allow us to make this distinction.

9.3.1 *Educational Field and Childlessness*

In Figs. 9.1 and 9.2 we present the percentages of women who were childless (at ages 40+ and of the cohorts 1955–1959) in Sweden and in Austria according to their educational orientation and educational level. In both countries, women who were educated to work in the education or health care sector are less likely to be childless than women with other types of education. In Austria, only women with an education in agriculture have lower rates of childlessness than women who were educated to work in the education or health care sector at all educational levels. On the whole, women who were educated to work in the education or health care sector are not only less likely to be childless than other women with the same level of education but in a different field; they are also less likely to be childless than women who were educated in a different field but at a lower level. For instance, Austrian women with a post-secondary degree that qualifies them to teach in primary and lower-secondary

---

[6] Austria has many more educational fields than these 650, but in many of these fields not a single woman from the cohorts born in 1955–1959 had completed a course of study. The smaller number of educational fields in our Austrian data reflects the strong concentration of women in a select group of educational fields.

[7] There were a few types of education in Sweden (e.g., library science and law enforcement) that did not exist (in a similar and recorded form) in Austria, and vice versa (for example, tourism studies are common in Austria, but there was no corresponding category in our Swedish data). We chose to retain educational fields in our analysis if they had been chosen by a sufficiently large number of women; or if their inclusion contributes to our understanding of the connection between education and childlessness, even if they were present in the data of only one of the two countries.

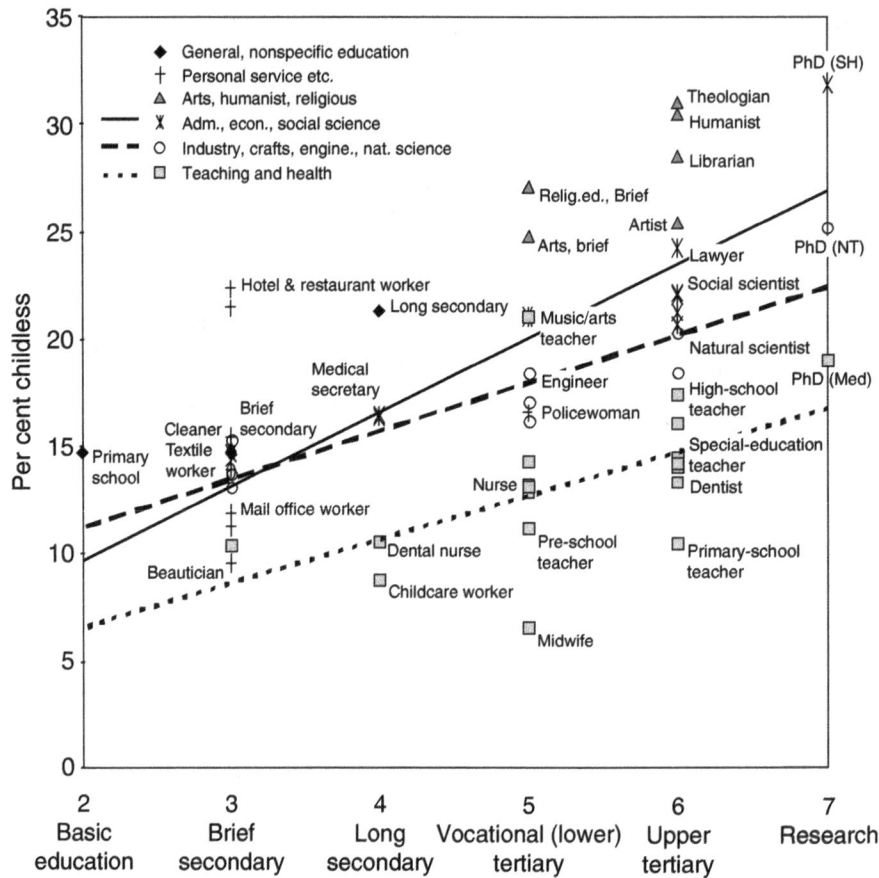

Fig. 9.1 Per cent childless in the birth cohorts 1955–1959, by educational level and educational field (Sweden) (Source: Hoem et al. 2006)

schools (Volks- und Hauptschule) are less likely to be childless (16 %) than women who had completed an apprenticeship in the beauty business, in the insurance or bank sector, or in book selling; or women who completed high school (Gymnasium) or who earned an upper-secondary vocational diploma that qualifies them to work in the textile or chemical industry, in communication technology, or in tourism. We get similar results when we compare the childlessness rates of women who were educated to work in the health care sector with the childlessness rates of women who were educated in a different field.

In Sweden, we see much larger differentials in childlessness than in Austria between women who were educated to work in the education or health care sector and women who were educated in other fields, even if they spent less time in education. Thus, Swedish women with a tertiary education that qualifies them to teach home economics or pupils with special needs (14 %) or to practice medicine as a medical doctor (14 %) have the same level of childlessness as women who left school after the compulsory minimum, or who left after earning a 2-year upper-secondary qualification without any particular vocational education.

By contrast, women who were educated in journalism, the social sciences, the humanities, theology, or the fine arts have high rates of childlessness in both

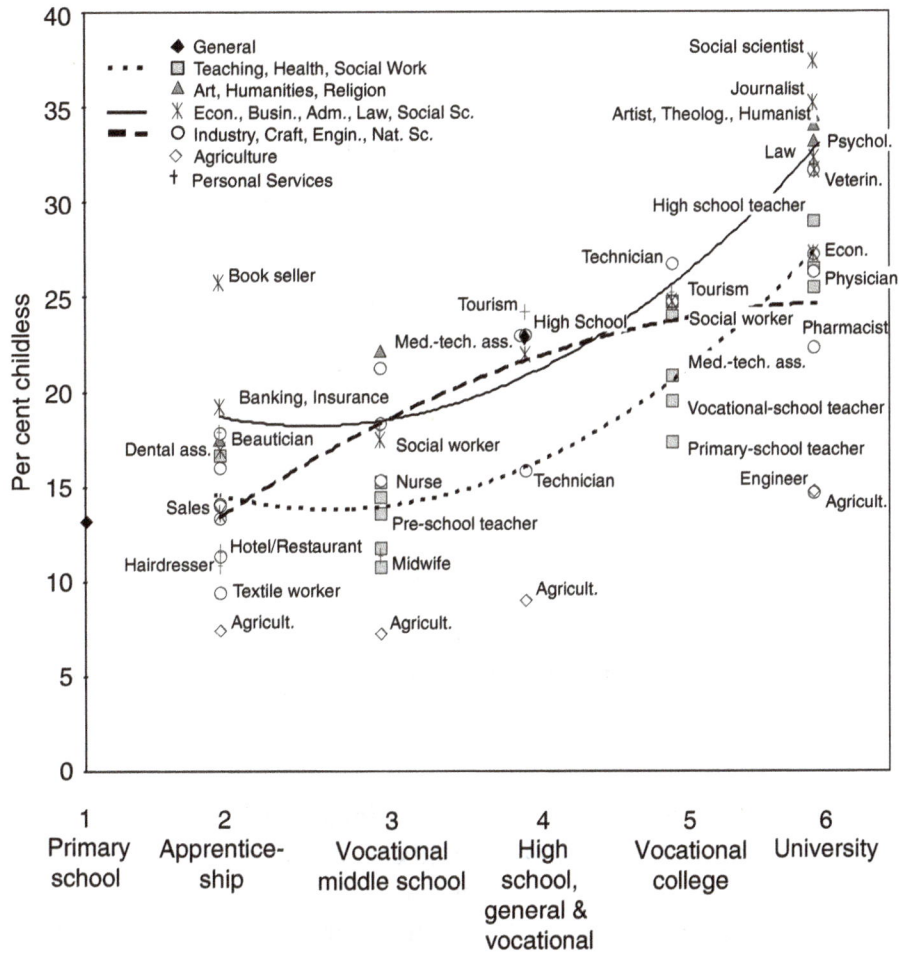

Fig. 9.2 Per cent childless in the birth cohorts 1955–1959, by educational level and educational field (Austria) (Source: Neyer and Hoem 2008)
Note: To facilitate interpretation of the figure, the trend lines refer to the larger groups of education)

countries. A woman who was educated in one of these fields (e.g., as artist or historian) is more likely to be childless than a woman with an education degree in the same field of study (e.g., as arts teacher or history teacher). Similarly, women who studied in fields closely aligned with the humanities, such as book selling (in Austria) or library science (in Sweden), are much more likely to be childless than women who were educated in other fields at the same level.

9.3.2 Educational Level and Childlessness

In both Sweden and Austria, the cohorts of women born in 1955–1959 have the same ultimate level of childlessness; namely, 15.7 %. This is somewhat surprising since we would expect to see different levels of childlessness given the institutional and educational differences in the two countries. However, national differences

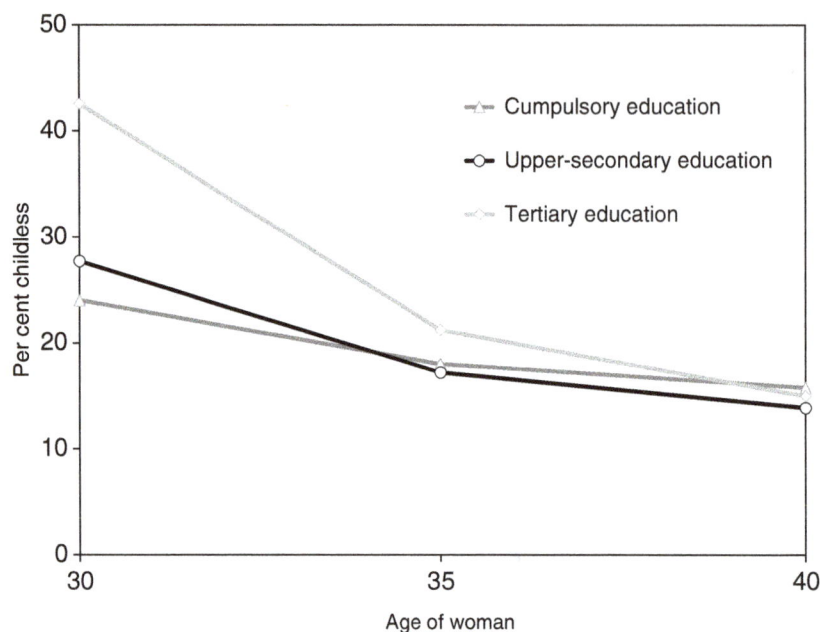

Fig. 9.3 Per cent childless by age attained and educational level, Swedish women born in 1955–1959 (Source: Andersson et al. 2009)

become evident when we take the level of educational attainment into account. If we only consider the three most commonly used educational levels – namely, compulsory education, secondary education, and tertiary education – we see no marked differences in childlessness between these three groups in Sweden, although the highly educated women tend to have their children later than less educated women (Fig. 9.3). Even more surprising is the finding that women with only a compulsory education have a slightly higher level of childlessness (15.8 %) than the most educated women (15.0 %) (Andersson et al. 2009).

In Austria, differences in rates of childlessness by education do not level out over the life course of women. The gap in the childlessness rates of women with only a compulsory education (13.0 %) and women with a tertiary education (23.2 %) was ten percentage points. When we use more refined groups of educational attainment (Fig. 9.4), the differences in the patterns in the two countries become even more striking. In Sweden, there are hardly any differences in rates of childlessness between women at the various levels of attainment below the advanced university levels. Only women with a master's degree (19 %) and women with a licentiate or doctorate (25 %) have higher rates of childlessness than other educational groups, but the rate of childlessness among these very highly educated women is still much lower than the rate among all tertiary-educated women in Austria (29 %). While in Sweden only women with the highest educational attainment are more likely than other women to remain childless, in Austria rates of childlessness are elevated even among women who have an upper-secondary school qualification (Matura). One-fifth (22.2 %) of the women for whom the Matura is their highest level of education remain childless; this rate is eight percentage points higher than the rate among

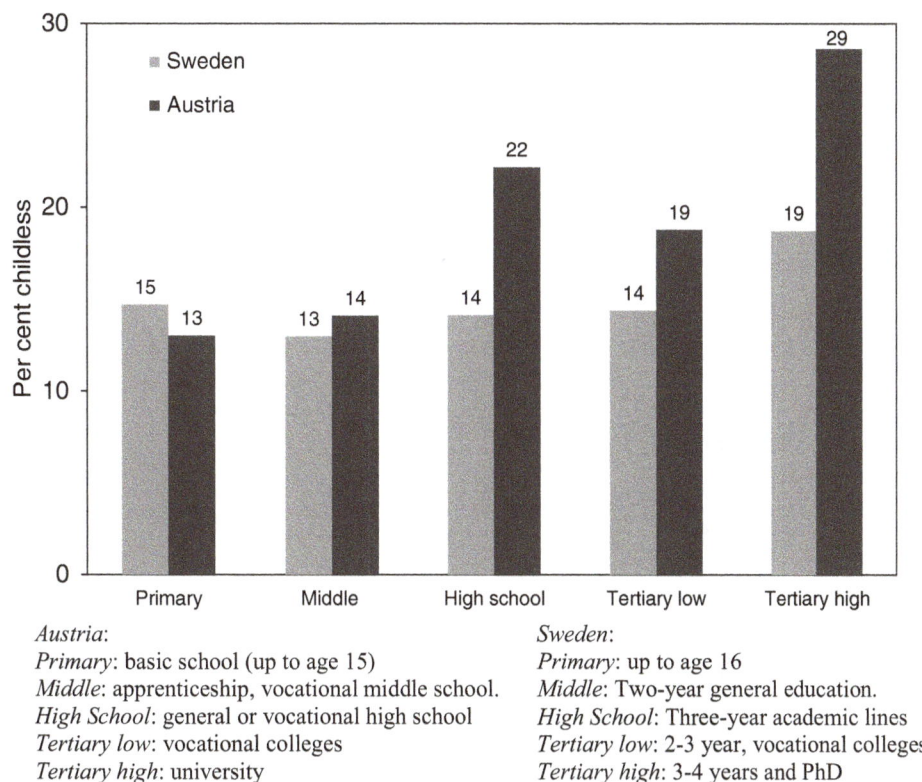

Austria:
Primary: basic school (up to age 15)
Middle: apprenticeship, vocational middle school.
High School: general or vocational high school
Tertiary low: vocational colleges
Tertiary high: university

Sweden:
Primary: up to age 16
Middle: Two-year general education.
High School: Three-year academic lines
Tertiary low: 2-3 year, vocational colleges.
Tertiary high: 3-4 years and PhD

Fig. 9.4 Childlessness according to educational attainment in Sweden and in Austria (Source: Neyer and Hoem 2008)

Austrian women who completed vocational middle school or an apprenticeship, and eight percentage points higher than the rate among Swedish women with the same educational attainment. As Figs. 9.1, 9.2, and 9.4 show, childlessness increases more strongly with educational level in Austria than in Sweden. There seems to be a clearer differentiation by educational attainment in Austria at each level of attainment, with the Matura being the boundary between women with average levels of childlessness and those with much higher levels of childlessness.

The distinctly higher rates of childlessness among Austrian women with an advanced education than among the corresponding Swedish women can be seen in Table 9.2. In the table, the childlessness rates of select groups of Swedish and Austrian women with equivalent education (level and field) are presented. The patterns of childlessness among women who were educated to work in the education or health care sector most clearly demonstrate the fundamental differences between Austria and Sweden. At each level of education, Austrian women with this educational background are more likely to be childless than similar women in Sweden, even though some of the requirements for these educational levels are higher in Sweden than in Austria (e.g., for kindergarten/pre-school teachers). The most obvious differences are among women at the university level. More than one-quarter of all Austrian women with a university-level degree in education or health are childless at age 40. Their childlessness rate is more than ten percentage points higher than that of Swedish women with the same educational background, and ten

Table 9.2 Childlessness of select groups of women by educational field and level in Sweden and Austria (per cent childless, women born 1955–1959)

	Austria	Sweden
Education		
Pre-school teacher child carers	13.5	11.0
Primary school teacher	16.5	10.3
High school teacher	29.1	17.3
Health		
Midwife	10.6	6.4
Nurse	14.5	13.0
Medical doctor	25.4	15.9
Education without *Matura*/ 2-year upper-secondary education		
Beautician/hairdresser	12.7	9.6
Textile specialist	10.6	13.9
Apprenticeship	9.3	
Vocational middle school	15.2	
Hotel/restaurant business	12.7	22.4
Apprenticeship	11.7	
Vocational middle school	17.9	
Home economics	11.4	21.6
Agriculture	7.4	15.5
University		
Social sciences	37.3	32.9
Theology	33.9	30.9
Humanities	33.1	30.4
Psychology	32.5	32.7
Technical university/natural sciences		
Engineers/technical professions	14.6	19.0
Natural sciences	26.2	22.0

Source: Hoem et al. (2006) and Neyer and Hoem (2008)

percentage points higher than that of Austrian women who were educated in the same field but at a lower level of attainment.

There are similar differentials by educational attainment in other areas of education, such as in fields of education that prepare women to work in the textile, leather, or clothing industries; in hotels and restaurants; in tourism, or in social work. For all of these fields the fraction of Austrian women who are childless increases from around 10 % among women who have completed an apprenticeship, to 15–18 % among women who have a vocational middle school qualification, and to 25 % among those who have a higher vocational school qualification. In Sweden childlessness also increases with educational level, but this relationship is less strong than the relationship between educational field and childlessness (Hoem et al. 2006).

In some areas of education, the results for Austria and Sweden diverge from our initial expectations. This is particularly the case for work in the hotel and restaurant sector, in home economics, or in agriculture. Swedish women who were educated in these fields are considerably more likely to be childless at age 40 than their counterparts in Austria (Table 9.2, Neyer and Hoem 2008). It is not clear why this is the case. These differences may be attributable to the number of women who pursue these courses of study, or to the structure or nature of the occupations associated with these courses. For instance, more than twice as many women in Austria as in Sweden finished a middle-level certificate that qualifies them to work in the hotel and restaurant industry. The hotel and restaurant sector is much larger in Austria than in Sweden, and the vast majority of businesses are small and family-owned. Thus, many Austrian women work in their own family business. In Sweden, an education in home economics prepares students to administer large (institutional) households, while in Austria education in home economics aimed at preparing women for housekeeping and motherhood. An apprenticeship or vocational middle school qualification with an agricultural orientation is also three times more common in Austria than in Sweden, and these courses often cover home economics, as well.

As we mentioned above, the rates of childlessness among women educated in the humanities, arts, psychology, and theology are similar in Austria and Sweden. The low rates of childlessness in both countries among women who have a university degree in engineering are surprising, particularly as in Austria these women have the lowest rates of childlessness among all university graduates (15 %); even lower than those among women in the same field but with a lower qualification, and considerably lower than women with a degree in the natural sciences. (Fig. 9.2 and Table 9.2).

9.4 Education and Childlessness: Discussion and Conclusions

The differences and the similarities in the patterns of childlessness in Sweden and Austria lead us to ask the question of what factors produced them. The present investigation cannot give a definitive answer, because the available data only contain information about whether a woman is childless, and not about the determinants of childlessness. Nevertheless, we will outline what we believe are the most important potential determinants, with a focus on institutional aspects, especially on the educational system, the links between education and labour market, as well as on the role of individual choice and self-selection.

9.4.1 Educational System and Childlessness

As we have outlined, the Austrian and Swedish educational systems have very different goals and structures. The Swedish system is oriented towards promoting the educational advancement of each individual throughout her/his life course. A woman therefore has the flexibility to arrange her educational career so that it fits with her other life goals, including having children. It appears that women often make use of this flexibility: in almost one-third of the 60 types of educational fields we analysed, women completed their (final) educational qualification after the birth of their first child (Hoem et al. 2006). More than half of these women were educated to work in the education or health sector, or in another public sector. From the data we have available, we cannot conclude whether it is easier to combine motherhood and education in these fields than in others, or whether the effect we see is attributable to re-education or to continued education after the arrival of the first child. Tesching (2012) showed that in Sweden childless women are twice as likely as mothers to change their educational field. She also showed that mothers who were educated in a female-dominated field that leads to stable employment with strong job protections, mostly in the public sector (e.g., education, health care, and welfare), have much lower risks of changing their field of education than mothers in general and/or mothers who were educated in another field. The risk of pursuing a course of study in another field after becoming a mother is very high among women who were educated in the humanities, the social sciences, journalism, law, and the fine arts and media (Tesching 2012). These findings suggest that women who were educated in these fields find it difficult to continue to work in their chosen occupation after they have become a mother. The findings also indicate that the flexibility of the Swedish educational system, which offers women the option of continuing their education later in life or of retraining for a job that can be more easily combined with raising children, explains at least in part the lower rates of childlessness among Swedish women with specific educational backgrounds and higher educational attainment.

By contrast, as we have noted repeatedly, the Austrian educational system is closed, and is organised in a rather fixed sequential order in which education precedes employment and family formation. Thus, the educational system does not accommodate childbearing. For instance, for apprentices (of our cohorts) who were pregnant or had a child, the maternity and parental leave regulations in the workplace were not coordinated with the rules for vocational school attendance. As a consequence, it was often impossible for female students to complete their apprenticeship if they became pregnant and had a child. At all levels of education, the only way for most women to avoid dropping out was to postpone motherhood until they had completed their desired level of education.

Overall, our results suggest that a flexible educational system is more conducive to parenthood than a closed system: it seems to reduce childlessness among women with long courses of study, as becoming a parent does not threaten the student's possibility to take her final examinations. It allows women (and men) to adapt their educational field to the demands of childrearing, and it makes it easier for them to update their qualifications following interruptions. It can therefore reduce the risk that women will remain childless for educational or occupational reasons.

9.4.2 Education and Labour Market

The outcomes of our investigation lead us to believe that the ways in which education and the labour market are intertwined may influence childbearing behaviour. All of these connections are underpinned by family and gender policies. On the basis of their findings for Swedish women Hoem et al. (2006) identified five clusters of education, each of which is connected to specific labour market and occupational areas. They analysed how each of these clusters leads to a different level of childlessness. The results were later partly confirmed in a cohort study for Norway by Rønsen and Skrede (2010). With our Austrian data, we can check whether the clusters hold for a conservative welfare state, as well.

Educational Fields of Study That Lead to Jobs in the Public Sector

In both Sweden and Austria, educational fields that prepare students to work in education, health, social work, and law often lead to jobs in the public sector. In both countries, the public sector offers increased job protection, a more stable and secure income, and better parental leave conditions than the private sector. We would therefore expect to find that women who were educated in fields that lead to jobs in the public sector have lower levels of childlessness. However, we find that, first, childlessness rates are lower only among women who are educated to work in female-dominated occupations in the public sector, such as education, health, and social work; whereas women who were educated to work in more male-dominated public sector areas – like law (Austria and Sweden), law enforcement, and library science (Sweden) – do not have childlessness rates that are much lower than those of other women with the same level of education (see also Ohlsson-Wijk 2015). Second, Austrian women with an upper-secondary (Matura), post-secondary, or tertiary degree in educational fields that lead to female dominated jobs in the public sector (such as a degree in high school education) are more likely to be childless than we would expect. This may be in part because for our cohorts, tenure and careers in the public sector were tied to uninterrupted, full-time employment. Taking parental leave or moving to a part-time schedule was incompatible with these requirements.

Fields of Education That Lead to Feminised Occupations in the Private Sector

Many fields of education lead to jobs in private sector industries in which most of the employees are female: e.g., the food production industry, the textile industry, business administration, personal services (such as the beauty and hairdressing business), and the hotel and restaurant industry. In both Austria and Sweden, women with these educational backgrounds are rarely childless, although there are some differences in childlessness rates between the countries (see Figs. 9.1 and 9.2). It appears that Swedish women are more likely to be childless if they are educated to work in an occupational field with high levels of employee turnover and with non-standardised working hours, such as the hotel and restaurant industry; and they are less likely to be childless if they are educated to work in sectors with more standardised working conditions. In Austria these relationships seem to be inverted. One reason for this difference could be that in Austria jobs with standardised working conditions usually have higher social status, better working conditions, and higher wages. We generally find that Austrian women with educational backgrounds that lead to occupations with these characteristics are more likely to be childless than women who were educated to work in occupations with lower levels of social prestige and professional gratification.

Gender-Mixed Lines of Education with Little Occupational Specialisation

In both countries childlessness rates are above average among women who chose a gender-mixed line of education without a specific occupational profile. This category includes women who left the educational system after primary school or after a general upper-secondary education without a vocational specialisation. It also includes women with a (non-education) degree in the humanities, fine arts, or general social sciences. Women who have completed educational lines with no specific vocational qualifications tend to find it harder to enter the labour market than women who chose an occupation-specific field of education (Korpi et al. 2003; Lassnig 2013). These uncertainties seem to discourage childbearing.

Gender-Mixed Lines of Education with a High Degree of Occupational Specialisation

A broad spectrum of educational lines are assigned to this category, including preparation to work in secretarial and administrative occupations, and in sectors such as banking and insurance, business administration, business economics, law, journalism, and tourism. These women have been educated for jobs with very different employment prospects, career paths, income levels, and degrees of occupational feminisation. In both countries, women with these educational backgrounds have higher rates of childlessness than comparable women with other educational backgrounds. We assume that women who work in an occupation with a balanced gender distribution face more competition from men and greater (direct or indirect) discrimination at work than women in a more female-dominated occupation, and that these factors may discourage them from having children.

Male-Dominated Lines of Education

Male-dominated educational lines frequently provide students with the skills needed to work in the private sector, such as in occupations related to engineering, technology, and the natural sciences. Women who are educated in these fields face greater difficulties in entering the labour market than women with other educational backgrounds: specifically, they tend to have a longer job search after completing their education, fewer secure job offers, and fewer opportunities to maintain their employment (Smyth 2003). Contrary to expectations, we find that women who were educated in a male-dominated – and especially in a technical – field are slightly (Sweden) to decidedly (Austria) less likely to be childless than women who were educated in a gender-balanced field. Job uncertainties and the experiences associated with being a "token woman" may account for the particularly low result in Austria, but studies in this country have also shown that women with a technical education often have highly educated parents (Fischer-Kowalski 1985). It is possible that women with university-educated parents find it easier than other women to combine work and family.

9.4.3 Choice of Education, Self-Selection, and Social Environment

The observed variations in childlessness by type of education in both Austria and Sweden suggest that women factor in their plans for having a family when they choose a specific educational line. Scholars often assume that women who want to have children tend to choose an educational field that will enable them to combine work and motherhood in their preferred form (Hakim 2000). This process may be expected to result in a concentration of women who want to have children in specific educational and occupational fields, which may in turn promote a social environment and social norms which support childrearing (Elster 1991). However, historical investigations of childlessness among women with specific types of education have shown that individual preferences play out differently in different contexts. As a consequence, the levels of childlessness among women with the same educational backgrounds may vary considerably depending on the circumstances in which these women live (Jensen 1973; Cookingham 1984). This leads us to take a more nuanced view of how self-selection and social norms may work:

First, because of the structural differences in the educational systems, the selection processes into educational lines may be quite different in Austria and in Sweden. For instance, the stronger segmentation of the educational system in Austria may mean that not every type of (secondary) education or apprenticeship was available in every region. In these circumstances, parents may send their children to the closest school, and pupils may choose an apprenticeship based on availability.

Second, differences in the organisation of the educational system, in parental leave, in childcare availability, and gender policies may lead to different selection processes. For example, in Austria women (of our cohorts) who wanted to have children may have tended to opt for shorter educational lines and to avoid longer courses of study. By contrast, in Sweden fertility considerations may play a smaller role in women's educational choices.

Third, the social environment during education and thereafter may lead women to change their preferences regarding childbearing, and to adjust their childbearing behaviour to the norms in their respective educational or occupational field. These shifts in attitudes and behaviour may partly explain the high rates of childlessness among women who were educated in the humanities, the fine arts, or the social sciences; as well as in library science or book selling. In the 1970s and 1980s, these disciplines generated feminist theories which raised fundamental questions about whether reproduction should be the norm for women.

Fourth, differences in social norms may explain the different distributions of childlessness in Sweden and in Austria. The largely uniform pattern of childlessness across educational levels in Sweden suggests that having children is the social norm for all women (and men) in this country, while in Austria remaining childless is a socially acceptable behaviour for highly educated women. Social pressure to have children appears to be stronger and more universal in Sweden than in Austria (Oláh and Bernhardt 2008; Prskawetz et al. 2008). The Swedish education, family, and gender policies tend to encourage conformity with the norm of having children. In Austria, there seems to be more leeway to opt out of or resist the social norm of having children, at least for the highly educated (Oláh and Hobson 2006).

9.4.4 Education and Childlessness: Should There Be an Individual-Level or an Institutional Approach?

As we noted in the introduction, the bulk of literature on education and childlessness stresses individual choices over institutional conditions. This may be attributable in part to the dominance of particular theories (like rational choice), but it may also be a consequence of empirical restrictions. Surveys usually contain too few cases to allow scholars to differentiate sufficiently by educational attainment, and comparative research across many countries does not allow researchers to adequately consider differences in educational systems. For our study, we had detailed information about the educational and childbearing histories of all of the women of certain cohorts in two countries. Thus, we had a dataset that was sufficiently large to allow us to distinguish between many educational lines. Focusing on two countries provided us with the opportunity to factor in the structures and the aims of the institutions that are assumed to shape childbearing behaviour. Our results clearly show that commonly reported findings on the link between education and childlessness should not be taken at face value and accepted as being indicative of universal patterns. In line with other scholars, we do not find that highly educated women have always had higher rates of childlessness than less highly educated women. Our results also do not provide unconditional support for the assumption that preferences regarding children guide women's educational choices. Instead, our findings support the view that institutional conditions modify preferences and behaviour. Our results also underline that an institutional approach which focuses only on family policies is too narrow to explain differentials in childlessness and fertility patterns. It is essential that one adopts a life course perspective on the role of institutions in family formation; i.e., that one considers the different institutions which shape childbearing behaviour over a person's life course. This calls for both a broadening of the institutional approach beyond family policies, as well as a more detailed consideration of institutions beyond the concept of the welfare state. Such an approach would allow scholars to link individual behaviour and institutional conditions with greater confidence, and in ways that provide us with a deeper understanding of childbearing decisions and of the variation in fertility patterns across social groups and across countries.

Acknowledgement The authors want to express their indebtedness to Britta Hoem, who started the line that we pursue in this paper, but did not live to develop her ideas into empirical research. We are grateful for financial support from the Swedish Research Council (Vetenskapsrådet) via the Linnaeus Center on Social Policy and Family Dynamics in Europe (SPaDE), grant 349-2007-8701, and the Swedish Initiative for Research on Microdata in the Social and Medical Sciences (SIMSAM), grant 340-2013-5164.

Literature

Andersson, G., Rønsen, M., Knudsen, L.B., Lappegård, T., Neyer, G., Skrede, K., Teschner, K., & Vikat, A. (2009). Cohort fertility patterns in the Nordic countries. *Demographic Research, 20*, 313–352. http://www.demographic-research.org/volumes/vol20/14/20-14.pdf

Bagavos, C. (2010). Education and childlessness: The relationship between educational field, educational level, employment and childlessness among Greek women born in 1955–59. *Vienna Yearbook of Population Research, 8*, 51–75.

Becker, G. S. (1960). An economic analysis of fertility. In National Bureau of Economic Research (Ed.), *Demographic and economic change in developed countries. A conference of the Universities-National Bureau Committee for Economic Research* (pp. 209–240). Princeton: Princeton University Press.

Begall, K., & Mills, M. (2012). The influence of educational field, occupation, and occupational sex segregation on fertility in the Netherlands. *European Sociological Review, 31*, 720–742.

Bergqvist, C., & Nyberg, A. (2002). Welfare state restructuring and child care in Sweden. In S. Michel & R. Mahon (Eds.), *Child care policy at the crossroads. Gender and welfare state restructuring* (pp. 287–308). New York/London: Routledge.

Bergqvist, C., Borchorst, A., Christensen, A.-D., Ramstedt-Silén, V., Raaum, N. C., Styrkársdóttir, A. (Eds.). (1999). *Equal democracies? Gender and politics in the Nordic countries*. Oslo: Scandinavian University Press.

Biffl, G. (1997). Schule – Wirtschaft – Frauen. In L. Lassnig & A. Paseka (Eds.), *Zum Geschlechterverhältnis im Bildungswesen* (pp. 234–239). Innsbruck: Studienverlag.

Blossfeld, H.-P., & Huinink, J. (1991). Human capital investment or norms of role transition? How women's schooling and career affect the process of family formation. *American Journal of Sociology, 97*, 143–168.

Cigno, A. (1991). *Economics of the family*. Oxford: Clarendon Press.

Cookingham, M. E. (1984). Bluestockings, spinsters and pedagogues: Women college graduates, 1985–1910. *Population Studies, 38*, 349–364.

Culpepper, P. D. (2007). Small states and skill specificity. Austria, Switzerland, and interemployer cleavages in coordinated capitalism. *Comparative Political Studies, 40*, 611–637.

Duvander, A.-Z., & Ferrarini, T. (2010). Earner-carer model at the crossroads: Reforms and outcomes of Sweden's family policy in comparative perspective. *International Journal of Health Services, 40*, 373–398.

Elster, J. (1991). Rationality and social norms. *Archive Européenne de Sociologie, 32*, 109–129.

Erikson, R., & Jonsson, J. O. (1996). The Swedish context: Educational reform and long-term change in educational inequality. In R. Erikson & J. O. Jonsson (Eds.), *Can education be equalized? The Swedish case in comparative perspective* (pp. 65–93). Boulder: Westview Press.

Esping-Andersen, G. (1990). *The three worlds of welfare capitalism*. Princeton: Princeton University Press.

Estévez-Abe, M. (2005). Gender bias in skills and social policies. The varieties of capitalism perspective on sex segregation. *Social Politics, 12*, 180–215.

Estévez-Abe, M., Iversen, T., & Soskice, D. (2001). Social protection and the formation of skills. A reinterpretation of the welfare state. In P. Hall & D. Soskice (Eds.), *Varieties of capitalism. The institutional foundation of comparative advantage* (pp. 143–184). Oxford: Oxford University Press.

Fischer-Kowalski, M. (1985). *Bildung. Bericht über die Situation der Frau in Österreich. Frauenbericht 1985*. Band 2. Wien: Bundeskanzleramt.

Graf, L., Lassning, L., & Powell, J. (2012). Austrian corporatism and institutional change in the relationship between apprenticeship training and school-based VET. In M. Busemeyer & C. Trampusch (Eds.), *The political economy of collective skill formation* (pp. 150–178). Oxford: Oxford University Press.

Gustafsson, S. (2001). Optimal age at motherhood. Theoretical and empirical considerations on postponement of maternity in Europe. *Journal of Population Economics, 14*, 225–247.

Hakim, C. (2000). *Work-lifestyle choices in the 21st Century. Preference theory*. Oxford: Oxford University Press.

Hall, P., & Soskice, D. (Eds.). (2001). *Varieties of capitalism. The institutional foundation of comparative advantage*. Oxford: Oxford University Press.

Halldén, K. (2008). The Swedish educational system and the ISCED-97. In S. Schneider (Ed.), *The International Standard Classification of Education. An evaluation of content and criterion validity in 15 European countries* (pp. 253–267). MZE: Mannheim.

Henz, U. (2001). Family formation and participation in higher education: cross-cutting life events? In J. O. Jonsson & C. Mills (Eds.), *Cradle to grave. Life-course change in modern Sweden* (pp. 45–69). Durham: Sociology Press.

Hobcraft, J., & Kiernan, K. (1995). *Becoming a parent in Europe*. Welfare state program discussion paper series No. 116. London: Suntory and Toyota International Centres for Economics and Related Disciplines.

Hoem, J. M., Neyer G., & Andersson, G. (2006). Education and childlessness. The relationship between educational field, educational level, and childlessness among Swedish women born in 1955–59. *Demographic Research, 14*, 331–380. http://www.demographic-research.org/volumes/vol14/15/14-15.pdf

Hoem, J. M., Prskawetz, A., & Neyer, G. (2001). Autonomy or conservative adjustment? The effect of public policies and educational attainment on third births in Austria. *Population Studies, 55*, 249–261.

Jensen, R. (1973). Family, career, and reform. In M. Gordon (Ed.), *The American family in social-historical perspective* (pp. 267–280). New York: St. Martin's Press.

Jonsson, J. O. (1999). Explaining gender differences in educational choice: An empirical assessment of a rational choice model. *European Sociological Review, 15*, 391–404.

Kantorova, V. (2004). Education and entry into motherhood. The Czech Republic during state socialism and the transition period (1970–1997). In G. Andersson & G. Neyer (Eds.), *Contemporary research in European fertility. Perspectives and developments* (pp. 246–270). Demographic Research. Special Collection 3, http://www.demographic-research.org/special/3/10/s3-10.pdf

Katzenstein, P. (1985). *Small states in world politics*. Ithaca: Cornell University Press.

Kiernan, K. (1989). Who remains childless? *Journal of Biosocial Science, 21*, 387–398.

Korpi, W. (2000). Faces of inequality. Gender, class, and patterns of inequality in different types of welfare states. *Social Politics, 7*, 127–189.

Korpi, W., de Graaf, P., Hendrickx, J., & Layte, R. (2003). Vocational training and career employment. Precariousness in Great Britain, the Netherlands and Sweden. *Acta Sociologica, 46*, 17–30.

Kravdal, Ø. (2001). The high fertility of college educated women in Norway. An artifact of the separate modeling of each parity transition. *Demographic Research, 5*, 187–216. http://www.demographic-research.org/volumes/vol5/6/5-6.pdf

Kreyenfeld, M. (2004). Fertility decisions in the FRG and GDR. An analysis with data from the German Fertility and Family Survey. In G. Andersson & G. Neyer, (Eds.), *Contemporary research in European fertility. Perspectives and developments* (pp. 275–318). Demographic Research. Special Collection, 3. http://www.demographic-research.org/special/3/11/s3-11.pdf

Lappegård, T., & Rønsen, M. (2005). The multifaceted impact of education in entry into motherhood. *European Journal of Population, 21*, 31–49.

Lassnig, L. (2013). Austria's success on the youth labour market – not systematic but voluntaristic. *Lifelong Learning in Europe (LLineE)*, http://www.lline.fi/en/article/policy/20135/what-are-they-doing-right-3-cases#title0

Lassnig, L., & Paseka, A. (Eds.). (1997). *Zum Geschlechterverhältnis im Bildungswesen.* Innsbruck: Studienverlag.

Leitner, S. (2003). Varieties of familialism. *European Societies, 5*, 353–375.

Lindahl, L. (2011). Improving the school-to-work transition for vocational students – what can we learn from research? Swedish Institute for Social Research (SOFI), Working Paper 13/2011.

Marten, C., Neyer, G., & Ostner, I. (2012). Neue soziale Risiken, neue Politiken – Familienpolitischer Wandel in Deutschland, Österreich und der Schweiz. In H. Bertram & M. Bujard (Eds.), *Soziale Welt. Sonderband 19. Zeit, Geld, Infrastruktur. Zur Zukunft der Familienpolitik* (pp. 115–138).

Martín-García, T., & Baizan, P. (2006). The impact of the type of education and of educational enrolment on first births. *European Sociological Review, 22*, 259–275.

Maul, K. (2012). *Der Einfluss der beruflichen Tätigkeit auf die Familiengründung.* Würzburg: Ergon Verlag.

Michelmore, K., & Musick, K. (2014). Fertility patterns of college graduates by field of study, US women born 1960–79. *Population Studies, 68*, 359–374.

Neyer, G. (2003). Family policies and low fertility in Western Europe. *Journal of Population and Social Security (Population)*, 1, Supplement: 46–93, http://www.ipss.go.jp/webj-ad/webjournal.files/population/ps03_06.asp

Neyer, G. (2009). Bildung und Kinderlosigkeit in Österreich und in Schweden. *Zeitschrift für Familienforschung, 21*, 286–309.

Neyer, G. (2010). Familienpolitik in Österreich zwischen Beharrung und Veränderung. *Revue d'Allemagne et des pays de langue allemande, 42*, 57–70.

Neyer, G., & Hoem, J. M. (2008). Education and permanent childlessness: Austria vs. Sweden. A research note: In J. Surkyn, P. Deboorsere, & J. Van Bavel (Eds.), *Demographic challenges for the 21st century. A state of the art in demography* (pp. 91–112). Brussels: VUP Press.

Neyer, G., Hoem, J. M., & Andersson, G. (2013). Kinderlosigkeit, Bildungsrichtung und Bildungsniveau. Ergebnisse einer Untersuchung schwedischer und österreichischer Frauen der Geburtenjahrgänge 1955–59. In D. Konietzka & M. Kreyenfeld (Eds.), *Ein Leben ohne Kinder. Ausmaß, Strukturen und Ursachen von Kinderlosigkeit* (pp. 101–135). Wiesbaden: Springer VS.

Obinger, H., & Tálos, E. (2010). Janus-faced developments in a prototypical Bismarckian welfare state. Welfare reforms in Austria since the 1970s. In B. Palier (Ed.), *A long goodbye to Bismarck? The politics of welfare reform in continental Europe* (pp. 101–128). Amsterdam: Amsterdam University Press.

Oláh, L. S., & Bernhardt, E. (2008). Sweden: Combining childbearing and gender equality. *Demographic Research, 19*, 1105–1144. http://www.demographic-research.org/volumes/vol19/28/19-28.pdf

Oláh, L. S., & Hobson, B. (2006). Birthstrikes? Agency and capabilities in the reconciliation of employment and family. *Marriage and Family Review, 39,* 197–227.

Ohlsson-Wijk, S. (2015). *Family formation at the turn of the new millenium* (Stockholm University Demography Unit Dissertation Series 13). Stockholm: Acta Universitatis Stockholmiensis.

Oppenheimer, V. K. (1994). Women's rising employment and the future of the family in industrial societies. *Population and Development Review, 20,* 293–342.

Prskawetz, A., Sobotka, T., Buber, I., Engelhardt, H., & Gisser, R. (2008). Austria: Persistent low fertility since the mid-1980s. *Demographic Research, 19,* 293–360. http://www.demographic-research.org/volumes/vol19/12/19-12.pdf

Rindfuss, R. R., & Bumpass, L. L. (1976). How old is too old? Age and the sociology of fertility. *Family Planning Perspectives, 8,* 226–230.

Rindfuss, R. R., Morgan, S. P., & Offutt, K. (1996). Education and the changing age pattern of American fertility: 1963–1989. *Demography, 33,* 277–290.

Rösler, W. (2012). *Strukturwandel und Fertilität. Wie die höhere Berufsbildung der Frau die Geburtenrate beeinflusst. Quantitative Analysen im Zeitverlauf des „zweiten demografischen Übergangs",* Dissertation. Humboldt University, Berlin.

Rønsen, M., & Skrede, K. (2010). Can public policies sustain fertility in the Nordic countries?. *Demographic Research 22,* 321–346. http://www.demographic-research.org/Volumes/Vol22/13/22-13.pdf

Seidl, M. (1993). *Einkommensunterschiede zwischen Männern und Frauen im Bundesdienst.* Wien: Wirtschaftsuniversität (Diplomarbeit).

Smyth, E. (2003). Gender differentiation and early labour market integration across Europe. In I. Kogan & W. Müller (Eds.), *School-to-work transitions in Europe: Analyses of the EU LFS 2000 Ad Hoc Module* (pp. 55–88). Mannheim: Mannheimer Zentrum für Europäische Sozialforschung.

Statistik Austria. (2014). *Kindertagesheimstatistik 2013/2014.* Wien.

Surkyn, J., & Lesthaeghe, R. (2004). Value orientation and the second demographic transition (SDT) in Northern, Western and Southern Europe: An update. In G. Andersson & G. Neyer (Eds.), *Contemporary research on European fertility: Perspectives and developments. Demographic Research. Special Collection* 3 (pp. 43–86). http://www.demographic-research.org/special/3/3/s3-3.pdf

Tesching, K. (2012). *Education and fertility. Dynamic interrelations between women's educational level, educational field and fertility in Sweden.* (Stockholm University Demography Unit Dissertation Series 6). Stockholm: Acta Universitatis Stockholmiensis.

van Bavel, J. (2010). Choice of study discipline and the postponement of motherhood in Europe: The impact of expected earnings, gender composition, and family attitudes. *Demography, 47,* 439–458.

van de Kaa, D. J. (1996). Anchored narratives: The story and findings of half a century of research into the determinants of fertility. *Population Studies, 50,* 389–432.

Chapter 10
Childlessness and Fertility Dynamics of Female Higher Education Graduates in Germany

Hildegard Schaeper, Michael Grotheer, and Gesche Brandt

10.1 Introduction

This paper examines the process of family formation, defined as the birth of the first child, of female higher education graduates belonging to different graduate cohorts. Focusing on this particular population allows us to take a closer look at a phenomenon which, although known to exist for some time, has only recently started to receive significant attention in the media and in research: namely, the declining and low birth rates among women with a higher education degree.

For a long time, exact figures for Germany on the proportion of female graduates who were permanently childless were not available. The number of actual births among this group was first recorded by the microcensus of 2008, which provides a more accurate picture of childlessness among women than was previously available (Pötzsch 2010). Analyses of these data have concluded that the share of female graduates who are childless is 29.5%, and far higher than the 19.5% share among other women. There is little indication that this difference is chiefly attributable to a lower desire for children among university graduates. Although there is some evidence suggesting that female higher education graduates are slightly less likely than women with lower educational levels to want children (Dorbritz and Ruckdeschel 2013), and that they have a tendency to subordinate this desire to other aspirations (Passet 2011), women of different educational levels vary much less in their desire to have children than in their actual childbearing. In other words, the gap between

The more detailed German version of this paper was published under the title "Familiengründung von Hochschulabsolventinnen. Eine empirische Untersuchung verschiedener Examenskohorten" (Schaeper et al. 2013).

H. Schaeper (✉) • M. Grotheer • G. Brandt
German Centre for Higher Education Research and Science Studies, Deutsches Zentrum für Hochschul- und Wissenschaftsforschung (DHZW), Hanover, Germany
e-mail: schaeper@dzhw.eu; grotheer@dzhw.eu; g.brandt@dzhw.eu

M. Kreyenfeld, D. Konietzka (eds.), *Childlessness in Europe: Contexts, Causes, and Consequences*, Demographic Research Monographs, DOI 10.1007/978-3-319-44667-7_10

desire and reality is especially large among highly educated women (Eckhard and Klein 2012).

Both theoretical analyses and empirical studies have pointed out a number of factors which explain why large shares of German women are failing to realise their desire to have children, e.g., the lack of childcare options (especially in western Germany), the lack of a partner (especially among highly qualified women), and the growing significance of paid employment. Whereas in the past a woman's life course tended to be organised predominantly around the family, the social institutions central to the typical female life course now also include career and the labour market. Decisions in one of these spheres are not made in isolation, but depend on developments, decisions, aspirations, and structures in the other sphere.

Thus, in this paper we investigate how and to what extent employment and the labour market affect the transition to motherhood among higher education graduates. Based on theoretical considerations presented in Sect. 10.2, we examine these questions empirically using the graduate studies undertaken by the German Centre for Higher Education Research and Science Studies (DZHW). In Sect. 10.3, we provide further information on these datasets and on the applied statistical methods and variables. The results of the empirical analyses are presented in two parts in Sect. 10.4. First, we examine the process of family formation from the age of 14 onwards. Second, we examine in detail the relationship between occupational career and family formation, focusing exclusively on the period after the first degree was awarded.

10.2 Theoretical Basis

10.2.1 General Theoretical Assumptions from a Life Course Perspective

The analysis of the transition to motherhood is based on life course theory. According to this perspective, actions which are biographically significant and associated with status changes are, like all actions, embedded in the life course and have multiple time references. Such actions take place in the present and are shaped by the current context. But they also refer both subjectively ("in-order-to motives", Schütz 1971: 80) and objectively (intended and unintended consequences) to the future, and in particular to the past: i.e., to biographical experiences, accumulated resources, and decisions and circumstances of the preceding life history. These factors shape biographies and subjectively prompt action ("because motives", ibid.).

From a diachronous perspective, the life course resembles a sequence of events, states, or status passages. However, in view of the multidimensional nature of life courses or their synchronous integration in several life domains, it is more appropriate to follow René Levy's (1996: 73) conceptualisation of the life course as a "sequence of participation-position-role configurations." Assuming further that developments in various areas of life are interdependent (Huinink 1995: 154), family formation can be regarded as a process which depends on the woman's occupational career, as well as other factors, such as her educational and union history.

Furthermore, the life course is part of a social multi-level process (Huinink 1995: 154–155). The actors are situated at the micro level, where they act in relation to their individual, but nonetheless collectively shaped aspirations and preferences; as well as in response to the prevailing opportunities and restrictions. The conceptualisation of these actions as rational—i.e., driven by cost-benefit deliberations and the objective of maximising utility—has become a dominant paradigm in analyses and explanations of fertility decisions. Empirical studies have indicated that the model of rational action has, indeed, a role to play in explaining behaviour (Schaeper and Kühn 2000) and that especially among female graduates family formation is to a large extent the result of a deliberate process of planning, decision-making, and evaluation (Herlyn et al. 2002). In this process, women weigh not only the direct economic costs and the psychological costs (e.g., stress, emotional burdens) of having children, but also the indirect (opportunity) costs, which are related to the forgone benefits of alternative uses of time (e.g., time spent in employment). Women may also consider the benefits of having children: While in modern societies children are seldom seen as sources of income or old-age insurance, they are especially thought to provide psychological and emotional benefits (e.g., personal fulfilment, life enrichment, affection).

When choosing a course of action, individuals refer to their immediate social context; i.e., to partners, peers, and members of their family of origin. This implies, for example, that actors are required to coordinate their life course, decisions, and plans with those of other people ("linked lives"). Furthermore, the individual's actions are embedded in a regional context which provides a variety of opportunity structures (e.g., labour market opportunities, childcare options) and socio-cultural orientation patterns. Finally, actions are framed by the structural and cultural conditions of the society through generally applicable opportunity structures, overarching norms, and interpretive schemes; as well as through largely binding institutions, such as school/university, labour market/occupation, and family.

10.2.2 Specific Assumptions About the Transition to Motherhood Among Female Higher Education Graduates

The effects of general structural and cultural changes on the timing of family formation and the extent of childlessness are usually assessed by taking the birth year as a proxy variable. Several studies (e.g., Blossfeld and Rohwer 1995) have demonstrated that the transition to motherhood was taking place at progressively higher average ages among women born after the middle of the twentieth century. Accordingly, we would also expect a trend towards fertility postponement among higher education graduates. However, the graduate cohorts included in our study represent only a relatively short historical period. Furthermore, Blossfeld and Rohwer (1995) found that the cohort effect disappears entirely if educational participation is controlled for. Given the brevity of the historical observation window and the small degree of variability in terms of both the participation in and the duration of education among the graduate cohorts studied, we expect to see only slight cohort differences.

The studies which have investigated the influence of participation in education on family formation have all found that the transition to motherhood is unlikely to take place as long as the prospective mother is in education (e.g., Blossfeld and Rohwer 1995; Schröder and Brüderl 2008; Buhr et al. 2011; Maul 2012). Research has shown that since 1991 the share of higher education students who have children has been around 6–7 % (Middendorff 2008). There are two main reasons why so few students have children. First, because of insufficient economic resources family formation during education appears to be inopportune (Huinink 1995). Second, most young people do not occupy themselves with family-related questions while in education, as they are concentrating on education-related biographical tasks (ibid.). If students give any thought to such matters, they generally associate family formation with high opportunity costs and competing demands on their time. Education calls for a large investment of time, and is therefore difficult to reconcile with family commitments (ibid.). Students who have children, and especially female students, can expect to take longer to complete their education, or may even be forced to drop out (Middendorff 2008; Heublein et al. 2010). As dropping out of education can have far-reaching negative implications for an individual's future income and career opportunities, having children while in education can give rise to high indirect costs.

These general observations apply to the social conditions prevailing in the Federal Republic of Germany (FRG). We therefore expect to find a significantly reduced inclination towards childbearing during the period of study among both western German respondents and eastern German study participants of the more recent cohorts. It should be noted, however, that the policies of the German Democratic Republic (GDR) attenuated the resource, compatibility, and prospects problems, and, according to Huinink (2000: 216), may have even incentivised starting a family early. In the GDR, several measures were specifically designed to support female students with children. In addition, the financial burdens of supporting a child in the GDR were negligible given the low cost of living, the availability of affordable childcare and housing, and the financial security provided by scholarships, which were augmented by a child benefit (Leszczensky and Filaretow 1990). For these reasons, we can expect to find that the institution effect was much less pronounced among eastern German female higher education graduates who belong to earlier graduate cohorts and began their studies before 1990 or shortly thereafter than among their western German counterparts.

Comparisons of the family formation process and family forms in eastern and western Germany clearly illustrate that significant differences persist, even though alignment processes are taking place in many spheres (Goldstein et al. 2010). A larger proportion of eastern German than western German women have children, and easterners tend to make the transition to motherhood earlier than westerners (Buhr et al. 2011). However, the proportions of childless women who do not wish to become mothers, and perceptions concerning the ideal family size, have started to converge between east and west (ibid. 187). We therefore assume to find persisting differences, but also increasing similarities between the family formation behaviour of women of the more recent eastern German graduate cohorts and those of their western German counterparts.

Our hypothesis that behaviour patterns are converging is based on the fact that after German reunification, the "gender order" (Pfau-Effinger 1998) and institutional environment of western Germany were introduced in eastern Germany, implying a "structural incompatibility" or, at best, "sequential compatibility" of family and career (Dornseiff and Sackmann 2003). The hypothesis of the enduring difference is supported by the persistence of a specifically eastern German "gender culture". According to the prevailing role model of the "working housewife and mother", for example, a woman was expected to be in continuous full-time employment, with only brief interruptions for family leave, while simultaneously maintaining her traditional responsibilities in the home. The transfer of the western German gender order gave rise to a cultural lag in eastern Germany; i.e., the gender culture lagged behind structural change. According to the literature cited by Maul (2012), the "cultural heritage" of the GDR continues to exert an influence up to today.

For western Germany as well, we can assume that the cultural and social structures did not develop in parallel. The FRG's organisations and institutions of the welfare state, the labour market, and the family have long lagged behind the modern paradigm of womanhood—which is oriented towards independence, employment, and a "double conduct of life" (Pfau-Effinger 1998; Born 2001). This "structural lag" and corresponding "compatibility dilemma" especially applied to well-educated western German women with high career ambitions who consider the usual models for reconciling work and family life, such as taking career breaks and moving to part-time work, as being hardly compatible with their aspirations.

Because of this compatibility issue we can expect to find that a woman may postpone the decision about whether to have a family until the time-consuming process of establishing and consolidating a career, which calls for flexibility and mobility, has been completed; and that this postponement can easily lead to unintended or deliberate childlessness. In view of the resource problem and the problem of prospects, we, in addition, can assume that for a highly educated woman, having a stable and sustainable professional position may be seen as a prerequisite for making the transition to motherhood. We would therefore expect to find, for example, that having a permanent employment contract would positively influence the inclination to form a family. However, the results of empirical studies examining this hypothesis, which is based on educationally diverse samples, is ambiguous. Schmitt (2008) found on the basis of data from the German Socio-Economic Panel (GSOEP) that fixed-term contracts have a negative effect on the entry into motherhood. The analyses of Gebel and Giesecke (2009), on the other hand, indicated that having a temporary employment contract does not have an impact on the transition to

parenthood for either men or women; and Brose (2008) came to the same conclusion for women only.

However, according to the theory of the value of children proposed by Friedman
et al. (1994), insecurity or a lack of certainty concerning biographical prospects can
also have the opposite effect. To reduce uncertainty, women whose chances of having a stable professional career are poor could have children earlier and more frequently. This assumption is substantiated in family economics by the argument that,
for women with diminished career resources, the opportunity costs associated with
motherhood—i.e., the temporary loss of earnings and the long-term detrimental
impact on a career and social security—are relatively low. Both arguments imply
that a mismatch between occupational position and education, or the experience of
downward occupational mobility, tends to accelerate family formation; and that
having full-time gainful employment and an elevated professional position tends to
delay the transition to motherhood. It is, however, possible that the influence of
biographical prospects differs depending on educational attainment. Kreyenfeld
(2010) found, for instance, that perceiving the economic situation to be uncertain
and having concerns about job security has negative effects on family formation
among women with high levels of education, but positive effects among women
with lower levels of education.

Women's orientations regarding family and career generally are not directly
included in quantitative analyses because they are rarely measured before the start
of the process being examined. In many cases, researchers can use only rough indicators which are known to correlate with the phenomenon of interest, such as social
origin (see below), religious affiliation, educational attainment, or subject area. A
number of studies (e.g. Heine et al. 2005) have, for example, found that students
who pursue a degree in medicine or teaching tend to have a strong social orientation
and relatively weak career ambitions; whereas students who study law, business, or
economics tend to be highly materialistic and career-oriented. At the same time,
different types of degrees open up different career opportunities. These observations
suggest that family formation rates among graduates in different disciplines are
likely to vary considerably. Indeed, research conducted in other countries has shown
that the field of study is a better predictor of fertility behaviour than the level of
education (Neyer et al. in this volume). In light of sometimes competing theoretical
arguments and opposing effects of career orientations and resources in some fields
of study, it is difficult to put forward a hypothesis regarding the direction of the
differences.

Occupational careers continue to be influenced by social origin, irrespective of
the level of qualification attained. With respect to higher education graduates, studies have shown (e.g. Hemsing 2001) that parents' social status and education not
only have an indirect effect on career success of their children (resulting from the
association between choice of subject, higher education institution and social origin); they also have a direct, independent effect. In addition, the social position of
the family of origin exerts an influence on the children's career orientation, aspirations, and expectations. We can therefore assume—in line with previous studies

(Blossfeld and Rohwer 1995)—that graduates whose parents have a high social position are more likely than others to postpone family formation.

In recent years, a series of policy measures have been introduced which were designed to alleviate the resource, incompatibility and prospects problems, and thus to increase the birth rate. However, the impact of these policies may take one to two decades to become apparent (Bujard 2011: 37). We therefore do not expect to observe an effect of these measures on the cohorts of female graduates who are the subject of the present study.

10.3 Data and Methods

10.3.1 Data

The analyses of the family formation process among female higher education graduates are based on the panel studies of higher education graduates conducted by the German Centre for Research on Higher Education and Science Studies (*Deutsches Zentrum für Hochschul- und Wissenschaftsforschung*, DZHW). The DZHW graduate studies cover the entire range of subjects, and include all state-run and state-approved higher education institutions, with minor exceptions.

The survey programme currently spans six graduate cohorts with up to three panel waves. In the survey of the 1989 cohort (who graduated in winter semester 1988/1989 or summer semester 1989 from a higher education institution in the pre-unification territory of the Federal Republic of Germany), 2898 women were observed over an average period of 42 months after graduation. The survey of the 1993 cohort, which for the first time included graduates from eastern Germany, yielded data of 2617 women for an average period of 66 months after graduation. In the surveys of the 1997, 2001 and 2005 cohort, 2739 respectively 3307 and 3828 women were observed over an average period of 70 months after graduation. Finally, in the first and only survey to date of the 2009 cohort, 2980 female graduates who completed a bachelor's degree course were surveyed alongside 3418 female graduates who attended traditional courses which concluded with either a state examination, a *Diplom* degree, or a *Magister* degree. The observation period of this cohort covers an average of 14 months after graduation.

10.3.2 Approach and Method

In order to obtain a descriptive overview of the process concerned, the survival functions for all of the graduate cohorts were estimated using the Kaplan-Meier method. The multivariate analyses used techniques of event history analysis. We estimated exponential models assuming a constant rate over time. The time-dependence of the processes being analysed was taken into account by integrating time-varying covariates (such as current age and educational participation). First, we estimated separate models for eastern Germany and western Germany. Second, we tested the east-west effect in a joint model. All of the results presented here were preceded by a comprehensive examination of theoretically possible interaction effects. In the interests of parsimony and simplicity, only significant interaction effects were included in the final models. Since the DZHW surveys consist in part of disproportionately stratified random samples of graduates, the analyses were performed with Stata statistical software using sampling weights.

10.3.3 Model Specification

Two perspectives are adopted in the analysis of the transition to motherhood. The first strand of analysis looks at all of the graduate cohorts and examines the transition to motherhood from the age of 14 onwards. The process time is therefore the age of the woman. Because of their particular biographies, graduates who belonged to older birth cohorts (pre-1960 cohorts in the west and pre-1965 cohorts in the east) or who qualified for entry into higher education abroad were disregarded. After application of these selection criteria, the sample for the survival analyses consists of 16,233 western German and 3835 eastern German women. The following variables were included in the multivariate models:

Graduate Cohort For the most part, the graduate cohorts correspond to specific birth cohorts. In the vast majority of cases, the women in the 1989 graduate cohort were born between 1960 and 1964, and the women in the 1993 graduate cohort were born between 1965 and 1969. However, the subsequent graduate cohorts are somewhat less homogeneous in age. The 2009 cohort also includes graduates of the new, shorter bachelor's degree programmes. These bachelor's degree graduates are on average 2 years younger than the graduates of traditional degree courses. For reasons which will be explained later, the results for the 1989 and 2009 graduates are reported in the survival analyses only.

Participation in Education We use two indicators for measuring the effect of being in education: (1) the annually adjusted time-dependent variable "studying for a first degree" (labelled "in first degree course"), which assumes the value one for as long as the respondents meet this criterion (and the value zero upon completion of the first degree); and (2) the annually adjusted time-varying variable "pursuing further higher or professional education (after having completed the first degree)" (labelled "in further education"). Because the effects did not differ, studying for a doctoral degree, studying for a second degree, and participating in professional training were grouped together in this variable.

Subject of First Degree and Degree Type For the type of degree, university degrees are distinguished from degrees awarded by universities of applied sciences. For the subject or field of study, three groups are distinguished: (1) social work (universities of applied sciences), teaching, and human medicine; (2) law, business, and economics; and (3) all other subjects.

Parents' Education This variable is defined as the educational attainment of the higher status parent. It is represented by three dummy variables: (1) lower secondary school leaving certificate/no school leaving certificate; (2) intermediate school leaving certificate/higher education entrance qualification; and (3) higher education degree.

Regional Origin Women graduates who obtained their higher education entrance qualification in the western German federal states are compared with their counterparts from the eastern German states.

Age To control for the well-known non-monotonic, bell-shaped age dependence of the rates of entry into first motherhood, two time-varying age variables—log(current age−13) and log(45−current age)—are included.

The method of episode splitting is used to introduce time-varying covariates into the model. The process time is measured in annual intervals only, and the age variables are adjusted annually. The imprecise measurement of the process time may give rise to an underestimation of the events in the right-censored survey years. For this reason, the models of the first strand of analysis are estimated for the 1993, 1997, 2001, and 2005 cohorts only, as their observation windows are of similar length (number of cases: 9074 western German and 2284 eastern German female respondents providing data for all variables).

The second strand of analysis looks at higher education graduates of the years 1997, 2001, and 2005 who were childless when they finished their studies, and who were born after 1960 for western German women or after 1965 for eastern German women (number of cases: 6470 western German and 1866 eastern German study participants with complete data). The subject of this analysis is the transition to motherhood after graduation, with a focus on the impact of career development and employment situation. In this case, therefore, the process time starts with graduation, and is recorded on a monthly basis. The cohort 1989 and 1993 had to be excluded from the analyses because the questionnaires addressed only the current employment situation. The 2009 cohort was excluded because the observation window of 14 months was too short to allow us to adequately examine the influence exerted by the graduates' employment history and employment situation.

Career progression and the employment situation are represented by the following characteristics:

Economic Inactivity (time-dependent), which is contrasted with economic activity and takes on different values: (1) periods of economic inactivity before starting the first job or commencing further training or education ("transitional phase"), (2) further higher or professional education (further training phases, studying for a doctorate or second degree; labelled "further education"), (3) other periods of economic inactivity lasting no more than 3 months ("interruption of up to 3 months"), and (4) other periods of economic inactivity lasting more than 3 months ("interruption of more than 3 months"). Women in gainful employment who were simultaneously participating in education are deemed to be economically inactive during such periods; those who are formally participating in an apprenticeship or an internship were likewise classified as economically inactive.

Education-Job Mismatch at Labour Market Entry (time-constant variable "negative start"), which is given when the first employment position after graduation clearly had a lower status than is warranted by the graduate's educational qualifications (e.g., unpaid family worker; unskilled, semi-skilled, or skilled worker; lower or middle-grade civil servant; low-level employee).

Length of Time Between Graduation and First Permanent Employment Contract (time-constant variable "permanent contract"), for which we distinguish four categories: (1) no permanent contract throughout the entire observation period, (2) first permanent contract obtained in the first 12 months after completion of studies, (3) first permanent contract obtained in the second or third year after graduation, and (4) first permanent contract obtained at a later date.

Self-Employment (time-constant) with two categories: never self-employed, and self-employed at least once during the observation period.[1]

Full-Time Gainful Employment (time-varying), contrasted with part-time employment.

Career Development (time-varying), for which we distinguish between lateral career paths, upward mobility, downward mobility, and discontinuous career patterns. Career development is reconstructed by arranging the employment positions in a hierarchical order: Unpaid family workers; unskilled and semi-skilled workers (Level 1), skilled workers, lower and middle-grade civil servants, low-level employees (Level 2), skilled employees, self-employed individuals with a contract for services/fee contract (Level 3), academically qualified employees without managerial responsibility, high-grade civil servants (Level 4), academically qualified professional employees with intermediate managerial responsibility, self-employed professionals, senior civil servants (Level 5), executive employees, independent entrepreneurs (Level 6).

---

[1] Self-employment (excluding contracts for work and services and fee contracts) ranks among the types of employment which—at least during the initial period—entail a certain degree of biographical uncertainty, and which are, as a rule, very time-consuming. It is to be assumed that this time pressure also applies in periods preceding, and during interruptions of, self-employment. The self-employment variable was therefore included as a time-constant characteristic.

Upward and Downward Mobility are defined as a job change that was accompanied by an increase or a decrease in rank or position. The initial attainment of a higher ranking position following a mismatch between educational qualification and job status at the time of labour market entry is not, however, classified as an upward move. The time-varying dummy variables retained the value one if the first upward move (downward move) is followed by a second upward move (downward move), or the professional position is no longer subject to change. If a downward move was followed by a step up the career ladder, or an upward move was followed by a downward move, the career was thereafter deemed to be erratic; the variables "upward/downward move" and "downward/upward move" are coded one, irrespective of the subsequent career development. Lateral career paths are therefore employment histories with neither upward nor downward moves.

Employment Position (time-varying) based on the results of estimates using the multi-level ranking of occupational positions and for the sake of a clear presentation of results, a distinction is made between only two aggregated categories: the extreme levels 1, 2, and 6; and the intermediate ranks on the career ladder (levels 3, 4, and 5; compare the career levels described above).

Region of Work (time-varying). This variable distinguishes between the western German states, the eastern German states, and other countries.

Work Experience This control variable has to be included to ensure that for all time-constant variables of the employment history, the reference category consisted exclusively of women who were economically active at least once in the observation period.

Graduate Cohort, Subject Area and Type of Degree, Parents' Education, Age and Regional Origin These variables are constructed as described above.

All of the covariates of the employment history and career path that are designed as time-varying characteristics are adjusted on a monthly basis. Since the focus of the analysis of the transition to motherhood is on the moment of decision-making, consideration is given not to the graduate's current employment situation, but to the situation 9 months earlier.

10.4 Empirical Findings on the Transition to Motherhood of Higher Education Graduates

10.4.1 Family Formation in Different Cohorts

Figure 10.1 depicts the survival functions for different graduate cohorts, which provide information on the probability of the graduates remaining childless up to a given age. The graph reveals that there are relatively small differences between cohorts of western German female graduates. However, these differences become

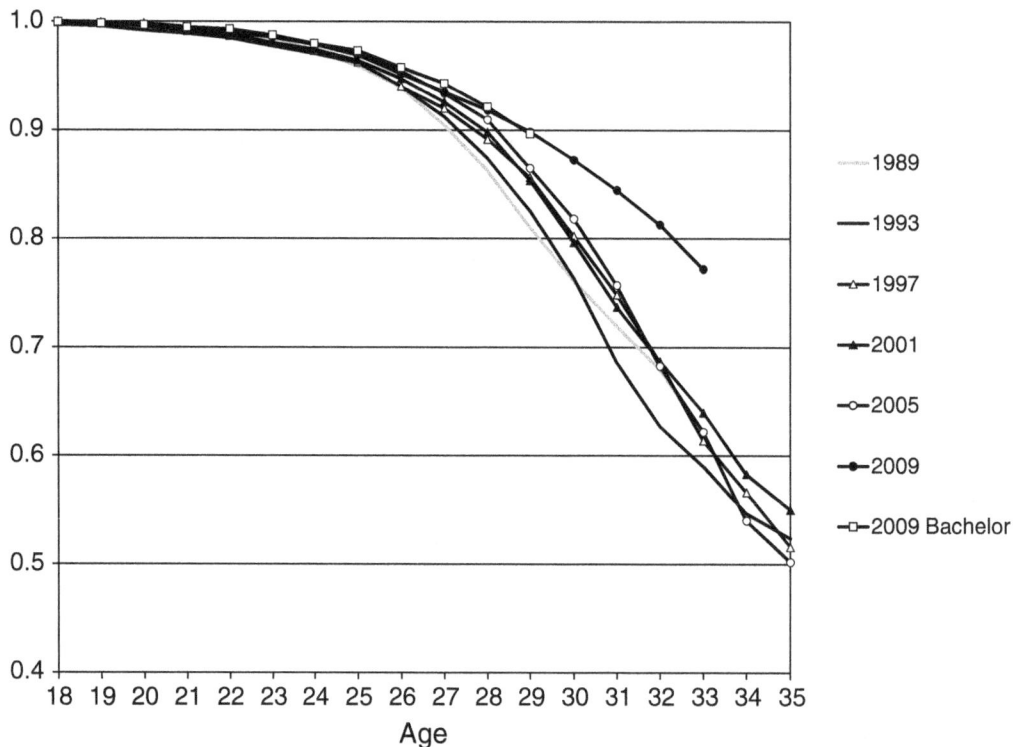

Fig. 10.1 The transition to motherhood of western German higher education graduates in different graduation cohorts (Kaplan-Meier survival function) (Source: DZHW graduate surveys 1989–2009)

pronounced for the 1997 cohort onwards. Almost 25 % of the "quickest" graduate cohorts—namely, those of 1989 and 1993, for whom the survival functions do not differ significantly—had made the transition to motherhood up to the age of 30, and almost 40 % (1993 cohort) up to the age of 32. In the subsequent graduate cohorts, childbearing was increasingly delayed. In the cohorts 1997, 2001, and 2005, only around 20 % of the women had given birth to a child at the age of 30, and only around 30 % had made the transition to motherhood at the age of 32 (measured against the 1993 cohort, the differences are significant with an error probability of less than .05). The significantly delayed family formation of western German women who graduated from a traditional degree programme in 2009 is particularly striking. An estimated 80 % of them were still childless at the age of 32. We can assume, however, that the differences will be reduced once the observation period for the 2009 cohort more or less matches those currently available for the older cohorts.[2] In the 2009 cohort, no differences can be observed between western

---

[2] Given the imprecise process time, events which took place at the time of the survey (i.e., at right-censored ages) are underestimated. The second panel waves have shown that, at the ages which were right-censored at the time of the first survey, a series of further events (births) occurred. In addition, the number of births increased sharply in the observation period of the second panel waves. Since the 2009 cohort has been surveyed only once thus far, this means that, for instance, women who were 30 years old at the time of the first survey 1 year after graduation (2009 cohort)

German graduates with a traditional degree and with a bachelor's degree, despite the fact that the majority of women who earned a bachelor's degree subsequently undertook a further period of study.

The trend towards fertility postponement was stronger among higher education graduates in the eastern German states than among their western German counterparts (Fig. 10.2). Only the differences between the 2001 and 2005 cohorts are insignificant. It follows from this finding that, as expected, the first birth rates of eastern and western German graduates are becoming more similar. The changes which took place between the 1993 and 1997 cohorts are striking. Between these two cohorts the probability of giving birth to a first child by the age of 27 dropped from more than 30 % to 20 %. Between the 1997 and 2001 graduate cohorts, a further reduction of six percentage points can be observed. Despite the convergence of cohorts, the east-west differences within cohorts were highly significant for all cohorts. Among the eastern German bachelor's degree graduates in the 2009 cohort, who are even more likely than their western German counterparts to have undertaken a second course of study, family formation was a rare event in the observation period.

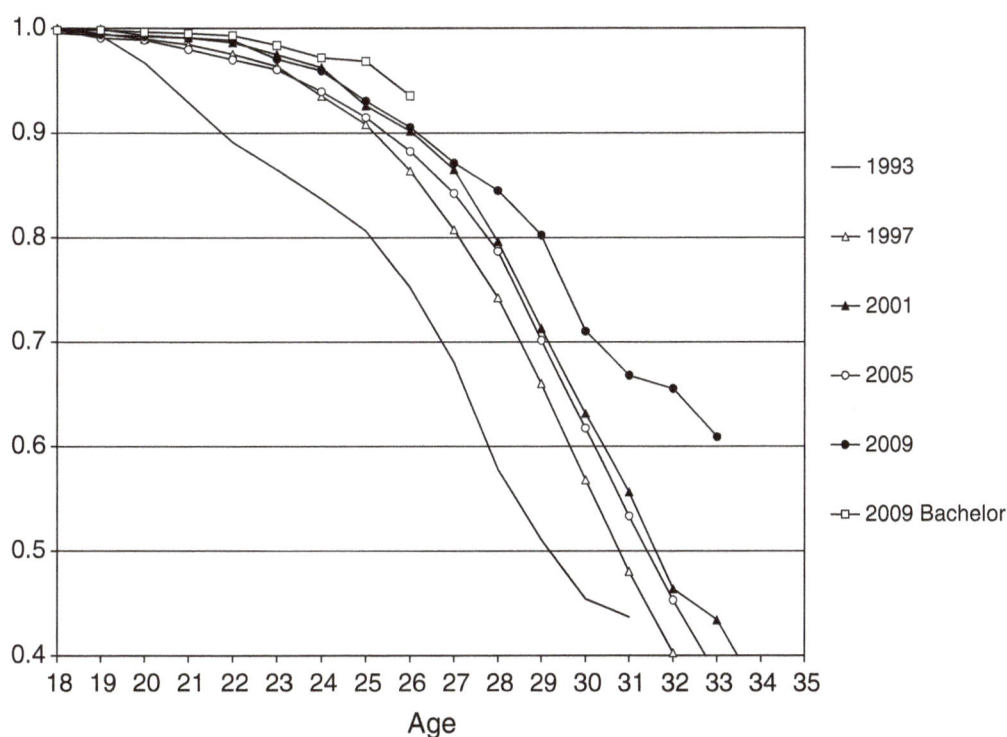

Fig. 10.2 The transition to motherhood of eastern German higher education graduates in different graduation cohorts (Kaplan-Meier survival function) (Source: DZHW graduate surveys 1993–2009)

had given birth to fewer children to date than women who were 30 years old at the time of the second survey 5 years after graduation (other cohorts). These considerations also apply, albeit to a lesser extent, to the 1989 cohort (average observation window of three and a half years). In view of these data artifacts, the 1989 and 2009 cohort were excluded from the multivariate models.

Table 10.1 The transition to motherhood of higher education graduates in different cohorts (exponential rate models), beta coefficients

	Western Germany Model I		Eastern Germany Model II		Combined Model III		Combined Model IV	
Graduate cohort (*ref.: 1993*)								
1997	−0.09		−0.01		−0.12	*	−0.09	
2001	−0.15	*	−0.24		−0.19	**	−0.18	**
2005	−0.15	*	−0.15		−0.17	**	−0.16	**
In first degree course[a] (*ref.: no*)	−0.67	**	−1.09	**			−0.72	**
In first degree course[a] × cohort 1993	−0.11		1.24	**				
In first degree course[a] × east × cohort 1993							1.19	**
In first degree course[a] × law/business/economics	−0.58	**	0.41				−0.32	
In further education[a] (*ref.: no*)	−0.47	**	−0.35	**			−0.44	**
Subject of first degree (*ref.: other subjects*)								
Teaching/medicine/social work (univ. of appl. sciences)	0.43	**	0.32	**			0.40	**
Law/business/economics	−0.06		−0.29	*			−0.11	
University degree (*ref.: awarded by univ. of appl. sc.*)	−0.05		0.27	**			−0.05	
University degree × east							0.34	*
Parents' education (*ref.: lower secondary school leaving cert./no school leaving cert.*)								
Intermediate school leaving cert./Higher education entrance qualification	−0.06		0.19				0.08	
Higher education degree	0.13	*	0.19				0.13	**
Log(age-13)[a]	5.41	**	4.32	**	5.42	**	5.08	**
Log(45-age)[a]	2.55	**	2.14	*	2.31	**	2.36	*
Regional origin eastern (*ref.: western*)					0.73	**	0.46	**
East × cohort 1993					0.41		0.02	
Constant	−25.03	**	−20.41	**	−24.42	**	−23.57	**
Cases	9074		2284		11,398		11,358	
Events	2979		1032		4022		4011	
Log likelihood initial model	−4650		−914		−5645		−5623	
Log likelihood final model	−2146		−312		−2700		−2473	

Source: DZHW graduate surveys 1993–2005

Note: [a] time-varying; * p < .05, ** p < 0.01

According to the multivariate analysis (Table 10.1, Model I) the cohort differences for western German graduates are similar to those estimated by survival analysis (only the difference between the 1993 and 1997 cohort is not significant). However, the marked differences between the eastern German graduates in the 1993 cohort and those in the later cohorts disappear (Table 10.1, Model II). This result is attributable to the conditional effect of studying which varied in eastern Germany with the year of graduation. While this institution effect is highly significant in the west and has the expected negative sign—indicating that the inclination to make the transition to motherhood is significantly reduced during a period of study—a similar effect in the east is observable only in the more recent graduate cohorts. As indicated by the highly positive interaction effect "in first degree course × cohort 1993", the institution effect among those in the 1993 graduate cohort—the majority of whom began their studies before German reunification—did not play a role. The second institution effect, which refers to a further phase of education after the first degree, is significant and negative for all eastern German graduates, but is less pronounced than among western German graduates.

As anticipated, graduates from different fields of study have very different family formation rates. Graduates in western and eastern Germany who earned a teaching or a medical degree, or a degree in social work awarded by a university of applied sciences, tend to make the transition to motherhood far sooner than graduates in other subjects. This result, which is in line with analyses of other datasets for Germany (Maul 2012) and for other countries (synoptic overview in Maul 2012, see also Neyer et al. in this volume), is found even without controlling for the birth-postponing effect of undertaking a further phase of education.

As we also expected, graduates of law, business, and economics have significantly lower transition rates. However, in western Germany the reduced inclination of these graduates to form a family exists only for the period of study for the first degree (see the negative and significant interaction effect "in first degree course × law/business/economics"). Once they have completed their studies, western German law, business and economics graduates give birth to their first child only marginally later than graduates of the study programmes grouped together in the reference category. However, the difference to graduates who studied social subjects remained significant. By contrast, among eastern German law, business, and economics graduates, the transition rates are a little higher during the period of study for the first degree, and are significantly lower afterwards. In this case as well, the family formation rates are much lower than among graduates of social subjects.

Contrary to our assumption that, given their greater career resources and aspirations, women from a family with a higher social status would postpone family formation to a greater extent, parents' qualifications actually produce only a slight and sometimes even an opposite effect among higher education graduates. For example, western German graduates born to parents with a higher education degree make the transition to motherhood slightly, but still significantly more often than other western German women.

In keeping with all of the other known studies, the age of higher education graduates has the expected non-monotonic effect on the family formation rate. This age dependence reflects a conglomeration of different factors which influence the timing of family formation. Apart from the biological limits of fertility, they include social and milieu-specific age conventions, the current state of career development (more on this below), and, finally, psychological preconditions. Personal maturity appears to be a major prerequisite for motherhood: for example, the reasons students give for not starting a family while studying include that they are "too young and inexperienced, and were still developing their personalities or finding their way in life", and are thus not yet "ready or able to accept the responsibility for a child" (Middendorff 2003: 22). The increasing participation in education may therefore have triggered an increasing postponement of family formation, not only because it is considered difficult or inopportune to have a baby while in education and training, but also because prolonged participation in education has contributed to an extension of adolescence.

Although the survival analyses detected an east-west difference in family formation among higher education graduates as well, they also showed that a partial alignment has taken place over time. This finding is confirmed by the multivariate analyses: higher education graduates from the eastern German federal states, even if they belong to the younger graduate cohorts (from 1997), continue to have their first child earlier than western German graduates (Table 10.1, Model III). The fertility behaviour of eastern and western German degree holders has, however, converged. As indicated by the positive interaction effect "east × cohort 1993", the east-west difference in the transition rate is significantly larger in the older graduate cohorts than in the more recent ones. To a large extent, however, this convergence is a result of a marked decrease in the inclination of women to make the transition to motherhood while in education. This insight was provided by the fourth estimation model, which took into account the fact that in the east the institution effect varies with the year of graduation, and therefore included the interaction "first degree × east × cohort 1993". In this model, the interaction effect "east × cohort 1993" was no longer significant. Once they had completed their studies, eastern German graduates belonging to the more recent graduate cohorts were not making the transition to motherhood any later than women in the older cohorts. Although the east-west effect itself was smaller in the combined model that included all of the variables (Table 10.1, Model IV), it remained significant at the one per cent level.

10.4.2 Family Formation and Employment History

Theoretical approaches which refer to one of the rational choice models of behaviour, and which posit that parenthood can be a strategy for reducing uncertainty, have suggested that because of economic uncertainty or lower opportunity costs associated with family formation, women with fewer career resources and opportunities have their first child earlier than women with good career and income prospects. This hypothesis is supported by our finding that the women in the sample of the western German degree holders who experienced downward occupational mobility or were unable to obtain a permanent employment contract were more inclined to start a family (Table 10.2, Model I). Also in line with these theoretical predictions is the finding that the transition to motherhood is delayed among women who have a very high professional position (level 6 on the career ladder). On the other hand, upwardly mobile women do not have lower transition rates than female higher education graduates with lateral employment paths. Interruptions of employment and a career start which do not match the graduates' level of education did not accelerate family formation. Women who have a low professional position do not have their first child earlier than those who were employed in a higher position. These findings tend to support the hypothesis that the reliability of both *career* and *economic* prospects is a precondition of motherhood for highly qualified women (Kreyenfeld (2010) reached a similar conclusion).

Even after the characteristics of the employment history and professional situation are controlled for, the analysis indicate that the 2001 and 2005 graduate cohorts had their first child a little bit later than the 1997 cohort; however, the effect was not always significant.

The overall effect of economic inactivity on the timing of the first birth is negative: employed women are the first to make the transition to motherhood. When looking at the reasons for interruptions in employment, we find that participation in education is the most important factor in the west. Among female higher education graduates from eastern Germany, however, this "institution effect" is considerably and significantly weaker. This is indicated by the interaction effect "further phase of education × east Germany" estimated in the combined model (Table 10.2, Model III). For eastern German graduates, participation in education do not delay family formation to the same extent as it do among western German women. The transition to motherhood is similarly unlikely to have taken place in the transitional phase between graduation and starting a first job or a further phase of education. Relatively brief periods of economic inactivity for other reasons do not significantly reduce the inclination to form a family, but prolonged interruptions in employment for other reasons have a strong negative effect.

It has been shown that the transition to fatherhood is not affected by uncertainty in the employment biography arising from temporary employment contracts (Tölke 2005; Schmitt 2008). For highly qualified women, the situation appears to be different. The transition to motherhood is fostered by both very insecure employment conditions (no permanent employment contract throughout the entire observation period) and an early stabilisation of the employment situation.

Our analysis shows that the sooner graduates from both western and eastern Germany are in permanent employment, the more likely they are to start a family. Family formation is also positively influenced by the attainment of an intermediate professional position. By contrast, self-employment, which generally entails a substantial time commitment and—at least in the initial start-up period—biographical uncertainties, exert a negative influence.

Furthermore, the transition rate is lower among western German women who are working full time 9 months before giving birth, possibly because of high opportunity costs. In the eastern German federal states, however, the number of hours female higher education graduates were working does not play a significant role. Compared with western German graduates, the family formation behaviour of eastern German women was less dependent on their career path and employment pattern. The east-west effect estimated in the combined model (Table 10.2, Modell III)

Table 10.2 The transition to motherhood after graduation in different cohorts: the effect of career development (exponential rate models), beta-coefficients

	Western Germany		Eastern Germany		Combined	
	Model I		Model II		Model III	
Graduate cohort (ref.: 1997)						
2001	−0.11		−0.22		−0.13	*
2005	−0.07		−0.12		−0.09	
Economic inactivity[a] (ref.: economic activity)						
Transitional phase	−1.25	**	−0.97	**	−1.18	**
Further education	−1.64	**	−0.88	**	−1.63	**
Interruption of up to 3 months	−0.29		−0.04		−0.24	
Interruption of more than 3 months	−1.03	**	−0.93	*	−1.00	**
Further education × east Germany					0.63	**
Negative start (ref.: no)	0.02		−0.23		0.04	
Permanent contract (ref.: never)						
Within 12 months after graduation	−0.28	**	−0.41	**	−0.31	**
2–3 years after graduation	−0.43	**	0.68	**	−0.5	**
Later	−1.00	**	−1.31	**	−1.06	**
Self-employment (ref.: no)	−0.31	**	−0.30		−0.30	**
Full-time employment[a] (ref.: part-time)	−0.25	**	0.06		−0.18	**
Intermediate occupational position[a] (ref.: levels 1, 2 & 6)	0.32	**	0.26		0.30	**
Career development[a] (ref.: no change)						
Upward move	0.15		0.05		0.13	
Downward move	0.33	*	−0.26		0.22	
Upward/downward move	0.17		0.69	*	0.28	
Downward/upward move	−0.12		0.32		0.01	
Region of work[a] (ref.: western Germany)						
Eastern Germany	0.47	**	0.31	**	0.33	**
Abroad	−0.21		−0.53		−0.29	
Subject of first degree (ref.: other subjects)						
Teaching/medicine/social work (univ. of appl. science)	0.41	**	0.17		0.35	**
Law/business/economics	0.02		−0.26		−0.05	
University degree (ref.: awarded by univ. of appl. science)	−0.07		0.23	*	−0.00	
Parents' education (ref.: lower secondary school leaving cert./no school leaving cert.)						
Intermediate school leaving cert./Higher education entrance qualification	0.16	**	0.04		0.14	*
Higher education degree	0.18	**	−0.10		0.15	*
log(age−13)[a]	7.08	**	1.67	**	6.29	**
log(45−age)[a]	3.96	**	—[b]		3.56	**
No work experience (ref.: work experience)	2.25	**	2.05	**	2.20	**

(continued)

Table 10.2 (continued)

	Western Germany		Eastern Germany		Combined	
	Model I		Model II		Model III	
Regional origin eastern Germany (ref.: western Germany)					0.42	**
Constant	−35.75	**	−9.24	*	−32.41	**
Cases	6470		1866		8336	
Events	1744		747		2491	
Log likelihood initial model	−4939		−1218		−6198	
Log likelihood final model	−4168		−1021		−5205	

Source: DZHW graduate surveys 1997–2005
Note: [a] time-varying, [b] not useful to estimate because of the small age range observed; * p < .05; ** p < .01

is significant even after controlling for all of the included career characteristics. In other words, the transition to motherhood among the female graduates from eastern Germany continues to be more natural and less dependent on the fulfilment of pre-conditions than among their western German counterparts.

In terms of career development, the effects of downward mobility are most notable: compared with other mobility patterns, western German graduates make the transition to motherhood much earlier if they experience a downward move without a subsequent or prior upward move. Among eastern German graduates, the transition to motherhood is more likely when a downward move was preceded by an upward move.

Finally, we comment on the region of employment. While being employed abroad tends to reduce the transition rate, the differences between working abroad and working in western Germany are not significant. For both eastern and western German female higher education graduates, economic activity in eastern Germany increase the inclination to start a family. It appears plausible that this finding is related to the more favourable opportunity structures in the east, especially the greater availability of public childcare.

Our empirical findings on the association among female higher education graduates in Germany between fertility behaviour on the one hand and the occupational career and the employment situation on the other are inconsistent with several theoretical explanations. They are not in line with arguments originating from family economics, the claim that family formation reduces uncertainty, or the argument that family formation depends on secure career and economic prospects. Instead, the results suggest that there is a more differentiated explanation for fertility behaviour: in the years immediately after graduating, women tend to focus on consolidating their career and securing their occupational and economic positions. In the current conditions, career-minded women—and, as a general rule, female graduates are career-oriented—risk the long-term impairment of their employment opportunities if they have a child before embarking on a career or entering permanent employment. In order to establish a career path that can be taken up again after family formation, women hold off on motherhood until they have attained a stable employment position. Only if there appears to be little or no prospect of consolidating and stabilising their employment situation—or if it seems unlikely that further postponement of family formation will result in the desired employment security—will graduates make the transition to motherhood more frequently and quickly.

10.5 Summary and Discussion

Adopting a multi-level life-course perspective and using quantitative analyses, this paper has examined the relationship between the fertility behaviour of highly qualified women and their educational and employment histories, as well as their current employment status and career situation.

Reflecting the general trend, we found that female higher education graduates were delaying the birth of their first child to an increasing extent. At first glance, the results for the 2009 graduate cohort, which suggest a considerably lower propensity to make the transition motherhood, were particularly striking. It is, however, important to note that the analyses were based on a very short observation period, and that the imprecise process time, which was measured in years, resulted in an underestimation of the family formation rate.

While we found that differences between the family formation processes of eastern and western German women persist, we also observed a convergence. However, the approximation was solely attributable to the behaviour of eastern German graduates who entered higher education after German reunification, and who were much less likely to have had their first child while enrolled in higher education. This institution effect played only a marginal role among eastern German higher education graduates who began their studies during the GDR era. However, for subsequent generations of students it appears to be as relevant as for western German students. As a consequence of this relationship of interdependence and mutual exclusion between participation in education and family formation, highly qualified women are not starting to plan a family until they reach an age when the most biologically opportune time for the transition to motherhood has already ended.

To some extent, the sharp decline in the inclination of eastern German students to start a family before graduating can be attributed to the increased opportunity costs of family formation while in education. As the forms of support provided to students with children in the GDR have been eliminated, and the financing of participation in higher education has become less secure, many student parents in eastern Germany now also have to shoulder not only the double burden of attending university and childcare, but often the triple burden of studying, raising a child, and having a job. The increased uncertainty of the career prospects of higher education graduates is likely another contributor to the cautious attitude towards starting a family among eastern German undergraduates. As they are no longer guaranteed a job upon graduating, they must prepare for the possibility of unemployment. Thus, students face an exacerbated resource problem which threatens the economic basis of family formation.

Despite the greater uncertainty of their career prospects, graduates from eastern Germany still make the transition to motherhood more quickly and frequently than western German higher education graduates. This finding can be explained by the persistence of the eastern German gender culture, in which working mothers and institutional childcare are viewed as normal, and by the greater availability of child-care in eastern Germany.

Qualitative analyses have shown that women's deliberations concerning family formation are shaped to a large extent by this question of how to reconcile work and family. They have also described how this compatibility problem can give rise to an ambivalent attitude among career-focused women, and ultimately to fertility post-ponement (Kühn 2004). A solution to the reconciliation issue is complicated not only by inadequate childcare services and the expectation that highly qualified employees will be flexible and mobile, but also by the prevailing labour market conditions governing career development. Part-time employment has negative con-notations, and is associated with a lack of commitment, availability, and motivation; as well as by a lack of professional or career ambition. It is not surprising, therefore, that women with elevated professional aspirations or abundant career resources postpone family formation, or even forego having children; or that, conversely, women reduce their career development efforts in anticipation of the transition to motherhood. This relationship between family formation on the one hand and pro-fessional ambition and career development and resources on the other was also reflected to some extent in our results on the fertility decisions of female higher education graduates. However, our findings also pointed to another, more important aspect of the timing of family formation: namely, the issue of career consolidation and the establishment of stable professional prospects. A woman's decision about if and when to make the transition to motherhood essentially depends on whether she has achieved a stable employment status and has been able to accumulate sufficient work experience. Only if these conditions are met is she likely to assume that her career ambitions can again be pursued after having a child. On the other hand, atten-tion may turn to family formation if over a prolonged period of time a women has had negative experiences in the labour market which indicate that her outlook for attaining stable employment is poor, and that attaining a secure and challenging occupation is likely to remain out of reach. Unless a highly qualified woman clearly prioritises having a family, the tendencies mentioned above, together with participa-tion in further qualification phases, may mean that family formation will not become a focal point of her biographical reflections until several years after graduation.

It remains to be seen whether family policy measures that have been adopted will have the desired impact on female degree holders as well, motivating and allowing them to have children earlier and more often. Given the very significant role career consolidation plays in shaping the fertility behaviour of women (and men), and the growing prevalence of fixed-term employment contracts (Rehn et al. 2011), a scep-tical view of the ability of family policy measures alone to halt or even reverse the trend towards the progressive postponement of family formation appears to be justified.

Literature

Blossfeld, H.-P., & Rohwer, G. (1995). West Germany. In H.-P. Blossfeld (Ed.), *The new role of women: Family formation in modern societies* (pp. 56–76). Boulder: Westview Press.

Born, C. (2001). Modernisierungsgap und Wandel. Angleichung geschlechtsspezifischer Lebensführungen? In C. Born & H. Krüger (Eds.), *Individualisierung und Verflechtung. Geschlecht und Generation im deutschen Lebenslaufregime* (pp. 29–53). Weinheim/München: Juventa.

Brose, N. (2008). Entscheidung unter Unsicherheit – Familiengründung und -erweiterung im Erwerbsverlauf. *Kölner Zeitschrift für Soziologie und Sozialpsychologie, 60,* 34–56.

Buhr, P., Huinink, J., Boehnke, M., & Maul, K. (2011). Kinder oder keine? Institutionelle Rahmenbedingungen und biographische Voraussetzungen für die Familiengründung und -erweiterung in Ost- und Westdeutschland. In J. Brüderl, L. Castiglioni, & N. Schumann (Eds.), *Partnerschaft, Fertilität und intergenerationale Beziehungen. Ergebnisse der ersten Welle des Beziehungs- und Familienpanels* (pp. 175–201). Würzburg: Ergon.

Bujard, M. (2011). *Familienpolitik und Geburtenrate. Ein internationaler Vergleich.* Berlin: BMFSFJ.

Dorbritz, J., & Ruckdeschel, K. (2013). Kinderlosigkeit – differenzierte Analysen und europäische Vergleich. In D. Konietzka & M. Kreyenfeld (Eds.), *Ein Leben ohne Kinder. Ausmaß, Strukturen und Ursachen von Kinderlosigkeit* (2nd ed., pp. 253–278). Wiesbaden: Springer VS.

Dornseiff, J.-M., & Sackmann, R. (2003). Familien-, Erwerbs- und Fertilitätsdynamiken in Ost- und Westdeutschland. In W. Bien & J. H. Marbach (Eds.), *Partnerschaft und Familiengründung. Ergebnisse der dritten Welle des Familien-Survey* (pp. 309–348). Opladen: Leske + Budrich.

Eckhard, J., & Klein, T. (2012). Rahmenbedingungen, Motive und die Realisierung von Kinderwünschen. Erkenntnisse aus dem westdeutschen Familiensurvey. In H. Bertram & M. Bujard (Eds.), *Zeit, Geld, Infrastruktur – zur Zukunft der Familienpolitik* (pp. 231–251). Baden-Baden: Nomos.

Friedman, D., Hechter, M., & Kanazawa, S. (1994). A theory of the value of children. *Demography, 31,* 375–401.

Gebel, M., & Giesecke, J. (2009). Ökonomische Unsicherheit und Fertilität. Die Wirkung von Beschäftigungsunsicherheit und Arbeitslosigkeit auf die Familiengründung in Ost- und Westdeutschland. *Zeitschrift für Soziologie, 38,* 399–417.

Goldstein, J., Kreyenfeld, M., Huinink, J., Konietzka, D., & Trappe, H. (2010). *Familie und Partnerschaft in Ost- und Westdeutschland. Ergebnisse im Rahmen des Projektes „Demographic Differences in Life Course Dynamics in Eastern and Western Germany".* Rostock: Max-Planck-Institut für demografische Forschung. http://www.demogr.mpg.de/publications\files\3988_1287680847_1_familie_und_partnerschaft_ost_west.pdf. Accessed 8 Aug 2014.

Heine, C., Spangenberg, H., Schreiber, J., & Sommer, D. (2005). *Studienanfänger in den Wintersemestern 2003/04 und 2004/05.* Hannover: HIS.

Hemsing, W. (2001). *Berufserfolg im Lebenslauf. Der Einfluss von Humankapitalinvestitionen, privaten Bindungen und Arbeitsmarktstrukturen auf den Berufserfolg ehemaliger Gymnasiasten.* Doctoral Dissertation, Universität Köln. http://kups.ub.uni-koeln.de/684/1/11w1431.pdf. Accessed 7 Aug 2014.

Herlyn, I., Krüger, D., & Heinzelmann, C. (2002). Späte erste Mutterschaft – erste empirische Befunde. In N. F. Schneider & H. Matthias-Bleck (Eds.), *Elternschaft heute. Gesellschaftliche Rahmenbedingungen und individuelle Gestaltungsaufgaben* (Sonderheft zur Zeitschrift für Familienforschung, Vol. 2, pp. 121–162). Opladen: Leske + Budrich.

Heublein, U., Hutzsch, C., Schreiber, J., Sommer, D., & Besuch, G. (2010). *Ergebnisse einer bundesweiten Befragung von Exmatrikulierten des Studienjahres 2007/08. Ursachen des Studienabbruchs in Bachelor- und in herkömmlichen Studiengängen.* Hannover: HIS.

Huinink, J. (1995). *Warum noch Familie? Zur Attraktivität von Partnerschaft und Elternschaft in unserer Gesellschaft.* Frankfurt/Main: Campus.

Huinink, J. (2000). Bildung und Familienentwicklung im Lebensverlauf. *Zeitschrift für Erziehungswissenschaft, 3,* 209–227.

Kreyenfeld, M. (2010). Uncertainties in female employment careers and the postponement of parenthood in Germany. *European Sociological Review, 26,* 351–366.

Kühn, T. (2004). *Berufsbiografie und Familiengründung. Biografiegestaltung junger Erwachsener nach Abschluss der Berufsausbildung.* Wiesbaden: VS Verlag für Sozialwissenschaften.

Leszczensky, M., & Filaretow, B. (1990). *Hochschulstudium in der DDR. Statistischer Überblick.* Hannover: HIS.

Levy, R. (1996). Zur Institutionalisierung von Lebensläufen. Ein theoretischer Bezugsrahmen. In J. Behrens & W. Voges (Eds.), *Kritische Übergänge. Statuspassagen und sozialpolitische Institutionalisierung* (pp. 73–113). Frankfurt/Main: Campus.

Maul, K. (2012). *Der Einfluss der beruflichen Tätigkeit auf die Familiengründung.* Würzburg: Ergon.

Middendorff, E. (2003). *Kinder eingeplant? Lebensentwürfe Studierender und ihre Einstellung zum Studium mit Kind* (HIS-Kurzinformation A, Vol. 4). Hannover: HIS.

Middendorff, E. (2008). *Studieren mit Kind. Ergebnisse der 18. Sozialerhebung des Deutschen Studentenwerks durchgeführt durch HIS Hochschul-Informations-System.* Bonn: Bundesministerium für Bildung und Forschung.

Passet, J. (2011). Kinderlosigkeit im Lebensverlauf: Wie wichtig ist das Lebensziel, Kinder zu bekommen, im Vergleich mit anderen Lebenszielen? *Bevölkerungsforschung Aktuell, 32,* 7–11.

Pfau-Effinger, B. (1998). Arbeitsmarkt- und Familiendynamik in Europa – Theoretische Grundlagen der vergleichenden Analyse. In B. Geissler, F. Maier, & B. Pfau-Effinger (Eds.), *FrauenArbeitsMarkt. Der Beitrag der Frauenforschung zur sozio-ökonomischen Theorieentwicklung* (pp. 177–194). Berlin: Edition sigma.

Pötzsch, O. (2010). Cohort fertility: A comparison of the results of the official birth statistics and of the Microcensus survey 2008. *Comparative Population Studies – Zeitschrift für Bevölkerungswissenschaft, 35,* 185–204.

Rehn, T., Brandt, G., Fabian, G., & Briedis, K. (2011). *Hochschulabschlüsse im Umbruch. Studium und Übergang von Absolventinnen und Absolventen reformierter und traditioneller Studiengänge des Jahrgangs 2009.* Hannover: HIS.

Schaeper, H., & Kühn, T. (2000). Zur Rationalität familialer Entscheidungsprozesse am Beispiel des Zusammenhangs zwischen Berufsbiographie und Familiengründung. In W. R. Heinz (Ed.), *Übergänge. Individualisierung, Flexibilisierung und Institutionalisierung des Lebensverlaufs* (Zeitschrift für Soziologie der Erziehung und Sozialisation, Beiheft 3, pp. 124–145). Weinheim: Juventa.

Schaeper, H., Grotheer, M., & Brandt, G. (2013). Kinderlosigkeit – differenzierte Analysen und europäische Vergleich. In D. Konietzka & M. Kreyenfeld (Eds.), *Ein Leben ohne Kinder. Ausmaß, Strukturen und Ursachen von Kinderlosigkeit* (2nd ed., pp. 47–80). Wiesbaden: Springer VS.

Schmitt, C. (2008). *Labour market integration and the transition to parenthood. A comparison of Germany and the UK.* (SOEPpapers on Multidisciplinary Panel Data Research No. 119). Berlin: Deutsches Institut für Wirtschaftsforschung. http://www.diw.de/documents/publikationen/73/diw_01.c.88337.de/diw_sp0119.pdf. Accessed 8 Aug 2014.

Schröder, J., & Brüderl, J. (2008). Der Effekt der Erwerbstätigkeit von Frauen auf die Fertilität: Kausalität oder Selbstselektion? *Zeitschrift für Soziologie, 37,* 117–136.

Schütz, A. (1971). Das Wählen zwischen Handlungsentwürfen. In A. Schütz (Ed.), *Gesammelte Aufsätze, Bd. 1: Das Problem der sozialen Wirklichkeit* (pp. 77–110). Den Haag: Nijhoff. English edition: Schütz, A. (1962). Choosing among projects of action. In A. Schütz (Ed.), *Collected papers 1: The problem of social reality*. The Hague: Nijhoff.

Tölke, A. (2005). Die Bedeutung von Herkunftsfamilie, Berufsbiografie und Partnerschaften für den Übergang zur Ehe und Vaterschaft. In A. Tölke & K. Hank (Eds.), *Männer – das, vernachlässigte 'Geschlecht in der Familienforschung* (pp. 98–126). Wiesbaden: VS Verlag für Sozialwissenschaften.

Part IV
Fertility Ideals, Biographical Decisions and Assisted Reproduction

Chapter 11
Fertility Ideals of Women and Men Across the Life Course

Anne-Kristin Kuhnt, Michaela Kreyenfeld, and Heike Trappe

11.1 Introduction

"Ich möchte niemals **Kinder** sind für mich das Größte" ("I do not want **children** are the most important thing to me") was a slogan of the insurance company Swiss Life in 2015. The slogan ridicules the volatility of people's preferences regarding children and family life. Having children may evolve from being a subordinate issue to being the focal point of attention in a person's life. In our paper, we explore the volatility of women's and men's fertility ideals across time. In particular, we examine how fertility ideals evolve as people age, how patterns differ by gender, and whether other factors—such as changes in an individual's partnership or employment domain—lead to changes in fertility ideals. Our study contributes to the large body of literature that has explored different concepts of fertility desires and intentions in Germany (e.g., Buhr and Kuhnt 2012; Heiland et al. 2008; Keim et al. 2009; Kuhnt 2013; Kuhnt and Trappe 2013; Lutz et al. 2013; Marbach and Tölke 2013; Rost 2005; Ruckdeschel 2007), for other countries (e.g., Bernardi et al. 2015; Iacovou and Tavares 2011; Klobas and Ajzen 2015; Liefbroer 2009; Miller 2011;

A.-K. Kuhnt (✉)
Institute of Sociology, University of Duisburg-Essen, Duisburg, Germany
e-mail: anne-kristin.kuhnt@uni-due.de

M. Kreyenfeld
Hertie School of Governance, Berlin, Germany

Max Planck Institute for Demographic Research, Rostock, Germany
e-mail: kreyenfeld@hertie-school.org

H. Trappe
Institute of Sociology and Demographic Research, University of Rostock, Rostock, Germany
e-mail: heike.trappe@uni-rostock.de

© The Author(s) 2017
M. Kreyenfeld, D. Konietzka (eds.), *Childlessness in Europe: Contexts, Causes, and Consequences*, Demographic Research Monographs, DOI 10.1007/978-3-319-44667-7_11

Morgan 1982; Quesnel-Vallée and Morgan 2004; Spéder and Kapitány 2015; Thomson 1997; Thomson and Hoem 1998; Vignoli et al. 2013) or across countries (e.g., Balbo and Mills 2011; Kapitány and Spéder 2013; Philipov et al. 2006; Puur et al. 2008; Régnier-Loilier et al. 2011; Testa 2007; Testa and Basten 2014).

While there are a large number of studies on this issue, little research has been done on the stability of fertility preferences. Most of the existing literature on fertility preferences has focused either on short-term fertility intentions (e.g., Billari et al. 2009; Dommermuth et al. 2011; Goldstein et al. 2003; Gray et al. 2013; Hayford 2009) or on the extent to which fertility intentions are realised (e.g., Berrington and Pattaro 2014; Schoen et al. 1999; Spéder and Kapitány 2009, 2015; Toulemon and Testa 2005). In our study, we investigate how the fertility ideals of women and men in Germany of the cohorts 1971–73, 1981–83, and 1991–93 evolved over a 5-year period spanning 2008/2009–2013/2014. Thus, our study covers a longer time period than most previous research. Fertility preferences are measured using the following question: "Under ideal circumstances, how many children would you like to have?" The aim of this question is to survey personal fertility ideals, rather than societal family size ideals, which were, for example, surveyed in the Eurobarometer (Testa 2007). The concept of personal fertility ideals is also different from the concept of fertility intentions, which is usually measured by asking respondents about their concrete plans for having a child within a narrowly defined time frame of, for example, 2 years (Miller 2011; Thomson 2001). It is, however, related to the widely used concept of fertility desires, which is usually measured by asking respondents how many children they wish to have (Thomson 2001: 5347). Compared to fertility intentions, fertility desires or ideals are probably more stable across time (Miller 1994, 2011). This is particularly the case given the first part of our question: the qualifier "under ideal circumstances" prompts the respondents to disregard the current conditions. We test whether significant changes in a person's life, such as the loss of a job or of a partner, affect his or her fertility ideals. We also examine whether the birth of a child (or the lack thereof) leads a person to adjust his or her fertility goals upwards or downwards. Here we draw upon the psychological literature that shows that people tend to revise their long-term goals if they are unable to accomplish them. For the sake of readability, we use the terms "fertility ideals" and "fertility preferences" interchangeably. The paper is structured as follows. In Sect. 11.2, we provide the theoretical background and review prior research findings. In Sect. 11.3, we describe the data we use, which come from the German Family Panel (pairfam) and cover respondents of the birth cohorts 1971–73, 1981–83, and 1991–93. Furthermore, we present our method and analytical strategy in this section. In Sect. 11.4, we present our descriptive results. In Sect. 11.5, we discuss our findings from the multivariate analyses, which consist of a pooled OLS regression and fixed-effects modelling. The dependent variable is the respondent's ideal number of children, and the main covariates are the respondent's partnership status, employment status, and number of children. In Sect. 11.6, we discuss the implications of our findings.

11.2 Theoretical Considerations and Prior Findings

The life course has been described as a self-referential process within which an individual acts or behaves based on his or her prior experiences and resources (Mayer 2004). Values, convictions, and emotions are part of the internal opportunity structure that guides individual behaviour (Huinink and Feldhaus 2009). Fertility ideals can be seen as fundamental and quite general value orientations, or as expressions of family size norms (Iacovou and Tavares 2011; Thomson 2001). However, there is some debate among researchers about how stable such value orientations are across the life course. According to the socialisation hypothesis, convictions and values are formed in late childhood and adolescence, and remain relatively stable thereafter. These values can be viewed as the concepts and scripts that guide an individual's future life plans (Inglehart 1977), or as mere lifestyle preferences (Hakim 2003). Others have raised concern over the stability of preferences across the life course. A person's values measured at a given moment in time not only influences action, but that action affects attitudes, values, and aspirations. The only way researchers can separate the causal linkage between attitudes and behaviour is by using panel data (Lesthaeghe and Moors 2002).

An important behavioural model that is often employed in the study of fertility preferences is the model of reasoned action developed by Ajzen and Fishbein (Ajzen 1991; Fishbein and Ajzen 2010). This concept distinguishes between desires and intentions (e.g., Bühler 2012; Miller 2011; Thomson 2001). Desires are "internal factors", such as motivations, attitudes, and beliefs (Miller 1994: 228). If desires become more manifest, they materialise into intentions, which will in turn be translated into behaviour if conditions are favourable. In our study, we analyse "fertility ideals", which are not examined as a distinct category in the Ajzen and Fishbein model. While it is clear that ideals are not the same as intentions, it is important to note that although fertility ideals are related to fertility desires, ideals and desires are not identical. Thus, previous findings on the volatility of fertility intentions and fertility desires may not be transferable to the study of the volatility of fertility ideals. We assume that fertility ideals, as measured by the phrase in our survey question "under ideal circumstances", are more stable than intentions, because ideals do not depend on actual living conditions (Miller 2011). Thus, a change in partnership status or economic circumstances may lead to a change in fertility intentions, but not necessarily in fertility ideals. However, if the adaptation argument applies, we can assume that the individual's achieved biographical status will affect his or her fertility ideals, as a person's current circumstances rarely align with his or her initial ideal scenario. For example, a woman might increase her ideal number of children so that it corresponds with the number of children she already has. Miller and Pasta (1995) have suggested that the birth of a first child can trigger in the parent an increase in his or her positive motivations for childbearing, as there is a biological mechanism that enhances the parent's positive responses to the baby, and thus strengthens his or her desire to have another child. Fertility preferences may also be adjusted upwards if an individual has an unplanned birth, or if his or her children do not have the desired gender. These scholars have also posited that there are mechanisms that counterbalance this positive feedback loop, such as delays or negative motivations. Fertility ideals might be adjusted downwards if, for example, a woman who is growing older perceives that it is unlikely that her initial ideals will be fulfilled (Gray et al. 2013).

11.2.1 Previous Findings

Relatively few studies have examined the stability of fertility ideals, desires, or intentions. Of the studies on the evolution of fertility expectations that exist, the most comprehensive was conducted by Hayford (2009) for women in the US. Hayford's analysis of 10 years of panel data collected between 1979 and 1994 showed that women tend to have relatively stable fertility expectations across their life course. For Europe, longitudinal studies on the stability of fertility desires or intentions have been conducted for the United Kingdom, France, Germany, and the Netherlands (Buhr and Kuhnt 2012; Heiland et al. 2008; Iacovou and Tavares 2011; Liefbroer 2009; Ní Bhrolcháin and Beaujouan 2011; Ní Bhrolcháin et al. 2010). However, most of these studies covered only two survey waves, and thus did not examine the evolution of fertility preferences across a longer period of time. These studies also differed considerably in terms of the concepts they used to measure fertility preferences. For example, some used fertility desires, while others used fertility expectations or intentions in assessing the "ideal family size". Despite the many conceptual differences between these studies, the following commonalities emerge.

Demographic factors, and especially age, have been shown to influence the stability of fertility intentions across an individual's life course. Fertility preferences seem to decline with increasing age (Gray et al. 2013; Hayford 2009; Heiland et al. 2008; Ní Bhrolcháin et al. 2010). Buhr and Kuhnt (2012: 291) found for Germany that over a period of 1 year, women and men in their early thirties are more likely than women and men in their early twenties to adjust the number of children they expect to have. Using data from the Netherlands, Liefbroer (2009: 363) showed that among both women and men, there is a downward adjustment in fertility intentions with increasing age. Using British panel data, Ni Bhroichain et al. (2010: 14) and Iacovou and Tavares (2011: 119) found a similar pattern: i.e., that the expected family size declines with increasing age. An intervening variable in this context may be fecundity, which also declines over time. Individuals who realize that they are infecund may adjust their fertility preferences in recognition of their biological constraints (Heiland et al. 2008; Liefbroer 2009; Régnier-Loilier 2006).

There is also longitudinal evidence that having a child leads to changes in fertility preferences. Heiland et al. (2008: 150) found that the fertility expectations of parents increase after the birth of an additional child. Similarly, Iacovou and Tavares (2011: 119) found that having a child is associated with upward and downward revisions in fertility expectations. However, their findings did not indicate that the birth of a first child has a greater effect on expectations than a subsequent birth.

There is also consistent evidence that changes in the partnership domain of the life course lead to changes in fertility preferences (Buhr and Kuhnt 2012; Iacovou and Tavares 2011; Spéder and Kapitány 2009). Buhr and Kuhnt (2012: 288) found considerable changes in the fertility intentions of men and women whose partnership situation had changed in the preceding year. Meanwhile, Hayford (2009: 777) found that married women have more stable fertility expectations than women who are single. Similarly, Heiland et al. (2008: 148) found that divorce or separation has a negative effect on the stability of the number of desired children among women. The findings of Iacovou and Tavares (2011: 119) indicate that having no partner or being separated from a partner is associated with a downward revision of fertility expectations across time.

Other studies have explored how changes in the employment domain of the life course relate to changes in fertility preferences. Heiland et al. (2008: 147) reported that unemployment has a negative, but insignificant effect on changes in the desired number of children. Buhr and Kuhnt (2012: 290) were unable to produce any statistically significant results supporting the notion that changes in labour force status affect fertility expectations. Iacovou and Tavares (2011: 119) studied the effect of income on fertility preferences. Their results show that while a man's income is not correlated with changes in the expected number of children, if a woman has a high income she tends to adjust her expected number of children downwards.

In summary, fertility preferences seem to be quite sensitive to changes in partnership status, but less sensitive to changes in economic circumstances. However, the psychological literature tells us that people may adjust their long-term goals based on the likelihood that they will achieve them. We therefore assume that the birth of (further) children may lead individuals to adjust their fertility ideals upwards.

11.3 Data and Analytical Strategy

This study uses data from the first six waves (2008/09–2013/14) of the German Family Panel (pairfam) and its supplement DemoDiff, release 6.0 (Brüderl et al. 2015). The German Family Panel (pairfam) is a panel survey that provides data on the formation and development of intimate relationships and families in Germany (Brüderl et al. 2015; Huinink et al. 2011). DemoDiff is a survey of residents of eastern Germany that is designed to complement the German Family Panel (Kreyenfeld et al. 2012). The pairfam and DemoDiff interviews are conducted annually with individuals from eastern and western Germany of the cohorts 1971–73, 1981–83, and 1991–93. The total number of respondents in wave 1 was 13,891. Overall attrition from wave 1 to wave 6 was about 46 %, which is within the normal range for panel studies in Germany with this duration (Müller and Castiglioni 2015). In our investigation, we have omitted respondents with invalid information on our key variables of interest, and especially those who failed to provide valid information on the ideal number of children or who said they were uncertain if they wanted children. The final sample includes 13,645 observations and 51,653 person-years of data.

11.3.1 Method & Analytical Strategy

The empirical analysis consists of two parts. In a first step, we provide descriptive statistics that depict the development of fertility preferences by age and gender. Moreover, we employ OLS-regression that examines the determinants of fertility preferences. The dependent variable is the reported fertility ideal. In order to account for the multiple observations of individuals in the sample, we calculate robust standard errors. Moreover, we employ fixed-effects modelling to gain a better understanding of the causal determinants of fertility preferences. The great advantage of using fixed-effects modelling is that it allows us to account for individual-specific time-constant heterogeneity (Allison 2009; Andreß et al. 2013; Schmidt 2013; Brüderl and Ludwig 2014). The drawback is that only characteristics that vary over time may be included in the analysis as covariates. Our main focus in the multivariate analysis is on the effects on fertility preferences of the respondents' employment status, partnership status, subjective financial situation, and number of children. A further control variable is the respondents' age. In the OLS-regression, we also include region, and migration status.

Our main variable of interest is the response to the fertility ideals measured by the following question: Under ideal circumstances, how many children would you like to have? The dependent variable has a mean of 2.2 and ranges from zero to seven children.[1] Figure 11.1 shows that a majority of the respondents reported that they prefer to have two children. This finding is in line with those of previous studies on western Europe that showed that most people report that their ideal number of children is 2 (Goldstein et al. 2003; Testa 2007). The differences between women and men were minor: Men were more likely than women to say they prefer to have two children (men: 60 %; women: 55 %), while women were slightly more likely than men to say they prefer to have three or four children. Among both men and women, just six per cent reported that they see childlessness as the ideal (see Fig. 11.1).

The independent variables in our analysis are the respondent's age, partnership status, employment status, number of children, and subjective assessment of the financial situation of his or her household. Age is treated as a categorical variable broken down by the following age groups: 14–19, 20–29, 30–39, and 40–42. Partnership status is a dummy variable that distinguishes between being single and being in partnership, regardless of whether the respondent is living with the partner. We also control for the number of children, and distinguish between respondents who are childless, have one child, have two children, or have three or more children. Employment status is distinguished using the following categories: in education, full-time employment, part-time employment, unemployment, and other activities. The subjective assessment of the financial situation is an ordinal scaled variable that

---

[1] A few of the respondents in the initial data set reported an ideal number of children that was higher than seven. Since there were only a few such observations, and because they may have biased our analyses, we excluded them from our analytic sample.

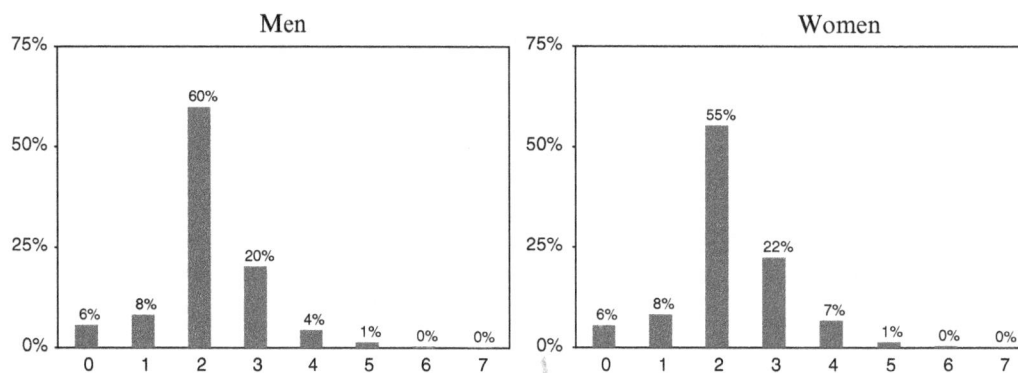

Fig. 11.1 Ideal number of children by gender (Source: German Family Panel (pairfam) wave 1–6, Release 6.0, weighted estimates)

ranges from zero (not satisfied) to 10 (absolutely satisfied). While unemployment is an objective variable used to measure economic conditions, the perception of financial satisfaction is a more subjective variable. In the OLS-regression, we also control for (largely) fixed covariates, such as region (eastern or western Germany), migration background (born in Germany or born in a different country), and level of education. In generating the level of education, we use the ISCED-97 classification to distinguish between respondents with low (ISCED 0–2), medium (ISCED 3–4), and high levels of education (ISCED 5–6). Table 11.1 reports the sample statistics.

11.4   Descriptive Results

In a first step, we analyse the mean ideal number of children by age for men and women (see Fig. 11.2). Please note that we do not yet exploit the within variation, and that the graphs in Fig. 11.2 merely give the mean values of fertility ideals by the age of the respondents. We have separated the graphs by birth cohorts and gender. Among men in their early twenties, the average ideal number of children is 2.1. These values increase modestly to 2.2 children over the life course. On the whole, however, the fertility ideals of men do not seem to change much with age. Likewise, we see little variation in the ideal number of children among women. Whereas the ideal number of children increases slightly across the life course among men, the number decreases slightly among women. When they are in their twenties, women have an ideal number of children that is slightly higher than that of men. This number increases to 2.3 when they are in their thirties, and then declines to 2.1 when they are in their forties. However, the fluctuations are modest and are within the range of the statistical error margin of 95 %. We conclude that fertility ideals at an aggregate level of the cohorts under study are relatively stable, even though some variation exists.

In a second step, we examine the within variation of fertility ideals. Table 11.2 reports the between and within variation for fertility preferences by gender and

Table 11.1 Composition of the sample by person-years, column per cent

	Men	Women
Ideal number of children (Mean & std. error)	2.17 (0.07)	2.23 (0.06)
Satisfaction with financial situation of household (Mean & std. error)	6.57 (0.02)	6.45 (0.02)
Age		
14–19	26 %	24 %
20–29	33 %	31 %
30–39	31 %	35 %
40–42	10 %	11 %
Region		
West	72 %	73 %
East	28 %	27 %
Country of birth		
Born in Germany	91 %	89 %
Not born in Germany	9 %	11 %
Number of children		
Childless	68 %	53 %
1 child	13 %	18 %
2 children	14 %	20 %
3 and more children	6 %	9 %
Partnership status		
No Partner	41 %	29 %
Partner	59 %	71 %
Level of education		
Low	40 %	37 %
Medium	39 %	42 %
High	21 %	21 %
Missing	0 %	0 %
Employment status		
In education	3 %	3 %
Employed full-time	85 %	56 %
Employed part-time	3 %	22 %
Unemployed	6 %	5 %
Other	3 %	15 %
Person years	24,586	27,067
Subjects	6,628	7,017

Source: German Family Panel (pairfam) wave 1–6, Release 6.0

region. The most important finding displayed in this table is that variation between individuals is much larger than variation within an individual. But there is still substantial within variation, which suggests that a considerable fraction of the population under study change their fertility ideals over survey waves. While men and women do not seem to differ, some differences are found between eastern and western Germany. On average, fertility ideals are higher in western than in eastern Germany, and are more stable in eastern than in western Germany.

Cohorts 1991-93, men

Cohorts 1991-93, Women

Cohorts 1981-83, men

Cohorts 1981-83, Women

Cohorts 1971-73, men

Cohorts 1971-73, Women

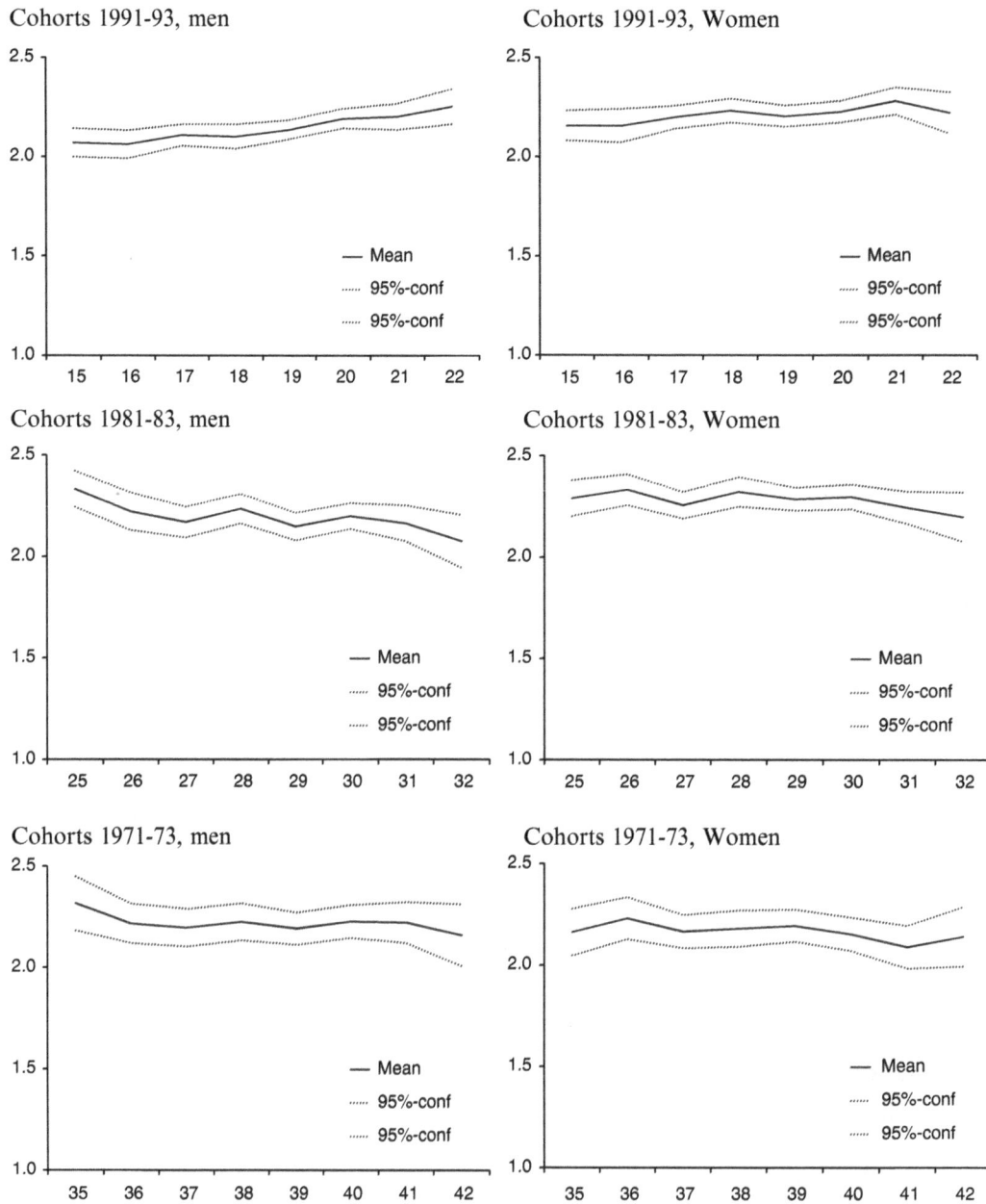

Fig. 11.2 Ideal family size by age, cohort and sex, mean and 95 % confidence level. (Source: German Family Panel (pairfam) wave 1–6, Release 6.0, weighted estimates)

11.5 Multivariate Results

Table 11.3 displays the results from the OLS models, separately for men and women. We start by discussing our findings on partnership status and economic conditions. With respect to partnership status, we find that men with a partner have a significantly higher fertility ideal than men without a partner. This association does not hold for women, however. Respondents who are (still) in education have higher fertility preferences than those in full-time employment. This finding might

Table 11.2 Within and between variation of fertility ideals

| | Mean | St. Dev. | | | Person-years |
		Overall	Between	Within	
All	2.20	0.96	0.87	0.49	51,653
Gender					
Men	2.16	0.93	0.85	0.50	24,586
Women	2.23	0.98	0.89	0.49	27,067
Region					
West Germany	2.24	0.97	0.89	0.51	37,230
East Germany	2.08	0.90	0.82	0.45	14,423

Source: German Family Panel (pairfam) wave 1–6, Release 6.0

be a reflection of the respondents' life course stage, rather than of their economic situation. Unemployment does not seem to be associated with lower fertility preferences, as we do not find statistically significant differences in the preferences of respondents depending on whether they are employed. We also find that fertility preferences do not appear to be associated with satisfaction with the household's financial situation. In addition, we find that the level of education matters for fertility preferences: The respondents who are highly educated are more likely to prefer having a large family than their less educated counterparts. This result for women is particularly surprising, as we know from other studies that highly educated women in Germany are more likely than other women to remain childless (see Kreyenfeld and Konietzka in this volume).

When we look at the effect of age, we find that fertility preferences decline significantly across the life course. On average, men's fertility preferences at age 40–42 are by 0.36 units lower than at ages 14–19. Among women, there is even a reduction by 0.59 units, which may be indicative of a stronger awareness of biological constraints. Please note that this stands in some contrast to the descriptive findings that did not show a strong age-gradient. Thus, the control variables seem to be suppressors in the relationship between age and fertility preferences. The ideal number of children is lower among eastern than western Germans. This result is consistent with previous descriptive findings indicating that most eastern Germans prefer to have a smaller family (Buhr and Huinink 2010). In line with previous studies on the fertility behaviour of foreigners and migrants in Germany, we find that ideal number of children is higher among foreign-born than native-born respondents (Helfferich et al. 2011; Schmid and Kohls 2011). The number of children also has a very strong effect on preferred fertility, as men and women who already have three or more children have a higher ideal number of children than other respondents. This finding is not surprising. First, we can assume that respondents who are more family-oriented and have a large number of children at the time of the interview will also report that they have a high "fertility ideal". Second, as their number of children increases, respondents will adjust their ideal to their family situation. These two mechanisms cannot be disentangled in the OLS-regression, but they can be addressed in the fixed-effects models below. Taken together, the findings from the

Table 11.3 Results from OLS regression, dependent variable: fertility ideals, beta coefficient and standard errors, (standard errors are adjusted for clustering in id)

	Men			Women		
	b	Std. err.		b	Std. err.	
Age						
14–19	1			1		
20–29	0.02	0.02		−0.06	0.02	**
30–39	−0.20	0.03	***	−0.42	0.04	***
40–42	−0.36	0.04	***	−0.59	0.04	***
Region						
Western Germany	1			1		
Eastern Germany	−0.13	0.02	***	−0.14	0.02	***
Migration status						
Born in Germany	1			1		
Born in other country	0.19	0.04	***	0.08	0.04	**
Number of children						
Childless	−0.17	0.03	***	−0.25	0.03	***
1 child	1			1		
2 children	0.32	0.03	***	0.39	0.03	***
3 or more children	1.35	0.05	***	1.33	0.05	***
Partnership status						
No Partner	1			1		
Partner	0.04	0.02	***	−0.02	0.02	
Level of education						
Low	−0.14	0.03	***	−0.11	0.03	***
Medium	1			1		
High	0.05	0.03		0.10	0.03	***
Other/Missing	0.86	0.05	***	−		
Employment status						
In education	0.15	0.07	**	0.16	0.05	***
Employed full-time	1			1		
Employed part-time	0.03	0.05		0.01	0.03	
Unemployed	0.01	0.07		−0.05	0.04	
Other/Missing	0.07	0.07		0.02	0.03	
Satisfaction with financial situation of household	0.002	0.00		0.007	0.00	*
Constant	2.24	0.07	***	2.40	0.05	***
R squared	0.17			0.19		
N (Person-years)	24,586			27,067		

Source: German Family Panel (pairfam) wave 1–6, Release 6.0
Notes: *** p<0.01, ** p<0.05, * p<0.1

OLS-regression reveal only weak associations between current living conditions, partnership status, and fertility ideals.

Next, we turn to the results from the fixed-effects model (Table 11.4). Fixed-effects modelling accounts for unobserved heterogeneity by "de-meaning" the data. Because fixed-effects analysis only draws on the within variation of individuals, the power of the model is lower than that of OLS-regressions. It is therefore more difficult to generate significant results with fixed-effects regressions than with OLS-modelling. However, even if we allowed for a very generous level of significance, the coefficients for partnership status or economic conditions do not come close to having an acceptable level of statistical significance. From this analysis, we conclude that neither

Table 11.4 Results from fixed-effects model, dependent variable: fertility ideals, beta coefficient and standard errors

	Men			Women		
	b	Std. err.		b	Std. err.	
Age						
14–19	1			1		
20–29	0.02	0.02		−0.01	0.02	***
30–39	0.01	0.02		−0.06	0.02	***
40–42	−0.02	0.03		−0.13	0.03	***
Number of children						
Childless	−0.09	0.03	**	−0.09	0.04	***
1 child	1			1		
2 children	0.19	0.04	***	0.13	0.03	***
3 or more children	0.41	0.07	***	0.48	0.06	***
Partnership status						
No Partner	0.02	0.02		0.02	0.02	
Partner	1			1		
Employment status						
In education	0.00	0.05		0.00	0.04	
Employed full-time	−0.04	0.03		−0.02	0.02	
Employed part-time	−0.02	0.04		0.01	0.03	
Unemployed	1			1		
Other/Missing	−0.02	0.04		−0.04	0.02	*
Satisfaction with financial situation of household	0.002	0.00		0.002	0.00	
Constant	2.18	0.05	***	2.24	0.04	***
R square						
Within	0.01			0.01		
Between	0.14			0.19		
Overvall	0.11			0.15		
N (Person-years)	24,586			27,067		

Source: German Family Panel (pairfam) wave 1–6, Release 6.0
Notes: *** $p<0.01$, ** $p<0.05$, * $p<0.1$

changes in partnership status nor changes in economic conditions impact fertility preferences. What does seem to matter, however, is the number of children a respondent has. Since fixed-effects models exploit the within variation, the coefficients tell us that the respondents whose number of children changed across the panel waves also changed their fertility preferences. As their number of children increased, the respondents adjusted their preferences upwards. This finding is fully in line with the argument by Miller and Pasta (1995) that the birth of a first child in particular increases the motivation for further childbearing. This may be attributable to a justification mechanism whereby each child born will be treated as if he or she was intended. Another potential explanation is that the respondents became more knowledgeable about the advantages and disadvantages of parenthood after the birth of a child, and that those who experienced parenthood as an overwhelmingly positive event came to associate having a larger number of children with more gains, and thus increased their fertility ideals. Interestingly, in the fixed-effects model the negative impact of age on fertility ideals disappears among men, and is found among women only. Among women, age has a negative effect on fertility preferences. This suggests that as women age they adjust their fertility ideals downwards, most likely because they become aware that it is unlikely that they will be able to achieve their initial goals.

11.6 Conclusion

In this paper, we investigated the evolution of fertility preferences in Germany across six waves of panel data. Preferences were measured using the following question: "Under ideal circumstances, how many children would you like to have?" We find that, on average, men and women prefer to have 2.2 children. The average number of "preferred children" slightly declines with increasing age. We also find that there is some variation in fertility ideals within individuals across time. We examined if these individual-level variations in fertility ideals would be related to changes in the respondent's partnership status or economic or employment situation. In a pooled OLS-regression, we show that satisfaction with the economic situation is positively related with fertility preferences among women, while having a partner has a positive impact on fertility ideals among men. However, the fixed-effects model that accounts for individual time-invariant heterogeneity did not confirm these findings. A major result of our analysis is therefore that fertility preferences, measured as "personal ideals," are relatively unaffected by short-term changes in life circumstances. These results support the findings of previous studies that showed that economic conditions do not significantly affect fertility preferences (e.g., Heiland et al. 2008; Iacovou and Tavares 2011). However, they are at odds with the findings of studies that found that partnership dissolution affects the desired number of children (Gray et al. 2013). The discrepancies between these findings may be explained by how fertility preferences are operationalised in our study. We used "fertility ideals" as a dependent variable. In the interview, the respondents were asked to report their desired number of children "under ideal circumstances." Because the respondents were asked to disregard their current circumstances, they may not have factored in their current employment situation or their partnership status.

While our findings indicate that partnership and economic conditions do not alter fertility ideals, they also show that an increase in the number of children in the respondent's family is associated with an upward adjustment of fertility preferences. Among women, increasing age is associated with a downward adjustment. This in turn suggests that individual-level variation in fertility ideals is largely explained by factors that are closely linked to goal achievement, such as the number of children already born and the woman's age. These findings are consistent with psychological theories of goal adjustment: i.e., that individuals will revise their fertility preferences if they perceive that it is unlikely that their initial goal will be realised, and that they will also change their preferences if they have more children than they had initially considered ideal. In sum, fertility ideals seem to be unaffected by short-term changes in the respondents' partnership status and employment situation, but they are sensitive to the achievement of long-term goals. In order to gain a more comprehensive understanding of the volatility of fertility ideals, we therefore need to have data that capture a long-term perspective. Only by using a sufficiently long-term panel will we be able to unravel the process through which people adjust their preferences based on their life course experiences. We were fortunate to have had access to 5 years of panel data. However, even this time horizon is short, as it captures only a snap-shot of the life course of an individual. For example, we were unable to produce any statistically significant results on the effects of union dissolution or unemployment on fertility preferences. We were also unable to explore whether previous disruptions in an individual's union or employment career affected the evolution of his or her fertility preferences. Unemployment or the lack of a suitable partner may not have an immediate impact on fertility preferences, but having a long history of economic hardship or complex partnerships may result in a downward or upward adjustment of fertility ideals at later ages. A direction for future research would be a systematic study of the long-term impact of the economic and partnership situations of individuals on their fertility preferences based on different concepts, such as personal ideals, desires, and intentions.

Literature

Ajzen, I. (1991). The theory of planned behavior. *Organizational Behavior and Human Decision Processes, 50*, 179–211.

Allison, P. D. (2009). *Fixed effects regression models*. Thousand Oaks: Sage.

Andreß, H.-J., Golsch, K., & Schmidt, A. (2013). *Applied panel data analysis for economic and social surveys*. New York: Springer.

Balbo, N., & Mills, M. (2011). The effects of social capital and social pressure on the intention to have a second or third child in France, Germany, and Bulgaria, 2004–05. *Population Studies, 65*, 335–351.

Bernardi, L., Mynarska, M., & Rossier, C. (2015). Uncertain, changing and situated fertility intentions. In D. Philipov, A. C. Liefbroer, & J. Klobas (Eds.), *Reproductive decision-making in a macro-micro perspective* (pp. 113–139). Dordrecht: Springer.

Berrington, A., & Pattaro, S. (2014). Educational differences in fertility desires, intentions and behaviour: A life course perspective. *Advances in Life Course Research, 21*, 10–27.

Billari, F. C., Philipov, D., & Testa, M. R. (2009). Attitudes, norms and perceived behavioural control: Explaining fertility intentions in Bulgaria. *European Journal of Population/Revue européenne de Démographie, 25*, 439–465.

Brüderl, J., & Ludwig, V. (2014). Fixed-effects panel regression. In H. Best & C. Wolf (Eds.), *SAGE handbook of regression analysis and causal inference* (pp. 327–359). London: Sage.

Brüderl, J., Hajek, K., Herzig, M., Huyer-May, B., Lenke, R., Müller, B., Schüzte, P., & Schumann, N. (2015). *Pairfam data manual, Release 6.0*. München: Universität München.

Bühler, C. (2012). *How to measure preferred family size? A discussion of different approaches.* Leibniz Universität Hannover: Unpublished manuscript.

Buhr, P., & Huinink, J. (2010). Kinderwünsche von Männern und Frauen. In J. Goldstein, M. Kreyenfeld, J. Huinink, D. Konietzka, & H. Trappe (Eds.), *Familie und Partnerschaft in Ost- und Westdeutschland – Ergebnisse im Rahmen des Projektes Demographic differences in life course dynamics in eastern and western Germany* (pp. 18–19). Rostock: Max-Planck-Institut für demografische Forschung.

Buhr, P., & Kuhnt, A.-K. (2012). Die kurzfristige Stabilität des Kinderwunsches von Kinderlosen in Ost-und Westdeutschland: eine Analyse mit den ersten beiden Wellen des deutschen Beziehungs-und Familienpanels. *Zeitschrift für Familienforschung, Sonderheft, 2012*, 275–297.

Dommermuth, L., Klobas, J., & Lappegård, T. (2011). Now or later? The theory of planned behavior and timing of fertility intentions. *Advances in Life Course Research, 16*, 42–53.

Fishbein, M., & Ajzen, I. (2010). *Predicting and changing behavior: The reasoned action approach.* New York: Taylor & Francis.

Goldstein, J., Lutz, W., & Testa, M. R. (2003). The emergence of sub-replacement family size ideals in Europe. *Population Research and Policy Review, 22*, 479–496.

Gray, E., Evans, A., & Reimondos, A. (2013). Childbearing desires of childless men and women: When are goals adjusted? *Advances in Life Course Research, 18*, 141–149.

Hakim, C. (2003). A new approach to explaining fertility patterns: Preference theory. *Population and Development Review, 29*, 349–374.

Hayford, S. R. (2009). The evolution of fertility expectations over the life course. *Demography, 46*, 765–783.

Heiland, F., Prskawetz, A., & Sanderson, W. C. (2008). Are individuals' desired family sizes stable? Evidence from West German panel data. *European Journal of Population/Revue européenne de Démographie, 24*, 129–156.

Helfferich, C., Klindworth, H., & Kruse, J. (2011). *frauen leben – Familienplanung und Migration im Lebenslauf*. Köln: Bundeszentrale für gesundheitliche Aufklärung.

Huinink, J., & Feldhaus, M. (2009). Family research from the life course perspective. *International Sociology, 24*, 299–324.

Huinink, J., Brüderl, J., Nauck, B., Walper, S., Castiglioni, L., & Feldhaus, M. (2011). Panel analysis of intimate relationships and family dynamics (pairfam): Conceptual framework and design. *Zeitschrift für Familienforschung, 23*, 77–101.

Iacovou, M., & Tavares, L. P. (2011). Yearning, learning, and conceding: Reasons men and women change their childbearing intentions. *Population and Development Review, 37*, 89–123.

Inglehart, R. (1977). *The silent revolution*. Princeton: Princeton University Press.

Kapitány, B., & Spéder, Z. (2013). Realization, postponement or abandonment of childbearing intentions in four European countries. *Population, 67*, 599–629.

Keim, S., Klärner, A., & Bernardi, L. (2009). Qualifying social influence on fertility intentions composition, structure and meaning of fertility-relevant social networks in Western Germany. *Current Sociology, 57*, 888–907.

Klobas, J. E., & Ajzen, I. (2015). Making the decision to have a child. In D. Philipov, A. C. Liefbroer, & J. E. Klobas (Eds.), *Reproductive decision-making in a macro-micro environment* (pp. 41–78). Dordrecht: Springer.

Kreyenfeld, M., Huinink, J., Trappe, H., & Walke, R. (2012). DemoDiff: A dataset for the study of family change in eastern (and western) Germany. *Schmollers Jahrbuch, 132*, 653–660.

Kuhnt, A.-K. (2013). Ja, nein, vielleicht? Der Einfluss der Partnerschaftsqualität auf die Übereinstimmung der Elternschaftsabsichten von Paaren. *Zeitschrift für Familienforschung, 25*, 365–388.

Kuhnt, A.-K., & Trappe, H. (2013). *Easier said than done: Childbearing intentions and their realization in a short term perspective* (MPIDR working paper WP 2013–018: Max Planck Institute for Demographic Research). Rostock: Rostock Max-Planck-Institut für demografische Forschung.

Lesthaeghe, R., & Moors, G. (2002). Life course transitions and value orientations: selection and adaptation. In R. Lesthaeghe (Ed.), *Meaning and choice: Value orientations and life course decisions* (pp. 1–44). Brussels: CBGS.

Liefbroer, A. C. (2009). Changes in family size intentions across young adulthood: A life-course perspective. *European Journal of Population/Revue européenne de Démographie, 25*, 363–386.

Lutz, K., Buhr, P., & Boehnke, M. (2013). Die Bedeutung der Erfahrungen mit dem ersten Kind für die Intention zur Familienerweiterung. *Zeitschrift für Soziologie der Erziehung und Sozialisation, 33*, 169–186.

Marbach, J. H., & Tölke, A. (2013). Frauen, Männer und Familie. Lebensorientierung, Kinderwunsch und Vaterrolle. In D. Konietzka & M. Kreyenfeld (Eds.), *Ein Leben ohne Kinder: Ausmaß, Strukturen und Ursachen von Kinderlosigkeit* (pp. 281–310). Wiesbaden: Springer VS.

Mayer, K. U. (2004). Whose lives? How history, societies and institutions define and shape life courses. *Research in Human Development, 1*, 161–187.

Miller, W. B. (1994). Childbearing motivations, desires, and intentions: A theoretical framework. *Genetic, Social, and General Psychology Monographs, 120*, 223–258.

Miller, W. B. (2011). Differences between fertility desires and intentions: Implications for theory, research and policy. *Vienna Yearbook of Population Research, 9*, 75–98.

Miller, W. B., & Pasta, D. J. (1995). How does childbearing affect fertility motivations and desires? *Social Biology, 42*, 185–198.

Morgan, S. P. (1982). Parity-specific fertility intentions and uncertainty: The United States, 1970 to 1976. *Demography, 19*, 315–334.

Müller, B., & Castiglioni, L. (2015). Attrition im Beziehungs- und Familienpanel pairfam. In J. Schupp & C. Wolf (Eds.), *Nonresponse Bias* (pp. 383–408). Wiesbaden: Springer.

Ní Bhrolcháin, M., & Beaujouan, É. (2011). Uncertainty in fertility intentions in Britain. *Vienna Yearbook of Population Research, 9*, 99–129.

Ní Bhrolcháin, M., Beaujouan, E., & Berrington, A. (2010). Stability and change in fertility intentions in Britain, 1991–2007. *Population Trends, 141*, 13–35.

Philipov, D., Spéder, Z., & Billari, F. C. (2006). Soon, later, or ever? The impact of anomie and social capital on fertility intentions in Bulgaria (2002) and Hungary (2001). *Population Studies, 60*, 289–308.

Puur, A., Oláh, L. S., Tazi-Preve, M. I., & Dorbritz, J. (2008). Men's childbearing desires and views of the male role in Europe at the dawn of the 21st century. *Demographic Research, 19*, 1883–1912.

Quesnel-Vallée, A., & Morgan, S. P. (2004). Missing the target? Correspondence of fertility intentions and behavior in the US. *Population Research and Policy Review, 22*, 497–525.

Régnier-Loilier, A. (2006). Influence of own sibship size on the number of children desired at various times of life: The Case of France. *Population (english edition), 6*, 165–194.

Régnier-Loilier, A., Vignoli, D., & Dutreuilh, C. (2011). Fertility intentions and obstacles to their realization in France and Italy. *Population, 66*, 361–389.

Rost, H. (2005). Kinder – Wunsch und Wirklichkeit. *Zeitschrift für Familienforschung, 17,* 8–20.

Ruckdeschel, K. (2007). Der Kinderwunsch von Kinderlosen. *Zeitschrift für Familienforschung, 19,* 210–230.

Schmid, S., & Kohls, M. (2011). *Generatives Verhalten und Migration – Eine Bestandsaufnahme des generativen Verhaltens von Migrantinnen in Deutschland.* Nürnberg: Bundesamt für Migration und Flüchtlinge.

Schoen, R., Astone, N. M., Kim, Y. J., Nathanson, C. A., & Fields, J. M. (1999). Do fertility intentions affect fertility behavior? *Journal of Marriage and the Family, 61,* 790–799.

Spéder, Z., & Kapitány, B. (2009). How are time-dependent childbearing intentions realized? Realization, postponement, abandonment, bringing forward. *European Journal of Population/ Revue européenne de Démographie, 25,* 503–523.

Spéder, Z., & Kapitány, B. (2015). Influences on the link between fertility intentions and behavioural outcomes. In D. Philipov, A. C. Liefbroer, & J. Klobas (Eds.), *Reproductive decision-making in a macro-micro perspective* (pp. 79–112). Dordrecht: Springer.

Testa, M. R. (2007). Childbearing preferences and family issues in Europe: Evidence from the Eurobarometer 2006 survey. *Vienna Yearbook of Population Research, 5,* 353–377.

Testa, M. R., & Basten, S. (2014). Certainty of meeting fertility intentions declines in Europe during the 'Great Recession'. *Demographic Research, 31,* 687–734.

Thomson, E. (1997). Couple childbearing desires, intentions, and births. *Demography, 34,* 343–354.

Thomson, E. (2001). Family size preferences. In N. J. Smelser & P. B. Baltes (Eds.), *International encyclopedia of the social & behavioral sciences* (pp. 5347–5350). Oxford: Pergamon.

Thomson, E., & Hoem, J. M. (1998). Couple childbearing plans and births in Sweden. *Demography, 35,* 315–322.

Toulemon, L., & Testa, M. R. (2005). Fertility intentions and actual fertility: A complex relationship. *Population and Societies, 415,* 1–4.

Vignoli, D., Rinesi, F., & Mussino, E. (2013). A home to plan the first child? Fertility intentions and housing conditions in Italy. *Population, Space and Place, 19,* 60–71.

Chapter 12
Childless at Age 30: A Qualitative Study of the Life Course Plans of Working Women in East and West Germany

Laura Bernardi and Sylvia Keim

12.1 Introduction

In Germany, the low birth rate and the difficulties women face in reconciling work and family life are frequently discussed by policy-makers. At the heart of the current debate on these issues is the legal entitlement of children under 3 years of age to a place in nursery school, which has been in effect on the national level since August 2013. The qualitative improvement in childcare and the increase in the uptake rate of Elterngeld (parental benefits) for both parents are also high on the political agenda. The aim of these policies is to facilitate the reconciliation of work and family life and the re-entry of mothers into employment as early as possible after childbirth, and thus to make it easier for young adults to pursue an employment career without having to forgo parenthood.

However, the interplay of employment history and fertility behavior, and the ways in which the subjective meanings attached to work trajectories are connected to thoughts and decisions about starting a family, are issues that have so far been little researched (Witzel and Kühn 2001: 56). Relatively few authors have examined the question of whether differences in meanings can explain the differences in

L. Bernardi (✉)
LIVES, Faculty for the Social and Political Sciences, University of Lausanne,
Lausanne, Switzerland
e-mail: laura.bernardi@unil.ch

S. Keim
Institute of Sociology and Demographic Research, University of Rostock,
Rostock, Germany
e-mail: sylvia.keim@uni-rostock.de

M. Kreyenfeld, D. Konietzka (eds.), *Childlessness in Europe: Contexts,
Causes, and Consequences*, Demographic Research Monographs,
DOI 10.1007/978-3-319-44667-7_12

behavior between young adults in East Germany and their counterparts in West Germany.[1] The work biographies and the family formation patterns of East and West Germans, especially of women, differed considerably. The focus of our analysis is on young women who grew up in the two different systems, and were thus exposed to contrasting family models. How do these differences in upbringing influence the life course plans and arrangements of these women after unification? How do these women envisage combining family formation and employment? Do these women have the same values, norms, attitudes, and behaviors as those of their parents' generation? According to Bourdieu, this legacy of the past could be regarded as an "inertial effect". He stressed that because socialization affects the formation of attitudes and values, as well as the meanings attached to certain behaviors and the range of action, values and behavior may persist after the macro-societal conditions have changed.

Our analysis in this chapter is based on the life stories of young employed women who were socialized in the former East and West Germany, experienced unification as teenagers, and were around age 30 at the time of interview. Over the course of four qualitative case studies we compare East and West German women who are still childless but who want to have children. We examine which family formation pathways these women prefer, the reasons why they have so far remained childless, and their attitudes and perceptions regarding the compatibility of motherhood and paid employment.

In the following section we briefly describe the institutional and demographic peculiarities of the two German states before and after reunification. In the third section we outline the theoretical background of our investigation and introduce our empirical data. In the fourth section we present four case studies of childless women from East and West Germany. In the concluding section we discuss our results and suggest topics for future research.

12.2   The Legacy of Different Socio-political Systems: Starting a Family in West and in East Germany

Before German unification, fertility behavior of East and West Germans differed profoundly; thus, we are dealing with two distinct demographic regimes. The term regime implies that these differences in family behavior were shaped by different institutional contexts. One of the most important differences in the realm of family behavior was that the East German government supported maternal full-time employment by providing extensive and easily accessible childcare services.

---

[1] Andreas Witzel and Thomas Kühn, for instance, examined the life courses of young adults from two regions in West Germany that have different labor market conditions. They found that women, especially after reaching age 30, experience an increased subjective pressure to have children. Career-oriented women "look for solutions which are compatible with family life via 'decelerated' careers" (Witzel and Kühn 2001: 78).

The centrally planned economy guaranteed that both men and women would have reliable and stable employment. Most women had their first child early in their life course, and returned to full-time work after the so-called "Babyjahr". In most cases mothers interrupted their employment for 1 year only. Women seldom had the option of taking a longer break from employment or of shifting to a part-time schedule, and few women spent more than short periods of time as a full-time homemaker (Falk and Schaeper 2001: 188). In contrast, the institutional framework in West Germany supported the model of the married couple with a gendered division of work: i.e. the husband was the principal earner while the wife was a homemaker and mother who was employed part-time or not at all. On average, women in West Germany were considerably older than their counterparts in East Germany at the time of family formation. About 20 % of the women in West Germany remained childless, compared with just 10 % in East Germany (Kreyenfeld and Konietzka, in this volume).

Under the terms of the Unification Treaty, the East German institutional, economic, and political systems were replaced by the West German systems. However, the eastern German Länder remained distinct from West Germany in a number of ways. In particular, in the eastern German Länder childcare services, organized and financed mainly by the municipalities, continued to be widely available (Kreyenfeld 2003; Statistische Ämter des Bundes und der Länder 2015). The annual birth rate fell dramatically in the years immediately after unification (Eberstadt 1994; Witte and Wagner 1995). Although the total fertility rate in East Germany converged with the West German rate after a few years, and even surpassed it slightly since 2008 (Statistisches Bundesamt 2012: 15), some differences between the two parts of the country in the average age at first birth remain. Moreover, women in East Germany are still less likely to be childless than women in West Germany. In addition to being younger when they have their first child, women in East Germany are more likely than women in West Germany to be living in a non-marital partnership at the time of family formation (Kreyenfeld and Konietzka 2010; Huinink et al. 2012; Statistisches Bundesamt 2012). Meanwhile, women in West Germany, who tend to have negative opinions of working mothers, are considerably less likely than women in East Germany to be in full-time employment (Wenzel 2010; Huinink et al. 2012). Given these differences, we conclude that despite the convergence of the political and institutional frameworks of the two parts of the country, two distinct demographic regimes continue to exist. It can, however, also be argued that these differences are merely symptomatic of the critical transitional period, and that behavioral patterns in East and West Germany will eventually converge (Witte and Wagner 1995; Beck-Gernsheim 1997; Kreyenfeld 2004). Yet when and how this assimilation process might occur is currently unclear. The hypothesis of assimilation fails to provide an explanation for the persistent differences in behavioral patterns between the two parts of the country, such as the much higher ratio of unmarried births in East than in West Germany.

In this paper, we contribute to the debate surrounding this ongoing East-West gap in fertility behavior by focusing specifically on the attitudes and life course plans of women who were socialized in the former East and West Germany, and who reached their teenage years around the time of German unification. How has the experience of being socialized in a particular regime shaped the life course plans of women in the two Germanies? Is there a legacy of the former East German regime that is visible in the attitudes and behavior of young East Germans, similar to an 'inertial effect' of socialization as described by Bourdieu (1984)? Or was German Reunification able to override particular features and attitudes of the "Reunification Cohorts"?

12.3   Theoretical and Empirical Background

Based on the concept of habitus, Pierre Bourdieu posited that socialization has an "inertial effect" (1984). Bourdieu used habitus to describe a permanent behavioral disposition that emerges through socialization in a given social environment. By means of his or her habitus, the individual is supposed to incorporate the social norms of the environment, to set his or her preferences, and to act accordingly. It is therefore assumed that the individual's range of action is not restricted by material living conditions alone. Instead, the individual's internalized norms regulate his or her perceptions of which actions are or are not appropriate. It is further assumed that the habitus is very stable, because the individual's perceptual categories and preferences are largely shaped in an unconscious manner through the socialization process.

The concept of ideology developed by Göran Therborn points in the same direction. He emphasized that behavior is limited not just by external circumstances, but also by the imagination of "what exists," "what is good," and "what is possible and impossible" (Therborn 1980: 18); and that multiple ideologies may exist simultaneously within a single culture.

The inertial effect is also conceptualized in the schema theory by Roy D'Andrade. This theory seeks to explain how the socialization process (e.g., acculturation) within a certain social (or cultural) group translates into wishes, motivations, and strategies for action. D'Andrade also stressed the resistance to change: a schema is crystallized in the memory and appears to be prototypical (D'Andrade 1997: 29). Like the concept of habitus, the schema theory posits that the individual perceives socially determined dispositions on an individual basis only. All of these theories assert that the individual behavioral repertoire is restricted by (a) the availability of material resources; as well as by (b) subjective perceptions of possible and appropriate behavior, which originate from the individual's experiences during socialization and in a certain social environment.

The availability of material resources can be analyzed empirically using indicators such as the individuals' socioeconomic characteristics and access to infrastructure. Meanwhile, the complex interaction of consciously chosen and internalized behavior, as described by the term habitus, can be better captured by an interpretative analysis of unstructured interviews in which the individual reconstructs his or her own biographical experiences and makes predictions about his or her future development.

As part of our research project on social influences on family foundation in East and West Germany, we conducted qualitative interviews with more than 100 young women and men in 2004 and 2005. The interviewees grew up in either Lübeck or Rostock, and had either an intermediate or a higher educational degree. We chose these two cities because they are similar in many respects, despite having been subject to two different political regimes for 40 years during the division of Germany. For example, both are port cities in northern Germany that were part of the Hanseatic League. The dominant religion in both cities is Protestant. Moreover, both Lübeck and Rostock have approximately 200,000 inhabitants, and the unemployment rate in both was relatively high during the period of our fieldwork (13.8 % in Lübeck compared to 7.6 % in West Germany; 18.2 % in Rostock compared to 17.7 % in East Germany in 2002). During the interviews, the respondents were encouraged to provide an account of their life up to that point, and to describe their plans for the future. The respondents were also asked systematic questions about the issue of family formation.[2]

Our analyses show that women who live in Rostock and Lübeck have very different ideas about what kinds of employment situations and levels of economic security are prerequisites for having a child (Bernardi et al. 2006). Of particular interest to us in this chapter are the views on starting a family and the reconciliation of work and family life among women who are highly qualified and in full-time employment. We focus on childless women who want to have children.[3] Since socioeconomic characteristics, such as educational level and income, have a considerable influence on both the material resources and the attitudes and perceptions of the individual, we restrict our study to women with similar socioeconomic profiles. Our sample selection allows us to attribute different narrations, especially those related to material life conditions, to different perceptions, attitudes, and values regarding family formation.

12.4 Childless Women from East and West Germany: A Comparison

How did these childless women, who were socialized in different fertility regimes and were about to enter their thirties, see their previous life experiences and their future life path? What similarities and differences are revealed in our interviews of women from East and West Germany? Based on our hypothesis of an inertial effect, is it possible to attribute these differences to differences in socialization in East and West Germany?

---

[2] Detailed information on the selection of the interviewees and the data collection method can be found in Bernardi et al. (2014).

[3] Only a few of our interviewees said that they definitely do not want to have children. We conducted a separate analysis of these interviewees, and therefore excluded them from this essay.

To allow us to focus on narrations of a complete life path, instead of on fragmented aspects of each story, we confine our investigation to four case studies: two women from Rostock and two women from Lübeck, who are similar in many ways. This approach helps to ensure that the differences in views on family formation are not primarily attributable to differences in living conditions. The first two women we compare both had a safe employment situation and moderate career ambitions. At the time the interview was conducted neither of the women was in a relationship suitable for starting a family (the interviewee from Lübeck was single while the respondent from Rostock was in a relationship which she considered unstable). The other two women we compared were similar in terms of their mobility experiences and career ambitions. At the time of the interview they had been in the same partnership for multiple years and wanted to have children with their partner. Thus, while each woman has her own story, our case studies exemplify the main differences between all of the interviewees from Lübeck and Rostock.

12.4.1 Antje from Rostock: Refusal to Engage in Family Planning: "I Hate Planning"

Antje is 29 years old. She grew up in Rostock, and graduated from high school and university in the city. She would have preferred to have stayed there, but—like many other women her age—she moved to nearby West Germany 5 years previously to take a job. When her first employer went bankrupt 2 years later, she looked for and easily found a new job. She is currently employed full-time and has a high disposable income. Although she does not consider her work to be exciting ("a lot of paperwork"), she describes her job as safe and her salary as appropriate. While she sometimes looks half-heartedly for another job, she expects to stay where she is for at least the next few years:

> "It's a rather safe place, but I do not really want to say that I want to grow old there. I feel I am still too young to stay in such an administrative position for years."

Antje has been in a relationship for 3 years, but does not live with her partner, although he would like to cohabit. She describes her relationship as a "pending action" and is not certain how it will develop:

> "I do not really have a plan, I honestly have to say. Maybe it's because the relationship is not that good at the moment, or maybe I simply have a little tick, that I don't want this [moving in together]. On the other hand I kind of like it this way [as it is]."

Antje states that having her own family will become an issue "certainly at some point in time," but not at the moment: "I am only 29 years old." Yet, she reports having an increased interest in children:

> "I find children very, very beautiful (…) maybe it's my hormones; one likes to look [at little children]. Don't ask why, it's like that."

She takes it for granted that she will continue to work after becoming a mother. She complains about the poor "childcare in the West," and hopes that in the future companies will do more to help women balance work and family life. Antje's image of a family coincides with the traditional family model in the former East Germany, which featured a full-time working mother. Antje's demand for adequate public childcare and for more family-friendly company policies also draw on this family model.

Throughout her narration, Antje refuses to make long-term plans. This systematic rejection of planning for the future is evident in almost all parts of the interview in which she talks about her work life or her partnership:

> "For the love of God, I hate planning. I would start panicking if things did not work out accordingly [laughs]. (...) Well, because then the people, if they plan, obviously also become frustrated eventually, if it doesn't happen the way they hoped. And then the life crises start [laughs]."

Even when asked about a possible timeframe for starting a family, she refuses to make any specific plans:

> "I don't want to somehow choose a time now, but I also don't want to be an old maid."

Although she wants to have a child, Antje cites her age as the main reason for her childlessness, as she believes she can wait a few years before having a child. However, the instability of her partnership also seems to play a role in her indecision, as the following quote illustrates:

> "I think if the circumstances were right, maybe I wouldn't plan things that precisely. But at the moment, I wouldn't like to have it [the child] by myself right now. (...) The partner should be right at least, I don't just need some sperm donor (...) and I also think that one should also live together. Yes, I think the relationship should be in place."

According to Antje, the "right circumstances" for motherhood include being in a harmonious partnership: if she had a suitable partner, she would not need to have a precise plan for starting a family. It is clear that she does not consider her current partner to be the "right" one. She does not, however, explain what bothers her about her current partner, or describe what qualities a suitable partner would have. She mentions her job as being another factor in her decision about when to start a family:

> "In my current job, I think I could take a break at any point for a certain period of time and then go back. I wouldn't worry too much about that."

Since her current job allows her to take parental leave and come back afterwards, the criterion of having a job suitable for starting a family has already been met. Thus, for Antje the issue of how to reconcile work and family life has been resolved.

As a counterpart to Antje's story, we now look at the story of a young woman from Lübeck. She has a very different image of the family, and describes a precise set of conditions under which she hopes to start a family.

12.4.2 Miriam from Lübeck: Family Planning Based on the Main Breadwinner Model: "I Envision it Like This, That I Will Definitely Stay Home"

Miriam is single, 30 years old, and has an open-ended full-time job. Although she is proud of her occupational achievements, she ascribes them more to coincidence or to external pressure than to her own efforts. She sees herself as lazy, and is not interested in any career objectives. She has considered continuing her education, but has repeatedly postponed doing so because she believes it would be too arduous. She is very happy with her current job, and has become friends with her boss and some of her colleagues. She currently views her job as relatively safe, but given the high rate of unemployment in Lübeck, she is aware that this can change quite quickly.

Miriam has wanted to have children for some time, and the main topic in this interview is her lack of a partner with whom she can start a family. When she talks about family, Miriam has the traditional West German family model in mind: the woman is a full-time homemaker or works part-time, while the husband is the main breadwinner.

> "If everything is great and all of the preconditions are met, I actually envision that I will definitely stay home and play mom as long as I feel like it. And then I can go back to work. I don't think that these three years are enough for me. I think I could even go longer."

This plan seems to reflect the experiences of her own mother, who raised four children while her husband worked, and did not have a job until the youngest child became a teenager. Miriam believes that taking care of children is the responsibility of the mother. She rejects the idea of involving her male partner in childcare (e.g., paternity leave) or putting her children in day-care:

> "If I actually give birth to a child, I would also like to enjoy it somehow."

Since having a secure financial foundation is very important for Miriam, she wants her partner to have a salary that is large enough to allow her to stay home:

> "By all means, if I actually plan this, if I plan to have children, then I absolutely would like to be financially secure so that I don't have to sacrifice so much."

Here it becomes evident that she would like to have a firm foundation before starting a family. Her planning also extends to the life of her partner: he is supposed to have career ambitions as well as a job (or the prospect of a job) which provides financial security and a good income. Her former partners were not suitable because they were not sufficiently career-oriented, they did not want to have children, or they did not want to take on the role of the main breadwinner:

> "I would have provided him with all the opportunities; we could have moved into a smaller apartment so he could study. But he didn't want to. (…) I have always, well we have also spoken about it, what we would do if we had children now, how would we finance this. I would have had to have gone back to work immediately. (…) That was another thing which bothered me, because it was never clear what happens then. (…) And yes, at this age, at 30,

one starts to think. I thought about whether I really wanted to have a family, children with him. Nah! I didn't."

As she wants to have children, Miriam attributes her childlessness to the lack of the right partner. Her goal is to find a partner who shares her views concerning role allocation within the family and the preconditions for starting a family, and who is able to provide the desired financial security.

The case studies of Antje and Miriam illustrate that the family models that were dominant in the former East and West Germany persist after unification, and that views on long-term life course planning can differ considerably in the two parts of the country. The following two case studies of women who have been living in a partnership for years are similar to the first two case studies. They also show that women in the East and the West differ in their views on family models and long-term family planning. Both women are highly qualified university graduates with excellent career prospects. Now they are facing the issue of how to reconcile work and family life.

12.4.3 Kristin from Rostock: Egalitarian Gender Roles and the Impossibility of Reconciling Work and Family Life: "A Great Job and Family—How is that Supposed to Work Out?"

Kristin is 29 years old and grew up in Rostock. After graduating from high school she moved several times. First she moved to another town in East Germany to attend university, and then to a town in West Germany to attend a different university. After graduating from university she moved to yet another town to enroll in a doctoral program. She got a full-time job a few months previously, and again lives in a town in East Germany. She has been in a partnership for 7 years. She and her partner have lived together for certain periods of time, while in other periods they have had a long-distance relationship and saw each other only on the weekends. They have been living together for 9 months now:

"I have reached the point at which we have been living together for a longer period of time than we commuted, if I don't move again [laughs]."

The main issue she raises in her interview is the difficulties she faces in combining the demands of her career, including the need to move frequently, with her desire to live with her partner:

"On the one hand I would like to have a great job, on the other hand I want to live together."

She is always forced to make compromises. Although she lives with her partner, her workplace is relatively far (70 km) from their home, and she is not completely satisfied with her job:

"It was clear to me beforehand that this isn't my dream job, but rather an attempt to somehow reconcile everything (...) Since we are living together at the moment, I am sticking with it for now. On the other hand if the job becomes very frustrating, at some point I will start thinking about living apart again."

As she has so far failed to find a way to combine living with her partner with having the right job, starting a family seems even less possible to her:

"And if one wants to have something like a family, [should the parents then] travel? How is this supposed to work? Should the parents decide to live alone as 'voluntarily single parents'? (...) I find this very, I can't, well I find this very, very difficult at the moment. (...) We actually want to have children. (...) And a relationship based on traveling, like I said: who takes the children? Me or you or maybe in the middle? How does one organize something like this?"

Like Antje from Rostock, Kristin takes for granted that she will continue to work and pursue her professional ambitions after becoming a mother. And like Antje, she does not want to have to plan to start a family, and lacks precise ideas about how and when to have a child. While she recognizes that the amount of time she has to become pregnant is limited, this thought does not inspire her to engage in more precise planning:

"So far I have always felt young enough, that the edge is still far away."

The young woman from Lübeck we will introduce in the following case study has also faced challenges in reconciling her career ambitions and her desire to become a parent. However, unlike Kristin, she has developed a plan which incorporates the typical family model in West Germany.

12.4.4 Karen from Lübeck: Planning a Family with a Gender-Related Role Allocation: "It Will be One of Those Modern Relationships, Where the Husband Works Somewhere else During the Week and Comes Home Over the Weekend"

Karen is 30 years old and lives in a town in West Germany not far from Lübeck. She has been with her partner for 7 years, and after years of seeing each other only on the weekends they have been living together for the past 3 years. At the time the interview took place she was certain that he was going to take up a new post soon, and that they would again see each other only on the weekends.

After graduating from high school Karen attended a business school in Lübeck. She then attended university in another town in West Germany. As she was unable to choose a single field of study, she pursued multiple fields. With such broad qualifications it was easy for her to find a job after she had completed her studies. Although this job was not well paid, it offered her the opportunity for further training over several years, and was a very good career move. Nevertheless, she left the job after 3 months:

"I did it for three months, and enjoyed it (…) but then I thought, nah, this way is somehow too long for me, again three, four years of further training, so little money the whole time (…) it was just such a long way, and slowly but surely the idea emerged that I want a family at some point. If I take this long before I can even start, then I am eventually 35 and then I want children, then I finally want to start having children."

Karen then found another temporary job which promised to advance her career. However, she left this position as well after a short time as it seemed to be incompatible with her desire to have a child in the near future. She now has an open-ended job which does not offer great career opportunities, but which provides the perfect conditions for having a child:

"One reason I took this job was because it was open-ended, which means I have a certain security and can switch to part-time anytime I want, and that I am staying here [in the town where I currently live], so the next thing in line is having children, planning a family. And I can foresee doing this within the next year, somehow. The next deadline—because it didn't work out by 29—is now to have the first child by 32 at the latest."

This ideal of working part-time (if at all) after becoming a mother is in line with the traditional family model in West Germany. Karen, like Miriam from Lübeck, has a precise plan for becoming a parent, and has already put a great deal of effort into pursuing this objective. She has adhered to her plan of finishing her studies, then securing the right job, and then becoming a parent. This applies to her partner as well. From his interview we know that initially he did not want to start a family, and did not plan his career with the goal of supporting a family. He gradually changed his attitude, in part because he was persuaded by his girlfriend. He made job-related changes to ensure that he could fulfill his role as the breadwinner of the family. He reports:

"It is really like this, that I was at least implicitly as well as explicitly raised to believe that the most important goal is to have a job and to have money. And actually I was opposed to this view in the 90s; previously I was afraid that I would become unemployed, because in school I was interested in subjects like history, which are not really relevant for work…I have always been a potential candidate for unemployment. And this has indeed left a mark on me, so I went back and forth [from fear of unemployment to opposing a well-paid and secure but boring job]."

After completing vocational training, he did not work in his profession, but became a freelance artist:

"And then it was actually important to me to live as an artist, well to get around a lot, but I haven't thought that I could support a family, because it was obvious that I can only take care of myself then. But this has changed now, since I got together with Karen. Yes at first I was still a bit uncertain, but since I got together with Karen the model of having a family is there for me. That means responsibility for others, that also means that money has to be earned. (…) Now it is more important for me that I also earn money and that I am taken up on my duties as a father. This is my perspective, especially now. That is also the most important to me. We want to start a family, and that is great."

This interview excerpt shows how Karen's partner came to accept the expectation that he would take on the role of the main breadwinner when he became a father, even though he had rejected the role for years after having grown up with it. He now believes that he has found an opportunity to combine his desire to have an interesting and varied job with his role as the family breadwinner by pursuing a career as a scientist. Under the couple's long-term plan, Karen and the child will live in Lübeck or in the town where they are currently living, while her partner will live elsewhere during the week in order to pursue his career. At the center of the plan is the mother-child-home unit, which will remain in one place. Karen refers to it as "the principal life residence." In contrast to Kristin from Rostock, Karen is not worried at the prospect of being a single mother during the week.

Karen has already talked to her parents and friends about her plans for having a family, and knows that she will be supported by them. In addition, the career and stable income of her husband are more important to her than being able to live with him. Using this approach, she expects to succeed in combining the traditional West German family model with the flexibility and mobility currently demanded in the labor market. Unlike Kristin from Rostock, who has been unable to find a way to follow the egalitarian family model by pursuing a career in science while being a parent, Karen has found a solution by modifying the traditional West German family model. She is willing to give up her own career and living with her partner, and has asked her husband to focus on his career instead. Her husband's willingness to sacrifice spending time with his children in order to pursue his career and fulfill his role as the family's breadwinner is also in line with this model.

12.5 Shared Living Conditions: Differing Conceptions and Behavioral Patterns

The women from East and West Germany who were interviewed in this study were similar in terms of their initial positions and their current material living conditions: they described having difficulties related to their uncertain employment situations, including having to take temporary jobs and make frequent moves. The women also complained of challenges in figuring out how to reconcile having a family life with having an active and satisfactory work life. Nonetheless, we found that the women in the East and the West had very different ideas and behavioral patterns which, given these living conditions, could lead to childlessness.

Our comparison of four individual case studies sheds light on some behavioral patterns that have emerged from the different socialization contexts that prevailed in Germany prior to unification. In particular, we have been able to illustrate that the family models that were dominant in the former East and West Germany were still very present in the narrations of the women interviewed. While the East German women assumed that both parents would have a job, their West German counterparts assumed that there would be an asymmetric role allocation: i.e., that the man would be the main breadwinner and the woman would be primarily responsible for homemaking. It is thus apparent that women from East Germany see work and family life as being two parallel tracks, neither of which should have priority. There was no indication that they had even considered following the West German family model.

Given the current levels of economic uncertainty and the labor market demands that workers remain flexible as well as mobile, the East German family model has the potential to result in childlessness, as it is difficult to ensure under these conditions that both partners will be able to reconcile their work life with parenthood. Yet the West German model, in which the man's job is the sole focus, could also lead to childlessness if the male partner is unable to be the main breadwinner due to adverse labor market conditions. Thus, the East German egalitarian model seems to be more advantageous because both partners are contributing to the family income.

Another difference between the interviewees from East and West Germany was the degree to which they had planned how they would start their family. The West German women developed clear ideas about how they would like to reconcile work and family life, and about the role their partner was supposed to play. The East German women, by contrast, considered having a family to be a project that was independent of their work life, and did not develop any special plans regarding their own career or their partner's choice of profession or career (as was the case with Miriam and Karen from Lübeck). In line with the habitus concept, we reason that this difference may be traced back to the fact that women in the GDR did not have to engage in long-term planning to advance their own career and to ensure that they could reconcile employment and family life. The young women from Rostock lacked the experience of normative pressure, including the example of the preceding generation, which may have otherwise led them to formulate long-term plans even before they were ready to have children (Antje). Thus, they were not prepared to address the issue of how to reconcile work and family life when they were ready to start a family (Kristin). It is also conceivable that the absence of long-term planning was a response to unification and its consequences, as this event was both unexpected and uncontrollable for the individual. The fundamental social changes induced by unification shook up the current lives of many East Germans, as well as their expectations concerning their future lives. Having witnessed how quickly biographical continuity can be destroyed may have led them to avoid making long-term plans. Given the ongoing labor market uncertainties in Germany and the increasing demands for individual flexibility and mobility, following a long-term plan may seem difficult. Overly rigid biographical plans—e.g., setting subjective preconditions which must be fulfilled prior to family formation—may cause women to postpone parenthood, and to end up childless. However, an absence of long-term planning can also hamper the spontaneous realization of parenthood. By hoping the circumstances will be better at some point in the future, starting a family may be perpetually delayed.

These results confirm our hypothesis that an inertial effect of socialization under different political regimes is having long-term effects on the life paths of the generation under study. Although their current life conditions are similar, their different socialization contexts lead women to cope with these conditions differently. To gain a better understanding of different paths to childlessness, we therefore have to take into account the different perspectives and behavioral patterns that have persisted in East and West Germany even after unification. The interesting question which follows from these observations is how durable this inertial effect is likely to be. Will we see fundamental changes in the cohort who are currently thinking about family formation, and who have been raised in unified Germany? Or will the inertial effect linger until the following generation—i.e., the young adults whose parents have not experienced a divided Germany—start having children? These are interesting issues for future research.

Acknowledgement   The authors thank Holger von der Lippe, Andreas Klärner, Christin Schröder, and Tina Hannemann for their valuable comments on this essay. This publication benefited from the support of the Swiss National Centre of Competence in Research LIVES—Overcoming vulnerability: life course perspectives, which is financed by the Swiss National Science Foundation. The authors are grateful to the Swiss National Science Foundation for its financial assistance.

References

Beck-Gernsheim, E. (1997). Geburtenrückgang und Kinderwunsch—die Erfahrung in Ostdeutschland. *Zeitschrift für Bevölkerungswissenschaft, 22*, 59–71.

Bernardi, L., von der Lippe, H., Klärner, A. (2006). *Perceptions of job (in)stability and parenthood perspectives. Case studies in eastern and western Germany.* Paper presented at the Population Association of America 2006 Meeting.

Bernardi, L., Keim, S., & Klärner, A. (2014). Social networks, social influence, and fertility in Germany: Challenges and benefits of applying a parallel mixed methods design. In S. Domínguez & B. Hollstein (Eds.), *Mixed-methods social networks research. Design and applications* (pp. 121–152). Cambridge: Cambridge University Press.

Bourdieu, P. (1984). *Distinction. A social critique of the judgement of taste.* Cambridge, MA: Harvard University Press.

D'Andrade, R. (1997). Schemas and motivation. In R. D'Andrade & C. Strauss (Eds.), *Human motives and cultural models* (pp. 23–44). Cambridge: Cambridge University Press.

Eberstadt, N. (1994). Demographic shocks after communism: Eastern Germany, 1989–1993. *Population and Development Review, 20*, 137–152.

Falk, S., & Schaeper, H. (2001). Erwerbsverläufe von ost- und westdeutschen Müttern im Vergleich: ein Land—ein Muster? In C. Born & H. Krüger (Eds.), *Individualisierung und Verflechtung. Geschlecht und Generation im deutschen Lebenslaufregime* (pp. 181–210). Weinheim/München: Juventa.

Huinink, J., Kreyenfeld, M., & Trappe, H. (2012). Familie und Partnerschaft in Ost- und Westdeutschland. Eine Bilanz. In J. Huinink, M. Kreyenfeld, & H. Trappe (Eds.), *Familie und Partnerschaft in Ost- und Westdeutschland. Ähnlich und doch immer noch anders* (pp. 9–28). Opladen: Budrich.

Kreyenfeld, M. (2003). Crisis or adaptation—reconsidered: A comparison of East and West German fertility patterns in the first six years after the "Wende". *European Journal of Population, 19*, 303–329.

Kreyenfeld, M. (2004). Fertility in the FRG and GDR. *Demographic Research, Special Collection, 3*, 67–318. http://www.demographic-research.org.

Kreyenfeld, M., & Konietzka, D. (2010). Nichteheliche Geburten. In J. Goldstein, M. Kreyenfeld, J. Huinink, D. Konietzka, & H. Trappe (Eds.), *Familie und Partnerschaft in Ost- und Westdeutschland* (pp. 8–9). Rostock: Max-Planck-Institut für demografische Forschung.

Statistische Ämter des Bundes und der Länder (Federal Statistical Office and the statistical offices of the Länder). (2015). Kindertagesbetreuung regional 2014. Ein Vergleich aller 402 Kreise in Deutschland. Wiesbaden.

Statistisches Bundesamt (Federal Statistical Office). (2012). *Geburten in Deutschland. Ausgabe 2012. Wiesbaden.* https://www.destatis.de/DE/Publikationen/Thematisch/Bevoelkerung/Bevoelkerungsbewegung/BroschuereGeburtenDeutschland0120007129004.pdf.

Therborn, G. (1980). *The ideology of power and the power of ideology.* London: Verso.

Wenzel, S. (2010). Konvergenz oder Divergenz? Einstellungen zur Erwerbstätigkeit von Müttern in Ost- und Westdeutschland. *Gender, 2,* 59–76.

Witte, J. C., & Wagner, G. G. (1995). Declining fertility in East Germany after unification: A demographic response to socioeconomic change. *Population and Development Review, 21,* 38–48.

Witzel, A., & Kühn, T. (2001). Biographiemanagement und Planungschaos. Arbeitsmarktplatzierung und Familiengründung bei jungen Erwachsenen. In C. Born & H. Krüger (Eds.), *Individualisierung und Verflechtung. Geschlecht und Generation im deutschen Lebenslaufregime* (pp. 55–82). Weinheim/München: Juventa.

Chapter 13
Assisted Reproductive Technologies in Germany: A Review of the Current Situation

Heike Trappe

13.1 Introduction

As assisted reproductive technologies have become increasingly prevalent, and the issues surrounding the use of ART are discussed in the public media, a sweeping social change with ethical, cultural, and demographic consequences has been set in motion. According to some commentators, the decoupling of procreation and pregnancy seems to have suspended the "fundamental law of human reproduction" (Bahnsen and Spiewak 2008: 35). Other observers have noted that fertility treatments have created the illusion of extended fecundity through the partial transcendence of the limitations set by nature (Correll 2010: 36).

The first "test tube baby" was Louise Joy Brown, born in England on 25 July 1978. Her birth represents the cornerstone in the development of assisted reproduction[1] (Steptoe and Edwards 1978). The first "IVF baby" in Germany was born at the university hospital in Erlangen in spring of 1982 (Berlin-Institut für Bevölkerung und Entwicklung 2007: 23). In 2010, Robert Edwards, a co-founder of the first in vitro fertilisation (IVF) programme, was awarded the Nobel Prize in Physiology or Medicine. Thus, reproductive medicine, a subfield of medicine which deals with human reproduction and its dysfunctions, is still quite young. Reproductive technologies have, however, been developing rapidly, and social acceptance of fertility treatments has been growing. Worldwide, more than four million individuals have

---

This contribution is a partly updated and reworked version of the article by Trappe (2015).

[1] The terms assisted reproduction and reproductive medicine are being used interchangeably in this chapter.

H. Trappe (✉)
Institute of Sociology and Demographic Research, University of Rostock,
Rostock, Germany
e-mail: heike.trappe@uni-rostock.de

© The Author(s) 2017
M. Kreyenfeld, D. Konietzka (eds.), *Childlessness in Europe: Contexts, Causes, and Consequences*, Demographic Research Monographs,
DOI 10.1007/978-3-319-44667-7_13

been conceived through the use of ART (Beier et al. 2012). Since the systematic registration of ART began in Germany in 1997, there have been around 202,000 live births to parents who used these technologies – a figure which approximates the number of inhabitants of medium-sized German cities like Kassel or Rostock (Deutsches IVF-Register (DIR) 2014: 261).

Physicians of reproductive medicine in Germany seek to support both women and men, most of whom are in heterosexual partnerships, in fulfilling their desire to have a child. Freedom of reproduction is seen as a fundamental human right. Fertility treatment is usually preceded by the diagnosis of one or more biologically caused fertility limitations. In diagnosing these limitations, the physician distinguishes between sterility and infertility in both the male and the female partner. Infertility is defined as the inability to carry a pregnancy to term and to deliver a live birth, whereas sterility indicates the inability to conceive or to father a child. Most of the couples who undergo fertility treatment are not absolutely sterile, but have an unspecified restriction of fertility (Ludwig et al. 2013: 2). As a rule, subfertility is assumed after at least 1 year of regular sexual intercourse without contraception within which no pregnancy has been achieved (Beier et al. 2012). Since 1967 the World Health Organisation (WHO) has classified permanent involuntary childlessness as an illness with potentially severe psychological consequences (Robert Koch-Institut 2004). The extent of involuntary childlessness is difficult to estimate because of its age dependence, and because of the lack of clear boundaries between voluntary and involuntary childlessness (Kreyenfeld and Konietzka 2013: 18; Sobotka in this volume). Existing data tend to underestimate the extent of biologically based childlessness because it is assumed that an appropriate diagnosis has been confirmed.

13.2 Legal Framework and Rules for the Assumption of Costs for ART

The Embryo Protection Act (ESchG), which went into effect in Germany in 1991, established the legal framework for providers of reproductive medicine (Diedrich 2008). The main purpose of the legislation was to ensure the preservation of the embryo, and to mandate penalties for noncompliance.[2] ESchG also stipulated that ART should be used to optimise the success of a pregnancy, and not for other purposes. "The core rule related to the realisation of these goals is the so-called 'rule of three': physicians are only allowed to fertilise the egg cells which will be transferred within a single treatment cycle, and the number of embryos which may be transferred in each cycle is limited to three" (Riedel 2008a: 11 – own translation). ESchG lists a number of misuses of ART, including egg cell donation (i.e., the

---

[2] An embryo is defined as "fertilized human egg capable of developing from the time of fusion of the two nuclei, and each totipotent cell removed from an embryo that is capable of dividing or developing into an individual human being if the necessary conditions prevail" (ESchG § 8 (1)).

transfer of an unfertilised egg cell from one woman to another), surrogate mother-hood, and the utilisation of egg or sperm cells after the death of the owner. The only major fertility treatments not mentioned in the legislation are the donation of sperm cells (Berlin-Institut für Bevölkerung und Entwicklung 2007: 33) and the donation of "surplus" embryos (Ahr and Hawranek 2014) unless the ART treatment had been undertaken with the purpose to donate embryos (Möller 2013: 588).

Since the ESchG first went into effect, researchers in Germany have been calling for the passage of a comprehensive law which regulates all aspects of assisted human reproduction (Diedrich and Griesinger 2006; Riedel 2008b; DIR 2014). So far, these efforts have been unsuccessful (Riedel 2008a), most likely because the proposal of new legislation would incite another round of public debate on the status of embryos and the beginning of human life (Spiewak 2009). On the one hand, the fact that assisted reproduction in Germany is only partially regulated implies that there are no clear instructions to providers on how to manage some important aspects of ART, such as the handling of "supernumerary" embryos.[3] On the other hand, a large number of directives and laws have been approved which regulate certain aspects of reproductive medicine. For instance, the standards of quality and safety for egg cells, sperm cells, oocytes, and embryos were established in the Tissue Act of 20 July 2007. The Stem Cell Act of 28 June 2002, which outlined the conditions for the import of and research on embryonic stem cells, mandated a high level of protection for human gametes. Meanwhile, German physicians of reproductive medicine have argued that, because of legal restrictions, the types of treatment they can offer their patients are not keeping up with the most recent developments in medical science and technology. For example, physicians have asserted that the prohibition on embryo selection, and thus of the elective transfer of a single embryo, often results in unwanted multiple pregnancies (Beier et al. 2012: 364).

As was noted above, the donation of sperm cells, including the use of sperm cells which do not come from the female patient's male partner (heterologous or third party donation), is generally allowed in Germany. The only requirement for using donated sperm is a written declaration of consent by the future parents and the sperm donor. While the use of anonymous sperm or a mixture of sperm cells from different donors is not punishable by law, many people believe it is immoral because it violates a child's right to know her or his genetic ancestry (Revermann and Hüsing 2010: 199). To date, a sperm donor in Germany is not fully protected from legal claims that he is obliged to provide financial and other forms of support for any children who are conceived from his donation (Beier et al. 2012: 365). Two other laws are relevant in this context: the Transplantation Law of 2007 and the Children's Rights Improvement Act of 2002. "The former law prescribes that all documents in relation to human tissue have to be stored for at least 30 years … The second law stipulates that paternity cannot be contested by the male partner or the mother if they have agreed to artificial insemination by a third party donor, but only by the child after she or he reaches the age of majority" (Wischmann 2012: 121 – own

---

[3] These are embryos which were produced through IVF and which were left over after the treatment had been finished (Riedel 2008a).

translation). This gives children conceived by third party sperm donation the option as adults to gain access to the data of the former donor, and thus to acquire full knowledge of their ancestry.

According to guidelines which are binding on all medical professionals, access to ART services is granted to all married couples, but it is granted to cohabiting heterosexual couples only under exceptional circumstances (No. 3.1.1. of the Guideline of the Medical Chamber, Bundesärztekammer 2006). The reasoning for this restriction is that a child's welfare is best ensured within the legal bonds of matrimony. Some observers have called this restriction an example of the "power of the norm of heterosexual families with biological children" (Correll 2010: 36), while others have claimed it represents unconstitutional discrimination of same-sex couples and single women (Revermann and Hüsing 2010: 200; Möller 2013: 595).

The reasoning for the controversial prohibition of egg cell donation is to avoid ambiguity about who the mother is, and to prevent a separation of the genetic and gestational components which might result in identity problems for the child. The differences in the regulation of egg cell and sperm donation have been justified by the different "depths" involved in collecting male and female gametes (Revermann and Hüsing 2010: 200). From a social science perspective, it is relevant that ambiguity about the identity of the father of a child has long been tolerated, whereas uncertainty about the identity of a child's mother has not. Meanwhile, reproductive medical professionals have been calling for a reasonable policy on egg cell donation in Germany to support the 3–4 % of women under age 40 who are unable to conceive for genetic or other reasons (Kentenich and Griesinger 2013: 273).

The diagnostic options related to ART are also regulated under ESchG and subsequent interpretations of the law. For example, polar body diagnosis, elective single embryo transfer (eSET), and pre-implantation diagnostics (PID) are legally permitted in Germany, but only within strict limits. These procedures and the legal framework surrounding them cannot be described in detail here (see Revermann and Hüsing 2010; Beier et al. 2012). The law on PID (PräimpG) went into effect on 21 November 2011, but the corresponding by-laws with important details (PIDV) did not become effective until February 2014. A PID procedure in connection with IVF is permitted only in specially authorised centres, and only after the couple have filed an application which has been approved by an interdisciplinary ethics panel. To qualify for a PID procedure, the couple must be able to show that they carry a serious genetic disease, or that the woman is likely to die or miscarry if she becomes pregnant (PräimpG § 3a(2) and PIDV).

"The reimbursement of the costs associated with ART varies between private and statutory health insurance. Overall, there are tendencies to limit reimbursement or to deny it" (Revermann and Hüsing 2010: 209 – own translation). "Until December 2003, up to four treatment cycles were fully covered by statutory health insurance. Since January 2004, the law for the modernisation of statutory health insurance (GMG) applies. Since then only 50 % of the treatment costs for a maximum of three treatment cycles are reimbursed.[4] For couples to qualify for coverage they must be married; women must be between 25 and 40 years of age and men must be between 25 and 50 years of age" (Passet-Wittig et al. 2014: 6). Before the treatment starts, couples have to undergo mandatory counselling on the medical and psycho-social aspects of ART with a physician who does not provide the treatment. For the relatively small share of women and men with private health insurance, the situation is somewhat different. Generally, private insurance provides full coverage for three treatment cycles based on the costs-by-cause principle, which implies that in a couple the insurance of the person who is considered "responsible" for the fertility problems has to cover the full costs (Revermann and Hüsing 2010).

"Since the implementation of the GMG, some statutory health insurance providers have individually increased coverage of fertility treatments for their customers" (Passet-Wittig et al. 2014: 7). A few selected federal states, like Saxony, Saxony-Anhalt, Lower Saxony, Mecklenburg-Western Pomerania, and Thuringia, support state residents who seek fertility treatments by limiting their co-payment to 25% (Passet-Wittig et al. 2014). This means that a couple's statutory health insurance provider and their place of residence have become significant factors in the size of their ART co-payments. The reduction in reimbursement by the GMG has had severe consequences for the great majority of couples with fertility problems.[5] The number of fertility treatments fell sharply after the passage of the law, and is only slowly returning to previous levels (DIR 2014, see section 13.3.5). In the political realm, the public financing of ART treatments is a matter of dispute. Proponents argue that permanent involuntary childlessness is an illness, and point to the tenuous demographic situation in Germany. Critics question the assertion that fertility problems are an illness, and argue that the fulfilment of the desire to have children should not be considered a form of social security. Rauprich (2008: 46) offered a further perspective on public financing of fertility interventions, asserting that having a child is a fundamental need, and that the question of how to pay for these treatments is one of equality of opportunity.

Across Europe, the financing mechanisms for ART vary greatly. While the costs associated with fertility treatments are fully covered by insurance in some countries (e.g., Spain), couples must bear the full costs themselves in others (e.g., Switzerland). The legal framework and the regulation of the criteria for access also vary considerably across Europe (Rauprich 2008; Revermann and Hüsing 2010; Küpker 2013). In Germany, some couples choose to pay for the fertility treatments themselves or to seek treatment abroad, presumably because of the legal restrictions in Germany and the challenges they face in gaining timely access to treatment. According to one

---

[4] A constitutional complaint about the reduction in reimbursement was rejected by the Federal Constitutional Court (Bundesverfassungsgericht 2009).

[5] "The costs associated with fertility treatments are considerable. In Germany, the cost of a standard IVF cycle including medication is about 3000 euros. An intracytoplasmatic sperm injection (ICSI), which is necessary in cases of male subfertility, costs about 3600 Euro. The rate of success varies according to the age of the woman and other factors … Based on this, a rough estimate of the cost of a live birth is about 15,000 euro" (Rauprich 2008: 32).

estimate, around 1000 German couples each year engage in "fertility tourism" in countries with less restrictive fertility treatment regulations (such as Belgium, the Czech Republic, and Spain) or with lower costs for ART (such as Hungary and Slovenia) (Revermann and Hüsing 2010: 221).[6]

13.3   Assisted Reproductive Technologies (ART)

In this section, I provide brief descriptions of the medical procedures and technologies which are currently being used to help couples with fertility problems fulfil their desire to have a child. While these descriptions do not include medical details, they should make it easier to understand the temporal developments in their use, and the extent to which these procedures have been successful in Germany (see section 13.3.5).

13.3.1   Intrauterine Insemination (IUI)

After the timing of a woman's ovulation is determined through regular ultrasound monitoring, a "washed" sperm sample is placed directly inside the woman's uterus using a sterile soft catheter. This procedure considerably shortens the distance the sperm must normally travel; i.e., from the vagina through the cervix and the uterus and into the fallopian tube. IUI can be performed with or without hormonal stimulation to trigger ovulation. As this treatment usually does not cause any pain, it can be performed without the use of anaesthesia (Wischmann 2012: 75). As the fertilisation takes place within the woman's body, it is a relatively simple form of ART. IUI has a long tradition (Dorn 2013), and has been practiced for a much longer period of time than the more extensive procedures that involve an extracorporeal fertilisation.

13.3.2   In Vitro Fertilisation (IVF)

IVF is the joining of an egg and sperm outside of the woman's body. The actual fertilisation and the initial process of cell division take place in vitro in a nutrient liquid. This eliminates the need for the embryo to pass through the fallopian tube. IVF is the most basic form of all of the extracorporeal ART procedures, which can be understood as being special cases of IVF. "IVF can be described as follows: After

---

[6] Other sources cite much higher numbers (Spiewak 2011). An ethnographic study by Bergmann (2011) provides insights into the complex motivations for fertility tourism to Spain, Denmark, and the Czech Republic.

a hormonal stimulation to trigger a woman's ovulation, multiple eggs are retrieved using a transvaginal technique. In the laboratory, the identified and prepared eggs are incubated together with the washed sperm. After successful fertilisation, the resulting embryos are cultivated and transferred to the patient's uterus" (Revermann and Hüsing 2010: 37 – own translation). It is important to note that the retrieval of mature follicles is done under conscious sedation or general anaesthesia, which has certain risks. In most cases, 6–10 eggs are removed from the woman at once, and the man's semen is collected, prepared, and washed on the same day. To initiate the fertilisation, the egg and the sperm are incubated together, and the embryos are cultivated for about 2 days in an incubator. This process is monitored microscopically, and the quality of the embryos is judged according to morphological criteria.[7] No later than 5 or 6 days after fertilisation a maximum of three promising embryos are transferred into the woman's uterus, in line with the rules set out in ESchG. Any "leftover" fertilised eggs which are at the stage prior to the fusion of the two nuclei (2-PN stage) are often cryopreserved in liquid nitrogen (Revermann and Hüsing 2010: 37). Interestingly, over time there has been an extension in the duration of the period prior to the transfer of the embryo. The purpose of this "German compromise", which is based on a liberal interpretation of the ESchG, is to limit the number of transferred embryos to a maximum of two, while still achieving pregnancy rates comparable to those in other countries (DIR 2011).[8] The decision about whether to use an IVF procedure often depends on the quality of the man's sperm and medical indications of the woman.

13.3.3   Intracytoplasmic Sperm Injection (ICSI)

The intracytoplasmic sperm injection procedure was first developed in the early 1990s. The only difference between ICSI and conventional IVF is the fertilisation itself. This technique involves the insemination of a mature egg cell by the microinjection of a single sperm cell into it. The steps before and after insemination are exactly the same as those in a conventional IVF procedure without ICSI. Therefore, the success of the treatment does not depend on the number and mobility of sperm. ICSI was originally developed to treat cases of male infertility or abnormalities in

---

[7] Judging the embryo's stage of development according to morphological criteria is an indirect method, and is thus subject to prognostic vagueness. The selection and further culturing of the embryos has to be done at the stage of the impregnated fertilized egg, under the Embryo Protection Act (ESchG) (Revermann and Hüsing 2010: 41). Therefore, this morphological evaluation is not comparable to the eSET.

[8] "In each individual case, the criteria for determining how many fertilized eggs should be cultivated longer so that after 5 days in vitro a maximum of three promising embryos can be transferred will depend on the characteristics and medical history of the couple (age, number, and outcome of previous treatments). However, more than three fertilized eggs may be kept prior to the fusion of the nuclei (2-PN stage). Thus, this practice is beneficial only for couples who have a certain number of fertilised eggs at their disposal" (DIR 2011: 12 – own translation).

sperm, and since then has proved to be a major advance in the treatment of subfertility of male origin. In the application of this technique, healthy women need to
undergo fertility treatment. Today, ICSI is routinely used to fertilise cryopreserved
eggs or treat idiopathic infertility, or in cases in which conventional IVF has not
been successful. Worldwide and in Germany specifically, ICSI is now used more
often than conventional IVF. A basic disadvantage of ICSI relative to IVF is that
natural selection of sperm in the fertilisation of the egg is replaced by artificial
selection. This could be associated with an elevated risk of genetic disorders,
although the different studies which have investigated this question have generated
contradictory results (Revermann and Hüsing 2010: 39).

13.3.4   Cryopreservation

Human gametes and embryos can be preserved through a process of freezing at
around −196°C. This process, called cryopreservation, is a widely used assisted
reproduction technique. The cryopreservation of embryos and impregnated egg
cells has become increasingly common in countries around the world, provided
their legal norms permit the procedure. "In Germany, the cryopreservation of
impregnated egg cells is practiced extensively, in particular because of the prohibition on creating and preserving 'leftover' embryos" (Revermann and Hüsing 2010:
43 – own translation).[9] The advantage to cryopreserving supernumerary fertilised
egg cells at the stage prior to the fusion of the two nuclei (2-PN stage) is that there
is no need for the repeated hormonal stimulation of women's ovulation and a
retrieval of mature eggs, or for the use of the expensive ICSI method. While today
the cryopreservation of sperm is routinely done, the cryopreservation of unfertilised
egg cells is still technically challenging because of their sensitiveness (Griesinger
et al. 2008). But the new technique of vitrification, in which egg cells are frozen
within a few seconds, appears to represent a breakthrough (Spiewak 2013).
Cryopreservation can also be applied to female and male gametes, and is thus also
a method for preserving fecundity in patients preparing to undergo radiation or
chemo therapy. For social reasons, interest in the freezing of egg cells or embryos
seems to be growing (Lawrence 2010): "More attention might be given to so-called
social freezing (highlighted originally – H.T.), because many women feel pressured
by their 'biological clock' and are concerned about the diminishing quality of their
egg cells and the declining likelihood of motherhood" (Beier et al. 2012: 372 – own

---

[9]In the majority of European countries, the cryopreservation of leftover human embryos is the
preferred procedure (Griesinger et al. 2008: 27). If the "rule of three" in the Embryo Protection Act
(ESchG) is strictly followed, "supernumerary" embryos can be generated only exceptionally,
while this is regularly the case if eSET or PID is being used (Riedel 2008b). In many countries with
more liberal laws than those of Germany, the fate of a great number of frozen embryos currently
poses complex problems (Grady 2008).

translation).[10] The cryopreservation of egg cells is legal in Germany, but the high costs of the procedure and the short optimal age span for extracting a supply of egg cells are obstacles to even wider use (Spiewak 2013).

13.3.5 Temporal Development of ART and Measures of Success

Among the aims of the German IVF registry is to ensure the quality of ART by collecting data and setting national standards. The registry has been collecting data since 1982, the year when the first IVF baby was born in the Federal Republic of Germany.[11] While participation by IVF centres in the collection of data for the registry was mandatory under the guidelines of the Medical Chamber from 1998 to 2012, since 2012 clinics are no longer required to collect data (DIR 2013). Nevertheless, the registry will continue to provide IVF centres with a wealth of data. The German IVF registry collects electronically all of the data needed for a quality assessment of each initiated treatment cycle. "The prospective documentation as well as the cycle-by-cycle data collection are of particular value" (DIR 2014: 237). Unlike in some other countries (e.g., Human Fertilisation and Embryology Authority in Great Britain), the IVF registry in Germany is an association which relies on the voluntary participation of professional organisations, and thus lacks a statutory basis (Griesinger et al. 2008). The registry collects data on extracorporeal fertilisation only, and not on intrauterine forms of insemination in which the fertilisation takes place within the woman's body. So far, there is no insemination registry in Germany.[12] In 2013, 130 out of 131 IVF centres which participate in the German IVF registry had exported their data into the registry (DIR 2014: 9).

Over the past 10 years, the practice of endocrinology and reproductive medicine in Germany has been moving out of the universities and into the private sector. The main reasons for this shift appear to be the lower remuneration of ART practitioners by the universities and increasing economic pressure. As a result, more than 80 % of ART treatments are taking place in the private sector (Beier et al. 2012: 351).

---

[10] This is the topic of the Dutch documentary "Eggs for later", which was produced in 2010 (http://www.imdb.com/video/wab/vi1370856473/). A 2013 poll conducted by the Cologne market research institute YouGov in Germany found that 27 % of the 536 women surveyed said they could imagine having their egg cells frozen to ensure that they can fulfil their desire to have a child (YouGov 2013). The debate on social freezing gained momentum when in 2014 the large US-based companies Facebook and Apple announced that they would pay for the social freezing of their employees' egg cells (Groll 2014).

[11] In 1984 the first IVF baby was born in the German Democratic Republic (Revermann and Hüsing 2010: 48).

[12] Estimates indicate that since 1970 more than 100,000 children have been born in western Germany following insemination by third party donors. Currently, about 1000 children per year in Germany are conceived through this method (Katzorke 2008: 98).

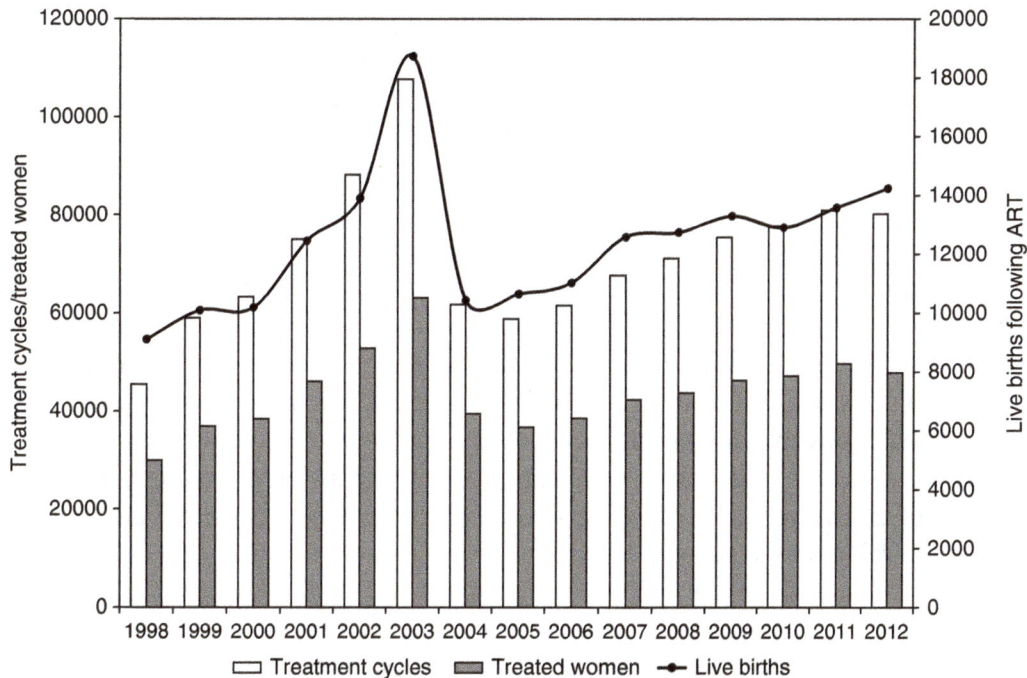

Fig. 13.1 The development of ART in Germany, 1998–2012 (Source: DIR 1999–2014 (own calculations))

"International lab networks are on the rise, and the takeover of IVF centres by private investors is nothing new" (DIR 2012: 13).

Figure 13.1 provides an overview of the development of ART over time since the beginning of reliable data collection. Up to 2003, the number of treatment cycles and the number of treated women[13] rose continuously. Over the same period, the number of live births resulting from fertility treatments also increased. Growth was particularly strong between 2002 and 2003, as couples and physicians were aware of the upcoming reduction in reimbursement levels. Physicians thus appear to have been performing treatments in that period which otherwise might have been performed the next year. The decline between 2003 and 2004 was especially large. Since then, the absolute numbers have reflected the consequences of the changes in reimbursement mandated in the GMG. In 2013, there were about as many treatment cycles as there were between 2001 and 2002. The mean age at fertility treatment among both women and men has increased rapidly: in 2013, it was 35.2 years for women and 38.6 years for men (DIR 2014: 28). In addition, some observers have argued that the rise in the use of treatments which are not covered by statutory health insurance is a sign that many couples are turning to privately financed treatments.[14] Since 2004, there has again been a steady increase in the number of treat-

---

[13] Even in cases in which the male partner is the cause of subfertility, the registry counts only fertility treatments among women.

[14] More detailed analyses of the reduction in reimbursement related to ART have shown that it is necessary to distinguish between short-term and long-term effects on use (Connolly et al. 2009).

ment cycles and in the number of live births following ART. The number of treatment cycles was roughly proportional to the number of treated women; on average, the number of treatment cycles per woman was between 1.5 and 1.7. Particularly telling is the share of live births resulting from ART among all live births: the share was largest in 2003, when it reached 2.6 %; whereas by 2012, the share was 2.1 % (own calculation).[15]

The IVF registry data clearly show that the success of ART is age dependent: "The likelihood of a pregnancy following ART is about 27 % per cycle after age 35 and it declines to 15 % per cycle at age 40" (Beier et al. 2012: 353 – own translation). This pattern is accompanied by increasing rates of miscarriage among women ages 35 and older (DIR 2014: 22–23). Overall, miscarriage rates have fallen over time. Another positive trend is that because of improvements in the quality of stimulation and in oocyte treatment, along with changes in transfer technology, the mean number of transferred embryos decreased by about 25 % between 1998 and 2012.

This development is associated with a further reduction in the share of multiple deliveries. Between 1998 and 2012, the proportion of triplets among all IVF newborns decreased by almost 80 %. In 2012, an average of less than two embryos were transferred per treatment cycle, which may be expected to improve the chances of a successful pregnancy (DIR 2014: 18).[16] The fact that transferring more than one embryo at a time increases the likelihood of multiple pregnancies is often seen as the most problematic aspect of ART. Compared with single pregnancies, multiple pregnancies are associated with higher morbidity and mortality risks for embryos and infants and increased health-related risks for women. Moreover, multiple births can have serious mental, social, and economic consequences for families.[17] In many countries, the use of diagnostic options like eSET is encouraged in an effort to limit the number of multiple pregnancies. For instance, in Sweden eSET is widely used to transfer only one embryo in each cycle (Revermann and Hüsing 2010). Of the live births resulting from ART in Germany in 2012, 66.5 % were singletons, 31.9 % were twins, and 1.6 % triplets (DIR 2014: 31).[18] Births following the use of ART therefore accounted for about 20 % of all multiple deliveries (own calculation).

The most common indicator of the success of ART is the pregnancy rate, defined as the percentage of clinical pregnancies per treatment. The data needed to track clinical pregnancies can be collected relatively quickly and completely, whereas the

---

[15] The last European comparison of data on ART for 2010, conducted by the European Society of Human Reproduction and Embryology (ESHRE), found that in Germany the share of infants conceived through ART relative to all births was about 2.1 %. The countries with larger shares were Denmark (5.9 %), Slovenia (5.1 %), and Iceland (4.4 %) (Kupka et al. 2014: 2104).

[16] It is noteworthy that the trend towards transferring fewer embryos did not stop when the GMG took effect: "The decision about the number of embryos that should be transferred was influenced by personal, health-related, and economic considerations" (Revermann and Hüsing 2010: 98).

[17] If there are strong medical reasons, multiple pregnancies have to be reduced. To prevent extreme preterm births and to limit related risks, fetal reduction is carried out via induced abortion of single embryos. In 2012 in Germany, this was done in 254 cases affecting 380 embryos (DIR 2014: 14).

[18] Of all live births in Germany (2012), only 3.5 % were from multiple deliveries (Statistisches Bundesamt 2014).

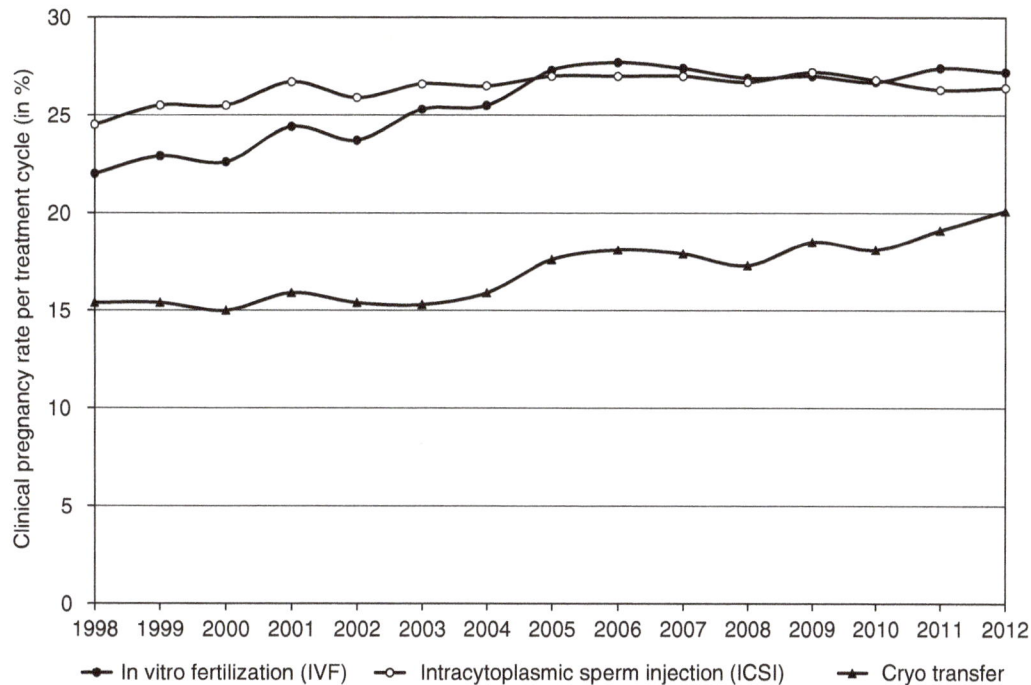

Fig. 13.2 The development of clinical pregnancy rates following ART in Germany, 1998–2012 (Source: DIR 1999–2014 (own calculations))

data on births following ART are often incomplete because it is difficult to link the data on the women who received treatment to information on subsequent births (Revermann and Hüsing 2010).

Figure 13.2 shows a clear increase in pregnancy rates following ART between 1998 and 2012. The rates rose for so-called fresh cycles (IVF, ICSI), but also for cryo transfers (frozen-thawed transfer, mostly in the 2-PN stage). It is important to note that pregnancy rates were higher following IVF and ICSI treatments than they were following cryo transfers. ICSI seems to have performed somewhat better than IVF from 1998 to 2004; thereafter, however, the pregnancy rates resulting from each of the two treatments can hardly be distinguished. Nonetheless, since 1998 ICSI has been used far more frequently in Germany than conventional IVF. Thus, the profiles of the patients who were treated with the respective methods might have shifted (Revermann and Hüsing 2010).

For couples and their attending physicians, a far more important indicator of the success of ART is the so-called "baby take-home rate", or the percentage of live births per treatment cycle. This rate is considerably lower than the clinical pregnancy rate (Fig. 13.3).

The trend of the baby take-home rate more or less reflects the temporal development of the pregnancy rates, but at a lower level. In 2012, a baby take-home rate of about 18 % after IVF or ICSI had been achieved. The rate was far lower following cryo transfers, as this method is associated with lower pregnancy rates and higher miscarriage rates. Overall, the baby take-home rate rose slightly between 1998 and 2012. This is remarkable because the mean age of the women and the men seeking

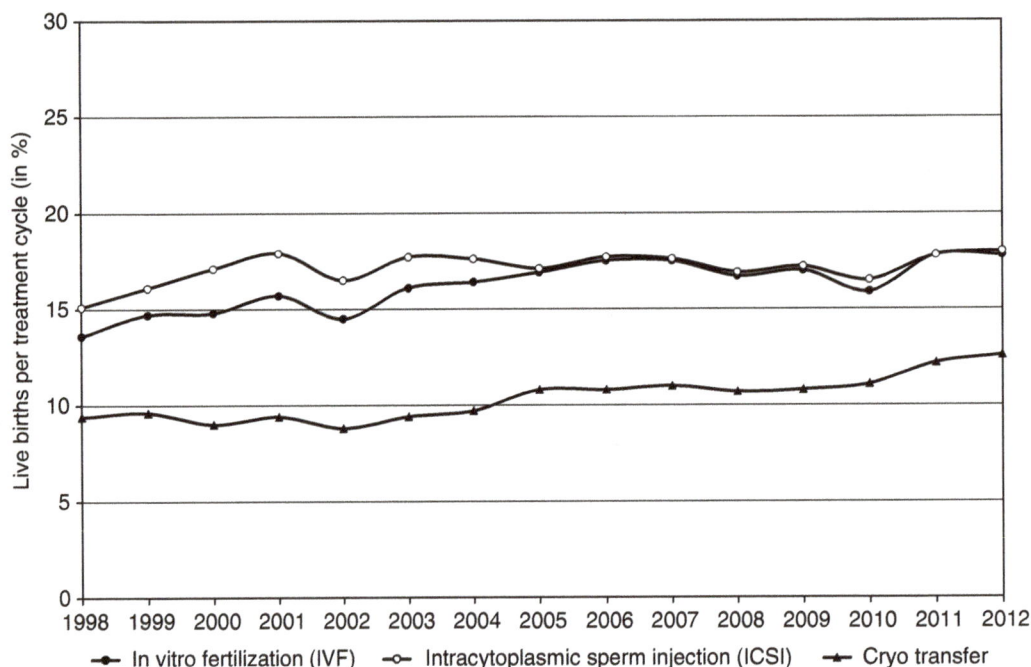

Fig. 13.3 The development of the baby take-home rate following ART in Germany, 1998–2012 (Source: DIR 1999–2014 (own calculations))

fertility treatment had been increasing rapidly and continuously during this time (DIR 2014: 28). Currently, the mean pregnancy rate after ART in Germany is only slightly below the European average, while the baby take-home rate corresponds to the European average.[19] Internationally, the further decline in the share of multiple pregnancies and deliveries and the reduction in the proportion of preterm births are considered signs of success, particularly among physicians of reproductive medicine (Wischmann 2012: 86). Due to improved medical and technical options, the use of ICSI and cryopreservation is increasing and the number of embryos transferred per cycle is declining, not only in Germany and across Europe, but also in other countries around the world (Revermann and Hüsing 2010).

The estimates of the rates of childlessness for bio-medical reasons vary widely for Germany. Revermann and Hüsing (2010: 18) have vaguely stated that between 0.5 and 1.5 million, or between three and 10 % of German couples, are involuntarily childless. Meanwhile, other scholars have estimated that between 1.2 and 1.5 million German couples are unable to conceive (Diedrich 2008). According to Sütterlin (2009: 1), every seventh German couple, or around 14 % of couples, experience involuntary childlessness. This value is closer to the figure mentioned by Michelmann (2008: 2), of between 10 and 15 % of all couples.[20] It should be noted, however, that

---

[19] Compared to Germany, the baby take-home rate is higher in the UK, Slovenia, Sweden, Norway, Iceland, and some formerly socialist countries (Revermann and Hüsing 2010: 96; Kupka et al. 2014: 2104).

[20] Beier et al. (2012) calculated based on a microsimulation model that the increase in the average age of women at first birth between 1985 and 2007 in West Germany contributed to an increase in involuntary childlessness from 3.5 % to 6.5 %.

all of these estimates of the extent of involuntary childlessness are based on data on the demand for ART, and are thus affected by the blurred lines between temporary and permanent childlessness. Given the lack of reliable data on involuntary childlessness, self-assessments by individuals of their own fecundity can be very informative. In the German Family Panel (pairfam), which covers certain birth cohorts (Huinink et al. 2011),[21] both the male and the female respondents had been asked whether it was possible for them and their partner to procreate by natural means. In the first wave (2008/09), between eight and nine per cent of women and men aged 35–39 replied that natural conception was probably or definitely not possible for them. Meanwhile, between 7 and 8 % of the respective partners of these respondents concurred with these assessments. Among the study participants who were 10 years younger, 3 % reported having fertility problems. Overall, it appears that the share of the German population who are concerned about their prospects for biological procreation is sizeable.

The question of whether – and, if so, to what extent – ART can contribute to a stabilisation or an increase in cohort fertility is difficult to answer. Based on complete fertility histories for Danish women, Sobotka et al. (2008: 95) estimated that for women of the birth cohort 1978 the net effect of ART is between 3 and 4 %. Among the factors which contribute to this relatively strong effect are easy access to ART treatments, public awareness of treatment options, increasing subfertility linked to the continued postponement of childbearing, and the relatively frequent use of ART among younger women and among mothers trying to have another child. At the same time, the authors expressed scepticism about suggestions that ART should be integrated into pronatalist policies, in part because they believe that promoting the illusion that fecundity is possible at higher reproductive ages could prove problematic.[22] Based on their analyses for West Germany, Beier et al. (2012) concluded that if the provision of ART continues at around current levels, the extent to which these treatments can compensate for the postponement of fertility will be negligible from a demographic perspective. Nevertheless, as the data on the temporal development of the baby take-home rate (Fig. 13.3) have shown, reproductive medicine can make an important contribution at the individual level by helping couples fulfil their desire to have a child. This is particularly relevant because involuntary childlessness is still a social taboo which can have grave psychological and mental implications for individuals (Hyatt 2012).

---

[21] This paper uses data from the German Family Panel pairfam, coordinated by Josef Brüderl, Karsten Hank, Johannes Huinink, Bernhard Nauck, Franz Neyer, and Sabine Walper. Pairfam is funded as long-term project by the German Research Foundation (DFG).

[22] This argument has also been put forward by Rainer et al. (2011), who emphasised that if ART was widely available, women might be tempted to postpone the births of their children until even later in the life course. This "behavioural effect" of postponement is likely to reduce the fertility rate in countries with high fertility in particular.

13.4   Discussion

"The declared ethos of reproductive medicine acknowledges the significance of the individual desire to have a child, and it affirms the right of couples to make their own procreation decisions" (Beier et al. 2012: 359 – own translation). Currently, the ability of German couples to make their own fertility treatment decisions is subject to legal restrictions, including prohibitions on the use of certain techniques, like egg cell donation, surrogacy, and reproductive cloning. However, in light of global changes in technologies and values, the debate about these legal obstacles may be expected to continue among experts and the public. Thus, in time, many of these restrictions will likely be challenged and overturned. A multifaceted societal debate is highly desirable, as it touches on fundamental aspects of the protection of human dignity, including questions about the beginning of human life and the essence of a life worth living. On the other hand, the freedom of individuals to make their own procreation decisions may be restricted in practice if access to ART services is limited. This is especially likely to be the case for economically disadvantaged population groups. ART has been relatively expensive in Germany particularly since the passage of the GMG in 2004, which substantially increased the co-payments for fertility treatments. Moreover, the legally and professionally defined criteria for access to reproductive medicine tend to exclude some social groups, including unmarried couples, same-sex couples, and singles. This tendency towards exclusion is attributable in part to the fact that the legal status of a sperm donor relative to any children conceived through his donation has not been fully clarified, particularly if the children are born out of wedlock. But the main reason certain social groups are excluded is the continued dominance of traditional cultural ideals of the family, which dictate that children should grow up in a home with two married biological parents (Herrmann-Green 2008). Groups who are not permitted to access ART services in Germany often have to seek out services in hospitals abroad.[23] The allocation of access to ART services in Germany privileges particular living arrangements, and is based on the cultural ideal of a "normal family" rooted in the interrelation of marriage and procreation. The more this family ideal comes under pressure due to on-going social changes, the more people will demand a liberalisation of access to reproductive medicine. Thus, the debate over access to assisted reproduction has the potential to challenge well-established attitudes about the family, and in so doing to unsettle deeply entrenched concepts about reproduction, motherhood, fatherhood, and kinship. The extent to which this actually occurs depends on the specific social conditions. In the case of Germany, it is interesting from a social science perspective to observe that social fatherhood and motherhood are still perceived differently by

---

[23] Worldwide, the rising demand for and the increasing shortage of egg cells has led to an international market in egg cells and fertility tourism. "The development of reproductive tourism is related to an extension of the supply as well as to the structural and economic inequities between countries and regions" (Berg 2008: 244 – own translation). Egg cell donation and surrogacy are aspects of the global commercialisation of the female body (Rudrappa 2012).

the legal system, with sperm donation by a third party donor being allowed while egg cell donation is prohibited.

Reproductive medicine is barely 40 years old, and is thus a young discipline which is still developing extremely rapidly. Not surprisingly, certain problems related to reproductive medicine remain unresolved. These problems often result from particular legal situations and corresponding value conflicts (Riedel 2008b). The unintended consequences of certain ART treatments did not become obvious until the first generation of children conceived by ART grew older. Now, however, it is generally recognised that allowing children to know their genetic origin is essential, not only for medical reasons, but also for reasons of personal identity. This presupposes that children will be told about their conception, that reproductive donations will not occur anonymously, and that the relevant data on donors will be stored and preserved in a central location. Revermann and Hüsing (2010: 228) have pointed out that the safety, the risks, and especially the consequences of ART over time have not been subjected to the same investigative rigour as the medical techniques. From an ethical standpoint, new courses of action always entail new responsibilities (Kreß 2013).

To evaluate the potential of ART, a broad societal debate about the opportunities and implications of these technologies is certainly needed. At present, the success rates of fertility treatments tend to be overstated, while the emotional strain of undergoing these treatments is often underestimated (Revermann and Hüsing 2010). The desire to have a child at any age cannot be fulfilled. Education and counselling should help to lower the barriers to seeking fertility treatment, and to alleviate widespread social biases regarding subfertility, particularly among men (Thorn 2008). In the future, topics like the "social freezing" of egg cells and new diagnostic options for preserving embryos may be expected to dominate the debate on the socially acceptable and desirable implications of ART. On the one hand, reproductive medicine can be seen as expression of a deeply rooted human desire to achieve emancipation from nature. But on the other, these technologies break taboos and call into question traditional ideas of what it means to be human (Rauprich and Siegel 2003).

Literature

Ahr, N., & Hawranek, C. (2014, October 9). Reproduktionsmedizin: Die gespendeten Kinder [Reproductive medicine: The donated children]. *Die Zeit, 40.*

Bahnsen, U., & Spiewak, M. (2008, May 29). Reproduktionsmedizin: Die Zukunftskinder [Reproductive medicine: Children of the future]. *Die Zeit, 23.*

Beier, H. M., van den Daele, W., Diedrich, K., Dudenhausen, J. W., Felberbaum, R., & Gigerenzer, G., et al. (2012). Medizinische und biologische Aspekte der Fertilität [Medical and biological aspects of fertility]. In G. Stock, H. Bertram, A. Fürnkranz-Prskawetz, W. Holzgreve, M. Kohli, & U. M. Staudinger (Eds.), *Zukunft mit Kindern: Fertilität und gesellschaftliche Entwicklung in Deutschland, Österreich und der Schweiz* [Future with children: Fertility and social development in Germany, Austria, and Switzerland] (pp. 294–391). Frankfurt/New York: Campus.

Berg, G. (2008). Die Eizellspende – eine Chance für wen? [The donation of egg cells – a chance for whom?] In G. Bockenheimer-Lucius, P. Thorn, & C. Wendehorst (Eds.), *Umwege zum eigenen Kind: Ethische und rechtliche Herausforderungen an die Reproduktionsmedizin 30 Jahre nach Louise Brown* [Detours to a child of one's own: Ethical and legal challenges of reproductive medicine 30 years after Louise Brown] (pp. 239–253). Göttingen: Universitätsverlag.

Bergmann, S. (2011). Fertility tourism: Circumventive routes that enable access to reproductive technologies and substances. *Signs, 36*, 280–289.

Berlin-Institut für Bevölkerung und Entwicklung. (2007). *Ungewollt kinderlos – Was kann die moderne Medizin gegen den Kindermangel in Deutschland tun?* [Involuntarily childless – What can be done by modern medicine against the shortage of children in Germany?] Berlin: Berlin-Institut für Bevölkerung und Entwicklung.

Bundesärztekammer (Medical Chamber). (2006). *(Muster-)Richtlinie zur Durchführung der assistierten Reproduktion* [Guideline on the realization of assisted reproduction]. http://www.bundesaerztekammer.de/downloads/AssRepro.pdf. Accessed 9 Mar 2015.

Bundesverfassungsgericht (Federal Constitutional Court). (2009). Pressemitteilung [Press release] Nr. 24/2009. http://www.bverfg.de/pressemitteilungen/bvg09-024.html. Accessed 9 Mar 2015.

Connolly, M. P., Griesinger, G., Ledger, W., & Postma, M. J. (2009). The impact of introducing patient co-payments in Germany on the use of IVF and ICSI: A price-elasticity of demand assessment. *Human Reproduction Update, 24*, 2796–2800.

Correll, L. (2010). *Anrufungen zur Mutterschaft* [Invocations to motherhood]. Münster: Westfälisches Dampfboot.

Diedrich, K. (2008). Einleitung [Introduction]. In K. Diedrich, R. Felberbaum, G. Griesinger, H. Hepp, H. Kreß, & U. Riedel (Eds.), *Reproduktionsmedizin im internationalen Vergleich – Wissenschaftlicher Sachstand, medizinische Versorgung und gesetzlicher Regelungsbedarf* [Reproductive medicine in international comparison – Scientific state of affairs, medical provision, and necessity for legal regulation] (pp. 8–10). Frankfurt: Friedrich-Ebert-Stiftung.

Diedrich, K., & Griesinger, G. (2006). Deutschland braucht ein Fortpflanzungsmedizingesetz [Germany needs a comprehensive law for all aspects of assisted human reproduction]. *Geburts- und Frauenheilkunde, 66*, 345–348.

DIR – Deutsches IVF-Register (German IVF registry). (2014). *Jahrbuch 2013 sowie zurückliegende Jahrgänge* [Annual 2013 and earlier annuals]. http://www.deutsches-ivf-register.de. Accessed 9 Mar 2015.

Dokumentarfilm (Documentary) „Eggs for later": http://www.imdb.com/video/wab/vi1370856473/. Accessed 9 Mar 2015.

Dorn, C. (2013). Inseminationsbehandlung [Assisted insemination]. In Diedrich, K., Ludwig, M., & Griesinger, G. (Eds.), *Reproduktionsmedizin* [Reproductive medicine] (pp. 197–207). Wiesbaden: Springer VS.

EschG – Gesetz zum Schutz von Embryonen (Embryonenschutzgesetz, The Embryo Protection Act). http://www.auswaertiges-amt.de/cae/servlet/contentblob/480804/publicationFile/5162/EmbryoProtectionAct.pdf. Accessed 9 Mar 2015.

Grady, D. (2008, December 4). Parents torn over fate of frozen embryos. *New York Times*.

Griesinger, G., Felberbaum, R., Hepp, H., & Diedrich, K. (2008). Reproduktionsmedizin in Deutschland und im internationalen Vergleich [Reproductive medicine in Germany and in international comparison]. In K. Diedrich, R. Felberbaum, G. Griesinger, H. Hepp, H. Kreß, & U. Riedel (Eds.), *Reproduktionsmedizin im internationalen Vergleich – Wissenschaftlicher Sachstand, medizinische Versorgung und gesetzlicher Regelungsbedarf* [Reproductive medicine in international comparison – Scientific state of affairs, medical provision, and necessity for legal regulation] (pp. 22–61). Frankfurt: Friedrich-Ebert-Stiftung.

Groll, T. (2014, October 20). Social Freezing: Der eingefrorene Lebensentwurf [Social freezing: The frozen script of life]. *Die Zeit,* online.

Herrmann-Green, L. (2008). Lesben mit Kinderwunsch: Eine ethische Herausforderung für die Reproduktionsmedizin? [Lesbians with a desire to have a child: An ethical challenge for reproductive medicine?] In G. Bockenheimer-Lucius, P. Thorn, & C. Wendehorst (Eds.), *Umwege zum eigenen Kind: Ethische und rechtliche Herausforderungen an die Reproduktionsmedizin*

30 Jahre nach Louise Brown [Detours to a child of one's own: Ethical and legal challenges of reproductive medicine 30 years after Louise Brown] (pp. 217–237). Göttingen: Universitätsverlag.

Huinink, J., Brüderl, J., Nauck, B., Walper, S., Castiglioni, L., & Feldhaus, M. (2011). Analysis of intimate relationships and family dynamics (pairfam): Conceptual framework and design. *Zeitschrift für Familienforschung, 23*, 77–101.

Hyatt, M. (2012). *Ungestillte Sehnsucht: Wenn der Kinderwunsch uns umtreibt* [Unsettled longing: When the desire for a child is always on our mind]. Berlin: Ch. Links Verlag.

Katzorke, T. (2008). Entstehung und Entwicklung der Spendersamenbehandlung in Deutschland [Emergence and development of sperm donation in Germany]. In Bockenheimer-Lucius, G., Thorn, P., & Wendehorst, C. (Eds.), *Umwege zum eigenen Kind: Ethische und rechtliche Herausforderungen an die Reproduktionsmedizin 30 Jahre nach Louise Brown* [Detours to a child of one's own: Ethical and legal challenges of reproductive medicine 30 years after Louise Brown] (pp. 89–101). Göttingen: Universitätsverlag.

Kentenich, H., & Griesinger, G. (2013). Zum Verbot der Eizellspende in Deutschland: Medizinische, psychologische, juristische und ethische Aspekte [On the proscription of egg cell donation in Germany: Medical, psychological, legal, and ethical aspects]. *Journal für Reproduktionsmedizin und Endokrinologie, 10*, 273–278.

Kreß, H. (2013). Ethik: Reproduktionsmedizin im Licht von Verantwortungsethik und Grundrechten [Ethics: Reproductive medicine in light of ethics of responsibility and fundamental rights]. In Diedrich, K., Ludwig, M., & Griesinger, G. (Eds.), *Reproduktionsmedizin* [Reproductive medicine] (pp. 651–670). Wiesbaden: Springer VS.

Kreyenfeld, M., & Konietzka, D. (2013). Kinderlosigkeit in Deutschland. Theoretische Probleme und empirische Ergebnisse [Childlessness in Germany. Theoretical problems and empirical results]. In Konietzka, D., & Kreyenfeld, M. (Eds.), *Ein Leben ohne Kinder: Ausmaß, Strukturen und Ursachen von Kinderlosigkeit* [A life without children: Extent, structures, and causes of childlessness] (pp. 13–44). Wiesbaden: Springer VS.

Kupka, M. S., Ferraretti, A. P., de Mouzon, J., Erb, K., D'Hooghe, T., Castilla, J. A., et al. (2014). Assisted reproductive technology in Europe, 2010: Results generated from European registers by ESHRE. *Human Reproduction Update, 29*, 2099–2113.

Küpker, W. (2013). Regulation der Reproduktionsmedizin im europäischen Vergleich [Regulation of reproductive medicine in European comparison]. In Diedrich, K., Ludwig, M., & Griesinger, G. (Eds.), *Reproduktionsmedizin* [Reproductive medicine] (pp. 631–637). Wiesbaden: Springer VS.

Lawrence, G. E. St. (2010, July 6). By freezing embryos, couples try to utilize fertility while delaying parenthood. *Washington Post*.

Ludwig, M., Diedrich, K., & Nawroth, F. (2013). Was ist „Sterilität"– eine Begriffsbestimmung [What is „sterility"– a definition]. In Diedrich, K., Ludwig, M., & Griesinger, G. (Eds.), *Reproduktionsmedizin* [Reproductive medicine] (pp. 1–7). Wiesbaden: Springer VS.

Michelmann, H.-W. (2008). Reproduktionsmedizin im Jahre 2008: Probleme – Wünsche – Lösungsansätze [Reproductive medicine in 2008: Problems – desires – methods of resolution]. In G. Bockenheimer-Lucius, P. Thorn, & C. Wendehorst (Eds.), *Umwege zum eigenen Kind: Ethische und rechtliche Herausforderungen an die Reproduktionsmedizin 30 Jahre nach Louise Brown* [Detours to a child of one's own: Ethical and legal challenges of reproductive medicine 30 years after Louise Brown] (pp. 1–8). Göttingen: Universitätsverlag.

Möller, K.-H. (2013). Rechtliche Regelung der Reproduktionsmedizin in Deutschland [Legal regulation of reproductive medicine in Germany]. In Diedrich, K., Ludwig, M., & Griesinger, G. (Eds.), *Reproduktionsmedizin* [Reproductive medicine] (pp. 583–606). Wiesbaden: Springer VS.

Passet-Wittig, J., Letzel, S., Schneider, N. F., Schuhrke, B., Seufert, R., Zier, U., et al. (2014). *The PinK study – Methodology of the baseline survey of a prospective cohort study of couples undergoing fertility treatment*. Wiesbaden: Federal Institute for Population Research.

PIDV – Verordnung zur Regelung der Präimplantationsdiagnostik (By-laws on the regulation of PID). http://www.bmg.bund.de/fileadmin/dateien/Downloads/P/PID/PIDVE_121114.pdf. Accessed 9 Mar 2015.

PräimpG – Gesetz zur Regelung der Präimplantationsdiagnostik (Law on PID) (Präimplantationsdiagnostikgesetz). http://www.bundesgerichtshof.de/SharedDocs/Downloads/DE/Bibliothek/Gesetzesmaterialien/17_wp/PID/bgbl.pdf;jsessionid=7A29046574 C95F59D0ACCBAC657246D4.2_cid354?__blob=publicationFile. Accessed 9 Mar 2015.

Rainer, H., Selvaretnam, G., & Ulph, D. (2011). Assisted reproductive technologies (ART) in a model of fertility choice. *Journal of Population Economics, 24*, 1101–1132.

Rauprich, O. (2008). Sollen Kinderwunschbehandlungen von den Krankenkassen finanziert werden? Ethische und rechtliche Aspekte [Shall ART treatments be publicly financed? Ethical and legal aspects]. In G. Bockenheimer-Lucius, P. Thorn, & C. Wendehorst (Eds.), *Umwege zum eigenen Kind: Ethische und rechtliche Herausforderungen an die Reproduktionsmedizin 30 Jahre nach Louise Brown* [Detours to a child of one's own: Ethical and legal challenges of reproductive medicine 30 years after Louise Brown] (pp. 31–47). Göttingen: Universitätsverlag.

Rauprich, O., & Siegel, S. (2003). Der Natur den Weg weisen: Ethische Aspekte der Reproduktionsmedizin [To show nature the path: Ethical aspects of reproductive medicine]. In A. Ley, & M. M. Ruisinger (Eds.), *Von Gebärhaus und Retortenbaby. 175 Jahre Frauenklinik Erlangen* [On delivery houses and test tube babies. 175 years of gynecological hospital Erlangen] (pp. 153–171). Nürnberg: Verlag W. Tümmels.

Revermann, C., & Hüsing, B. (2010). Fortpflanzungsmedizin – Rahmenbedingungen, wissenschaftlich-technische Fortschritte und Folgen [Reproductive medicine – Conditions, scientific progress, and consequences]. Berlin, Büros für Technikfolgenabschätzung beim Deutschen Bundestag. Arbeitsbericht Nr. 139.

Riedel, U. (2008a). Vorgeschichte und Stand der Gesetzgebung [Pre-history and state of legislation]. In K. Diedrich, R. Felberbaum, G. Griesinger, H. Hepp, H. Kreß, & U. Riedel (Eds.), *Reproduktionsmedizin im internationalen Vergleich – Wissenschaftlicher Sachstand, me-dizinische Versorgung und gesetzlicher Regelungsbedarf* [Reproductive medicine in international comparison – Scientific state of affairs, medical provision, and necessity for legal regulation] (pp. 11–21). Frankfurt: Friedrich-Ebert-Stiftung.

Riedel, U. (2008b). Notwendigkeit eines Fortpflanzungsmedizingesetzes (FMG) aus rechtlicher Sicht [Necessity of a comprehensive law for all aspects of assisted reproduction (FMG) from a legal perspective]. In K. Diedrich, R. Felberbaum, G. Griesinger, H. Hepp, H. Kreß, & U. Riedel (Eds.), *Reproduktionsmedizin im internationalen Vergleich – Wissenschaftlicher Sachstand, medizinische Versorgung und gesetzlicher Regelungsbedarf* [Reproductive medicine in international comparison – Scientific state of affairs, medical provision, and necessity for legal regulation] (pp. 88–111). Frankfurt: Friedrich-Ebert-Stiftung.

Robert Koch-Institut. (2004). *Gesundheitsberichterstattung des Bundes* [Health report by the Federal government], Themenheft 20 „Ungewollte Kinderlosigkeit". Berlin: Robert Koch-Institut.

Rudrappa, S. (2012). India's reproductive assembly line. *Contexts, 11*, 22–27.

Sobotka, T., Hansen, M. A., Jensen, T. K., Pedersen, A. T., Lutz, W., & Skakkebæk, N. E. (2008). The contribution of assisted reproduction to completed fertility: An analysis of Danish data. *Population and Development Review, 34*, 79–101.

Spiewak, M. (2009, July 16). Medizin – Die Ausweitung der Grauzone [Medicine – The extension of the twilight zone], *Die Zeit, 30*.

Spiewak, M. (2011, July 3). Eizellspende – Für ein Baby nach Prag [Egg cell donation – For a baby to Prague], *Die Zeit, 45*.

Spiewak, M. (2013, July 11). Später Kinderwunsch – Die biologische Uhr anhalten [Late desire for a child – Stopping the biological clock], *Die Zeit, 29*.

Statistisches Bundesamt. (2014). *Natürliche Bevölkerungsbewegung* [Natural changes of population] – Fachserie 1, Reihe 1.1. Wiesbaden: Statistisches Bundesamt.

Steptoe, P. C., & Edwards, R. G. (1978). Birth after the reimplantation of a human embryo. *Lancet, 312*, 366.

Sütterlin, S. (2009). Ungewollte Kinderlosigkeit [Involuntary childlessness]. Online-Handbuch Demografie des Berlin-Instituts für Bevölkerung und Entwicklung: http://www.berlin-institut. org/online-handbuchdemografie/bevoelkerungsdynamik/auswirkungen/ungewollte-kinderlosigkeit.html. Accessed 9 Mar 2015.

Thorn, P. (2008). Samenspende und Stigmatisierung – ein unauflösbares Dilemma? [Sperm donation and stigmatizaion – an inextricable dilemma?] In G. Bockenheimer-Lucius, P. Thorn, C. Wendehorst (Eds.), *Umwege zum eigenen Kind: Ethische und rechtliche Herausforderungen an die Reproduktionsmedizin 30 Jahre nach Louise Brown* [Detours to a child of one's own: Ethical and legal challenges of reproductive medicine 30 years after Louise Brown] (pp. 135–155). Göttingen: Universitätsverlag.

Trappe, H. (2015). Reproduktionsmedizin in Deutschland: Eine Bestandsaufnahme aus bevölkerungssoziologischer Sicht [Reproductive medicine in Germany: An inventory from a perspective of population sociology]. In Niephaus, Y., Kreyenfeld, M., & Sackmann, R. (Eds.), *Handbuch Bevölkerungssoziologie* [Handbook population sociology] (forthcoming). Wiesbaden: Springer VS.

Wischmann, T. (2012). *Einführung Reproduktionsmedizin: Medizinische Grundlagen – Psychosomatik – Psychosoziale Aspekte* [Introduction reproductive medicine: Medical foundation – psychosomatic – psychosocial aspects]. München/Basel: Ernst Reinhardt Verlag.

YouGov. (2013). Künstliche Befruchtung: Jede vierte Frau würde sich ihre Eizellen einfrieren lassen [Assisted reproduction: Every fourth woman would freeze her egg cells]. http://yougov.de/ news/2013/10/15/kunstliche-befruchtung-jede-vierte-frau-wurde-sich/. Accessed 9 Mar 2015.

Chapter 14
Assisted Reproductive Technology in Europe: Usage and Regulation in the Context of Cross-Border Reproductive Care

Patrick Präg and Melinda C. Mills

14.1 Introduction

Involuntary childlessness, or infertility, is a condition that affects a sizeable number of couples around the world (Mascarenhas et al. 2012). Assisted reproductive technologies (ART) represent an important set of techniques for addressing involuntary childlessness. While it has always been difficult to make a precise distinction between voluntary and involuntary childlessness, the main reasons for childlessness, such as the perceived lack of a suitable partner or problems associated with balancing work and family, can be seen as both voluntary and involuntary (Sobotka 2010). The current trend of fertility postponement in European societies (Mills et al. 2011) has exacerbated the issue of involuntary childlessness. While it is clear that female fecundity declines sharply at higher ages, because the pace of fecundity loss varies greatly between women, it can be difficult for an individual woman to ascertain how long she can postpone childbearing (te Velde and Pearson 2002; te Velde et al. 2012).

ART is increasingly perceived as being one way to alleviate the problems of involuntary childlessness. Between the birth in 1978 of Louise Brown, the first live ART baby (Steptoe and Edwards 1978), and the awarding of the Nobel Prize in Physiology or Medicine to Robert G. Edwards for the development of *in vitro* fertilization in 2010, ART had become a standard medical practice and a profitable commercial enterprise for thousands of firms in Europe. An estimated five million babies have been born with the help of assisted reproduction in the past four decades (Adamson et al. 2013), a sizable share of them in Europe.

ART generally refers to treatments in which gametes or embryos are handled *in vitro* ("in glass;" i.e., outside of the body) to establish a pregnancy. A key technique

P. Präg (✉) • M.C. Mills
Department of Sociology and Nuffield College, University of Oxford, Oxford, UK
e-mail: patrick.prag@sociology.ox.ac.uk; melinda.mills@sociology.ox.ac.uk

M. Kreyenfeld, D. Konietzka (eds.), *Childlessness in Europe: Contexts, Causes, and Consequences*, Demographic Research Monographs, DOI 10.1007/978-3-319-44667-7_14

of ART is *in vitro fertilization* (IVF). In IVF, oocytes are fertilized using sperm in a laboratory and the embryo is surgically implanted in the woman's womb. IVF was invented to treat cases of female infertility. When only a single sperm cell is injected into the oocyte during IVF, the procedure is referred to as *intracytoplasmic sperm injection* (ICSI). ICSI was developed to tackle male fertility problems, such as a low sperm count or poor sperm quality, but has in recent years become a standard form of fertilization in ART. A *frozen* or *thawed embryo transfer* is an IVF procedure in which embryos that have been cryopreserved for storage are transferred (as opposed to a "fresh" transfer of never-frozen embryos). This procedure is often used because obtaining oocytes from a woman is a rather invasive act. Thus, after a hormonal treatment, several oocytes are collected at the same time, fertilized, and frozen for later use in case the first embryo transfer fails—which is likely, given the relatively low success rate of ART (Malizia et al. 2009). In an alternative collection strategy, immature eggs are collected from a woman and are then matured in a lab (*in vitro maturation*). This procedure may be indicated when a woman is at risk of reacting adversely to the fertility drugs given before the oocytes are collected.

Frozen oocyte replacement is a technique in which oocytes are retrieved, frozen, stored (oocyte cryopreservation), and fertilized only after they have been thawed for transfer. This technique provides women with the option of having genetically related children later in life, even if no suitable father is present at the time of cryopreservation. Frozen oocyte replacement was first used in cancer patients, who had oocytes retrieved and frozen before undergoing forms of chemo- or radiotherapy that could damage their ovaries. But because this technique can also be used for delaying motherhood for any reason, including the desire to pursue a career, it has attracted substantial public attention in recent years, and is sometimes referred to as "social freezing" (Mertes and Pennings 2011). Large companies, such as Facebook and Apple, have recently offered social freezing as a benefit for female employees, offering them up to $20,000 to cover the cost of egg freezing (Tran 2014).

When prospective parents are concerned about passing on hereditary diseases like cystic fibrosis, it can be useful to conduct *preimplantation genetic diagnosis* (PGD) or *screening* (PGS). PGD involves examining an embryo to determine whether specific genetic and structural alterations are present. In PGS, an embryo is examined to ascertain whether any aneuploidy, mutation, or DNA rearrangement has taken place. In cases of *egg donation*, an oocyte from a woman is fertilized and then transferred to another woman's womb. Donation may be done in cases of *surrogate motherhood* for prospective parents who are unable to carry a child, such as a gay male couple; or when a woman is unable to have her own oocytes fertilized, often because she is older. Another type of egg donation is called "egg sharing:" women who underwent ART can share any non-used frozen oocyte with other women, sometimes in exchange for a discount on their ART treatments.

Globally, Europe has the largest number of ART treatments. In 2005, the most recent year for which global data are available, 56 % of ART aspirations[1] were in

---

[1] Aspirations are initiated ART cycles in which one or more follicles are punctured and aspirated, irrespective of whether oocytes are retrieved. See Footnote 2 for more details on the metrics with which ART treatments are recorded.

Europe, 23 % were in Asia, and 15 % were in North America (Zegers-Hochschild et al. 2014). As many European countries have been characterized as having "lowest-low" fertility (Kohler et al. 2002), ART represents not just a means of alleviating the suffering of individuals who are involuntarily childless, but also a potential policy lever for raising fertility rates in Europe. Thus, there is substantial interest in ART among policy-makers. Another key aspect of ART in Europe is the stark variation in the rates of ART uptake and in the regulation of ART, both across countries and over time. This variation in regulations between and within European countries allows us to make comparisons that could yield important insights into the antecedents and outcomes of ART usage and could have implications for ART across the globe.

The first aim of the current study is to present comparative data on ART usage in Europe, demonstrating the wide variability across European countries. In a second step, we will explore forms of ART governance across European countries, illustrating the variation in how ART is regulated and in who gets access to which techniques. We then turn to the specific case of surrogacy, which often falls outside the scope of national ART legislation. We conclude with a related discussion on cross-border reproductive care, which is sometimes characterized as "reproductive tourism." In the concluding section, we will summarize the findings, discuss the implications, and point to areas for future research.

14.2 Usage of Assisted Reproductive Technologies in European Countries

The usage of ART varies considerably across European countries. Although diagnostic and treatment services are currently available in all European countries, the variation in ART usage indicates that there are substantial differences in equity of access. To explore these differences, we analyze data collected by the European IVF Monitoring (EIM) Consortium of the European Society of Human Reproduction and Embryology (ESHRE). The EIM data go back to 1997, and are based on information from national registries (with the voluntary or mandatory participation) of European countries; or, if those are not available, stem from information reported by clinics. In our analysis, we primarily focus on information from the most recent report, which contains data for the year 2010 (Kupka et al. 2014), and present information from the countries that have complete or almost complete figures.

In Fig. 14.1, we can see the high degree of variation in ART usage across Europe. The figure shows the number of treatments[2] by the main group of potential ART

---

[2] There are different metrics for recording ART treatments. The term "initiated ART *cycle*" refers to the menstrual cycle in which a woman receives ovarian stimulation (or, in the rare case of natural-cycle IVF, receives monitoring) with the intention of conducting ART, regardless of whether a follicular aspiration is attempted. The term "*aspiration*" refers to an attempt to retrieve oocytes from one or more follicles, regardless of whether oocytes are successfully retrieved. The term

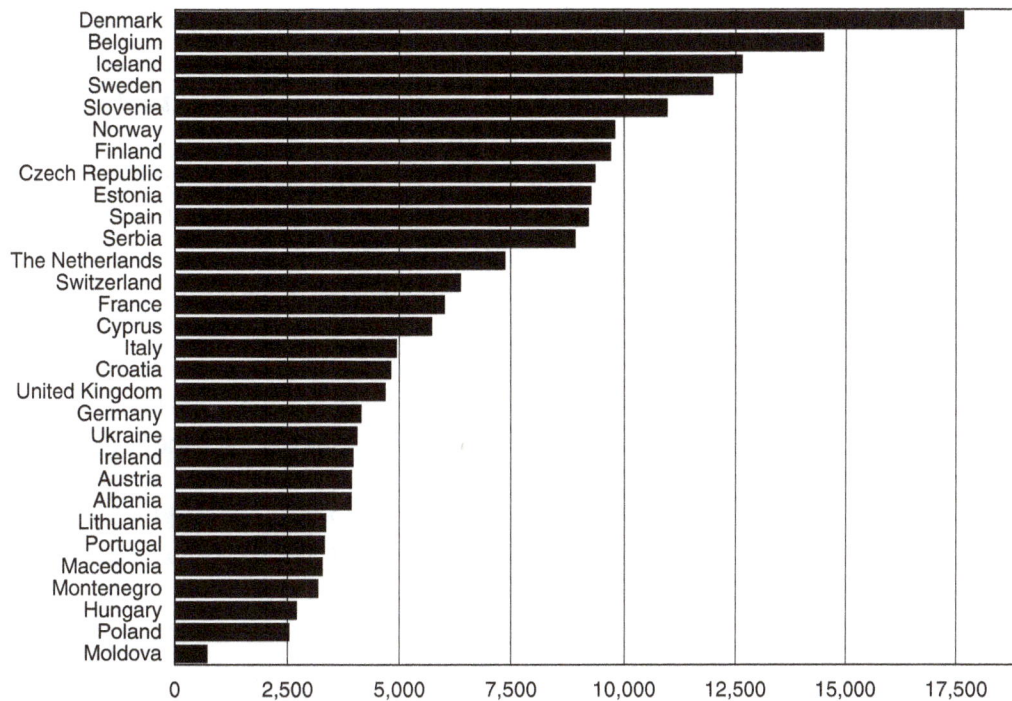

Fig. 14.1 ART cycles per million women age 15–45 per country, 2010 (Sources: Ferraretti et al. (2012, 2013) and Kupka et al. (2014). Notes: The values for Albania, Estonia, Ireland, Lithuania, Poland, Spain, Serbia, Switzerland, and Ukraine refer to 2008; the values for Croatia, Cyprus, and France, and Denmark refer to 2009. ART cycles include IVF, ICSI, frozen embryo replacement (thawings), preimplantation genetic diagnosis and screening, egg donation (donation cycles), in vitro maturation, and frozen oocyte replacement (thawings))

patients in a country; namely, women between the ages of 15 and 45. Denmark, Belgium, Iceland, Sweden, and Slovenia are the countries where the largest numbers of ART cycles are initiated. A comparison of these four countries shows that there is substantial heterogeneity at the top of the distribution. ART treatments are considerably more common in Belgium and Denmark than in Iceland, Sweden, and Slovenia. It is also striking that the top group is not completely dominated by affluent western European countries. In addition to Slovenia, the Czech Republic, Estonia, and Serbia are also in the upper half of the distribution; well ahead of wealthy nations such as Switzerland, the Netherlands, or Germany. When we look at the bottom of the distribution, it is apparent that ART is no more widespread in Germany, Austria, or Ireland than it is in Ukraine or in Albania.

A number of studies have attempted to explain the very large differences in ART usage across countries. Several factors have emerged. ART costs and affordability appear to play an important role. Belgium and Denmark are known for their comparatively generous reimbursement policies for couples and individuals under-

---

"*transfer*" refers to a procedure in which embryos are placed in the uterus or Fallopian tube, irrespective of whether a pregnancy is achieved (Zegers-Hochschild et al. 2009). However, for frozen embryo replacements, frozen oocyte replacements, and egg donations, cycles and aspirations are usually not recorded; here, *thawings* and *transfers* are the relevant metrics.

going ART. In a cross-national study, Chambers et al. (2014) found that greater affordability of ART—measured as the net cost of an ART cycle in a country as a share of the average disposable income in that country—is associated with greater ART utilization. Remarkably, this finding holds even after accounting for important factors such as GDP per capita, the number of physicians, and the number of ART clinics in a country. Studies that have looked at variation within countries and over time (e.g., Hamilton and McManus 2012) have also found evidence that affordability is an important driver not only of utilization, but also of the use of safer ART practices.

Norms and beliefs also seem to play an important role for cross-national differences in ART usage. Billari et al. (2011) found that there is a large positive association between higher social age deadlines for childbearing—i.e., generally shared assumptions about when one is too old to have children—and the availability of ART in European countries. The higher the social age norm for childbearing, the greater the availability of ART clinics. Kocourkova et al. (2014) showed that ART use and the total fertility rate in a country are correlated, which they interpret as being a sign of increasing demand for children. This interpretation is plausible, as most studies have found that the net impact of ART on fertility rates is actually small (Präg et al. 2015). Mills and Präg (2015) have suggested that beliefs about the moral status of a fertilized egg—i.e., whether a human embryo is seen as a human being immediately after fertilization—are associated with ART utilization. Generally, in countries where the belief that an embryo becomes a human being right after fertilization is less widespread, ART is used more often.

In addition to the differences in the extent of ART usage in Europe, there is also considerable variation in the range of ART techniques that are utilized. Figure 14.2 reports the share of single ART treatments among all ART treatments for selected countries in 2010. The classical form of ART, *in vitro* fertilization, is no longer the most popular type of ART procedure. The share of IVF treatments among all ART treatments ranges from less than 10% in Spain to slightly more than 40% in Denmark. ICSI, a method invented more recently (Palermo et al. 1992) to treat male factor infertility, has overtaken IVF in recent years as the method of choice for ART (Kupka et al. 2014). The reasons for this development are not fully understood, especially because the leading professional organizations of reproductive health providers discourage the routine practice of ICSI in the absence of male factor infertility diagnoses (Boulet et al. 2015). It is likely related to what demographic researchers have called the "absent and problematic men" issue in fertility research and infertility diagnoses, as collecting data on men and establishing male factor infertility is difficult (Greene and Biddlecom 2000). Nonetheless, in virtually all of the countries displayed in Fig. 14.2, the share of ART procedures that are ICSI treatments is larger than the share of procedures that are IVF treatments. Only in Denmark is the share of ART procedures that are IVF treatments slightly larger (42%) than the share that are ICSI treatments (35%). In the United Kingdom, IVF and ICSI are used to a similar extent (37 and 40%, respectively). The substantial differences between countries have been noted in the literature, yet explanations for

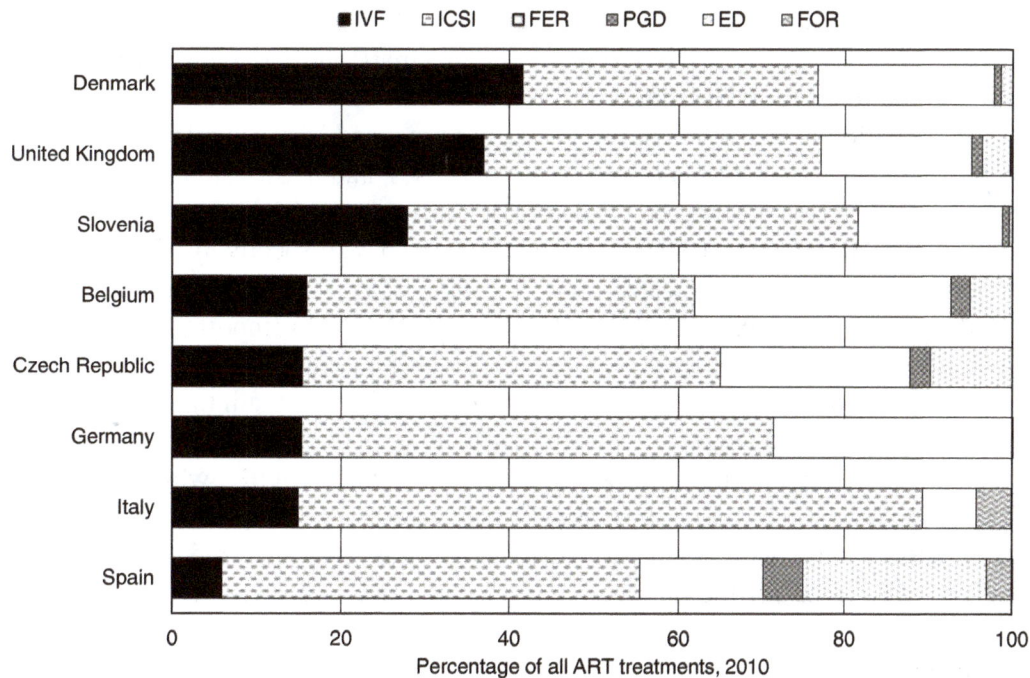

Fig. 14.2 ART treatments in selected countries, 2010 (Notes: *IVF* in vitro fertilization (cycles), *ICSI* intracytoplasmic sperm injection (cycles), *FER* frozen embryo replacement (thawings), *PGD* preimplantation genetic diagnosis (cycles), *ED* egg donation (donations), *FOR*: frozen oocyte replacement (thawings). In vitro maturation (aspirations, 0.0–0.1 % per country) not displayed. Source: Kupka et al. (2014))

these differences are still lacking (Nyboe Andersen et al. 2008). It is, however, clear that IVF and ICSI together make up the bulk of treatments in all countries.

The third-most popular form of ART treatment is frozen embryo replacement, making up between 6 % (Italy) and 31 % (Belgium) of ART treatments. The low uptake of FER in Italy is attributable to a national law that prohibited embryo cryo-preservation (except under exceptional circumstances) from 2004 to 2009 (Benagiano and Gianaroli 2010). The relative popularity of FER in Germany is surprising, as German regulations regarding embryo freezing are fairly restrictive: i.e., the non-emergency freezing of embryos is banned, and the freezing of fertilized eggs is allowed only in the earliest stages of development. Preimplantation genetic diagnosis (PGD), which has been practiced since the early 1990s (Simpson 2010), is likely the ethically most controversial form of ART. PGD has clear benefits, as it can help parents avoid passing on inheritable disorders to their children, and it is generally considered to be safe and to have a low rate of errors (Ory et al. 2014). However, fears about the creation of "designer babies" and moral concerns about the use of PGD for non-medical purposes (such as sex selection) are often expressed in public discussions about ART. The data show that very few ART procedures involve PGD: the share of all ART treatments in a country that involve PGD ranges from no reported cases (in Germany and Italy) to 4.7 % of cases (in Spain). The share is around 1 % in Denmark, Slovenia, and the United Kingdom; and is around 2 % in Belgium and the Czech Republic. Given the controversy surrounding PGD, it is interesting to note that the procedure is generally allowed in all of the countries listed in Fig. 14.2 (Ory et al. 2014); however, Denmark and Slovenia restrict its use to screening for specific hereditary disorders.

Egg donation is also a technique that is not practiced in all countries, as can be seen in Fig. 14.2. Germany and Italy report no cases, and in Slovenia and Denmark egg donation makes up less than 2 % of ART procedures. In the United Kingdom and Belgium, the shares are slightly higher (3.3 and 5 %, respectively). In the Czech Republic and Spain a significant share (9.7 and 22 %) of ART treatments involve egg donation. As we will discuss in more detail below, it is important to note that these differences between countries are attributable in part to cross-border reproductive care. Couples and single women who are unable to obtain the desired treatment in their home country are sometimes willing to travel abroad to obtain that treatment in another country. Frozen oocyte replacement (FOR), which builds on fertilizing thawed oocytes, is a relatively rare form of ART: FOR treatments are reported only in the United Kingdom, Spain, and Italy (0.1, 3.1, and 4.1 %, respectively). One reason for the relative popularity of FOR in Italy is that the cryopreserving of embryos was banned, which created incentives to further develop and refine technologies for cryopreserving oocytes.

14.3 Regulation of Assisted Reproductive Technology in Europe

Europe is the only continent where the legal regulation of ART is widespread. Other major countries where ART is used, such as India, Japan, and the U.S., largely rely on voluntary guidelines. While ART regulation is sometimes portrayed as a novel phenomenon, there is a long history of government interference in the reproductive realm. For example, countries have long had laws pertaining to marriage and divorce, contraception, births out of wedlock, adoption, and abortion (Spar 2005).

There are three major ways of regulating the practice of and the access to ART. First, ART can be regulated via *guidelines*, or sets of rules that practitioners are expected to follow voluntarily. These guidelines are generally issued by professional organizations, such as associations of obstetricians and gynaecologists. Second, as an alternative or a supplement to these guidelines, ART is also often subject to governmental *legislation*. Thus, rules for using ART are codified in the law, and penalties for the violation of these rules are imposed. A third route that regulates access to ART is *insurance coverage*: given the high cost of infertility treatments, the level of coverage can be seen as an indirect regulation of access to ART. However, because infertility is now seen as a condition leading to disability (WHO and World Bank 2011), infertile individuals should have a right to treatment.

The International Federation of Fertility Societies (IFFS) provides information on ART guidelines, regulations, and insurance coverage in their triennial

"Surveillance Reports," which have been published since 1999 (Jones and Cohen 1999). The data in these reports are based on surveys of experts from national fertility societies. The IFFS data are organized into relatively broad categories, and are sometimes incomplete or inconsistent. Nonetheless, these reports provide a useful overview of the differences in ART governance across Europe. In the following, we present data from the most recent IFFS Surveillance Report (Ory et al. 2014), which refers to the year 2013. We include all of the European countries featured in the report, plus a number of contrasting non-European cases.

The left column of Table 14.1 reveals that in all European countries, ART is regulated under the law. In about half of the countries, governmental regulation is supplemented by voluntary guidelines. By contrast, for two of the three non-European cases listed at the bottom of the Table (India and Japan), ART is fully governed by voluntary guidelines. While the distinction between legislation and guidelines does not reveal the scope and extent of the actual regulation, it roughly illustrates how important ART is to the respective government. The second column shows that ART legislation is a salient issue for governments, as half of the countries have introduced new ART legislation in the relatively short period of 4 years.

When it comes to the financing of ART treatments, virtually all European countries offer some assistance. Only Belarus, Ireland, and Switzerland do not provide their citizens with any form of coverage. Whereas most countries provide coverage via national health plans, some mandate that private insurers provide coverage. Six countries—Denmark, France, Hungary, Russia, Slovenia, and Spain—offer complete coverage through national health plans. A comparison with the results from Fig. 14.1 reveals that Denmark, Slovenia, and Spain are among the countries with particularly high ART utilization rates. In the countries where partial coverage is provided, the extent of the coverage varies considerably. For example, two-thirds of the costs are covered by the national health system in Austria, but only 40 % of the costs are covered in Finland. Furthermore, the level of insurance coverage usually depends on patient characteristics. In Spain, for example, coverage is only available for women up to age 40. Slovenia covers six cycles for the first child and four cycles after a first live birth, but only for women up to age 42. In some parts of the United Kingdom, women who are obese are being denied coverage. In the U.S., there is substantial heterogeneity in coverage across the states, with a few states providing rather generous coverage, and the vast majority providing no coverage.

Couple and sexuality requirements represent a socially relevant aspect of ART policies, as they govern access to ART treatments over and above the financial restrictions that infertile couples and individuals face. Table 14.2 lists the couple and sexuality requirements, as reported by Ory et al. (2014) for all European countries and India, Japan, and the U.S. It should be noted that these requirements can stem from both legislation and guidelines. The first column of Table 14.2 reveals that marriage is a requirement for ART treatment in most countries. Only six out of 22 European countries in Table 14.2 report that marriage is not a requirement for ART access. However, apart from Turkey (and Japan), all of the European countries listed also provide treatment to couples who live in a stable relationship. Ory et al. (2014) acknowledged that "stable relationship" is a poorly defined concept open to

Table 14.1 Types of ART regulation in Europe, India, Japan, and the U.S., 2013

Country	Type of ART governance	New ART legislation since 2009	Type of coverage	Extent of coverage
Austria	Legislation and guidelines	No	National health plan	Partial
Belarus	Legislation and guidelines	No	No coverage	None
Belgium	Legislation only	Yes	National health plan and private insurance	Partial
Bulgaria	Legislation only	Yes	National health plan	Partial
Croatia	Legislation only	Yes	National health plan and private insurance	Partial
Czech Republic	Legislation only	Yes	National health plan	Partial
Denmark	Legislation only	Yes	National health plan	Complete
Finland	Legislation only	No	National health plan	Partial
France	Legislation and guidelines	Yes	National health plan	Complete
Greece	Legislation only	No	National health plan	Partial
Hungary	Legislation only	No	National health plan	Complete
Iceland	Legislation only	No	National health plan	Partial
Ireland	Legislation and guidelines	No	No coverage	None
Italy	Legislation and guidelines	Yes	National health plan	Partial
Latvia	Legislation and guidelines	Yes	National health plan	Partial
Norway	Legislation and guidelines	No	National health plan	Partial
Portugal	Legislation only	Yes	National health plan	Partial
Russia	Legislation and guidelines	Yes	National health plan	Complete
Slovenia	Legislation only	No	National health plan	Complete
Spain	Legislation and guidelines	No	National health plan and private insurance	Complete
Sweden	Legislation and guidelines	No	National health plan	Partial
Switzerland	Legislation and guidelines	No	No coverage	None
Turkey	Legislation and guidelines	Yes	National health plan	Partial
United Kingdom	Legislation and guidelines	Yes	Private insurance	Partial

(continued)

Table 14.1 (continued)

Country	Type of ART governance	New ART legislation since 2009	Type of coverage	Extent of coverage
India	Guidelines only	No	No coverage	None
Japan	Guidelines only	No	National health plan	Partial
United States	Legislation and guidelines	No	Private insurance	Partial

Source: Ory et al. (2014)

Table 14.2 Couple and sexuality requirements for ART in Europe, India, Japan, and the U.S., 2013

	Marriage required	Stable relationship permitted	Singles permitted	Lesbians permitted
Austria	Yes	Yes	No	No
Belgium	Yes	Yes	Yes	Yes
Bulgaria	Yes	Yes	Yes	Yes
Croatia	Yes	Yes	No	No
Czech Republic	Yes	Yes	No	No
Denmark	Yes	Yes	Yes	Yes
Finland	No	Yes	Yes	Yes
France	No	Yes	No	No
Greece	No	Yes	Yes	No
Hungary	Yes	Yes	Yes	No
Ireland	No	Yes	No	No
Italy	Yes	Yes	No	No
Latvia	Yes	Yes	Yes	Yes
Russia	Yes	Yes	Yes	No
Slovenia	No	Yes	No	No
Spain	Yes	Yes	Yes	Yes
Sweden	Yes	Yes	No	No
Switzerland	No	Yes	No	No
Turkey	Yes	No	No	No
United Kingdom	No	Yes	Yes	Yes
India	Yes	Yes	Yes	No
Japan	Yes	No	No	No
United States	No	Yes	Yes	Yes

Source: Ory et al. (2014)

interpretation, yet it is widely embraced across countries. Countries are somewhat more restrictive in their rules regarding unpartnered women who want to undergo ART treatment. Only 10 of the 22 European countries, along with India and the U.S., permit singles to utilize ART services. Moreover, only seven European countries and the U.S. allow lesbian women to have access to ART.

To better illustrate how European countries vary in their approach to regulating forms of ART, we examine the particularly controversial ART variant of surrogacy. There are several forms of surrogacy (see the notes below Table 14.3). The most prominent form is a traditional variant that uses the surrogate mother's egg. By contrast, in gestational surrogacy, the egg is provided by the intended mother or a donor, fertilized via IVF, and then transferred to the surrogate mother's womb.

The first central difference between countries lies in whether they prohibit (Table 14.3, column 1) or heavily regulate surrogacy (Table 14.3, column 3). Surrogacy is prohibited in many countries, such as France, Germany, Italy, Spain, and Portugal. Surrogate motherhood is explicitly allowed in Belgium, Belarus, Denmark, Greece, Ireland, the Russian Federation, Ukraine, and the United Kingdom. A second difference refers to compensation of the surrogate mother. When surrogacy is permitted, in some countries the prospective parents are not allowed to pay the surrogate mother beyond covering her "altruistic costs." Conversely, commercial surrogacy is legal in certain U.S. states, as well as in India, Ukraine, and the Russian Federation. In countries where surrogacy is prohibited, stakeholders have produced evidence that prospective parents may travel to other countries that allow commercial surrogacy.[3] A third difference between countries relates to access to surrogacy. Since some countries require that both partners provide gametes when surrogates are used, singles are generally unable to have a child via surrogacy in these countries.

Finally, due to the frequent cross-border nature of surrogacy, highly contentious ethical and legal debates have arisen about the citizenship and parental rights of surrogate and adoptive parents. The media have recently reported numerous cases of babies who have been left without citizenship or parents. A famous case that demonstrates the legal problems that can arise is that of twins who were born to a gay male British couple, of whom one was the biological father, with the help of an anonymous egg donor and a Ukrainian surrogate mother (Henderson 2008). Because of conflicts between British and Ukrainian laws, the British father was not treated as a parent of the twins, and his children were not allowed to enter the United Kingdom. Conversely, the Ukrainian surrogate mother had waived all rights to custody of her biological offspring in a surrogacy agreement, which was, however, only recognized under Ukrainian law, and not under British law. In the end, the British couple were able to gain custody of the twins following a decision in a British court of law. Similar cases have been reported in Germany: for example, babies who were born outside of the country using surrogacy have been denied citizenship, even though the German parents were named on the birth certificate (The Local 2011). Concerns have been raised about the "Baby Gammy" case, in which a child with Down's syndrome who was born to a Thai surrogate mother was abandoned by the intended Australian parents. The child was recently granted Australian citizenship, and remains under the care of the Thai surrogate mother (Farrell 2015). The legal mechanisms for granting parenthood status remain unclear and differ depending on where the surrogate mother is located, or on a court's opinion regarding the best interests

[3] See, e.g., Surrogacy UK, http://www.surrogacyuk.org/

Table 14.3 Overview of legal approaches to surrogacy, Europe and selected other countries, 2013

	General prohibition	Commercial surrogacy allowed or prohibited?	Special law on surrogacy?	Adoption rules or recognition of citizenship of children from cross-border surrogacy
Austria	Egg donation prohibited; gestational surrogacy allowed	No specific prohibition for traditional surrogacy	No for traditional surrogacy	No recognition of child's citizenship
Belarus	Allowed	Unknown	Unknown	Unknown
Belgium	Allowed[b]	Prohibited on public policy grounds	No for altruistic surrogacy	Adoption required to transfer legal parenthood
Bulgaria	Prohibited	n/a	No, but draft legislation under consideration	n/a
Cyprus	Allowed	Allowed/no prohibition	Yes	Surrogate mother and biological father listed on birth certificate
Czech Republic	Allowed	Allowed/no prohibition	Yes	Unknown
Denmark	Allowed[b]	Prohibited	No for altruistic surrogacy	Adoption required to transfer legal parenthood
Estonia	Allowed	Allowed/no prohibition	Yes	Unknown
Finland	Prohibited for IVF	No specific prohibition for traditional surrogacy	No for traditional surrogacy	Unknown
France	Prohibited	n/a	n/a	Unknown
Germany	Prohibited	n/a	n/a	No recognition of child's citizenship
Greece	Allowed	Allowed/no prohibition	Yes: altruistic gestational surrogacy subject to restrictions	Surrogate mother and biological father listed on birth certificate
Hungary	Allowed	Prohibited	No for altruistic surrogacy	

(continued)

Table 14.3 (continued)

	General prohibition	Commercial surrogacy allowed or prohibited?	Special law on surrogacy?	Adoption rules or recognition of citizenship of children from cross-border surrogacy
Ireland	Allowed[b]	Prohibited	No for altruistic surrogacy but formal guidelines for cross-border surrogacy agreements	Adoption required to transfer parents; genetic intended parents' names as legal parents on birth registry
Italy	Prohibited	n/a	n/a/	Unknown
Latvia	Allowed	Prohibited	No for altruistic surrogacy	Unknown
Lithuania	Allowed	Allowed/no prohibition	Yes	Unknown
Luxembourg	Allowed	Allowed/no prohibition	Yes	Unknown
Malta	Prohibited	n/a	n/a	Unknown
Norway	Prohibited	n/a	No	
Netherlands	Allowed[b]	Prohibited	Yes altruistic gestational surrogacy required by law to abide by professional guidelines	No special law for parenthood: adoption required
Poland	Allowed	Allowed/no prohibition	Yes	Surrogate mother and biological father listed on birth certificate
Portugal	Prohibited	n/a	n/a	Unknown
Russian Fed.	Allowed	Allowed/no prohibition	Unknown	Unknown
Slovakia	Allowed	Allowed/no prohibition	Yes	Unknown
Slovenia	Allowed	Allowed/no prohibition	Yes	Unknown
Spain	Prohibited	n/a	n/a	Unknown

(continued)

Table 14.3 (continued)

	General prohibition	Commercial surrogacy allowed or prohibited?	Special law on surrogacy?	Adoption rules or recognition of citizenship of children from cross-border surrogacy
Sweden	Prohibited for fertility clinics to make surrogacy arrangements	Prohibited	No law for privately arranged surrogacy; Swedish Council Medical Ethics recently recommended altruistic surrogacy should be permitted	Adoption required to transfer parenthood
Switzerland	Prohibited	n/a	n/a	No recognition of child's citizenship
Turkey	Prohibited	n/a	n/a	Unknown
Ukraine	Allowed	Allowed/no prohibition	Unknown	Intended parents' names on birth certificate
United Kingdom	Allowed[b]	Prohibited	No for altruistic surrogacy	Parenthood only transferred in certain circumstances
India	Allowed	Allowed/no prohibition	Yes	Parents' names on birth certificate, Indian surrogates cannot be named as mother
Japan	Prohibited	n/a	n/a	Unknown
Canada	Allowed[b]	Prohibited	Unknown	Unknown
United States	Allowed[a]	Allowed/certain prohibitions	Yes	Parents' names on birth certificate

Notes: In traditional surrogacy, the surrogate mother is the genetic mother, as one of her eggs is inseminated using the sperm of the intended father or donated sperm (either IVF or insemination). In altruistic surrogacy, the surrogate mother is paid nothing or only enough to cover her expenses. In commercial surrogacy, the surrogate mother is paid a fee that may exceed her expenses

Source: Brunet et al. (2013), Ory et al. (2014), Families Thru Surrogacy (2015). When expert interviews from IFFS data from Ory et al. (2014) differed from legal and clinical survey data reported by Brunet et al. (2013), the latter data were adopted over the expert interviews

[a]Allowed in California, Maryland, Massachusetts, Ohio, Pennsylvania, South Carolina, Alabama, Arkansas, Connecticut, Illinois, Iowa, Nevada, North Dakota, Oregon, Tennessee, Texas, Utah, and West Virginia

[b]Allowed only for non-commercial surrogacy (i.e., the mother is not paid or is paid only enough to cover her expenses)

of the child. It appears that when many ART laws were initially written or amended, surrogacy was often excluded or barely acknowledged.

14.4 Cross-Border Reproductive Care in Europe

As we touched upon in our discussion on surrogate motherhood, the variation in regulations in Europe has given rise to the phenomenon of cross-border reproductive care (Shenfield et al. 2010; Nygren et al. 2010). Cross-border reproductive care refers to couples or individuals seeking assisted reproduction treatments in a country other than their country of permanent residence.[4] Although practitioners, patients, and policy-makers appear to be aware of this phenomenon, there is little empirical research on the actual extent of cross-border reproductive care. The review article by Hudson et al. (2011) tellingly reported that the number of commentaries on the topic greatly exceeds the number of empirical studies.

So far, researchers have been unable to generate reliable estimates of the incidence of cross-border reproductive care. The most ambitious attempt to conduct a global survey of this form of care was by Nygren et al. (2010), who collected information from experts in 23 countries. Virtually all of the reports were based on estimates by informants rather than empirical data, and the authors concluded that their efforts yielded "little, if any, solid data" on cross-border reproductive care. The estimates of Nygren et al. suggest that most cross-border reproductive care in Europe involves traveling to other European countries, not to other continents.

The largest study of patients undergoing cross-border reproductive care in Europe was conducted in 2008/09 by Shenfield et al. (2010). They surveyed all women from other countries who were undergoing treatment in 44 fertility clinics in Belgium, the Czech Republic, Denmark, Switzerland, Slovenia, and Spain. The main countries of origin of the women seeking care were Italy (32 %), Germany (15 %), the Netherlands (12 %), and France (9 %). Geographic and cultural proximity is a driving factor in the choice of treatment country: the majority of Italians traveled to Spain and Switzerland, most of the Germans traveled to the Czech Republic, the majority of the Dutch and French women went to Belgium, and most of the Norwegian and Swedish women traveled to Denmark. Shenfield and colleagues suggest that a conservative estimate of cross-border reproductive care (i.e., crossing country borders in order to undergo ART) in 2008/2009 would be one of 11,000–14,000 patients and 24,000–30,000 treatment cycles in the six countries alone. When confronted with the number of ART cycles (2008: 532,000; 2009: 537,000) counted in all of Europe at that time (Ferraretti et al. 2012; Ferraretti et al. 2013), this is a small, yet substantial share of patients and cycles.

---

[4] This phenomenon is also sometimes referred to as "reproductive tourism" or "reproductive exile" (Pennings 2005), but given the charged nature of both terms, we follow Shenfield et al. (2010) in their use of the more descriptive and neutral term "cross-border reproductive care."

The reasons for seeking cross-border reproductive care are diverse, with patients reporting a combination of factors (Culley et al. 2011). The main reasons cited were legal restrictions, difficulties in accessing ART treatments (e.g., long waiting lists), the expectation of better quality treatment in the destination country, and the failure of previous treatments in the patient's country of origin. A number of studies have described the legal reasons why ART patients seek treatment in other countries. For example, egg donation is a form of assisted reproduction that is banned in some European countries, including Germany. Thus, some German couples travel to the Czech Republic or Spain for egg donation (Bergmann 2011). In France, single women and lesbian couples lack access to donor sperm (see Table 14.2). Thus, these women sometimes travel to Belgium to seek treatment (van Hoof et al. 2015; Rozée Gomez and de La Rochebrochard 2013). Certain countries, like the United Kingdom, have long waiting lists for donor gametes, and patients who wish to avoid lengthy waiting periods seek treatment in countries where donor gametes are more readily available (Culley et al. 2011). These long waiting periods have arisen for a number of reasons. For example, some countries (e.g., Finland, Sweden, and the United Kingdom) have banned anonymous gamete donation, which tends to discourage donation. There is also considerable variation across countries in the amounts donors are paid. Patients from countries such as Italy hope to receive better quality treatments abroad (Zanini 2011; Shenfield et al. 2010), while other patients go abroad because the previous treatments they received in their country of residence failed (Shenfield et al. 2010; Culley et al. 2011). In their comparative study of patients seeking treatment abroad, Shenfield and colleagues (2010) found evidence that supports the assumption that differences in regulations are important drivers of cross-border fertility care. Between 57 and 80 % of patients from Italy, Germany, Norway, France, and Sweden cited legal restrictions as one of the reasons why they were seeking fertility treatment abroad. By contrast, only 32 % of patients from the Netherlands and 9 % of patients from the United Kingdom cited legal barriers. However, 53 % of patients from the Netherlands reported that they went abroad to obtain better quality treatment (compared to an average of 43 % across the six countries surveyed), while 34 % of the patients from the United Kingdom said they went abroad because of access difficulties (compared to an average of 7 % across the six countries surveyed).

While the extent to which European patients cross borders to obtain reproductive care appears to be limited, cross-border care has far-reaching consequences and implications for ART regulation, access, and treatment success rates. Because it is relatively easy and inexpensive for Europeans to travel across borders to obtain care, the value of legal restrictions on ART is largely symbolic (van Beers 2015). Furthermore, as patients can easily circumvent national regulations by seeking treatment abroad, patient groups and other national stakeholders may have reduced incentives to make their interests known in the policy-making process. This lack of pressure allows policy-makers to impose more onerous restrictions than they would have if they had been facing more resistance from stakeholders (Storrow 2010). Furthermore, cross-border reproductive care has implications for equity of access to ART. Rozée Gomez and de la Rochebrochard (2013) have reported that lower income French patients seek fertility treatment in Greece for financial reasons. This might in turn affect access to ART within Greece, as local patients might be "priced out" of the market for ART services.

14.5 Discussion

This study has shown that there is marked variation in ART usage levels across Europe, and that the highest levels are not just in affluent countries such as Denmark and Belgium, but also in Slovenia, the Czech Republic, Estonia, and Serbia. The reasons for this variation include affordability, reimbursement levels, and the social and cultural norms surrounding childbearing. A striking shift has been the move away from IVF as the dominant form of ART, and toward ICSI, a method used primarily to treat male infertility. We also show that the mix of treatments used varies across countries.

Currently, all of the European countries have laws on ART, and virtually all (with the exception of Belarus, Ireland, and Switzerland) provide some sort of financial assistance for treatments. The countries where the cost of treatments is completely covered by national health plans—such as Denmark, Slovenia, and Spain—have the highest ART utilization rates. Coverage also differs by patient characteristics, such as the age of the prospective mother and how many children she already has. In many countries, patients who seek ART treatments must be legally married or in a stable partnership. Currently only half of European countries permit single women to have ART treatments, and even fewer countries grant access to lesbian women.

We also looked at the increasingly relevant issue of surrogacy and cross-border reproductive care. Surrogacy is strictly prohibited in many countries, and where it is allowed, there are often restrictions on commercial surrogacy. Due to the frequent cross-border nature of surrogacy, there is considerable confusion about which laws apply when determining the citizenship of the child and the parental rights of the surrogate and the adoptive parents. The growth in cross-border reproductive care means that restrictive national regulations can be easily circumvented, but it raises questions about equity of access. Cross-border reproductive care is a transnational phenomenon that forces social scientists and policy-makers to think beyond the confines of the nation-state (Mau and Verwiebe 2010; Wimmer and Glick Schiller 2002). Notwithstanding all of the problems related to patients crossing borders to achieve fertility treatment, it is important to acknowledge that women have been crossing borders in Europe for a long time to abort pregnancies, exploiting country differences in reproductive legislation.

Recently, there has been a rise in the uptake of techniques such as the "social freezing" of eggs, and it has even been suggested that ART could help countries raise their fertility levels. However, we would be reluctant to argue that it is an upcoming policy to reconcile career and family aspirations, such as measures that encourage flexible work schedules (Präg and Mills 2014) or improve access to public childcare (Mills et al. 2014). Because ART treatments tend to have low success rates at higher ages, they cannot be expected to reverse the "biological clock" (Präg et al. 2015; Wyndham et al. 2012).

This study also showed some strong limitations in what we are able to conclude, which is due to the lack of data about ART in Europe. In the future, researchers should first attempt to standardize the collection of data on ART treatments and their outcomes, as this would improve our knowledge of the individual antecedents and effects of ART. Second, researchers should develop national databases to collect quantitative information that can be linked across countries, as cross-border reproductive care needs to be properly registered. Third, we need these initiatives to not only monitor cross-border reproductive care in Europe, but also to support caregivers in providing help for patients both undergoing and returning from cross-border fertility care in these often legally diffuse situations.

Although Europe is currently the biggest market for ART in the world, it is important to note that the demand for ART is relatively low in Europe. Paradoxically, involuntary childlessness is most prevalent (and is perceived by infertile women as most pressing) in Africa, where fertility levels are the highest in the world. Given the increasing international recognition of the problem and the push for the low-cost provision of ART (Ombelet 2014), the "globalization of ART" has yet to be achieved (Inhorn and Patrizio 2015).

Acknowledgements The research leading to these results has received funding from the European Union's Seventh Framework Program (FP7 2007–2013) under grant agreement no. 320116 for the research project Families and Societies (familiesandsocieties.eu).

Literature

Adamson, G. D., Tabangin, M., Macaluso, M., & de Mouzon, J. (2013). The number of babies born globally after treatment with the assisted reproductive technologies (ART). *Fertility and Sterility, 100*, S42.

Benagiano, G., & Gianaroli, L. (2010). The Italian constitutional court modifies Italian legislation on assisted reproduction technology. *Reproductive Biomedicine Online, 20*, 398–402.

Bergmann, S. (2011). Reproductive agency and projects. Germans searching for egg donation in Spain and the Czech Republic. *Reproductive Biomedicine Online, 23*, 600–608.

Billari, F. C., Goisis, A., Liefbroer, A. C., Settersten, R. A., Aassve, A., Hagestad, G., et al. (2011). Social age deadlines for the childbearing of women and men. *Human Reproduction Update, 26*, 616–622.

Boulet, S. L., Mehta, A., Kissin, D. M., Warner, L., Kawwass, J. F., & Jamieson, D. J. (2015). Trends in use of and reproductive outcomes associated with intracytoplasmic sperm injection. *JAMA, 313*, 255–263.

Brunet, L., Carruthers, J., Davaki, K., King, D., Marzo, C., & McCandles, J. (2013). *A comparative study on the regime of surrogacy in EU member states.* Brussels: European Parliament.

Chambers, G. M., Hoang, V. P., Sullivan, E. A., Chapman, M. G., Ishihara, O., Zegers-Hochschild, F., et al. (2014). The impact of consumer affordability on access to assisted reproductive technologies and embryo transfer practices. *Fertility and Sterility, 101*, 191–198. e194.

Culley, L., Hudson, N., Rapport, F., Blyth, E., Norton, W., & Pacey, A. A. (2011). Crossing borders for fertility treatment. Motivations, destinations, and outcomes of UK fertility travelers. *Human Reproduction Update, 26*, 2373–2381.

Families Thru Surrogacy. (2015). *Surrogacy by country*: http://www.familiesthrusurrogacy.com/surrogacy-by-country. Accessed 20 Aug 2015.

Farrell, P. (2015, January 19). Baby gammy, born into Thai surrogacy scandal, granted Australian citizenship. *The Guardian*. http://www.theguardian.com/australia-news/2015/jan/20/baby-gammy-born-into-thai-surrogacy-scandal-granted-australian-citizenship. Accessed 20 Aug 2015.

Ferraretti, A. P., Goossens, V., de Mouzon, J., Bhattacharya, S., Castilla, J. A., Korsak, V., et al. (2012). Assisted reproductive technology in Europe, 2008. Results generated from European registers by ESHRE. *Human Reproduction Update, 27*, 2571–2584.

Ferraretti, A. P., Goossens, V., Kupka, M., Bhattacharya, S., De Mouzon, J., Castilla, J. A., et al. (2013). Assisted reproductive technology in Europe, 2009. Results generated from European registers by ESHRE. *Human Reproduction Update, 28*, 2318–2331.

Greene, M. E., & Biddlecom, A. E. (2000). Absent and problematic Men. Demographic accounts of male reproductive roles. *Population and Development Review, 26*, 81–115.

Hamilton, B. H., & McManus, B. (2012). The effects of insurance mandates on choices and outcomes in infertility treatment markets. *Health Economics, 21*, 994–1016.

Henderson, M. (2008, December 12). British surrogacy ruling saves baby twins from Ukraine orphanage. *The Times*. http://www.thetimes.co.uk/tto/law/article2212834.ece. Accessed 20 Aug 2015.

Hudson, N., Culley, L., Blyth, E., Norton, W., Rapport, F., & Pacey, A. (2011). Cross-border reproductive care. A review of the literature. *Reproductive Biomedicine Online, 22*, 673–685.

Inhorn, M. C., & Patrizio, P. (2015). Infertility around the globe. New thinking on gender, reproductive technologies, and global movements in the 21st Century. *Human Reproduction Update, 21*, 411–426.

Jones, H. W., Jr., & Cohen, J. (1999). IFFS Surveillance 1998. *Fertility and Sterility, 71*, S1–S34.

Kocourkova, J., Burcin, B., & Kucera, T. (2014). Demographic relevancy of increased use of assisted reproduction in European countries. *Reproductive Health, 11*, 37.

Kohler, H.-P., Billari, F. C., & Ortega, J. A. (2002). The emergence of lowest-low fertility in Europe during the 1990's. *Population and Development Review, 28*, 641–680.

Kupka, M. S., Ferraretti, A. P., De Mouzon, J., Erb, K., D'Hooghe, T., Castilla, J. A., et al. (2014). Assisted reproductive technology in Europe, 2010. Results generated from European registers by ESHRE. *Human Reproduction Update, 29*, 2099–2113.

Malizia, B. A., Hacker, M. R., & Penzias, A. S. (2009). Cumulative live-birth rates after In Vitro fertilization. *New England Journal of Medicine, 360*, 236–243.

Mascarenhas, M. N., Flaxman, S. R., Boerma, T., Vanderpoel, S., & Stevens, G. A. (2012). National, regional, and global trends in infertility prevalence since 1990. A systematic analysis of 277 health surveys. *Plos Medicine, 9*, e1001356.

Mau, S., & Verwiebe, R. (2010). *European societies. Mapping structure and change*. Bristol: Policy.

Mertes, H., & Pennings, G. (2011). Social egg freezing. For better, not for worse. *Reproductive Biomedicine Online, 23*, 824–829.

Mills, M., & Präg, P. (2015). *Norms, politics, and assisted reproductive technology (ART) policies. A cross-national comparative analysis*. Paper presented at the annual meeting of the population association of America, San Diego.

Mills, M., Rindfuss, R. R., McDonald, P., & te Velde, E. (2011). Why do people postpone parenthood? Reasons and social policy incentives. *Human Reproduction Update, 17*, 848–860.

Mills, M., Präg, P., Tsang, F., Begall, K., Derbyshire, J., Kohle, L., et al. (2014). *Use of childcare services in the EU member states and progress towards the Barcelona targets*. Brussels: European Commission DG Justice.

Nyboe Andersen, A., Carlsen, E., & Loft, A. (2008). Trends in the use of intracytoplasmatic sperm injection. Marked variability between countries. *Human Reproduction Update, 14*, 593–604.

Nygren, K., Adamson, D., Zegers-Hochschild, F., & de Mouzon, J. (2010). Cross-border fertility care. International committee monitoring assisted reproductive technologies global survey. 2006 data and estimates. *Fertility and Sterility, 94*, e4–e10.

Ombelet, W. (2014). Is global access to infertility care realistic? The Walking Egg project. *Reproductive Biomedicine Online, 28*, 267–272.

Ory, S. J., Devroey, P., Banker, M., Brinsden, P., Buster, J., Fiadjoe, M., et al. (2014). IFFS surveillance 2013. Preface and conclusions. *Fertility and Sterility, 101*, 1582–1583.

Palermo, G. D., Joris, H., Devroey, P., & Van Steirteghem, A. C. (1992). Pregnancies after intracytoplasmic injection of single spermatozoon into an oocyte. *Lancet, 340*, 17–18.

Pennings, G. (2005). Reproductive exile versus reproductive tourism. *Human Reproduction Update, 20*, 3571–3572.

Präg, P., & Mills, M. (2014). *Family-related working schedule flexibility across Europe*. Brussels: European Commission DG Justice.

Präg, P., Mills, M., Tanturri, M. L., Monden, C., & Pison, G. (2015). *The demographic consequences of assisted reproductive technologies*: Deliverable D4.6 of 'Families and Societies'.

Rozée Gomez, V., & de La Rochebrochard, E. (2013). Cross-border reproductive care among French patients. Experiences in Greece, Spain, and Belgium. *Human Reproduction Update, 28*, 3103–3110.

Shenfield, F., de Mouzon, J., Pennings, G., Ferraretti, A. P., Nyboe Andersen, A., de Wert, G., et al. (2010). Cross-border reproductive care in six European countries. *Human Reproduction Update, 25*, 1361–1368.

Simpson, J. L. (2010). Preimplantation genetic diagnosis at 20 years. *Prenatal Diagnosis, 30*, 682–695.

Sobotka, T. (2010). Shifting parenthood to advanced reproductive ages. Trends, causes and consequences. In J. C. Tremmel (Ed.), *A young generation under pressure? The financial situation and the "rush hour" of the cohorts 1970–1985 in a generational comparison* (pp. 129–154). Berlin: Springer.

Spar, D. (2005). Reproductive tourism and the regulatory map. *New England Journal of Medicine, 352*, 531–533.

Steptoe, P. C., & Edwards, R. G. (1978). Birth after the reimplatation of a human embryo. *Lancet, 312*, 366.

Storrow, R. F. (2010). The pluralism problem in cross-border reproductive care. *Human Reproduction Update, 25*, 2939–2943.

te Velde, E. R., & Pearson, P. L. (2002). The variability of female reproductive ageing. *Human Reproduction Update, 8*, 141–154.

te Velde, E. R., Habbema, D., Leridon, H., & Eijkemans, M. (2012). The effect of postponement of first motherhood on permanent involuntary childlessness and total fertility rate in six European countries since the 1970's. *Human Reproduction Update, 27*, 1179–1183.

The Local. (2011, April 28). Surrogate children have no right to German Passport, Court Rules. *The Local*. http://www.thelocal.de/20110428/34681. Accessed 20 Aug 2015.

Tran, M. (2014, October 15). Apple and Facebook offer to freeze eggs for female employees. *The Guardian*. http://www.theguardian.com/technology/2014/oct/15/apple-facebook-offer-freeze-eggs-female-employees. Accessed 20 Aug 2015.

van Beers, B. C. (2015). Is Europe 'Giving in to Baby Markets?' Reproductive tourism in Europe and the gradual erosion of existing legal limits to reproductive markets. *Medical Law Review, 23*, 103–134.

van Hoof, W., Pennings, G., & de Sutter, P. (2015). Cross-border reproductive care for law evasion. A qualitative study into the experiences and moral perspectives of French women who go to Belgium for treatment with donor sperm. *Social Science and Medicine, 124*, 391–397.

WHO, World Bank. (2011). *World report on disability*. Geneva: WHO.

Wimmer, A., & Glick Schiller, N. (2002). Methodological nationalism and beyond. Nation-state building, migration, and the social sciences. *Global Networks, 2*, 301–334.

Wyndham, N., Marin Figueira, P. G., & Patrizio, P. (2012). A persistent misperception: Assisted reproductive technology can reverse the 'aged biological clock.'. *Fertility and Sterility, 97*, 1044–1047.

Zanini, G. (2011). Abandoned by the state, betrayed by the church. Italian experiences of cross-border reproductive care. *Reproductive Biomedicine Online, 23*, 565–572.

Zegers-Hochschild, F., Adamson, G. D., de Mouzon, J., Ishihara, O., Mansour, R., Nygren, K. G., et al. (2009). International committee for monitoring assisted reproductive technology (ICMART) and the World Health Organization (WHO) revised glossary of ART terminology, 2009. *Fertility and Sterility, 92*, 1520–1524.

Zegers-Hochschild, F., Mansour, R., Ishihara, O., Adamson, G. D., de Mouzon, J., Nygren, K. G., et al. (2014). International committee for monitoring assisted reproductive technology. World report on assisted reproductive technology, 2005. *Fertility and Sterility, 101*, 366–378.

Part V
Consequences of Childlessness

Chapter 15
What's a (Childless) Man Without a Woman? The Differential Importance of Couple Dynamics for the Wellbeing of Childless Men and Women in the Netherlands

Renske Keizer and Katya Ivanova

15.1 Introduction

Parenthood is often seen as being a core element of a "normal" adult life (Dykstra and Hagestad 2007). This notion has coloured both scientific and societal views on people who will never make the transition to parenthood. Childless individuals, especially childless women, are depicted as "others", and even as deviants (Letherby 2002). They are also perceived as being disadvantaged and as having weaker support networks. It is often assumed that childless adults are more likely than parents to suffer from isolation, loneliness, and physical and mental ill health (see for review Dykstra and Hagestad 2007).

Since being a parent is considered to be more central to the life of a woman than to the life of a man (Veevers 1980; Hird and Abshoff 2000; Letherby 2002; Bulcroft and Teachman 2003), the ramifications of not having taken on a parental role are generally assumed to be more disadvantageous for a childless woman than for a childless man. Scholars have often asserted that among men, circumstances and behaviours in the domain of paid employment have a much stronger influence on their identity and wellbeing than those in the domain of family life (e.g., Gilford 1986; Thomson and Walker 1989). Most studies on the impact of childlessness have

Both authors contributed equally to this chapter

R. Keizer (✉)
Department of Sociology, Erasmus University of Rotterdam, Rotterdam, The Netherlands

Department of Child Development, University of Amsterdam, Amsterdam, The Netherlands
e-mail: keizer@fsw.eur.nl

K. Ivanova (✉)
University of Amsterdam, Amsterdam, The Netherlands
e-mail: k.o.ivanova@uva.nl

313

M. Kreyenfeld, D. Konietzka (eds.), *Childlessness in Europe: Contexts, Causes, and Consequences*, Demographic Research Monographs, DOI 10.1007/978-3-319-44667-7_15

therefore examined the effects on women only, and have overlooked or simply neglected men (for a review, see Greene and Biddlecom 2000). Recent studies which have investigated the extent to which men's lives are affected by remaining childless have concluded that the implications of childlessness are no less significant for men than for women, but that the effects may be different (e.g., Eggebeen and Knoester 2001; Keizer et al. 2010).

These studies have revealed that the impact of childlessness among men is conditioned to a much larger extent by partner status than it is among women (Dykstra and Wagner 2007; Kendig et al. 2007; Wenger et al. 2007; Umberson et al. 2010). For example, Kendig et al. (2007) showed that never-married and formerly married childless men were more likely than married childless men to report being in poor physical health, whereas among women there were no significant differences in self-reported health among childless women based on partner status. Other studies have shown that the life outcomes of never-married childless women are much more favourable than those of their married counterparts (Koropeckyj-Cox and Call 2007). Taken together, these findings suggest that the presence of a partner is more important to the wellbeing of childless men than of childless women. If the presence of a partner indeed plays a bigger role in the life outcomes of childless men than of childless women, then are childless men also more affected by couple dynamics than childless women? Moreover, does relationship satisfaction have a greater impact on the overall wellbeing of childless men than on that of childless women?

Understanding the importance of couple dynamics for relationship satisfaction and, subsequently, overall wellbeing is important, especially for middle-aged and elderly couples. With increasing age, the social network of an individual becomes smaller and the relative importance of the partner increases (Carstensen 1992). This may be particularly true for childless couples, whose social networks are already more limited because of the absence of children and grandchildren. By studying the potential gender differences in the effects of couple dynamics and relationship satisfaction, our work addresses the pertinent issue of whether there are particular individuals within the childless population who are "at risk" of maladjustment.

Using a couple perspective, we investigate in the current study the differential importance of couple dynamics for relationship satisfaction among childless couples. Subsequently, we investigate whether relationship satisfaction has different effects on the well-being of the male partner and of the female partner in a given couple. As studies on the impact of parenthood on the wellbeing of adults have shown that the consequences of having or of not having children are not necessarily uniform across life outcomes (Dykstra and Wagner 2007; Kendig et al. 2007; Wenger et al. 2007), we focus on both physical and mental wellbeing. In our analysis, we use of multi-actor data from the Netherlands Kinship Panel Study (NKPS), a nationally representative survey conducted in 2002–2004.

15.2 Theoretical Background

15.2.1 Gendered Benefits of Marriage?

Being in a relationship is thought to be beneficial for individuals because a partnership represents an important source of both social support and financial stability, factors which are linked to higher levels of physical and mental health (e.g., Stimpson and Peek 2005). Bernard (1972) was one of the first scholars to explore the idea that relationships are more beneficial for men than for women. Based on her belief that marriage oppresses women because the wife is subordinate to the husband, she concluded that women tend to be less satisfied with marriage than men. Bernard (1972) also argued that men derive greater health benefits from marriage than women, and that marriage is harder on women than on men because women shoulder the majority of the household and childcare tasks.

In Bernard's work, which was published in the 1970s, gender balance and an equal division of tasks were the key factors used to explain the differences between men's and women's levels of satisfaction with marriage. Today, however, there is a much greater degree of gender equality in relationships than was the case in the period in which Bernard wrote her seminal studies (Sullivan 2006). The overwhelming majority of contemporary mothers are no longer confined by the role of housewife, but are actively involved in the labour market. In addition, while women still shoulder the majority of childcare duties, men have taken on a greater share of household and childcare tasks (e.g., Hook 2006). These trends suggest that couples today are much more gender-equal than they were four decades ago. Thus, based on the argumentation of Bernard, we would expect to find that gender differences in marital satisfaction are weaker today than they were in previous generations. Indeed, recent meta-analyses (Jackson et al. 2014) have reported that within non-clinical samples, no gender differences in marital satisfaction could be found. In line with these findings, and given that childless couples are viewed as being more gender-egalitarian than couples with children (e.g., Grunow et al. 2012; Schober 2012), we should not observe any gender differences in relationship satisfaction levels among contemporary childless couples. However, the question of whether experiences *within* the partnership might affect the two partners differently remains.

15.2.2 Gender Differences in the Importance of Relationship Characteristics

Following up on the arguments of Bernard, numerous studies have investigated the implications of partner status for wellbeing (e.g., Coombs 1991; Kiecolt-Glaser and Newton 2001). Recently, however, scholars have shifted their attention to investigating the impact on wellbeing of *within*-relationship dynamics. The majority of these studies have shown that positive marital relations (characterised by support and closeness) are protective for relationship satisfaction and wellbeing, whereas negative marital relations (characterised by disagreement and distress) are associated with poor outcomes for one or both members of the couple (e.g., Acitelli and Antonucci 1994; Ducharme 1997; Miller et al. 2004; Henry et al. 2005; Whisman et al. 2006).

Scholars have argued that what is going on in the relationship tends to have a greater impact on the female partner's than on the male partner's satisfaction with the relationship (e.g., McRae and Brody 1989). They often explain this difference by claiming that women tend to do more of the emotional work in the relationship than men (Thomson and Walker 1989), i.e., that women are generally more aware than men of the emotional climate of the relationship, and are more likely to monitor the relationship's emotional quality. While it has been shown that the perception of problems is associated with lower levels of relationship satisfaction and higher levels of stress among both women and men, women have been found to be more likely than men to perceive problems in the relationship (McRae and Brody 1989). In line with these findings, other studies have revealed that women initiate relationship therapy and file for divorce more frequently than men (e.g., Rokach et al. 2004). Scholars have further observed that a woman tends to be at a double disadvantage in a relationship relative to her male partner, not only because she is more likely to perceive problems in their relationship, but because these problems are more likely to have a detrimental impact on her wellbeing (e.g., Gove and Hughes 1979; McRae and Brody 1989). In other words, as Rae and Brody (1989) have put it: "Women's marriages are more negative than men's marriages and the negatives translate into more distress for women than men" (ibid.: 246).

Most studies which have examined the extent to which characteristics of the relationship affect relationship satisfaction have focused on negative marital relations, such as relationship problems and conflicts (for a critique, see Cramer 2004). Although the ways in which partners experience conflict and handle relationship problems are strong predictors of satisfaction with the relationship, recent studies have found that the ways in which partners provide emotional support to one another may be equally or even more important determinants of satisfaction (e.g., Cramer 2004; Hilbert et al. 2013). Findings in this area complement the findings on the impact of conflict and problems in the relationship: i.e., a woman's level of relationship satisfaction is not only more likely than a man's to be negatively affected by relationship conflict and problems; it is also more likely to be positively affected by partner support (e.g., Julien and Markman 1991).

Furthermore, scholars have argued that the physical and mental wellbeing of a woman is more strongly affected than that of a man by relationship quality because marriage is considered a more central component of a woman's than a man's life (Gilford 1986). Women are socialised to derive their wellbeing from close interpersonal relationships, whereas men are encouraged to derive their sense of self through more autonomous pathways, such as paid labour (Quirouette and Gold 1992). It has therefore been posited that while men tend to benefit from marriage regardless of the quality of the relationship, women may derive mental and physical health benefits from marriage only if the relationship is satisfying (Hess and Soldo

1985). Some scholars have even found that positive relationship characteristics such as high levels of closeness, while beneficial for a woman, are actually detrimental to the wellbeing of a man, as intense intimacy with a partner may interfere with the man's ability or desire to maintain his autonomy (Quirouette and Gold 1992).

15.2.3 Is the Picture Different for Childless Couples?

Although the literature has shown that childless couples exhibit higher levels of relationship satisfaction than parents (see Wagner et al. 2015 for a recent exception), it is not yet clear whether the previously described gender differences in the effects of relationship characteristics on relationship satisfaction – and, subsequently, on wellbeing – also apply to childless couples. Although childless couples (perhaps in part because of the greater degree of gender equality in their relationship) may be expected to report having fewer relationship conflicts and problems, there is no basis for assuming that the existence of relationship problems or conflicts would have different effects on the relationship satisfaction levels of childless couples than on those of parents. Therefore, we hypothesise that the link between relationship satisfaction and both positive and negative relationship dynamics will be stronger for childless women than for childless men (*H1*).

In terms of the effects of relationship satisfaction on physical and mental wellbeing, the literature suggests that previous findings for couples with children should not be extrapolated to childless couples. Compared to childless men, childless women are often better off economically and have substantially larger networks (e.g., Dykstra and Hagestad 2007). This might indicate that the overall wellbeing of childless women is less dependent than that of childless men on what is going on in their romantic relationship. We therefore hypothesise that the link between relationship satisfaction and both physical and mental wellbeing will be stronger for childless men than for childless women (*H2*).

In the current study we address two main questions: (1) do relationship dynamics have different effects on the relationship satisfaction levels of childless women than of childless men; and, (2) does the link between relationship satisfaction and mental and physical wellbeing differ between childless men and childless women? These questions were investigated by estimating couple-level random effects models using data on 163 Dutch childless couples from the first wave of the nationally representative Netherlands Kinship Panel Study (NKPS). Our work therefore helps to answer the question of whether previous findings on the importance of relationship dynamics and relationship satisfaction for couples with children also apply to the rather distinct population of childless partnerships.

15.3 Method & Method

15.3.1 Data

The data used in this chapter come from the first wave of the Netherlands Kinship Panel Study (NKPS; Dykstra et al. 2005). The NKPS is a longitudinal, nationally representative study. In wave one of the NKPS, 8161 individuals aged 18–79 participated. The respondents (also referred to as "anchors") were selected from a random sample of private addresses in the Netherlands. The first wave was conducted in 2002–2004 and had a response rate of 45% (Dykstra et al. 2005), which is not atypical for the Netherlands. Dutch response rates tend to be lower than elsewhere and have been declining over time, likely because the Dutch are particularly sensitive about privacy issues (De Leeuw and De Heer 2001 (fehlt); Stoop 2005 (fehlt)). The anchor data were collected via computer-assisted face-to-face interviews, as well as through separately completed questionnaires. Data were also collected from a number of significant others (also referred to as "alters"), including the anchors' current partner.

For our analyses, we focused on anchors who had partners at the time of the first wave of data collection, and whose partners were also participating in the NKPS (51.4% of the wave one sample, $n = 4194$). We further restricted our sample to couples in which neither partner was a parent (i.e., neither had children, including with an ex-partner) and the female partner was age 40 or older at the time of the interview. This restriction was made because we were interested in the couple dynamics of permanently childless individuals. Earlier research has shown that the proportion of couples who make the transition to parenthood after the age of 40 is small (Landry and Forrest 1995; Garssen et al. 2001). These selections resulted in a final sample of 163 childless couples. In our work, we used the data provided by both partners; thus, our sample consisted of 326 individuals nested in 163 couples.

15.3.2 Measures

Relationship Satisfaction Both partners provided answers to the following four items: "We have a good relationship", "The relationship with my partner makes me happy", "Our relationship is strong", and "The relationship with my partner is very stable". The responses were coded from 1 = *strongly agree* to 5 = *strongly disagree*. Developed specifically for the NKPS, the reliability and validity of this scale were tested during pilot studies (Verweij 2002), and it has been used successfully in other studies (Komter et al. 2012). The scale was created based on the mean of the items ($\alpha = .95$ for anchors and $\alpha = .92$ for alters). The items were recoded so that a higher value represented higher relationship satisfaction. The correlation between the partners' answers was $r = .55$, $p < .05$.

Self-Reported Health The partners' health was assessed based on the following question: "How is your health in general?" The respondents could choose from 1=*excellent* to 5=*very poor*. Self-assessed health has been shown to be a strong indicator of general health (Ferraro and Farmer 1999; McHorney 2000), and this NKPS item in particular has been validated in previous research on the link between family of origin and health (e.g., Monden 2010). The question was recoded so that a higher value corresponded to better health. The correlation between the partners' responses was $r=.05, p>.05$.

Mental Well-Being The partners' mood in the past 4 weeks was assessed using the following five questions: "How often have you felt particularly tense in the past 4 weeks?", "How often have you felt so down in the dumps in the past 4 weeks that nothing could cheer you up?", "How often have you felt calm and peaceful in the past 4 weeks?", "How often have you felt downhearted and miserable in the past 4 weeks?", and "How often have you felt happy in the past 4 weeks?". The answer categories ranged from 1=*all the time* to 6=*never*. Two of the items were recoded so that a higher value on this scale indicated a better mental wellbeing. The scale was created based on the mean of the items ($\alpha=.82$ for anchors and $\alpha=.85$ for alters). The correlation between the partners' answers was $r=.24, p<.05$.

Support from the Partner Both the anchor and the alter provided information about the level of support they received from their partner by answering the following five questions: "To what extent does your partner support you: (a) in decisions about your work or education; (b) when you have worries or health problems; (c) in your leisure time activities and social contacts; (d) with all kinds of practical things you need to do; and (e) in personal matters that are on your mind?" (1=*no support* to 4=*a lot of support*). The scale was created based on the mean of the items. The reliability of the measure was high both for the anchors and alters ($\alpha=.84$ for both). The correlation between the partners' responses was $r=.30, p<.05$.

Relationship Conflict The level of conflict in the relationship was assessed using the following three items: "Please indicate whether the following situations have occurred between you and your partner in the past 12 months: (1) heated discussions between you and your partner; (2) one of you putting down and blaming the other; and (3) you didn't want to talk to each other for a while". Both partners responded to these questions on a scale from 0=*not at all* to 2=*several times*. The scale was created based on the mean of the items. The reliability of the scale in our analytical sample was slightly under the conventionally established .70 threshold, but was still acceptable ($\alpha=.63$ for anchors and $\alpha=.66$ for alters). The correlation between the partners' answers was $r=.48, p<.05$.

Control Variables In all of our analyses, we controlled for the age of the reporting partner (in years), the highest attained level of education of the reporting partner (coded as 1=*(incomplete) elementary only/lower vocational/lower general secondary*, 2=*intermediate general secondary/upper general secondary/intermediate* *vocational*, and 3 = *higher vocational/university/post-graduate*), and for the duration of the current relationship in years (from the start of the partnership to the date of the interview).

In the analyses focusing on self-reported health, we also controlled for the reporting spouse's informal social capital and level of agreement with child-endorsing norms. The informal social capital of each partner was measured based on four questions which referred to the extent to which the anchor/alter was able to rely on his or her friends ("When I am troubled, I can always discuss my worries with my friends", "I place confidence in my friends", "Should I need help, I can always turn to my friends", and "I can always count on my friends"; rated from 1 = *strongly agree* to 5 = *strongly disagree*). The items were recoded so that a higher value corresponded to a large amount of informal social capital. A similar scale based on the NKPS data has been successfully used in earlier works on the impact of social contexts on romantic relationships (e.g., Hogerbrugge et al. 2012). The reliability of the scale was high both for the anchor and alter ($\alpha = .92$ for anchors and $\alpha = .93$ for alters). Finally, our measure of child-endorsing norms was constructed based on the partners' responses to the following four statements: "A person's life is not complete if s/he has not had children", "People have a duty to society to have children", "I believe that in this world a person can feel totally at ease only in his or her own family with children", and "If a person never has children, s/he can never be really happy" (rated on a scale from 1 = *strongly agree* to 5 = *strongly disagree*). The items were recoded so that a higher value corresponded to a higher level of agreement with the child-endorsing norm. The reliability of the scale was high for both partners ($\alpha = .77$ for anchors and $\alpha = .87$ for alters). Table 15.1 displays descriptive information about all of the variables used in the analyses.

Table 15.1 Descriptive statistics for variables used in the analyses

	Female partners		Male partners	
	n	M (SD)	n	M (SD)
Relationship satisfaction	161	4.57 (0.53)	160	4.64 (0.56)
Self-reported health, 1 (lowest)-5 (highest)	163	3.91 (0.86)	163	4.03 (0.72)
Mental wellbeing, 1 (lowest)-6 (highest)	161	4.90 (0.70)	162	4.98 (0.74)
Support from partner, 1 (lowest)-4 (highest)	159	3.40 (0.55)	159	3.49 (0.48)
Relationship conflict, 0 (lowest)-2 (highest)	159	0.40 (0.42)	156	0.43 (0.41)
Age (in years)	163	51.29 (8.99)	163	53.02 (10.52)
Informal social capital, 1 (lowest-5 highest)	162	3.92 (0.67)	162	3.78 (0.71)
Child-endorsing norm, 1 (lowest-5 highest)	161	1.41 (0.54)	161	1.45 (0.63)
Duration of the partnership (in years)	163	24.92 (13.43)	163	24.92 (13.43)
	n	**% of n**	**n**	**% of n**
Educational attainment	163		163	
Elem only, lower voc, lower general secondary		43.6%		30.7%
Intermediate, upper general secondary, interm. voc.		16.6%		27.0%
Higher voc., university, postgraduate		39.9%		42.3%

15.3.3   Analytical Approach

We carried out our analyses in two steps. In the first step, we examined whether gender differences could be observed in the association between aspects of the relationship (i.e., conflict and support) and relationship satisfaction (*H1*). In the second step, we examined whether the link between relationship satisfaction and self-rated physical and mental health differed between the male and the female partners (*H2*). The research questions were addressed using linear regression models with couple-level random effects. We did not estimate fixed-effects models because there was little variation in the covariates of interest *within* couples (e.g., level of conflict, support from the partner), which could have resulted in standard errors which were too large (Allison 2009). The models were fitted using *xtreg* in STATA, Version 13.1. In all of the models we included control variables for the age of the partner whose relationship satisfaction/wellbeing was being examined, as well as his/her educational level and the duration of the relationship. Additionally, in the models which addressed the link between relationship satisfaction and wellbeing we controlled for the individual's level of agreement with child-endorsing norms (as a proxy for whether the respondent's childless status was (in)voluntary) and social capital.

To test the hypotheses, we included interaction terms in our models (i.e., between the gender of the partner and the covariate of interest, such as conflict, support, or relationship satisfaction). To facilitate the interpretation of the significant interaction terms, we used the *margins* command in STATA to estimate and plot the marginal effects at representative values for the female and the male partners. All of the marginal effects were estimated for the reference categories of the categorical control variables, and the continuous variables were kept at the sample mean.

15.4   Results

Detailed descriptive information about the measures used in this study is displayed in Table 15.1. The table clearly shows that, by and large, the childless NKPS participants reported rather high levels of relationship satisfaction (*M* for female partners = 4.57 (*SD* = .53) and *M* for male partners = 4.64 (*SD* = .56)). Furthermore, there were no gender differences in the mean levels of any of the central covariates of interest (i.e., relationship satisfaction, self-reported health, mental wellbeing, support from the partner, and relationship conflict).

In the first step of our analyses we focused on the question of whether there were gender differences in the association between relationship dynamics and relationship satisfaction. The results addressing this question are displayed in Table 15.2. The first two models in the table display the main effects of gender (Model 1) and of support from the partner and relationship conflict (Model 2). As was mentioned earlier, the gender of the partner was not associated with the self-reported level of

Table 15.2 Estimates from relationship-level Random-Effects Regression Models with relationship satisfaction as dependent variable

	Model 1		Model 2		Model 3		Model 4	
	Gender		Relationship dynamics		Interaction with support		Interaction with conflict	
	B	SE	B	SE	B	SE	B	SE
Gender (ref. = female partner)	0.05	(0.04)	0.01	(0.04)	−0.17	(0.30)	0.10+	(0.06)
Support from partner			0.45**	(0.05)	0.43**	(0.06)	0.45**	(0.05)
Relationship conflict			−0.19**	(0.07)	−0.19**	(0.07)	−0.09	(0.08)
Interactions								
Gender × support from partner					0.05	(0.09)		
Gender × relationship conflict							−0.21*	(0.10)
Controls								
Age (in years)	0.01	(0.00)	0.01+	(0.00)	0.01+	(0.00)	0.01+	(0.00)
Educational level (ref. = highest)								
Lowest	0.05	(0.07)	−0.03	(0.06)	−0.03	(0.06)	−0.04	(0.06)
Middle	0.00	(0.07)	−0.01	(0.06)	−0.01	(0.07)	−0.02	(0.06)
Duration of relationship (in years)	−0.00	(0.00)	−0.00	(0.00)	−0.00	(0.00)	−0.00	(0.00)
Constant	4.23**	(0.20)	2.80**	(0.25)	2.88**	(0.28)	2.77**	(0.25)
Miscellaneous parameters								
Residual SD of random intercept (sigma_u)	0.42		0.31		0.31		0.31	
Residual intraclass correlation (rho)	0.58		0.47		0.47		0.47	
R^2 within unions	0.03		0.16		0.16		0.17	
R^2 between unions	0.01		0.39		0.39		0.41	
R^2 overall	0.01		0.31		0.32		0.33	

Note. + $p<0.10$, * $p<0.05$, ** $p<0.01$

relationship satisfaction, whereas the self-reported level of support received from the partner and the level of relationship conflict were associated with relationship satisfaction in the manner predicted (i.e., a one point increase in partner support was linked to a .45 point increase in the dependent variable, and a one point increase in relationship conflict was linked to a .19 decrease in relationship satisfaction). Our first research question is, however, addressed in the subsequent models, which included an interaction between the gender of the partner and the indicators of relationship dynamics (Model 3 for support and Model 4 for conflict). All of the results discussed below were found after accounting for the individual and relationship level control variables.

As can be seen in Model 3, the association between the level of support received from the partner and the level of self-reported relationship satisfaction did not differ between the male and the female childless partners. In other words, we did not find evidence that childless women were more strongly affected than childless men by the positive aspects of their relationship. While we did find evidence of gender differences in the association between conflict and relationship satisfaction, these differences were not in the expected direction (Model 4 of Table 15.2). For ease of interpretation, the estimated marginal effects at representative values are plotted in Fig. 15.1. A post-estimation examination of the slopes for the two groups showed that only the slope for the male partners ($b=-.31$, $SE=.08$, 95 % CI [$-.47 - -.14$]) was significant (slope for female partners: $b=-.09$, $SE=.08$, 95 % CI [$-.25 - .06$]). An additional check demonstrated that the difference between the partners was significant ($p<.05$) only at particularly high levels of conflict (i.e., two), and that the magnitude of the difference was not large (i.e., a difference of .32 points at *frequency of conflict*$=2$).

The subsequent models addressed the second research question: namely, whether there were gender differences in the link between relationship satisfaction and the partners' wellbeing. Our findings are displayed in Table 15.3, Model 2 and Fig. 15.2 for physical health; and in Table 15.3, Model 4 and Fig. 15.3 for mental health. Model 2 of Table 15.3 and Fig. 15.2 show that relationship satisfaction was found to be positively associated with self-rated health, but only among the childless men. A post-estimation examination of the slopes indicated that whereas the slope for the male partners was significant ($b=.25$, $SE=.11$, 95 % CI [.03 -- .47]), the slope for the female partners was not ($b=-.08$, $SE=.12$, 95 % CI [$-.30 - .15$]). Our findings in Model 4 of Table 15.3 also demonstrated that there was a (borderline) significant gender interaction for the link between relationship satisfaction and self-rated mental wellbeing. Once again, whereas the slope for the male partners was significant ($b=.33$, $SE=.10$, 95 % CI [.14 - .52]), the slope for the female partners was not ($b=.09$, $SE=.10$, 95 % CI [$-.11 - .29$]; also see Fig. 15.3). In other words, our results indicated that the link between (physical) wellbeing and relationship satisfaction was stronger for the male than for the female childless partners.

15.5   Discussion

In this chapter, our goal was to test to what extent gender differences in couple dynamics exist within childless couples. In our analyses we found that male and female childless partners reported similar levels of relationship satisfaction, a result which is in line with the findings of recent studies on gender differences in marital satisfaction of partners with children (e.g., Jackson et al. 2014). The key

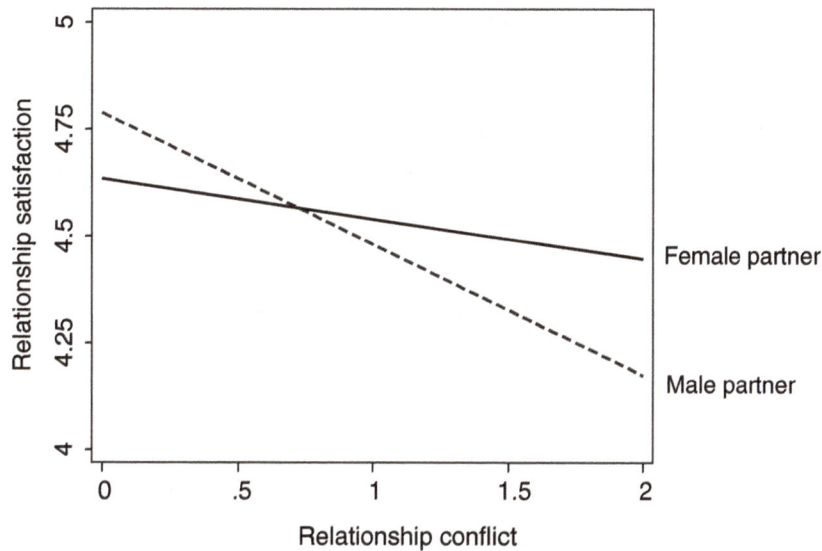

Fig. 15.1 Plot of estimated values for relationship satisfaction, based on estimates from Model 3, Table 15.2 (control variables at representative value)

contribution of our work however, is our finding that there were gender differences in the link between relationship dynamics and relationship satisfaction and in the link between relationship satisfaction and wellbeing.

First, in contrast to our expectations, we found that the link between relationship conflicts and relationship satisfaction was stronger for the childless men than for the childless women. Interestingly, no gender differences were found in the link between partner support and relationship satisfaction. In other words, the positive aspects of the partnership were equally important for both the male and the female childless partners studied. These findings were surprising, as most of the previous literature has stressed that female partners are more strongly affected by both the positive and the negative aspects of their romantic relationships (e.g., McRae and Brody 1989). Our finding concerning relationship conflict could be interpreted in two ways. As we noted above, compared to childless men, childless women have been reported to be economically better off and, even more importantly, to have larger networks (Dykstra and Hagestad 2007). Therefore, it is possible that childless men depend heavily on their intimate partnerships, and are thus, more sensitive to the internal dynamics of these relationships than childless women. Another possible interpretation of this finding is that it is not the case that childless *men* are more strongly affected by relationship conflicts, but rather that childless *women* are less strongly affected by conflicts. In other words, we suggest that previous evidence that mothers are more sensitive than fathers to relationship conflict might be attributable to a heightened preoccupation among mothers with the potential impact of those conflicts on the wellbeing of their children. As childless women do not face this concern, they might be less sensitive to conflicts. These interpretations are, however, highly speculative. Future research may want to examine whether the gender difference we found here is robust, and to investigate to what extent it is driven by a

Table 15.3 Estimates from relationship-level Random-Effects Regression Models with self-reported health and mental wellbeing as the dependent variables

| | Model 1 | | Model 2 | | Model 3 | | Model 4 | |
| | Gender | | Relationship dynamics | | Interaction with support | | Interaction with conflict | |
	B	SE	B	SE	B	SE	B	SE
Gender (ref. = female partner)	0.16+	(0.09)	−1.34+	(0.72)	0.12	(0.07)	−1.00	(0.63)
Support from partner	0.09	(0.08)	−0.08	(0.12)	0.22**	(0.07)	0.09	(0.10)
Relationship conflict			0.33*	(0.16)			0.24+	(0.14)
Interactions								
Gender × support from partner	0.06	(0.07)	0.07	(0.07)	0.20**	(0.06)	0.20**	(0.06)
Gender × relationship conflict	−0.17*	(0.08)	−0.16*	(0.08)	−0.12+	(0.07)	−0.12+	(0.07)
Controls								
Age (in years)	−0.01*	(0.01)	−0.01*	(0.01)	0.00	(0.01)	0.00	(0.01)
Educational level (ref. = highest)	−0.09	(0.10)	−0.09	(0.10)	−0.06	(0.09)	−0.05	(0.09)
Lowest	−0.16	(0.12)	−0.15	(0.12)	−0.09	(0.10)	−0.08	(0.10)
Middle	0.00	(0.00)	0.01	(0.00)	0.00	(0.00)	0.00	(0.00)
Duration of relationship (in years)	4.13**	(0.50)	4.90**	(0.63)	3.07**	(0.46)	3.65**	(0.56)
Constant	4.23**	(0.20)	2.80**	(0.25)	2.88**	(0.28)	2.77**	(0.25)
Miscellaneous parameters								
Residual SD of random intercept (sigma_u)	0.18		0.20		0.27		0.24	
Residual intraclass correlation (rho)	0.06		0.07		0.17		0.14	
R^2 within unions	0.10		0.12		0.04		0.04	
R^2 between unions	0.04		0.04		0.14		0.18	
R^2 overall	0.06		0.07		0.11		0.12	

Note. $^+ p < 0.10$, $^* p < 0.05$, $^{**} p < 0.01$

heightened sensitivity to relationship dynamics among childless men or by a lower sensitivity to relationship dynamics among childless women.

The second main finding of our work concerned the link between relationship satisfaction and self-reported mental and physical wellbeing. In line with our hypothesis, we found that the association between relationship satisfaction and health was stronger for the childless men than for the childless women, and that this

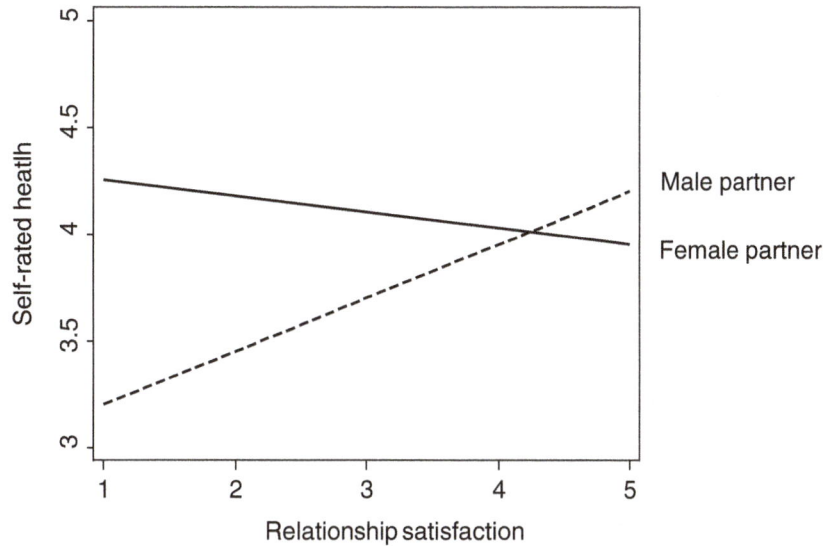

Fig. 15.2 Plot of estimated values for self-rated health, based on estimates from Model 2, Table 15.3 (control variables at representative values)

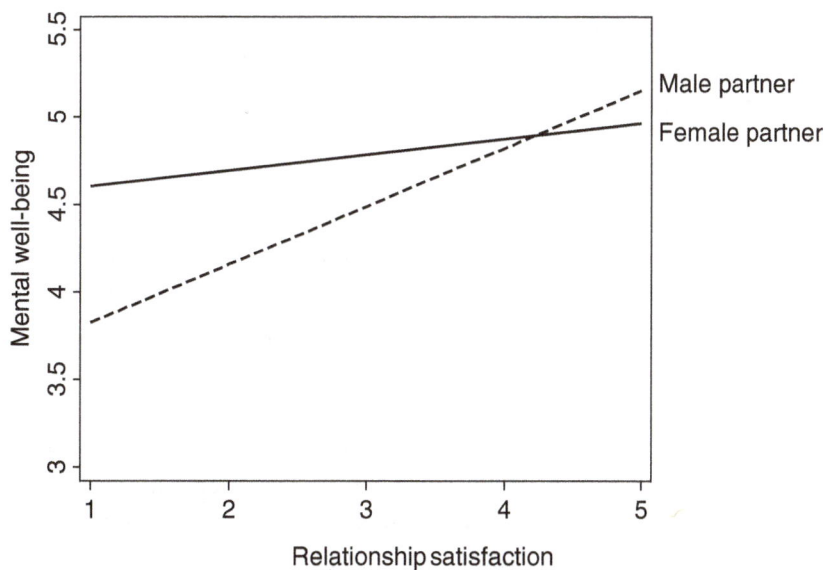

Fig. 15.3 Plot of estimated values for mental well-being, based on estimates from Model 4, Table 15.3 (control variables at representative values)

difference was particularly evident when the levels of relationship satisfaction were low. These results indicate that when they are in unsatisfying romantic relationships, childless men are at greater risk than childless women of physical and mental ill health. Again, future research should investigate in detail the mechanisms underlying this pattern. Are childless men indeed more affected by being in an unsatisfying relationship because they rely on their wife as their chief source of social support (Pugliesi and Shook 1998), and are these men therefore especially vulnerable when that support weakens or dissipates? Or is it the case that compared to fathers and childless women, childless men place a higher value on their romantic relationship than on other domains of life, and are therefore be more affected by what is going on in their relationship? Yet regardless of the underlying mechanisms, our study reveals that when childless men are dissatisfied with their romantic relationship, they are at risk of physical and mental maladjustment.

Some limitations of our study should be mentioned here. First, it is important to note that we did not strictly compare each childless man to his *own* female partner, who was also childless. As was previously stated, the optimal way to test for possible gender differences in the link between relationship dynamics and relationship satisfaction, and between relationship satisfaction and wellbeing, is to utilize couple-level fixed effects. However, given the very limited variability in the constructs of interest which we observed *within* our units of analysis (i.e., the partnerships) and due to concerns about the possibility of inflated standard errors, we opted to run random effect models (Allison 2009).

Another methodological concern which might be raised about our work is the fact that we did not address the question of possible reverse causality. In other words, we cannot exclude the possibility that what we are seeing is, for example, a gender difference in the impact of mental and physical wellbeing on relationship satisfaction. We chose to use data from the Dutch NKPS survey because they provide high-quality, *dyadic* information on the concepts of interest. However, as the data were cross-sectional in nature, we have taken great care throughout our work to avoid implying that we have found evidence of any causal links.

Despite these limitations, our results suggest that childless men may be more affected than childless women by negative couple dynamics. Using a rich couple-level data set, we showed that the link between relationship conflict and relationship satisfaction was stronger among the childless men than among the childless women. In addition, we found that the childless men who reported experiencing low levels of relationship satisfaction were also in worse physical and mental health than the childless women. Currently, approximately one in five men will remain childless (Keizer 2010), and divorce rates remain high. Thus, it appears that entry into fatherhood could become even more selective in the future (e.g., Rønsen and Skrede 2006). Future studies should therefore investigate in greater detail how childless men of middle and older ages function in romantic relationships.

Acknowledgement   The present study was supported by a grant from the Netherlands Organization for Scientific Research to Renske Keizer (NWO MaGW VENI; grant no. 016.125.054).

Literature

Acitelli, L. K., & Antonucci, T. C. (1994). Gender differences in the link between marital support and satisfaction in older couples. *Journal of Personality and Social Psychology, 67*, 688–698.
Allison, P. D. (2009). *Fixed effects regression models*. Newbury Park: Sage.

Bernard, J. (1972). *The future of marriage*. New York: Bantam.

Bulcroft, R., & Teachman, J. (2003). Ambiguous constructions: Development of a childless or childfree life course. In M. Coleman & L. H. Ganong (Eds.), *Handbook of contemporary families: Considering the past, contemplating the future* (pp. 116–135). London: Sage.

Carstensen, L. L. (1992). Social and emotional patterns in adulthood: Support for socioemotional selectivity theory. *Psychology and Aging, 7*, 331–338.

Coombs, R. H. (1991). Marital status and personal well-being: A literature review. *Family Relations, 40*, 97–102.

Cramer, D. (2004). Satisfaction with a romantic relationship, depression, support, and conflict. *Psychology and Psychotherapy: Theory, Research and Practice, 77*, 449–461.

De Leeuw, E. D., & de Heer, W. (2001). Trends in household survey nonresponse: A longitudinal and international comparison. In R. M. Groves, D. A. Dillman, J. L. Eltinge, & R. J. A. Little (Eds.), *Survey nonresponse* (pp. 41–54). New York: Wiley.

Ducharme, F. (1997). Conjugal support, coping behaviours and mental health of elderly couples: A three-wave longitudinal panel study. *Health Care in Later Life, 2*, 155–165.

Dykstra, P. A., & Hagestad, G. O. (2007). Childlessness and parenthood in two centuries: Different roads – Different maps? *Journal of Family Issues, 28*, 1518–1532.

Dykstra, P. A., & Wagner, M. (2007). Pathways to childlessness and late-life outcomes. *Journal of Family Issues, 28*, 1487–1517.

Dykstra, P. A., Kalmijn, M., Knijn, T. C. M., Komter, A. E., Liefbroer, A. C., & Mulder, C. H. (2005). *Codebook of the Netherlands Kinship panel study, a multi-actor, multimethod panel study on solidarity in family relationships, wave 1* (No. 4). Den Haag: NIDI

Eggebeen, D. J., & Knoester, C. (2001). Does fatherhood matter for men? *Journal of Marriage and Family, 63*, 381–393.

Ferraro, K. F., & Farmer, M. M. (1999). Utility of health data from social surveys: Is there a gold standard for measuring morbidity? *American Sociological Review, 64*, 303–315.

Garssen, J., de Beer, J., Cuyvers, P., & de Jong, A. (2001). *Samenleven. Nieuwe feiten over relaties en gezinnen. [Living together. New facts about relationships and families]*. Voorburg/Heerlen: CBS.

Gilford, R. (1986). Marriages in later life. *Generations, 10*, 16–20.

Gove, W. R., & Hughes, M. (1979). Possible causes of the apparent sex differences in mental health. *American Sociological Review, 44*, 59–81.

Greene, M. E., & Biddlecom, A. E. (2000). Absent and problematic men: Demographic accounts of male reproductive roles. *Population and Development Review, 26*, 81–115.

Grunow, D., Schulz, F., & Blossfeld, H.-P. (2012). What determines change in the division of housework over the course of marriage? *International Sociology, 27*, 289–307.

Henry, R. G., Miller, R. B., & Giarrusso, R. (2005). Difficulties, disagreements, and disappointments in late-life marriages. *International Journal of Aging and Human Development, 61*, 243–264.

Hess, B., & Soldo, B. (1985). Husband and wife networks. In W. J. Sauer & R. T. Coward (Eds.), *Social support networks and the care of the elderly: Theory, research and practices* (pp. 67–92). New York: Springer.

Hilbert, P., Bodemann, G., Nussbeck, F. W., & Bradbury, T. N. (2013). Predicting relationship satisfaction in distressed and non-distressed couples based on a stratified sample: A matter of conflict, positivity or support? *Family Science, 4*, 110–120.

Hird, M., & Abshoff, K. (2000). Women without children: A contradiction in terms? *Journal of Comparative Family Studies, 31*, 347–366.

Hogerbrugge, M. J. A., Komter, A. E., & Scheepers, P. (2012). Dissolving long-term romantic relationships: Assessing the role of the social context. *Journal of Social and Personal Relationships, 30*, 320–342.

Hook, J. (2006). Care in context. Men's unpaid work in 20 countries, 1965–2003. *American Sociological Review, 71*, 639–660.

Jackson, J. B., Miller, R. B., Oka, M., & Henry, R. G. (2014). Gender differences in marital satisfaction: A meta-analysis. *Journal of Marriage and Family, 76*, 105–129.

Julien, D., & Markman, H. J. (1991). Social support and social networks as determinants of individual and marital outcomes. *Journal of Social and Personal Relationships, 8*, 549–568.

Keizer, R. (2010). *Remaining childless. Causes and consequences from a life course perspective.* Dissertation. Utrecht University. Enschede: Ipskamp.

Keizer, R., Dykstra, P. A., & Poortman, A.-R. (2010). Life outcomes of childless men and fathers. *European Sociological Review, 26*, 1–15.

Kendig, H., Dykstra, P. A., van Gaalen, R. I. A., & Melkas, T. (2007). Health of aging parents and childless individuals. *Journal of Family Issues, 28*, 1457–1486.

Kiecolt-Glaser, J. K., & Newton, T. L. (2001). Marriage and health: His and hers. *Psychological Bulletin, 127*, 472–503.

Komter, A. E., Keizer, R., & Dykstra, P. A. (2012). The men behind economically successful women: A focus on Dutch dual earner couples. *Multidisciplinary Journal of Gender Studies, 1*, 156–187.

Koropeckyj-Cox, T., & Call, V. R. A. (2007). Characteristics of older childless persons and parents: Cross-national comparisons. *Journal of Family Issues, 28*, 1362–1414.

Landry, D. J., & Forrest, J. D. (1995). How old are U.S. fathers? *Family Planning Perspectives, 27*, 159–161 + 165.

Letherby, G. (2002). Childless and bereft?: Stereotypes and realities in relation to "voluntary" and "involuntary" childlessness and womanhood. *Sociological Inquiry, 72*, 7–20.

McHorney, C. A. (2000). Concepts and measurement of health status and health-related quality of life. In G. L. Albrecht, R. Fitzpatrick, & S. Scrimshaw (Eds.), *Handbook of social studies in health and medicine* (pp. 339–358). Thousand Oaks: Sage.

McRae, J. A., Jr., & Brody, C. J. (1989). The differential importance of marital experiences for the well-being of women and men: A research note. *Social Science Research, 18*, 237–248.

Miller, B., Townsend, A. L., & Ishler, K. J. (2004). Change in marital dissatisfaction, health and depression in older married couples. *Journal of Mental Health and Aging, 10*, 65–77.

Monden, C. W. S. (2010). Do measured and unmeasured family factors bias the association between education and self-assessed health? *Social Indicators Research, 98*, 321–336.

Pugliesi, K., & Shook, S. L. (1998). Gender, ethnicity, and network characteristics: Variation in social support resources. *Sex Roles, 38*, 215–238.

Quirouette, C., & Gold, D. P. (1992). Spousal characteristics as predictors of well-being in older couples. *International Journal of Aging and Human Development, 34*, 257–269.

Rokach, R., Cohen, O., & Dreman, S. (2004). Who pulls the trigger? Who initiates divorce among over 45-year-olds? *Journal of Divorce & Remarriage, 42*, 61–83.

Rønsen, M., & Skrede, K. (2006). Nordic fertility patterns: Compatible with gender equality? In A. L. Ellingsæter & A. Leira (Eds.), *Politicising parenthood in Scandinavia: Gender relations in welfare states* (pp. 53–76). Bristol: Policy Press.

Schober, P. S. (2012). Gender equality and outsourcing of domestic work, childbearing, and relationship stability among British couples. *Journal of Family Issues, 34*, 25–52.

Stimpson, J. P., & Peek, M. K. (2005). Concordance of chronic conditions in older Mexican American couples. *Preventing Chronic Disease: Public Health Research, Practice and Policy, 2*, 1–7.

Stoop, I. A. L. (2005). The hunt for the last respondent. PhD Thesis. *Faculty of social sciences.* The Netherlands: Utrecht University.

Sullivan, O. (2006). *Changing gender relations, changing families: Tracing the pace of change over time.* New York: Rowman and Littlefield.

Thomson, L., & Walker, A. J. (1989). Gender in families: Women and men in marriage, work and parenthood. *Journal of Marriage and Family, 51*, 845–871.

Umberson, D., Pudrovska, T., & Reczek, C. (2010). Parenthood, childlessness, and well-being: A life course perspective. *Journal of Marriage and Family, 72*, 612–629.

Veevers, J. E. (1980). *Childless by choice.* Toronto: Butterworth.

Verweij, A. (2002). *Rapportage pilotstudy schriftelijke vragenlijst Netherlands Kinship Panel Study* [Report of the pilot study of the selfcompletion questionnaire of the NKPS] (No. 3).

Wagner, J., Wrzus, C., Neyer, F. J., & Lang, F. R. (2015). Social network characteristics of early midlife voluntarily and involuntarily childless couples. *Journal of Family Issues, 36*, 87–110.

Wenger, G. C., Dykstra, P. A., Melkas, T., & Knipscheer, K. C. P. M. (2007). Social embeddedness and late life parenthood: Community activity, close ties, and support networks. *Journal of Family Issue, 28*, 1419–1456.

Whisman, M. A., Uebelacker, L. A., Tolejko, N., Chatav, Y., & McKelvie, M. (2006). Marital discord and well-being in older adults: Is the association confounded by personality? *Psychology and Aging, 21*, 626–631.

Chapter 16
Fertility and Women's Old-Age Income in Germany

Tatjana Mika and Christin Czaplicki

16.1 Introduction

In Germany, the average woman earns far less than the average man (Finke 2011). This large gender gap in earnings is attributable in part to the tendency of German women to work part-time and to take employment breaks. So far, however, there has been little research on the "motherhood penalty": i.e., on the additional costs associated with having a child, relative to remaining childless (Waldfogel 1998). It is clear that the impact of having a child on a woman's life course goes beyond an immediate reduction in income when she withdraws from labour market after giving birth. The shift to part-time employment that many mothers make not only reduces a woman's gross income because she works fewer hours; it also damages her long-term career prospects (Brenke 2011). Moreover, even women who work full-time earn less on average than men, in part because they often choose to study disciplines that channel them into professions that are lower paid than those typically chosen by their male counterparts (Begall and Mills 2012; Busch and Holst 2011; Petersen and Morgan 1995; Trappe 2006).

The two regions of Germany have different histories with respect to female, and particularly maternal employment (Rosenfeld et al. 2004). In the German Democratic Republic (GDR) women were expected to work full-time and to return to work after taking a single year of leave; the so-called "Babyjahr" (Rosenfeld et al. 2004). Part-time work was not common in the GDR, and not encouraged by the government (Drasch 2011). In the Federal Republic of Germany (FRG), by contrast, women of the cohorts born around 1930 often exited the labour market upon marriage (Lauterbach 1994). Until 1972, a husband was allowed to forbid his wife to work if he was able to provide sufficient household income from his own salary. This had a

T. Mika (✉) • C. Czaplicki
Research and Development, German Pension Insurance, Berlin, Germany
e-mail: tatjana.mika@drv-bund.de; christin.czaplicki@drv-bund.de

© The Author(s) 2017   331
M. Kreyenfeld, D. Konietzka (eds.), *Childlessness in Europe: Contexts, Causes, and Consequences*, Demographic Research Monographs, DOI 10.1007/978-3-319-44667-7_16

negative effect on employment among married women in western Germany. Although western German women started entering the labour market in greater numbers starting in the 1970s, full-time employment continued to be rare among mothers (Allmendinger 2011: 47). Only a small minority of working-age women in western Germany were in continuous full-time employment (Simonson et al. 2011). Most women who had children returned to work after spending a shorter or a longer period of time raising children, or left the labour market permanently after having their first child (Stegmann and Mika 2013: 239). A large share of working mothers in western Germany were in "marginal" part-time employment. In most marginal employment arrangements, a worker's hours and income are capped (currently at 450 euros per month). Moreover, workers in these jobs accrue very little pension benefits.

After German reunification, the employment patterns of mothers continued to differ in the two parts of the country, as the full-time employment rates remained higher in eastern than in western Germany. In recent years, however, the rates of unemployment and of part-time employment among women have been increasing in the east, and women in eastern Germany have lower earnings than their western German counterparts. It is therefore very difficult to determine how the recent employment patterns of mothers in eastern and western Germany will affect their old-age pension benefits (Allmendinger 1994). In particular, it is unclear whether the welfare state will be able to buffer the adverse effects that career interruptions are expected to have on the old-age pensions of western German women.

Research on the effects of motherhood on employment has often focused on the years immediately after childbirth. In this paper, we focus on the lifetime employment and earning patterns of German women with and without children. We investigate the long-term effects of motherhood on women's earnings during their working years, and on their income in retirement. Because the employment patterns of mothers in eastern and western Germany have long differed, we conduct the analysis separately for the two parts of Germany. The data for this analysis come from a unique dataset that contains linked survey and register data. In this dataset the Survey of Health, Ageing, and Retirement in Europe (SHARE) is combined with information from the pension insurance records (SHARE-RV). Using these data, we are able to examine the lifetime employment patterns and earning profiles of the cohorts born between 1919 and 1982; although most of the women in our sample were born between 1930 and 1965. We explore the question of whether eastern German women who are more likely than western German women to be employed face a less severe "motherhood penalty" than their western counterparts. We map each woman's gross earnings (as recorded in the pension insurance data), as well as household information on her partner's income and earnings record. The last and major step in our investigation is an analysis of the lifetime income of women according to the number of children they have and the region where they live. For 2 years after a child is born, the German state provides mothers with relatively generous pension benefit subsidies. The benefits each woman accrues are equivalent to the national average income in those years. As most women earn less than the national average income, the benefits a mother accrues during this period may supplement her pension entitlement more than if she had continued to work. We analyse the question of to what extent these subsidies bridge the old-age income gap between mothers and childless women. We also seek to determine whether the loss of income among mothers is offset at the household level by the higher earnings of fathers.

16.2 Institutional Background

In Germany, the size of each individual's old-age statutory pension is mainly based on the compulsory contributions he or she has made while in paid employment. However, an individual may qualify for additional top-ups on the grounds of social hardship. For example, a person may be entitled to receive additional pension benefits if he or she has a low income, is caring for a child or another family member, or is engaged in military and civil service. In Germany, women have been included in the old-age pension scheme since it first began in 1895. However, women's pensions have always been smaller than those of men because the average woman has always earned less than the average man. After the Second World War, pension funds were structured differently in the GDR and in the FRG. In western Germany, contribution levels were raised from 1957 onward to allow for increases in old-age pension benefits. In eastern Germany, contribution levels were considerably lower, and pension benefits were correspondingly low. The old-age income levels of women in eastern and western Germany also differed because of the differences in the employment patterns of women in the GDR and the FRG.[1]

Under the German Unification Treaty, the eastern and western pension systems were largely harmonized. However, the old-age income levels of women in eastern and western Germany who are now reaching retirement age still differ because of their different employment and earning histories. Particularly notable is the high share of western German women who have spent many years in marginal employment arrangements with very low gross income. The income a worker earns in these so-called "mini-jobs" is usually exempt from taxation and full social security contributions, unless he or she makes these contributions voluntarily. Thus, mothers in western Germany who work primarily in marginal employment may be expected to have much lower old-age income levels than childless women who work full-time.

However, some of these differences in employment patterns are offset by the additional pension benefits women accrue after the birth of each of their children. The German pension insurance scheme awards mothers special benefits for each child they have. First, when each child turns 1 year old, the retired mother (or father)

---

[1] In the Federal Republic of Germany, a special provision in the social security code actually offered married women the option of cancelling their personal pension insurance account and getting a refund of the contributions they made while in socially insured employment. As a result, a considerable number of western German women from the cohorts born around 1930 had no pension fund account in their own name.

receives pension benefits equivalent to 2 years of the national average income (Dünn and Stosberg 2014). Since women's earnings are usually lower than the national average income, this credit typically compensates the mother for more than 2 years of complete income loss. In addition, the mother usually qualifies for a top-up for low-income individuals from a social insurance employment fund. Through 1991, the maximum pension insurance credit was equivalent to 75 % of the national average income. After 1992, a similar top-up was introduced for parents who work while their child is under age 12. Until the child turns 12, one person in the family is considered the child's main caregiver for the purposes of accruing pension insurance benefits. This is usually the mother.

16.3   Data, Variables, and Methods

16.3.1   Data

The data for our investigation comes from SHARE-RV. SHARE-RV stands for the direct linkage of survey data of the Survey of Health, Ageing, and Retirement in Europe (SHARE: www.share-project.org) with administrative data of the research data centre of the German Pension Insurance (FDZ-RV). The combination of information about different aspects of the respondents' life with accurate administrative data has several advantages, and can provide scholars with a wide range of research options. The survey data of SHARE are used in Germany for the direct linkage. For data protection reasons, administrative records are collected only for those respondents who gave their written consent during the interview.[2]

Launched in 2004, SHARE is an innovative and multidisciplinary panel survey that has so far collected micro-data on the health, the socio-economic status, and the social and family networks of more than 45,000 individuals aged 50 or older. Face-to-face interviews are conducted not only with each sampled individual, but also with each respondent's partner or spouse who lives in the same household. Instead of relying on a standard questionnaire that only collects current information, in the third wave (called SHARELIFE) the survey has used a retrospective questionnaire that covers each respondent's life from birth up to the time of the current interview (Schröder 2011). The longitudinal and multidisciplinary design of SHARE sheds light on how different areas of a respondent's life interact as he or she ages. As they are central elements of social life and economic security, the survey focuses on the respondents' family relationships and their level of integration into the labour market. To learn more about lives of older people, SHARE collects information on the respondents' partnership status, personal networks and intergenerational support, labour market participation, economic situation, and health (Malter and Börsch-Supan 2015).

---

[2] For more details on linking procedures see Korbmacher and Czaplicki (2013).

The FDZ-RV provides cross-sectional and longitudinal micro-data in areas such as retirement, disability, and rehabilitation. These data are available as scientific use files (SUFs) and as public use files (PUFs). The data are process-produced and were originally compiled for the purposes of administering pension insurance benefits. Because the statutory pension scheme is mandatory for all private sector employees and for some public sector workers, the FDZ-RV contains data on most German employees (Rehfeld and Mika 2006). The administrative data that are linked with SHARE have the same format and content, but refer only to those SHARE respondents who agreed to the linkage. The FDZ-RV provides SHARE with two different datasets: namely, the longitudinal dataset constructed according to the so called sample of the insured population (Versichertenkontenstichprobe, or VSKT) and cross-sectional pension data (Versichertenrentenbestand, or RTBN) on people who have already retired. The VSKT is one of the longitudinal data sources of the FDZ-RV, and includes information on individuals insured under the statutory pension scheme, and on their pension entitlements.[3] The data cover virtually all employees in Germany, with coverage being slightly higher in the eastern states because there are fewer civil servants and self-employed in this part of the country. As the VSKT contains information on all pension-relevant activities, it is the best source of information on the public pension benefits each individual has accrued. Moreover, because these activities are covered on a separate timeline, any overlapping activities can be analysed. The VSKT contains a wide range of information on each individual, including on his or her contributions to the pension system; his or her employment or unemployment status by month; and periods the individual spent outside of the labour market because of sickness, childrearing responsibilities, and education and training.

The monthly earnings biographies included in the data make it possible to analyse individual gross wages. The gross wages recorded in the VSKT are also linked to the official average income of the particular calendar year. Each pension insurance credit point that appears in a pension insurance record in a given year is equivalent to the national average income for the year. Because the official national average income is adjusted every year, the credit points are an adjusted measure of the individual's personal gross income over time. These credit points can be accumulated over the individual's life course until retirement, and represent the person's complete gross income from the start of his or her working career. However, the amount of income for which credit points can be earned is capped at about twice the national average income. Thus, on average men who retired in 2013 accumulated 40 credit points. Among the women, who spent fewer years in employment and earned less than men, the average number of credit points accumulated for those who retired in 2013 was 23.

The longitudinal information ends when the individual transitions into retirement, but it is supplemented with cross-sectional pension data. These data, which

---

[3] A few categories of employees, like civil servants, have their own pension systems, and thus do not appear in the social security data; or, like miners and employees of the federal railways, are treated differently from other insured individuals.

include information on the pension payments made by the German pension insurance and the concrete steps followed in the pension calculation, allow us to analyse the respondents' pension income after they have retired. In particular, information on the size of each respondent's pension is useful for evaluating the individual's economic situation. With a few exceptions e.g., for individuals who were self-employed throughout their life and for people who refused to participate in the data linkage pension insurance data are available for all of the SHARE respondents who have a record, regardless of whether they are still actively insured or have retired.

SHARE-RV shows that combining survey and administrative data is useful, as doing so enables us to benefit from the advantages associated with different data sources. The administrative data enrich the survey data as they include very detailed information on, for example, lifelong earnings broken down by month. In addition, because some types of information are included in both datasets (like an individual's job history), combining the data make it possible to validate retrospectively collected data. The administrative data are also improved through the linkage with the survey data. Previous analyses focused on how the labour biography or accrued benefits of individuals influenced their income in old age. Important information is also added on all sources of individual and household income, partnership, or health status.

16.3.2 Variables

A great advantage of using SHARE-RV for fertility analysis is that it contains fertility, employment, and household information (Czaplicki and Post 2015). One of our key variables of interest in the analysis is the number of children per woman. A peculiarity of the information in the dataset on children is that in SHARE's first, second, fourth, and fifth waves, only information on living children was gathered. Because deceased children were not reported, a fertility analysis may be expected to underestimate the number of children born. Moreover, the administrative data include information on the children in a given family for only one of the parents; in most cases the mother. Thus, in a first step we validate both types of information and create a valid number of children. Since the number of children in the register data is verified in the process of account clarification, we use VSKT's information on children as basic information for the retirees as well as for the individuals for whom the data in SHARE indicate that they have more children, but for whom no account clarification has yet taken place. In all other cases, we determine the number of children based on information from SHARE.

In order to examine the effects of having children on the lifetime employment patterns and earning profiles of mothers, we use the employment and earnings information from the longitudinal register data of the VSKT. We narrow our focus to women's regular employment, as workers in regular employment make social insurance contributions. We also include women's lifetime income from employment. One pension insurance credit point is equivalent to the average annual income of a

Table 16.1 Number of children, eastern and western German women

	Western German women (%)	Eastern German women (%)
No children	11	5
1 child	20	25
2 children	40	46
3 or more children	29	25

Source: FDZ-RV, SHARE-RV-3-0-0, n = 1,943, own calculations

full-time, year-round employee. On average, men earn one credit point per year, and women earn less than one point. The differences between the credit points earned in eastern and western Germany are harmonized in order to make the income analysis comparable.[4]

For the multivariate analysis, we also consider the highest level of education. As the information on education in the register data is often not available due to missing information from the employer, we take it from the survey. We distinguish between individuals with a low level of education (no degree, primary school, eighth-grade polytechnic high school), a medium level of education (secondary school), and a high level of education (high school). To control for work experience we use the years of employment, which are generated by counting the number of months of employment subject to social security contributions, and dividing this sum by 12.

The analysis is carried out separately for eastern and western Germany. The region is identified by the place of residence at the date of data collection. The SHARE-RV sample contains 3717 cases, or 1983 women and 1734 men born between 1919 and 1982. Thus, 40 % of the sample (1502) are western German women and 13 % (481) are eastern German women. While 54 % of the total sample are retired, the share is lower for the women in the sample because they are usually the younger partner in the relationship. The sample consists of 1121 couples, and register and survey data are available for both partners. In addition, we have data on 862 women (43 %) and 609 men (35 %) who either have no partner in the linked dataset, or who have a partner who did not give his or her consent for the linkage. Table 16.1 shows the distribution of the number of children in the sample in western and eastern Germany: 11 % of the western German women and 6 % of the eastern German women are childless, 20 % of the western German women and 25 % of the eastern German women have one child, 40 % of the western German women and 46 % of the eastern German women have two children, and 29 % of the western German women and 25 % of the eastern German women have three or more children.

---

[4] The income ceiling (set roughly at double the national average income) for insurance contributions is lower in eastern Germany. Western German women therefore reach the highest income levels only. Since very few women in Germany earn double the national average income, the point at which the upper limit has been set, this difference does not affect our analysis much.

16.3.3   Methods

Our analysis consists of a descriptive part and a multivariate part. In the descriptive part, we map labour market participation rates and earnings across the life course. The labour market participation rate is defined as the ratio of individuals who are in the labour force to the total working-age population. Thus, this rate measures the extent to which an economy's working-age population are actually working. In order to investigate the influence of childbearing on employment patterns, we group labour market participation rates by the number of children. In addition, we generate individual wage histories and group these histories by the number of children. We then compare these profiles with the reference average wage from 2013. In the multivariate analysis, we use OLS regression to investigate the effects of having a certain number of children on the number of points a woman earns over her lifetime. The dependent variable is the sum of the points earned over the woman's whole employment career from spells of employment subject to social insurance contributions. To account for east-west differences in income dynamics and employment patterns, all of the models are estimated separately for eastern and western German women. The regression analysis consists of three parts. In the first step, we use OLS regression to study the effects of having children on women's lifetime earnings. In a second step, we investigate how the results change if the pension insurance points women earn for childrearing periods are accounted for. In the final step, we also consider the income of the male partner.

16.4   Descriptive Results

16.4.1   Mothers' Labour Market Participation in Eastern and Western Germany

Figure 16.1 maps the employment patterns of western German women between the ages of 25 and 60 by their final number of children. We have chosen to disregard periods under age 25 because most women are in education or training at this age, and are thus not employed. Similarly, we have chosen to disregard periods over age 60, as most women at this age are retired.

Figure 16.1 shows that some of the women had already reached retirement age at the time of the SHARE interview. For the others, the calculation of the participation rate is shown until the actual age is reached. The four lines represent women with zero, one, two, or three or more children. The lines differ greatly by age. At ages 25–45, the employment participation rate is around 75 % among childless women, and is around 60 % among women with one child. However, among women with two or more children the pattern is more irregular: their labour market participation rate declines until they reach their mid-thirties, and increases gradually there-after.

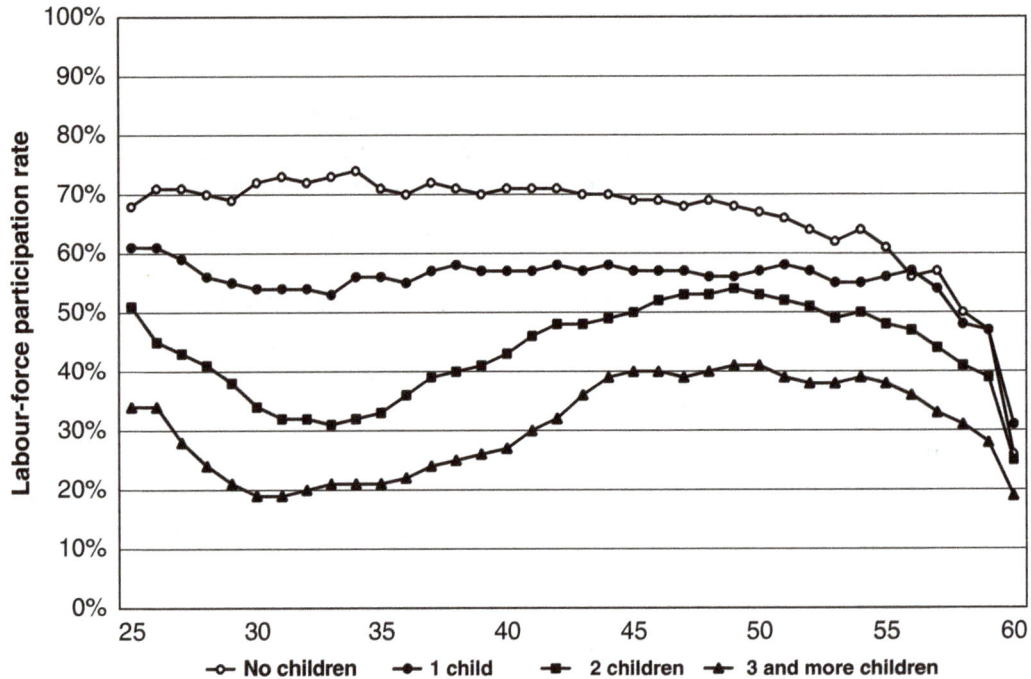

Fig. 16.1 Labour market participation of western German women by number of children (Source: FDZ-RV, SHARE-RV-3-0-0, n = 1,486, own calculations)

At age 35, only about 30 % of the women with two children and 20 % of the women with three or more children are working.

Figure 16.2 shows the labour market participation patterns for eastern Germany. Because fewer eastern than western German women participated in the SHARE survey, the line for eastern Germany fluctuates more than the line for western Germany. It is also important to note that the cohorts born from 1930 to 1950 had their children and spent most of their working years in the German Democratic Republic (GDR). These parts of the life course are included in this analysis. In the GDR, a woman was entitled to a maternity leave (Babyjahr) of 12 months after the birth of a first or a second child, and of 18 months after the birth of a third or a subsequent child (Drasch 2011). The labour market participation rates of women between the ages of 25 and 33 who had no children or fewer than three children were roughly the same in the GDR. Only women who had three or more children had lower labour market participation rates.

However, the proportion of eastern German women in employment decreased after age 55. This is because after 1990 unemployment was more common in eastern than in western Germany, and women with low qualification levels had difficulties finding employment (Bielenski et al. 1995; Diewald and Sorensen 1996). This effect was particularly strong among childless women.

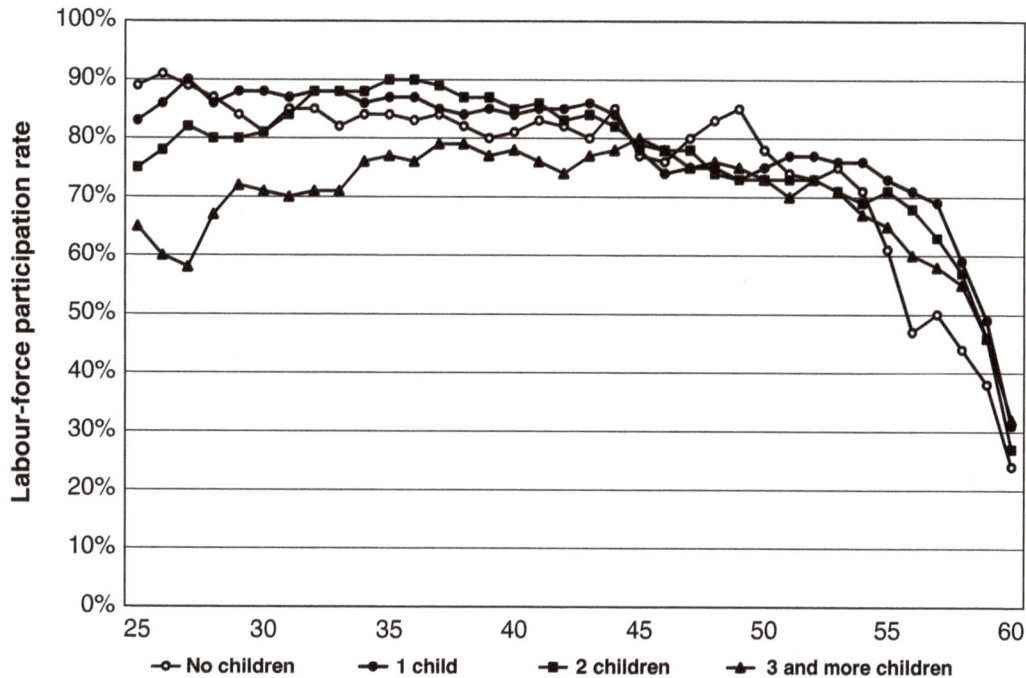

Fig. 16.2 Labour market participation of eastern German women by number of children (Source: FDZ-RV, SHARE-RV-3-0-0, n = 497, own calculations)

16.4.2 The Earnings of Mothers Compared to the Earnings of Childless Women

The statutory pension insurance records contain information on the gross income of each individual who works in socially insured employment. The income is then measured each year against the average income, which is set by the Ministry for Social Affairs based on national-level income trends. A worker with the average gross income earns one credit point in his or her personal record. These points are therefore not affected by inflation, and can be compared over the life course and between different birth cohorts. Figure 16.3 shows the development of income across the life course of western German women, by their number of children. The average income is represented as the dotted line. For the sake of illustration, the income is standardized by the average gross yearly income of 2013; the year the survey was conducted. The calculation for the average income of each group includes only those women who were participating in the labour market at this age. The women who were not employed were not included in the calculation. As the gross income is not adjusted for the number of hours worked, it is not a measure of hourly wages.

Childless women, who are represented by the top line, had the highest average annual income by far. The line shows that having a steady career path is associated with increasing wages. At age 30, the earnings of childless women had reached the

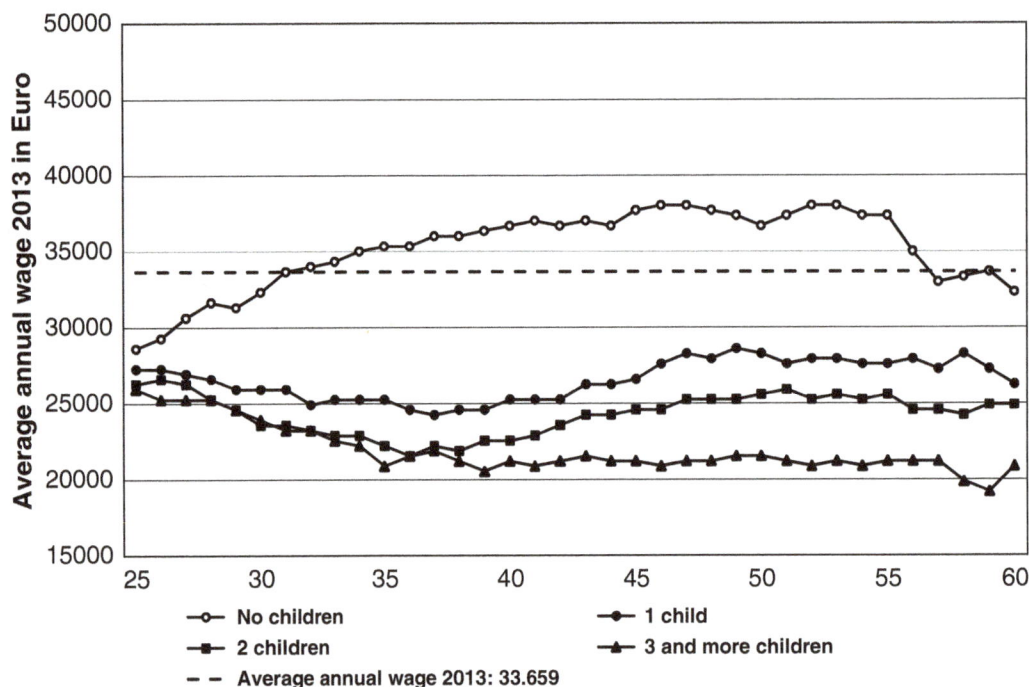

Fig. 16.3 Average income of western German women by number of children (Source: FDZ-RV, SHARE-RV-3-0-0, n = 1,486, own calculations)

level of the national average income. Moreover, at around age 45, childless women were earning as much as the average man (Fachinger and Himmelreicher 2008). Mothers with one child, whose labour market participation levels were not much lower than those of childless women, nonetheless saw their wages decline between the ages of 25 and 40, and increase slightly at later ages. They never came close to having the average income, which is represented by the dotted line. The income trajectories of mothers with two children were similar to those of mothers with one child, but their wages were lower. The steady decline in their income stopped at age 35, and their wages increased from that point onwards. Mothers with two children reached their highest earnings level, of about 60 % of the national average income, between ages 50 and 55. Mothers with three or more children had a distinct income path. Their income declined steadily until they reached age 40, and then remained at a low level of around half of the national average income. This suggests that the relatively small number of mothers with three or more children who were working were mainly in low-income jobs or part-time employment (Fig. 16.4).

The dotted line is again an indicator of the set value of the average gross income. At first glance, the graph appears to show that earnings of women in eastern Germany hardly ever reached the level of the national average income, regardless of the number of children they had. This was particularly true among women who were working in the GDR. Thus, the income differences between mothers and childless women were rather small. Only women with three or more children had consistently lower levels of gross income.

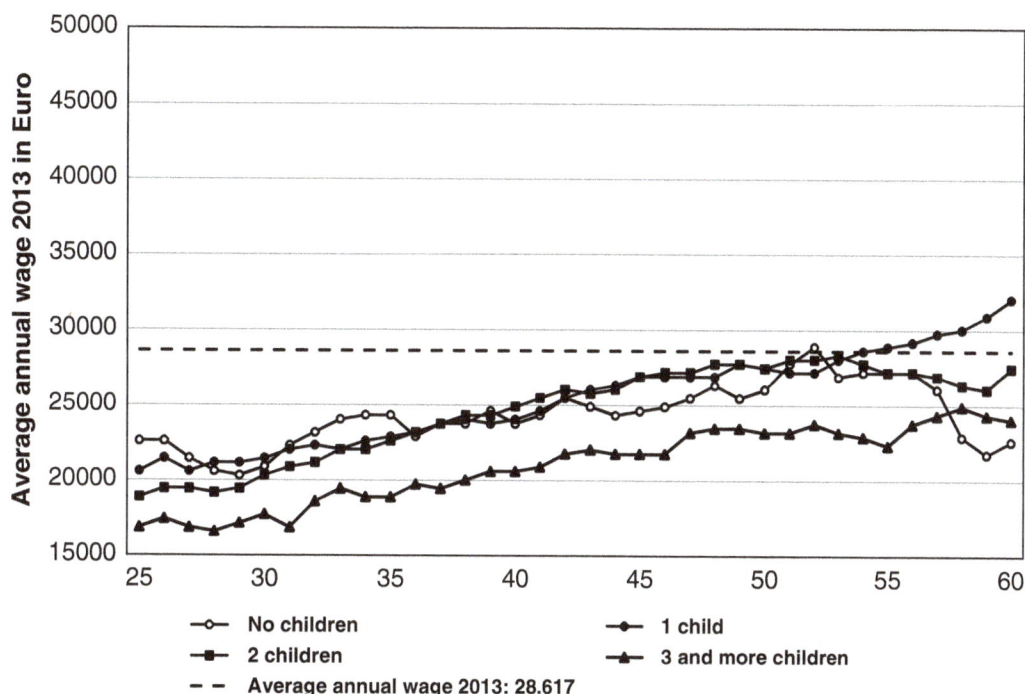

Fig. 16.4 Average income of eastern German women by number of children (Source: FDZ-RV, SHARE-RV-3-0-0, n = 497, own calculations)

In the pension insurance records, income in eastern Germany is measured on a different scale than income in western Germany. This was done in order to raise the pension benefits of eastern Germans to those of western Germans. To help offset the lower income levels in the former GDR and in eastern Germany after reunification, the scale is roughly 20 % higher. The scale on the left-hand side of the graph therefore shows different gross income levels for 2013.

16.5 Multivariate Analysis

16.5.1 Determinants of Lifetime Credit Points

Model 1 in Table 16.2 shows the effects of having children on a woman's lifetime gross income (measured in terms of credit points). The dependent variable is a measure of a woman's gross income from periods of socially insured employment over her entire insurance record, starting at age 14 and ending at age 67, or at the time of the interview. One year of full-time employment resulted in one credit point. Among men, the average number of years spent in employment was about 40 in western Germany and was slightly higher in eastern Germany.

The regression was conducted separately for eastern and western Germany, and controlled for the level of education. Having children had a negative impact on women's lifetime earnings. In western Germany, the lifetime earnings of a woman

Table 16.2 Linear regression with the lifetime earnings of women, as recorded in the pension insurance registers, as the dependent variable

| | Western Germany | | Eastern Germany | |
	Model 1	Model 2	Model 1	Model 2
Number of children				
No children	Ref.	Ref.	Ref.	Ref.
1 child	−8.530***	−6.200***	1.520	−1.986
2 children	−13.251***	−7.243*	0.016	−2.416*
3 or more children	−17.681***	−7.648***	−2.812	−3.024*
Education				
Low education	−2.117**	−4.189***	−7.223***	−10.652***
Medium education	1.600	−1.763***	−5.490***	−6.901***
High education	Ref.	Ref.	Ref.	Ref.
Years of employment		0.799***		0.905***
Years until retirement (65)		−0.041		0.068
Constant	27.769***	8.578***	25.654***	2.855
R^2	0.20	0.76	0.08	0.69

Source: FDZ-RV, SHARE-RV-3-0-0, own calculations
*** $p < 0.01$; ** $p < 0.05$; * $p < 0.10$

declined significantly with the birth of each additional child. In eastern Germany, having children did not have a significant effect on a woman's lifetime earnings. While the effect of education on lifetime earnings was more pronounced in eastern than in western Germany, it is important to note that the group of less educated eastern German women of these cohorts was still rather selective. Model 2 additionally controlled for the duration of employment over the life course. After these variables were included, the effect of having children on a western German woman's earnings was greatly reduced. In eastern Germany, the negative effect of having three children disappeared after duration of employment was controlled for. This suggests that in eastern Germany the average woman with a large number of children also had reduced earnings. The introduction of the length of employment into the regression also increased the effect of education. This shows that among the older cohorts of women in both parts of Germany, blue-collar workers spent more years in employment than white-collar workers. The fact that blue-collar workers were employed for more years helped to offset their lower gross wages.

16.5.2 Determinants of Lifetime Credit Points Including Child-Related Pension Points

In the next step, we explore how the results change if we consider the additional pension points women receive for having children (which we refer to as "child benefits" in the following). For each child registered in the pension insurance records, the mother receives two credit points. Table 16.3 shows the results of this analysis.

Table 16.3 Linear regression with lifetime earnings of women, as recorded in the pension insurance registers, by number of children and length of employment, including benefits for childrearing periods

	Western Germany		Eastern Germany	
	Model 3	Model 4	Model 3	Model 4
Number of children				
No children	Ref.	Ref.	Ref.	Ref.
1 child	−6580***	−4.277***	3.542	0.031
2 children	−9292***	−3.351***	4.049	1.605
3 or more children	−10,653***	−0.731	4.386*	4.161***
Education				
Low education	−1883	−3.963***	−7.017***	−10.490***
Medium education	1588	−1.755***	−5.468***	−6.863***
High education	Ref.	Ref.	Ref.	Ref.
Years of employment		0.791***		0.906***
Years until retirement (65)		−0.047		0.058
Constant	27.693***	8.754***	25.554***	2.803
R^2	0094	0.72	0071	0.69

Source: FDZ-RV, SHARE-RV-3-0-0, own calculations
*** $p < 0.01$; ** $p < 0.05$; * $p < 0.10$

The findings indicate that having children had a negative impact on the lifetime credit points of women in Germany. However, the effect is more modest than in the prior analysis. For example, the previous analysis showed that compared to their childless counterparts, western German women with three or more children had 18 fewer credit points. If we factor in the additional credit points these women received with the birth of each child, the difference shrinks to 11 credit points (see Model 1, western Germany). If we control for both length of employment and educational level (Model 2), we still find that the effect of having children was negative in western Germany. However, the coefficient for having three or more children is no longer significant, compared to the reference category of childless women. Thus, it appears that the old-age income of mothers with three or more children was boosted by the child benefits they received, and that their periods of non-employment and their lower income levels in times of employment were fully offset by these child benefits. However, the coefficient for one-child mothers in western Germany remains large and significant. These women suffered from a "motherhood penalty" on the labour market, but received little compensation for having raised a child.

For eastern Germany, the prior analysis showed that having children had a smaller impact on women's credit points. Only women with three or more children saw a significant reduction in their accumulated credit points. In this analysis, which factors in the credit points for children, we see that having children actually had a positive impact on the overall number of pension points women received. On average, mothers with three or more children had three more points than childless women because they received child benefits. Thus, the average childless woman appears to have collected a smaller number of pension points than the average woman with children. It is important to note, however, that childlessness was very uncommon among the eastern German cohorts we consider here. We can therefore assume that many of the childless women of these cohorts had a health impairment, which may have also affected their employment career.

16.5.3 Couples' Pension Income

Table 16.4 addresses the question of whether within a given family, a husband's old-age income can compensate for the lower old-age income of his wife. It is important to note that this part of the analysis is descriptive, and is also restricted to women and men who were living as a couple at the time of the interview in 2014. As we can see in the table, in western Germany the average personal statutory insurance old-age pension of a childless woman was higher than that of the average mother (865 euros versus 684 euros). These differences are hardly surprising given the higher lifetime income levels found among childless women in the regression analysis. The relationship between the number of children a woman had and the size of her pension appears to be almost linear: i.e., the more children that are registered in a woman's pension insurance account, the lower her statutory pension benefits. This is because the effects of low earnings are stronger than the effects of the childrearing benefits provided in the pension insurance scheme.

While having children had a negative impact on women's statutory pension benefits, this relationship did not exist for men. The average western German man with children had higher pension insurance benefits than the average childless man, even though he did not receive additional credit points from social insurance funds. Generally, the size of a man's old-age pension varied little depending on the number of children he had. The personal old-age pension benefits of western German men ranged from 1295 to 1342 euros per month. The old-age income levels of couples with no children or with one or more children also did not vary much. In eastern Germany, the overall effect of having children on the pension benefits of women was considerably weaker than it was in western Germany.

Table 16.4 Couples statutory pension income by region, gender, and number of children

Children registered in women's accounts	Western Germany			Eastern Germany		
	Women	Men	Couples	Women	Men	Couples
No children	871 €	1117 €	1904 €	(1012 €)	(1089 €)	(1971 €)
1 Child	713 €	1306 €	2025 €	893 €	1068 €	1954 €
2 Children	592 €	1249 €	1889 €	926 €	1074 €	1977 €
3 or more children	550 €	1231 €	1812 €	894 €	1017 €	1981 €
Number of cases	815	815	815	306	306	306

Source: FDZ-RV, SHARE-RV-3-0-0, own calculations, N = 1,121 couples. Pension calculation in Euro on the basis of pensions insurance credits points, including additional credit points granted after the "Mütterrente" reform in 2014. Numbers in brackets: Number of cases below 50

16.6   Conclusion

For both men and women, the number of years they spent in employment and their earnings over the course of their career forms the basis of their personal retirement income. For mothers, the pension credits they accrue through employment are supplemented by credits for childrearing periods. In Germany, the pension benefits of mothers have often been considered insufficient because they are on average lower than those of childless women. In this chapter, we examined the reasons why mothers tend to have a relatively small pension, and how having children affects their employment career. We also explored the question of whether public transfers are sufficient to offset the disadvantaged position of women with children.

The results of the descriptive analysis show that on average in western Germany, childless women had higher pension benefits than women with children, largely because their income increased more over their life course, especially up to age 45. By contrast, western German mothers had relatively low labour market participation levels and far lower average lifetime earnings. While the average mother with one child worked for most of her life course, she received just 60 % of the national average income. In many cases, this low earnings level was not just difficult to live on while the mother was employed; it also resulted in relatively low pension benefits. Thus, our first conclusion is that motherhood, even when the mother has only one child, exacts a high price in western Germany. Because most women earn less than the national average, they tend to be economically dependent on either their partner or the welfare state, and this dependency continues into old age.

The results of our analysis of eastern German women indicate that their employment histories differed far less than those of western German women depending on the number of children they had. First, mothers in eastern Germany were more likely than mothers in western Germany to have been employed. The only group of eastern German women with below-average levels of employment during certain parts of their life course were women who had three or more children; but even they had an employment level of nearly 85 % at age 35. The rates of participation in socially insured employment were consistently high among eastern German women. Thus, their biographies differ sharply from those of their western German counterparts. Moreover, the income levels of eastern German women were far less dependent than those of western German women on the number of children they had. However, while most eastern German women saw their gross income rise continuously over their life course, only a small share of these women were earning the national average income by the end of their career.

In the regression analysis, we explored the determinants of lifetime credit points. Our findings indicate that in the calculation of old-age pension benefits, western German women faced a heavy motherhood penalty. Between the ages of 25 and 40, when most workers are making career advancements, western German mothers with two or more children worked very little. It is therefore not surprising that mothers with two or more children had gross earnings that were one-third or one-quarter of the national average income. This gap is reduced if we consider the additional pension credit points women received for each childrearing period. On average, however, only women with three or more children were able to collect as many credit points as childless women. To a large degree, the old-age income of a mother with three or more children depended on the points she received from the statutory pension insurance fund for childrearing periods. Indeed, many of these women had little or no earned income across their life course. For these women, the points they received for childrearing periods represent not just a form of a compensation for their loss of income during the periods when their children were young, but an independent source of old-age income.

In eastern Germany, we find that mothers and childless women had similar numbers of life-time credit points. If we consider the additional credit points women collected for each childrearing period, we find that the average mother had more credit points than the average childless woman. Women with three or more children were especially likely to have accumulated more credit points than childless women. The policy measure that awards mothers the equivalent of the national average income for each childrearing period appears to have imposed a childlessness penalty on eastern German women. Thus, as a consequence of the latest pension insurance reform, motherhood has become a positive factor in old-age income in eastern Germany. However, this surprising finding should be put into context. Earnings in eastern Germany were and are much lower than in western Germany, and there is a gender gap in earnings across Germany. Thus, in eastern Germany, the earnings of women including of those with very few interruptions in their employment career rarely reach the national average.

Acknowledgments This paper uses data from SHARE Wave 5 release 1.0.0, as of March 31st 2015 (DOI: 10.6103/SHARE.w5.100) or SHARE Wave 4 release 1.1.1, as of March 28th 2013 (DOI: 10.6103/SHARE.w4.111) or SHARE Waves 1 and 2 release 2.6.0, as of November 29th 2013 (DOI: 10.6103/SHARE.w1.260 and 10.6103/SHARE.w2.260) or SHARELIFE release 1.0.0, as of November 24th 2010 (DOI: 10.6103/SHARE.w3.100). The SHARE data collection has been primarily funded by the European Commission through the 5th Framework Programme (project QLK6-CT-2001-00360 in the thematic programme Quality of Life), through the 6th Framework Programme (projects SHARE-I3, RII-CT-2006-062193, COMPARE, CIT5-CT-2005-028857, and SHARELIFE, CIT4-CT-2006-028812) and through the 7th Framework Programme (SHARE-PREP, N° 211909, SHARE-LEAP, N° 227822 and SHARE M4, N° 261982). Additional funding from the U.S. National Institute on Aging (U01 AG09740-13S2, P01 AG005842, P01 AG08291, P30 AG12815, R21 AG025169, Y1-AG-4553-01, IAG BSR06-11 and OGHA 04-064) and the German Ministry of Education and Research as well as from various national sources is gratefully acknowledged (see www.share-project.org for a full list of funding institutions).

Literature

Allmendinger, J. (1994). *Lebensverlauf und Sozialpolitik. Die Ungleichheit von Mann und Frau und ihr öffentlicher Ertrag*. Frankfurt am Main/New York: Campus.

Allmendinger, J. (2011). *Verschenkte Potentiale? Lebensläufe nicht erwerbstätiger Frauen*. Frankfurt am Main/New York: Campus.

Begall, K., & Mills, M. C. (2012). The influence of educational field, occupation, and occupational sex segregation on fertility in the Netherlands. *European Sociological Review, 28*, 1–23.

Bielenski, H., Brinkmann, C., & Kohler, B. (1995). *Erwerbsverläufe seit der Wende in Ostdeutschland: Brüche und Kontinuitäten. Ergebnisse des Arbeitsmarkt-Monitors über berufliche Veränderungen 1989 bis 1994* (IAB Werkstattbericht). Nürnberg: IAB.

Brenke, K. (2011). Anhaltender Strukturwandel zur Teilzeitbeschäftigung. *DIW Wochenbericht, 78*, 3–12.

Busch, A., & Holst, E. (2011). *Gender-specific occupational segregation, glass ceiling effects, and earnings in managerial positions: Results of a fixed effects model* (DIW Berlin discussion paper, No. 1101). Bonn: IZA.

Czaplicki, C., & Post, J. C. (2015). SHARE-RV: Neues Analysepotential für die Untersuchung des Zusammenhangs von Fertilität und Erwerbstätigkeit in den Lebensverläufen von Männern und Frauen. DGD-Online-Publikation, Nr. 01/2015, 97–104.

Diewald, M., & Sorensen, A. (1996). Erwerbsverläufe und soziale Mobilität von Frauen und Männern in Ostdeutschland: Makrostrukturelle Umbrüche und Kontinuitäten im Lebensverlauf. In M. Diewald & K. U. Mayer (Eds.), *Erwerbsverhalten in Ostdeutschland und ihre Auswirkungen auf das Wohlbefinden* (pp. 63–88). Opladen: Leske und Budrich.

Drasch, K. (2011). Zwischen familiärer Prägung und institutioneller Steuerung. Familienbedingte Erwerbsunterbrechungen von Frauen in Ost- und Westdeutschland und der DDR. In P. A. Berger, K. Hank, & A. Tölke (Eds.), *Reproduktion von Ungleichheit durch Arbeit und Familie* (pp. 171–200). Wiesbaden: VS Verlag für Sozialwissenschaften.

Dünn, S., & Stosberg, R. (2014). Was ändert sich durch das RV-Leistungsverbesserungsgesetz? *RV aktuell*, 156–165.

Fachinger, U., & Himmelreicher, R. K. (2008). Alters-Lohn-Profile und Einkommensdynamik von westdeutschen Männern im späten Erwerbsleben. *DRV Schriften, 55*, 212–232.

Finke, C. (2011). Verdienstunterschiede zwischen Männern und Frauen – Eine Ursachenanalyse auf Grundlage der Verdienststrukturerhebung 2006. *Wirtschaft und Statistik*, 36–48.

Korbmacher, J., & Czaplicki, C. (2013). Linking SHARE survey data with administrative records: First experiences from SHARE-Germany. In F. Malter & A. Börsch-Supan (Eds.), *SHARE wave 4: Innovations & methodology*. Munich: Munich Center for the Economics of Aging (MEA), Max-Planck-Institute for Social Law and Social Policy.

Lauterbach, W. (1994). *Berufsverläufe von Frauen*. Frankfurt/Main: Campus.

Malter, F., & Börsch-Supan, A. (Eds.). (2015). *SHARE wave 5: Innovations & methodology*. Munich: Munich Center for the Economics of Aging (MEA), Max-Planck-Institute for Social Law and Social Policy.

Petersen, T., & Morgan, L. A. (1995). Occupation-establishment sex segregation and the gender wage gap. *American Journal of Sociology, 101*, 329–365.

Rehfeld, U. G., & Mika, T. (2006). The research data centre of the German statutory pension insurance (FDZ-RV). *Schmollers Jahrbuch, 126*, 121–127.

Rosenfeld, R. A., Trappe, H., & Gornick, J. C. (2004). Gender and work in Germany: Before and after reunification. *Annual Review of Sociology, 30*, 103–124.

Schröder, M. (2011). *Retrospective data collection in the survey of health, ageing and retirement in Europe. SHARELIFE methodology*. Munich: Munich Center for the Economics of Aging (MEA), Max-Planck-Institute for Social Law and Social Policy.

Simonson, J., Romeu Gordo, L., & Titova, N. (2011). Changing employment patterns of women in Germany: How do baby boomers differ from older cohorts? A comparison using sequence analysis. *Advances in Life Course Research, 16*, 65–82.

Stegmann, M., & Mika, T. (2013). Kinderlosigkeit, Kindererziehung und Erwerbstätigkeitsmuster von Frauen in der Bundesrepublik und der DDR und ihre Auswirkungen auf das Alterseinkommen. In D. Konietzka & M. Kreyenfeld (Eds.), *Ein Leben ohne Kinder* (pp. 213–252). Wiesbaden: Springer VS.

Trappe, H. (2006). Berufliche Segregation im Kontext. Über einige Folgen geschlechtstypischer Berufsentscheidungen in Ost- und Westdetuschland. *Kölner Zeitschrift für Soziologie und Sozialpsychologie, 58,* 50–78.

Waldfogel, J. (1998). Understanding the "family gap" in pay for women with children. *Journal of Economic Perspectives, 12,* 137–156.

Chapter 17
Childlessness and Intergenerational Transfers in Later Life

Marco Albertini and Martin Kohli

17.1 Introduction

After reaching a low point among the 1935–1945 birth cohort, childlessness has increased significantly in recent decades in most European societies (Rowland 2007; OECD 2010; Tanturri et al. 2015). In previous research on childlessness, a recurring theme has been the consequences for an individual's risk of social isolation and insufficient informal support, particularly in later life (Kohli and Albertini 2009). From the perspective of public policy, childless elderly people are usually seen as a problem group. It has been shown that parent-child relations are central to the social embeddedness of elderly people. Thus, it is generally assumed that compared to adults who have children, childless adults are at higher risk of lacking the social and emotional support they will need when they become frail and dependent. Citing the negative effects of the absence of children on social inclusion, policy makers have expressed concerns that increasing rates of childlessness among the elderly population will lead to increasing demands for public social care and health services.

There are, however, two reasons why this assumption may be flawed. First, childless elderly people are not only on the receiving end of support; they also give to their families and to society at large by establishing strong linkages with next-of-kin relatives, investing in non-family networks, and participating in voluntary and

M. Albertini (✉)
Department of Political and Social Sciences, University of Bologna, Bologna, Italy
e-mail: marco.albertini2@unibo.it

M. Kohli
Department of Social and Political Sciences, European University Institute, Florence, Italy

Bremen International Graduate School of Social Sciences, Bremen, Germany
e-mail: martin.kohli@eui.eu

© The Author(s) 2017
M. Kreyenfeld, D. Konietzka (eds.), *Childlessness in Europe: Contexts, Causes, and Consequences*, Demographic Research Monographs,
DOI 10.1007/978-3-319-44667-7_17

charitable activities. Taking these transfers and activities into account, we have found that the differences in the support exchange behaviours between parents and childless adults are small (Albertini and Kohli 2009). Second, childless elderly people are not a homogenous group. Childlessness should be seen as a life course process across a series of decision and bifurcation points (Kreyenfeld and Konietzka 2007). The social consequences of being childless in later life depend on the specific paths into childlessness (Dykstra and Hagestad 2007; Keizer et al. 2010; Mynarska et al. 2015), and they may also depend on the specific family and kinship constellations of each childless individual.

The aim of the present chapter is to address these two points. We report the results of a new study that deals with the social consequences of childlessness in later life by looking at the support given *and* received, and that examines parenthood and childlessness not as two exclusive alternatives, but as a continuum across a range of intermediate statuses. Thus, we analyse not only the financial and social support childless elderly people receive, but also the support they provide to their kin and friends, and to the society in which they live; and we map the patterns of support onto the different types of parental and childlessness status.

17.2 Social Consequences of Childlessness: Patterns of Support

The social consequences of childlessness in old age are multiple and complex. They vary with the specific institutional setting, and, at the individual level, with the specific motivation for and the pathway to childlessness. *How* someone ends up with no children may be more important than not having a child *per se*. Choosing not to have children, being unable to find a partner, not being fecund, surviving the death of one's children, and being socially childless because of early divorce represent different paths to childlessness, and each of these paths has different connotations. Marital history and gender also mediate the consequences of childlessness for individuals, as do the usual cleavages of education, income, and health.

Raising children requires the investment of substantial financial and time resources by parents, and there is a general recognition that the costs associated with parenthood outweigh the benefits, at least while children are young (for a literature review on the costs of children see Folbre 2008). At the same time, research on well-being in old age has shown that adult children have a positive impact overall on parents' well-being (for a review of studies on parenthood and well-being over the last decade, see Umberson et al. 2010) and even on mortality: People tend to live longer if they have a surviving adult child. This effect of children on life expectancy is mediated by people's perceptions of the emotional and social support that is available to them in case of need. The effect also extends to parents who have survived, abandoned, or lost contact with their children (Weltoft et al. 2004). One explanation for parents' higher life expectancy may be the healthier behaviour that parenthood encourages (Dykstra and Hagestad 2007).

According to an influential theory of the modern transition to low fertility, one of the main reasons why people had children in the past was because the children were expected to provide social and economic support when the parents became old and frail and were no longer able to be self-sufficient (Caldwell 1976); whereas today older people no longer depend on the support of their descendants in old age because they can now rely on pensions, health care, and social services provided by the welfare state (Nuget 1985). Some authors have argued that such old-age security motives for having children – ensuring material support and care in old age – still apply today, not just in low-welfare developing societies, but to some extent also in affluent societies with extensive welfare states (Kreager and Schröder-Butterfill 2004; Boldrin et al. 2005). While this controversy has yet to be resolved, it has been documented that elderly people in affluent societies continue to be embedded in dense intergenerational family networks of support, especially between parents and their children (Albertini et al. 2007; Kohli et al. 2010). Apart from providing direct support, children can serve as important intermediaries between their parents and health and social care services, and can thus help their parents gain access to the public resources available to the aged population (Choi 1994).

Given that adult children continue to represent an important source of support for elderly parents, we may assume that childless older people have a higher risk than parents of lacking social and moral support when they become frail and dependent. The evidence to date only partially confirms this expectation. Generally, the childless do not appear to have larger support deficits than parents (Albertini and Mencarini 2014). Childless people tend to compensate for the absence of exchanges with adult children by having frequent contact with neighbours and friends, and by developing strong ties with other family members, including with their parents, their siblings, and their nephews and nieces (Albertini and Kohli 2009; Schnettler and Woehler 2015). Moreover, despite the stigma that may still be attached to voluntary childlessness and the distress that may accompany involuntary childlessness (Dykstra and Hagestad 2007), recent empirical evidence does not support the assumption that childless older people have lower levels of economic, psychological, or social well-being than their counterparts who have children (Hank and Wagner 2013).

However, the evidence also indicates that when intensive support is needed, these compensatory strategies work only partially. When they become frail and limited in their ability to carry out the activities of daily living, childless people receive less support and are more likely to enter residential care, and do so at lower levels of dependency compared with people who have children (Wenger 2009). If the share of the childless population increases, we may expect that the share of those who lack family support – and thus the demand for public health and social care services – will also grow. Given the constraints on welfare state spending, it is possible that this additional demand will not be met, and that childless older people will have to look to the private market for alternative solutions. Even in an advanced welfare state such as Sweden, public home help services have not been able to fully compensate for the lack of family support among the childless (Larsson and Silverstein 2004).

At the same time, however, the debate about the effects of increasing levels of childlessness on the future demand for social care has neglected the opposite flows of support: How the absence of children affects what older people give. Contrary to widespread perceptions, on balance elderly people make more transfers and provide more support than they receive (Kohli et al. 2010). We have shown that although childless elderly people are less likely than parents to provide financial transfers and social support to others, these transfers and supports are still substantial (Albertini and Kohli 2009). A study conducted in the United States found that compared with parents, childless older people are more likely to make financial transfers to other kin, friends, and neighbours; and that they transfer larger amounts (Hurd 2009). A considerable share of these transfers still go to descendants such as nephews and nieces, and can therefore be considered intergenerational giving. Moreover, because they have a greater need to construct social networks outside of their families, childless people may be expected to give more of their time and money to charitable and community activities, and thus contribute more to society at large. Hurd (2009) shows that childless older people in the U.S. indeed donated larger amounts of money to charities than parents. To the extent that these organizations focus on young people, this type of giving is again intergenerational.

17.3   Parenthood as a Continuum

As we noted above, a large body of previous research on childless people has treated non-parents and parents as two homogeneous groups, distinguishing only between those who had and those who did not have living children at the time of the interview. There is, however, increasing evidence that there are different pathways to childlessness, and that the consequences of childlessness vary depending on these pathways and their endpoints. The same is true for parents. There is no straightforward distinction between being or not being a parent: a person can become a parent as the result of having a natural child (with or without the help of assisted reproduction technologies), but also by adopting a child or becoming a stepparent of a partner's child. Thus, people can have children through different routes and at different points in their life course. A person can also cease to be a parent. The most obvious case in which this occurs is when a parent has survived his/her children. But there are also parents who, due to life events such as a divorce or an intense family conflict, have lost track of their children and no longer have contact with them. Other parents have children who live very far away (see Schnettler and Woehler 2015). These situations may have different effects on support networks and exchanges. Our empirical analysis is a first step towards taking these different situations into account. We distinguish between those who have natural children and stay in contact with them; those who have had natural children but have survived them, have lost contact with them, or live far away from them; those who did not have natural children but have adopted, foster, or stepchildren; and, finally, those who never had any children, natural or otherwise. Thus, we conceptualise parenthood and childlessness not as two fully separate conditions, but as a continuum of parental statuses.

17.4 Analytic Approach, Data, and Variables

The data for this analysis is drawn from the first three regular waves of the Survey of Health, Ageing and Retirement in Europe (SHARE) collected in 2004, 2007, and 2011; and from the retrospective third wave (SHARELIFE) collected in 2009. We use data from the 11 European countries that participated in the first wave of SHARE: Austria, Belgium, Denmark, France, Germany, Greece, Italy, the Netherlands, Spain, Sweden, and Switzerland.

SHARE is a longitudinal, cross-national survey representative of the population aged 50 and older; the partners of the respondents (regardless of their age) are also included. SHARE contains detailed information on the financial transfers and social support (including formal and informal care) given and received during the 12 months prior to each interview. Using the combined information of SHARE and SHARELIFE, we were able to distinguish between different types of parenthood and childlessness. We created six subgroups of respondents: (a) those who never had natural children and had no adopted, foster, or stepchildren at the time of the interview (*fully childless*); (b) those who had natural children, but no living children at the time of the interview (*survived all children*); (c) those who never had natural children, but who at the time of the interview had adopted, foster, or stepchildren who were living less than 500 km away with whom they had contact at least once a month (*social parents*); (d) those who had natural children, and who at the time of the interview still had at least one child who was living less than 500 km away with whom they had contact at least once a month (*natural parents*); (e) those who had at least one living child at the time of the interview (natural, step, adopted, or foster), but who had lost contact with all of their children (i.e., less than one contact per month or no contact at all during the 12 months prior to the interview) (*parents no contact*); and (f) those who had at least one living child at the time of the interview (natural, step, adopted, or foster), but who were living more than 500 km away from their nearest child (*parents geographical distance*).

Our final sample consists of 50,358 person years of data. Table 17.1 provides the main descriptive statistics. Of the cases in the sample, 85 % are parents, 9 % are fully childless, and 4 % are social parents. A further 3 % can be considered "de facto childless": those who had survived all of their children, those who had children but had no contact with them, and those who were living at a considerable geographical distance from their nearest child each make up around 1 % of the sample.

Table 17.1 Sample characteristics, column per cent

	%
Female	40.9
Parental status	
Fully childless	9.1
Survived all children	0.9
Social parents	3.5
Natural parents	84.7
Parents who have lost contact with children	1.2
Parents who live at >500 km away from children	0.7
Marital status	
Married or in registered partnership	73.0
Separated/divorced	7.7
Widowed	14.0
Never married	5.4
Education	
None (ISCED 0)	4.7
Low (ISCED 1 & 2)	43.7
Intermediate (ISCED 3 & 4)	30.7
High (ISCED 5 & 6)	20.9
Has at least one limitation	58.8
Age (mean, SD)	65.5 (10.0)
Household equivalent income (ppp), (mean, SD)	23,311 (27,787)
Household per-capita wealth (ppp), (mean, SD)	146,041 (309,684)
Person-years	50,358

First, we report some descriptive statistics on the support networks of the six types of parents/non-parents. The second step consists of multivariate analyses of support exchange. The previous literature has consistently shown that elderly parents and non-parents differ systematically in their characteristics, such as economic resources, health, and partnership status. These characteristics are also important factors that influence personal support networks. Therefore, in order to analyse the relationship between parental status and support exchange, we need to control for a number of possible compositional effects. We introduce the following control variables into our multivariate analyses: age, marital status (i.e., married or in a registered partnership, separated or divorced, widowed, never married), educational level (measured according to the ISCED-97 scale), health status (measured as the presence of at least one limitation on the Global Activity Limitation Index [GALI], or on the Activities of Daily Living [ADL] or Instrumental Activities of Daily Living [IADL] indicators, or on the indicator of mobility and fine motor limitations), the natural logarithm of household equivalent income, household net per capita wealth, and the country of residence.

The multivariate analyses are carried out by using population-averaged logit and linear regression models for binomial and continuous variables, respectively, on the unbalanced sample of respondents taking part in at least one of the first three regular waves of SHARE. We consider several dependent variables: the likelihood of giving/receiving social support (i.e., help with paperwork, household chores, personal care) to/from non-coresiding individuals; the natural logarithm of the amount of social support given/received expressed as the estimated number of hours per year (this variable is only available for the first two waves of the survey); the likelihood of giving/receiving financial support to/from others; the likelihood of participating in the activities of charitable or voluntary organizations in the 4 weeks prior to the interview, and the likelihood of providing this support on a weekly or daily basis (these variables are only available for the first two waves of the survey); and the likelihood of receiving professional or paid home help, or of staying overnight in a nursing home in the last 12 months (this variable is only available for the first two waves of the survey). Because the previous literature has shown that the lack of children has different effects for men and women, we estimate separate models for these two groups. Due to space limitations we report below only the regression coefficients for the different parental statuses, while omitting those for the controlling variables.[1]

17.5 Results

Even though they are largely overlooked by the literature, the contributions of non-natural parents to family, friends, and society at large are far from negligible (Table 17.2). Thus, for instance, while they were less likely than natural parents to have provided support to others, 17 % of the fully childless respondents in our sample gave financial support in the 12 months prior to the interview, and more than 30 % helped with household work or personal care – a share that is very close to that of natural parents. The shares of respondents who performed charitable or voluntary work were similar across the different parental status groups (with the exception of parents who had lost contact with their children), and the analysis of the amount of this work provided some surprising results: 70 % of the fully childless who participated in these activities contributed to their community on a daily or weekly basis; a share that is higher than the figure found among natural parents.

Moving the focus to the support received, Table 17.2 indicates that contrary to expectations, non-natural parents and parents who had lost contact with their children were more likely than natural parents to have been receiving social support. These groups, together with the group of parents who were living more than 500 km away from their children, were also more likely to have been receiving formal care support.

Clearly, all of these differences between the types of parenthood or childlessness could be the result of systematic compositional differences. For instance, natural and social parents might, on average, be younger and/or in better economic and

---

[1] The full regression results are available from the authors upon request.

Table 17.2 Characteristics of the respondents' support network by parental status

Childlessness typology	Fully childless	Survived all children	Social parents	Natural parents	Parents no contact	Parents geo distance
Support given						
% Giving economic support	17.2	16.7	35.8	32.9	17.2	33.8
% Giving social support	31.4	26.5	32.8	33.5	23.5	31.1
Mean amount of social support given	484	326	468	563	1474	245
% Participating in charitable or voluntary work	14.7	13.6	14.8	15.0	9.7	12.4
% Participating in charitable or voluntary work on a daily or weekly basis	70.7	64.3	62.6	65.1	65.9	57.5
Support received						
% Receiving economic support	4.5	3.6	4.9	6.1	4.9	8.0
% Receiving social support	23.6	25.3	16.5	18.8	29.2	19.4
Mean amount of social support received	279	596	280	495	531	354
% Receiving professional or paid care support (home care or nursing home)	8.8	10.3	4.2	5.1	14.9	13.8

health conditions than the other respondents, and these differences could explain why they were less likely to be receiving formal and informal social support. For this reason, the next step of our analysis is to investigate the relationship between childlessness and support networks in a multivariate framework.[2]

17.5.1 What Childless People Give

One of the most overlooked topics in the study of childless elderly people is the extent to which they contribute to others (relatives and non-relatives) and to society at large. Most of the previous research on elderly non-parents has focused on the challenges they face later in life. As we have shown (Albertini and Kohli 2009), however, the amount of support provided by non-parents to others is far from

---

[2] Given the small size of some of our groups, the statistical power of the data set is low. We will therefore show and comment on coefficients that are significant at the 5 or 10 % level.

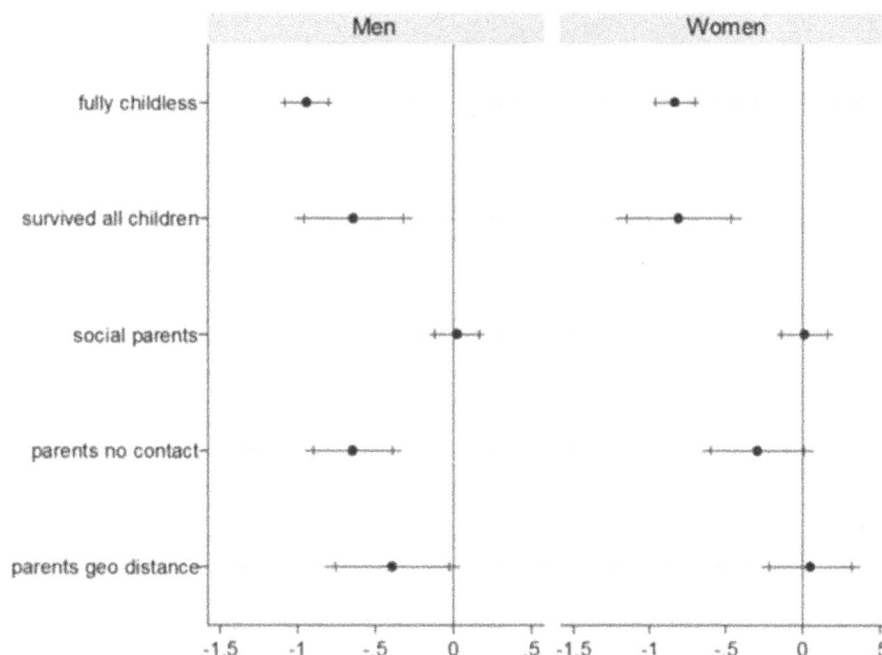

Fig. 17.1 Effects of parental status (reference: natural parents) on the likelihood of making a financial transfer to others, by respondent's gender. Beta coefficients and 90 and 95 % confidence intervals from logit models (Note: Further variables in the models are: marital status, educational level, health status, income, wealth, country of residence)

negligible. In the present section, we want to address this issue by examining the contributions of elderly people based on their parental status.

The multivariate analyses on the financial support provided to others confirm that, in general, the fully childless were giving less than natural parents (Fig. 17.1). Among fathers, only those who had step or adopted children were providing financial help to others to the same extent as natural fathers; those who had lost contact with their children or lived more than 500 km away were significantly less likely to have been providing financial support. Among women, only those who were fully childless or who had survived their children were less likely to have been doing so. In other words, among parents who lived far away from their children or had lost contact with them, the transfer behaviour of the mothers was similar to that of natural mothers, whereas the transfer behaviour of the fathers was in-between that of fully childless men and natural fathers.

With regard to social support provided to others, the differences between parents and non-parents were either very small or absent (Fig. 17.2). There is no clear polarisation of transfer behaviour between the fully childless and natural parents, and there is no clear gradient among the different parental statuses. Only two groups provided significantly lower levels of social support than natural parents: namely, social fathers and mothers who had lost contact with their children. Marginally significant negative effects are also found for social mothers and mothers who were living more than 500 km away from their children. The weakness of the relationship between parental statuses and the provision of social support is further confirmed by

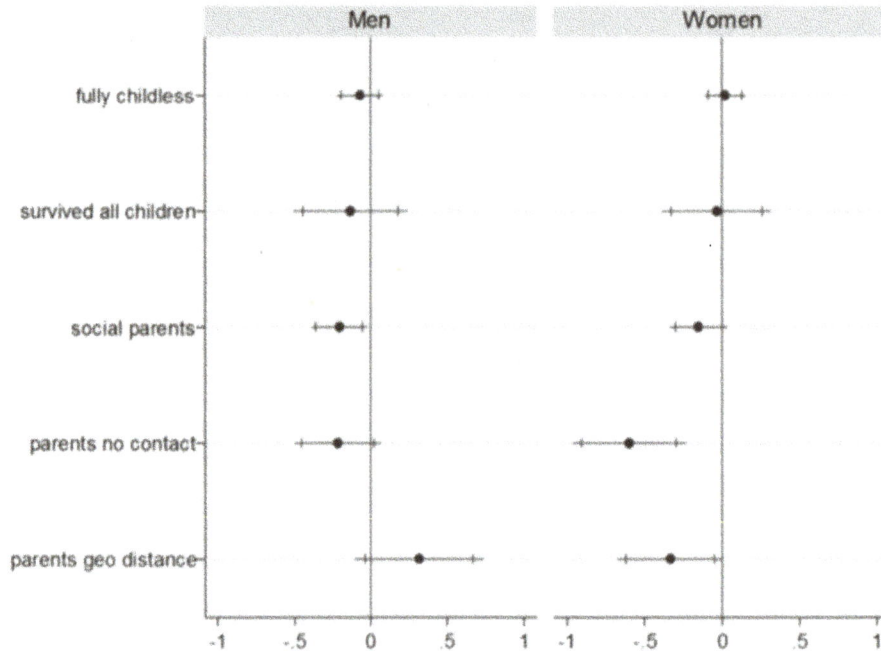

Fig. 17.2 Effects of parental status (reference: natural parents) on the likelihood of providing social support to others, by respondent's gender. Beta coefficients and 90 and 95 % confidence intervals from logit models (Note: For further variables in the models, see Fig. 17.1)

the finding that in terms of the hours of social support provided, just one subgroup is significantly different from natural parents: Fully childless women transferred less time to others than natural mothers (Fig. 17.3).

Providing social or financial support to family and friends is not the only way in which individuals can contribute to society. As we have argued previously (Kohli and Albertini 2009), childless elderly people may be the pioneers of a new form of post-familial civic engagement in which they devote their resources to public instead of private concerns by donating to foundations, participating in the activities of charitable organizations, or doing voluntary work. However, the results of the present analysis provide only weak support for this hypothesis. SHARE has no information on charitable donations, so the analysis is restricted to participation in the activities of charitable or voluntary organizations. As is shown in Fig. 17.4, the behaviour of the different subgroups is similar. Only mothers who survived their children seem to be slightly more likely to have participated in the activities of charitable or voluntary organizations. Fathers who had lost contact with their children tended to participate less than the other fathers. When we look at the intensity of support provided to others through this type of participation (Fig. 17.5), we find that – partially in line with our hypothesis and with previous findings – there is a marginally significant (10 % level) positive relationship between being a fully childless man and engaging in the activities of voluntary organizations on a daily or weekly basis. In other words, fully childless men may be the only group who compensated for the absence of children by involving themselves more intensively than natural parents in these forms of post-familial civic engagement.

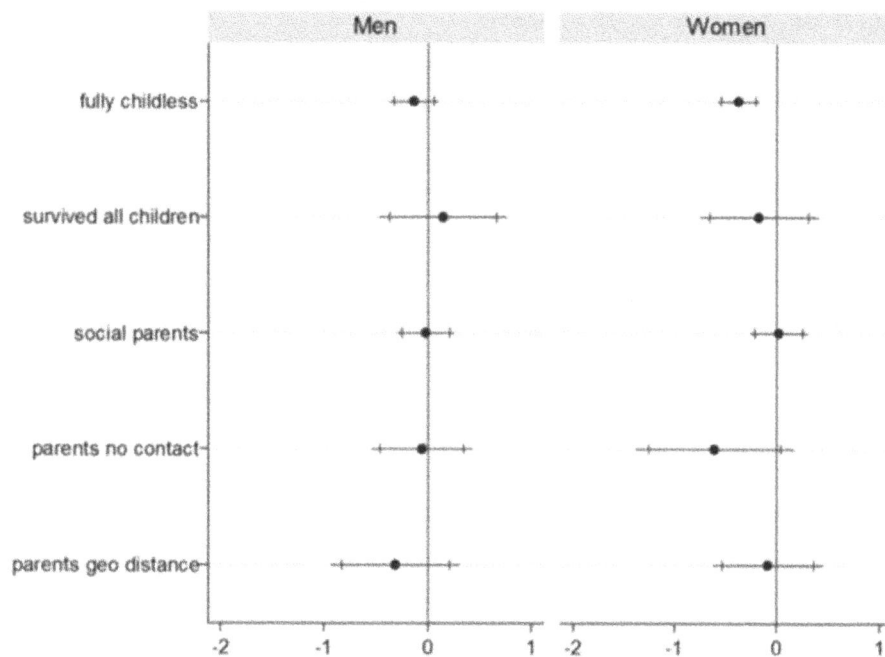

Fig. 17.3 Effects of parental status (reference: natural parents) on the amount of social support provided to others (as the natural log of hours per year), conditional on having provided at least 1 h of support, by respondent's gender. Beta coefficients and 90 % and 95 % confidence intervals from OLS regressions (Note: For further variables in the models, see Fig. 17.1)

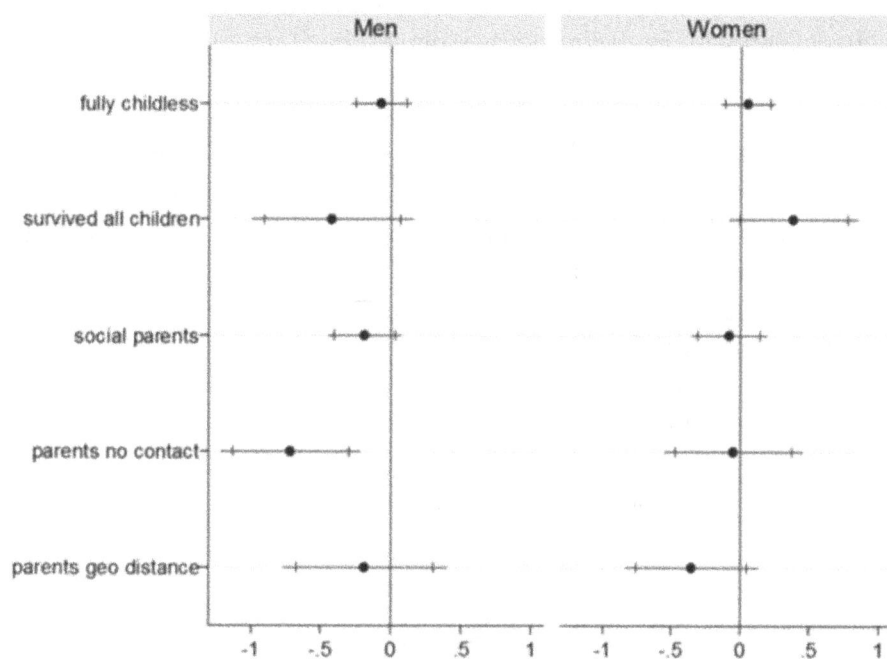

Fig. 17.4 Effects of parental status (reference: natural parents) on the likelihood of participating in the activities of charitable or voluntary organizations in the 4 weeks prior to the interview, by respondent's gender. Beta coefficients and 90 % and 95 % confidence intervals from logit models (Note: For further variables in the models, see Fig. 17.1)

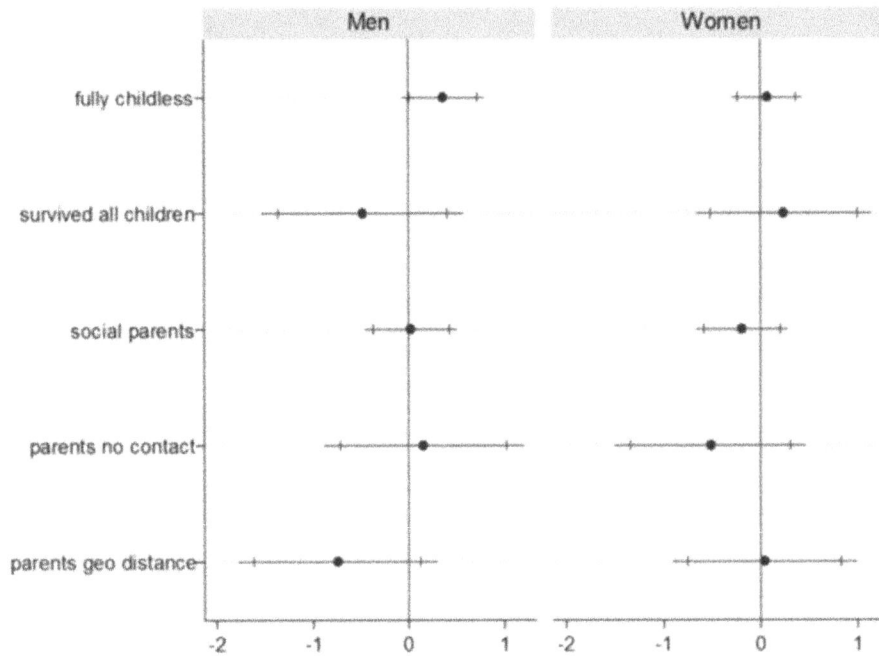

Fig. 17.5 Effects of parental status (reference: natural parents) on the likelihood of participating in the activities of charitable or voluntary organizations at least on a daily or weekly basis (vs. less often) in the 4 weeks prior to the interview, by respondent's gender. Beta coefficients and 90 % and 95 % confidence intervals (Note: For further variables in the models, see Fig. 17.1)

In sum, these results show that the likelihood of financial support to others is clearly associated with having or not having children, and that for fathers whether they had regular contact with their children is also a factor. Generally, the fully childless, those who had survived their children, and those who had lost contact with them are less likely to have been making financial transfers than parents. It seems that the two latter groups of fathers are located between the two extremes of the financial transfer behaviour of natural fathers and fully childless men. In contrast, social support is less clearly connected with the presence of children, except among fully childless women and mothers who had lost contact with their children. The results for participation in charitable or voluntary work are similar: while we find little evidence that the childless were playing a special role in these forms of social engagement beyond their immediate circle of family and friends, our findings do contradict the common assumption that childless people are ego-centred and isolated members of contemporary societies.

17.5.2   *What Childless People Receive*

As was mentioned above, most previous research on the social networks of the childless has focused on what they lack in terms of informal social support. Here we complement this approach by including in our analysis both the formal and the

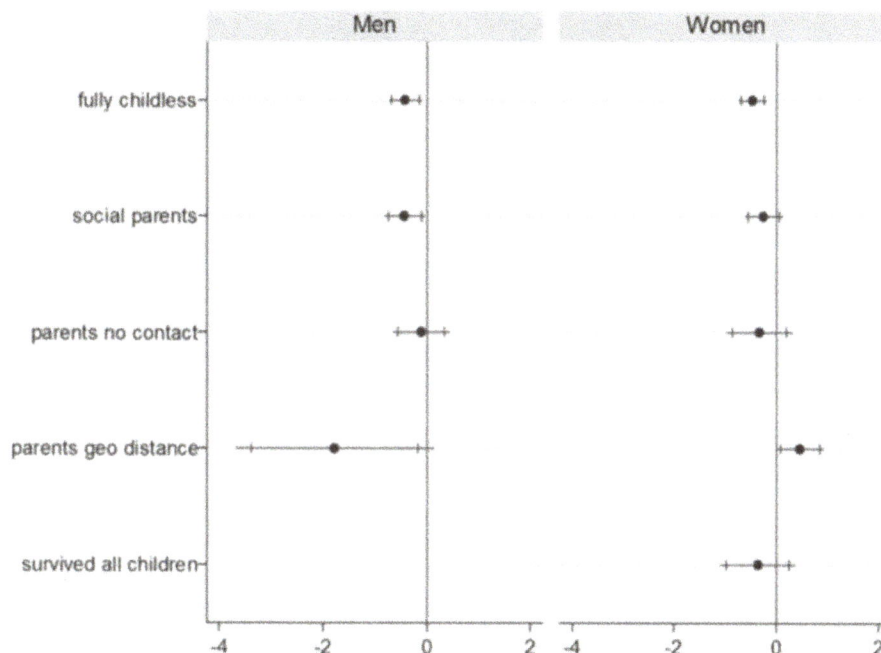

Fig. 17.6 Effects of parental status (reference: natural parents) on the likelihood of receiving a financial transfer from others, by respondent's gender. Beta coefficients and 90 % and 95 % confidence intervals from logit models (Note: For further variables in the models, see Fig. 17.1)

informal types of support the childless receive, and by investigating how the levels and the types of support they receive differ across the range of parental statuses.

Figure 17.6 shows that our results for the financial support given – namely, that the absence of children is negatively associated with it – also applies to some extent to the flow of resources in the other direction. We find a significant negative relationship between having received financial support and having been fully childless for both women and men, as well as for social fathers and for fathers who were living more than 500 km away from their children. This latter finding mirrors the finding that these fathers are also less likely to have been providing economic support to others. An opposite pattern is found for mothers: i.e., mothers who were living far away from their children are more likely to have been receiving financial support.

Regarding the likelihood of having received informal social support (Fig. 17.7) we find that the patterns differ between men and women. While both fully childless men and fathers who had lost contact with their children are more likely than natural parents to have been receiving social support, among women none of the subgroups' coefficients is significant. In other words, motherhood status does not affect the likelihood of having received help from outside of the household. The picture becomes more complex when we also take into consideration the intensity of these time transfers (Fig. 17.8). For both fully childless men and fathers with no contact with their children we observe a significant negative coefficient; thus, while they are

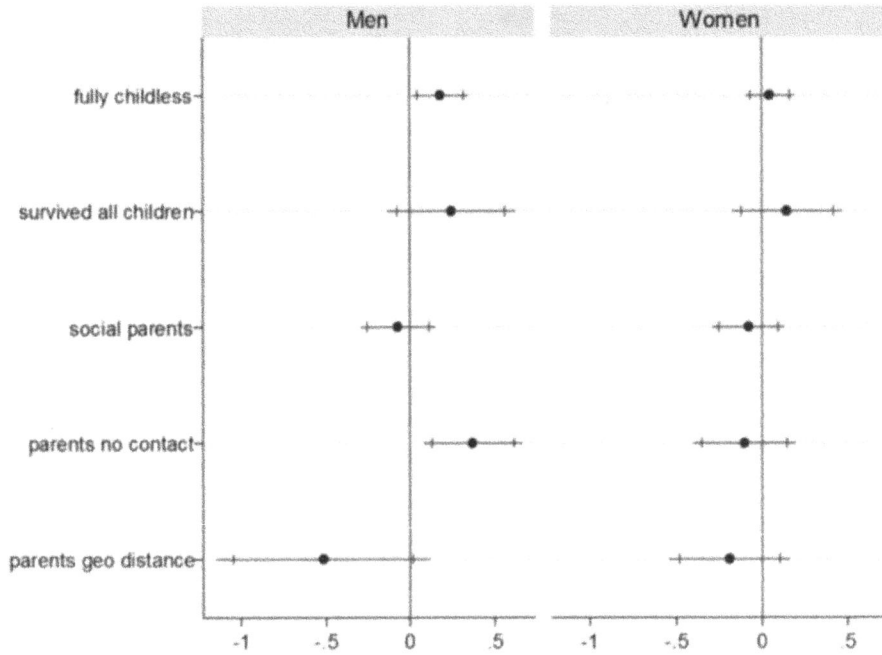

Fig. 17.7 Effects of parental status (reference: natural parents) on the likelihood of receiving social support from others, by respondent's gender. Beta coefficients and 90 % and 95 % confidence intervals from logit models (Note: For further variables in the models, see Fig. 17.1)

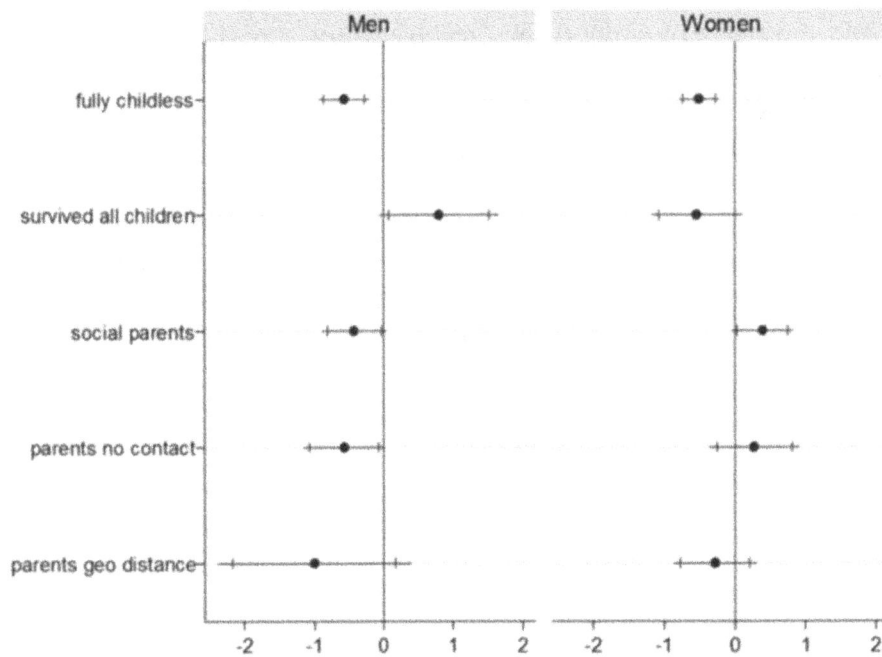

Fig. 17.8 Effects of parental status (reference: natural parents) on the amount of social support received from others (as the natural log of hours per year) conditional on having received at least 1 h of support, by respondent's gender. Regression coefficients and 90 % and 95 % confidence intervals (Note: For further variables in the models, see Fig. 17.1)

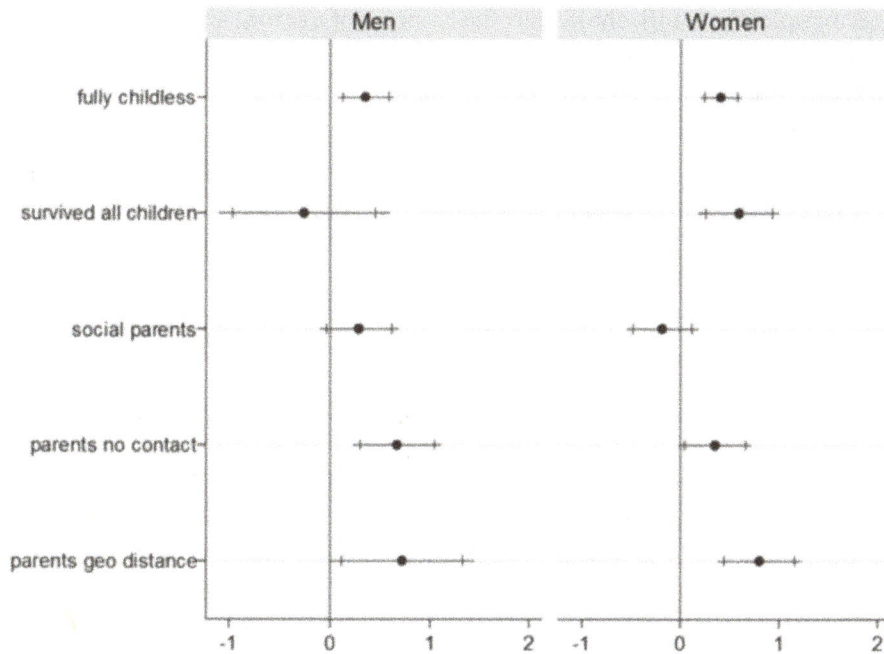

Fig. 17.9 Effects of parental status (reference: natural parents) on the likelihood of receiving professional or paid home care or staying overnight in a nursing home, by respondent's gender. Beta coefficients and 90 % and 95 % confidence intervals (Note: For further variables in the models, see Fig. 17.1)

more likely than natural parents to have received help, among those who did receive it the number of hours of help was significantly lower. A marginally significant negative association is also observed for mothers who survived their children and for social fathers, whereas a positive association is found for fathers who survived their children and for social mothers. In sum, when we look at the likelihood of having received support we can see that none of the different groups of parents and non-parents is disadvantaged relative to natural parents, with some even being more likely to have received help. On the other hand, some weakness in the support networks of the non-parents can be seen when we shift the focus to the intensity of the support received: fully childless men and women received a significantly lower amount of social support than natural parents.

It is clear from our results that some types of elderly non-parents are more likely than natural parents to lack informal social support when they become old and frail. This finding resonates with results from previous research. The question then arises whether someone else provides the non-parents with the help they need when they get old. The answer is given in Fig. 17.9. The fully childless men and women are more likely than natural parents to have spent some time in an old-age home or to have received some professional or formal care support (acquired on the market or received from public institutions). This is also the case for women who have survived their children, parents who do not have contact with their children any more and parents who live far away from their children[1]. For long-term care policies, it is thus not only the increasing number of fully childless people that will challenge the supply of formal care services, but also the increasing number of parents who do not live close to their children or have lost contact with them.

[1] The latter finding confirms the results of a recent study of the elderly Dutch population by van der Pers et al. (2015) which showed that having children living close by was negatively associated with the likelihood of moving to a care institution.

17.6   Conclusions

Childlessness in later life is a topic that has been attracting increased levels of attention from researchers and policy makers. It is also still the subject of widely held misconceptions. Two of the most misleading ones are that childless elderly people are only or mainly at the receiving end of intergenerational exchanges, and that they are all of one kind. Contrary to these assumptions, we find that elderly childless people give as well as receive support, and that parental status is a continuum, ranging from full childlessness across several intermediary conditions to full current natural parenthood.

In a study of the elderly population across 11 European countries, we have shown that non-parents make significant contributions to their social networks of family and friends through financial and time transfers, and that their contributions of time in particular differ little from those of natural parents. The same applies to participation in charitable and voluntary work. Different parental statuses are significantly associated with the various dimensions of giving and receiving. The patterns across these dimensions and statuses need to be examined in detail, but two general results stand out. The first is that social parents (i.e., people who have no natural children but who have adopted, foster, or stepchildren) are more similar to natural parents than to non-parents. Family recomposition thus does not seem to inhibit intergenerational exchanges as long as social parents have sufficient contact with their social children. The second result is that parents who have lost contact with their children – natural or otherwise – are an overlooked group in terms of their heightened demand for formal care in later life. As this group may be increasing in size, it represents a special challenge for policy.

Literature

Albertini, M., & Kohli, M. (2009). What childless older people give: Is the generational link broken? *Ageing and Society, 29*, 1261–1274.

Albertini, M., & Mencarini, L. (2014). Childlessness and support networks in later life: New pressures on familialistic welfare states? *Journal of Family Issues, 35*, 331–357.

Albertini, M., Kohli, M., & Vogel, C. (2007). Intergenerational transfers of time and money in European families: Common patterns – Different regimes? *Journal of European Social Policy, 17*, 319–334.

Boldrin, M., De Nardi, M., & Jones, L. E. (2005). *Fertility and social security* (NBER working paper No. 11146). Cambridge, MA: National Bureau of Economic Research.

Caldwell, J. C. (1976). Toward a restatement of demographic transition theory. *Population and Development Review, 2*, 321–366.

Choi, N. G. (1994). Patterns and determinants of service utilization: Comparisons of the childless elderly and elderly parents living with or apart from their children. *The Gerontologist, 34*, 353–362.

Dykstra, P. A., & Hagestad, G. O. (2007). Roads less taken: Developing a nuanced view of older adults without children. *Journal of Family Issues, 28*, 1275–1310.

Folbre, N. (2008). *Valuing children*. Cambridge, MA: Harvard University Press.

Hank, K., & Wagner, M. (2013). Parenthood, marital status and well-being in later life: Evidence from SHARE. *Social Indicators Research, 114*, 639–653.

Hurd, M. (2009). Intervivos giving by older people in the United States: Who received financial gifts from the childless? *Ageing and Society, 29*, 1207–1225.

Keizer, R., Dykstra, P. A., & Poortman, A. R. (2010). Life outcomes of childless men and fathers. *European Sociological Review, 26*, 1–15.

Kohli, M., & Albertini, M. (2009). Childlessness and intergenerational transfers: What is at stake? *Ageing and Society, 29*, 1171–1183.

Kohli, M., Albertini, M., & Künemund, H. (2010). Linkages among adult family generations: Evidence from comparative survey research. In P. Heady & M. Kohli (Eds.), *Family, kinship and state in contemporary Europe* (Perspectives on theory and policy, Vol. 3, pp. 195–220). Frankfurt am Main: Campus.

Kreager, P., & Schröder-Butterfill, E. (Eds.). (2004). *Ageing without children: European and Asian perspectives*. Oxford: Berghahn.

Kreyenfeld, M., & Konietzka, D. (2007). Die Analyse von Kinderlosigkeit in Deutschland: Dimensionen – Daten – Probleme. In D. Konietzka & M. Kreyenfeld (Eds.), *Ein Leben ohne Kinder: Kinderlosigkeit in Deutschland* (pp. 11–41). Wiesbaden: VS Verlag für Sozialwissenschaften.

Larsson, K., & Silverstein, M. (2004). The effects of marital and parental status on informal support and service utilization: A study of older Swedes living alone. *Journal of Aging Studies, 18*, 231–244.

Mynarska, M., Matysiak, A., Rybińska, A., Tocchioni, V., & Vignoli, D. (2015). Diverse paths into childlessness over the life course. *Advances in Life Course Research, 25*, 35–48.

Nuget, J. B. (1985). The old-age security motive for fertility. *Population and Development Review, 11*, 75–97.

OECD. (2010). OECD family database Paris. OECD – Social Policy Division – Directorate of Employment, Labour and Social Affairs. SF2.5: Childlessness.

van der Pers, M., Mulder, C. H., & Steverink, N. (2015). Geographic proximity of adult children and the well-being of older persons. *Research on Aging, 37*, 524–551.

Rowland, D. T. (2007). Historical trends in childlessness. *Journal of Family Issues, 28*, 1311–1337.

Schnettler, S., & Woehler, T. (2015). No children in later life, but more and better friends? Substitution mechanisms in the personal and support networks of parents and the childless in Germany. *Ageing and Society*, pre-publication view.

Tanturri, M. L., Mills, M., Rotkirch, A., Sobotka, T., Takacs, J., Miettinen, A., Faludi, C., Kantsa, V., & Nasiri, D. (2015). *State-of-the-art report. Childlessness in Europe* (Families and societies working paper series, 32).

Umberson, D., Pudrovska, T., & Reczek, C. (2010). Parenthood, childlessness, and well-being: A life course perspective. *Journal of Marriage and Family, 72*, 612–629.

Weltoft, G. R., Burstrom, B., & Rosen, M. (2004). Premature mortality among lone fathers and childless men. *Social Science and Medicine, 59*, 1449–1459.

Wenger, G. C. (2009). Childlessness at the end of life: Evidence from rural Wales. *Ageing and Society, 29*, 1241–1257.

Index

www.ingramcontent.com/pod-product-compliance
Lightning Source LLC
Chambersburg PA
CBHW080244030426
42334CB00023BA/2694